Paris &
Versailles

Delia Gray-Durant and Ian Robertson

B L U E   G U I D E

A&C Black • London
WW Norton • New York

Ninth edition May 1998 © Delia Gray-Durant and Ian Robertson

Published by A&C Black (Publishers) Limited
35 Bedford Row, London WC1R 4JH

1st (post-war) and 2nd editions by L. Russell Muirhead © Ernest Benn Limited 1951, 1960
3rd edition by Stuart Rossiter © Ernest Benn Limited 1968
4th and 5th editions by Ian Robertson © Ernest Benn Limited 1977
6th, 7th and 8th editions by Ian Robertson © A & C Black (Publishers) Limited 1985, 1989, 1992
9th edition © Delia Gray-Durant and Ian Robertson

ISBN 0 7136–4447 8

'Blue Guides' is a registered trademark.

Illustrations © Olivia Brooks. Title page illustration: detail of the Fontaine de l'Observatoire.
Cover photograph: Gate to the Palace of Versailles by Neil Beer/Corbis.
Maps and plans © A&C Black. Street map and maps on pp by John Flower updated for this edition by Map Creation Ltd; plans on pp 139, 146, 282, 299 by Robert Smith

A CIP catalogue record of this book is available from the British Library.

Published in the United States of America by
WW Norton & Company, Inc
500 Fifth Avenue, New York NY 10110

Published simultaneously in Canada by
Penguin Books Canada Limited
10 Alcorn Avenue, Toronto, Ontario M4V 3B2

ISBN 0–393–31803–6 USA

The authors and the publisher have done their best to ensure the accuracy of all the information in Blue Guide Paris and Versailles; however, they can accept no responsibility for any loss, injury or inconvenience sustained by any traveller as a result of information or advice contained in this guide.

Delia Gray-Durant has updated this edition of the Blue Guide. She has lived and worked in Paris, and also had a home in the French Midi. As well as writing Blue Guides—she is also the author of Blue Guide Midi-Pyrénées—translates French art history publications and has contributed to British art publications. For several years she has devised and led art history and cultural tours.

Ian Robertson was the original author of the Blue Guide. He currently lives in France and is the author of Blue Guide France.

Printed and bound in Great Britain by Butler & Tanner, Frome and London

Contents

Ile de la Cité and Ile-St-Louis

The South or Left Bank: La Rive Gauche

The Right Bank

Around Paris

Further Afield

Maps and Plans

Paris

Outside Paris

Introduction

I have been visiting Paris for many years, and, to me, it has never looked so beautiful. Following a tremendous programme to present itself to the best possible advantage, many monuments have been overhauled and numerous domes and statues regilded, with the result that it is more dazzling than ever at the approach to the 21C. Equally encouraging is the way that the visitor is better catered for and made more welcome than before.

The ninth edition of the Blue Guide Paris and Versailles has been thoroughly revised. The general overall format of the previous edition has been retained, while the layout and accessibility have been improved and practical information expanded, so that it can be used both to plan a visit from beginning to end and as a companion guide during a stay in the city. Now that Paris is a mere three-hour train journey from London, it is even more accessible from Britain. Whether you plan a brief or extended visit, whether your are new to Paris or know it well, there is a vast number of new experiences and improvements to the old ones. Worthy of special mention are the improvements to the parks and gardens over the last decade and a half.

The detailed art-historical content, on which the Blue Guides' reputation rests, has been revised and expanded where appropriate to cover the numerous changes that have occurred in Paris since the last edition. This applies particularly to the Musée du Louvre where the Grand Projet du Louvre is nearing completion. The Richelieu wing opened in November 1993, with its two large courtyards, Marly and Puget, glazed and terraced providing a magnificent setting for former royal commissions for sculpture. Other French sculpture is in the galleries around the courtyards. In the same wing are French paintings up to the 17C and paintings from the Northern Schools, as well as Objets d'Art which incorporates the Apartments of Napoléon III.

The Oriental Antiquities collections are also in the Richelieu wing, in galleries around the Cour Khorsabad and include the very fine section devoted to Islamic Art. The Egyptian Department reopened in 1997. Italian Paintings, in the Denon wing, as well as the smaller collections of Spanish and English Paintings, are being reorganised and will be in place by 1998. Likewise, work on the new layout and displays in the Department of Greek, Etruscan and Roman Antiquities, in Denon and Sully, will be finished by 1998. The Prints and Drawings sections have been totally rearranged, and are exhibited with the national schools of painting to which they correspond.

Some exciting new museums have been opened in Paris since the last edition of this guide. The Musée Maillol, the private collection of Dina Vierny, is beautifully presented in the 18C Hôtel de Bouchardon in Rue de Grenelle. The brand new Musée de la Musique opened at the end of 1996 in the Cité de la Musique in La Villette Park.

There have also been a number of reopenings, notably the Musée Jacquemart André in 1996, after a long closure and extensive renovations. The work on the Musée Carnavalet is finally complete, and several rooms now show off to even greater effect the 17C and 18C interiors salvaged from Parisian mansions. Other museums that have been renovated or reorganised include the Musée Delacroix and the Musée du Moyen Age-Thermes et Hôtel de Cluny (formerly known as the Musée de Cluny). Work is continuing in some, which are likely to be entirely or partly closed for the next few years. The Musée des Arts Décoratifs and the Musée des Arts Asiatiques-Guimet may have sections on view until their total reopening in 1999, as may the Musée des Arts et Métiers which has a tentative opening date of 1998.

The Pompidou Centre, which celebrated its twentieth anniversary in 1997, has undergone major renovations to the exterior, and work on the interior is scheduled to be completed to coincide with the new millennium. Meanwhile, one gallery of the Pompidou Centre remains accessible in the main building and the rebuilt Studio of Constantin Brancusi on the piazza is open to visitors. Works from the collection of modern art have gone on display in other museums in Paris and in the French provinces.

A remarkable transformation is the refurbished Grande Galerie de l'Evolution, which reopened in 1994 after 30 years' closure. This tells the story of evolution and the relationship between human beings and nature in a splendid setting, with an inspired use of modern techniques and museology in a 19C building.

Of architectural interest is the new—and highly controversial—Bibliothèque Nationale de France François Mitterand on the Tolbiac site in the 13e arrondissement, part of which opened to readers at the end of 1996 and the rest in 1997. The most brilliant church restoration is that of St-Etienne du Mont.

Some of the sites further afield which are covered in this guide have also undergone improvement. The Apartments of Napoléon I at the Château de Fontainebleau are resplendent after lengthy renovation work. The Neoclassical decorations of certain rooms at the Château de Malmaison have been restored, and the Château de Sceaux, which contains the Musée de l'Ile de France, has also undergone thorough restoration and reorganisation.

It has become even easier, with the extended RER system and improved bus connections, to visit the sites on the edge of or outside Paris, which make a pleasant half day or day's visit. There are stimulating contrasts to be discovered. For example, on the immediate periphery of Paris, the complex of La Défense grows defiantly taller while the suburb of St-Denis has undergone sensitive urban renewal and is a much more attractive place to visit than it used to be. Recommended is a visit, possible in a half day, to the beautiful 16C Château of Ecouen north of Paris, home to the lesser known but superbly laid-out Musée de la Renaissance, which carries on from where the Musée du Moyen Age ends. The section devoted to the Château de Versailles has been rearranged to explain more clearly the complex range of visits available so that you can make a selection in advance and maximise your time spent there.

Another welcome improvement is the increasing number of cafés and restaurants inside museums and galleries, not only in the larger ones like the Louvre, the Musée d'Orsay and La Villette, but also in the smaller ones, for example, the Musée Jacquemart André and in the Musée Maillol.

Parks, Gardens and Open Spaces

There are about 400 public gardens in the city. Since 1977, 103 hectares have been given over to create a remarkable 126 new parks and gardens. The publicity about all green spaces has improved, with information posters and documents and recently introduced guided tours of gardens. A bonus are the free concerts in about 20 of the city's parks and gardens between May and September.

Most innovative are the new gardens. Parc Citroën in the 15e arrondissement, inaugurated in 1992, is a perfect formal landscape covering the banks of the Seine on a site where cars were once manufactured. Also in the 15th is a slightly earlier and very successful creation (1977–85) Parc Georges-Brassens, in the former parish of Vaugirard. One particular garden novelty is the Jardin Atlantique (1992–94), planted on top of a station, the Gare de Montparnasse serving the Atlantic coast; an even newer creation is the Parc de Bercy (1992–95) in the 12e arrondissement where wine warehouses once stood. The Parc Georges-Brassens, Parc de Bercy and the tiny Clos de Montmartre all cultivate vines as a souvenir of the traditions of the district, whereas the Jardins de Luxembourg has a fruit garden on the south side, recalling a former monastery orchard on this site. Parc Belleville in the 20th (1988) enjoys some of the best views over Paris, and the Parc de la Villette, established in 1990–91, the largest in Paris, covers 35 hectares where the abattoirs of Paris once stood, between the Cité des Science et de l'Industrie and the new Cité de la Musique. This is a fascinating combination of large green areas crossed by the Canal de l'Ourcq and the Canal St-Denis and futuristic or thematic gardens, designed by Bernard Tschumi.

Other well-established gardens build on what they already do beautifully, such as the Jardin des Plantes, the Parc de Bagatelle and the Parc Florale, while work has been carried out the Tuilleries Gardens in conjunction with the Grand Projet du Louvre. One of the older (1860s) but less well-known gardens, the Parc des Buttes-Chaumont (in the 19th), makes picturesque use of former gypsum quarries.

Not only gardens, but avenues and river and canal banks have been enhanced. The Avenue des Champs-Elysées has been planted with about 300 extra trees to soften its outline, which look magical at Christmas when the trees are festooned with lights. The gardens of the port of the Arsenal, near Pl. de la Bastille, and the banks of the canal St-Martin almost make an alternative to the Seine's banks. Particularly original are the two promenades plantées (planted walkways), one established on 4.5km of a disused railway line between Vincennes and Bastille, and another in the Batignolles area above the RER track. The many famous cemeteries of Paris (e.g. Montparnasse, Montmartre, Père Lachaise) provide an outdoor curiosity with their serried ranks of tombs and bizarre monuments.

Delia Gray-Durant, 1998

Acknowledgements

I would like to thank Nicolle Roques-Lagier and her colleagues at the Office de Toursime de Paris; also members of the Office de Tourisme St-Denis, the Comité Régional de Tourisme de 'Ile de France, and the Comités Départmentaux de l'Oise and des Yvelines for setting up visits and introductions, and providing practical information. My special thanks go to Marijke Naber at the Musée du Louvre and Julia Fritsch at the Musée National de la Renaissance, Ecouen. A great number of experts from cultural organisations, monuments, museums and galleries in and around Paris have generously contributed information, advice and time to help bring this book up to date, and, while too numerous to mention individually, I would like to express my sincere appreciation for the help offered by each one. A huge personal debt of gratitude is due to Yvonne Laugier and her family who have nurtured, advised and assisted in every way my time in Paris, as well as to Serena Poisson and family and to Marie Eymard, who have also given me their personal support. I am very grateful to Gemma Davies at A & C Black for the opportunity to revise Blue Guide Paris and Versailles. And thank you Will and Siân for your encouragement.

Delia Gray-Durant, 1998

Paris Surveyed

Paris lies on both banks of the Seine, near the centre of the Paris Basin, between 25 and 130m above sea-level and 150km (or over 320km by the windings of the river) from the sea. The Seine, the third in length of the four great rivers of France, enters this part of the Paris Basin some 500km from its source.

The great loop of the Seine divides the city into Left Bank (Rive Gauche) on the south and Right Bank (Rive Droite) on the north. It washes two islands, the Ile de la Cité, cradle of Paris, and the smaller Ile St-Louis. Spanned by numerous bridges, and lined by rapid thoroughfares, traffic roars alongside it and across it. But the Quais, lined with elegant façades, trees, bouquinistes, gardens, and historic monuments, remain the place for a leisurely walk and, between Pont de Sully and Pont d'Iéna, were declared a UNESCO World Heritage site in 1992. The river and its banks serve as a pleasant introduction to Paris while the sightseeing launches on the Seine offer unusual and attractive low-level views.

Paris in the 19C was bounded by a line of ramparts which, although they have long been demolished (tiny sections are still visible in places) and their sites built over, served to contain the population, denser than in any other European city (recently over 20,200 inhabitants per square kilometre) in an area of 7800 hectares. The line of the 19C walls can be imagined by following the exterior Blvd Périphérique.

Pl. du Parvis-Notre-Dame on the Ile de la Cité, from which kilometric distances in France are measured, is a good starting point for exploring Paris. However, the carefully planned vistas from one bank of the river to the other are more obvious from Place de la Concorde. To the north west is the most famous of avenues, the Champs Elysées leading to the Arc de Triomphe and La Défense beyond, while in the opposite direction, through the trees of the gardens of the Tuileries, is the immense bulk of the Louvre. This is flanked, to the north, by Rue de Rivoli and its continuation, Rue St-Antoine, ending at Pl. de la Bastille; and further east, by the Rue du Faubourg St-Antoine, leading to Pl. de la Nation, and ultimately to Vincennes.

It is essential to take into account museum and monument opening times. Many are closed on either Monday or Tuesday and on certain Public Holidays. It is becoming more usual for opening times to be adjusted for the summer or the winter season. Many of the main sights have one or two late-night openings. Weekend times may differ from weekday times. The information on opening times given at the beginning of the description of each museum or monument will help you to plan your route. The index and atlas section will help you to devise an itinerary of your own. The chapters in this Guide have been designed to assist you to explore the city systematically by district.

There are always many tourists, and the high season is not always when might expect it. July and August are strange months in Paris, when Parisians desert their city in favour of the coast or countryside. Although it is possible to travel more easily by car during that period, some entertainments (such as theatres) and neighbourhood shops or restaurants are likely to be closed.

Ile-de-France

La Région d'Ile-de-France which includes and surrounds Paris, consists of eight départements, as follows (with their postal prefix). The **Ville-de-Paris** (75) divided into arrondissements (see below) at the core. The three that lie immediately outside the periphery (*la proche banlieue*) are **Hauts-de-Seine** (92; préfecture Nanterre) to the west, **Seine-St-Denis** (93; préfecture Bobigny) to the north-east, and **Val-de-Marne** (94; préfecture Créteil) to the south-west. A second band around these (*la grande banlieue*) is made up of **Val-d'Oise** (95; préfecture Cergy-Pontoise) to the north, **Yvelines** (78; préfecture Versailles) to the west, **Essonne** (91; préfecture Évry) to the south, and **Seine-et-Marne** (77; préfecture Melun) to the east. Some highlights of these départements are covered (Versailles, Fontainebleau, Ecouen, St-Germain-en-Laye) in the last section of the Guide.

The Arrondissements

These municipal districts, of which there are 20 in central Paris, each with its Maire and Mairie, or town hall, are important administrative and topographical entities. You can make yourself familiar with the position of some of them: see plan on pp 2-3 of the Atlas. Their numbering follows a spiral working out clockwise from the centre. When addressing correspondence to Paris the arrondissements are written 75001, 75002, etc. (rather than 1er, 2e., etc. as before), the prefix 75 indicating the département. The arrondissements touched on, in whole or in part, are indicated at the beginning of each Route.

75001   Louvre: the western half of the Cité, the Louvre, Pl. Vendôme, Palais-Royal and St-Eustache.
75002   Bourse: also the Bibliothèque Nationale, Richelieu.
75003   Temple: comprising the north half of the Marais, the Temple and Archives.
75004   Hôtel de Ville: includes the eastern half of the Cité, with Notre-Dame, the Ile St-Louis and the Centre Pompidou, the southern part of the Marais with Pl. des Vosges, and bounded by the Pl. de la Bastille to the east.
75005   Panthéon: the Quartier Latin, with the Sorbonne, Panthéon, Val-de Grâce and Jardin des Plantes.
75006   Luxembourg: with St-Germain-des-Prés, St-Sulpice and the Palais du Luxembourg.
75007   Palais-Bourbon: comprising the Faubourg St-Germain, the Musée d'Orsay, Les Invalides, the Ecole Militaire and bounded to the west by the Eiffel Tower.
75008   Elysée: with the Pl. de la Concorde, the Madeleine, the Champs-Elysées and Faubourg St-Honoré, and including the Parc Monceau to the north, and containing the Av. George-V to the west.
75009   Opéra: reaching up to the Blvd de Clichy and Pl. Pigalle.
75010   Enclos St-Laurent: with the Gares du Nord and de l'Est, and Hôpital St-Louis.

75011	Popincourt: the area north east of the Pl. de la Bastille and reaching to Pl. de la Nation.
75012	Reuilly: the area south east of the Pl. de la Bastille, including the Gare de Lyon and Bercy.
75013	Gobelins: the area south of the Gare d'Austerlitz, including the Gobelins and Pl. d'Italie.
75014	Observatoire: including the Cimetière de Montparnasse, Parc de Montsouris and Cité Universitaire.
75015	Vaugirard: the area south west of the Tour Montparnasse and Av. de Suffren.
75016	Passy: between the Seine and Bois de Boulogne, its northern half crossed by the Avenues Foch, Victor-Hugo and Kléber, radiating from the Étoile, and containing the districts of Chaillot, Passy and Auteuil.
75017	Batignolles Monceau: the area north west of the Étoile.
75018	Butte Montmartre: the area north east of the Pl. de Clichy and reaching as far east as the Rue d'Aubervilliers.
75019	Buttes-Chaumont: including La Villette.
75020	Ménilmontant: including Père Lachaise.

Métro stations. A list of convenient métro stations is given at the beginning of most chapters: see also Atlas, pp 4–5.

Statistics

The total municipal population of Paris, according to provisional estimations at 1 January 1995, are—in round figures—2,155,000, with 11,000,000 in greater Paris, while the total population of France in 1990 was 57,685,603. (A century or so earlier the figures were 2,269,000 for Paris and 39,238,000 for France.) Those interested in such figures and many other statistics should contact the INSEE Info Service, Tour Gamma A, 195 Rue de Bercy, 75582 Paris Cedex 12, ☎ 01 41 17 50 50, information ☎ 01 41 17 66 11 (easily approached from the level of the Gare de Lyon).

Practical Information

When to go

Parisian weather is changeable, particularly in the winter and spring, although long periods of fine weather occur each year. It can occasionally be oppressively hot in summer (30°C) for a few days, and bitterly cold in winter. The average number of days a year on which the temperature falls below freezing-point is about 35; the number of days of snowfall has averaged 15 in recent decades. Although spring in Paris is most peoples' ideal, the autumn can be glorious.

Planning your trip

There are various ways of getting to Paris from Great Britain, by rail, air, sea and rail or sea and coach. A car is not essential for getting around Paris and to its immediate surroundings as public transport is excellent (see below). In fact a car can be a liability in central Paris except perhaps in August when the city is relatively empty. Car hire facilities are available at the airports and rail termini or in central Paris.

Tourist Offices

General information, including how to get to Paris from the **UK**, with suggestions for accommodation and how to travel around, may be obtained from the French Government Tourist Office, Maison de la France, 178 Piccadilly, London W1V 0AL, ☎ 0891 244 123 (all calls charged at 50p per minute), fax 0171 493 6594. Maison de la France compiles a very useful Reference Guide for the Traveller in France which can be obtained at 178 Piccadilly or by sending four first-class stamps. The Tourist Office has opened a travel centre at the site which includes a bank, travel agent, bookshop, and Air France, Brittany Ferries and SeaFrance centres.

In the **USA** Government Tourist Office are at 444 Madison Av., 16th floor, New York, NY 10022, ☎ 212 838 7800, fax 212 838 7855, with branches at 676 North Michigan Av., 3360 Chicago, Il. 60611, ☎ 312 751 7800, 312 337 6339; 9454 Wilshire Blvd, Suite 715, Beverly Hills, Ca. 90212-2967, ☎ 310 271 6665, fax 310 276 2835. Their **Canadian** office is at 1981 Avenue McGill College, Suite 490, Montreal, Quebec H3A 2W9 ☎ 514 288 4264, fax 514 845 4868, with a branch at 30 St-Patrick Street, Suite 700, Toronto, Ontario M5T 3A3, ☎ 416 593 4723, 416 979 7587.

Visit the French tourist office's web sites at www.franceguide.com and www.fgtousa.org/ta.htm.

Travel Agents and Tour Operators

Any accredited member of the Association of British Travel Agents will sell tickets and book accommodation. There are numerous excellent package deals offered by agents specialising in Paris. Look in the national press for special offers.

UK based tour operators specialising in holidays to Paris are: *Aeroscope*, Scope House, Hospital Road, Moreton-in-Marsh GL56 0BQ, ☎ 01608 650 103; *Airtours*, Wavell House, Holcombe Road, Helmshore BB4 4NB, ☎ 01706 260 000; *AT Mays Citybreaks*, Unit B, Blair Court, Clydebank Business Park, Clydebank G81 2LA, ☎ 0141 951 8411; *Inghams*, 10/18 Putney Hill, London SW15 6AX, ☎ 0181 780 4400; *Just France*, 10–18 Putney Hill, London SW15 6AX, ☎ 0181 780 0303; *Paris Travel Service*, Bridge House, 55–59 High Road, Broxbourne EN10 7DT, ☎ 01992 456 000; *Thomson Citybreaks*, ☎ 0990 502555; *Travelscene Ltd*, 11/15 St Ann's Road, Harrow HA1 1AS, ☎ 0181 427 4445.

USA based tour operators include *B&V Associates*, ☎ 212 688 9538, fax 212 688 9467; *Barclay, International Group*, ☎ 212 832 3777, fax 212 753 1139; *Golden Tulip*, ☎ 212 557 3555, fax 212 557 3355; *HSA Voyages*, ☎ 212 689 5400, fax 212 689 5435; *Paris Accommodation*, ☎ 800 446 1090, fax 617 863 0119; *Parisotel*, ☎ 800 462 7274, 800 GO 2 PARIS, fax 408 395 4443.

Passports

Passports are necessary for all British and American travellers entering France. British passports, valid for ten years, are issued at five regional Passport Offices in the UK and Clive House, 70 Petty France, London SW1H 9HD. For all information, ☎ 0990 21 04 10. Passport forms are available from main Post Offices, Lloyds Bank and some travel agents. **Visas** are not required for British or American visitors to France.

If you are from an EU country and intend staying in France for more than three months, you should apply in advance for a *carte de séjour* to the nearest French Consulate, or if already in France, to the Préfecture de Police, Ile de la Cité (Salle Sud).

British subjects wanting to work in France should write to the Consular Section of the Embassy (see below) who will advise on the procedure to be followed, according to the status of the person concerned under EU regulations. It should be emphasised that it acts neither as an employment agency nor an accommodation agency.

Customs

Travellers by air pass through customs at the airport of arrival; EU travellers between EU countries may go through the blue exit and therefore do not need to go through Customs. However, selective checks are carried out. If travelling on international expresses, luggage may be examined on the train. If travelling by road, luggage may be checked at the frontier or at ports of departure and disembarkation.

In general, there are no limits on quantities of goods carried from one European Union country to another, provided tax has been paid on them in the country of origin, and provided they are for personal use, but there are guidance levels: cigarettes, 800, cigarillos, 400, cigars, 200, smoking tobacco, 1 kg.; spirits, 10 litres; fortified wine (port, sherry) 20 litres, wine, 90 litres (not more than 60 litres of sparkling), beer 110 litres. For passengers from outside the EU, the restrictions will vary and it is advisable to check with your local travel agent about allowances.

Getting to Paris

By air

Regular scheduled air services between England and France are operated by Air France working in conjunction with British Airways. Full information about flights from London and Gatwick and other cities in the UK to Paris Charles de Gaulle and Orly can be obtained from **British Airways**, 156 Regent St, London W1R 5TA, ☎ 0171 434 4700, and from **Air France**, 10 Warwick Street, Piccadilly, London W1, ☎ 0181 742 6600. **British Midland**, Donnington Hall, Castle Donnington Derby DE74 SB, ☎ 0345 554 554, offers several flights a day from Heathrow and from the East Midlands, as well as from Aberdeen via East Midlands, and Belfast, Edinburgh and Glasgow, via Heathrow or East Midlands. **Air UK** operates flights from Stansted and Leeds, ☎ 0141 221 5227.

For charter flights, check the national press.

For details of flights available from the **USA** contact the following airlines:
American Airlines, ☎ 800 624 6262. Departures from Boston, Chicago, Dallas, Miami, JFK New York,
Continental Airlines, ☎ 800 231 0856. Departures from Houston, Newark New York.
Delta Airlines, ☎ 800 241 4141. Departures from Atlanta, Cincinnati, JFK New York.
Air France, ☎ 800 AF PARIS. Departures from Chicago, Houston, Los Angeles, Miami, JFK New York, San Francisco, Washington.
Northwest Airlines, ☎ 800 225 2525. Departures from Detroit.
TWA, ☎ 800 892 4141. Departures from JFK New York, Saint-Louis.
United Airlines, ☎ 800 538 2929. Departures from Chicago, Los Angeles, San Francisco, Washington.

British Airways has a Paris office at 13–15 Blvd de la Madeleine, 75009, ☎ 0801 63 66 00. **Air France** has an office at 119 Av. des Champs-Elysées, ☎ 01 44 08 22 22.

Internal or domestic services are operated by **Air Inter**, 116 Av. des Champs-Elysées, ☎ 01 47 23 59 58, and branches.

Paris is served by two international airports: **Roissy-Charles de Gaulle** (CDG), ☎ 01 48 62 22 80, 23km north east of the capital, comprising two separate terminals; and **Orly** (south and west), ☎ 01 49 75 15 15, 14km south of the city.

Charles de Gaulle is linked by a **shuttle** and **RER** train service with the Gare du Nord; Orly with the Gare d'Austerlitz.

They are also connected by an **Air France bus service**, ☎ 01 49 38 57 57, leaving each terminal every 12 minutes. CDG to Etoile/Porte Maillot, between 05.40 and 23.00. Orly to Les Invalides air terminal and Montparnasse Station, between 05.50 and 23.00. The Roissy Bus runs every 15 minutes between CDG and Rue Scribe (near Opéra Garnier), 05.45 to 23.00. The Orly Bus every 12 minutes between Orly and Denfert-Rochereau, 06.00 to 23.00. ☎ 08 36 68 77 14 for both.

Taxis can be found at the airports and car-hire firms have offices there.

By rail

The opening of the **Channel Tunnel** has transformed rail travel to Paris (and to Lille and Brussels) for those coming from Britain. For foot passengers, the easiest way to travel is by Eurostar from Waterloo International Terminal, which brings you in just three hours to Paris Gare-du-Nord; or from the Ashford International Terminal, Kent, in two hours. Information can be obtained and reservations made direct with **Eurostar** on ☎ 0345 30 30 30, and from most main line stations. The Eurostar faxback information service number for up-to-date timetabling etc., is ☎ 0660 600 600 (49p per minute); to call Eurostar from abroad, ☎ 1233 617 575. In North America, British Rail International, ☎ 1212 382 3737.

General and up-to-date information and bookings for rail-sea connections can be also made through International Rail, Victoria Station, London SW1, ☎ 0990 848 848. The Paris office of BRI is at Maison de la Grande Bretagne, 19 Rue des Mathurins, 75009, ☎ 01 44 51 06 14.

For passengers and vehicles, the **Shuttle** drive-on, drive-off service, terminal in England is at Cheriton, just west of Folkestone, M20 (Junction 11a); the French terminal is near Coquelles, some 5km south west of Calais, A16 (Junction 13). There are up to three Shuttles per hour during the day (less frequent at night). The journey takes 35 minutes from platform to platform (25 minutes in the tunnel). For information, special offers and reservations, ☎ 0990 35 35 35, departure information: ☎ 0891 55 55 66; brochures ☎ 0990 700 800; for coach services: ☎ 01303 272 70; disabled helpline: ☎ 01303 27 37 47. In France, information and reservations: ☎ 03 21 00 61 00; coach: ☎ 03 21 00 65 43.

The French Railways Ltd (SNCF, or Société Nationale des Chemins de Fer Française), The Rail Shop, 179 Piccadilly, London W1V 0BA, ☎ 0990 300 003 (next to the French Government Tourist Office) for information and bookings on all French rail services.

Railway termini in Paris. The main stations are all on métro lines, and most have left-luggage offices (*consignes*) or lockers, trolleys, information bureaux, etc. Some, such as Gare d'Austerlitz and Gare du Nord, are also connected by regular bus services. SNCF information and reservations: main line, ☎ 08 36 35 35 35, in English: ☎ 08 36 35 35 39; Ile-de-France, ☎ 01 53 90 20 20 (French only).

The main stations of the SNCF, are:
Gare d'Austerlitz (Pl. 15; 6-8), serving the Région Sud-Ouest (Tours, Bordeaux, Toulouse, Bayonne, the Pyrenees) and Spain and Portugal.
Gare de l'Est (Pl. 9; 3) for the Région Est (Reims, Metz, Strasbourg) and Luxembourg, Germany, Austria and Switzerland and Eastern European countries.
Gare de Lyon (Pl. 15; 6) for the Région Sud-Est (Lyon, Dijon, Provence, Côte d'Azur) and Italy, Switzerland, Greece. TGV Sud-Est.
Gare Montparnasse (Pl. 12; 8), terminus for the Région, Ouest (Brittany, La Rochelle, etc.), and Aquitaine (the west-south-west of France). TGV Atlantique.
Gare du Nord (Pl. 9; 3) for the Région Nord (Lille, Brussels, Amsterdam, Cologne, Hamburg, etc.), and also for boat-trains to Boulogne, Calais and Dunkerque). Eurostar terminus for London. TGV Thalys (Northern Europe).
Gare St-Lazare (Pl. 7; 4), another terminus of the Région Ouest (Normandy

lines, Rouen, and boat-trains from Dieppe, Le Havre, Cherbourg, etc.).
There is also an Interprovincial service around Paris linking the TGV network.
Note: French Railways do not have ticket control at platform barriers. Passengers purchasing a ticket in France **must** punch-and-date-stamp (or *composter*) their ticket in an orange-red-coloured machine at the platform entrance before boarding the train or risk paying a supplementary fee or fine. This procedure does not apply to tickets purchased outside France.

By sea
Hoverspeed Ferries, frequent crossings (approximately 9 per day) taking 35 minutes, ☎ 0990 240 241. Stena Line operates the Lynx service (catamaran), Dover-Calais, taking 45 minutes, ☎ 0900 707 070. Ferry crossings run between Dover and Calais: P & O Ferries, ☎ 0990 98 09 80, Stena Line, ☎ 0990 707 070, and Sea France ☎ 0990 711 711. Between Ramsgate and Dunkerque, Sally Lines, ☎ 01843 595 522 or 595 566; between Portsmouth and Le Havre, P & O (as above), and Portsmouth and Caen, Brittany Ferries, ☎ 0990 360 360.

By bus/coach
There are regular bus or coach services from the UK to Paris, and details may be obtained from Eurolines Victoria Coach Station, 164 Buckingham Palace Rd, London SW1, ☎ 0990 808 080 or 01582 404511.

By car
Motorists driving to Paris may apply to any of the automobile associations for information on necessary documents, routes, rules of the road, restrictions on caravans and trailers, availability of spare parts, insurance etc. **AA**, Norfolk House, Priestley Way, Basingstoke, Hants RG24 9NY, ☎ 345 555 557; the **RAC**, P.O. Box 100, Bartlett Street, South Croydon, Surrey CR2 6XW, ☎ 0800 55 00 55. The **American Automobile Association** is at 1000 AAA Drive, Heathrow, Florida 32746-5063, ☎ 1407 444 7000.

Comprehensive motor insurance is advisable. Driving on a provisional licence is not allowed. At junctions, where there are no signs, traffic from the right has priority.

Insurance facilities are available from Europ Assistance, Sussex House, Perrymount Road, Haywards Heath, West Sussex RH16 1DN, ☎ 0181 680 1234.

The use of safety belts is compulsory, crash helmets must be worn by motorcyclists; children under ten may not travel in the front seat (unless the car has no back seat); vehicles should carry spare bulbs for headlights, left hand external mirror and warning lights or advance warning signal (triangle).

The area between the French Channel ports and Paris is described in detail in Blue Guide France.

The most rapid route from **Calais** or **Boulogne** to Paris is to take the A26 as far as Arras and then the A1. There are tolls (*péages*) to pay on these roads. From Dunkerque take the A25 to Lille and join the A1 at Lille.

An alternative road is the A16 from Calais to Boulogne, then the N1 bypassing Montreuil, to Abbeville, the D901 to Beauvais (bypass) and on to the N1 for Paris. Alternatively, from Abbeville: the continuation of the N1 via Amiens and Breteuil to Beauvais; or from Amiens on the D934 to meet the A1 motorway 108km north of Paris; or bear south east from Breteuil via Clermont to either Chantilly or Senlis (see Ch. 39) for Paris.

If disembarking in **Le Havre** or **Caen**, the A13 brings you in to the west of Paris. This is a convenient route from southern England for those who might prefer to be based on the outskirts of Paris at, for example, St-Germain-en-Laye, Versailles or Fontainebleau.

If driving into central Paris, it is as well to check the number of the exit (*sortie*) from the motorway that you are aiming for prior to embarking on the Blvd Périphérique. Exits are usually well indicated, but take care you get into the correct lane well in advance. The Blvd Périphérique is the efficient but often very crowded, inner ring road, around Paris. Likewise it is important that make sure you know which exit you need from the Périphérique (these are described as Portes, e.g. Porte Maillot, Porte de Vincennes).

Maps

For Paris and its immediate surroundings the following are recommended to supplement the Atlas section at the end of this Guide.

Michelin, **Plan de Paris** (No. 10, at 1:10,000), also available with street references as No. 12. Perhaps more convenient when walking, and containing métro and bus maps is their Paris Plan (No. 11). Nos 10, 11 and 12 show the position of underground car-parks and 24-hour petrol stations. Other maps published annually by Michelin are **Outskirts of Paris** (No. 101, at 1:50,000), **Environs of Paris** (No. 106, at 1:100,000), **Paris Region** (No. 237, at 1:200,000). The **suburbs of Paris** (with street indexes) are covered in nos 18, 20, 22 and 24. Map no. 9 concentrates entirely on forms of transport in Paris.

The **Institut Géographique National** (IGN) map of the **Environs de Paris** (No. 90, at 1:100,000) gives a good indication of contour and the general lie of the land. Paris is covered in detail in **Série Bleue** (No. 2314 est, and ouest, at 1:25,000); and the environs by **Série Verte** at 1:100,000, Maps Nos 8, 9, 20 and 21. The IGN map of **Région d'Ile de France: patrimoine artistique** at 1:150,000, will help to pin-point monuments; covering a more extensive area is No. 103 in their **Série Rouge** (Carte de l'Environnement Culturel et Touristique) at 1:250,000.

Travelling to or from Paris, Michelin's No. 236 is recommended, and also **France-Grandes Routes** (No. 989), or the IGN **France-Routes: autoroutes** (No. 901), both at 1:1,000,000. Also available are the Michelin **Motoring Atlas France** at 1:200,000, and their hardback **Road Altas France**. Collins publish a **Road Atlas France** at 1:250,000, based on IGN maps.

The latest editions of maps can be found in London at Stanfords, 12–14 Long Acre, London WC2E 9LP: ☎ 0171 836 1321, fax: 0171 836 0189; and at most good booksellers in the UK, USA or France.

The London offices of the Michelin Tyre plc are at Davy House, Lyon Road, Harrow, Middlesex, HA1 2DQ.

In Paris the offices of Pneu Michelin are at 46 Av. de Breteuil, south of Les Invalides. IGN's Paris address is 107 Rue La Boétie (the Champs-Elysées end of the street: Métro. Franklin Roosevelt).

Tourist Information in Paris

The **Office de Tourisme de Paris**, has its Head Office at 127 Av. des Champs-Elysées, 75008, ☎ 01 49 52 53 54, fax 01 49 52 53 00. It is open daily from 09.00–20.00 (Nov–March, Sun and public holidays, 11.00–18.00, closed 01/05). There are English-speaking staff who will answer queries concerning Paris and the environs, make hotel reservations for the same day, reservations for exhibitions, shows and concerts, tickets by sightseeing coaches or boats, brochures, currency exchange, etc. It sells for a small sum a number of useful booklets on museums and monuments, hotels, restaurants and annual events (*Calendreis des Manifestations*). You can also purchase a Paris Museum Pass here (see Museums, p 362).

There are subsidiary branches of the Tourist Office at the main stations, Gare du Nord, ☎ 01 45 26 94 82; Gare de l'Est, ☎ 01 46 07 17 73; Gare de Lyon, ☎ 01 43 43 33 24; and Gare Montparnasse, ☎ 01 43 22 19 19, all open May–Oct. 08.00–21.00, Mon–Sat, Nov–Apr 08.00–20.00. Gare d'Austerlitz, 08.00–15.00 Mon–Sat, ☎ 01 45 84 91 70; Tour Eiffel, May–Sep 11.00–18.00. ☎ 01 45 51 22 15; Mairie de Paris, 29 Rue de Rivoli, 70004, 09.00–18.00 Mon–Sat, closed public holidays, ☎ 01 42 76 43 43.

For information on the Ile-de-France as a whole, the Regional Tourist Bureau is in the Galerie du Carrousel du Louvre, 99 Rue de Rivoli, 754001. Tourist Bureau of Vieux Montmartre, 21 Pl. du Tertre, 75018, ☎ 01 42 62 21 21. Most towns in the environs of Paris have a Tourist Information Office.

Transport in Paris

Buses and the métro

Buses (*autobus*) and the underground railway (*métro*) in Paris are controlled by the RATP (Régie Autonome des Transports Parisiens), with offices at 53 bis Quai des Grands-Augustins (south of Pont Neuf) and Pl. de la Madeleine (east of the church) For all information on métro, bus and RER, call ☎ 08 36 68 41 14 (English), ☎ 08 36 68 77 14 (French). The RATP issues useful maps of the métro, bus and RER networks (see p 22), and a leaflet giving details of various summer excursions. The Michelin Map No. 9 (Paris Transports) is handy.

Travel Passes and Tickets. The RATP sell a 1-day travel pass, **Formula 1**, or 2, 3 or 5-day travel passes, **Paris-Visite**, at variable tariffs depending on the zone, which can be used for unlimited trips by métro, RER, bus, suburban SNCF trains, Montmartre Funicular, and the St-Denis/Bobigny tram. These can be purchased at the Paris Tourist Office at 127 Av. des Champs-Elysées, in the main métro, RER and SNCF stations, and at airports. In England they are on sale at Eurostar ticket desks at Waterloo and Ashford terminals, and at French Railways in London (179 Piccadilly). This is an economical and efficient system if you are going to use public transport frequently. (The *Paris Visite* card also entitles you to reductions for certain museums or monuments.)

Tickets, valid on both métro and buses, are sold in a book (*carnet*) of ten tickets at all stations. Tickets, which operate a turnstile, should be retained until the end of the journey as they may be checked or necessary to operate an an exit or interchange turnstile. The fare is the same for any distance on the main inner network, including all necessary changes, making long journeys reasonably inexpensive in comparison to the shorter distances covered. Visitors staying more than a few days and planning to use public transport frequently are advised to buy (at any métro station) a **Carte Orange**, for a week (*hebdomadaire*) or for a month (*mensuel*), for which you will need a passport-size photograph. You will be issued with an SNCF identification card, which you use to buy further weekly or monthly tickets. It is important to write the number of that card on your ticket.

The **Métro** (*Métropolitan*) provides a rapid means of transport throughout Paris from 05.30 to 00.30, and its modernisation continues. The most convenient métro stations are listed at the beginning of each route described in this Guide. Trains glide silently on rubber wheels through stations approx. 500m apart. Platforms at certain stations (e.g. Louvre, Hotel de Ville, Varenne) are decorated with reproductions of objects from nearby museums or sites. As in most large cities, avoid travelling alone late at night, and beware of bag-snatchers and pickpockets.

The first line of the métro was opened in 1900, and certain stations, notably the Bois de Boulogne entrance of Porte Dauphine, retain their Art Nouveau decoration. The various lines are called by the names of the terminal stations: e.g. Ligne 1, Château de Vincennes–Pont de Neuilly. The direction in which the train is running is indicated by a sign naming the terminal station. At interchange stations, the passages leading to the line concerned are clearly indicated by an orange-lighted sign marked *Correspondance*, followed by the name of the terminal stations of the connecting line. Certain correspondances necessitate a long walk.

RER (*Réseau Express Régional*) The fast overground lines of the RER have been extended.

Line A runs west to east across Paris, between St-Germain-en-Laye (**A1**), Poissy (**A5**), and Cergy-le-Haut (**A3**) to Boissy St-Léger (**A2**) and Marne-la Vallée/Chessy (Parc Disneyland) and is connected to the Métro at Etoile, Auber, Châtelet-Les Halles, Gare de Lyon and Nation.

Line B runs south-west through Châtelet-Les Halles and Denfert-Rochereau to Robinson (and Sceaux) (**B2**) and St-Rémy-lès-Chevreuse (**B4**) (link from Antony to Orly airport), and north from Châtelet-Les Halles via the Gare du Nord, to the airport of Roissy-Charles de Gaulle (**B3**), or Mitry-Claye (**B5**).

Line C, serves the western section, north through Porte Maillot to Montigny-Beauchamp (**C1**) and Argenteuil (**C3**), west following the Left Bank of the Seine through St-Michel Notre-Dame, to Versailles-Rive Gauche (**C5**), St-Quentin-en-Yvelines (**C7**) and Versailles Chantiers (**C8**), and south to Pont de Rungis-Orly (**C2**), Dourdan-la-Forêt (**C4**) and St-Martin d'Etampes (**C6**).

Line D through Châtelet-Les Halles north to Orry-la-Ville-Coye (**D1**) and south to Melun (**D2**) and Malesherbes (**D4**).

The métro ticket is valid on these lines within Central Paris but if travelling further afield a separate one must be bought at the interchange stations, which have elaborate automatic ticket machines.

Buses. This is the pleasantest means of travelling around Paris, and made relatively easy as bus routes are usually marked at bus-stops and inside the buses. All bus stops are request stops (*arrêt facultatif*), and each is indicated by its name on the stop itself. All forms of travel pass and ticket mentioned above (*métro, Formule 1, Paris Visite, Carte Orange*) will cover any journey on the Paris bus network. One métro ticket from a carnet is valid for any one journey by bus (without changes) which should be punched (*composté*) in the small machine at the front of the bus. However, if you have one of the multi-voyage tickets, you can jump on and off buses with abandon (but do not punch your pass). Owing to the large number of one-way streets, buses do not necessarily return along the same route, which can be confusing.

Daytime bus schedules run from around 07.00 to 20.30; some routes do not function on a Sunday; there is an evening service between 20.30 and 00.30; the **Balabus** takes you to the main tourist sites from April to September—bus stops marked Balabus (Bb). The **Monmatrobus** takes you on a round trip of Montmartre between the Mairie du 18C and Pigalle. **La Petite Ceinture** runs between the *Portes de Paris*, just inside the Blvd Périphérique. The **29 bus** (from Gare St-Lazare to Porte de Montempoivre, via the Marais) is a new version of the old buses with an open platform at the back.

Smoking is forbidden on both buses and the métro. The worst of the rush hour is between 08.00–09.00, and 17.30–19.30, and in some areas traffic is heavy between 12.00 and 14.00.

By car
Parking is severely restricted in central Paris and prohibited in many streets. Pay and display machines (*horodateurs*) dispense tickets either in exchange for coins or for cards purchased in *tabacs*. There are underground car-parks (e.g. Champs-Elysées, Place Vendôme, Louvre) but they are expensive. For information on street parking, ☎ 01 43 46 98 30. Michelin maps indicate car parks.

Badly-parked foreign cars are towed away as ruthlessly as native ones, and may take hours to recover from one of the eight *fourrières* or pounds, and at a considerable charge; there will also be a heavy fine to pay. Alternatively, a clamp or sabot may be attached to a wheel. In either case, the owner should apply to the nearest Police Station (Commissariat).

River trips on the Seine
Batobus is river transport between the main sights with five stopovers but no commentary (Eiffel Tower, Musée d'Orsay, Passerelle des Arts et Musée du Louvre, Notre-Dame and Hôtel-de-Ville), ☎ 01 44 11 33 44. There are several companies offering cruises with commentary, both during the day and after dark, April–September: **Les Bateaux-Mouches** from Pont de l'Alma, ☎ 01 42 25 96 10; **Bateaux Parisiens**, Quai Montebello (St Michel) ☎ 01 43 26 92 55, or **Eiffel Tower**, ☎ 01 44 11 33 44; **Vedettes de Paris**, Port de Suffren (Bir Hakeim) ☎ 01 47 05 71 29; and **Vedettes du Pont-Neuf**, Sq. du Vert-Galant, Ile de la Cité, ☎ 01 46 33 98 38.

Canal trips are a less well-known means of discovering Paris, on the Canal St-Martin between the Arsenal Dock (Bastille) and Parc de la Villette: **Canauxrama** (all year), runs from the Arsenal Port to the Park of La Villette, returning to the Bassin de la Villette, ☎ 01 42 39 15 00; **Paris Canal**, between Musée d'Orsay to La Villette, ☎ 01 42 40 96 97; **Ourcq Loisirs**, boat hire, ☎ 01 42 40 82 10.

Sightseeing by coach. The following companies run tours with commentaries: **Paris Vision**, 214 Rue de Rivoli, ☎ 01 42 60 30 01; **Cityrama**, 4 Pl. des Pyramides, ☎ 01 44 55 60 00; **Tas Voyages**, 7 Rue Jules Vernes, St Ouen, ☎ 01 40 12 88 08; **Parisbus**—les Cars Rouges, from the Eiffel Tower, tickets valid for two days, ☎ 01 42 30 55 50; **Paris Bus service** (minibus exclusively), 22 Rue de la Prévoyance, Vincennes, ☎ 01 43 65 55 55.

By taxi

Taxis, which are not excessively expensive, can be hailed from the street or found at a taxi rank. (Each taxi rank has a phone number.) There are also phone cabs. Three tariffs apply (A, B, C), displayed inside the vehicle, in Paris: A— 07.00–19.00, B—19.00–07.00, Sundays and public holidays; Immediate suburbs: B—07.00–19.00, C—19.00–07.00, Sundays and public holidays; outside suburban limits, tariff C. Taxi drivers expect a tip of 10 per cent in addition to the charge on the meter. There is an additional charge for luggage, pick up from railway termini, fouth adult passenger, large packages and pets.

Any complaints should be addressed to the Service des Taxis, Préfecture de Police, Service des Taxis, 36 Rue des Morillons, 75015 Paris, ☎ 01 55 76 20 00.

Food and Drink

Restaurants. Paris has a staggering 8000 or so eating establishments of every kind and category and eating is a serious pastime. Restaurants of all types are indicated with each chapter, summarily described (e.g., haute cuisine, traditional, bistrot or brasserie) to give some idea of the type of restaurant. The prices for a meal will vary from anything between an average of 800F per person à la carte to 400F set menu at the haute cuisine category restaurants, to 200F and 80F at the other end of the scale. £ (inexpensive), ££ (moderate), £££ (expensive) have been used to give some indication of price. All restaurants have to display menus and prices outside.

The set menu, *à prix fixe*, or *formule*, often with one or two choices, including the dish of the day (*plat du jour*), can be good value, particularly for lunch, when you may find a good three-course meal for as little as 60F or 70F. Take care, if on a budget, with à la carte, as an additional vegetable, for example, might bump the bill up considerably.

There are, of course, a number of specialised French gastronomic guides listing or recommending a great range of eating-places in Paris and elsewhere detailing the quality, price, type of food and setting. The Paris Tourist Office also publishes a booklet on Restaurants. Unfortunately it becomes harder to find the typical simple French bistrot, but it does still exist. The fashionable chefs in Paris—Jacques Cagna, Guy Savoy and Michel Rostang—all have their bistrots as well as their gastronomic restaurants. Many restaurants are closed on Sundays, and during August. It is advisable to book in advance at the better-known or more fashionable restaurants.

Restoration rapide/menu rapide is fast food, and there are several chains specialising in this; e.g. the French equivalent of MacDonalds is **Quick**. There are many chains of restaurants in operation, some classy, like the **Brasseries Flo**, and others which will give you a good, reasonable but standardised meal, such as the chain **Léon de Bruxelles** which specialises in mussels and chips, or the **Bistros Romain** with reasonably priced two-course menus, often including carpaccio *à volonté* (as much as you can eat) and expensive desserts; **Bar à Huitres** has seafood; **Batifol**, bistrot-type food; **La Dame Tartine**, open sandwiches and snacks; **Hippopotamus**, grills, open until 5 am, etc. Like everywhere else in Europe, pizzerias abound.

The Parisians have woken up to the fact that restaurants in galleries and museums or monuments are very welcome: the Louvre has quite a choice; the Musée d'Orsay has a couple; and there are a number at the Cité des Sciences et de l'Industrie (La Villette) and the Cité de la Musique. The Pompidou Centre, the Palais de Tokyo, the Grand Palais, the Musée de l'Armée, the Grand Galerie de l'Evolution, all have restaurants. There is a cafeteria in the garden of the Musée Rodin, a charming Salon de Thé in the Musée Jacquemart André, and in the Musée Maillol. Restaurants with views are found in the Eiffel Tower, the Institut Arabe, in the department store La Samaritaine (Le Toupary), and the Tower Montparnasse. In several of the public gardens of Paris there are restaurants, cafés or snack bars: for instance, in the Bois de Boulogne, the Bagatelle gardens, the Tuileries, the Parc des Buttes Chaumont, and so on. Look in the list accompanying each route for details.

Wines. *Rouge, blanc* or *rosé* wine, can vary from excellent to pretty rough. The mark-up on wine is very high, but in the more modest restaurants, house wine is still served in a *pichet* or *carafe* (*litre, demi* or *quart*) for a very reasonable price. Always check your bill (*l'addition*). A service charge of 15% will be added, but it is up to you whether you leave an additional tip.

The **Cafés** of Paris are legion and always popular, especially when it is fine enough to sit outside on the pavement (or *terrasse*). Take heed, prices are usually higher on the terrace than sitting down inside, and it is cheaper still to stand at the bar for your coffee or drink. A glass of ordinary wine (*un petit blanc/un petit rouge*) or a beer in a standard café may be cheaper than a coffee, a sparkling water or a coca cola. A small draught beer is a *un demi pression*.

Cyber Cafés are among the 'in places' to be seen—such as **UGC World Net Café** in the Forum des Halles, Pl. Carrée, **Web Bar**, 32 Rue de Picardie, 75003, or **Bistrot Internet** in Galeries Lafayette (1st floor of the Galfa Club).

If you simply order *un café* you will get an expresso. A *café crème/café au lait* is with hot milk and usually large and drunk at breakfast. Some cafés (but not all) serve *un petit crème*. If you would prefer coffee with cold milk, ask for *un (grand/petit) café avec un peu de lait froid*. Tea is usually served as a tea bag with separate hot water, and with milk (*thé au lait*), lemon (*thé citron*) or plain (*thé nature*). Chocolate (*chocolat chaud*) is a popular drink, especially in the morning.

A Continental breakfast (*petit déjeuner*) is served in the mornings at many cafés and will consist of fresh baguette or rolls and/or croissants, brioches etc., with a choice of coffee, tea or chocolate. The breakfasts in hotels are improving, and the more expensive hotels often serve a buffet breakfast.

Sample Menu

Many French culinary terms and processes are universally known, but to assist those not so well acquainted with some of the more common foods, there follows a list with English equivalents.

Les Potages ~ Soups

Bouillon, broth
Consommé, clear soup
Crème, thick soup

Hors-d'oeuvre and Salads

Crudités, raw vegetables, usually sliced, chopped, or grated
Tapénade, a purée of black olives, capers, anchovies, tuna fish, etc., from the provençal tapéno, for capers
Salade Niçoise, with tomato, anchovy, onions and olives Salade Cauchoise, of potatoes, celery and ham
Salade panachée, mixed salad
Salade verte, green salad; also Salade simple, or *de saison*
Salade de riz aux tomates, rice and tomato salad
Salade Lyonnaise consists of a variety of meats, seasoned and with an oil, vinegar, shallot and parsley dressing, and served on separate dishes.

Les Oeufs ~ eggs (including some hot hors d'oeuvre)

à la coque, soft-boiled; *mollets*, medium-boiled; *durs*, hard-boiled; *sur le plat*, or *au plat*, fried; *pochés*, poached; *en cocotte*, baked in a ramekin; *brouillés*, scrambled
Omelette aux fines herbes, savoury omelette; *au jambon*, ham omelette, etc., and an infinite variety of others
oeufs durs soubise, hard-boiled eggs with an onion and cream sauce
Pissaladière, provençal onion and anchovy pie Gratin Dauphinois, sliced potatoes cooked in cream
Gratin savoyard, similar, but with the addition of eggs and cheese

Les poissons, les coquillages et crustacés (or fruits de mer) ~ fish and shellfish

cuisses de grenouilles, frogs' legs
escargots, snails
alose, shad
anchois, anchovies
anguille, eel
bar, bass
barbou, brill
baudroi, angler fish
bellon, a type of oyster
blanchaille, whitebait, a dish of which is friture, deep fried
brochet, pike, often the base of quenelles Calmars, inkfish
carpe, carp
chipirones, squid

colin, hake
coquilles St.-Jacques, scallops
crevettes, prawns or shrimps
daurade, sea bream
ecrevisse, fresh-water crayfish
encornet, squid
eperlans, smelts
espadon, swordfish
harengs, herrings
homard, lobster Huîtres, oysters
lamproie, lamprey
langouste, crawfish or lobster
langoustine, Dublin Bay prawn
lotte, burbot, monkfish
loup, a kind of sea bass

maquereau, mackerel
merlan, whiting
mérou, brill
morue, salt cod (see brandade, below);
fresh cod is *cabillaud*
moules, mussels
mulet, grey mullet
palourdes, clams; also *praires*
poulpe, octopus
raie, skate (often served '*au beurre noir*', with black butter)

rouget, red mullet
St-Pierre, John Dory
saumon, salmon; *fumé*, smoked
thon, tuna
truite, trout
aïoli, a mayonnaise of vinegar, oil and pulverised garlic, often eaten with fish
quenelles, fish (often pike) or meat dumpling roll, served in a sauce

Les viandes ~ meat

agneau, lamb; *gigot*, leg of lamb; *carré d'agneau*, cutlets
boeuf, beef; *queue de boeuf*, ox-tail; *rosbif*, roast beef; (bifteck is a franglais word which has been in use since 1786)
cochon de lait, sucking-pig
mouton, mutton
porc, pork; see below
veau, veal; *ris de veau*, sweetbreads
viandes froides, cold meats
    Meat may be ordered *bleu*, very rare; *saignant*, underdone; *à point*, medium; or *bien cuit*, well done
daube, a stew; other forms are *pot-au-feu* and *marmite*
cassoulet, a stew of mutton, pickled pork, sausages and possibly goose, and haricot beans, originating in Castelnaudary
    Some general terms are:
basquaise, with tomato and pimento
bercy, with wine and shallots
Bourguignonne, cooked in red wine, with bacon, mushrooms and small onions
cauchoise, with cream, calvados and apples
chasseur or *forestière*, with mushrooms Lyonnaise, with onions
à la meunière, cooked slowly in butter
à la nivernaise, with a glazed carrot and onion garnish Normande and cream sauce
parmentier, with potatoes Périgourdine, with truffles and/or foie gras
Provençale, with oil, tomatoes and garlic

La charcuterie ~ pork products and cooked meats

andouille, smoked chitterling sausage; andouillettes, a smaller version
boudin, black pudding (or white if pork-based)
boudin blanc, chicken mousse
cervelles, brains
foie, liver
jambon, ham; *jambon cuit*, York ham; *fumé* or *cru*, smoked; *de Bayonne*, salt-cured
pieds de porc, pigs' trotters
rillettes, potted shredded pork; in *rillons* the pieces of pork are larger
rognons, kidneys
saucisses, sausages; *saucisson*, salami sausage
terrines, potted meats

Les volailles et *le gibier* ~ poultry and game

alouettes, larks
bécasse, woodcock
caille, quail
canard, duck
canard sauvage, wild duck
caneton, duckling (those of Duclair and Nantes are reputed)
cerf or *chevreuil*, venison
dinde or *dindon*, female and male turkey
faisan, pheasant
grives, thrushes

lapin, rabbit
lièvre, hare
oie, goose; *paté de foie gras* is made from goose liver; a *confit d'oie* is a conserve of goose preserved in its own fat
palombes, wood-pigeons
perdreau or *perdrix*, partridge
pintade, guinea-fowl
poulet, chicken; *poularde*, capon
sanglier, wild boar; *marcassin*, a young wild boar
sarcelle, teal

Les légumes et aromates ~ vegetables and herbs

ail, garlic; *aïoli*, a mayonnaise of pulverised garlic, vinegar, oil, etc.
artichauts, globe or leaf artichokes; *fonds*, hearts; *Topinambours*, Jerusalem artichokes
asperges, asparagus
betterave, beetroot
blettes, chard
céleris, celery
carottes, carrots
céleri-rave, celeriac; *céleri-rave rémoulade*, in mustard sauce
cerfeuil, chervil
champignons, cultivated mushrooms. Other common edible fungi are *cèpes* (boletus edulis), *chantarelles* or *girolles*, and *morilles chicorée*, Belgian endive (or *witloof*); *chicorée frisée* or *scarole*, curly chicory
chou, cabbage; *chou rouge*, red cabbage; *choux de Bruxelles*, Brussels sprouts
choucroute, sauerkraut
choufleur, cauliflower
ciboulettes, chives
concombre, cucumber
cornichon, gherkin
courge, marrow
cresson, watercress

echalotes, shallots
epinards, spinach
estragon, tarragon
fenouil, fennel
fèves, broad beans
genièvre, baies de, juniper berries
haricots blancs, white haricot beans; *haricots verts*, French beans; *flageolets*, green beans
huile d'olive, olive oil; *huile de noix*, walnut oil
laitue, lettuce; *salade*, green salad
lentilles, lentils
miche, lamb's-lettuce or corn-salad
navets, turnips
oignons, onions
oseille, sorrel
persil, parsley
petits pois, green peas
pissenlits, dandelions
poireaux, leeks
pois chiches, chick peas
poivre, pepper
poivrons, sweet peppers (pimentos)
pommes de terre, potatoes
raifort, horseradish
riz, rice
romarin, rosemary

Les fromages ~ cheeses

There are numerous regional varieties and all are made from cow's milk unless marked *e* for ewe (*brebis*) or *g* for goat (*chèvre*). Only some of the more usual types are listed.

Normandy: Bondon, Camembert, Livarot, Pont-l'Evêque, Boursin.
Northern France and Ile-de-France: Mimolette, St.-Paulin, Brie, Coulommiers.
Brittany: Port-du-Salut.
Touraine and Poitou: St-Paulin, Chabicou (*g*), Ste-Maure (*g*).
Berry and Burgundy: Valençay (*g*), St-Florentin and Epoisse.
The Pyrenean region produces several, mostly cow, but also ewe-cheeses.
The Causses in the south west produce the renowned Roquefort (*e*) and Pelardon des Cévennes (*g*).
The Auvergne is noted for the Bleu-d'Auvergne, Cantal, St-Nectaire and Fourme-d'Ambert.
Alsace and Lorraine: Carré-de-l'Est, Munster and Rocollet.
The Franche-Comté produces the Comté, and further south, the Bleu-de-Bresse.
Savoy is noted for Beaufort, Emmental, Reblochon and Tomme); in the Lyonnais. and Dauphiny, the Rigotte-de-Condrieu; the Picodon and St-Marcellin (both *g*) are reputed; and in Provence, the Banon (*g*).
There are also many varieties of cream cheeses, such as the Petit-Suisse, and numerous processed forms, some encrusted with grape-pips, or walnuts, or dusted with pepper, etc.
The Fondue Savoyarde consists of melted cheese (often the Vacherin), wine and kirsch, kept at a sizzling temperature, into which cubes of bread are dipped.

Note that cheese is always eaten before the dessert in France.

Les desserts

abricots, apricots
ananas, pineapples
bananes, bananas
cannelle, cinnamon
cassis, blackcurrant
cerises, cherries
citron, lemon
coings, quinces
figues, figs
fraises, strawberries; *fraises des bois*, wild strawberries
framboises, raspberries
fruits confits, crystallised fruit
fruits en compote, stewed
groseilles, red or white currants
groseilles à Maquereau, gooseberries
marrons, chestnuts; *marrons glacés*, candied chestnuts
mendiant, a plate of mixed almonds, raisins, etc.
miel, honey
mûres, mulberries

mûres de ronce, blackberries
myrtilles, bilberries
noisettes, hazel-nuts
noix, walnuts
pamplemousse, grapefruit
pêches, peaches
poires, pears
pommes, apples
pruneaux, prunes
prunes, plums; *mirabelles*, small yellow plums
reine-claudes, greengages
raisins, grapes; *raisin sec*, raisin
sucre, sugar
crème brulée, caramelised cream
crémets, a confection of thick cream and egg yolks
flan, cream caramel
glaces, ice-creams
pâte d'amande, almond paste or marzipan; *pâte des prunes*, plum paste; *pâte de coings*, quince paste

Patisseries et confiseries ~ **pastries, cakes and confectionery**
berlingots, pyramid-shaped sweets
confiture, jam; *confiture d'orange*, marmalade
crêpes dentelles, pancakes
dragées, sugared almonds
en brioche, baked in dough
galettes, a biscuit
gâteaux secs, biscuits
gaufres, waffles
macarons, almond paste macaroons
nougatines, caramelised ground almonds
pain d'epices, spiced honey-cake or gingerbread
petits fours, fancy biscuits
pain, bread, is usually bought at *boulangeries*; there are numerous forms and varieties, the most common perhaps being the *baguette*, a long roll of medium thickness, also thinner, known as a *ficelle*; the *épi* is of more irregular shape; there is also the larger *pain campagne*.

Embassies and Consulates
French Embassy, 58 Knightsbridge, London SW1X 7JT, ☎ 0171 201 1000. French Consulate, 21 Cromwell Road, London SW7, ☎ 0171 838 2000; Visa Dept 6a Cromwell Place, ☎ 0891 88 77 33/0171 838 2050; French Chamber of Commerce, 197 Knightsbridge, ☎ 0171 304 4040.

British Embassy, 35 Rue du Faubourg St-Honoré, 75008 (☎ 01 44 51 31 00); British Consulate, 16 Rue d'Anjou (Visa Office), (near the Embassy) ☎ 01 44 51 31 00; visas: ☎ 01 44 51 33 01/01 44 51 33 03; passports: ☎ 01 40 39 80 64; resident permits: ☎ 01 40 39 80 65. The Chamber of Commerce, 8 Rue Cimarosa, 75016; British Council, 9 Rue De Constantine, 75007.

US Embassy, 2 Av. Gabriel, 75008 (just north of the Pl. de la Concorde), ☎ 01 43 12 22 22; Canadian Embassy, 35 Av. Montaigne, 75008, ☎ 01 44 43 29 00; Australian Embassy, 4 Rue Jean Rey, 75015, ☎ 01 40 59 33 00; New Zealand Embassy, 7ter Rue Léonard-de-Vinci, 75016, ☎ 01 45 00 24 11; Irish Consultate, 4 Rue Rude, 75016, ☎ 01 45 00 20 87.

Money and banks
The monetary unit is the **franc**, subdivided into 100 **centimes**. Bank notes of 20, 50, 100, 200 and 500 francs are in circulation, and there are also coins of 5, 10, 20 and 50 centimes, 1, 2, 5, 10 and 20 francs.

Branches of most French **banks** are open from 09.00 to 17.00 Monday to Friday; most branches close on Saturday morning. Not all banks have a foreign exchange service, but if they do, central branches of the principal banks may have a bureau de change open from 09.00 to 12.00. Most banks shut at noon on days preceding public holidays as well as on the holiday. **Bureaux de change**: at the main train stations (Gares du Nord, de Lyon, de l'Est, de Montparnasse, St-Lazare, Austerlitz), are open daily from about 06.30 to 22.00 or 23.00. Those at the international airports operate a daily service from 06.00 to 23.00.

Larger hotels will also accept and exchange travellers' cheques, but usually at a lower rate of exchange than banks or bureaux de change. It useful to have enough French currency for incidental expenses on arrival, particularly during a weekend. It is worth shopping around for different rates of exchange and some bureaux de change do not charge commission. Most credit cards are generally accepted and cash may be obtained from cash dispensing machines bearing the Carte Bleue/Visa or Mastercard logo, the Eurocard symbol and from American Express machines. However, it is recommended that dispensing machines are only used when the banks are closed or in an emergency, as the machines have a tendency to swallow cards at the slightest provocation. Some main Post Offices have change facilities.

Currency Regulations. There is no restriction on the amount of sterling you can take out of Great Britain. At present, you can take up to 50,000 francs out of France without declaring it. Visitors from outside the EU can claim back VAT (about 14%) (TVA) on certain articles worth more than 1200 francs (enquire at the shop) but need to acquire a *Bordereau de vente* form which has to be stamped by Customs on the way out of France.

Insurance
As members of the EU, British subjects are entitled to French health services but must have a form E111 (available from DHSS offices and post offices) as this is necessary for any refund you will apply for in France. Note that it is essential to have the form signed by the doctor and keep prescriptions and all receipts for consultations, treatments and medicines. The average refund of medical expenses is about 70 per cent. You are also strongly advised to take out private insurance (available from travel agents and banks) which will not only cover the cost of any medical expenses but also loss of luggage, cash and other valuables.

Emergencies
In an emergency, ☎ 17 for the police, and ☎ 15 for SAMU (*Service Aide Médicale d'Urgence*). Other emergency services are: medical ☎ 01 47 07 77 77; dental ☎ 01 43 37 51 00; anti-poison centre ☎ 01 40 37 04 04; children's burn unit, ☎ 01 44 73 62 54; adult burn centre, ☎ 01 42 34 17 58; public ambulance service ☎ 01 43 78 26 26.

Late-night chemists. Pharmacie St-Germain, 149 Blvd St-Germain, open until 01.00, métro: St-Germain-des-Prés; Pharmacie Dhéry, 84 Av. des Champs-Elysées, 24 hours, métro: George V; Drugstore Champs-Elysées, 133 Av. des Champs-Elysées, to 02.00, métro: Charles-de-Gaulle Etoile; Pharmacie Azoulay, 5 Pl. Pigalle, 75009, to 00.30, métro: Pigalle; Pharmacie Opéra, 6 Blvd des Capucines, to midnight, métro: Opéra; Pharmacie des Arts, 106 Blvd du Montparnasse, to midnight, métro: Vavin; Pharmacie Mozart, 14 Av. Mozart, 75016, to 22.00 weekdays, métro: La Muette.

Medical Services
Hospitals. Hospitals with English-speaking staff: the Franco-British Hospital, 3 Rue Barbès, 92300-Levallois-Perret, north west of the Porte de Champerret ☎ 01 46 39 22 22 (métro: Anatole France); and the American Hospital in Neuilly ☎ 63 Blvd Victor-Hugo, 92202-Neuilly ☎ 01 46 41 25 25.

Disabled travellers

Anyone with a mobility problem will find *Access in Paris* by Gordon Couch and Ben Roberts (Quiller Press) useful (published in 1993). This booklet is available from bookshops or from RADAR, 12 City Forum, 250 City Road, London EC1 V8AF, ☎ 0171 250 3222. RADAR can also give helpful advice on all aspects of travel. The Paris Tourist Office has an excellent free pamphlet, *Touristes Quand Même* (but only in French); it also sells *Paris-Ile de France pour tous*.

Personal Security

As in any large city, do not leave objects of any value inside parked cars and beware of bag-snatchers and pickpockets in various guises, who are particularly common in the most touristy areas. Note that any parcels or luggage left about and apparently abandoned may be destroyed by the authorities. Most hotels have a safe-deposit system; sometimes there is a charge for this service, but it worth the peace of mind.

You should carry official identification with you at all times (i.e. a passport or identity card). It hardly needs to be added that it is wise to leave a note of your passport details in a safe place. Identification is also necessary for changing travellers' cheques.

Lost or Stolen Property

If identity papers are mislaid, in whatever circumstances, make a declaration at the nearest police station as a receipt will be needed for any further steps. Likewise for the loss of articles of value, a receipt will be needed for insurance claims. Lost or stolen credit cards should be reported to: Carte bleue, ☎ 01 42 77 11 90; Diner's Club, ☎ 01 47 62 75 00; American Express: ☎ 01 47 77 72 00; American Express Travellers Cheques: ☎ 05 90 86 00.

Articles lost on the métro or in buses are held for claiming for the first 48 hrs at the terminus of the route concerned. Property lost on trains, at stations, on planes and at airports should be reclaimed at the lost property office of the terminus or airport in question.

When items have been lost in the street, theatres or cinemas, etc., enquire at the Bureau des Objets Perdus, Préfecture de Police, 36 Rue des Morillons, 75015 (open Mon, Wed, Fri 08.30–17.00. Tues and Thurs 08.30–20.00); métro Convention ☎ 01 55 76 20 00.

Working hours

In France, small shops (e.g. *tabacs, boulangeries*) open earlier than in the UK (although most offices do not). Parisian cafés are open for a quick espresso on the way to work, and lunch is often at 12 noon (although less so in Paris than in the French provinces), whereas dinner is eaten late. Most food shops are open on Sunday mornings, and remain open until 18.00 or 19.00 on weekday evenings; but they are likely to be shut on Mondays.

Public Holidays ~ *jours feriés*

1 January (*Jour de l'An*); Easter Monday; Whit Monday (*Pentecôte*); Ascension Day; 1 May (with Lily-of-the-Valley sold in the streets) Labour Day (*Fête de Travail*); 8 May (commemorating the end of World War Two in Europe); 14 July

(*Fête Nationale*; Bastille Day); 15 August Assumption; 1 November (*Toussaint*; All Saints' Day); 11 November (Armistice Day); and 25 December (*Noël*; Christmas).

Language

Increasingly many Parisians speak English and are often only too pleased to get some practice, but an effort to speak French is usually appreciated.

Hello/good day *bonjour*
Goodbye *au revoir*
See you later *à plus tard/à tout à l'heure*
Good morning/afternoon *Bonjour*
Good evening *Bon soir*
Good night (on retiring) *Bonne nuit*
Yes/no *oui/non*
OK/all right *OK/d'accord/ça va*
please *s'il vous plaît/s'il te plaît*
thank you (very much) *merci (beaucoup)*
today *aujourd'hui*
tomorrow *demain*
yesterday *hier*
now *maintenant*
later *plus tard*
in the morning *dans la matinée*
in the afternoon/evening *dans l'après midi/au soir*
at night *dans la nuit*
cold/hot *froid/chaud*
with/without *avec/sans*
open/closed *ouvert/fermé*
cheap/expensive *bon marché/cher*
left/right/straight on *à gauche/à droite/tout droit*
railway station *la gare*
bus station *la gare d'autobus/la gare routière*
airport *un aéroport*
ticket *le billet*
police station *le commissariat de police/la gendarmerie*
hospital *un hôpital*
doctor *le medecin*
dentist *le dentiste*
aspirin *une aspirine*
What is your name? *Quel est votre nom/quel est ton nom. Comment vous appellez-vous?/Comment t'appelles-tu?*

My name is ... *Mon nom est .../Je m'appelle...*
I would like ... *Je voudrais.../J'aimerais...*
Do you have ... *Avez vous..?/Est-ce-que vous avez..?*
Do you speak English? *Parlez-vous anglais?/Parles-tu anglais?*
I don't understand *Je ne comprends pas*
Where are the toilets? *Où se trouvent les toilettes?*
Where is...? *Où est...?/Où se trouve...?*
What time is it? *Quelle heure est-il?*
At what time? *à quelle heure?*
How much is it? *ça coûte combien?/c'est combien?*
the bill *l'addition/la note*

Monday *lundi*
Tuesday *mardi*
Wednesday *mercredi*
Thursday *jeudi*
Friday *vendredi*
Saturday *samedi*
Sunday *dimanche*
January *janvier*
February *février*
March *mars*
April *avril*
May *mai*
June *juin*
July *juillet*
August *août*
September *septembre*
October *octobre*
November *novembre*
December *décembre*
spring *le printemps*
summer *l'été*
autumn *l'automne*
winter *l'hiver*

1 *un* 2 *deux* 3 *trois* 4 *quatre*
5 *cinq* 6 *seize* 7 *sept* 8 *huit*
9 *neuf* 10 *dix* 11 *onze* 12 *douze*
13 *treize* 14 *quatorze* 15 *quinze*
16 *seize* 17 *dix-sept* 18 *dix-huit*

19 *dix-neuf* 20 *vingt* 30 *trente*
40 *quarante* 50 *cinquante*
60 *soixante* 70 *soixante-dix*
80 *quatre-vingt* 90 *quatre-vingt-dix*
100 *cent*

Manners

The French, especially the older generation, may still be quite formal by Anglo-Saxon standards, and handshaking is still generally practised at meeting and parting. It is safer to use the *vous* form of address with people you do not know although the French *tu-toi* each other more readily than they used to. It is also polite to use *Monsieur, Madame* or *Mademoiselle* as a form of address (without the surname, which is fortunate when you have forgotten a name) even after some acquaintance. While, overall, manners are becoming more relaxed, courtesy to foreign visitors, especially in museums, seems to have greatly improved.

Post Offices

Post Offices, indicated by the sign **PTT**, are open from 08.00 to 19.00 on weekdays, and until 12.00 on Saturdays. The main post office in Paris is at the Hôtel des Postes, 52 Rue du Louvre, 75001, which operates a 24-hour 7-day service. The post office at 71 Av. des Champs-Elysées, 75008, is open from 08.00 until 22.00 Mon–Sat, and 10.00–12.00, 14.00–20.00 Sun. Postal enquiries, 08.00–19.00 weekdays and to 12.00 Saturday, ☎ 05 05 02 02. Postage-stamps (*timbres*) are on sale at all post offices and tobacconists (*tabacs*). **Letter-boxes** are painted yellow.

The main post office is the destination of letter marked '*Poste Restante, Paris*' without an arrondissement number. With an arrondissement number, it will go to the main post office in the appropriate district. Take identification (passport) to claim such mail, and a fee will be charged. Registered (*recommandé*) mail will only be delivered with proof of identity.

Telephone telegrams in English may be telephoned to ☎ 05 33 44 11. There are telex offices at 7 Rue Feydeau and 9 Pl. de la Bourse, both 75002; many post offices now have fax machines.

Telephones

Public call-boxes can be found at most post offices, métro stations, cafés, restaurants and at some bus stops (taxiphones). The majority of booths take only *Télécarte* (50 or 120 units), which you can buy at post offices, France Telecom agencies, tobacconists and railway stations. Reversed-charge calls (PVC) are accepted. Note that the charge for calls made from hotels may be as much as 40 per cent higher than for those made from public telephone boxes.

When calling abroad, dial 00 (international) followed by the country code. Since 18 October 1996 all French phone numbers are 9 digits, prefixed by 0 when calling inside France. Paris is prefixed by 01. Phone calls are less expensive in the evenings and at weekends.

Telephone rates within France: at present the full tariff applies from 08.00–12.30, 13.30–18.00 on week days, and until 12.30 on Saturday. It is less expensive between 12.30–13.30 and 18.00–21.30 Monday–Friday and between 12.30–13.30 on Saturday; there are further reductions between

06.00–08.00 and 21.30–22.30 Monday–Friday, 06.00–08.00 and 13.30–22.30 on Saturday and 06.00–23.00 on Sunday; the cheapest rate of all applies between 22.30–06.00 daily (or rather, nightly). Reduced rates to the UK and Northern Ireland apply between 21.30 and 08.00 Monday–Friday, from14.00 Saturday and all day Sunday and public holidays. To the US and Canada, the most economical rate is from 02.00–12.00 Monday–Friday; the next cheapest rate is 12.00–14.00 and 20.00–02.00 Monday–Saturday, and from 12.00–14.00 on Sunday and public holidays.

For directory information in France, ☎ 12; for international information ☎ 00 33 12 plus country code; for the operator ☎ 13; telecom services (complaints etc.) ☎ 14; SAMU (ambulance) ☎ 15; police ☎ 17; fire ☎ 18. Minitel, an information service linked to the phone, is available in most post offices: for telephone directory information, ☎ 36 11 (in English, ☎ 36 14); telex, telefax, fax directory: ☎ 36 16 SCRIP; follow-up and reception of telexes: ☎ 36 17 MONTELEX.

Directories. Almost any address can be found in *Le Bottin* (the Annuaire-Almanach du Commerce et de l'Industrie Didot-Bottin), which may be consulted at post offices, hotels, restaurants, shops, etc.

Entertainment

For up-to-date information on theatres, cinemas, cabarets, night clubs, cultural events, sporting events, fairs, exhibitions and shows, consult the Tourist Office publications: *Paris Saisons* for annual events, and *Paris Selection* for monthly events. Weekly information can be found in *Pariscope* or *l'Officiel des Spectacles* on sales at news-stands.

Theatre/Opera/Ballet. The national, or state-subsidised, theatres are the Comédie-Française, Pl. André-Malraux, 75001 (☎ 01 40 15 00 15); the Théâtre de l'Odéon), Pl. Paul-Claudel, 75006 (☎ 01 44 41 36 36); Théâtre National Populaire (TNP), Palais de Chaillot, 75016 (☎ 01 47 27 81 15); Théâtre National de la Colline, 17 Rue Malte-Brun, 75020 (☎ 01 44 62 52 52); Théâtre de la Ville, Pl. du Châtelet, 75004 (☎ 01 42 74 22 77), theatre, dance, variety; Théâtre du Châtelet, 75004 (☎ 01 40 28 28 40) concerts, opera, variety; Opéra National de Paris, Palais Garnier, 75009 (☎ 01 40 01 17 89, dance, opera, cinema; Opéra National de Paris Bastille, 75012 (☎ 01 44 73 13 00); Opéra-Comique, Salle Favart, Pl. Boïeldieu, 75002 (☎ 01 44 73 13 00).

Some theatres close for some weeks in the summer and on one evening a week, usually Monday or Tuesday. Smoking is forbidden. Note that tickets bought through an agency will cost as much as 25 per cent more than at the box-office of the theatre concerned, usually open between 11.00 and 18.30 or 19.00.

Concerts take place at the Salle Pleyel, 252 Rue du Fb. St-Honoré, 75008 (☎ 01 45 61 53 00); Théâtre des Champs-Elysées, 15 Av. Montaigne 75008 (☎ 01 49 52 50 50); Théâtre du Châtelet (see above); Salle Gaveau, 45 Rue La Boétie, 75008 (☎ 01 49 53 05 07); the Maison de l'ORTF (or de la Radio), 116 Av. du Président-Kennedy, 75016 (☎ 01 42 30 22 22) Cité de la Musique, 221 Av. Jean Jaurès, 75019 (☎ 01 44 84 44 84), and elsewhere. For information on free concerts in the city's garden (May–September), contact the Tourist Office, the Mairie Information Office, or ☎ 01 40 71 76 47.

Cafés-Théâtres/Chansonniers, for informal revues or pithy political satire, for which a fairly thorough knowledge of the language and latest *argot* is needed, still exist, one of the most famous being Au Lapin Agile in Montmartre.

Cabarets/Dinner shows, for which Paris is famous, vary from 'artistically exotic or erotic' to grossly vulgar. Among the more up-market establishments of long-standing are Crazy Horse Saloon, 12 Av. George V, 75008 (☎ 01 47 23 32 32); Lido, 116bis Av. des Champs-Elysées, 75008 (☎ 01 40 76 56 10); Folies Bergère, 32 Rue Richer, 75009 (☎ 01 44 79 98 98), Moulin Rouge, 82 Blvd de Clichy, 75018 (☎ 01 46 06 0 19), etc.

Cinemas abound (the French are great cinema goers), and Paris claims nearly 350 screens, showing films of all kinds. Programmes normally change on Wednesdays. Prices charged in the better-known cinemas can be high but the seats are very comfortable. Many cinemas show films in VO (*vérsion originale*), i.e. foreign-language films which are not dubbed.

Church music and organ recitals are frequently held at such churches as Notre-Dame, St-Eustache, St-Germain-des-Prés, St-Louis des Invalides, St-Séverin, St-Sulpice, St-Roch, St-Clotilde, St-Étienne-du-Mont and the Madeleine, and special concerts are usually well advertised.

Art exhibitions. Although smaller shows devoted to individual artists can be seen at any number of galleries and art-dealers' shops, many of them in the 6e arrondissement, the more important temporary exhibitions are held in the Grand Palais, Petit-Palais, Musée d'Orsay, Palais de Tokyo, Musée des Arts Décoratifs, Centre National d'Art et de Culture Georges Pompidou, and most art galleries.

Sports. General information about a variety of sporting events, sporting facilities, addresses of tennis-clubs, squash-courts, golf-courses, swimming-pools, etc. in Paris and environs, may be obtained from the Office de Tourisme de Paris, 127 Av. des Champs-Elysées, and its branches, and from the Direction de la Jeunesse et des Sports, 17 Blvd Morland, 75004. They can also advise on the capacities of the French sporting federations to assist the visitor; however, you are recommended to apply well in advance to the offices of your own home club or sporting organisation which may well be able to give more practical information.

Shopping and markets
The really smart shops and designer boutiques are in the 1er, 6e, 8e and 16e arrondissements, particularly around Rue du Faubourg-St-Honoré. But in fact every district of central Paris has good and less pricey shops. The best known department stores are: *Les Galeries Lafayette* and *Au Printemps*, at 40 and 69 Blvd Haussmann respectively (métro: Havre Caumartin, Chaussée d'Antin); *Samaritaine* (métro: Louvre, Châtelet, Les Halles); and popular with Parisians are the two Marks & Spencer stores (Rue de Rivoli, métro: Châtelet), and Blvd

Haussmann (métro: Havre Caumartin). The *Carrousel du Louvre*, 99 Rue de Rivoli (closed Tuesdays), is a fashionable covered shopping centre.

The main, and expensive, antique centre is *Le Louvre des Antiquaries*, Pl. du Palais Royal, 75001. Many antique shops and *brocanteurs* (second-hand dealers) are in the 6e; the so-called *Village Suisse* (shut Tuesday–Wednesday); west of the Ecole Militaire (métro: La Motte Piquet), Village Saint-Paul (métro: St-Paul) and *Carré Rive Gauche* (métro: Rue du Bac). The extensive and best known *Marché aux Puces* (open Saturday–Monday), a few minutes' walk north of the Porte de Clignancourt métro), sometimes produces bargains among the bric-à-brac.

A Paris kiosk

Auctions are held regularly at the rebuilt *Salle Drouot*, 6 Rue Rossini, 75009. Nearby, in the Rue Drouot and further south in the arcades of the Palais-Royal, are the haunts of philatelists; while an open-air stamp market is held Thursday–Sunday, at Av. Matignon, Rond-Point des Champs-Elysées.

Art and craft work is found at the *Viaduc des Arts*, 9–129 Av. Daumesnil, not far from the Bastille.

Colourful **markets** devoted to flowers are held in the Pl. Louis-Lépine (not far east of the Conciergerie), on the east side of the Madeleine, at the Pl. des Ternes, and Pl. de la République. On Sundays the flowers of the Pl. Louis-Lépine give way to a bird market, while opposite, on the Quai de la Mégisserie, is a pet market.

On the north side of the Pl. de la Madeleine are some superb **food shops**, but one of the delights of Paris is the high quality fromageries, pâtisseries, choco-latiers and charcuteries all over the city, with mouth watering displays of merchandise.

Outdoor markets not too far from the centre are at Rue de Montorgueil (leading north from Les Halles métro); the Rue Mouffetard, 75005; Rue des Martyrs, 75009; Rue de Lévis (north east of the Parc de Monceau); Rue Cler, 75007; and Rue de Buci (just north of the Odéon métro); Av. Président Wilson; Place Monge, Rue Daguerre (Denfert-Rochereau), and many others. There are often lively neighbourhood food markets on a Sunday morning.

Covered arcades, built at the end of the 18C or in the 19C, seem to have come back into fashion, among them: Passage des Pavillons, 6 Rue du Beaujolais, 75001 (métro: Pyramides); Galerie Véro-Dodat (1826), 75001 (métro: Palais-Royal); Passage du Caire (1798), 75002, (métro: Sentier).

If you are determined to shop 'til you drop, try a Paris shopping tour, with fashion brands at low prices (☎ 01 42 94 13 87, or Shopping Plus, by shopping theme (☎ 01 47 53 91 17).

Bookshops

Bookshops continue to proliferate throughout central Paris, but differ widely in the range of books stocked, and in the quality of their service. English newspapers and magazines can be found at a price at many kiosks near the centre. A selection of books in English is provided by Brentano (37 Av. de l'Opéra),

Galignani (224 Rue de Rivoli: near the Tuileries métro) and W.H. Smith (248 Rue de Rivoli), among others.

Gardens

There are guided visits to the Gardens of Paris, either thematic (e.g. historic gardens, modern gardens, cemeteries, etc.), and a half-day coach tour of the gardens. For information, ring the Service des Visites des jardins de la Ville de Paris, ☎ 01 40 71 75 23 (groups ☎ 01 40 71 75 60). The programme is available at the Office de Tourisme, at the Hôtel de Ville, and recorded information: ☎ 01 40 71 76 47.

Children's Paris

Zoos: Parc Zoologique de Paris, Bois de Vincennes; Ménagerie du Jardin des Plantes; Parc zoologique du Château de Thoiry. **Parks and Gardens**: Jardin d'enfants des Halles, Jardin du Luxembourg, Parc Floral de Paris, Vincennes; Aquaboulevard, in the 15e arrondissement; Jardin d'Acclimatation; Parc de la Vilette (Porte de Pantin); **Theme Parks**: Parc Astérix, Plailly; Disneyland Paris; France Miniature (Elancourt). **Science areas**: La Cité des Sciences et de l'Industrie; Palais de la Découverte; Grande Galerie de l'Evolution. **Video Games**: Centre Séga.

Paris from above

There are several monuments or buildings which offer spectacular views over Paris (some free, some to be paid for). These include: the Eiffel Tower, the Grande Arche de la Défense, Butte Montmartre and the Basilica of Sacré Coeur, the Towers of the Cathedral of Notre Dame, the Arc de Triomphe, the Pompidou Centre, the Panthéon, the Tour Montparnasse, La Samaritaine (department store), the Institut du Monde Arabe and Parc de Belleville (20e arrondissement).

Accommodation

There is a vast choice of hotels and other accommodation (*Résidences de tourisme*) in Paris. Nowhere within Paris is far from the centre by métro and it can be agreeable to stay in districts which are less touristy and more residential. Listed below are hotels in Paris and in the areas around Paris which are covered by this guide.

Apart from direct booking, accommodation can be reserved through central reservation numbers (see below), through travel agencies or, in Paris, through branches of the Office de Tourisme de Paris (see 21) who will make advance bookings with a written confirmation and deposit, and on-the-spot reservations for the same night. These are automatically cancelled if not taken up within 1.5 hours. They also provide an up-to-date *Guide des Hôtels* for Paris and region.

It is wise to book rooms in advance, particularly during the high seasons which are: during the fashion salons in January and the start of July; the most popular tourist seasons of Easter, September and October; and during the course of exhibitions and other trade fairs. Low season is mid-December, the rest of January, the second half of July and August. In between these periods the season is described as 'normal' with patches of peak demand.

Useful publications are the Red Michelin guide to *Paris and environs: Hotels and Restaurants*, and *Michelin, Kléber,* and *Gault-Millau* guides, or the *Guide des Relais Routiers*. Local Tourist Information Offices provide lists of hotels in their area.

Hotels

All hotels are officially classified and are graded by stars awarded by the French Tourist Board, depending on their amenities and the type of hotel.

L**** very high class, de luxe (1050 francs upwards)
*** very comfortable (500–1050 francs)
** comfortable (250–750 francs)
* and without star (HT) simple with basic comforts (180–350 francs)

The prices quoted above are approximate. Prices vary according to the position of the hotel, its grading and amenities, and also to the time of year.

Only a proportion of hotels in the one and two-star categories have rooms with private bath and WC en suite, although many provide shower and bidet. Similarly, many hotels have no restaurant, although almost all provide a continental breakfast (breakfast is usually charged extra).

In most hotels (especially when quoting *en pension* terms) a service charge of 15 per cent is added to the bill. When the bill is marked *service et taxes compris* (s.t.c.) no additional gratuity is expected. Additional is the *Taxe de Séjour*, a visitor's tax (introduced in Paris in 1994) on persons not liable for resident tax, which applies to all forms of paying accommodation from luxury hotels to camp sites, with rates varying from 1 to 7 francs per day per person.

Résidences de tourisme. These are furnished apartments in collective units or separate housing, available for the day, week or month, but not as permanent residence. They are a good alternative for visitors who want to cater for themselves. In some cases, the deal improves relative to the length of the stay.

Booking. Each reservation should be confirmed in writing, as should any cancellations. The hotel will normally ask for a deposit for each reservation. At certain times a total payment in advance may be required. In the event of a cancellation, the deposit will normally be kept. Hotels are not obliged to accept credit cards, but they usually do. It is the duty of the hotel management to issue an invoice for each payment. Do not leave valuables in the room, but place them in the hotel safe.

The list of hotels below is organised by *arrondissement* (the postal districts in Paris), and by rating. It is not definitive, but offered as a guideline to finding a place to stay in Paris. Most of the more expensive hotels in Paris are situated in the 1ere, 6–10e and 16–17e arrondissements. Large hotels outside the centre tend to be used by groups and those attending trade fairs.

Hotels in Paris

75001 ~ **the Louvre**: the western half of the Cité; the Louvre; Pl. Vendôme; Palais-Royal and St-Eustache

Luxury 4-star and 4-star
Cambon, 3 Rue Cambon, ☎ 01 42 60 38 09
Castille, 37 Rue Cabon, ☎ 01 44 58 44 58
France et Choiseul, 239 rue Saint Honoré, ☎ 01 42 44 50 00
Inter Continental Paris, 3 Rue de Castiglione, ☎ 01 44 77 11 11
Lotti, 7 Rue de Castiglione, ☎ 01 42 60 37 34
Meurice, 228 Rue de Rivoli, ☎ 01 44 58 10 10
Régina, 2 Pl. des Pyramides, ☎ 01 42 60 31 10
Ritz, 15 Pl. Vendôme, 75001, ☎ 01 43 16 30 30
Royal Saint-Honoré, 221 Rue St-Honoré, ☎ 01 42 60 32 79
Saint James et Albany, 202 Rue de Rivoli, ☎ 01 44 58 43 21

3-star
Brighton, 218 Rue de Rivoli, ☎ 01 42 60 30 03
Britannique, 20 Avenue Victoria, ☎ 01 42 33 74 59
Costes, 239 Rue St-Honoré, ☎ 01 42 44 50 00
Duminy-Vendôme, 3–5 Rue du Mont-Thabor, ☎ 01 42 60 32 80
Grand Hotel de Champagne, 17 Rue Jean-Lantier, ☎ 01 42 36 60 00
Louvre Saint-Honoré, 141 Rue St-Honoré, ☎ 01 42 96 23 23
Montana Tuileries, 12 Rue St-Roch, ☎ 01 42 60 35 10
Novotel Paris Les Halles, 8 Pl. Marguerite-de-Navarre, ☎ 01 42 21 31 31
Relais du Louvre, 19 Rue des Prêtres St-Germain-l'Auxerrois, ☎ 01 40 41 96 42
Tuileries, 10 Rue St-Hyacinthe, ☎ 01 42 61 04 17
Place du Louvre, 21 Rue des Prêtres St-Germain-l'Auxerrois, ☎ 01 42 33 78 68

2-star
Agora, 7 Rue de la Cossonnerie, ☎ 01 42 33 46 02
Ducs d'Anjou, 1 Rue Ste-Opportune, ☎ 01 42 36 92 24
Ducs de Bourgogne, 19 Rue du Pont-Neuf, ☎ 01 42 33 95 64
Londres et Stockolm, 13 Rue St-Roch/300 Rue St-Honoré, ☎ 01 42 60 15 62
Montpensier, 12 Rue de Richelieu, ☎ 01 42 96 28 50
Prince Albert, 5 Rue Saint-Hyacinthe ☎ 01 42 61 58 36, fax. 42 60 04 06

75002 ~ Bourse
Luxury 4-star and 4-star
Edouard VII, 39 Av. de l'Opéra, ☎ 01 42 61 56 90
Westminster, 13 Rue de la Paix, ☎ 01 42 61 57 46
3-star
Noailles, 9 Rue de la Michodière, ☎ 01 47 42 92 90
2-star
Grand Hotel de Besançon, 56 Rue Montorgueil, ☎ 01 42 36 41 08

75003 ~ Temple: the north half of the Marais
4-star
Pavillon de la Reine, 28 Pl. des Vosges, ☎ 01 42 77 96 40
3-star
ALHotel Vertus, 5 Rue des Vertus, ☎ 01 44 61 89 50
Chevaliers, 30 Rue de Turenne, ☎ 01 42 72 73 47
2-star
Belle Vue et Charoit d'Or, 39 Rue de Turbigo, ☎ 01 48 87 45 60
Marais, 2bis Rue Commines, ☎ 01 48 87 78 27

75004 ~ Hôtel de Ville: the eastern half of the Cité and the southern part of
the Marais
4-star
Jeu de Paume, 54 Rue St-Louis-en-l'Ile, ☎ 01 43 26 14 18
3-star
Bastia Speria, 1 Rue de la Bastille, ☎ 01 42 72 04 01
Axial Beaubourg, 11 Rue du Temple, ☎ 01 42 72 72 22
Bretonnerie, 22 Rue Ste-Croix-de-la-Bretonnerie, ☎ 01 48 87 77 63
Caron de Beaumarchais, 12 Rue Vieille-du-Temple, ☎ 01 42 72 34 12
Deux Iles, 59 Rue St-Louis en l'Ile, ☎ 01 43 26 13 35
Lutèce, 65 Rue St-Louis-en-l'Ile, ☎ 43 26 23 52
Hotel de Notre Dame, 19 Rue Maître Albert, ☎ 01 43 26 79 00,
fax 01 46 33 50 11
Panthéon, 19 Pl. du Panthéon, ☎ 01 43 54 01 81, fax 01 43 44 64 13
Saint-Louis, 75 Rue St-Louise-en-l'Ile, ☎ 01 46 34 04 80
Saint-Louis Marais, 1 Rue Charles V, ☎ 01 48 87 87 04
Saint-Merry, 78 Rue de la Verrerie, ☎ 01 42 78 14 15
2-star
Castex, 5 Rue Castex, ☎ 01 42 72 31 52, fax 01 42 72 57 91
Grand Hotel Jeanne d'Arc, 3 Rue Jarente, ☎ 01 48 87 62 11
Grand Hotel Malher, 5 Rue Malher, ☎ 01 42 72 6092
Place des Vosges, 12 Rue de Birague, ☎ 01 42 72 60 46, fax 01 42 72 02 64
Nice, 42 bis Rue de Rivoli, ☎ 01 42 78 55 29, fax 01 42 78 36 07`
Sansonnet, 48 Rue de la Verrerie, ☎ 01 48 87 96 14, fax 01 42 78 68 26
Septième Art, 20 Rue St-Paul, ☎ 01 42 77 04 03
Vieux Marais, 8 Rue du Plâtre, ☎ 01 42 78 47 22

75005 ~ the 'Latin Quarter'
4-star
Rives de Notre Dame, 15 Quai St-Michel, ☎ 01 43 54 81 16, fax 01 43 27 09
3-star
Colbert, 7 Rue de l'Hôtel-Colbert, 75005, ☎ 01 43 25 85 65,
fax 01 43 25 80 19
Elysa Luxembourg, 6 Rue Gay-Lussac, ☎ 01 43 25 31 74, fax 01 46 34 56 27
Grands Hommes, 17 Pl. du Panthéon, ☎ 01 46 34 19 60, fax 01 43 26 67 32
Jardin de Cluny Best Western, 9 Rue Sommerard, ☎ 01 43 54 22 66,
fax. 01 40 51 03 36
Jardins de Luxembourg, 5 Impasse Royer Collard, ☎ 01 40 46 08 88,
fax 01 40 46 02 28
Nations, 54 Rue Monge, ☎ 01 43 26 45 24, fax 01 46 34 00 13
Notre Dame, 19 Rue Maître-Albert, ☎ 01 43 26 79 00, fax 01 46 33 50 11
Panthéon, 19 Pl. du Panthéon, ☎ 01 43 54 32 95, fax, 01 43 26 64 65
Parc Saint-Severin, 22 Rue de la Parcheminerie, ☎ 01 43 54 32 17,
fax 01 43 54 70 71
Résidence Saint-Christophe, 17 Rue Lacepède, ☎ 01 43 31 81 54,
fax 01 43 31 12 54
Royal Saint-Michel, 3 Blvd St-Michel, ☎ 01 44 07 06 06, fax 01 44 07 36 25
Select Hotel, 1 Pl. de la Sorbonne, ☎ 01 46 34 14 80, fax 01 46 34 51 79
2-star
Hotel du Collège de France, 7 Rue Thénard, ☎ 01 43 26 78 36,
fax 01 46 34 58 29
Familia, 11 Rue des Ecoles, ☎ 01 43 54 55 27, fax 01 43 29 61 77
Trois Collèges, 16 Rue Cujas, ☎ 01 43 54 67 30, fax 01 46 34 02 99
Saint-Séverin, 40 Rue St-Séverin, ☎ 01 46 34 05 70, fax 01 46 33 84 47
1-star
Esmeralda, 4 Rue St-Julien-le-Pauvre, 75005, ☎ 01 43 54 19 20

75006 ~ Luxembourg
4-star
L'Hotel, 13 Rue des Beaux-Art, ☎ 01 43 25 27 22, fax 01 43 25 64 81
Littré, 9 Rue Littré, ☎ 01 45 44 36 68, fax 01 45 44 88 13
Manoir de St-Germain des Prés, 152 Blvd St-Germain, ☎ 01 42 22 21 65,
fax 01 45 48 22 25
3-star
l'Abbaye St-Germain, 10 Rue Cassette, ☎ 01 45 44 38 11, fax 01 45 48 07 86
Angleterre St-Germain-des-Prés, 44 Rue Jacob, ☎ 01 42 60 34 72,
fax 01 42 60 16 93
Atelier Montparnasse, 49 Rue Vavin, ☎ 01 46 33 60 00, fax 01 40 51 04 21
Buci Latin, 34 Rue de Buci, ☎ 01 43 29 07 20, fax 01 43 29 67 44
Danemark, 21 Rue Vavin, ☎ 01 43 26 93 78, fax 01 46 34 66 06
Danube, 58 Rue Jacob, ☎ 01 42 60 34 70, fax 01 42 60 81 18
Ferrandi, 92 Rue du Cherche-Midi, ☎ 01 42 22 97 40, fax 01 45 44 89 97
Fleurie, 32 Rue Grégoire-de-Tours, ☎ 01 43 29 59 81, fax 01 43 29 68 44
La Perle, 14 Rue des Canettes, ☎ 01 43 29 10 10, fax 01 46 34 51 04
Latitudes St-Germain des Prés, 7–11 Rue St-Benoit, ☎ 01 42 61 53 53,
fax 01 49 27 09 33

Madison, 143 Blvd St-Germain, ☎ 01 40 51 60 00, fax 01 40 51 60 01
Louis II St-Germain, 2 Rue St-Sulpice, ☎ 01 46 33 13 80, fax 01 46 33 17 29
Lutétia, 45 Blvd Raspail, ☎ 01 49 54 46 46, fax 01 49 54 46 00
Prince de Conti, 8 Rue Guenegaud, ☎ 01 44 07 30 40, fax 01 44 07 36 334
Quality Inn Paris Rive Gauche, 91 Rue de Vaugirard, ☎ 01 42 22 00 56,
fax 01 42 22 05 39
Relais Medicis, 23 Rue Racine, ☎ 01 43 26 00 60 fax 01 40 46 83 39
Relais Saint-Germain, 9 Carrefour de l'Odéon, ☎ 01 43 29 12 05,
fax 01 46 33 45 30
Relais de Vieux-Paris, 9 Rue Gît-le-Coeur, ☎ 01 43 54 41 66, fax 01 43 26 00 15
Saint-Germain des Prés, 36 Rue Bonaparte, ☎ 01 43 26 00 19,
fax 01 40 46 83 63
Saint-Grégoire, 43 Rue de l'Abbé-Grégoire, ☎ 01 45 48 23 23,
fax 01 45 48 33 95
Saint-Paul, 43 Rue Monsieur-le-Prince, ☎ 01 43 26 98 64, fax 01 46 34 58 60
Saints-Pères, 65 Rue des Saints-Pères, ☎ 01 45 44 50 00, fax 01 45 48 67 52
2-star
Atlantis St-Germain-des-Prés, 4 Rue du Vieux Colombier, ☎ 01 45 48 31 81,
fax 01 45 48 35 16
Perryve, 63 Rue Madame, ☎ 01 45 48 35 01, fax 01 42 84 03 30
Rive Gauche, 25 Rue des Saints-Pères, ☎ 01 42 60 34 68, fax 01 42 61 29 78
1-star
Saint-André-des-Arts, 66 Rue St-André-des-Arts, ☎ 01 43 26 96 16,
fax 01 43 29 73 34

75007 ~ **Palais-Bourbon**: Faubourg St-Germain; the Musée d'Orsay; Eiffel
Tower
4-star
Cayré, 4 Blvd Raspail, ☎ 01 45 44 38 88, fax 01 45 44 98 13
Elysées Maubourg Best Western, 35 Blvd Latour-Maubourg, ☎ 01 45 56 10 78,
fax 01 4705 65 08
Tourville, 16 Av. de Tourville, ☎ 01 47 05 62 62, fax 01 47 05 43 90
3-star
Académie, 32 Rue des Saints-Pères, ☎ 01 45 48 36 22, fax 01 45 44 75 24
Bac St-Germain, 66 Rue du Bac, ☎ 01 42 22 20 03, fax 01 45 48 52 30
Bersoly's, 28 Rue de Lille, ☎ 01 42 60 73 79, fax 01 49 27 05 55
Duc de Saint-Simon, 14 Rue de St-Simon, ☎ 01 44 39 20 20,
fax. 01 45 48 68 25
Jardins d'Eiffel, 8 Rue Amélie, ☎ 01 05 46 21, fax 01 45 55 28 08
Lenox, 9 Rue de l'Université, ☎ 01 42 96 10 95, fax 01 42 61 52 83
Suède, 31 Rue Vaneau, ☎ 01 47 05 00 08, fax 01 47 05 69 27
Université, 22 Rue de l'Université, ☎ 01 42 61 09 39, fax 01 42 60 40 84
Varenne, 44 Rue de Bourgogne, ☎ 01 45 51 45 55, fax 05 45 51 86 63
Verneuil Saint-Germain, 8 Rue de Verneuil, ☎ 01 42 60 82 14,
fax 01 42 61 40 38
2-star
Centre, 24bis Rue Cler, ☎ 01 47 05 52 33, fax 01 40 62 95 66
Empereur, 2 Rue Chevert, ☎ 01 45 55 88 02, fax 01 45 51 88 54
Solférino, 91 Rue de Lille, ☎ 01 47 05 85 54, fax 01 45 55 51 16

75008 ~ Elysée: Place de la Concorde, the Madeleine, the Champs-Elysées and Faubourg St-Honoré

Luxury 4-star and 4-star

Balzac, 6 Rue Balzac, ☎ 01 44 35 18 00, fax 01 42 25 24 82

Le Bristol, 112 Rue du Faubourg-St-Honoré, ☎ 01 42 66 91 45, fax 01 42 66 34 16

Château Frontenac, 54 Rue Pierre-Charron, ☎ 01 53 23 13 13, fax. 01 53 23 13 01

Chateaubriand Copatel, 6 Rue Chateaubriand, ☎ 01 40 76 00 50, fax 01 40 76 09 22

Claridge Bellman, 37 Rue François-Ier, ☎ 01 47 23 54 42, fax 01 47 23 08 84

Crillon, 10 Pl. de la Concorde, ☎ 01 44 71 15 00, fax 01 44 71 15 02

Etoile Friedland Best Western, 177 Rue du Faubourg St-Honoré, ☎ 01 45 63 64 65, fax 01 45 63 88 96

George V, 31 Av. George-V, ☎ 01 47 23 54 00, fax 01 37 20 40 00

Golden Tulip Saint-Honoré, 218-220 Rue St-Honoré, ☎ 01 49 53 03 03, fax 01 40 75 02 00

Plaza Athénée, 25 Av. Montaigne, ☎ 01 47 23 78 33, fax 01 47 20 20 70

Prince de Galles Sheraton, 33 Av. George V, ☎ 01 47 23 55 11, fax 01 47 20 96 92

Résidence Maxim's de Paris, 42 Av. Gabriel, ☎ 01 45 61 96 33, fax 01 42 89 06 07

Royal Monceau, 37 Av. Hoche, ☎ 01 42 99 88 00, fax 01 42 99 89 90

San Régis, 12 Rue Jean Goujon, ☎ 01 44 95 16 16, fax 01 45 61 05 48

3-star

Bradford Elysées Best Western, 10 Rue St-Philippe-du-Roule, ☎ 01 45 63 20 20, fax 01 45 63 20 07

Colisée Best Western, 6 Rue du Colisée, ☎ 01 43 59 95 25, fax 01 45 63 26 54.

Concorde Saint-Lazare, 108 Rue St-Lazare, ☎ 01 40 08 44 44, fax 01 42 93 01 20

Folkestone Best Western, 9 Rue de Castellane, ☎ 01 42 65 73 09, fax 01 42 65 64 09

Galileo, 54 Rue Galilée, ☎ 01 47 20 66 06, fax 01 47 20 67 17

Lido Best Western, 4 Passage de la Madeleine, ☎ 01 42 66 27 37, fax 01 42 66 61 23

Massena, 16 Rue Tronchet, ☎ 01 42 68 07 93, fax 01 40 07 07 05

Ministère, 31 Rue Surène, ☎ 42 66 21 43 , fax 01 42 66 96 04

La Trémoille, 14 Rue la Trémoille, ☎ 01 47 23 34 20, fax 01 40 70 01 08

Résidence Monceau, 85 Rue du Rocher, ☎ 01 45 22 75 11, fax 01 45 22 30 88

Tronchet, 22 Rue Tronchet, ☎ 01 47 42 26 14, fax 01 49 24 03 82

2-star

d'Albion, 15 Rue de Penthièvre, ☎ 01 42 65 84 15, fax 01 49 24 03 47

75009 ~ Opéra, as far as Blvd de Clichy and Pl. Pigalle

Luxury 4-star and 4-star

Scribe, 1 Rue Scribe, ☎ 01 44 71 24 24, fax 01 42 65 39 97

Grand Hotel Inter Continental, 2 Rue Scribe, ☎ 01 40 07 32 32, fax 01 42 66 12 51

3-star

Ambassador, 16 Blvd Haussmann, ☎ 01 44 83 40 40, fax 01 42 46 19 84
Chateaudun, 30 Rue de Chateaudun, ☎ 01 49 70 09 99, fax 01 49 70 06 99
Leman, 20 Rue de Trévise, ☎ 01 42 46 50 66, fax 01 48 24 27 59
Opéra Cadet, 24 Rue Cadet, ☎ 01 48 24 05 26, fax 01 42 46 68 09
Pré, 10 Rue Pierre Semard, ☎ 01 42 81 37 11, fax 01 40 23 98 28
Tour d'Auvergne, 10 Rue de la Tour d'Auvergne, ☎ 01 48 78 61 60,
fax 01 49 95 99 00

2-star

des Arts, 7 Cité Bergère, ☎ 01 42 46 73 30, fax 01 48 00 94 42
Chopin, 49 Passage Jouffroy (10 Blvd Montmartre), ☎ 01 47 70 58 10,
fax 01 42 47 00 70
Confort, 3/5 Rue de Trévise, ☎ 01 42 46 12 06, fax 01 48 01 09 82
Croisés, 63 Rue St-Lazare, ☎ 01 48 74 78 24, fax 01 49 95 04 43
Riboutté Lafayette, 5 Rue Riboutté, ☎ 01 47 70 62 36, fax 01 48 00 91 50

75010 ~ Gare du Nord and Gare de l'Est

3-star

Abotel Garden Opéra, 65 Rue du Château-d'eau, ☎ 01 47 70 40 75,
fax 01 47 70 07 41
Hotel Français, 13 Rue du 8-Mai-1945, ☎ 01 40 35 94 14, fax 01 40 35 94 14
Horset Pavillon, 3 Rue de l'Echiquier, ☎ 01 42 46 92 75, fax 01 42 47 03 97
Libertel Terminus Nord, 12 Blvd de Denain, ☎ 01 42 80 20 00,
fax 01 42 80 63 89
Plaza La Fayette, 175 Rue La-Fayette, ☎ 01 44 89 89 10, fax 01 40 36 00 30

2-star

Apollo, 11 Rue de Dunkerque, ☎ 01 48 78 04 98, fax 01 42 85 08 78
Résidence Magenta, 35 Rue Yves-Toudic, ☎ 01 42 40 17 72,
fax 01 42 02 59 66

75011 ~ north east of the Pl. de la Bastille to Pl. de la Nation

4-star

Holiday Inn Paris République, 10 Pl. de l République, ☎ 01 43 55 44 34,
fax 01 47 00 32 34

3-star

Abotel Beauséjour République, 1 Rue de la Fontaine-au-Roi, ☎ 01 43 57 34 01,
fax 01 48 05 70 17
Résidence Trousseau, 13 Rue Trousseau, ☎ 01 48 05 55 55,
fax 01 48 05 83 97

2-star

Campanile Paris Bastille, 9 Rue du Chemin-Vert, ☎ 01 43 38 58 08,
fax 01 43 38 52 28
Ibis Paris Bastille, 15 Rue Bréguet, ☎ 01 43 38 65 65, fax 01 43 38 09 33
Lyon-Mulhouse, 8 Blvd Beaumarchais, ☎ 01 47 00 91 50, fax 01 47 00 06 31

75012 ~ south east of the Pl. de Bastille (including the Gare de Lyon and Bercy)

3-star

Belle Epoque, 66 Rue de Charenton, ☎ 01 43 44 06 66, fax 01 43 44 10 25

Claret Comfort Inn Bercy Lyon, 44 Blvd de Bercy, ☎ 01 46 28 41 31, fax 01 49 28 09 29

Modern Hotel Lyon, 3 Rue Parrot, ☎ 01 43 43 41 52, fax 01 43 43 81 16

Pavillon Bastille, 65 Rue de Lyon, ☎ 01 43 43 65 65, fax 01 43 43 96 52

Le Zephyr, 31 bis Blvd Diderot, ☎ 01 43 46 12 72, fax 01 43 41 68 01

2-star

Nouvel Hotel, 9 Rue d'Austerlitz, ☎ 01 43 42 15 79, fax 01 43 42 31 11

75013 ~ Gobelins: south of the Gare d'Austerlitz, including the Gobelins and Pl. de l'Italie

3-star

Confort Inn Les Gobelins, 57 Blvd St-Marcel, ☎ 01 43 31 79 89

Vert Galant, 41 Rue Croulebarbe, ☎ 01 44 08 83 50, fax 01 44 08 83 69

2-star

Résidence les Gobelins, 9 Rue des Gobelins, ☎ 01 47 07 26 90, fax 43 31 44 05

no star (HT)

Hotel Tolbiac, 122 Rue de Tolbiac, ☎ 01 44 24 25 54, fax 01 45 85 43 47

75014 ~ Observatoire

4-star

Méridien Montparnasse, 19 Rue du Cdt-Mouchotte, ☎ 01 44 36 44 36, fax 01 44 36 49 00

Sofitel Saint-Jacques, 17 Blvd St-Jacques, ☎ 01 40 78 79 80, fax 01 40 78 79 04

3-star

Lenox, 15 Rue Delambre, ☎ 01 43 35 34 50, fax 01 43 20 46 64

l'Orchidée, 65 Rue de l'Ouest, ☎ 43 22 70 50, fax 01 42 79 97 46

Orléans Palace Hotel, 185 Blvd Brune, ☎ 01 43 39 68 50, fax 01 45 43 65 64

Le Parnasse, 79 Av. du Maine, ☎ 01 43 20 13 93, fax 01 43 20 95 60

Raspail-Montparnasse, 203 Blvd Raspail, ☎ 01 43 20 62 86, fax 01 43 20 50 79

2-star

Istria, 29 Rue Campagne-Première, ☎ 01 43 20 91 82, fax 01 43 22 48 45

Parc Montsouris, 4 Rue du parc Montsouris, ☎ 01 45 89 09 72, fax 01 45 80 92 72

1-star

Bains Montparnasse, 33 Rue Delambre, ☎ 01 43 20 85 27, fax 01 42 79 82 78

Floridor, 28 Pl. Denfert-Rochereau, ☎ 01 43 21 35 53, fax 01 43 21 35 53

75015 ~ Vaugirard: south west of the Tour Montparnasse and Av. de Suffren

4-star

Hilton, 18 Av. de Suffren, ☎ 01 44 38 56 00, fax 01 44 38 56 10

3-star

Adagio Paris Vaugirard, 257 Rue de Vaugirard, ☎ 01 40 45 10 00, fax 01 40 45 10 10

Frantour Paris Suffren, 20 Rue Jean Rey, ☎ 01 45 78 50 00, fax 01 45 78 91 42

Nikko de Paris, 61 Quai de Grenelle, ☎ 01 40 58 20 00, fax 01 45 75 42 35

Résidence Saint-Lambert, 5 Rue E. Gibez, ☎ 01 48 28 63 14, fax 01 45 33 45 50

Sofitel Paris Porte de Sevres, 8–12 Rue Louis-Armand, ☎ 01 40 60 30 30, fax 01 45 57 04 22

Yllen, 196 Rue de Vaugirard, ☎ 01 45 67 67 67, fax 01 45 67 74 37

75016 ~ Passy: between the Seine and the Bois de Bologne, including the districts of Passy, Chaillot and Auteuil

Luxury 4-star and 4-star

Le Raphaël, 17 Av. Kléber, ☎ 01 44 28 0 28, fax 01 45 01 21 50

Baltimore (Westin Demeure), 88 bis Av. Kléber, ☎ 01 44 34 54 54, fax 01 44 34 54 44

Majestic Paris, 29 Rue Dumont d'Urville, ☎ 01 45 00 83 70, fax 01 45 00 29 48

Le Parc (Westin Demeure), 55-57 Av. R.-Poincaré, ☎ 01 44 05 66 66, fax 01 44 05 66 00

Pergolèse, 3 Rue Pergolèse, ☎ 01 40 67 96 77, fax 01 45 00 12 11

La Villa Maillot, 143 Av. de Malakoff, ☎ 01 45 01 25 22, fax 01 45 00 60 61

3-star

Belmont, 30 Rue de Bassano, ☎ 01 47 23 72 41, fax 01 47 23 09 70

Libertel Elysées Bassano, 24 Rue de Bassano, ☎ 01 47 20 49 03, fax 01 47 23 06 72

Longchamp, 86 Rue de Longchamp, ☎ 01 47 27 13 48, fax 01 47 55 68 26

Sévigné, 6 Rue de Belloy, ☎ 01 47 20 88 90, fax 01 40 70 98 73

2-star

Boileau, 81 Rue Boileau, ☎ 01 42 88 83 74, fax 01 46 47 57 49

Hameau de Passy, 48 Rue de Passy, ☎ 01 42 88 47 55, fax 01 42 30 83 72

75017 ~ Batignolles Monceau: north west of the Étoile

4-star

Méridien Etoile, 81 Blvd Gouvion-Saint-Cyr, ☎ 01 40 68 34 34, f fax 01 40 68 31 31

3-star

Banville, 166 Blvd Berthier, ☎ 01 42 67 70 16, fax 01 44 40 42 77

Concorde Layfayette, 3 Pl. du Général Koenig, ☎ 01 40 68 50 68, fax 01 40 68 50 43

Courcelles Etoile Best Western, 184 Rue de Courcelles, ☎ 01 47 63 65 30, fax 01 46 22 49 44

Eber Monceau, 18 Rue Léon-Jost, ☎ 01 46 22 60 70, fax 01 47 63 01 01

Etoile Park, 10 Av. MacMahon, ☎ 01 42 67 69 63, fax 01 43 80 18 99

Etoile Pereire, 146 Blvd Pereire, ☎ 01 42 67 60 00, fax 01 42 67 02 90

Magellan, 17 Rue J-B.-Dumas, ☎ 01 47 72 44 51, fax 01 40 68 90 36

Regent's Garden Best Western, 6 Rue P.–Demours, ☎ 01 45 74 07 30, fax. 01 40 55 01 42

Ternes Arc de Triomphe, 97 Av. des Ternes, ☎ 01 53 81 94 94, fax 01 53 81 94 95

75018 ~ Butte Montmartre: north east of the Pl. de Clichy as far east as Rue d'Aubervilliers

4-star

Terrass, 12 Rue Joseph-de-Maistre, ☎ 01 46 06 72 85, fax 01 42 52 29 11

2-star
Eden, 90 Rue Ordener, ☎ 01 42 64 61 63, fax 01 42 64 11 43
Ermitage, 24 Rue Lamarck, ☎ 01 42 64 79 22, fax 01 42 64 10 33
Prima Lepic, 29 Rue Lepic, ☎ 01 46 06 44 64, fax 01 46 06 66 11
Regyn's Montmartre, 18 Pl. des Abbesses, ☎ 01 42 54 45 21,
fax 01 42 23 76 69
Tim Hotel Montmartre, 11 Rue Ravignan (Pl. E. Goudeau), ☎ 01 42 55 74 79,
fax 01 42 55 71 01

75019 ~ Buttes-Chaumont, La Villette
4-star
Holiday Inn Paris Pantin La Villette, 216 Av. Jean-Jaurès, ☎ 01 44 84 18 18,
fax 01 44 84 18 20
3-star
Forest Hill Paris La Villette, 28 ter Av. Corentin-Cariou, ☎ 01 44 72 15 30,
fax 01 44 72 15 80
2-star
Butts Chaumonts, 4 Av. Secrétan, ☎ 01 42 55 33 81, fax 01 42 45 60 40
Le Laumière, 4 Rue Petit, ☎ 01 42 06 10 77, fax 01 42 06 72 50
Rhin-et-Danube, 3 Pl. du Rhin-et-Danube, ☎ 01 42 45 10 13
fax. 01 42 06 88 82

75020 ~ Ménilmontant
3-star
Timhotel Nation, 110 Rue des Orteaux, ☎ 01 40 09 28 28, fax 01 40 09 73 14
2-star
Pyrénées Gambetta, 12 Av du Père-Lachaise, ☎ 01 47 97 76 57,
fax 01 47 97 17 61

Hotel Groups with central reservation facilities
(Bookings usually taken up until 3 pm for the same night.)

Abotel	☎ 0181 876 2420, fax 0181 392 9124
Balladins	☎ 0171 287 3181, fax 0171 434 1870
Best Western	☎ 0181 446 0126, fax 0181 446 0196;
	USA ☎ 800 528 12344200, fax 602 780 6099
Campanile	☎ 0181 569 6969, fax 0181 814 0887
Châteaux Hôtels Indépendants, France, ☎ 01 47 57 23 67, fax 01 47 57 32 50	
Cidotel, France	☎ 44 70 24 24, fax 01 44 70 24 51
Climat de France	☎ 0171 287 3171, fax 0171 434 1870
Concorde Hotels	☎ 0800 181 591, fax 0171 630 0391;
	USA ☎ 800 888 4747, 212 752 8916
Frantour, France	☎ 01 45 19 12 12, fax 01 45 19 15 71
Hilton	☎ 05 90 75 46, UK ☎ 0990 445 866,
	fax 01923 218 548; USA ☎ 800 445 8667, 212 820 1700; Canada ☎ 800 268 9275
Holiday Inn	☎ 0800 897 121; USA ☎ 212 355 2660, 800 331 3831; fax 2112 980 6783
Hotels l'Horset	☎ 0181 951 39 99, fax 0181 905 61 70;
	France: Paris ☎ 01 42 25 00 88, fax 01 49 53 90 04;

	USA/Canada, ☎ 800 847 4249, ☎ 800 255 3393
Ibis-Arcade	☎ 0171 724 1000, fax 0181 748 9116;
	France, ☎ 01 60 77 52 52; UK, ☎ 0181 746 3233
Intercontinental	☎ 0181 847 3711, fax 0181 568 9555
Inter Hotel	☎ 0171 287 3171, fax 0171 434 1870
Lotti	☎ 0800 282 729, fax 01923 896 071
Mercure	☎ 0171 724 1000, fax 0181 748 9116;
	Paris ☎ 01 60 77 22 33; USA ☎ 800 MERCURE
Méridien	☎ 0129 681 391, fax 0171 439 1244
Novotel	☎ 0181 748 3433; France, ☎ 01 60 77 87 65;
	USA ☎ 800 NOVOTEL
Prince de Galles, Sheraton	☎ 0800 353 535, fax 353 21 359 352
Sofitel UK	☎ 0171 724 1000, France, ☎ 01 60 77 87 65,
	Paris, ☎ 01 60 77 87 65, USA, ☎ 800 SOFITEL
TimHotel	☎ 0990 300 200, fax 0181 661 1234
UTELL	USA ☎ 402 398 3200, 800 44 UTELL, fax 402 398 5484

Residences de Tourisme

75001 ~ Louvre: the western half of the Cité
Hall'Studios, 4 Rue des Halles, ☎ 01 40 13 85 80, fax 01 40 13 85 78
Orion Paris Les Halles, 4 Rue des Innocents, ☎ 01 40 39 76 00,
fax 01 45 08 40 65

75002 ~ Bourse
4-star
Metropole Opéra, 2 Rue de Gramont, ☎ 01 42 96 91 03, fax 01 42 96 22 46
3-star
Citadines Paris Opéra, 18 Rue Favart, ☎ 01 44 50 23 23, fax 01 44 50 23 50
Au Montorgueil, 55 Rue St-Sauveur, ☎ 01 40 98 01 28, fax 01 40 28 92 01

75006 ~ Luxembourg
3-star
Citadines Raspail Montparnasse, 121 Blvd du Montparnasse, ☎ 01 43 35 46 35,
fax 01 40 47 43 01
Du Residence du Golf, 23 rue Guisarde, 75006, ☎ 01 40 46 07 99,
fax 01 43 26 62 10

75008 ~ Elysée: the Pl. de la Concorde, the Madeleine, the Champs-Elysées and
Faubourg St-Honoré
****Beverly Hills, 35 Rue de Berri, ☎ 01 53 77 56 00, fax 01 42 56 52 75
****Libertel Elysées Ponthieu, 20 Rue du Colisée, ☎ 01 42 25 68 70,
   fax 01 42 25 80 82
****Relais Carré d'Or, 46 Av. George V , ☎ 01 40 70 05 05,
fax 01 47 23 30 90
****Residential Chambiges, 8 Rue Chambiges, ☎ 01 44 31 83 83,
   fax 01 40 70
95 51
****Suites Saint-Honoré, 13 Rue d'Aguesseau, ☎ 01 44 51 16 35,
fax 01 42 66 35 70

Citadines Prestige Haussmann, 129–131 Blvd Haussmann, ☎ 01 53 77 07 07, fax 01 45 63 46 64

Claridge, 74 Av. des Champs-Elysées, ☎ 01 44 13 33 33, fax 01 42 25 04 88

Times Square Saint-Honoré, 218–110 Rue du Fb.–St-Honoré, ☎ 01 49 53 03 03, fax 01 40 75 02 00

75009 ~ **Opéra**
Alba Opéra, 34 ter Rue de la Tour-d'Auvergne, ☎ 01 48 78 80 22, fax 01 42 85 23 13

Eurotel Fontaine, 29 Rue Fontaine, ☎ 01 49 95 03 04, fax 01 49 95 03 06

Bergère Opéra, 6 Cité Bergère, ☎ 01 44 21 80 20, fax 01 44 21 80 21

75010 ~ **Gare de l'Est**
Vacantel Paris Gare de l'Est, 5/7 Passage Dubail, ☎ 01 44 98 66 70, fax 01 40 37 55 97

75011 ~ **north east of the Place de la Bastille**
***All Suite Hotel First Class Home Plazza, 74 Rue Amelot, ☎ 01 40 21 22 23, fax 01 47 00 82 40

***Citadines Paris République, 75 bis Av. Parmentier, ☎ 01 43 14 17 17, fax. 01 43 14 90 30

All Suite Hotel First Class Home Plazza, 289 bis Rue du Fb. St-Antoine, ☎ 01 40 09 40 00, fax 01 40 09 11 55

Hotel du Monde, 15 Rue Pasteur, ☎ 01 48 05 24 73, fax 01 47 00 71 09

Orion Bastille, 35–39 Blvd R. Lenoir, ☎ 01 53 36 22 22, fax 01 53 36 22 00

Trousseau, 13 Rue Trousseau, ☎ 01 48 05 55 55, fax 01 48 05 83 97

75012 ~ **south east of the Place de la Bastille**
***Citadines Paris Bastille, 14–18 Rue de Chaligny, ☎ 01 40 01 15 15, fax 01 40 01 15 20

75013 ~ **Gobelins**
***Citadines Paris Austerlitz, 27 Rue Esquirol, ☎ 01 44 23 51 51, fax 01 45 86 59 76

***Orion Place d'Italie, 18 Pl. d'Italie, ☎ 01 40 78 15 00, fax 01 40 78 16 99

**Amhotel-Inn City Choisy, 96 Av. de Choisy, ☎ 01 44 23 22 02, fax 01 45 82 71 05

Times Square Pascal, 71 Rue Pascal, ☎ 01 40 79 53 00, fax 01 40 79 53 94

Vacantel Facotel, 15 Rue de Tolbiac, ☎ 01 53 61 62 00, fax 01 53 61 62 02

75014 ~ **Observatoire**
***Citadines Maine Montparnasse, 67 Av. du Maine, ☎ 01 40 47 41 41, fax 01 43 27 29 94

Amhotel Ripoche, 35 Rue M. Ripoche, ☎ 01 44 12 55 00, fax 01 44 12 55 01

Citadines Paris Didot, 94 Rue Didot, ☎ 01 40 52 54 54, fax 01 40 52 54 52

75015 ~ **Vaugirard**
Pierre et Vacances, 20 Rue Oradour-sur-Glane, Porte de Versailles, ☎ 01 45 54 97 43, fax 01 45 57 28 43

Flatotel International, 14 Rue du Théâtre, ☎ 01 45 75 62 20,
fax 01 45 79 73 30
Plaza Mirabeau, 10 Av. Emile-Zola, ☎ 01 45 77 72 00, fax 01 45 77 57 87

75016 ~ **districts of Passy, Chaillot, Auteuil**
***Citadines Paris Trocadero, 29 bis Rue St-Didier, ☎ 01 44 34 73 73,
fax 01 47 04 50 07
***Espace Greuze, 30 Rue Greuze, ☎ 01 40 56 99 50, fax 01 40 56 99 69
Times Square Alma Marceau, 5-7 Rue Jean Giraudoux, ☎ 01 47 20 60 06,
fax 01 40 70 06 70

75017 ~ **Batignolles Monceau**
Amhotel Aeriel, 138 Av. de Clichy, ☎ 01 44 85 00 50, fax 01 44 85 03 10
Hotel Malesherbes, 129 Rue Cardinet, ☎ 01 44 15 85 00,
fax 01 44 15 85 29

75018 ~ **Butte-Montmartre**
***Pierre et Vacances, 10 Pl. Charles Dullin, ☎ 01 42 57 14 55,
fax 01 42 54 48 87
Citadines Paris Montmartre, 16–18 Av. Rachel, ☎ 01 53 42 43 44,
fax 01 45 22 59 10
Eurotel Montmartre, 9 Rue Paul-Albert, ☎ 01 42 54 45 00, fax 01 42 54 36 36
Hotel Pacific, 77 Rue du Ruisseau, ☎ 01 42 62 53 00, fax 01 46 06 09 82
Residel Residence Baudelique, 24 Rue Baudelique, ☎ 01 42 55 60 60,
fax 01 42 55 24 70

75019 ~ **Butte-Chaumont, La Villette**
***Maeva La Villette, 28 bis Av. Corentin-Cariou, ☎ 01 44 72 42 00,
fax 44 72 42 42

Résidences de Tourisme, central booking
Claridge, ☎ 01 44 13 33 33, fax 01 42 25 04 88
Citadines, ☎ 01 41 05 79 79, fax 01 47 59 04 70
Orion, ☎ 01 40 78 54 54, fax 01 40 78 54 55; USA. ☎ 800 755 8266/212
688 9526, fax 212 688 9467
Paris Appartements Services, 69 Rue d'Argout, 75002, ☎ 01 40 28 01 28,
fax 01 40 28 92 01

Hotels in Ile de France
Neuilly-sur-Seine (92200, Hauts de Seine)
****Parc Neuilly, 4 Blvd du Parc, ☎ 01 46 24 32 62, fax 01 46 40 77 31
***International de Paris, 58 Blvd VIctor Hugo, ☎ 01 47 59 80 00,
fax 01 47 59 80 01
**Paris Neuilly, 1 Av. de Madrid, ☎ 01 47 47 14 67, fax 01 47 47 97 42

Paris La Defense (92060, Hauts de Seine)
****Sofitel Paris La Defense Centre, 34 Cours Michelet, ☎ 01 47 75 44 43,
fax 01 47 73 72 74

Rueil Malmaison (92500, Hauts-de-Seine)
***Atria Novotel Rueil Malmaison, Rue Edouard-Belin, ☎ 01 47 16 60 60, fax 01 47 52 09 29

Sceaux (92330, Hauts-de-Seine)
**Colbert, 20 Av. de Camberwell, ☎ 01 46 60 02 21, fax 01 47 02 95 78

Fontainebleau/Barbizon (77300/77630, Seine-et-Marne)
****Grand Hotel de l'Aigle Noir, 27 Pl. Nap.-Bonaparte, Fontainebleau, ☎ 01 60 74 60 00, fax 01 60 74 60 01
****Grand Hotel Mercure Royal Fontainebleau, 41 Rue Royale, ☎ 01 64 69 34 34, fax 01 64 69 34 39
***Hotel Legris et Parc, 36 Rue Paul Séramy, Fontainebleau, ☎ 01 64 22 24 24, fax. 01 64 22 22 05
***Hotel de Londres, Pl. Gen. de Gaulle, Fontainebleau, ☎ 01 64 22 20 21, fax 01 60 72 39 16
***Hotel Napoléon, 9 Rue Grande, Fontainebleau, ☎ 01 64 22 20 39, fax. 01 64 22 20 87
**Hotel Victoria, 112 Rue de France, Fontainebleau, ☎ 01 60 74 90 00, fax 01 60 74 90 10
Le Bas Bréau, 22 Rue Grande, Barbizon, ☎ 01 60 66 40 05, fax 01 60 69 22 89
Interhotel de la Dague, 5 Grande Rue, Barbizon, ☎ 01 60 66 40 49, fax 01 60 69 24 59
Hostellerie Les Pléiades, 21 Rue Grande, Barbizon, ☎ 01 60 66 40 25, fax 01 60 66 41 68

Champs (77420, Seine-et-Marne)
**Comfort Inn Primevere Champs sur Marne, 34 Allée des Fresnes, Quartier de Nesles, ☎ 01 64 68 33 36, fax 01 64 68 16 68

St-Germain-en-Laye (78100, Yvelines)
****Cazaudehore et La Forestière, 1 Av. du Président-Kennedy, ☎ 01 39 73 36 60, fax 01 39 73 73 88
Le Pavillon Henri IV, 19–21 Rue Thiers, ☎ 01 39 10 15 15, fax 01 39 73 93 73
Ermitage des Loges, 11 Av. des Loges, ☎ 01 39 21 50 90, fax 01 39 21 50 91
**Coqvert, 45 Blvd de la Paix, Coteaux du Bel-Air, ☎ 01 30 61 48 48, fax 01 39 72 83 36

Versailles (78000, Yvelines)
L**** Trianon Palace, 1 Blvd de la Reine, ☎ 01 30 84 38 00, fax. 01 39 49 00 77
****Sofitel, 2 bis Av. de Paris, ☎ 01 39 53 30 31, fax 01 39 53 87 20
***Versailles, 7 Rue Ste-Anne, ☎ 01 39 50 64 54, fax 01 39 02 37 85
Angleterre, 2 bis Rue de Fontenay, ☎ 01 39 51 43 50, fax 01 39 02 37 85
**Clagny, 6 impasse de Clagny, ☎ 01 39 50 18 09, fax. 01 39 50 85 17
Home Saint-Louis, 28 Rue St-Louis, ☎ 01 39 50 23 55, fax 01 30 21 62 45
Paris Hotel, 14 Av. de Paris, ☎ 01 39 50 56 00, fax 01 39 50 56 00

Ecouen (95440, Val-d'Oise)
Campanile Paris Nord Ecouen, La Redoute du Moulin, RN16,   01 39 94 46 00,
fax 01 39 94 18 59

Picardy
Chantilly (60500, Oise)
*Les Balladins, ZAC du Coq-Chantant (RN 16) ☎ 03 44 58 13 12, fax 03 44 57
64 47
**Campanile, Route de Creil (RN 16), ☎ 03 44 57 39 24, fax 03 44 58 10 05
**Hotel Restaurant de la Gare, Pl. de la Gare, ☎ 03 44 62 56 90,
fax 03 44 62 56 99
***Hotel du Parc-Best Western, 35 Av. du Maréchal-Joffre, ☎ 03 44 58 20 00,
fax 03 44 57 31 10
Gouvieux-Chantilly (60270, Oise)
***Le Château de la Tour, Chemin de la Chaussée, ☎ 03 44 57 07 39,
fax 03 44 57 31 97
Senlis (60300, Oise)
**Le Point du Jour, 1 Rue de la République, ☎ 03 44 53 01 22,
fax 03 44 53 13 01
**Hotel du Nord, 110 Rue de la République, ☎ 03 44 53 01 16,
fax 03 44 53 60 60
**Hostellerie de la Porte Bellon, 51 Rue Bellon, ☎ 03 44 53 03 05,
fax 03 44 53 29 94

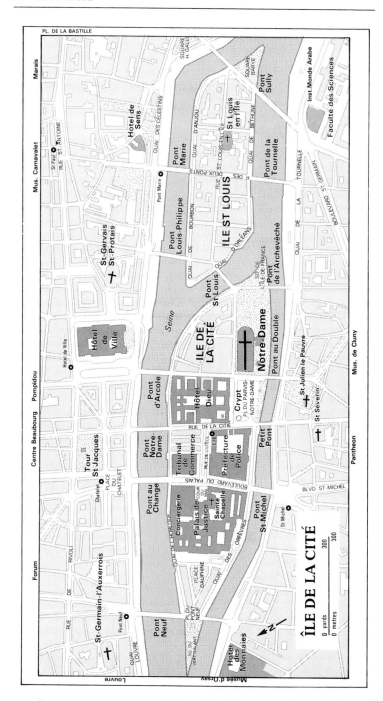

ÎLE DE LA CITÉ

Ile de la Cité and Ile-St-Louis

1 · The Ile de la Cité

■ Arrondissements: 75001, 75004.
■ Métros: Cité, Pont-Neuf-La Monnaie; RER: St-Michel-Notre-Dame, Châtelet-Les Halles.

Restaurant

Chez Paul, 15 Place Dauphine, Ile de la Cité, ☎ 01 43 54 21 48, long established. Traditional. £

The Ile-de-la-Cité, at the heart of Paris, contains three major monuments, The Sainte-Chapelle, best known for its wonderful 13C stained glass, and the rather dreary and infamous Conciergerie, where hundreds were imprisoned and died during the Revolution are described in Chapter 1. The Cathedral of Notre-Dame is covered in Chapter 2.

The Ile de la Cité (Pl. 14; 2-4 and opposite), the earliest inhabited part of Paris, lies in the river like a ship—the *pointe* its prow and Notre-Dame its poop—moored to both banks by numerous bridges. The freighted vessel on a sea argent has figured in the arms of Paris since the '*sceau des marchands de l'eau*' (the seal of the water merchants) became the seal of the first municipal administration at the time of St Louis in the 13C, with its device '*fluctuat nec mergitur*' (tossed but not engulfed). In its stylised form as the logo of the Mairie de Paris it is found all over the city.

The Cité was the site of the original Gallic settlement of *Lutèce* or *Lutetia Parisiorum*, and after the destruction of the later Roman city on the Left Bank, became the site of Frankish Paris. It remained the royal, legal and ecclesiastical centre, with fourteen parishes in the Middle Ages, long after the town had extended onto both river-banks. Despite the incursions of the 19C, its historic importance is still evident and some of the most important monuments of Paris are concentrated in this small area: the Cathedral of Notre-Dame de Paris, the Conciergerie and the Sainte-Chapelle. There are also the delights of the flower market (see p 60) on the north, the quiet charm of Place Dauphine to the west and the gardens of Square Jean XXIII behind the cathedral.

The Cité derives its importance from its situation at the crossroads of two natural routes across northern France. The Capetian kings were the great builders of the Cité, and it remained little changed from 1300 to the Second Empire, when Haussmann, after massive demolition, left it more or less with its present appearance.

From the Quai du Louvre the picturesque **Pont-Neuf** crosses the western extremity of the island. It is, in spite of its name, the oldest existing bridge in Paris, begun by Baptiste du Cerceau, completed in 1607, and repaired several times since. It was also the first to be built without houses lining each side, and with pavements. This Pointe de la Cité is occupied by Sq. du Vert-Galant, whose name alludes to the amorous adventures of Henri IV. Steps lead down behind the statue of the gallant King (Lemot, 1818), to a small shaded garden from where you have fine panoramas of the mainland buildings. The Vedettes du Pont-Neuf (sightseeing boats) depart from here.

East of the Pont-Neuf, entered by Rue Henri-Robert, is the **Pl. Dauphine**, retaining two rows of houses, some dating from the reign of Louis XIII, but many have been altered since. This little square contains one or two restaurants. Unfortunately the east wing of the triangle was demolished in 1874 to provide an unmerited view of Louis Duc's west façade of the Palais de Justice (see below).

Other **bridges** connecting the Cité to the Right Bank of the Seine are **Pont au Change** (1860), a name it acquired in the 12C when goldsmiths and moneylenders set up shop on the medieval bridge, the present one replacing a 17C stone bridge lined with buildings; **Pont Notre-Dame**, rebuilt in 1913 on the site of the main Roman bridge; and beyond, **Pont d'Arcole** (1855), named after a youth killed in 1830 leading insurgents against the Hôtel de Ville.

To the south, the island is connected to the Left Bank by **Pont St-Michel**, rebuilt several times since the late 14C (last in 1857), affording a fine view of the façade of Notre-Dame. Beyond is the Petit Pont (1853), on the site of another Roman bridge. Until 1782 it was defended at the southern end by the Petit Châtelet, the successor of the Tour de Bois, which in 886 held Viking or Norman marauders at bay. From the west front of Notre-Dame, the **Pont-au-Double** (1882) replaced a mid 17C bridge where the toll of a diminutive coin known as a double was charged; while from the eastern extremity of the Cité, near the site of the archbishop's palace (pulled down in 1831), **Pont de l'Archevêché** (1828), offers a good view of the apse of Notre-Dame, with its profusion of flying buttresses.

The Conciergerie

Follow the Quai de l'Horloge (north of the Palais de Justice), just beyond twin towers (see below), to find the entrance to one of the world's most infamous prisons, the **Conciergerie** (CNMHS), open 09.30–18.30, winter 10.00–17.00, closed 1/1, 1/5, 1/11, 11/11, 25/12, ☎ 01 53 73 78 50.

The Conciergerie occupies part of the lower floor of the Palais de la Cité, originally the servants quarters and then residence of the Concierge, an executive of the Parlement. Its historical associations are numerous and grisly, particularly during the Revolution when a succession of the celebrities of the day, both Royalist and Jacobin, including Marie-Antoinette, Mme du Barry, Camille Desmoulins, Charlotte Corday, Danton, André Chénier and Robespierre, passed their last days in the Conciergerie. 250–350 prisoners perished here in the massacres of September 1792, which marked the start of the Revolutionary Terror.

The visit starts in the Salle des Gardes, a handsome vaulted room of the 14C (restored 1877). This room contains two staircases, one ascending to the Tour de César (no access), the other to the Tour d'Argent (no access). Behind a red door in the right-hand corner of the room is a spiral staircase supposedly climbed by Marie-Antoinette and some 2275 other prisoners on their way from their cells to the Tribunal (see below).

The Conciergerie, Ile de la Cité

The impressive four-aisled Gothic **Salle des Gens-d'Armes**, constructed 1302–13 (restored in the 19C), originally served as a refectory for the servants of the royal household. It is often used today for concerts and private receptions. Near the far end, to the left, is a curious spiral staircase leading to the so-called Cuisines de St Louis, built in the 14C during the reign of Jean II Le Bon, a vaulted room containing four huge fireplaces.

Returning to the first bay, you turn left onto Rue de Paris, an area reserved for the *pailleux* (prisoners who slept on straw, being unable to pay for their term in jail) and enter the Galerie des Prisonniers which looks out onto the Cour des Femmes where the female prisoners took exercise, the supposed scene of the massacres of September 1792. In the Cour, a small sectioned-off area was reserved for those awaiting their fate at the guillotine. Further along the Galeries des Prisonniers is a small room, La Toilette, where prisoners were prepared for their execution and had their hair shorn. At the end is the iron wicket which was the only way in and out of the Conciergerie in Revolutionary times. Upstairs, several rooms show memorabilia from the prison and reconstructions of cells; there is a guillotine blade on the wall of one room. Here you can watch a short video film with English subtitles.

Another sad reminder is a door said to have been that of Marie-Antoinette's second cell, where the queen remained from 12 September to 16 October 1793. The chapel where the Girondins were incarcerated has a gallery reserved for the prisoners in the 19C. Behind the altar is the other former cell of Marie-Antoinette, transformed into a chapel by Louis XVIII during the Restoration and restored in 1989.

A re-creation of Marie Antoinette's cell can be seen at the end of the visit to the Conciergerie.

On leaving the Conciergerie, turn right into Blvd du Palais passing beneath the Tour de l'Horloge. Unlikely as it may now seem now, the Cour du Mai, on the right, was named after the maypole set up here annually by the society of law clerks.

The **Palais de Justice**, a huge block occupying the whole width of the island, is a great but inglorious result of 19C rebuilding, the main architects of which were Duc and Daumet. Embraced within its precincts, as well as the Conciergerie, are the Sainte-Chapelle (see below). This, and the four towers on the northern side, are the oldest surviving parts.

The site was occupied as early as the Roman period by a palace in which Julian the Apostate was proclaimed emperor in 360; the Merovingian kings, when in town, divided their time between the Thermes (see p 75) and this Palais de la Cité within the city walls. Louis VI died in the palace in 1137 and Louis VII in 1180. St Louis altered the palace and built the Sainte-Chapelle. From 1431 it was occupied entirely by the Parlement, which had previously only shared it with the king, but it was at the Revolution that it acquired its present function.

Here, in the 16th Chambre Correctionelle, the trials of Flaubert's *Madame Bovary* and Baudelaire's *Les Fleurs du Mal* (29 January and 20 August 1857 respectively) took place.

The 18C buildings were greatly enlarged in 1857–68 and again in 1911–14. In the mid 19C, the 14C tower, at the north eastern corner, with a clock copied from the original dial designed c 1585 by Germain Pilon, was virtually rebuilt. Splendid to look at, this replaced the first public clock in Paris. Likewise, the upper part of the north façade was rebuilt in the 19C in an attempt to reproduce the original 14C work by Enguerrand de Marigny. The domed Galerie Marchande, dominating the Cour du Mai, is embellished with sculptures by Pajou.

The most interesting part of these law courts may be entered directly from the boulevard just north of the Cour du Mai, by stairs up to the **Salle de Pas-Perdus**. This magnificent hall, which replaced the great hall of the medieval palace (where in 1431 the coronation banquet of Henry VI of England was celebrated), was rebuilt in 1622 by Salomon de Brosse, and restored in 1878 after being burned by the Communards. At the far end of the room, divided in two by a row of arches, and to the right, is the entrance to the Première Chambre Civile, formerly the Grand Chambre or Chambre Dorée (restored in the style of Louis XII), a vestige of the old palace and perhaps originally the bedroom of Louis IX. Later it was used by the Parlement, in contempt of which Louis XIV here coined his famous epigram '*L'état, c'est moi*'.

Sainte-Chapelle

The Sainte-Chapelle (CNMHS), entered from Blvd du Palais, was built in 1248 by the saintly Louis IX. A remarkable building, best known for its stained glass and its exceptional lightness and delicacy, it was planned both as royal chapel and as resting place for precious and costly relics acquired from the Emperor of Constantinople, among them the Crown of Thorns and fragments of the True Cross. The importance attributed to these relics is reflected in the sumptuousness of the original building, whose design has been ascribed to Pierre de Montreuil (compare St-Denis and St-Germain-en-Laye). The west window was replaced in 1485 by a Flamboyant rose.

Open summer, 09.30–18.30, winter 10.00–17.00, closed 1/1, 1/5, 1/11, 11/11, 25/12 (☎ 01 53 73 78 51).

Damaged by fire in 1630, the chapel was slowly rebuilt only to be put under risk of demolition at the end of the 18C. Thankfully, enthusiasm for all things medieval, engendered by the Romantic movement in the 19C, resulted in a full-scale restoration between 1837–57 by Duban, Lassus (who reconstructed a leaden *flèche* in the 15C style; the fifth on this site),

Viollet-le-Duc (chief architect of the Monuments Historiques created in 1830 to safeguard the national heritage) and his successor Boeswillwald.

From the outside, the impression of great height, actually 42.50m, in proportion to its length (36m) and breadth (17m) is accentuated by the buildings which crowd in around it. The chapel in fact consists of two superimposed levels: the lower, a small proportion of the whole, was for the use of servants and retainers; the upper chapel, with its lofty windows and rich stained glass, was reserved for the royal family and court. The portal consists of two porches, one above the other; the statues are 19C restorations. The balustrade is decorated with a motif of fleurs de lys and carved on the pinnacle above the south tower is a Crown of Thorns.

The interior of the **Chapelle Basse**, with carved oak bosses and 40 columns supporting the upper chapel is darkened by the decoration of Emile Boeswillwald, who attempted to reproduce its medieval decor painted with the fleurs de lys of France and the towers of Castille. The glass is 19C and three-lobed arcades and medallions enhance the walls. There are a number of 14C–15C tombstones in the pavement.

A narrow spiral staircase leads to the **Chapelle Haute** (20.50m high); royalty had an entrance direct from the palace. In contrast to the gloominess of the lower chapel, the upper chapel is a revelation. A virtuoso achievement of the Middle Ages, the structure is reduced to clumps of tracery and supports, between walls of richly coloured glass. Linking the blind traceried arcades of the lower part and the soaring windows are statues of Apostles under baldaquins— the 4th and 5th on the left, and the 4th and 5th to the right, are 13C. The upper chapel, originally inlaid with gilt and glass to give the effect of enamels emphasised the relationship to a shrine or reliquary. Ideally, to take full advantage of the stained glass, the Sainte-Chapelle needs to be seen in bright daylight. The two deep recesses under the windows of the 3rd bay were the seats reserved for the royal family. On the south side is a small chapel built at the time of Louis XI to enable the monarch to participate in mass without being seen.

In the centre of the restored arcade across the apse is a wooden canopy beneath which the relics used to be exhibited on Good Friday; those few surviving the Revolution are in the treasury of Notre-Dame.

The **stained-glass** was skilfully restored in 1845 and although some glass has been lost, a large proportion dates from the 13C. The glass reads from left to right and from bottom to top, and binoculars are a great help. Of the three east windows, on the left are scenes from the life of *St John the Evangelist* and the *Childhood of Christ*; the central one, considered the most outstanding, dwells on *Christ's Passion*; and on the right are the stories of *St John the Baptist* and of *Daniel*. All the other windows, except one, deal with the Old Testament, reading from north-west: *Genesis, Exodus, Numbers, Deuteronomy* and *Joshua, Judges, Isaiah* and the *Rod of Jesse*. Then the three apse windows are followed by *Ezekiel* —92 of the 121 scenes are original—*Jeremiah* and *Tobiah, Judith* and *Job, Esther*, and the *Book of Kings*. The south-west window depicts the *Legend of the True Cross* with illustrations of the translation of the relics to Paris by St Louis. However, this is one of the least well preserved and contains only 26 of the original 67 scenes. The 86 panels from the *Apocalypse* in the large rose-window, which are the easiest to read, were a gift of Charles VIII.

You leave the Chapelle Haute by the second spiral stair.

Opposite the Cour du Mai, Rue de Lutèce leads between (right) the Préfecture de Police and (left) the domed Tribunal de Commerce (by Bailly; 1860–65), behind which the **Marché aux Fleurs** offers a colourful and sweetly scented contrast. A bird market is held here on Sundays.

The Quai des Orfèvres on the south side of the island owes its name to the goldsmiths who were established here between 1580 and 1643. Much later, as the site of the headquarters of the detective branch of the French police, the quartier became famous through Maigret, Georges Simenon's detective hero.

2 · Notre-Dame

■ Métro: Cité.

On the eastern side of Rue de la Cité, a right and a left turn brings you into **PL. DU PARVIS NOTRE-DAME** (a space which Baron Haussmann increased sixfold by his demolitions) and face-to-face with the oldest of Paris's emblems, the Cathedral of Notre-Dame de Paris, the ribcage of the Cité and of Paris, with all its associations from pre-Christian times, royal marriages, Quasimodo, and presidential funerals. The Parvis or forecourt is at the very heart of Paris, and road distances are calculated from a symbolic centre marked by a bronze flagstone engraved with the arms of the town and the four points of the compass.

On the left is the **Hôtel-Dieu**, the hospital for central Paris, rebuilt in 1868–78 to the north of the site where the first hospital was founded by St Landry, Bishop of Paris, c 660. The old Hôtel-Dieu, built at the same time as Notre-Dame (12C), was razed by Haussmann. In the past, ecclesiastical authorities brought condemned heretics to trial on the Parvis where they knelt to acknowledge their sin and beg absolution before execution.

Near the west end of the Parvis is the entrance to the **Crypte Archéologique** (CNMHS). Superimposed layers of architectural remains of all periods of the Cité's past were uncovered here in 1965 during excavation work for the adjacent underground carpark. The site is exceptionally well presented with dioramas and models explaining the growth of the district prior to the ravaging fire of 1772. Sections are illuminated by press-button lighting and explanatory notes are printed both in French and English. Open 09.30–18.30, winter 10.00–17.30, closed 1/1, 1/5, 1/11, 11/11, 25/12 (☎ 43 29 83 51)

> The path runs above the foundations of the late-3C Gallo-Roman rampart, more of which is seen later. Further to the east, beyond the excavated area, lie the foundations of the west end of the Merovingian cathedral of St-Etienne (6C). After passing display cases of artefacts from the dig, you follow the foundations of the demolished Hospice des Enfants-Trouvés and other medieval buildings which flanked Rue Neuve Notre-Dame—some on the right as you approach the exit date from as early as the 2C. On the left are vestiges of hypocausts, etc.

Notre-Dame

To the east of the Parvis or forecourt rises Notre-Dame (Pl.14; 4), an immensely important building in the history of the development of Gothic architecture. Started in 1163 when Gothic art was beginning to throw off the traditions of the Romanesque style, it developed the new style initiated at St-Denis. The west front, with its magnificent rose window, was completed in the 13C, and Notre-Dame was in its turn a major influence on church architecture in the Ile-de-France and all over Europe. Despite successive alterations, this building represents a text-book example of the evolution of the Gothic style from the 12C to the 14C. Open 08.00–19.00 (closed Sat 12.30–14.00, ☎ 01 42 34 56 10).

Bishop Maurice de Sully, who died in 1196, was the inspiration behind the move to replace two earlier churches, St-Etienne and Notre-Dame, by a single building on a much larger scale. St-Etienne, founded by Childebert in 528 (see above), replaced a Roman temple of Jupiter more or less on the site of the present cathedral. Tradition holds that the foundation stone of the new cathedral was laid by Pope Alexander III in 1163. Between that date and the consecration of the main altar on 19 May 1182 the choir and double ambulatory were finished except for the high vault. The second phase of work, which completed the transepts and most of the nave, extended from c 1178–1200. From 1190–1220 the west front was built up to the rose window and during this period the second nave aisle was being erected. The rose itself dates from 1220–25 and the towers from 1225–50.

However, modifications were already being made by c 1225 to the earlier sections, notably the enlargement of the clerestory windows all around the church. In 1235–50 a series of chapels was built between the nave buttresses. Around 1250 the north transept was extended and the porch built by Jean de Chelles (d. c 1260) who also began c 1258 the extension of the south transept which was completed by Pierre de Montreuil. Pierre de Chelles built the jubé at the beginning of the 14C and he, followed by Jean Ravy, was responsible for the chapels around the apse (1296–1330). The latter *maître d'oeuvre* began the flying buttresses which took the strain of the high vaults and whose dramatic proportions provoke comparisons with the rigging of a ship. Jean Ravy's successors, Jean le Bouteiller and Raymond du Temple, completed work on the great vessel by the second half of the 14C.

For some three centuries the fabric of the cathedral remained relatively untouched and provided the setting for many important events. The School of Music at Notre-Dame was influential during the late 12C and 13C. In 1176 Geoffrey Plantagenet (the son of Henry II) was buried here after his sudden death in Paris. Henry VI of England at the age of 10 was crowned king of France here in 1431. Many royal marriages were celebrated within its walls, including those of James V of Scotland to Madeleine of France in 1537, François II to Mary Stuart (1558), Henri of Navarre, the future Henri IV, to Marguerite de Valois (1572) and Charles I of England (by proxy) to Henrietta Maria (1625).

Changes in taste and emphasis during the reigns of Louis XIV and Louis XV brought about major alterations. Tombs and stained-glass were destroyed, the jubé and the stalls were condemned, and in 1771 Soufflot (1713–80) knocked down the trumeau and part of the tympanum of the central portal to allow a processional dais to pass through. Much of what survived this destruction was lost during the Revolution. But the cathedral was still used for great ceremonies: in 1804, Napoléon I was crowned Emperor by Pius VII; Napoléon III and Eugénie de Montijo were married here in 1853.

By 1844, due in great part to Victor Hugo's Romantic novel, *Notre-Dame de Paris* (1831), otherwise known as the Hunchback of Notre-Dame, which helped to engender an interest in Gothic architecture, Notre-Dame was thought worth a thorough restoration. This was begun under the direction of Lassus and Viollet-le-Duc.

A century later, on 26 August 1944, the thanksgiving service following Général de Gaulle's entry into liberated Paris took place at Notre-Dame. The cathedral continues to be the scene of occasional ceremonial functions, state funerals, etc., the latest of which was the state's adieu to François Mitterand, in January 1996.

Exterior

The **west front**, composed of three distinct storeys, is a model of clarity and harmony. A masterful design of verticals and horizontals divides the elevation into regular and complementary sections, its construction continued through the entire first half of the 13C. The central **Porte du Jugement**, c 1220, ruined by Soufflot, is medieval only in essence. The figure of Christ on the trumeau dates from 1885, the Last Judgement was restored by Viollet-le-Duc, and most of the other sculptures are also 19C.

The **Porte de la Vierge** on the left, slightly earlier, is a fine composition. The Virgin on the central pier is a restoration, and the statues of saints were remade by Viollet-le-Duc. However, the scenes relating to the Life of the Virgin in the tympanum are 13C: in the lower register, the Ancestors of the Virgin, in the middle, the Resurrection of the Virgin, and in the upper register, Her Coronation.

The sculptures of the **Porte de St-Anne** (right) are mostly of 1165–75, designed for a narrower portal, with additions of c 1240. On the pier is St Marcellus (19C); above are scenes from the life of St Anne and the Virgin, and the Virgin in Majesty, with Louis VII (right) and Maurice de Sully (left). The two side doors retain their medieval wrought-iron hinges.

In the buttress niches flanking the doors are modern statues of St Stephen, the Church, the Synagogue and St Denis. Above, across the full width of the façade, is the Gallery of the Kings of Judah, reconstructed by Viollet-le-Duc. Its 28 statues were destroyed in 1793 because the Parisians assumed they represented the kings of France but fragments discovered in 1977 are now in the Musée du Moyen Age. The magnificent rose-window, 9.6m in diameter, is flanked by double windows within arches. Higher still is an open arcade on slender columns.

The massive **towers** (CNMHS) never received the spires which were originally intended. It is possible to climb the 387 steps inside and it is worth the effort for the view of Viollet-le-Duc's flèche and the rooftops. You enter by the north tower. The great bell, Emmanuel, recast in 1686 and weighing 13 tonnes, can be seen in the south tower, recalling Quasimodo, Victor Hugo's bell-ringer. The suitably chimerical gargoyles were redesigned by Viollet-le-Duc. Open 09.30–18.30, winter 10.00–17.00, closed 1/1, 1/5, 1/11, 11/11, 25/12 (☎ 01 44 32 16 70).

Like the west front, the side façades and apse also consist of three distinct and receding storeys; the bold and elegant flying buttresses of the latter were an innovation by Jean Ravy. The **south porch**, according to a Latin inscription at the base, was begun in 1257 under the direction of Jean de Chelles. The story of St Stephen (a reference to the earlier church dedicated to him) in the tympanum and the medallions depicting student life, are original. The **north porch**, slightly earlier, has an original statue of the Virgin and, in the tympanum, the Story of Theophilius. Just to the east of this porch is the graceful Porte Rouge, probably by Pierre de Montreuil. To the left, below the windows of the choir chapels, are seven 14C bas-reliefs. The flèche (90m above the ground), a lead-covered oak structure, was rebuilt by Viollet-le-Duc in 1860, after the original was destroyed in the 18C.

Interior
The interior is fairly regular in its layout with only slight discrepancies, and the shift in axis between the nave and choir and the increased width of the latter (48m) over the former are hardly discernible. Despite the large clerestory windows with modern glass (1964), the interior tends to be rather sombre, and is usually very busy. On the left when entering is a bookstall, and visitors are encouraged not to enter the ambulatory except for devotional purposes.

The height of the ten-bay **nave**, 33m—very daring for the time—emphasised the prestige of the principal ecclesiastical building in Paris. The sheer elevations of the nave and shallow mouldings of the upper storey emphasise the wafer thinness of the walls relative to their height. In contrast, short cylindrical piers, a throw-back to St-Denis, surround the nave and the apse. Triple shafts of equal size rise uninterrupted from the capitals to the springing of the sexpartite vaults. The nave is flanked by double aisles and a double ambulatory surrounds the choir (five bays) and 37 chapels surround the whole. The total length of the cathedral is 130m. A vaulted triforium overlooks the nave whereas the gallery around the choir has double openings.

The change in master of works c 1178 resulted in a contrast between the piers with shafts on the east and the piers with pilasters to the west. The upper part of the transept bays and west bay of the choir were remodelled in the 19C to approximately their original 12C disposition.

The shallow transepts contain two of the three **rose-windows** which have retained some original 13C glass. The north is the finest and best preserved and represents kings, judges, priests and prophets around the Virgin. The south was much restored in 1737 and, with Christ at the centre, figures saints, apostles and angels, with the wise and foolish virgins. The rose in the west contains scenes of the labours of the months, the signs of the zodiac, vices, virtues and prophets, with the Virgin, but was almost entirely remade in the 19C.

In the **side-chapels** of the nave hang seven 17C paintings from an original 76 (by Charles le Brun, Sébastian Bourdon and others), presented by the Goldsmiths' Guild of Paris between 1630 and 1707. Against the south east pillar at the crossing stands a 14C image of the Virgin, known as Notre-Dame de Paris, and against the north east pillar is St Denis by Nicolas Coustou (18C).

The **choir**, completely altered in 1708–25 by Louis XIV in fulfilment of his father's vow of 1638, under the direction of Robert de Cotte, was not spared by

Viollet-le-Duc. Behind Viollet-le-Duc's altar is a Pietà (1723) by Nicolas Coustou, the base by Girardon, part of the Voeu de Louis XIII. The statue of Louis XIII (south) is also by Coustou; that of Louis XIV (north) by Coysevox (both 1715). Of the original 114 **stalls**, 78 remain, adorned with bas-reliefs from the designs of Jules Degoulon (1711–15) with canopied archiepiscopal stalls stand at either end. The bronze angels (1713) against the apse-pillars escaped the Revolutionary melting-pot.

In the first four bays of the choir are the remains of the mid 14C choir screen which, until the 18C, extended round the whole apse; the expressive reliefs on the exterior were unhappily restored and repainted by Viollet-le-Duc. In the blind arches below are listed some of the eminent people buried in the church.

The **ambulatory** contains the tombs of 18C–19C prelates. Behind the high altar is the tomb-statue of Bishop Matiffas de Bucy (died 1304). In the 2nd chapel south of the central chapel is the theatrical tomb, by Jean-Baptiste Pigalle, of the Comte d'Harcourt (died 1769); here also are the restored tomb-statues of Jean Jouvenel des Ursins and his wife (died 1431, 1451).

On the south side of the ambulatory is the entrance to the sacristy, now containing the **treasury**, a somewhat indifferent collection of ecclesiastical plate, reliquaries and cult objects. In the west is the main organ, 1733, by Cliquot rebuilt in 1868 by the Cavaillé-Coll workshops. Open 09.30–11.45, 12.30–17.30, Sat. 09.30– 11.45, 14.00–17.30, closed Christian feast days.

At No. 10 Rue du Cloître Notre-Dame is the Musée Notre-Dame de Paris with collections relating to the history of the cathedral. Open Wed, Sat and Sun, 14.30–18.00.

Rue Massillon turns north into Rue Chanoinesse. Parallel to the north, at 19 Rue des Ursins, stands part of the nave of St Aignan (1118). **Sq. Jean XXIII** is a pleasant little garden with a fountain and benches on the site of the 17C archbishop's palace. Further east, another garden, **Sq. de l'Ile-de-France**, was the Canons' Walk. At the extreme east end, down a flight of steps, is a stark but moving **Mémorial de la Déportation of 1962** by Henri Pingusson to some 200,000 Frenchmen deported to German concentration camps during the 1939–45 war.

3 · Ile St-Louis

■ Arrondissement: 75004.
■ Métros: Cité, Pont-Marie, Sully-Morland.

Restaurants and cafés

Auberge de la Reine Blanche, 30 Rue Saint-Louis en l'Île, ☎ 01 46 33 07 87. Traditional. £

Bertillon, 31 Rue Saint-Louis en l'Ile, ☎ 01 43 54 31 61. Ice cream parlour. £

Brasserie de l'Ile St-Louis, 55 Quai de Bourbon, ☎ 01 43 54 02 59. Alsatian fare. £

La Flore en l'Ile, Quai de Bourbon, ☎ 01 43 29 88 27. Café/tea shop. £

The Ile St-Louis boasts no major monuments but a harmonious architectural setting and river views for quiet contemplation.

Just a footbridge away from the Ile de la Cité is its smaller and younger sister, the **Ile St-Louis**. This tranquil and elegant backwater, with no métro station, is a sought-after residential area. It can be reached on foot from the Ile de la Cité via Pont St-Louis (dating from 1614, but replaced in 1969).

At the head of the bridge (the sunniest spot on the island) is the ***Brasserie de l'Ile St-Louis*** (see p 64), for decades a popular haunt of the British, and the island is well-known for the 116 flavours of ice cream made by ***Berthillon's ice-cream parlour***. There are also one or two pleasant hotels tucked away in this quiet spot.

The Ile St-Louis was formerly two islets which were not linked until the 17C when, as an annexe of the Marais to the north, it became the site of a number of imposing mansions, several designed by Louis Le Vau, the

Musicians playing on Ile St-Louis

leading French baroque architect. These jostle for place in the few narrow streets or present a dignified and subtly-hued cordon facing out to the river.

The island is connected to the north bank by **Pont Louis-Philippe** (rebuilt 1862); beyond stands **Pont Marie** (1635), named after the original developer of the island, Christophe Marie, crossing to Quai des Celestins. Further east, the island and river are intersected obliquely by **Pont de Sully** (1876), at the northern end of which, beyond Sq. H.-Galli, stands the striking Hôtel de Fieubet. On the south side of the island, **Pont de la Tournelle** of 1928 (the last of a succession since 1369), crosses from Rue des Deux-Ponts to the Quai de la Tournelle.

The main street, RUE ST-LOUIS-EN-L'ILE does not have the views of the river and its banks but has retained an aura of times past. It is endowed with one or two good buildings, including at No. 51 the **Hôtel Chenizot**, with a fine decorated doorway and balcony of 1726 by Pierre de Vigny.

The church of **St-Louis-en-l'Ile** could be passed by unnoticed if it were not for the curious openwork spire and the clock of 1741. Begun in 1664 to replace the by then outgrown original chapel, St-Louis-en-l'Ile was based on designs by the great architect Louis Le Vau. It was finished in 1726 by Jacques Doucet. The bright baroque interior has ornamental stone-carving executed under the direction of the painter Philippe de Champaigne's nephew Jean-Baptiste de Champaigne, who is buried here (d. 1681). As well as several 18C paintings and furnishings of some interest, the church contains a 16C Flemish polychromed wood relief of the *Dormition of the Virgin*, and six Nottingham alabaster reliefs.

Typical of the grander *hôtels particuliers* built on the eastern part of the island is the **Hôtel Lambert** at No. 2, begun in 1641 by Le Vau, the interior decorated by Eustache Le Sueur and Charles Le Brun, among others. It is now privately owned but the terraced garden and oval gallery designed by Le Vau can be glimpsed from the Quai d'Anjou.

The extreme easterly tip of the island is a tiny triangular Square, named after the sculptor Antoine-Louis Barye.

Across the Seine is a view of the Left Bank with the Institut du Monde Arabe to the south east (see p 80), and the adjacent Science Faculty Building, with its tower, built on the site of the old Halles aux Vins.

No. 3 Quai d'Anjou, on the north eastern side of the island, belonged to Le Vau; No. 9 was the home of the artist Honoré Daumier (1808–79) from 1846. No. 17 the **Hôtel de Lauzun**, 1657, attributed to Le Vau, was the residence in 1682–84 of the Duc de Lauzun, commander of the French forces at the Battle of the Boyne in 1690, when he was defeated by King William III of Britain. From 1842 it became a popular meeting place for artists and writers, and both Baudelaire and Théophile Gautier rented rooms here. The artists responsible for its splendid decoration were Le Brun, Le Sueur, Patel and Sébastien Bourdon. Visits are arranged through the CNMHS. Ford Madox Ford's literary periodical *Transatlantic Review* was published from No. 29.

Further west, 13 and 15 Quai de Bourbon, the Hôtel Le Charron (17C), has a mansard window with the old pulley used for hoisting goods. No. 1 was the cabaret or inn Franc-Pinot.

Turning south, you pass at No. 6 Quai d'Orleans, the **Musée Adam Mickiewicz**, with a Polish library and souvenirs of the poet (1798–1855), and also of Chopin.

The South or Left Bank: La Rive Gauche

4 · Quartier Latin

■ Arrondissement: 75005.
■ Métros: St-Michel, Cluny-La Sorbonne, Maubert-Mutualité, Card. Lemoine, Luxembourg. RER: Saint-Michel-Notre Dame.

Restaurants and cafés

Le Balzar, 49 Rue des Ecoles, ☎ 01 43 54 13 67. 1930s brasserie. £
Le Bar à Huîtres, 33 Rue St-Jacques, ☎ 01 44 07 27 37. Oyster bar. £
Bistrot d'à Côté St- Germain, Michel Rostaing, 16 Blvd St-Germain, ☎ 01 43 54 59 10. £
Grand Bistro, 7 Rue St-Séverin, ☎ 01 43 25 94 21. £
Les Bouchons de F. Clerc, 12 rue de l'Hôtel-Colbert, ☎ 01 43 54 15 34. Newish bistrot. £
Campagne et Provence, 25 Quai de la Tournelle, ☎ 01 43 54 05 17. Bistrot. £
La Cochonnaille, 21 Rue de la Harpe, ☎ 01 46 33 96 81. Traditional. £
La Cour aux Crêpes, 27 Rue Galande, ☎ 01 43 25 45 00. Crêpes. £
Les Fontaines, 9 Rue Soufflot. ☎ 01 43 26 42 80. Trendy café-restaurant. £
La Parcheminerie, Rue La Parchiminerie, ☎ 01 46 33 65 12. Traditional. £
La Rôtisserie du Beaujolais, 19 Quai de la Tournelle, ☎ 01 43 54 17 47. Traditional. £
La Tour d'Argent, 15 Quai de la Tournelle, ☎ 01 43 54 23 31. Haute cuisine. ££
Perraudin, 157 Rue St-Jacques, ☎ 01 46 33 15 75. Bistrot. £
Le Port du Salut, 163 bis Rue St-Jacques, modestly priced, no ☎. £

This chapter includes the two major Gallo-Roman remains of Paris—the Thermes de Cluny and the Arènes de Lutèce—and three of the most interesting lesser-known medieval churches: St-Séverin, St-Etienne-du-Mont, and St-Nicholas-du-Chardonnet. The Musée du Moyen Age is described in Ch. 5.

The Quartier Latin, associated with the young, is one of the oldest parts of Paris. It derives its name from the language spoken by scholars who began to congregate in the area in the 12C. The site of Roman Lutetia, on the south bank of the Seine opposite the Ile de la Cité (see Ch. 1), it developed after Abélard's removal in c 1100 from the school attached to Notre-Dame to the Montagne Ste-Geneviève. Originally known as the Université, the Quartier Latin still contains the majority of the educational and scientific institutions of Paris.

The quarter holds an irresistible yet vague attraction to many visitors, and cafés and bookshops abound, but the crass commercialism, fast-food restaurants and constant frenetic hustle and bustle of the main artery, the **BOUL MICH** (Blvd St-Michel) can be a disincentive to linger. The more picturesque character of the quartier is found in the side-streets where there are many reminders of the past. In the mid 19C, Blvd St-Germain was driven east through the old streets and many ancient buildings were swept away. During the student revolution of 1968, the old *pavés* (cobblestones) were used as missiles and have been replaced by dull slabs.

The Place St-Michel (Pl. 14; 4) is linked to the Cité by the Pont St-Michel, with the Fontaine St-Michel at its south end (1860), incorporating a memorial to the Resistance of 1944. From the Place, Blvd St-Michel leads south to the Carrefour de l'Observatoire, in part following the Roman Via Inferior. The boulevard was laid out by Haussman as a direct continuation of Blvd de Strasbourg and Blvd de Sébastopol, and shortly crosses Blvd St-Germain, running roughly parallel to the Seine.

Immediately to the east of the Pl. St-Michel, is a still decrepit corner of Old Paris penetrated by ancient streets or alleys such as Rue de la Huchette, Rue Xavier-Privas and Rue du Chat-qui-Pêche (named after an old shop-sign).

St-Séverin

Turn right along Rue de la Harpe, and take the first turning left, to arrive at St-Séverin, an interesting church, built from the 13C–16C combining early and late Gothic styles overlaid with various modifications of later periods.

The first simple church was built here in the 13C on the site of an oratory of the time of Childebert I in which Foulque of Neuilly-sur-Marne had preached the Fourth Crusade (c 1199). The church was enlarged at the end of the 13C and beginning 14C, but only the first three bays of the nave escaped a fire in 1448. Rebuilding work began in 1452 and went on until 1498. In the 17C the church was drastcially altered like many churches at the time. The jubé was demolished and the choir partially classicised at the request of Mlle de Montpensier.

The early 13C **west door**, carved with foliage in the hollows between the colonettes, was brought piecemeal from St-Pierre-aux-Boeufs in the Cité in 1837 (Virgin and Child 19C). The upper two storeys date from the 15C. On the left is a tower of the 13C, completed in 1487, with a door which was once the main entrance; the tympanum dates from 1853, but in the frame is a 15C inscription: 'Bonnes gens qui par cy passés, Priez Dieu pour les trespassés'. To the left of the tower, a niche holds a statue of St Séverin (1847). On the south are the galleries of the 15C charnel house, the only one left in Paris.

The **interior** is impressively broad compared to its length, with a double ambulatory but no transept. The difference in style between first three bays, built in the 13C, and the remainder, which are 15C, is quite obvious. The earlier bays contain late 14C glass from St-Germain-des-Prés, but much restored; from the fourth bay on, the glass is mid-15C. One of the subjects on the south side of the nave is the *Murder of Thomas à Becket*. The west rose-window contains a *Tree of Jesse* (c 1500) masked by the organ of 1745, once played by Fauré and Saint-Saëns.

The **double ambulatory** is a tour de force of Flamboyant architecture with a dynamic central column around which shafts spiral to burst into leaf in the vaults like a palm tree. The stained glass of the apse chapels is by Jean Bazaine (1966). Off the south-east chapel is the Holy Communion Chapel designed by Jules Hardouin-Mansart in 1673. The liturgical furnishings are by Georges Schneider (1985–89) and the chapel contains a series of engavings, *Miserere*, 1917–27, by Georges Rouault, exposed here since 1993.

On the far side of Rue St-Jacques is Rue Galande, one of the oldest streets in Paris (14C). It has retained traces of earlier times, and on No. 42 is a carved relief of the life of St Julian.

The church of **St-Julien-le-Pauvre** (right), rebuilt c 1170–1230 by monks of Longpont, a Cluniac abbey, stands on the site of a succession of chapels dedicated to St Julien the Hospitaller or the Poor Man. Despite degradation and many restorations it retains the air of a solid late-Romanesque country church and there are two original carved capitals in the chancel. It was used in the 13C–16C as a university church and in 1655–1877 by the former Hôtel-Dieu for various secular purposes, has been occupied by Melchites (Greek Catholics) since 1889 and an iconostasis obscures the east end. The present west front was built in 1651.

The small garden adjacent to the church, **Sq. René-Viviani**, is adorned not only with some architectural elements, possibly from Notre-Dame, but the oldest tree in Paris, a *robinier* (false acacia) planted in 1601. From here is a classic view of Notre-Dame.

From the north east side of this square runs Rue de la Bûcherie. **Shakespeare & Co.** at No. 37 established its reputation as the rendez-vous of interwar American writers and by publishing James Joyce's *Ulysses* in 1922, at its first home in Rue de l'Odéon. No. 13 was occupied by the École de Médecine from 1483 to 1775, with a rotunda built in 1745.

South of Sq. René-Viviani is Rue du Fouarre (named after the straw on which the students sat), the centre of four 14C schools of the University, and referred to by Dante who is reputed to have attended lectures here.

A short distance along the Rue Monge, leading south east, is (left) **St-Nicolas-du-Chardonnet**—its name a reminder that an earlier church was built in a field of thistles. The major part of the present church was built 1656–1709; only the tower (1625) remains of the previous building. Le Brun designed the finely carved door on Rue des Bernardins. In the 19C, Blvd St-Germain shaved the east of the church necessitating a rearrangement of the apsidal chapel, and the main façade on Rue Monge was not completed until this century.

The lucid **interior** space contains some interesting furnishings while the ornamental glass chandeliers add a decadent touch. In the first bay is Le Brun's painting of the *Martyrdom of St-John the Evangelist*, and in the first chapel on the right is Corot's study for the *Baptism of Christ*; in the transept are two paintings by Nicolas Coypel. Outstanding are a monument by Girardon of *Bignon*, the jurist, died 1656 (second chapel on the right of the choir), and the splendidly theatrical tomb of *Le Brun's mother*, designed by Le Brun (8th chapel round the apse); in the same chapel is a monument to *Le Brun* (d. 1690) *and his widow*, by the sculptor Antoine Coysevox.

Across Rue Monge under the wall of the former Ecole Polytechnique is a triangle of greenery, **Sq. Paul Langevin**. The fountain is 18C and the two headless statues are from the old Hôtel de Ville. The statue is of the poet François Villon (1431–63). Steps lead up to the Jardin Carré, a modern formal garden open to the public in the former college's courtyard (see below), embellished with a modern bronzes by Meret Oppenheim (1986), Mostaheim and Penone.

Turn left along Rue St-Victor to reach (left) Rue de Poissy. At No. 24 are the remains of the 14C refectory of the ancient Collège des Bernardines.

At the far end of this street, where it meets Quai de la Tournelle, stands the restored 17C **Hôtel de Nesmond** (Nos 55–57), containing the offices of La Demeure Historique. This association of owners of historic residences, founded in 1924, is devoted to promoting public interest in privately owned châteaux and publishes information about them.

At No. 47 is the former convent of the Miramiones or Filles Ste-Geneviève, founded by Mme de Miramion (died 1696). It has a small **museum** devoted to the history of the hospitals of Paris, the Musée de l'Assistance Publique (10.00–17.00, closed Sun, Mon, public hols & Aug, ☎ 01 40 27 50 05). No. 15 is **La Tour d'Argent**, one of the oldest top-class eating places in Paris built on the site of a tavern dating from 1582. The restaurant is on the top floor looking across to Notre-Dame, and below is the small Musée de la Table.

At 32 Rue du Card.-Lemoine, the next main street running south from the quai, stood the Collège des Bons-Enfants, where Vincent de Paul founded his congregation of mission-priests. Further south, No. 49 is the **Hôtel le Brun**, built by Gabriel Boffrand (1667–1754), and later occupied by Watteau and by Buffon.

Climbing south west at the junction of Rue du Card.-Lemoine with Rue Monge, you reach Rue Clovis, where a section of Philippe Auguste's 13C perimeter wall is visible.

65 Rue du Card.-Lemoine, the Institution Ste-Geneviève, was the **Collège des Ecossais** (Scots College), re-founded in 1662 by Robert Barclay. To visit, apply to the CNMHS. This street meets Rue des Ecoles and the quarter of the old schools.

At 5 Rue Descartes (running across Rue Clovis) is the entrance to the former **Ecole Polytechnique**, founded in 1794 for the training of artillery and engineer officers. This most prestigious of the *Grandes Ecoles* (colleges created by the Convention to provide technical experts needed by the Empire), transferred here in 1805 to the old buildings of the Collège de Navarre and the Collège de Boncourt, and moved to the outskirts of Paris in 1977. The gardens are open to the public (see above.).

At 34 Rue Montagne-Ste-Geneviève, further down the hill, are remains of the Collège des Trente-Trois, named after its 33 scholarships (one for each year of Christ's life).

At 23 Rue Clovis is the entrance to the **Lycée Henri-IV**, one of Paris's great schools, which took over the site of the old Abbaye Ste-Geneviève in 1796. Little remains of the original abbey demolished in 1802 except the courtyard tower, with Romanesque base and two Gothic upper storeys (14C–15C). The former refectory (now the chapel) is an over-restored 13C building. The kitchens are also medieval.

St-Etienne-du-Mont

On the right is St-Etienne-du-Mont (Pl. 14; 6), enhanced after recent restoration, an unusually pretty church with some original features. Essentially a late-Gothic structure with Renaissance decoration, it was almost continuously in construction from 1492 to1586. It has sheltered the shrine of Ste-Geneviève, the patron saint of Paris, since the destruction of the old church. But its most unusual asset is a rare jubé still in place.

> Originally St-Etienne adjoined the abbey church possibly accounting for the choir, nave and façade being on slightly different axes. In 1610, Marguerite de Valois laid the foundation stone of the façade which has three pedimented tiers with a small rose window in each of the upper ones in a curious combination characteristic of the transitional style of architecture from late Gothic to Renaissance. The statues are 19C. The tower, begun in 1492, was completed in 1628 and on the north flank is a picturesque porch of 1632.

The luminous **interior** gives an impression of height because of the tall aisles. Its originality lies in the elegant gallery which links the supporting pillars of the nave and choir. Several of the large windows contain original stained glass. The ambulatory is wide with ribbed vaulting and heavy pendant bosses, the longest above the crossing. The celebrated fretted stone **jubé**, built in 1525–35, is a virtuoso piece of stone carving with magnificent sweeping spirals at either side of the central pierced balustrade. The design is attributed to Philibert de l'Orme, and the work was probably carried out by Antoine Beaucorps. The date 1605 on the side refers only to the door to the spiral.

The organ, over the west door, has a richly carved case by Jean Buron dating from 1631–32, with *Christ of the Resurrection* at the summit. The works are 17C, renovated in the 19C. The pulpit is the work of the great sculptor Germain Pilon, with later sculptures designed by Laurent de la Hyre.

The **stained glass** ranges in date from c 1550 to c 1600; the high nave windows by N. Pinaigrier, date from 1587–88, and include scenes of the *Resurrection*, *Ascension* and the *Coronation of the Virgin*. The transept glass (1585–87), also by Pinaigrier with J. Bernard, include various saints and the *Crucifixion*. The high windows in the choir contain glass of the 1540s onwards, and in the ambulatory are fragments of 16C glass mixed with 19C work.

The church has many **furnishings** of note. Above the first chapel in the choir is an ex-voto to Ste Geneviève, with the provost and merchants of Paris, by François de Troy (1726), while higher, to the right, is a similar painting by Largillière of 1696. On either side of the chapel are the epitaphs of Pascal and Racine (by Boileau), whose graves are at the entrance to the Lady Chapel. Also buried in the church are Charles Rollin (1661–1741), the historian, and the artist Eustache le Sueur (1616–55). In the next chapel south of the choir is the copper-gilt shrine of Ste Geneviève (1853), containing a fragment of her tomb; her remains were burned by the mob in the Pl. de Grève (Pl. de l'Hôtel de Ville) in 1801.

From the next bay runs a corridor, at the end of which (right) is the presbytery, built in 1742 for Louis d'Orléans (son of the Regent), who died here in 1752. On the left is the **charnier**, or gallery of the graveyard, with 12 superb **windows** of 1605–09; the joy of these is that the glass panels are at eye level and the most notable are: 1. *The Miracle of Rue des Billettes*, 2. *Noah's Arc*, 9. *Manna from Heaven*, and 10. *The Mystic Wine-press*.

The Panthéon

To the south west of St-Etienne-du-Mont and across Pl.-Ste-Geneviève (Pl. 14; 6) is the unmistakable and grandiose bulk of the Panthéon (CNMHS), The building was inspired by the Pantheon in Rome with its dome and peristyled portico. Situated on the Mont de Paris, the highest point on the Left Bank (60m), this was the legendary burial-place of Geneviève (5C), the *pucelle* of Nanterre, later regarded as the patron saint of Paris. Open summer 10.00–19.30, winter 10.00–18.15, (last admission 45 mins before closing), closed 1/1,1/5,1/11, 11/11, 25/12.

> In 1744, lying ill at Metz, Louis XV vowed that if he recovered he would replace the abbey church of Ste-Geneviève, then in a ruinous state. The present building was begun 20 years later, although not completed until 1789. Its architect, Jacques-Germaine Soufflot, died of anxiety, it is said, because the construction showed signs of subsidence as its foundations were laid above Roman clay pits.
>
> In 1791, the Constituent Assembly decided that the building should be used as a Panthéon or burial-place for distinguished citizens, and the pediment was inscribed with the words *Aux Grands Hommes la Patrie reconnaissante*. From the Restoration to 1831 and from 1851 to 1885 it was reconsecrated, but on the occasion of Victor Hugo's interment in 1885 it was definitively secularised.

The Panthéon, built in the shape of a Greek cross, is 110m long, 82m wide and 83m high to the top of its majestic dome. The pediment above the portico of Corinthian columns contains a masterful relief by David d'Angers, representing *France between Liberty and History*, distributing laurels to famous men.

The **interior** is coldly Classical, using the giant Corinthian order, and Ste-Geneviève's tomb was originally intended to lie below the cupola. The vast space is enlivened with a series of huge (everything is colossal here) **murals**, made possible when 42 windows were walled up during the Revolution. The most notable of these is the series of the *Life of Ste Geneviève* by the Symbolist painter Puvis de Chavannes, recognisable by their calm dignity and quiet colours. The only true exponent of the technique of fresco painting to work in the Panthéon, and admirer of the art of the Quattrocento, this series, begun in 1874, gave Puvis the ideal setting in which to work and brought him general acclaim. Note in particular the panel showing the saint watching over Paris and bringing supplies to the city after the siege by the Huns.

The central part of the Panthéon is out of bounds because of danger from falling masonry. In the east end is a work representing the Convention, by Sicard. Against the central pillars are monuments to: (right) Jean-Jacques Rousseau by Bartholomé: left, to Diderot and the Encyclopaedistes by Terroir.

The **dome**, supported by four piers united by arches, contains three distinct cupolas, of which the first is open in the centre to reveal the second, with a fresco by Antoine Gros. Within the dome, in 1852, the physicist Léon Foucault gave the first public demonstration of his pendulum experiment proving the rotation of the Earth, dramatically reconstructed and commentated by audio-visual displays in the aisles.

The **crypt** (enter by the north east) contains the **tombs** of *Jean-Jacques Rousseau* (1712–78), *Voltaire* (1684–1778), and *Soufflot*, the architect. Of the famous men whose remains have been reinterred in the vaults, the most eminent are *Victor Hugo* (1802–85) and *Emile Zola* (1840–1902); *Marcelin Berthelot* (1827–1907), the chemist; *Jean Jaurès* the socialist politician (1859–assassinated 1914); *Louis Braille* (1809–52), benefactor of the blind; the explorer *Bougainville* (1729–1811); and *Jean Moulin* (1899–1944), the Resistance hero. The heart of *Léon Gambetta* (1838–82), one of the proclaimers of the Republic in 1870, is enshrined here. *Jean Monnet* (1888–1979), the 'Father of Europe', was buried in the Panthéon on the centenary of his birth, and most recently (1995) the remains of *Pierre and Marie Curie* and *André Malraux* were translated here.

It is now possible to climb up into **la colonnade** for an unusual and interesting view over historic Paris.

In the north west corner of the Pl. du Panthéon is the Law Faculty building, begun by Soufflot in 1771, and subsequently enlarged.

The **Bibliothèque Ste-Geneviève**, on the northern side of the Place (10 Place du Panthéon), originated in the library of the Abbaye Ste-Geneviève. On this site until the 19C stood the Collège de Montaigu, founded in 1314, where Loyola, Erasmus and Calvin were students. The present building (1844–50), by the great architect Henri Labrouste, is an important structure not only because it is an early example of a metal frame building, using both wrought and cast iron, but also for its highly original exterior, a cross between a 16C Florentine palace and a 19C railway station. (Visits on request: write or ☎ 01 44 41 97 97.)

The library contains c 2,000,000 vols (nearly 4000 MSS) and over 40,000 prints and engravings (including 10,000 portraits). Rooms are devoted to Scandinavian literature (c 90,000 vols) and the Bibliothèque Jacques Doucet, comprising c 25,000 vols of late 19C and 20C French authors, including MSS of Rimbaud, Verlaine, Baudelaire, Gide and Valéry.

In Rue Valette, next to the library, was the Collège Fortet (No. 21) where Calvin studied in 1531. At No.1 bis is the Museum of the History of the Prefecture of Police, with a room devoted to the Resistance and the Liberation of Paris (09.00–17.00, Sat 10.00–17.00, closed Sun and public holidays). Here are records of important conspiracies, arrests, famous characters, archives, unique weapons and uniforms, and evidence from famous criminal cases.

The other side of the library in Rue Cujas, is the Collège Ste-Barbe, founded in 1460, the oldest existing public educational establishment in France.

The RUE ST-JACQUES is an ancient and important thoroughfare which follows the course of the Roman road the Via Superior from Lutetia to Orléans, and formed part of the pilgrimage route to Santiago de Compostela in the Middle Ages. Its southern section is described on p 87.

Turn right into the Rue St-Jacques (several places to eat), and on the right is the **Lycée Louis-le-Grand**, formerly the Jesuit Collège de Clermont, founded in

1560 and rebuilt in 1887–96. Molière, Voltaire, Robespierre, Desmoulins, Delacroix and Hugo studied here.

The next building is the **Collège de France**, its entrance in the Pl. Marcelin-Berthelot (Pl. 14; 4–6). In the courtyard, with its graceful portico, is a statue of the scholar Guillaume Budé (Budaeus; 1468–1540), under whose influence it was founded by François I in 1530 with the intention of spreading Renaissance humanism and counteracting the narrow scholasticism of the Sorbonne. Independent of the University, its teaching was free and public. The present building was begun in 1610, completed by Jean-François Chalgrin c 1778 and has since been enlarged.

Sq. A.-Mariette-Pacha, next to the Collège de France, contains statues of Dante (1882), Ronsard (1928) and C. Bernard (1946), and in Impasse Chartière nearby is a monument to the Pléiade (a group of Renaissance poets), which originated in the vanished Collège Coqueret, founded on this site in 1418–1643.

The Sorbonne

To the west of the Collège de France is the Sorbonne, founded as a theological college in 1253 by Robert de Sorbon (1201–74), chaplain to Louis IX. It was rebuilt at Richelieu's expense by Jacques Lemercier in 1629 but, with the exception of the church, the present buildings date from 1885–1901.

The University of Paris, which disputes with Bologna the title of the oldest university in Europe, arose in the first decade of the 12C out of the schools of dialectic attached to Notre-Dame. Transferred by Abélard to the Montagne Ste-Geneviève, the university obtained its first statutes in 1208, and these served as the model for Oxford and Cambridge and other universities of northern Europe. By the 16C it comprised no fewer than 40 separate colleges.

Before the end of the 13C the Sorbonne had become synonymous with the faculty of theology, overshadowing the rest of the university and possessing the power of conferring degrees. It was noted for its religious rancour, supporting the condemnation of Joan of Arc, justifying the St-Bartholomew's Day massacre and refusing its recognition of Henri IV, a former Protestant. Nevertheless in 1469 it was responsible for the introduction of printing into France, by allowing Ulrich Gering and his companions to set up their presses within its precincts.

In the 18C it attacked the *philosophes* and in 1792 was itself suppressed to be refounded by Napoléon, to become in 1821 the seat of the University of Paris. The student revolution of May 1968 eventually brought about overdue reforms in the university system, and in 1970 the University of Paris was replaced by the formation of 13 autonomous universities in the region. Paris-IV and Paris III (Letters, French Civilisation and Human Sciences faculties) are based here.

The courtyard and galleries can be visited; the great staircase and amphitheatre, can be seen on application at the main entrance at 47 Rue des Ecoles (☎ 01 40 46 20 15).

The ponderous buildings, which still house the university library of 700,000 volumes, the Académie de Paris and minor learned institutions, include the

Grand Amphithéâtre or main lecture hall, containing the best work in the building, Puvis de Chavannes' mural, *Le Bois sacré*.

The **Chapel of the Sorbonne**, facing Pl. de la Sorbonne was founded in the 13C and rebuilt by Jacques Lemercier in 1635–42 at the expense of Richelieu. The dramatic **tomb** of the great cardinal (1585–1642) was designed by Le Brun and sculptured by Girardon (1694). The chapel is open only for temporary exhibitions or concerts.

5 · The Musée du Moyen Age

■ Arrondissement: 75005.
■ Métros: Cluny-La Sorbonne, Maubert-Mutualité, Odéon, St-Michel.
  RER: St-Michel-Notre Dame.

Opposite the entrance to the Sorbonne is the tiny Square Paul-Painlevé (Pl. 14; 3–4) with a statue of *Montaigne* by Landowski and of *Puvis de Chavannes* by Desbois; also a replica of the Roman *She Wolf*, given by Rome to Paris in 1962.

It is flanked to the north by the 15C Hôtel de Cluny, adjacent to the Gallo-Roman thermae. The 15C building is one of the finest extant examples of medieval French domestic architecture and houses the **Musée du Moyen Age-Thermes et Hôtel de Cluny**, formerly known as the Musée de Cluny, an intimate museum of special charm. As well as the Roman remains, a remarkably well-conserved vestige of antique Paris, there is a superb collection of the arts and crafts of the Middle Ages, from gold artefacts of the Visigoth and Merovingian periods, through remnants of stonecarving from Notre-Dame de Paris, to the celebrated series of 15C tapestries, *The Lady with the Unicorn*.

The entrance is in the right-hand corner of the courtyard, beyond an archway.

■ The museum is open 09.15–17.45, closed Tues and public holidays, ☎ 01 53 73 78 00, guided visits and cultural activities, ☎ 01 53 73 78 16, for group visits ☎ 01 53 73 78 30.

The property was bought in 1340 by Pierre de Chalus, Abbot of Cluny in Burgundy, to establish a residence in the area of the university. The mansion which replaced the earlier building was built c 1490 by Abbot Jacques d'Amboise, as the town house of the abbots who rarely occupied it. The building is important architecturally as an early example of a house standing between a courtyard and a garden. Louis XII's widow, Mary Tudor (1496–1533) lived here for a time.

At the Revolution, the mansion became national property but in 1833 it was taken over by Alexandre du Sommerard (1771–1842) and filled with the treasures which he spent his life collecting. These were bought by the State and supplemented by many new acquisitions during the long curatorship of his son, Edmond du Sommerard (d. 1889), and since. Subsequently the thermae became the repository of original stonework removed from major Parisian monuments during renovation.

Ground floor

The entrance and ground floor have recently been renovated. Outstanding in the first rooms is the collection of **tapestries**. Among them are *The Resurrection* (c 1420) the oldest tapestry in the museum, *The Grape Harvest* (early 15C) (with sound and touch equipment for the non-sighted) and *The Deliverance of St Peter*, 1460. The set of six scenes illustrating the activities of a noble household of c 1500, entitled **La Vie Seigneuriale** c 1500–25, hangs in **room 4** with other furnishings of the same period. Also displayed are the 15C *Altarpiece of the Passion*, in wood with painted panels, and a small statue of St Denis, holding his head in his hand according to the legend of his martyrdom.

The **textiles and embroidery** in **room 3**, range from 6C–14C. Some are Coptic or Byzantine others of French, Italian and Spanish origin, including examples of Hispano-Moresque fabrics. An example of the highly regarded English production of the earlier part of the 14C is the *Embroidery with Leopards*, the stylised creatures surrounded by foliage and young girls, embroidered in gold on velvet. Displayed in the small **room 5** are alabasters, mainly from Nottingham.

Room 6 displays precious panels of stained glass including the section of a circular medallion from St-Denis (before 1144); from Alsace, part of a window depicting *St-Timothy* (c 1160); a scene of the *Charity of St-Nicholas* from Troyes (c 1170-85), and various pieces from the Sainte-Chapelle, Paris (early to mid-13C).

In the corridor, **room 7**, where the medieval and antique buildings join, are various tombstones including that of Jean de Sathanay (1360) from the Cluny college chapel and Pierre de Montreuil's portal of the Chapel of the Virgin from the interior of St-Germain-des-Prés.

Turn right through the portal into **room 8**, Salle Notre-Dame-de-Paris, a light and spacious area arranged to exhibit sculptural fragments removed from Notre-Dame de Paris during the Revolution. These include the original 13C heads from the gallery of the Kings of Judah, discovered in 1977 during excavation work in Rue de la Chaussée d'Antin; a magnificent Adam, c 1260, a heavily restored yet vigorous nude figure, originally painted, and from the south transept; also fragments of statue columns from St-Anne's gate.

The rooms across the corridor (**rooms 9,10,11**) contain many carved ivories (4C–12C) among which is the sensual Ariadne (Constantinople, 6C), and an 8C English diptych remarkable in being carved on both sides. Having been reused in the 9C, the later decoration is typical of the Carolingian Renaissance. Also many fine examples of medieval statuary in wood and stone. Among important examples of Romanesque carving from Paris is a group of 12 capitals from the abbey church of St-Germain-des-Prés (mid-11C) and large, richly carved capitals from Ste-Geneviève-de-Paris (c 1100). Three early Gothic heads come from the abbey church of St-Denis. There are also two very moving 12C French Crucifixions in polychrome wood from provincial France.

Statues of the Apostles (1241–48) removed from the Sainte-Chapelle during restoration in the 19C remained in the museum and are on display along with a group of 12C Catalonian historiated capitals. Note the Gothic sway of the ivory Virgin and Child, determined by the shape of the tusk. Several fine carved stone retables from the Paris area include one of 1250–60 from St-Denis showing the Baptism of Christ and and of 1259–67 from St-Germer-de-Fly and a 14C altarpiece with Scenes of the Passion. Also to see are fragments of 12C mural paintings.

Below **room 12** is the **frigidarium** of the Gallo-Roman baths, remarkable in that it still retains its 2C vault, unique in France. The room (20m by 11.5m and 14m in height) with the Piscina on the northern side, is all that remains in its entirety of the baths, assumed to have been built during the 1C and modified later (212–17): only partial ruins remain of its Tepidarium and Caldarium and the palestras (gymnasiums) facing Blvd St-Germain, but the rest was demolished in the 16C and 19C. Underground chambers on the north side still exist. The museum's collection of Gallo-Roman sculpture is displayed here as well as some early medieval pieces of masonry and stone-carving. The area is regularly used for concerts (☎ 01 46 34 51 17).

First floor

On the first floor, in circular **room 13**, are displayed the series of six exquisite millefleurs tapestries known as **La Dame à la Licorne** (or Unicorn). This recently renovated gallery is equipped with fibre optic lighting deliberately kept dim for conservation reasons. There is also sound and touch equipment for the non-sighted (in French).

> These tapestries, probably designed by a Parisian artist but woven, in silk and wool, in Northern Europe between 1484 and 1500, were commissioned by Jean le Viste, a Lyonnais lawyer whose family arms—gules, a band azur with three crescents argent—are frequently repeated in the designs. The tapestries hung for a long time in the Château of Boussac in the Creuse until brought to public notice by both Prosper Mérimée, Inspector of Historic Monuments, and the writer George Sand. They were acquired by the museum in 1882 and have undergone a number of restorations.
>
> Visually stunning, with rich red backgrounds, blue islands of colour, and different types of trees, the panels are scattered with thousands of delicate flower, animal and bird motifs. In each the Lady appears differently attired, sometimes accompanied by her maid, and always flanked by the mythical, elusive Unicorn, symbol of purity, and a Lion. In several of the panels a monkey and a pet dog are also included.
>
> Five of the tapestries present the theme of the Senses. Taste: the Lady feeds the monkey and a parakeet from a bowl of sweetmeats; Hearing: in which the Lady plays a portable organ; Sight: in which the Unicorn gazes into the mirror held before him by the Lady; Smell, where the monkey sniffs a flower while the Lady weaves a garland and Touch: in which the Lady gently grasps the horn of the unicorn. Opposite and in isolation, the sixth tapestry in the series, known by the enigmatic motto A mon seul désir embroidered above the pavilion before which the Lady stands while returning jewels to a casket held by her maid. The iconography of this is still mysterious.

Among the late medieval religious works from all parts of Europe in the large gallery, **room 14**, are several altarpieces. The most noteworthy is the *Altarpiece of the Blessed Sacrament* from Averbode in Brabant (1513) the work of Jan de Molder, carved with the Mass of St Gregory in the centre and the Last Supper on the right. The numerous representations of Virgins and female saints include an early 16C *Virgin reading to the Child* from the Lower Rhine and a late-15C *St Mary Magdalen* from Brussels carved in wood with braided tresses. Also of note are a painted *Pietà* from Tarascon (mid 15C), the elegantly carved head of the funeral effigy of Jeanne of Toulouse (c 1280), and a disturbing wooden *Head of Christ*, c 1470, from Franconia. There is a rare example of an English painting of *Scenes of the Life of the Virgin*, c 1325, and this room also contains the elegantly animated Prodigal Son tapestries, c 1520.

In the corridor (**Room 15**) are various medieval domestic objects and examples of the locksmith's craft.

Room 16 is devoted to the arts of **goldsmiths and enamellers**. The centrepieces, part of the magnificent Treasure of Gurrazar, include three Visigothic votive crowns with their pendant crosses, dating from the late 7C; and the Golden Rose (1330), given by the Avignon Pope John XXII to a count of Neuchâtel. There is also Gallo-Roman and Merovingian jewellery, including gold torques, bracelets, buckles, ornamented belts and fibulas; late Roman and Byzantine cloisonné enamelwork; two rock crystal lionheads (4C–5C), from the Roman Empire; enamels from the Rhineland and Meuse.

Among the fine examples of late 12C–14C Limoges enamelwork, are reliquaries, chalices, pyxes, shrines, plaques, croziers and crucifixes; two reliquaries of St Thomas à Becket (1190–1200) with the scene of the Archbishop's assassination; the 13C *Reliquary of the Sainte-Chapelle* commissioned by Louis IX, like a miniature chapel and engraved with three decapitated saints; the *Picture-reliquary of Ste Geneviève*, c 1380, acquired in 1989, showing the patron saint of Paris and the legend of the candle; and a finely worked gilded silver Virgin with the Child standing on her knee which is the *Reliquary of the Umbillicus of Christ* (1407). The so-called Colmar Treasure consists of early 14C coins and jewellery found in a wall of the Rue des Juifs, Colmar in 1853. There are also processional crosses from Barcelona (mid 14C) and from Siena (mid 15C); a collection of cameos, intaglios and glyptics; and the *Reliquary of St Anne* (1472; by Hans Greiff of Ingolstadt). The finely engraved portable triptych showing the *Dormition of the Virgin* (Nuremberg, 15C) whose central plaque was found in London in 1994.

Room 17 has 14C and 15C stained glass and ivories; also ceramics and a fine collection of Hispano-Moresque ware and other lustreware from Manises (Valencia).

In **room 18** are the reassembled choir-stalls, with irreverently carved misericords, from the abbey of St-Lucien at Beauvais (1492–1500). Illuminated manuscripts with Book of Hours, signs of the Zodiac, a page of antiphons (end 11C) and the text of law written for Louis IX which can be leafed through.

Room 19 contains some choice pieces: the early-11C gold Antipendium (altar front) possibly intended as a donation for Monte Cassino from Emperor Henry II and Empress Cunegonde, who are portrayed as miniscule figures at the feet of Christ, but which in fact ended up in Basle Cathedral; the 12C Stavelot (Meuse) retable, with a Pentecostal scene of Christ and the Apostles; and a gospel binding of the 12C in nielloed and gilded silver.

Adjacent is the **chapel** (**room 20**), a masterpiece of Flamboyant vaulting from a central pillar, with a filigree of delicate moulding between the main ribs. There are two 14C fonts and a 15C carved wooden door from Provins.

Starting by the staircase and continuing in the adjoining room, is a series of **tapestries** depicting the *Life of St Stephen*, based on 23 scenes taken from The Golden Legend, woven c 1500 for Jean Baillet, Bishop of Auxerre for the Cathedral. The tapestries, brought to the museum in 1880, are in remarkable condition. Although they have never been restored, the colours still strong and every painstaking detail clearly revealed. Like a strip cartoon with captions, the scenes are arranged in alternate interior and exterior settings, the first part dealing with the life and martyrdom of St Stephen and the second with the legend of the relics.

In **room 21** you will find mainly **Italian works** such as three 14C polychrome wooden sculptures: a Tuscan *Angel of the Annunciation* (end 14C), the bust-reliquaries of *St Ursula* (c 1340) and one of her 11,000 maiden companions, *St Mabilla* (c1370–80), and a 14C Sienese *St John the Baptist*. There is a collection of gilded and engraved glass (*églomisé*). Other small artefacts include a collection of late medieval wooden combs with intricate decoration, embroidered alms purses, bakery moulds, etc. The tapestry has *Scenes of the Life of the Virgin*, with a Donor (late 15C). Hanging in **room 22** is a mid-15C painting of the *Jouvenel des Ursins family* standing in line, commissioned for their chapel in Notre-Dame de Paris. Two small examples of domestic stained glass include one of chess players (15C) and a small monogrammed roundel in grisaille, c 1450–60. New to the museum are two carvings from the late Middle Ages, from the school of Hans Geiler of Fribourg. In **room 23** are arms and armour in different materials and games pieces in ivory and bone, dating from 11C–12C to 1500. On the walls are three small tapestries depicting courtly culture (15C).

There is a helpful **bookshop** and boutique (☎ 01 53 73 78 22) with a large selection of information on the society, arts and music of the Middle Ages. Later objects, from the era of the Renaissance but part of the collections of this museum, are to be seen at Ecouen: see Ch. 38.

North of the Hôtel de Cluny, between Blvds St-Germain and St-Michel, is Square de Cluny, a public garden since 1971, with some shady trees and rose bushes, from which through the railings is another view of the Roman thermae. Against the wall of the chapel are two porches, all that remain of the church of St-Benoît-le-Bétourné (16C) and of the Collège de Bayeux (14C).

6 · South east of the Quartier Latin

■ Arrondissements: 75005, 75013.
■ Métros: Jussieu, Cardinal Lemoine, Maubert-Mutualité, Pl. Monge, St-Marcel, Gare d'Austerlitz, Les Gobelins, Censier-Daubenton. RER: Gare d'Austerlitz.

The sites described in this chapter range from the botanical gardens of Paris, the Jardin des Plantes with the Grand Galerie de l'Evolution which reopened in 1994, the Institut du Monde Arabe (1987), and the new and controversial Bibliothèque Nationale de France, to the historic Gobelins Tapestry Factory.

Restaurants and cafés

L'Anacreon, 53 Blvd St-Marcel, ☎ 01 43 31 71 18. Haute cuisine. £
Chez Françoise, 12 Rue de la Butte aux Cailles, ☎ 01 45 80 12 02. Périgordian. £
Grand Mère, 92 Rue Broca,☎ 01 47 07 13 65. Traditional. £
Restaurant Marty, 20 Av. des Gobelins, ☎ 01 43 31 39 51. Traditional brasserie. £
Moissonnier, Rue des Fossés-St-Bernard, ☎ 01 43 29 87 65. Well-established bistrot. £
Café de la Mosquée de Paris, ☎ 01 43 31 18 14. Tea shop. £
Café Mouffetard, 116 Rue Mouffetard. Good coffee and croissant. £
La Ferme du Périgord, 1 Rue des Fossés St-Marcel. Périgordian, ☎ 01 43 31 69 20. £
La Timbale St. Bernard, 16–18 Rue des Fossés-St-Bernard, ☎ 01 46 34 28 28. Traditional. £

At the east end of Rue des Ecoles rises the extensive utilitarian block and obtrusive tower, a product of the 1960s, housing Paris-VI and Paris-VII, the Faculty of Science of the University of Paris. On the north side, Rue des Fossés-St-Bernard descends towards the Seine and the Pont Sully. The **Collection of Minerals** of the university are displayed at 34 Rue Jussieu, open Wed–Mon, 13.00–18.00, closed Tues (☎ 01 44 27 52 88).

Here, until their transfer to Bercy, stood the huge bonded warehouses of the Halles aux Vins, itself on the site of the Abbaye de St-Victor. Dispersed in 1790, this was where Thomas à Becket and Abélard had resided and Rabelais had studied in its library.

The **Institut du Monde Arabe**, inaugurated in the autumn of 1987 at 23 Quai St-Bernard, was founded in 1980 to further cultural and scientific relations between France and some 20 Arab countries. The sleek and complex building, designed by Jean Nouvel, rises to a height of 32m. An attractive feature of the exterior of the south façade are the shutters of the windows. Like the iris of an eye, each aperture was intended to expand and contract in reaction to the sun's intensity through the medium of photo-electric cells; in fact they are now operated mechanically. A spiral of white marble is visible in the Book Tower. The public parts of the Institute includes a library, documentation centre and museum. Take the glass lift to the 9th floor for the restaurant and terrace with views of the Seine and Notre-Dame which rival those from the Tour d'Argent, whereas the price of a meal will not. Open Tues–Sun 10.00–18.00, closed Mon (☎ 01 40 51 38 38).

The museum, on five levels with space for temporary exhibitions, is dedicated to the art and civilisation of the Arab world from pre-Islamic time to the present day, presented chronologically. There are displays concerned with the development of the religion of Islam and of the part played by the Arab world in the history of science. The arts and crafts of Islam, from the 9C to the 19C, include ceramics, MSS, metalwork, ivories, fabrics and glass objects from throughout the Arab world.

Between the Quai St-Bernard and the Seine, in the Tino-Rossi gardens on the riverside, extends the **Musée de Sculpture en Plein Air** (Pl. 15; 5), created in 1980 with examples of mostly contemporary sculpture. There are works by some 29 artists, including César, Stahly, Ipousteguy, Nicolas and Olivier Debré as well as Brancusi and Zadkine. The most noticeable is Schöffer's gyrating metallic tower, with its struts and discs.

Bearing south from Rue Jussieu, you ascend Rue Linné, off which Rue des Arènes climbs right to the remains of the 1C amphitheatre, the **Arènes de Lutèce**, the second most important Gallo-Roman site in Paris (after the baths, see p 77), which fell into ruin in the 3C and was used as a necropolis in the 4C. Only discovered in 1869 and fully excavated since 1883, a large chunk was lost during the construction of Rue Monge and the site has suffered from over-enthusiastic restoration. The arena is surrounded by the gardens of **Sq. Capitan** named after Dr Capitan, who restored the ruins in 1917–18, and is a popular place for playing boules or eating sandwiches.

Jardin des Plantes

At the junction of Rue Linné with its continuation, Rue Geoffroy-St-Hilaire, stands the Fontaine Cuvier (1840), and the north-west entrance to the Jardin des Plantes, officially the **Muséum National d'Histoire Naturelle** (Pl. 15; 7). This delightful oasis of 28 hectares encompasses botanic gardens, a group of museums, and other attractions, several of which will entertain and inform younger visitors, notably the menagerie (zoo), the maze, and the revamped Grande Galerie de l'Évolution. As well as unrivalled collections of wild and herbaceous plants, are alpine, rose, and ecological gardens, tropical green-houses, and in May and June magnificent displays of peonies and iris.

■ The Jardin des Plantes is open from 7.30–20.00 (depending on sunset); the Menagerie Mon–Sat 09.00–17.00 or 18.00 (or sunset), April–Sept Sun 09.00–18.30; the greenhouses Mon–Fri 13.00–17.00, Sat, Sun 10.00–18.00, winter 17.00 (☎ 01 40 79 30 00). Métros: Jussieu, Monge, Censier-Daubenton and Gare d'Austerlitz.

There are other entrances in Rue Geoffroy-St-Hilaire and in the semicircular Pl. Valhubert to the east, opposite Gare d'Austerlitz. There are facilities for the handicapped and refreshments in the gardens and the Grand Galerie.

Founded in 1626 under Louis XIII for the cultivation of medicinal herbs by the royal physician Guy de la Brosse, the garden was first opened to the public in 1640. Its present importance is mainly due to the great naturalist, the Comte de Buffon (1707–88), who was superintendent from 1739 and greatly enlarged the grounds. Known until 1793 as the Jardin du Roi, it was then reorganised by the Convention under its present official title and provided at that time with 12 professorships. The National Museum of Natural History is a public institute with the triple role of research, conservation and dissemination of knowledge. The library owns a remarkable collection of botanical MSS, including the *Vélins du Roi*, illustrated by Nicolas Robert (1614–85) and others; also works by Redouté.

Several of the distinguished French naturalists who taught and studied here are commemorated by monuments in or near the garden. A statue of the naturalist J.-B. Lamarck (1744–1829), by Léon Fagel of the early 20C, faces the Place Valhubert entrance and another by the same artist of the chemist Eugène Chevreul (1786–1889) stands in the northern part of the gardens. Chevreul's research on the principles of harmony and colour contrasts had an important influence on the Impressionist painters' colour theories and he was, for a time, director of the dyeing department at Gobelins tapestry factory. Buffon's likeness faces the Grande Galerie.

Among other scientists associated with the Jardin des Plantes are the zoologist Geoffroy Saint-Hilaire (1772–1844), Louis Daubenton (1706–99), and the botanists Joseph de Tournefort (1656–1708) and Bernard de Jussieu (1690–1777).

The Maison de Cuvier, home of Georges Cuvier (1769–1832), zoologist and paleontologist, was later occupied by Heri Becquerel (1788–1878) who discovered radioactivity here in 1896. The Administrative Department is housed in the Hôtel de Magny, built in 1650.

From the Esplanade Milne Edwards in front of the Grande Galerie formal gardens bordered by plane trees create an orderly floral vista with a backdrop of modern Paris, while behind the northern avenue is a host of less regimented gardens.

On the right of the rue Linné entrance is the Butte, a charming hillock with a maze and the first cedar of Lebanon (from Kew Gardens) to be planted in France, in 1734. At the summit is the famous Gloriette, a metal structure of 1786 and sundial bearing the inscription *Horas non numero nisi serenas*: I only count the light hours.

Animals from the royal collection at Versailles and of street showmen formed the nucleus of a Menagerie in 1792. It now occupies most of the northern side of the gardens and contains more than 1000 animals. The Greenhouses, built in 1830–33—one known as 'Australian' and the other 'Mexican'—are in the western section

Gloriette, Jardin des Plantes

Grande Galerie de l'Evolution

Part of the Museum of Natural History (nearest entrance 36 Rue Geoffroy-St-Hilaire), the Grande Galerie de l'Evolution re-opened in 1994 after a closure of nearly 30 years. It was one of President Mitterand's 'grand projects' and offers an exciting visual experience besides the natural history content. Open Wed–Mon 10.00–18.00, Thur to 22.00, closed Tues; café on level 1 and facilities for the handicapped (☎ 01 40 79 30 00).

Originally the Zoological Gallery which opened in 1889, the building and the specimens, arranged according to zoological classification, deteriorated and the museum was closed in 1965. The architects of the renovation were Paul Chemetov and Borja Huidobro, assisted by the scenographer René Allio, and the present exhibition space uses the central nave, balconies and side galleries of the old building. The theme of the museum revolves around the History of

Evolution, whose drama unfolds through the different levels of the museum and the concepts of modern museology to convey a powerful scientific message in a magical way. The permanent exhibition combines carefully selected and restored specimens—the smaller ones suspended in transparent display cases to great effect—with audio visual presentations, models, etched glass, and a son et lumière at 11.00 and 16.00 each day. This condenses into an hour and 40 minutes different moments of the day from dawn to dusk.

The **ground floor**, excavated to reveal stone arcades, evokes the watery underworld and takes you across various marine zones, from the deep to the shallows and on to the coast and dry land. Arctic regions have to be crossed on the way to **level one** and a change in climate. Here, among other displays, are a cavalcade of animals across the African savannah and the tropical forests of South America. Lifts fly you past exotic birds to **level three** to be greeted by the oldest specimen in the museum, the rhinoceros that belonged to Louis XV. The balconies, devoted to the evolution of living organisms, provide a spectacular view down onto the nave of level one. The exhibition continues on **level two** with the science of selectivity and man's role in evolution, including some most disturbing effects on the environment. Behind the balcony on the east side is a gallery devoted to extinct and endangered species. This chapel-like room, with its original wooden display cabinets, is classified as an historic monument and contains a clock made for Marie-Antoinette.

Other public galleries, arranged along the southern side of the gardens, are open Wed–Mon 10.00–17.00, Sun 10.00–18.00; 10.00–17.00 winter; closed on public holidays. **Mineralogy** has an interesting collection including a group of giant crystals from Brazil, originally destined for industrial use, which amount to three-quarters of the world's known stock. **Entomology** (Wed–Fri, Mon 13.00–17.00) has 1500 examples of the most beautiful or most surprising insects. The **Paleontology and Compared Anatomy Gallery**, next to the Austerlitz entrance, is frequently mistaken for the Grande Galerie de l'Evolution. There is nothing modern here, but skeletons and fossils presented like 17C collection of curiosities, and due for renovation. However, the staircase which sweeps you to the upper floor has splendid metal bannisters with a chrysanthemum and fern motif.

To the west of Rue Geoffroy-St-Hilaire is a green-tiled mosque, the **Mosquée de Paris**, complete with minaret, inaugurated in 1926, which is open to the public 09.00–12.00 and 14.00–18.00, guided visits (entrance on Rue des Quatrefages). Still part of the mosque, but the opposite corner (Rue Daubenton/Rue G. St-Hilaire) is a tea-room and shop.

Another sombre 1960s example of utilitarian architecture west of Rue G. St-Hilaire, on Rue Censier, is the Faculty of letters, languages and sociology, Paris-III, Sorbonne nouvelle. Not far to the south, Blvd St-Marcel is reached and leads north east to meet Blvd de l'Hôpital.

To the right of this latter junction stands the huge **Hôpital de la Salpêtrière** (Pl. 15; 8), founded in 1656 as a home for aged or abandoned women. The criminal wing, built in 1684, is associated with Manon Lescaut, in the novel by Abbé Prévost.

The main building, by Le Vau and Pierre Le Muet, dates from 1657–63; the domed chapel of **St-Louis**, built in 1670–77 by Libéral Bruant, can hold 4000 people. Statues by Antoine Etex were added after 1832. As a whole, it is a notable example of the austere magnificence of the architecture of the period and may be compared to Les Invalides. In contrast, is the post-modernist Pavilion of the Child and Adolescent, 1985. Dr Jean-Martin Charcot (1825–93), the hypnotist, is commemorated by a monument to the left of the gateway; his consulting-room, laboratory and library have been preserved intact.

Adjacent to the south is the Hôpital de la Pitié, transferred in 1911 from Rue Lacépède, where it had been founded by Marie de Médicis in 1612.

To the north east is **Gare d'Austerlitz**, the main railway terminus for Tours, Bordeaux, Bayonne and Toulouse (see Pl. 15; 6). Between 1870 and 1871 (during the Siege of Paris), the station, then known as the Gare d'Orléans, was turned into a balloon factory.

The area immediately south east of the station has undergone drastic change as part of a larger, long-term project to renovate this district. Blvd St-Marcel has been extended north east, across Blvd de l'Hôpital, and the station to the southern end of the new Pont Charles-de-Gaulle. This will provide direct access between Gare d'Austerlitz and Gare de Lyon. A new road, Avenue de France, is planned over the Austerlitz train tracks.

Quai d'Austerlitz (facing the new buildings of the Ministère des Finances and Palais Omnisport on the far bank of the Seine) has been cleared and an avenue, flanked by new buildings, driven south west from the station. A footbridge spanning the river connects this bank with the new Parc de Bercy; see p 286.

Bibliothèque Nationale de France, François Mitterand

Opposite the footbridge, beside the Seine half way between the Pont de Bercy and the Pont de Tolbiac, is the new Bibliothèque de France, a veritable fortress for books to which the major part of the national collection will be transferred from the Bibliothèque Nationale, Cardinal de Richelieu (see p 198). At the centre of a new *quartier*, the area immediately surrounding the library is planned as a place for permanent access by the public. There are limited guided visits to the building Tuesday to Saturday from the East entrance at 14.00, Sunday 15.00 (☎ 01 33 79 59 59) and exhibitions. Métro: Quai de la Gare, Tolbiac-Masséna.

The last of Mitterand's grand projects, this mammoth construction is the design of Dominique Perrault and was begun in 1990. It consists of four L-shaped 80m-high towers, each of 20 storeys, simulating books opened at right angles, standing at the corners of a hollow rectangular podium. The whole Tolbiac site covers 7.5 hectares. The esplanade (60,000m²) and wide steps leading up to it are covered by silvery-grey hard-wood and decorated with evergreen bushes caged within rectangular metal frames. Only on reaching the top of the steps do the sunken gardens (12,000m²), planted with tall pines and silver birches, come into view. The 11 upper floors of each glazed tower-block, designed to contain the book stacks, are lined with wooden shutters for protection. Each floor is independently air conditioned. Together with the wings surrounding the reading rooms, there is a total storage capacity of over 15,000,000 volumes. The reading rooms themselves, which are arranged around the gardens and intended to evoke a vast, transparent cloister, cover a total area of 58,000m².

The **haut-de-jardin** (upper garden level) is open to the public (i.e. anyone over 16). This 1650-seat library provides open access to 300,000 specifically acquired volumes, not part of the patrimonial collection. The **rez-de-jardin** (garden level), which is scheduled to open 8 October 1998, has 2000 places for researchers who will have access to the closed stack collections as well as a collection on open access of some 400,000 volumes. The reading rooms and collections on both levels are organised into five departments, four of them thematic and one devoted to audio-visual material. The library has all the latest technological services and facilities, which will allow access to an extensive range of bibliographical information as well as conservation and restoration sections, and legal deposit offices.

The vast interior spaces are panelled in woven metal, wood and concrete and softened with hectares of rust colour carpet. The funishings are also Perrault's designs. There are two main entrances and two entrance halls to receive an estimated 12,000 people a day.

The present Bibliothèque Nationale at the Richelieu site will retain manuscripts, maps and plans, engravings, photographic material, coins and medals, and the performing arts and music collections; see p 198.

Blvd St-Marcel runs south west of Blvd de l'Hôpital to meet Av. des Gobelins, beyond which it divides to be continued by Blvd Arago (leading due west to Pl. Denfert-Rochereau) and Blvd de Port-Royal (eventually meeting Blvd du Montparnasse).

A short distance south of this junction stands (right) **La Manufacture Nationale des Gobelins** (CNMHS) (Pl. 14; 8), the famous tapestry factory which has been a state institution for over 300 years, and still retains some of its 17C buildings. Open Tues–Thurs by guided tour only at 14.00 and 14.15 (☎ 01 44 08 52 00)

The original factory at Fontainebleau was moved to Paris during the reign of Henri II. Suspended during the 16C Religious Wars, the industry was revived by Henri IV and installed in 1601 in the buildings of the Gobelins, named after Jean Gobelin (d. 1476), head of a family of dyers who made their reputation with the discovery of a scarlet dye, and who had set up their dye-works here on the banks of the Bièvre in 1443. In 1662, under Colbert, the royal carpet factory of the Savonnerie, established in 1604 in the galleries of the Louvre and subsequently moved to a *savonnerie* (soap-factory) at Chaillot, was placed under the same management. It was not until 1768 that private individuals were allowed to buy Savonnerie carpets. The factory transferred its workshops to the Gobelins in 1825. In 1667 Louis XIV added the royal furniture factory and Charles le Brun and then Pierre Mignard (in 1690) were appointed directors. The Beauvais tapestry workshops, destroyed in 1940, were also moved here.

The tapestry is still woven by hand on high-warp looms, several of which date from the time of Louis XIV. The weaver works on the reverse side of the tapestry; the painting which he is copying is placed behind him and reflected in a mirror. The average amount of tapestry that a weaver can produce in a day is $15cm^2$.

In the former chapel, restored in 1994, hang two tapestries specially made for it. The tour crosses Rue Berbier-du-Mets, behind the factory, which now covers the non-calcareous waters of the Bièvre, which used to flow between the dye-works and workshops. Another new building contains workshops for the weaving of carpets, where the original methods are still followed.

Adjacent is the Mobilier National (or National Furniture Store), and beyond are the gardens of Sq. René-le-Gall on the site of the former kitchen gardens of employees of Les Gobelins.

Av. des Gobelins ends to the south at **PL. D'ITALIE**, the hub of seven important thoroughfares.

Turning north down Av. des Gobelins, you approach picturesque **St-Médard** (Pl. 14; 8), dedicated to the St Swithin of France. The nave and west front are of the late 15C; the choir, in construction from 1550 to 1632, was classicised in 1784, when the Lady Chapel was added. The church was sacked by the Huguenots in 1561, and not much 16C glass survives.

The narrow, shabby but busy **RUE MOUFFETARD**, an ancient thoroughfare (the lower end is closed to traffic), climbs north through a tatty but picturesque district with a good street market and a village-like atmosphere. Several of the houses, although frequently altered, stand on medieval foundations. In Rue de l'Arbalète, at No. 3, Auguste Rodin was born in 1840. Eventually you pass (right) Pl. de la Contrescarpe, where No. 1 has a tablet commemorating the Cabaret de la Pomme-de-Pin, immortalised by Rabelais and the Pléïade.

Also in this district, but slightly to the west, in Rue Pierre-Brossolette, at the Ecole de Physique et de Chimie industrielles, Pierre and Marie Curie did their experimental work in 1883–1905. Further west, and best approached by Rue d'Ulm (leading south from the Panthéon), is the Maronite church of N.-D. du Liban, facing Rue Lhomond. The Collège des Irlandais, founded in 1578 by John Lee and re-founded in 1687 by English Catholics as a seminary, stands at the corner of the adjacent Rue des Irlandais.

At 45 Rue d'Ulm is the Ecole Normale Supérieure, established in 1794 for the training of teachers and sited here since 1843. Pasteur worked in laboratories here between 1864 and 1888.

7 · Val-de-Grâce and Montparnasse

■ Arrondissements: 75005, 75014, 75015.
■ Métros: Luxembourg, Port-Royal, Denfert-Rochereau, Vavin, Montparnasse-Bienvenue. RER: Cité-Universitaire, Denfert-Rochereau.

The lesser-known places to see around the former bohemian quarter of Montparnasse, with its famous cemetery, include the Baroque church of Val-de-Grâce, the Paris Observatory, the Cité Universitaire, the Tour Mont-parnasse, the Postal Museum, the former studio of the sculptor Bourdelle, and the Jardin Antlantique, with gardens planted on top of the mainline station of Montparnasse.

Restaurants and cafés

Bistro d'Antan, 21 Rue de la Gaîté, ☎ 01 43 20 67 67. Traditional. £
Bergamote, 1 Rue Niepce, ☎ 01 43 22 79 47. Provincial cooking. £
Le Bourdonnais, 29 Rue Delambre, ☎ 01 43 20 61 73. Traditional. ££
Le Dôme, 108 Blvd du Montparnasse, ☎ 01 43 35 25 81. Brasserie. ££
Chez Dumonet/Josephine, 117 Rue du Cherche-Midi, ☎ 01 45 48 52 40. Traditional. ££
Closerie des Lilas, 171 Blvd du Montparnasse, ☎ 01 43 26 70 50/ 43 54 21 68. 1930s brasserie. ££
La Coupole, 102 Blvd du Montparnasse, ☎ 01 43 20 14 20. Brasserie. £
Chez Marcel, 7 Rue Stanislas, ☎ 01 45 48 29 94. Lyonnais bistrot. £
Pavillon Montsouris, 20 Rue Gazan, ☎ 01 45 88 38 52. Belle Époque, near Park. ££
Au Vin des Rues, 21 Rue Boulard, ☎ 01 43 22 19 78. Lyonnais cooking.

Turn south from Rue Soufflot along the continuation of the ancient Gallo-Roman route, Rue St-Jacques (Pl. 13; 8; see pp 73, 87), which runs parallel to Blvd St-Michel and leads out of the Quartier Latin and into the Val-de-Grâce and Montparnasse area. At No. 195 is the Institut Océanographique, with the Centre de la Mer et des Eaux, which holds frequent exhibitions; open Tues–Fri, 10.00–12.30, 13.15–17.30, Sat, Sun 10.00–17.30.

A little further along on the right is **St-Jacques-du-Haut-Pas**. The west elevation of this plain classical building (1630–88) has recently been cleaned. Originally the site of a hospice for pilgrims on the road to Santiago de Compostela, the severe 17C building reflects its Jansenist connections. It was completed in 1712 with the help of the Duchesse de Longueville (1619–79) who is buried here), together with Jean Duvergier de Hauranne (1581–1643), the prominent Jansenist, and Jean-Dominique Cassini (1625–1712), the astronomer. It has a fine organ, with a case dating mainly from 1609, transferred here from the church of St-Benoît-le-Bétourné and entirely rebuilt by in 1971. It is frequently used for concerts.

No. 254, at the corner of Rue de l'Abbé-de-l'Epée, is the **Institut National des Sourds-Muets**, a hospital for the deaf and dumb, founded by the Abbé de l'Épée (1712–89) about 1760. It was taken over by the State in 1790 and reconstructed in 1823. In the courtyard is a statue of the Abbé by Félix Martin, a deaf and dumb sculptor (1789).

Further on, at No. 269 (left) is the **Schola Cantorum** (visitors admitted), a free conservatoire of music, established in 1896 by three pupils of César Franck, including Vincent d'Indy. The buildings (1674), by Charles d'Avilère, are those of the English Benedictine monastery of St-Edmund, founded in France in 1615, which occupied this site from 1640 until the Revolution and is still an English property. The salon and staircase are good examples of 17C decor, and the chapel, where the exiled James II's body lay in state in 1701, is now a concert hall.

At No. 284 (left), integrated into a modern building, is the entrance of a former distinguished Carmelite convent to which Louise de la Vallière, a mistress of Louis XIV, retired in 1674.

Rue St-Jacques widens opposite the impressive front of **Val-de-Grâce** (Pl. 13; 8), one of the best preserved examples of 17C architecture in Paris.

From 1624 it was the house of the Benedictine nuns of Val-Profond whose patroness was N.-D. du Val-de-Grâce; it has been a military hospital since 1790. The Army Medical School was added in 1850. The present more extensive buildings were erected by Anne of Austria in thanksgiving for the birth of Louis XIV in 1638 after 22 years of marriage without issue, and the first stone of the new works was laid by the young king in 1645. In the courtyard is a bronze statue of Napoléon's surgeon, Baron Larrey (1766–1842), by David d'Angers.

François Mansart (1598–1666) was replaced as architect before 1649 by Jacques Lemercier, and after 1654 the buildings were finished by Le Muet and Le Duc, the church being completed in 1667. The remains of royalty interred here, including Anne of Austria (wife of Louis XIII) and Marie-Thérèse (wife of Louis XIV), were dispersed at the Revolution.

The façade of the church (by Mansart) is a notable example of the Counter-Reformation style introduced by the Jesuits, and the lead and gilt **dome** (by Le Duc), one of the finest in France, shows the influence of Roman Baroque.

Inside, the painting in the dome *La Gloire des Bienheureux* (1663) is by Pierre Mignard and the sculptures by François and Michel Anguier, Pierre Sarazin and others. The high-altar, with its six huge twisted marble columns, is inspired by Bernini's baldacchino or canopy over the saint's tomb in St Peter's, Rome; the sculptured *Nativity* on it is a copy of Anguier's original (now at St-Roch). In the chapel on the right of the choir is a portrait of *Anne of Austria borne by an angel*; and in the Chapel of the Sacrament is the *Communion of the Angels*, by J.-B. de Champaigne. The St-Anne Chapel once contained the hearts of royalty. Val-de-Grâce was only one of the many religious houses which, until the Revolution, were established in this district and some of the neighbouring street names recall vanished convents: Rue des Ursulines and Rue des Feuillantines.

To the right on the far side of Blvd de Port-Royal, a maternity hospital has, since 1818, occupied the buildings of Port-Royal de Paris, a branch of the Jansenist abbey of Port-Royal-des-Champs (south west of Versailles), destroyed at the instigation of the Jesuits and its site ploughed over in 1709. However, the chapel completed by Le Pautre in 1647, still stands and has kept its 17C architecture and some of the furnishings including, in the chapter house, some good woodwork.

The extensive buildings of the Hôpital Cochin lie to the left of Rue Faubourg-St-Jacques. George Orwell and Samuel Becket were among its more famous patients. On the right, No. 38, is the Hôtel de Massa (1784), transferred here from the Champs-Elysées in 1927, re-erected, and now occupied by the Société des Gens de Lettres.

Next turn right into the pleasant Rue Cassini, lined with early 20C buildings in variations of the modern style; Nos 2–6 contain fragments of old masonry. Many of these houses were built as artists' studios and the English engraver, S.W. Hayter, lived at No. 12.

Observatoire

On the left is the Observatoire (Pl. 14; 7), the oldest working observatory in the world, founded by Louis XIV. On 21 June 1667 the meridian of Paris was established and determined the orientation of the building. It is indicated by a copper line embedded in the paving of the second floor (2-20'14" east of Greenwich). The Paris meridian was replaced by Greenwich in 1884. The four sides of the building face the cardinal points of the compass, and the latitude of the southern side is the recognised latitude of Paris (48-50'11" north) which, until 1912, was the basis for the calculation of longitude on French maps. The Observatoire is also the headquarters of the Bureau International de l'Heure, and a speaking clock is installed in its cellars.

The Observatoire was designed by Claude Perrault and completed in 1672, the year of his death. One of its directors was Jean Dominique Cassini (1625–1712), the first of the family of astronomers and cartographers. The famous Danish astronomer Olaf Römer (1644–1710), worked here from 1672.

Application to attend a guided tour (first Saturday of each month at 14.30) should be made in writing to the Secrétariat at 61 Av. de l'Observatoire, 75014 Paris (☎ 01 40 51 22 21).

In the entrance is the original speaking clock (1933). On the first floor of the main building is a Museum of Astronomical Instruments, and the contents of the Rotunda in the west tower illustrate the history of astronomy. From the second storey is a staircase to the terrace and in the east cupola is an equatorial telescope of 38cm aperture.

For the leafy **gardens** behind the Observatory, take Rue du Fb. St-Jacques to the entrance on Blvd Arago, open to the public from 1 April to 15 October, at 13.00. At No. 65 is a gate opening onto a hidden garden, known as the Cité Fleurie, which a group of artists studios constructed from scraps salvaged from the Universal Exposition of 1878.

In the angle between Rue Cassini, Av. de l'Observatoire and Av. Denfert-Rochereau is the former Couvent du Bon Pasteur, now a centre for handicapped children, encompassing the Pavillon Fontainiers (water tower) built in 1624 as part of the rebuilding of the Roman aqueduct carrying water from Rungis, restimulated by Marie de Médicis, to supply the Left Bank and the fountains of the Luxembourg Gardens. On Av. Denfert-Rochereau is the Hôpital St-Vincent-de-Paul, with a chapel of 1650–55.

Slightly further north on Blvd Raspail (No. 261) is the **Cartier Foundation for Contemporary Art**, in a building by Jean Nouvel opened in 1994, which organises exhibitions of contemporary art by international artists. It has a garden landscaped by Lothar Baumgarten. Open 12.00–20.00, closed Mon (☎ 01 42 18 56 67).

Where Blvd Arago and Av. Denfert-Rochereau meet is a large junction, PLACE DENFERT-ROCHEREAU, known as the Place d'Enfer until 1879, when it received its present name in honour of the defender of Belfort during the Franco-Prussian War. The earlier name originated as Via Inferior, the Roman road (now Blvd St-Michel) leading south to it from the Ile de la Cité, parallel to and west of the Via Superior (now Rue St-Jacques). In the centre of the Place is a copy, though smaller in size, of Bartholdi's sculpture of the *Lion of Belfort* and the area is cheered up by four small squares planted with trees. In Square Ledoux on the south-west side are the remnants of twin pavilions of the old Barrière d'Enfer where levies were collected. These heavily rusticated remains of the wall of the *fermiers généraux* (1784) were designed by the great neoclassical architect Claude-Nicholas Ledoux (1736–1806).

The eastern pavilion is the main entrance to **Les Catacombes**. This labyrinthine series of underground quarries, covering about 850 hectares, has provided building material for the city of Paris since Roman times. The 160km of tunnels extend from the Jardin des Plantes to the Porte de Versailles and into the suburbs of Montrouge, Montsouris and Gentilly. In the 1780s they were converted into a charnel-house for bones removed from disused graveyards, and most of the victims of the massacres of the Terror were later transferred here. In 1944 they served as a headquarters of the Resistance Movement.

Guided tours take place Tues–Fri between 14.00 and 16.00, and Sat–Sun 09.00–11.00; 14.00–16.00 (☎ 01 43 22 47 63). It is advisable to take a torch. The tour lasts over an hour, starting with the historic background, then a macabre series of galleries lined with bones and skulls leading to a huge ossuary containing the debris of over six million skeletons.

Leading south from Pl. Denfert-Rochereau, Av. René-Coty approaches the **Parc de Montsouris**, covering 16 hectares and laid out in 1875–78 as part of Haussmann's scheme to provide green spaces around the capital. The gardens imitate the informal English style with lawns and some 1400 trees in groups; near its north-east corner is a lake. As well as sculptures in stone and bronze, such as Etex's *Les Naufrages* (1882) and *Drame au désert* (1891) by Georges Gardet, there is also a bandstand, a café, and a marionnette theatre.

Facing the south side of the park spread over about a kilometre along Blvd Jourdan, is the **Cité Universitaire**, founded in 1922 on the site of the 19C fortifications. The Cité accommodates around 7000 students in some 37 national halls of residence, designed to evoke national characteristics, and the Maison Internationale (1936) financed by John D. Rockefeller. The architecture covers a wide spectrum of styles from 1922 to 1960. The most innovative building of the time was Le Corbusier's sleek Swiss Hall (1930–32) introducing revolutionary new elements, including *pilotis* (ie built on piles). A later example of Le Corbusier's work, in conjunction with Lúcio Costa, is the partly painted and more brutal Brazilian Hall (1952). Other important buildings are the Japanese pavilion, designed by P. Sardou, the Dutch hall, by M. Dudok, 1927, and the Fondation Avicenne, which is the most recent (1966–68) and exemplifies French architecture of the period.

Montparnasse

Returning to the Observatoire and continuing north, Av. Denfert-Rochereau brings you to the Carrefour de l'Observatoire. Straight ahead is the extravagant **Fontaine de l'Observatoire** (1875) by Davioud, with Carpeaux's group of figures representing the four quarters of the globe, and bronze horses and turtles by Frémiet. To the north west is François Rude's statue of Marshal Ney (1769–1815), who was shot close by for supporting Napoléon on his return from Elba. Behind it is the Closerie des Lilas, built in 1903, altered in 1925, one of the famous literary resorts of the 1920s.

From the Carrefour de l'Observatoire the long Blvd du Montparnasse leads north west across Blvd Raspail, where to the north stands Rodin's recently restored **statue of Balzac**. This junction is the centre of a quarter which partly supplanted Montmartre as the principal artistic and bohemian rendezvous. Both Henry Miller and Ernest Hemingway have described the café life, disreputable and otherwise, of the district in its heyday.

To the south west and parallel to Blvd du Montparnasse, is the Blvd Edgar-Quinet, with the main entrance of **Cimetière Montparnasse** (Pl. 13; 7), an 18-hectare site laid out in 1824. The list of the late and

Fontaine de l'Observatoire: one of the bronze horses by Emmanuel Frémiet

great buried here is impressive: Maupassant, Baudelaire, J.-K. Huysmans, Leconte de Lisle, Sainte-Beuve, Jean-Paul Sartre and Ionesco among writers; César Franck and Saint-Saëns among composers and musicians; Fantin-Latour, Gérard, Houdon, Rude, Soutine, Zadkine, Bourdelle, Bartholdi and Brancusi, among artists and sculptors; Pierre-Joseph Proudhon, the social reformer; Arago, the scientist and politician; Alfred Dreyfus; Charles Garnier, the architect; André Citroën, the car manufacturer. A plan is available at the office just inside the gate.

The district has inevitably changed since the 1920s retaining only fading associations with late-19C and early 20C artists and intellectuals who inhabited the area. As well as the writers and critics who inhabited the area (Sainte-Beuve, Rilke, Romain Rolland) Rodin, Carolus-Duran, Gauguin, Modigliani and Whistler at some point in their careers had studios in and around Montparnasse, and Trotsky frequented the Rotonde before 1917. It is still home to some artists, and the boîtes in Rue de la Gaité and elsewhere continue to attract visitors. The large brasseries, such as *Le Dôme*, *La Coupole* and *La Rotonde*, while altered in character, are still popular.

The area is now dominated by the obtrusive **Tour Montparnasse** (1973; 200m high), which has little to recommend it except for the impressive panoramic views (fee) from the 56th floor and its open-air terrace. Adjacent to the Tour, and forming part of the glass and concrete complex, is the **Gare Montparnasse** (Pl. 13; 7), 18 storeys high, surrounding the station platforms on three sides.

The station, which serves Brittany and the Atlantic coast, has been the subject of a long series of improvements not the least of which is **Le Jardin Atlantique**, built above the the station. Enter the garden from Place des Cinq-Martyrs-du-Lycée-Buffon or from the mainline station. This urban breathing space uses metal, wood, marble and granite structures, with a central lawn featuring an intermittent fountain, the Ile des Hespérides, evoking the sound of waves on a seashore, and a meteorological centre. There is a sandy area for children and coastal plants are used to harmonise with the theme. On the west is a sports area; on the east a raised walkway and a group of small thematic gardens organised around the pavilions of the Blue Waves and of the Pink Rocks, intended to evoke ocean and sky.

Entering from the Jardin Atlantique (the Tower end) are the resolutely modern Museums of Marshal Leclerc de Hauteclocque and of the Liberation of Paris, and of Jean Moulin, open 10.00–17.40, closed Mon and some public holidays (☎ 01 40 64 39 44).

At 34 Blvd de Vaugirard, flanking the station to the north west, is the recently renovated **Musée de la Poste**. The well-displayed collection explains the history of the French postal system from its earliest days, laid out in some 15 rooms, descending in stages from the 5th floor (lift). Sections are devoted to methods of communication and transport; to postmen themselves, illustrated by old costumes and prints; to letter-boxes; to stamps and their printing; and to telecommunication and the mechanisation of the service. The catalogue is well-produced and informative. Open 10.00–18.00, closed Tues and public holidays, (☎ 01 42 79 24 25).

Further to the west is Blvd Pasteur, off which runs Rue du Docteur-Roux, with (left) the Institut Pasteur, founded by Louis Pasteur (1822–95) in 1887 and built by private subscription.

At 16 Rue Antoine-Bourdelle, north of and parallel to Blvd de Vaugirard, is the discreet **Musée Bourdelle**, devoted to the sculptor Antoine Bourdelle (1861–1929), who lived and worked here from 1885 until his death. Open 10.00–17.40, closed Mon and public holidays (☎ 01 49 54 73 73).

Bourdelle's entire collection was donated to the Ville de Paris by his widow. The museum encompasses a small courtyard open to the street and the studios and furnished living apartments. A gallery for plaster models was added in 1961 and in 1990–92 a two-level extension was built for permanent and temporary exhibitions as well as a gallery for graphic arts (by appointment only) and a library. On display are studies, plaster casts and bronzes of his best known works. Bourdelle tended to work on a monumental scale and among models and casts for larger works are: the *Monument to General Alvear*, for Buenos Aires (1913–23); *Hercules the Archer*; and studies for the Hartmannweilerkopf crypt in Alsace; *Monument to Mickiewicz*; and *La France*. A pupil of Rodin, Bourdelle's earlier works, such as *Beethoven aux Grands Cheveux* (1891) show Rodin's influence while his later, more classical style, appears in the reliefs for the Théâtre des Champs-Elysées (1912–13), strongly influenced by the dances of Isadora Duncan.

8 · Faubourg St-Germain: eastern sector

■ Arrondissements: 75006, 75007.
■ Métros: Pont-Neuf, Odéon, Luxembourg, St-Sulpice, St-Germain-des-Prés, Mabillon.

Among the finest buildings in the district are the Institut de France, the Hôtel de la Monnaie, containing a museum of coins and medals, and the Palais du Luxembourg standing in the gardens of the same name. Also in the area is the small museum dedicated to the painter Eugène Delacroix, and two important churches, the ancient St-Germain-des-Prés and the neo-classical St-Sulpice.

Restaurants and cafés

La Bastide Odéon, 7 rue Corneille,☎ 01 43 26 03 65. Provençale cuisine. £
Restaurant des Beaux Arts, 11 Rue Bonaparte, ☎ 01 43 26 92 64. £
Bistrot d'à Côté St-Germain, 16 Blvd St-Germain, ☎ 01 43 54 59 10. Chef: Michel Rostang. £
Bistrot Mazarin, 42 Rue Mazarin, ☎ 01 43 29 99 01. £
Brasserie St-Benoît, 26 Rue St-Benoît, ☎ 01 45 48 29 66. £
Les Bookinistes, 53 Quai des Grands-Augustins, ☎ 01 43 25 45 94. One of chef Guy Savoy's other places. ££
La Cafetière, 21 Rue Mazarine, ☎ 46 33 76 90. Bistro. £
Restaurant Jacques Cagna, 14 Rue des Grands-Augustins, ☎ 01 43 26 49 39. Haute cuisine. £££
Chez Henri, 16 Rue Princesse, ☎ 01 46 33 51 12. Trendy bistro. ££
La Chope d'Alsace, 4 Carrefour de l'Odéon, ☎ 01 43 26 67 76. Alsatian cuisine and seafood. £
Coté Seine, 45 Quai des Grands-Augustins, ☎ 01 43 54 49 73. Elegant bistro. £
The Café des Deux Magots, 170 Blvd St-Germain, ☎ 01 45 48 55 25. £
L'Echaudé St-Gemain, 22 Rue l'Echaudé, ☎ 01 43 54 79 02. Rustic. £
L'Epi Dupin, 11 rue Dupin,☎ 01 42 22 64 56. £
Café de Flore, 172 Blvd St-Germain, ☎ 01 45 48 55 26. Café. £
Git le Coeur, 14 Rue Git le Coeur, ☎ 01 46 33 02 06. Traditional. £
La Grosse Horloge, 22 Rue St-Benoît, ☎ 01 42 22 22 63. £
Horse Tavern, 16 Carrefour de l'Odéon, ☎ 01 43 54 96 91. Traditional. £
Les Jardins St-Germain, Rue du Dragon, ☎ 01 45 44 72 82. £
Brasserie Lipp, 151 Blvd St-Germain, ☎ 01 45 48 53 91. 1920s brasserie. £
Relais de Montfaucon, 8 Rue de Montfaucon, ☎ 01 43 26 50 56. ££
Le Muniche, 7 Rue St-Benoît, ☎ 01 42 61 12 70. ££
Le Paris at the Hôtel Lutétia, 45 Blvd Raspail, ☎ 01 49 54 46 90. £
Le Petit St-Benoît, 4 Rue St-Benoît, ☎ 01 42 60 27 92. £
Le Petit Vatel, Rue Lobineau, ☎ 01 43 54 28 49. Reasonably priced. £
Le Petit Zinc, 11 Rue St-Benoît, ☎ 01 42 61 20 60. £
Polidor, at 41 rue Monsieur le Prince, ☎ 01 43 26 95 34. Traditional. £
Pralognan, 3 rue Hautefeuille, ☎ 01 43 54 35 46. Savoyard cuisine.
Le Procope, 13 Rue de l'Ancienne Comédie, ☎ 01 43 26 99 20. Paris's oldest café. £
Roger la Grenouille, 26–28 Rue des Grands Augustins, ☎ 01 43 26 10 55. Frogs' legs. ££
La Rotisserie d'en Face, Rue Christine, ☎ 01 43 26 40 98. Bistrot. £

As emblematic of Paris as the Quartier Latin or Montparnasse, but timelessly elegant and fashionable, Faubourg St-Germain fascinates every visitor. The oldest of the major churches of Paris, St-Germain-des-Prés, is close to cafés associated with the Romantic poets and Existentialist writers of the 19C and mid-20C (*Les Deux Magot*, *Le Flore*, *Brasserie Lipp*). Smart but discreet hotels and restaurants, antiquarians selling books and *bibelots*, modern galleries stand cheek-by-jowl with the best in fashion boutiques and one of the most colourful street markets in central Paris (Rue de Buci).

This district stretches south from the Seine opposite the Louvre, from the Institut de France on the east to Pont de la Concorde to the west. Much of this area, the property of the Abbaye St-Germain-des-Prés, was open country with a *bourg* which developed outside Philippe-Auguste's walls bounded in the 13C by Rues du Vieux-Colombier and des Saints-Pères. Early in the 14C more houses were built, and in the 17C the abbey enclosure was gradually dismantled. With the 16C–17C religious revival, several convents were built here and, in 1670, the Hôtel des Invalides was constructed on the west outskirts. By 1685 the new Pont Royal provided easy access to the Palais des Tuileries, the home of the court during the Regency (1715–21). This, together with the creation of the École Militaire, was the main reason for building this new aristocratic quarter, which gradually supplanted the Marais. About half the houses were built between 1690 and 1725, a quarter between 1725 and 1750, and most of the rest between 1750 and 1790. In style they are very similar; often the more handsome façades face the interior garden, and the gateway or *porte-cochère* from the street leads to the *cour d'honneur*.

Haussmann in the mid-19C created the main thoroughfares, Blvd St-Germain, Rue de Rennes, and Blvd Raspail, obliterating small streets, houses and hôtels particuliers. The most characteristic streets of the once noble faubourg are Rue de Lille, Rue de l'Université, Rue St-Dominique and Rue de Grenelle. About 100 old mansions remain, many of them converted to house embassies or government offices. The 6e and eastern half of the 7e arrondissements are still two of the most pleasant districts of Paris.

For convenience this large area is tackled in two sections: Ch. 8 describes the Luxembourg and St-Germain-des-Prés (from Blvd St-Michel to Rue des Saints-Pères and Blvd Raspail); Ch. 10 describes the rest of the 7th arrondissement.

Institut de France

Pl. de l'Institut, on the south bank of the Seine, facing the Louvre, is flanked by the curved wings of the Institut de France (Pl. 14; 1). These prestigious premises, with the newly-gilded dome, are among the most attractive on this reach of the *quais*. The building may be visited by prior arrangement with the Secrétariat, 23 Quai de Conti, ☎ 01 44 41 44 41.

The east wing of the Institut and the adjacent Hôtel de la Monnaie (see below) cover the site of the Hôtel de Nesle (13C), in which was incorporated the 13C Tour Nesle or Hamelin, the river bastion of Philippe Auguste's wall (which ran south east parallel to Rue Mazarine). The western part, known as the Petit-Nesle and the workshop of Benvenuto Cellini in 1540–45, was demolished in 1663. The eastern part, or Grand-Nesle, rebuilt in 1648 by François Mansart, became the Hôtel de Conti, and in 1770, the Hôtel de la Monnaie (Mint).

The present building was erected in accordance with the will of Cardinal Mazarin, who bequeathed 2 million *livres* in silver and 45,000 *livres* a year for the establishment of a college for 60 gentlemen of the four provinces acquired by the Treaty of the Pyrenees: Artois, Alsace, Roussillon and Piedmont (Pinerolo) hence known as the Collège des Quatre-Nations rather than by its official title, Collège Mazarin. Based on designs by Louis le Vau, on the axis of the Cour Carré of the Louvre, it was built between 1662–91, the architects Lambert and d'Orbay carrying on where le Vau left off. An outstanding edifice, without parallel in 17C France, the oval cupola and semi-circular façade embody characteristics typical of Roman Baroque. The Institut, founded in 1795 and installed first in the Louvre, acquired the building in 1806.

The Institut de France comprises five academies: the exclusive Académie Française, founded by Cardinal Richelieu in 1635 and restricted to 40 members, whose particular task was the editing of the dictionary of the French language; the Académie des Beaux-Arts (1816), founded by Mazarin in 1648 as the Académie Royale de Peinture et de Sculpture; the Académie des Inscriptions et Belles-Lettres, founded by Colbert in 1663; the Académie des Sciences, also founded by Colbert, in 1666; and the Académie des Sciences Morales et Politiques, founded in 1795 and reconstituted in 1832. The Institut is also responsible for several collections, among them the Musée Marmottan, and the Musée Condé at Chantilly (see p 331 and p 268. An annual general meeting of all five academies is held on 25 October (restricted admission).

The Académie Française holds special receptions for newly elected members who are known as *Les Immortels* (because their ranks are always refilled). Only in 1980 was the first woman member, the writer Marguerite Yourcenar, elected.

From the first octagonal courtyard, beyond which are two others, one of them the Kitchen Courtyard of the old college, an elegant staircase (1824) by Vaudoyer leads to the **Bibliothèque Mazarine**. Little changed little since the 17C, it contains c 450,000 vols, 4600 MSS and 2100 incunabula. Originally the Cardinal's personal library, opened to scholars in 1643, it became the first public library in France and was considerably augmented by other collections during the Revolutionary period. The Institut library is also in this wing, together with several rooms decorated with academic statues and busts of eminent academicians.

In the former chapel in the west wing is the Salle des Séances Solennelles. Restoration has undone the damage caused by Vaudoyer, and Mazarin's Tomb, by Coysevox, has been returned from the Louvre. The room contains some 400 seats (green for members of the Académie Française; red for the others), and is used for receptions and general meetings.

The riverside embankment here, as elsewhere in this reach of the Seine, is lined with the bookstalls of the *bouquinistes*. At 13 Quai de Conti is the Hôtel Guénégaud or de Sillery-Genlis, by François Mansart (1659), often visited by Napoléon as a young officer; Napoléon's surgeon, Baron Larrey, lived here from 1805 to 1832.

No. 11, the **Hôtel de la Monnaie**, the former Mint, is a dignified building by J.-D. Antoine (1771–75). The handsome doorway is ornamented with Louis XV's monogram and elegant bronze knockers; above is the fleur-de-lys escutcheon with Mercury and Ceres as supporters. From the vestibule, a notable example of 18C architecture, a double staircase on the right ascends to the

Musée de la Monnaie, containing an impressive collection of stamping presses, punches, medals and coins. Medals are for sale in the far wing. Open 13.00–18.00; closed Mon and some public holidays (☎ 01 40 46 55 33).

The Salle Guillaume Dupré, in the centre of the building, is (apart from the modern ceiling) representative of the best Louis XVI style; showcases display medals from the Renaissance to the present. The Salle Sage contains new acquisitions; the Salle Jean Warin, portraits of the Walloon medallist Warin (1604–72) and directors of the Mint. The Salle Denon, named after Baron Denon (1747–1825), the engraver and director general of French museums under Napoléon, is devoted to medals of the Consulate and Empire period and the Salle Duvivier displays examples of coins illustrating the evolution of French currency from Merovingian times. On the right of the second courtyard is the entrance to the ateliers or workshops, where you can see the processes of coin and medal production. In 1973 the minting of French coins was transferred to a new establishment at Pessac, near Bordeaux.

At No. 5, on the corner of Rue Guénégaud, Col de Margueerittes, of the Resistance, set up his headquarters while conducting operations for the liberation of Paris 19–28 August 1944.

At the end of the adjacent Rue de Nevers (entered below an arch), part of Philippe Auguste's wall is visible.

Continuing from the southern end of the Pont Neuf, **RUE DAUPHINE**, cut in 1607, runs through picturesque streets, passing on the left at 9 Rue Mazet the site of Chez Magny, a literary rendezvous in the 1860s. The Carrefour de Buci with its enticing **street market** is a veritable assault on the senses.

QUAI DES GRANDS-AUGUSTINS, between Pont St-Michel and the Pont-Neuf, built in 1313, is the oldest quai in Paris. It took its name from a convent situated here from 1293 until its demolition in 1797. The quay is bordered by fine mansions, from the 14C to 16C. Rue Séguier, lined with old houses, leads south to meet Rue St-André-des-Arts, also containing several notable 17C–18C buildings (Nos 27, 28 and 52). The cuisine of two of Paris's great restauranteurs, Jacques Cagna and Guy Savoy, can be sampled in this area—*Les Bookinistes*, 53 Quai des Grands-Augustins, is one of Guy Savoy's restaurants; *La Rotisserie d'en Face*, Rue Christine, is Jacque Cagna's place.

From Pl. St-André-des-Arts, to the east, Rue Hautefeuille leads south; No. 5, the Hôtel des Abbés de Fécamp, has a pretty turret. Also running south Rue de l'Eperon shortly meets (right) Rue du Jardinet. At the end of this the alley is the entrance to the Cour de Rohan (16C–17C), originally part of the palace of the Archbishop of Rouen. Turning left on passing through an archway, through the window of the boutique at No. 4 in the Cour de Commerce-St-André you see the base of one of Philippe Auguste's towers.

At No. 9, opposite, popular myth has it that Dr Joseph-Ignace Guillotin (1738–1814), professor of anatomy, perfected his 'philanthropic beheading machine', although in fact he merely proposed to the *Assemblée constituante* that beheading should be the only method of capital punishment, preferably by machine. A mechanic built one to the specifications of the secretary of the College of Surgeons, Dr Louis, which was put into operation on 25 April 1792, at first being known as the Louisette.

Rue de l'Ancienne Comédie (the next street to the west) takes its name from the Comédie Française of 1689–1770, which occupied No. 14, while opposite *Le Procope*, created in 1686, which claims to be the oldest café in Paris and was the favourite haunt of many generations of writers—Voltaire, Balzac, George Sand and Oscar Wilde among others—is still an attractive and popular place to eat.

At No. 42 Rue Mazarine, back towards the Institut, was the site of the *jeu de paume* de la Bouteille, where the Abbé Perrin established the Opéra in 1669–72; then occupied by Molière's company in 1673–80, and by the Comédie-Française in 1680–89, it is now a bistrot, *La Cafetière*. No. 12 is the site of another *jeu de paume*, where the Illustre Théâtre was opened in December 1643 by Molière's company. No. 30, known as the Hôtel des Pompes, was until 1760 the headquarters of the *pompiers* or fire brigade of Paris, founded in 1722.

In the mid-19C, Blvd St-Germain was cut through the meandering urban lanes leading south from the river. Opposite Rue de l'Ancienne Comédie, beyond the Pl. Henri-Mondor, is the Carrefour de l'Odéon (Pl. 14; 3), both busy crossroads. At the Café Voltaire, which stood there, a banquet was held in honour of Gauguin before he left for Tahiti in 1891.

To the east, at 12 Rue de l'Ecole de Médicine, is the old **Faculty of Medicine** on the site of the Collège de Bourgogne and Collège des Prémontrés. Gondouin was responsible in 1769–76 for the courtyard and pedimented entrance, a grandiose Classical structure, enlarged by Ginain between 1878–1900.

In the courtyard is a statue of the anatomist Xavier Bichat (1771–1802) by David d'Angers (1788–1856). The library contains c 600,000 vols and commentaries of the heads of the faculty from 1395 onwards. Also of interest are the lecture hall, the Musée d'Histoire de la Médecine (open 14.00–17.30, closed summer: Sat, Sun, winter: Thurs, Sun, and some public hols, ☎ 01 40 46 16 93), and the Salle du Conseil, hung with four Gobelins tapestries of the Louis XIV period, after Le Brun. Opposite is the entrance to the former refectory of the Couvent des Cordeliers, a 15C Franciscan house.

At No. 5, the Institut des Langues Modernes occupies the old domed Amphithéâtre du Jardin du Luxembourg St-Côme (1691–94), with an attractive portal. This was originally the lecture-hall of the College of Surgery. A plaque commemorates the birth of the actress Sarah Bernhardt (1844–1923).

Further east (left) at the corner of the southern section of Rue de Hautefeuille (No. 32), Gustave Courbet (1819–77) had his studio in the former chapel of the Collège des Prémontrés.

Rue de l'Ecole-de-Médecine narrows at the eastern end before meeting Blvd St-Michel. From its western end, a flight of steps ascends to Rue Monsieur-le-Prince (de Condé). To the left, on meeting Rue de Vaugirard, is the Lycée St-Louis, built by Bailly on the site of the Collège d'Harcourt (1280), where the writers Racine and Boileau studied. Its entrance faces Pl. de la Sorbonne.

Adjacent to the south end of Rue Monsieur-le-Prince is Pl. Edmond-Rostand, looking across to the Panthéon (see Ch. 4). To the south, on the right of Blvd St-Michel, the Ecole Supérieure des Mines occupies the Hôtel de Vendôme, an 18C building enlarged after 1840, its principal façade facing towards the Luxembourg Gardens. It contains a **Museum of Mineralogy and Geology**, open Tues–Fri 13.30–18.00, Sat 10.00–12.30, 14.00–17.00, closed Mon, Sun, public holidays (☎ 01 40 51 92 90).

The Jardin and the Palais du Luxembourg

One of many entrances to the **Jardin du Luxembourg** (Pl. 14; 5) is a few paces south of Pl. Edmond-Rostand. This extensive garden (23 hectares), embellished by more than 80 statues, two fountains and a pond, forms a pleasantly refreshing area in an arrondissement with few green spaces and has long been favoured by mothers with children. Laid out in the 17C, it was radically altered in 1782 and 1867, although the basic layout follows to some extent the one that was first created for Marie de Médicis. It is well equipped with facilities such as cafés, bandstand, carrousel, marionnette theatre and children's play area.

Steps descend from the east terrace to lawns surrounding an octagonal pond with a fountain. Beyond the formal west terrace is the Jardin Anglais enclosing a replica of the *Statue of Liberty* by Bartholdi, given to the United States in 1885. To the south west is a fruit garden. Due south, beyond Pl. André-Honnorat, the impressive perspective between the two branches of Av. de l'Observatoire was achieved at the cost of the Carthusian monastery demolished at the Revolution. Landscaped during the First Empire, these gardens have recently been renamed, Jardin Robert-Cavelier-de-la-Salle and Jardin Marco-Polo.

North of the central octagonal pond, on the right, at the end of an oblong pool, is the **Fontaine Médicis**, attributed to Salomon de Brosse (c 1627), in the style of an Italianate grotto. It was moved here in 1861. In the central niche is *Polyphemus about to crush Acis and Galatea*; on either side are Pan and Diana, the work of Augustin Ottin (1866). At the back is a low-relief, the Fontaine de Léda, brought from the Rue du Regard in 1855.

Among the scattered sculptures of varying quality are *Stendhal* by Rodin, *George Sand* by François Sicard, *Leconte de Lisle* by Denys Puech (1898), the *Seller of Masks* by Zacharie Astruc (1883), a monument to *Watteau* by Henri Gauquié, a bust of *Beethoven* by Bourdelle, and the monument to *Eugène Delacroix* by Dalou.

The **Palais du Luxembourg** was once a royal residence. Heavily rusticated, it is more attractive externally than internally. The northern façade, where the main entrance is surmounted by an eight-sided dome, is original; the south façade, facing the gardens, is a 19C copy by Gisors. The two wings, terminating in steep-roofed pavilions, with three orders of columns superimposed, are connected by a single-storeyed gallery.

The Luxembourg was built by Salomon de Brosse in 1615–27 for Marie de Médicis, widow of Henri IV, who, it is said, sought a refuge from the noisy Louvre to a more rural setting reminiscent of Tuscany and a palace recalling the Pitti Palace, her birthplace, in Florence. She acquired the mansion of the Duc de Tingry-Luxembourg (the Petit-Luxembourg; 1570–1612), hence its name. The building was altered in 1808 and enlarged in 1831–44.

After Louis XIII's death, the palace passed to her second son Gaston, Duc d'Orléans, and the Palais Médicis became known as the Palais d'Orléans. Subsequently, it belonged in succession to Mlle de Montpensier, the Duchesse de Guise (1672), Louis XIV (1694) and the Orléans family.

It was used as a prison during the Revolution and in 1794 the Directory transferred the seat of government from the Tuileries to the Luxembourg. In 1800 it became the Palais du Consulat, under the Empire it was the Palais du Sénat and later the Chambre des Pairs (House of Lords). Several important people were tried here, including Louis-Napoléon Bonaparte after his attempted coup in 1840. From 1852 to 1940, except for a short time, the Palais was the meeting-place of the Senate, the upper chamber of the French Republic. In 1940–44 it was occupied as the Luftwaffe's headquarters and reverted in 1958 to the Senate.

The **interior**, drastically remodelled by Jean Chalgrin (1739–1811) under Napoléon I, is decorated in the sumptuous 19C manner, replete with an indifferent group of statues and paintings, historical and allegorical. The celebrated series of paintings devoted to the *Life of Marie de Médicis*, by Rubens, which once hung in the palace, is now in the Louvre.

Notable is the luxuriously gilt Cabinet Doré, Marie de Médicis's audience chamber. Other rooms (on the first floor) occasionally open to the public are the Salles des Conférences, the hemicycle of the Salle de Séances and the library, overlooking the gardens, with magnificent **paintings by Delacroix**. Those above the window show *Alexander Placing the Poems of Homer in Darius's Golden Coffer* and, in the cupola, the *Limbo of Dante's Inferno.*

The adjoining **Petit-Luxembourg** (now the residence of the President of the Senate) was presented to Richelieu by Marie de Médicis in 1626. It includes the cloisters and chapel of the Filles du Calvaire, for whom the queen built a convent; the chapel is a charming example of the Renaissance style; the cloister forms a winter-garden. To the west is the Orangery, once occupied by a museum, some of the former contents of which now embellish the Musée d'Orsay.

A few paces to the north east of the Palais, in isolation and surrounded by arcades, stands the **Théâtre de l'Odéon**. It was built 1779–82 as the Théâtre-Français, in the form of a classical temple, by Wailly and Peyre in the garden of the demolished Hôtel de Condé. The Théâtre de l'Odéon was inaugurated in 1782 as the Théâtre-Français. It was rebuilt by Chalgrin after a fire in 1799 and re-opened in 1808. The ceiling of the auditorium was decorated by André Masson in 1965.

From its north entrance, Rue de l'Odéon, bordered by 18C houses, slopes downhill towards the Carrefour de l'Odéon. At No. 12 once stood the Librairie Shakespeare (Shakespeare and Co, see p 69), founded by Sylvia Beach, where in 1922 the first edition of James Joyce's *Ulysses* was published, in an edition of 1000 numbered copies.

The main entrance of the Palais du Luxembourg, is in RUE DE VAUGIRARD, the longest street in Paris, stretching from Blvd St-Michel to the Porte de Versailles. The Café Tabourey, which once stood at No. 20 was a famous literary rendezvous. The wide and stately RUE DE TOURNON, with its fine 18C façades and elegant shops, runs gently down to the Blvd St-Germain. It extends to the north by Rue de Seine, also flanked by a number of attractive houses, to the Institut.

The next street, turning right off Rue de Vaugirard, RUE BONAPARTE, becomes narrower and more interesting the other side of Blvd St-Germain as it approaches the Seine. A commercial street, it encourages lingering to admire the numerous antique shops and art galleries. Between Rue de Vaugirard and Pl. St-Sulpice (Pl. 13; 6) is a small garden, l'Allée du Seminaire, which takes its name from the neighbouring former seminary of St-Sulpice. Under the shady chestnuts is the fontaine de la Paix which was moved from Place St-Sulpice in 1824, went first to the Marché St-Germain, and came here in 1835. Rue Bonaparte skirts **PLACE ST-SULPICE**, since 1844 embellished with the Fontaine des Quatre-Evêques by Visconti with statues of four famous preaching bishops: Bossuet, Fénelon, Massillon and Fléchier. A charming and elegant part of the Left Bank, in June the square hosts an antiques fair.

At No. 6 is a dignified mansion by Servandoni (1754), the first of a range which never materialised. Although the merchandise in the shops in the neighbourhood is changing, traditionally this has always been the place to buy ecclesiastical artefacts.

St-Sulpice

The wealthiest church on the Left Bank, St-Sulpice is a fine classical building, imposing mainly for its size. The sober west front, like a Roman theatre, features a two-storey colonnade of superimposed Doric and Ionic orders. The north tower, topped by a balustrade, is 73m high; the unfinished south tower is 5m lower. Evident from Rue Palatine on the south flank, are the scale of the project and the change in style of the elevations, notably the Jesuit or Baroque characteristics of the transept arm.

A succession of masons and a succession of designs mark the character of this church. Begun in 1646 by Gamard, to replace an older church, it was continued on a larger scale by Gittard in 1670. After an interval from 1678 to 1719 work was resumed by Oppenordt, still on the designs of Gittard, but the tower added above the crossing had to be demolished after 1731. The building of the west front was entrusted to Giovanni Servandoni (1695–1766), a Florentine, who was replaced in 1766 by Maclaurin. His successor, Chalgrin, built the north tower in 1778–80, but the south tower was left incomplete.

In the form of a Latin cross, the **interior**, is spacious and regular in Counter Reformation style, measuring 115m long, 57m wide, and 33m high, with high arcades to the aisles. The organ, one of the largest in existence (6588 pipes), was built in 1781 and remodelled in 1860–62; the case was designed by Chalgrin with statues by Clodion and decoration by Duret. The church is noted for its music and organ recitals.

Among the furnishings are two huge Tridacna gigas shells serving as holy water stoups, presented to François I by the Venetian Republic; supporting them are rocks carved from marble and covered in naturalistic aquatic flora and fauna by Pigalle. The late-18C pulpit, designed by Wailly, bears gilded figures of Faith and Hope by Guesdon, and Charity by Dumont.

The lateral **chapels** are decorated with frescoes. The most important are the late works (1855–61) by **Delacroix** in the first chapel on the right. These vigorous images of spiritual conflict represent, in the vault, *St-Michael Vanquishing the Devil*, on the left, *Jacob Wrestling with the Angel*, and on the right *Heliodorus Chased from the Temple*. In the 5th chapel is the tomb, by Slodtz, of the curé Languet de Gergy (1674–1750), founder of the Enfants Malades, and responsible for the completion of the church.

In the paving of the south transept is a bronze table connected by a meridian line with a marble obelisk in the north transept. At noon the sun's rays, passing through an aperture in a blind window in the south transept, strike the meridian at specific points according to the time of year: during the winter solstice the sun strikes the obelisk, and during the spring and autumn solstice, the ray strikes the bronze table.

The **sacristy** on the south has some good 18C woodwork. The statues against the pillars of the choir are by Bouchardon and his workshop (1740), and the stalls are 18C. The high windows are 17C except the Sacré Coeur, which is of 1885. The sizeable, domed **Lady Chapel** was designed by Servandoni but, damaged by fire in 1762, its trappings were restored by Wailly in 1774. The original painting by F. Lemoyne (1731–32) in the cupola has undergone several alterations. The four easel paintings are by Carle van Loo (1746–51) and the subtly lit marble Virgin (placed here in 1774), in the niche behind the altar, is by Pigalle, with angels by Mouchy, and the bronze altar relief is by M.A. Slodtz (1730). Remains of the 16C church may be seen in the crypt.

Continue north to cross Rue du Four. Beyond is the busy intersection of **PLACE ST-GERMAIN-DES-PRÉS** (Pl. 13; 4). Diagonally opposite are the best-known and still popular cafés of Paris made famous by the artists, writers and existentialists who patronised them: *Café des Deux Magots* and *Café de Flore*; and close by is *Brasserie Lipp*.

St-Germain-des-Prés

Dominating the north of the square is the revered and reassuring tower of St-Germain-des-Prés. Although heavily rebuilt and restored, this is the oldest church in Paris and the only one retaining any considerable remains of Romanesque work.

A part of the great Benedictine abbey founded in 558 by Childebert I, who was buried there, as was St Germanus, Bishop of Paris (d. 576), it was also the burial place of the Merovingians. The church was rebuilt at the beginning of the 11C, and the nave completed up to the vaults by 1050. The base of the west tower dates from this time. Pope Alexander III consecrated the enlargement of the chancel in 1163 and in the 13C the master mason, possibly Pierre de Montreuil, came up with a solution to the long-standing problem of how to vault the curved section of an ambulatory. The ensemble was embellished at this time with a Gothic Lady Chapel and cloisters. A small sample of the cloisters stands in the gardens.

In the 17C, when it was the chief house of the reformed Congregation de St-Maur, the wooden roof of the nave was replaced by a neo-Gothic vault, the transepts were remodelled (c 1644) and the bell-chamber of the tower was added. Badly desecrated at the Revolution, drastic alterations in the 19C included the rebuilding of the Lady Chapel in 1819, the truncation in 1822 of the two towers flanking the choir and the restoration of the upper part of the west belfry.

The massive flying buttresses of the choir are among the earliest in France. The west porch dates from 1607, but retains the jambs of a 12C door and a battered

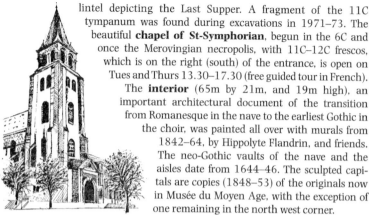

The Church of St-Germain-des-Prés

lintel depicting the Last Supper. A fragment of the 11C tympanum was found during excavations in 1971–73. The beautiful **chapel of St-Symphorian**, begun in the 6C and once the Merovingian necropolis, with 11C–12C frescos, which is on the right (south) of the entrance, is open on Tues and Thurs 13.30–17.30 (free guided tour in French).

The **interior** (65m by 21m, and 19m high), an important architectural document of the transition from Romanesque in the nave to the earliest Gothic in the choir, was painted all over with murals from 1842–64, by Hippolyte Flandrin, and friends. The neo-Gothic vaults of the nave and the aisles date from 1644–46. The sculpted capitals are copies (1848–53) of the originals now in Musée du Moyen Age, with the exception of one remaining in the north west corner.

To the right in the **south aisle** is a marble image of *N.-D. de Consolation*, presented to the Abbey of St-Denis by Queen Jeanne d'Evreux in 1340. In the south transept is the tomb, by Girardon, of Olivier and Louis de Castellan, killed in the king's service in 1644 and 1669.

The small marble columns in the triforium of the **choir** are re-used material from the 6C antecedent of this church, the abbey of St-Vincent and their bases and capitals are 12C. When cleaning work was done on the ambulatory in the 1950s, the 12C structure and capitals of some of the eastern chapels came to light. In the first ambulatory-chapel is the tomb of Lord James Douglas (1617–45; son of the first Marquess of Douglas), commander of Louis XIII's Scots regiment, killed near Arras. In the second chapel: tombstones of Descartes (1596–1650) moved from Ste-Geneviève in 1819 and of Mabillon; fourth chapel: has fragments of mid-13C stained glass. The Lady Chapel was rebuilt and decorated in the 19C.

In the **northern aisle** is the tombstone of Nicolas Boileau (1636–1711) transferred from the Sainte-Chapelle, and the tomb of William Douglas, 10th Earl of Angus (1554–1611), who died in the service of Henri IV. In the north transept are a statue of St Francisco Xavier, by G. Coustou; and the theatrical tomb, by G. and B. Marsy, of John Casimir V, King of Poland, Abbot of St-Germain in 1669, who died in 1672.

In the little gardens of Square L.-Prache to the north are fragments of sculptures from the Lady Chapel (1212–55) and Picasso's *Head of a Woman* given in 1959 in Hommage to Guillaume Apollinaire. In Square F.-Desruelles on the Blvd St-Germain side of the church is a statue of the potter, Bernard Palissy, and a monumental portico in ceramic and stone made at the Sèvres works by Risler for the Great Exhibition of 1900. In Rue de l'Abbaye, but further east, is the Abbot's Palace, erected c 1586 by Cardinal de Bourbon, behind which was the Prison de l'Abbaye (its site crossed by the present boulevard).

In 1857, six years before he died at 6 Rue de Furstenberg (or Fürstemberg) Delacroix built a studio in the adjoining Pl. de Fürstemberg, which with its four

Paulownias, is now less of a back-water than it once was. This was later shared by Monet and Bazille, and now contains the **Musée Delacroix**, open 09.45–17.00, closed Tues and some public holidays (☎ 01 44 41 86 50).

For streets radiating south west and west of the Pl. St-Germain-des-Prés, see below.

Rue Bonaparte continues north, intersecting Rue Jacob while the Hôtel du Marquis de Persan (Nos 7–9) was the birthplace of the painter Edouard Manet in 1832.

The main entrance of the **Ecole des Beaux-Arts** (Pl. 13; 4), is at 14 Rue Bonaparte. Begun in 1820 by Debret and finished in 1862 by Duban, it replaced the convent of the Petits-Augustins, founded in 1608, of which certain relics remain. It was here that Alexandre Lenoir (1762–1839) collected together numerous pieces of sculpture, saving them from destruction during the Revolutionary period (including the tomb of the kings from St-Denis). At the Restoration many, but not all, were returned to their place of origin or dispersed among museums. The building was further enlarged in 1885 on the acquisition of the Hôtel de Chimay (see below). The library contains c 120,000 volumes and 140,000 engravings and drawings.

The courtyard of the school can be seen from the street and is open at times (enquire at the office on the right). There are occasional visits arranged by the CNMHS.

The main points of interest are the former convent chapel (c 1600) with, re-erected against the south wall, the central part of the façade of the Château d'Anet (c 1540), by Philibert Delorme. This is cited as the earliest example in France of the correct use of the three orders of architecture according to Vitruvius. In the vestibule are more souvenirs of Anet. The adjoining Chapel des Louanges (occasionally used for temporary exhibitions) was built by Marguerite de Valois. The small hexagonal dome is the earliest built in Paris (1608). An arcade from the Hôtel de Torpane (c 1570) and the façade from the Hôtel de Chimay are also preserved. Scattered around the courtyards and inside the buildings are many pieces of sculpture, while the Salle de Melpomène is used to display the work of students when competing for the Grands Prix de Rome.

Leading south west from the Pl. St-Germain-des-Prés is Rue de Rennes, at the far end of which obtrudes the Tour Montparnasse (see p 91). A little way on the left is **Rue de Cassette**, one of the oldest in this district with some fine 18C houses. Turning right at the end of this street into Rue de Vaugirard, you pass the domed St-Joseph-des-Carmes, once the chapel of a Carmelite convent, dating from 1613–20, and containing several 17C canvases. In the crypt are the bones of some 120 priests massacred in the convent garden in September 1792. Joséphine de Beauharnais, later Madame Bonaparte, was one of many imprisoned here during the Terror.

Adjacent are the buildings of the Institut Catholique, founded in 1875, the most prestigious Catholic teaching establishments in France. Here, in 1890, radio waves were discovered by Edouard Branly (1844–1940).

This brings you to the crossroads with Rue d'Assas. Tucked away on the south (left) side of Rue d'Assas, at 100 bis, is the **Zadkine Museum** (10.00–17.30, closed Mon and public holidays (☎ 01 43 26 91 90). The studio from 1928 of the sculptor Ossip Zadkine (1890–1967), on exhibition are about 100 of the 300 works bequeathed by his widow. Renovated in 1991, this small museum demonstrates the range of Zadkine's sculptures, from his early Cubist inspired work to Expressionism and abstraction.

Turning right into Rue d'Assas, and recrossing Rue de Rennes, you reach RUE DU CHERCHE-MIDI which derives its name from an 18C sign on No. 19 representing an astronomer tracing a sundial and contains several attractive 17C–18C houses. The western section of Rue du Cherche-Midi is beyond the Blvd Raspail.

From the busy Carrefour de la Croix-Rouge (Pl. 13; 5), sporting a centaur sculpted by César as a *Hommage to Picasso* (1988), Rue de Sèvres leads south west. For the west section of Rue de Sèvres and Rue de Grenelle, which also starts at the Carrefour de la Croix-Rouge, see p 104.

Across this junction is Rue du Dragon, the possible site of the pottery workshop of Bernard Palissy (1510–89). Victor Hugo as a young man lived at No. 30. The next street along, Rue de Grenelle, parallel with Rue du Dragon, is Rue des Saints-Pères which runs north and crosses Blvd St-Germain. At No. 184 in the Boulevard is the Hôtel de la Société de Géographie, founded in 1821.

On the east side of Rue des Saints-Pères, after crossing St-Germain, is a miniscule garden, named after a Ukranian poet, Taras-Chevtchenko (1814–61). The Chapelle St-Pierre, rebuilt in 1611, is the sole relic of the Hôpital de la Charité, which stood on this site from 1605 to 1937. It is now the church of the Ukranian Catholic community in Paris (St-Vladimir-le-Grand).

Adjacent are buildings of the Faculty of Medicine (1936–53), while opposite, in the 18C Hôtel de Fleury, by Antoine, is the Ecole des Ponts et Chaussées, a civil engineering school founded in 1747. Further north, at the corner of Rue de Lille, is the Ecole des Langues Orientales, founded by the Convention in 1795. The artist Edouard Manet died at 5 Rue des Saints-Pères and at No. 45 is the Museum of Anatomy—Delmas-Orfila-Rouvière (to visit, ☎ 01 42 86 20 47).

The Quai Malaquais, leading east to the Institut, contains a number of 17C–18C mansions. Henrietta Maria (the widow of Charles I) lived at No. 17, part of the Hôtel de Chimay, built by François Mansart c 1640, and altered in the 18C. No. 9, at the corner of Rue Bonaparte, the Hôtel de Transylvanie, is a good example of Louis XIII architecture (1622–28).

9 · Musée d'Orsay

- Arrondissement: 75007.
- Métros: Musée d'Orsay, Solférino, RER: Musée d'Orsay.
- Open Tues–Sun, summer 09.00–18.00, winter 10.00–18.00, Sun 09.00–18.00, Thurs. until 21.45, closed Mon, 1/1, 1/5, 25/12. ☎ 01 40 49 48 14, recorded information, ☎ 01 45 49 11 11. The museum's address is 62 Rue de Lille, 75007, but the main entrance is at No. 1 Rue Bellechasse, at its west end.

Museum cafés and restaurants

Café des Hauteurs, ☎ 01 45 49 47 03. £
Restaurant de Musée, ☎ 01 45 49 47 03. £

The Quai d'Orsay is dominated by the huge and ornate bulk of the former Gare d'Orsay, still bearing the names of destinations it once served—Orléans, Bordeaux, Toulouse. It has two great clocks above the massive glazed arcades, and large allegorical figures look out from its façade across the river to the Tuileries Gardens.

The façade of Musée d'Orsay

The Musée d'Orsay was inaugurated in December 1986 (Pl. 13; 1). This remarkable metamorphosis of railway station into museum is extremely popular with art-loving Parisians. The aim of the museum is to continue, chronologically, where the Louvre leaves off, bringing together national collections of the second half of the 19C and the early 20C. It is an important record of the different themes of mid-19C art and follows the evolution of art through Impressionism and beyond. The works exhibited include all aspects of the visual arts: painting and drawing (including pastels), sculpture, decorative arts and photography, but the museum is probably best known for the collection of Impressionist paintings. The works assembled come from the Louvre, the Jeu de Paume, the Palais de Tokyo, the Musée de Luxembourg and provincial museums, and through donation and acquisition.

The building was originally the Gare and Hôtel d'Orsay, erected in 1898–1900 by Victor Laloux (1850–1937) on the site of the ancient Cour des Comptes, set ablaze in 1871 during the Commune. With a metal frame, intended to be both functional and decorative, the elevation towards the Seine was masked with stone to complement the Louvre on the opposite bank. The hotel façade faced west on Rue de Bellechasse. Edouard Detaille, the artist, remarked ironically at the time that the railway station looked exactly like a Palais des Beaux-Arts, but 86 years were to elapse before the transformation took place.

By 1939 the station had virtually outlived its usefulness because of its comparatively short platforms and had a succession of roles. The belated revival of interest in the conservation of 19C industrial architecture saved the condemned building, and the decision was taken to convert it into a museum. This was one of the *grands projets* of President Valéry Giscard d'Estaing, but inaugurated by President François Mitterand.

The architects chosen for the museum were Renaud Bardon, Pierre Colboc and Jean-Paul Philippon of ACT and the architect/designer responsible for the interior was Gae Aulenti. Certain rooms retain their original decoration of the 1900s.

The museum is also the site of frequent temporary exhibitions as well as concerts, films and lectures; brochures detailing forthcoming events are available. The **Belle Epoque restaurant** of the former hotel is now the museum restaurant, and also in the building are a rooftop café, bookshop, library, postcard shop and boutique (with access from the exterior); postal and exchange facilities are also available and for the disabled.

The Collections

The main permanent collection—approximately 2300 paintings, 250 pastels, 1500 sculptures, 1100 objets d'art and 13,000 photographs (exhibited in rotation)—is shown on three floors. Separate sections are devoted to individual collections, including the collections of Chauchard, Gachet, Kaganovitch, Mollard, Personnaz, and Moreau-Nélaton.

On the **forecourt** of the museum are bronzes commissioned for the first Trocadero Palace built for the Paris Universal Exposition of 1878, and on Rue de Lille are works of 1925 by Bourdelle.

The first impression of the **interior** is of space and light. The building is in total 220m by 75m and the coffered vault—with its 1600 rosettes—of the central hall alone, which once spanned the platforms, is 138m in length, 40m wide and 32m high. The architects wanted to create a museum on a human scale without losing the original perspectives. The new installations use a great deal of pale, polished Buxy stone and are designed neither to emulate nor to vie with the original building. The 16,000 square metres for permanent exhibitions is divided into some 80 separate sections or galleries and the layout can be confusing, particularly when finding the route to the upper galleries. A well planned visit will save both time and frustration.

The museum aims to present all aspects of the art of the period. A representative selection of sculpture produced in the 19C is shown to advantage in the **central aisle**. A large section is dedicated to the stiff and formal Salon paintings produced in quantity by less able followers of David, Ingres and Canova. Work of the Romantic era is well represented, as are early *plein air* painters, such as the Barbizon School, of Art Nouveau artefacts, and of Symbolism. In fact, all the art against which the Impressionists reacted, or from which Impressionism developed, and the art of the early 20C influenced by them. The remarkable collection of Impressionist works is in a series of rooms on an upper level.

On the **ground floor**, with its entrance below the great clock of the terraced central aisle, are displayed some of the more important sculptures by Rude, David d'Angers, Pradier, Préault and Barye. The 19C works come into their own in this large, lucid area which throws up the contrast between the marble and bronze and the severely geometric partitions which flank the aisle.

On the left as you enter is one of the most extreme examples of Romanticism, albeit in a classical guise: *Napoleon Awakening to Immortality* (1846), by François Rude (1784–1855), a plaster of the monument made for Fixin, Burgundy. The creative energies of Jean-Baptiste Carpeaux (1827–75), are given full recognition, and outstanding are the *Ugolin group* (1862), the *Four Quarters of the World* bearing the celestial sphere (1867–72) for the fountain on Avenue de l'Observatoire, and *La Danse* (1869), commissioned for the façade of the Opéra. Works by Rodin, Camille Claudel, Bourdelle, Maillol and Joseph Bernard are on the terraces around the central aisle and other sculptures are scattered through the galleries (see below).

Suggested tour around the museum

The route proposed below is for visitors wanting to work their way through the exhibits in a fairly logical order and is accompanied by a plan of rooms pp 108–9. The suggested itinerary starts in **room 1**, the first room on the right as you enter the central aisle, works from the period up to 1880 are in this section, including two dominant yet contrasting painters and their followers, the Neoclassical **Jean Auguste Dominique Ingres** (1780–1867) and the Romantic **Eugène Delacroix** (1798–1863). Representative of their works are Ingres' *La Source* (completed 1856), Delacroix's *The Lion Hunt*; *The Tepidarium* (1853) by Théodore Chassériau (1819–1856)—student of Ingres, admirer of Delacroix, and later the teacher of Moreau—was inspired by one of the thermae discovered at Pompeii. The technically competent but vacuous works of Salon painters such as Alexandre Cabanel (1808–79) and Bourguereau are in this section.

Facing the main aisle is a huge canvas by Thomas Couture (1815–79), *Roman Decadence* (1847), much praised in its time. The section immediately to the east (**room 9**) is devoted to the decorative arts of the period 1850–80.

Room 11 contains important works by **Puvis de Chavannes** (1824–98), a profound influence on many later painters including the Symbolists and Seurat. The museum owns *The Poor Fisherman* (1881), *Young Girls by the Sea* (1879), and *The Pigeon* and *The Balloon*, both painted during the Siege of Paris (1870–71). Close by are works by **Gustave Moreau** (1826–98). Early (i.e. before 1870) works by **Edgar Degas** (1834–1917), include the finely tuned family group, *The Bellelli Family* (1858/60), *Portraits of Hilaire de Gas*, the artist's grandfather (painted on a visit to Italy in 1857) and of *Thérèse de Gas* (1863), *Before the Race* (1862/80), *The Orchestra of the Opéra* (1868/69) and the unfinished *Semiramis Watching the Construction of Babylon* (1861).

Crossing the central aisle diagonally, **rooms 4 to 6** and the **Seine gallery** display work of the mid-19C. Not only are there paintings by **Honoré Daumier** (1808–79), such as *The Laundrywoman* (c 1863) but also his remarkable series of 36 painted clay caricature busts of Parliamentarians, modelled from 1831. The paintings of the 1860s, include Ernest Meissonier (1815–91), *Campagne de France*, and pleasant but undemanding rural scenes by Jules Breton, Rosa Bonheur, Constant Troyon, Félix Diem, Eugène Isabey, early Delacroix, and small animal bronzes by Bayre. From this period are the gentle silvery landscapes of **Jean-Baptiste Corot** (1796–1875); works by the Barbizon painters: Théodore Rousseau (1812–67), Charles Daubigny (1817–78), and Diaz de la Peña (1807–76), who paved the way for open-air painting; and the atmospheric and dignified canvases of **Jean-François Millet** (1814–75), including *The Gleaners* (1857), *The Angelus* (1858/9) and several portraits and landscapes. Many of the works in this section belong to the Chauchard collection.

Both controversial and influential were the large, and sometimes sombre, works of **Gustave Courbet** (1819–77), in **room 7**. Considered scandalous at the Salon of 1850, because of its blatant realism, is the *Burial at Ornans*. Its counterpart, equally huge and impressive, is *The Artist's Studio* (1855) with Baudelaire depicted on the right, reading. The museum's most recently acquired Courbet is the beautiful nude entitled *The Origin of the World* (1866).

The first of the two rooms (**14** and **18**) on the right of the Seine gallery is dedicated to **Edouard Manet** (1832–83) before 1870. This stunning group of paintings includes *Portraits of his Parents* (1860), *Lola de Valence* (1862), *Bullfight* (1865–66), *The Balcony* (c 1868–69), with Berthe Morisot in the foreground, the audaciously defiant *Olympia* (1863), and *Portrait of Zola* (1868), with the previous painting in the background. *The Fife-Player* (1866) contrasts the rigorous play of black and white with the red trousers of the musician. There are some delicious still lifes.

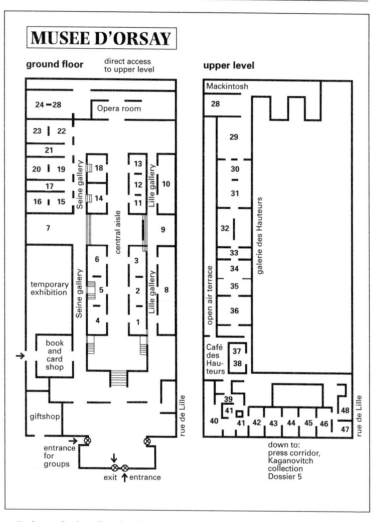

MUSEE D'ORSAY

ground floor direct access to upper level

upper level

Opera room

24 → 28

23 | 22

21

20 | 19

17

16 | 15

7

Seine gallery

18

14

central aisle

13

12

11

Lille gallery

10

9

6

5

4

Seine gallery

3

2

1

Lille gallery

8

temporary exhibition

book and card shop

giftshop

→

entrance for groups

↓

⊗ ⊗

exit ↑ entrance

rue de Lille

Mackintosh

28

29

30

31

32

33

34

35

36

galerie des Hauteurs

open air terrace

Café des Hauteurs

37

38

39

41

40

41

42

43

44

45

46

47

48

rue de Lille

down to:
press corridor,
Kaganovitch
collection
Dossier 5

Early works by **Claude Monet** (1840–1926), in the continuation of the Seine gallery and **room 18**, are shown with pre-1870 works of his friends and colleagues **Auguste Renoir** (1841–1919) and **Frédéric Bazille** (1841–70), and reveal the early experiments which led to Impressionism. By Monet are *Portrait of Mme Gaudibert*, two sections from *Le Déjeuner sur l'herbe* (1865/6), *Women in a Garden*, painted in the open air, and *The Magpie*, the black and white bird against the subtle whites of a snow-covered landscape. Here also are works executed before 1870 by Renoir, *Bazille Painting* (1867); and by Bazille, *Portrait of Renoir*.

Rooms 15 and 16 deal with painters close to the Impressionists or their forerunners. **Henri Fantin-Latour** (1836–1904), recorded the artistic milieu of the day in *The Studio in the Batignolles* (1870), showing Manet at the easle and grouped around him Monet, Bazille, Zola and Renoir and others; and in *A Corner of the Table* are the poets Verlaine and Rimbaud. There are also charming small **marine paintings** by Boudin (1824–98), Lépine (1836–92) and Jongkind (1819–91). Room 17 has rotating exhibitions of pastels.

Rooms 19 and 20 contain the Antonin Personnaz and Eduardo Mollard collections. In the former are 14 landscapes by **Camille Pissarro** (1830–1903) from 1870 to 1902: *Winter at Louveciennes* (c 1870) and green scenes such as *Landscape at Chaponval* (1880) and *Woman in an Enclosure* (1887), show the evolution of his later style. By **Monet**, *Bridge at Argenteuil* (1874); **Guillaumin** (1841–1927), *The Place Valhubert* and *Paris, Quai de Bercy in the Snow* (somewhat different from its present aspect, see Ch. 21); the only painting in the Orsay by the American, **Mary Cassatt** (1844–1926), *Woman Sewing* (c 1880/82).

In the adjacent room is the Mollard collection including Jongkind, *The Seine at Notre-Dame*; **Boudin**, the well-known *Beach at Trouville* (1864), and **Sisley's** (1839–99), *The Bridge at Moret-sur-Loing* (1893).

Room 21 houses part of the museum's fine **collection of pastels** (dimly lit for conservation reasons), by Millet, Puvis de Chavannes, Braquemond, Cassatt, and Degas; glorious blues in *Madame Manet on a Blue Sofa* (1874) by Manet; and swirling, foggy blues in *Waterloo Bridge, London*, c1899–1901 by Monet.

Room 22 is devoted to the harsh light of Realism with canvases by **Adolphe Monticelli** (1824–86), among others. Orientalism, in the adjoining room, refers to paintings inspired mainly by North Africa and Egypt. In the footsteps of Ingres and Gérôme are Guillaumet (1840–87) *Evening Prayer in the Sahara* (1863) and *The Desert* (1867); Fromentin, *The Land of Thirst*.

On leaving this section turn left to reach the eastern extremity of the museum. On the left, in **rooms 24 to 28**, is Richard Peduzzi's *Architectural Tower*. Successive elevations of the tower demonstrate architectural features of public and private constructions of the period 1850–1900, the vocabulary of the decorative elements, and the use of a variety of materials.

Below the main vault of the building, in the 'Opera' room, is a remarkable exhibit devoted to Charles Garnier (1825–98) and the construction of the Paris Opéra, started in 1862. This contains a maquette of the entire Opéra quarter at 1:100 as it was in 1914; a model of it shown as a cross-section; and a maquette of the stage of the Opéra built for the Universal Exhibition of 1900.

Upper level

A bank of escalators, discreetly tucked away and easy to miss, behind the Opéra display, ascends to the upper level and the galleries devoted to the main **Impressionists** (**room 29**). The majority of these works were moved here from the Jeu de Paume and are displayed in roughly chronological order. This very popular part of the museum is often crowded.

The first gallery contains the Etienne Moreau-Nélaton collection (other parts of this collection are dispersed in the Orsay, and in the Louvre). One of the most notorious picnics of all time is here, *Le Déjeuner sur l'Herbe* (1863) by **Manet**. The contrasting flesh and fabric, the juxtaposed still life and abandoned blue dress are still provocative.

This extraordinarily rich collection also includes an all-time favourite by **Monet**, *The Poppies*, a halcyon moment with intrusive 19C engineering in *The*

Railway Bridge at Argenteuil (c 1875). Also Fantin-Latour's *Hommage to Delacroix*, Sisley, *The Footbridge at Argenteuil*, and further works by Pissarro.

The following gallery contains **James Whistler** (1834–1903), *Arrangement in Grey and Black*, and *Whistler's Mother* (1871), composed with austere harmony. Tender are the two paintings by **Berthe Morisot** (1841–95), *The Cradle* (1872) and *Young Woman in a Ball Gown* (1879), whereas more vigorous is **Gustave Caillebotte** (1848–94), *Floor Planers* (1875). **Degas'** *The Absinthe Drinkers* (1876) is a moving portrayal of dejection.

Room 31 concentrates on work by **Manet** and **Degas**. Bronzes by the latter includes the 14-year-old *Dancer wearing her tutu*. Oblique or unusual glimpses by Degas are *The Dancing Class* (1873–76), *The Stock Exchange* (c 1878–79), the fatigue of *Women Ironing* (c 1884–86), and several horse-racing scenes. Manet is represented here by *On the Beach at Berck-sur-Mer* (1873), the marvellous *Lady with the Fans* (1873–74), and at his most impressionistic in the *Portraits of Mallarmé* and of *Clemenceau*.

Works before 1880, a turning point in Impressionism, include **Monet**'s *Regatta at Argenteuil* (c 1872), the *Fête in the Rue Montorgueil* (1878), and *St-Lazare Station* (1877). Landscapes by **Pissarro** include *Red Roofs*. The effects of dappled light are used by **Renoir** in paintings of 1876 such as *Dancing at the Moulin de la Galette* and *The Swing*; also, among his sculptures, are a bust of Mme Renoir.

Room 34 contains later Impressionist works. By **Monet**: *Woman with the Sunshade* (1886), five of the series of views of the *Cathedral at Rouen*, showing the effects of light at different times of day (1892–93), and blue iris in *The Garden at Giverny* (1900). By **Renoir**, are the joyful *Dance in the Country*, and the more restrained *Dance in the Town* of 1883, and *Girls playing the Piano*.

Room 35 has a large number of of the best-loved paintings by **Vincent van Gogh** (1853–90). From the dark and brooding early paintings, Van Gogh's work erupts into the vigorous impasto and intense colour of *The Portrait of Dr Paul Gachet* (1890), one of three portraits of the doctor who befriended the Impressionists and whose collection was donated to the museum by his children. The collection includes van Gogh's The *Bedroom at Arles* (1889); two *Self-portraits*, of 1887 and 1889, electrifying in the use of colour and the tense energy of the brushstrokes; and the intense *Church at Auvers-sur-Oise* (1890); *The Siesta*, after Millet, 1889–90, could be called rhapsody in blue and gold.

The museum possesses a significant cross-section of the works of **Paul Cézanne** (1839–1906), which are hung in **room 36**. From Cézanne's earlier period are the *Portrait of Achille Emperaire* (1869/70), the *Still Life with Soup Tureen* (c 1877) and *A Modern Olympia* (1873), a burlesque of Manet's painting. Examples of his monumental mature works include *The Card-players* and *Woman with a Coffee-pot*. Landscapes are represented by the *Bay at Estaque* (c 1878–79), the *Bridge of Maincy* (1879), and *Poplars* (1879–82). *Still Life with Onions* (1896/98), and *Apples and Oranges* (c 1899) combine the textures of voluptuous fruit and heavy fabrics. *Bathers* (c 1890), was his last and largest canvas of male nudes.

Next to room 36 are **Toulouse-Lautrec's** (1864–1901) panels for La Goulue's booth at the Foire du Trône. The later **pastels by Degas** (in **rooms 37 and 38**) include *A Dancer with a Bouquet taking a Bow* (c 1877), eerily bathed in a grey-green theatrical light; and nudes such as *The Tub* (1886) and the sensitive *After the Bath* (c 1895).

Adjacent to these rooms is the ***Rooftop Café***, providing a curious version of Paris through the hands of the huge clock, and panoramic views from the terrace.

Room 39 has late works by **Monet** and **Renoir**. By the former, *The Houses of Parliament*, London, *Sunlight in the Fog* (1904), *Lily Pond*, 1899 and 1900, and *Blue Waterlilies* (c 1916–18), and one example of the Haystacks series. **Renoir's** *Large Bathers* (c 1918–19) is considered the culmination of his art.

Room 40. Examples of **Odilon Redon's** (1840–1916) mysterious and luminous work include *The Buddha* (1906/07), pastel, and *Portrait of Gauguin* (1903/05). There are pastels by Ker-Xavier Roussel (1867–1944), Maurice Denis, Georges Rouault (1891–1959) and a watercolour by Piet Mondrian (1872–1944).

Rooms 41–43 at the western end of the museum include work by Pissarro, Guillaumin, and Monet. **Henri (le Douanier) Rousseau** (1844–1910) is represented by *Portrait of a Woman* (c1897) and the *Snake Charmer* (1907). Following these are **Emile Bernard** (1868–1941) and **Paul Sérusier** (1863–1927) at Pont-Aven, and **Paul Gauguin** (1848–1903), covering periods in Brittany and in the South Seas from 1875 through to 1903, from an impressiontistic style to an emphasis on flat patterning and symbolic use of colour: *Washerwomen in Pont-Aven* (1886), *La belle Angèle* (1889); *Tahitian Women on the Beach (1891), And the Gold of their Bodies* (1901); two Self Portraits, of 1883/93 and 1896.

Neo-Impressionism or Pointillism is represented by **Georges Seurat** (1859–91), **room 45**, in his preparatory sketches for *La Grande Jatte, Poseuses*, and *The Circus* of 1890/91; *Port-en-Bessin, avant-port, marée haute* (1888). **Room 46**. Pointillism or Divisionism becomes coarser and richer in the hands of **Paul Signac** (1863–1935), Henri Cross (1856–1910) and Maximilien Luce (1858–1941); **Henri Matisse** (1869–1954) adapts the technique in *Luxe, Calme et Volupté* (1904) to shimmering horizontal dashes captured within an outline.

Works by **Toulouse-Lautrec** in **room 47** include *Jane Avril Dancing* (c 1891), *La toilette* (1896), and *Cha-U-Kao* (the female clown) (1895); **room 48** is devoted to small format paintings by the Nabis, including Pierre Bonnard (1867–1947), Maurice Denis (1870–1943); Félix Vallotton (1865–1925) and Edouard Vuillard (1868–1940). (The larger works by these artists are on the floor below, the Middle Level.)

Escalators take you down to the Press Corridor, which traces the development of images in the press over the period, and to the Gallery of Dates. This brings you also to the Kaganovitch collection (**room 50**), including Gauguin's, *Breton Peasant Women*, and works by Monet, Sisley, Renoir, Pissarro and Van Gogh.

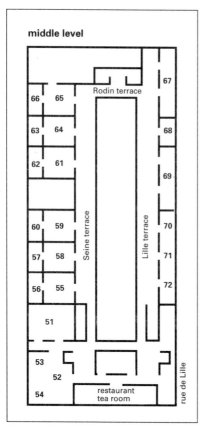

middle level

Rodin terrace

66 65

63 64

62 61

60 59

57 58

56 55

51

53

52

54

67

68

69

70

71

72

Seine terrace

Lille terrace

restaurant tea room

rue de Lille

Middle level

Cross the press corridor to reach escalators descending to the **middle level** of the museum. On this level is the grand *Belle Epoque Restaurant*, which is not unreasonably priced.

Rooms 51–54 present the **Decorative Arts of the Third Republic**. The former ballroom (Salle des Fêtes) of the station hotel has been restored to its former glitzy glory, with gilded mirrors and chandeliers. Large portraits of society beauties and frivolous paintings by William Bouguereau (1825–1905), mingle with sleek statues by Denys Puech (1854–1942) and Ernest Barrias (1841–1905). The stuccoed rooms in the north-west angle deal with the creation of public monuments, many of which still embellish Paris, through preparatory paintings, maquettes and models.

A footbridge brings you to the next section, the **Seine Terrace** overlooking the central aisle, with Monumental Sculpture 1870–1914 by Barrias, Coutain, Frémiet and Gérôme, mainly addressing themes of conflict, power or heroism, for example Frémiet's *Saint Michael*.

Leading off the terrace are a number of rooms (**55–58**) devoted to **Naturalism**. Among them are paintings by Bastien-Lépage (1848–84), Léon Bonnat (1833–1922), Jacques-Emile Blanche (1861–1942), Philip Wilson Steer (1860–1942) and Jean-Léon Gérôme's *bust of Sarah Bernhardt* (c 1895). There are also works by Sir Lawrence Alma-Tadema (1836–1912) and small bronzes by Dalou (1838–1902).

Among the **Symbolist** works in **rooms 59 and 60** are Burne-Jones (1833–98), *The Wheel of Fortune*; and paintings by Gustav Klimt (1862–1918), Edvard Munch (1863–1944) and James Ensor (1860–1949).

Adjacent is a fascinating section (**rooms 61–66**) containing **Art Nouveau** production from several European countries. There are samples of jewellery by René Lalique (1860–1945); glass, ceramics and enamel work by Emile Gallé (1846–1904) and the School of Nancy as well as Albert Dammouse (1848–1926); also stained glass by Louis Comfort Tiffany and Jacques Gruba (1870–1930). There is an interior design by Redon (1899).

There are also examples, perfectly crafted and sometimes exquisitely over-the-top, of **furniture and woodwork**. The craftsmen include Hector Guimard

(1867–1942), Alexandre Charpentier (1856–1909) dining room (1901), Jean Dampt (1854–1945), Louis Majorelle (1859–1926), including the bedroom suite, Nénuphars (c 1905), Eugène Vallin, and F.-R. Carabin (1862–1932); and Henry Van de Velde, through to chairs (c 1902) by Peter Behrens (1860–1940).

The Tour Guimard is devoted to international Art Nouveau furniture and the decorative arts.

Outside these rooms and on the east landing is an important collection of sculpture by **Auguste Rodin** (1840–1917). Among numerous busts is the marble, entitled *La Pensée*, of the Head of **Camille Claudel** (1864–1943), whose impressive bronze group entitled *L'Age mûr* (Maturity) is also in this section.

Rooms 67–69 are used for temporary thematic exhibitions. Sculpture continues on the Lille Terrace with **Émile Antoine Bourdelle** (1861–1929) and **Aristide Maillol** (1861–1944). Passing a section devoted to temporary exhibitions, you reach to the left, the last series of rooms containing paintings, largely post 1900, of work by the Nabis: Denis, Bonnard, Vuillard, Vallotton and Ker-Xavier Roussel. There are large decorative panels by **Edouard Vuillard**, as well as canvases: *In bed* (1891) and *Portrait of Thadée Natanson*. Among **Pierre Bonnard's** contributions are *The Croquet Party*, and others showing a heavy debt to Japanese art.

Among collections of **early photographs** are representative examples of the art of Eugène Atget, Edouard Baldus, L.-A. Humbert de Molard, Félix Nadar, Charles Nègre, Pierre Petit, George Charles Beresford, Julia Margaret Cameron, Lewis Carroll, Roger Fenton and George Shaw.

10 · Faubourg St-Germain: western sector

■ Arrondissement: 75007.
■ Métros: Solférino, Musée d'Orsay, Assemblée Nationale, Invalides, Varenne, Sèvres-Babylone, Rue du Bac. RER: Musée d'Orsay, Invalides.

Established in elegant hôtels particuliers in this part of St-Germain are two museums dedicated to the sculptors Auguste Rodin and Aristide Maillol, while the Palais Bourbon is home of the Assemblée Nationale.

From the Louvre, Pont du Carrousel crosses the Seine to QUAI VOLTAIRE (Pl. 13; 3), the continuation of Quai Malaquais (see p 104). Futher west extends Quai Anatole-France and the Quai d'Orsay. The former is dominated by the Musée d'Orsay; see Ch. 9. Several writers and artists lived and died in Quai Voltaire, including Voltaire (1694–1778) died at No. 27; Ingres died at No. 11 in 1867; Delacroix lived at No. 13 between 1829 and 1836 (as did Corot some time later). Baudelaire lived at No. 19 in 1856–58 while writing *Les Fleurs du Mal*, and Wagner completed the libretto of Die Meistersinger at the same address in 1861–62; later tenants included Sibelius and Oscar Wilde.

Opposite the west end of the Musée d'Orsay is the **Palais de la Légion d'Honneur**, flanked by a colonnade with bas-reliefs on the attic storey. The Corinthian portico in the courtyard is adorned with a frieze of arabesques with the motto *Honneur et Patrie*. Facing the quay is a rotunda with Corinthian columns and symbolic busts.

Restaurants and cafés

Arpège, 84 Rue de Varenne, ☎ 01 45 51 47 33. Haute cuisine. £££
Le Divelec, 107 Rue de l'Université, ☎ 01 45 51 91 96. Upmarket, fish. £££.
Les Ministères, 30 Rue du Bac, ☎ 01 42 61 22 37. Traditional. £££
Gaya Rive Gauche, 44 Rue du Bac, ☎ 01 45 44 73 73. Seafood. ££
Le Télégraph, 41 Rue de Lille, ☎ 01 40 15 06 65, in the former Maison des Dames des PTT, built by Bliault, 1905, retains much of its original decor—trendy. £
Le Recamier, 4 Rue Recamier, ☎ 01 42 22 51 75. Traditional. ££
Le Bourbon, Pl. du Palais Bourbon, ☎ 01 45 51 58 27. Brasserie. £
A La Petite Chaise, 36 rue de Grenelle, reputed to be the oldest restaurant in Paris, established in 1680, ☎ 01 42 22 13 35. Bistrot style. £
Le Bambouche, 15 Rue de Babylone, ☎ 01 45 49 14 40. Bistrot. ££
Au Pied de Fouet, 45 Rue de Babylone, ☎ 01 47 05 12 27. Bistrot. £
L'Epi Dupin, 11 Rue Dupin, ☎ 01 42 22 64 56. Bistrot. £
Musée Maillol cafeteria, ☎ 01 42 22 59 58. £
Musée Rodin cafeteria, ☎ 01 45 50 42 34. £

Built in 1782–86, the house became the Swedish Embassy in 1797 and Mme de Staël, the ambassador's wife, gave her famous receptions here. In 1804 it was bought by the government for the grand chancellory of the Legion of Honour and was restored to its original form in 1878, after being severely damaged by fire during the Commune.

The entrance to the Musée National de la Légion d'Honneur et des Ordres de Chevalerie, which exhibits medals, decorations, and the like, relating to the history of the Orders of Chivalry since Louis XI, together with foreign heraldic trappings, is at No. 2 in the adjoining Rue de Bellechasse. The first room has exhibits relating to the Royal Orders: the Ordres de Saint-Michel, du Saint-Esprit, de Saint-Louis, etc. The second room deals with the history of the Legion of Honour which replaced all the other honours after the Revolution. A non-hereditary order, it was instituted in May 1802 and comprises five classes in ascending order: Chevalier, Officier, Commandeur, Grand-Officier and Grand-Croix. Open 14.00–17.00, closed Mon (☎ 01 40 62 84 25.)

At 80 Rue de Lille (to the south) is the **Hôtel de Seignelay** by Gabriel Boffrand, in 1714. Boffrand, France's finest Rococo architect, also built the adjacent **Hôtel de Beauharnais** (1713), one of the finest in this area. Sold first to Jean-Baptiste Colbert, nephew of the Great Colbert, it was then acquired by Eugène de Beauharnais in 1803 and became the occasional the home of his sister Queen Hortense. In 1814 it became the Prussian legation, in 1871 the German Embassy, and is now the German ambassador's residence. The curious neo-Egyptian peristyle characterises a fashion that was introduced after Napoleon's Egyptian expedition of 1798.

A few minutes' walk west to the end of Blvd St-Germain brings you to the **Palais Bourbon**, seat of the Assemblée Nationale (pl. 12; 2), facing Pont de la Concorde (see Ch. 13). Guided tours when not in session, Sat 10.00, 14.00, 15.00, at 33 Quai d'Orsay, ID required, ☎ 01 40 63 77 77.

In 1722–28 a mansion was erected on this site for the Dowager Duchess of Bourbon, of which only the inner courtyard and main entrance (at 128 Rue de l'Université) have survived. The Prince de Condé enlarged the palace between 1764 and 1789, incorporating the Hôtel de Lassay. The Palais became national property at the Révolution and transformed into the meeting-place of the Council of Five Hundred, and was later occupied by the Archives (1799–1808). Since 1815 it has been used by the Chambre des Députés, the French equivalent to the House of Commons, its name being changed to the Assemblée Nationale in 1946.

In 1940–44 the Palais Bourbon was the headquarters of the German military administration of the Paris region. At the time of the Liberation considerable fighting took place in the neighbourhood, causing some damage to the building and the destruction of over 30,000 volumes in the library.

The north façade (1804–07), a neo-Hellenistic piece of imperial bombast designed principally to balance the Madeleine when seen from Pl. de la Concorde, is entirely decorative and consists of a portico of twelve Corinthian columns. The low reliefs on the wings are by Rude and Pradier. Inside, the semi-circular *salle de séances* (1828–32) retains bas-reliefs by Lemot (1798), statues by Pradier, Desprez and others, and a Gobelins tapestry after the School of Athens (Raphael). Other rooms contain historical paintings by Horace Vernet (1789–1863) and by Delacroix (in the Salon du Roi and library). The Galerie des Fêtes (1848) connects the building to the Hôtel de Lassay (1724), the official residence of the President of the Assembly.

Further along Quai d'Orsay stands the Ministère des Affaires Etrangères (Foreign Office), built in 1845. Adjacent, on the Esplanade des Invalides, is Gare des Invalides (1900) adapted in 1945 as the Air France Aérogare (Air Terminus). For the Hôtel des Invalides and Musée de l'Armée, see Ch. 11.

Turning east along Rue de l'Université, you shortly reach Pl. du Palais Bourbon, an elegant ensemble of Louis XVI houses built to the same pattern after 1776.

At 108 Rue de l'Université (entrance at 121 Rue de Lille, parallel to the north) in the former Hôtel Turgot (18C), is the Institut Néerlandais, with a good collection of Dutch and German drawings. Open to the public during exibitions and conferences.

Further east (on the far side of Blvd St-Germain), at 51 Rue de l'Université, is the magnificent **Hôtel de Soyécourt** (1707, by Lassurance), also known as the Hôtel Pozzi di Borgo; No. 24, the Hôtel de Sennecterre, has a notable courtyard façade. Rue de Bellechasse leads south to regain Blvd St-Germain, flanked to the west, at this point, by the extensive buildings of the Ministère de la Défense (by Bouchot; 1867–77), with a clock-tower at the corner of Rue de Solférino.

Nos 1, 3 and 5 Rue St-Dominique, running west from Blvd St-Germain, date from c 1710; Nos 10–12 (since 1804 part of the Ministère de la Défense) occupy the former Couvent des Filles de St-Joseph (1641). Nos 14–16, in the same block of buildings, the Hôtel de Brienne (1714 and 1730), was acquired by Lucien Bonaparte in 1802. No. 28 was the Hôtel Rochefoucauld-d'Estissac (1710), while further west, the Hôtel de Sagan (No. 57), built by Brongniart in 1784 for the Princess of Monaco, is now the Polish Embassy, and was the British Embassy prior to the purchase of the Hôtel de Charost: see Ch. 26.

South of Rue St-Dominique rises the uninspired Gothic-revival church of **Ste-Clotilde**, built in 1846–56, where César Franck was organist from 1858 until his death in 1890. In the little patch of greenery, Square Samuel-Rousseau, is a commemorative monument to Franck (1891) by Lenoir; and in the square, one of the last urinoirs in Paris.

It is easy to reach **RUE DE GRENELLE**, a street of numerous embassies and ministries, by following Rue de Bellechasse south. At No. 41, the Conseil de la Résistance and the Comité Parisien de la Libération organised operations for the rising of 19 August 1944.

To the left of the junction at No.106 Rue de Grenelle, is the Temple de Pentémont of the Reformed Church (1747–56) by Constant d'Ivry, originally the chapel of a Bernardine convent. No. 102, the very fine **Hôtel de Maillebois**, was remodelled by the architect Jacques-Denis Antoine in 1783. No. 87 is the Hôtel de Bauffremont (1721–36), with a curved façade. No. 85, the Hotel d'Avaray was built by Leroux 1718–23, and was tastefully renovated in 1920 when it became the Netherlands Embassy. No. 79, the pale yellow and white Hôtel d'Estrées, the Russian Embassy, was built by Robert de Cotte in 1713.

Retracing your steps towards the west, you pass No. 110, the Hôtel de Courteilles (1778); No. 116, the old Hôtel de Brissac, was rebuilt in 1709 for Marshal de Villars by Boffrand. No. 101, opposite, the former Hôtel Rothelin (or de Charolais), built by Lassurance in 1700; Nos 138 and 140 were built by Jean Courtonne in 1722 and decorated by Lassurance in 1735 for Mlle de Sens. Marshal Foch (1851–1929) died in the former; the latter is occupied by the Institut Géographique National. No. 127, the Hôtel du Châtelet, and one of the finest examples of the Louis-XV style, and was used as the Archbishop's Palace in 1849–1906. The Hôtel de Chanac, at No. 142, opposite (by Delamair; 1750), is now the Swiss Embassy.

Musée Rodin

Turn left along Blvd des Invalides, passing the north east corner of the Hôtel des Invalides (see Ch. 11), and left again into Rue de Varenne. Immediately on the right (No. 77), is the **Hôtel Biron** (Pl. 12; 4), host to the Musée Rodin.

■ The museum is open summer: 09.30–17.45, Park to 18.45; winter 09.30–16.45; closed Mon and 1/1, 25/12 (☎ 01 44 18 61 10). There is a garden café. Métro: Varenne.

This stately mansion and its gardens provide an ideal setting for the important and comprehensive collection of works by Auguste Rodin (1840–1917), which he donated to the State in 1916. Together with many original marbles and bronzes, there are plaster casts, maquettes, drawings and watercolours. There is also his personal collection of art, antiquities and furniture, together with some 8000 old photographs associated with the sculptor. Perhaps the most popular museum in Paris dedicated to a single artist, recent renovations contribute to the charm of the 18C building.

The Hotel Biron, home of the Rodin Museum

The mansion, built in 1728–30 by Aubert and Gabriel, was occupied by the Duc de Biron in 1753, and in 1820 by the aristocratic convent of the Sacré-Coeur who were expelled in 1904. Much of the painted and gilt panelling, which had been removed by the superior of the convent as ostentation, has been recovered and replaced. From 1908 Rodin rented a studio, along with other other artists and writers including the poet Rainer Maria Rilke, then his secretary. He gradually took over more rooms and lived here until his death.

Nearly 500 of Rodin's sculptures are on show in the museum, from early seminal works to his best known masterpieces, grouped chronologically and thematically. The presentation demonstrates the revolutionary nature of his art, in comparison with academic sculpture at the time, and his debt to Michelangelo. He opened new vistas in sculpture in much the same way as the Impressionists did in painting, although he was not as vigorously criticised.

In the **front courtyard** are several of his major commissions. Near the entrance, and seen from the street is the large group, the *Burghers of Calais*; on the right, among the conical yews, is the *Thinker*, while nearby is his *Balzac*. To the left are the *Gates of Hell*, based on Ghiberti's Baptistry Gates in Florence, the iconography inspired by Dante's Inferno. Intended for the Musée des Arts Decoratifs but never installed they were, in fact, cast only in 1926.

The **entrance hall** has portrait busts of *Rodin* by Bourdelle and Desbois and bronzes of *St John the Baptist* and the vigorous *L'Homme qui marche*. A visit begins to the left on the ground floor, past the shop, with rooms that have small and often pretty or ornamental works of the period (1860–80), including the terracotta, *Young Woman with a Flowered Hat*. The oval **Salon** with its original woodwork, contains *The Age of Bronze* (1875–76), his first freestanding figure of precise anatomical proportions which caused controversy at the time as it was erroneously reputed to have been cast from a live figure.

The next **two galleries** overlooking the garden concentrate on sculptures of couples and the human body—*Adam and Eve, Paolo and Francesca*, a version of his best known work, *The Kiss*, and examples of fragments of figures, such as *The Hand of God*; also examples of the technique based on Michelangelo's unfinished works, which Rodin brought to a state of perfection, where a highly polished figure emerges from rough hewn marble or stone.

In the room devoted to **Camille Claudel**, Rodin's pupil and lover, are compositions modelled on her such as *La France* and *l'Aurore*. Her exceptional and sensitive talent as a sculptress is demonstrated in *L'Age Mûr* (1898), *Gossips*, and

The Wave (1897–1902) in onyx and bronze (acquired in 1995). The next two rooms concentrate on women, in the symbolic sense, such as *Eve*, and portraits of women such as Eve Fairfax, the suffragette, Lady Sackville-West, and Mrs Potter-Palmer, some of them souvenirs of amorous adventures. The last room, 9, on the ground floor has rotating exhibitions of his drawings.

The *Gates of Hell* provided Rodin with a source of motifs such as the *Three Shades* on the staircase, and the first rooms of the **upper galleries** contain studies for and variations on the Gates of Hell. There is a room devoted to studies for the *Burghers of Calais*. The upper rooms overlooking the garden have preparatory works for public monuments, including clothed and unclothed versions of Balzac. The group of male busts—*Clemenceau, George Bernard Shaw, Gustav Mahler* and *Puvis de Chavannes*—reflects the sculptor's intellectual and political connections, and in his later years he was inspired by dancers, including Isadora Duncan who at one time occupied studios in this building. Among later works (1890–1905) is the gravity defying *Iris, Messenger of the Gods*, headless and leaping.

Among **paintings collected by Rodin** are three glorious works by Van Gogh: the celebrated *Portrait of Père Tanguy, Les Moissoneurs* and *La Vue du Viaduc à Arles*; there is also a female nude by Renoir, and Monet's *Paysage de Belle-Isle*.

The **gardens**, which can be visited independently, were remodelled in 1993. The formal layout, flanked by mature trees, frames to advantage the elegant south façade of the Hôtel. Scattered in the garden are more Rodin works, including *Whistler's Muse, Cybele, Bastien Lepage, Claude Lorrain* and, in the pool, *Ugolino and his Children*. On the west side is the pleasant cafeteria. The small building by the entrance is the 19C chapel of the former convent, used for temporary exhibitions.

There is an annexe to the museum at Meudon, Rodin's home, see p 292.

No. 72 in Rue de Varenne is the Hôtel de Castries (1700), and No. 69 is the Hôtel de Clermont by Leblond (1711). Just beyond is the **Hôtel de Matignon** (No. 57), built by Courtonne in 1721 and altered in the 19C. The Austro-Hungarian Embassy from 1888 to 1914, since 1935 it has been the residence of the Présidence du Conseil (or Prime Minister). One of the most beautiful hôtels in the faubourg, it has an unusually large garden. The statesman Talleyrand (1754–1838) lived here in 1808–11.

No. 50, the handsome Hôtel de Gallifet, with an Ionic peristyle built by Legrand in 1775–96, is now the Italian Institute; their embassy is at No. 47. (See below for the continuation of the route north from Rue du Bac.)

To the south, Nos 118–120 Rue du Bac, the Hôtel de Clermont-Tonnerre, are two matching mansions of the early 18C with doors designed by Toro. No.128 the Séminaire des Missions Etrangères, founded in 1663, protects relics of martyred missionaries and has a leafy garden open to the public. Nos 136–140 are the Hôtel de la Vallière, with handsome portals, occupied by the Soeurs de Charité. The chapel of the Médaille Miraculeuse (which can be visited) is an important shrine.

To the left is the Grands Magasins du Bon Marché, built on the site of an asylum, the Petites Maisons. To the east is Sq. Boucicaut (Pl. 13; 5), named after the founder of Bon Marché with an imposing monument by Moreau-Vauthier, of 1914. To the west is the Jardin de Babylone, which opened to the public in

1978, in part of the park of the former hôtel de la Vallière.

A short distance to the south west, at 42 Rue de Sèvres, is the Hôpital Laënnec, formerly a women's hospice, founded c 1635, with its original courtyard and chapel. At No. 95 is the Eglise des Lazaristes, with a silver shrine containing the body of Vincent de Paul (1576–1660), canonised in 1737.

Running parallel to Rue de Sèvres, is Rue du Cherche-Midi (eastern section, see Ch. 8). At No. 38 (No. 56 Blvd Raspail) is the Maison des Sciences de l'Homme, built in 1968 on the site of the Prison Militaire du Cherche-Midi, where many French patriots were imprisoned between 1940 and 1944. At No. 85, the Hôtel de Montmorency (1743), is the **Musée Hébert**, open Wed–Mon 12.30–18.00, Sat, Sun and some public holidays, 14.00–18.00; closed Tues, certain public holidays (☎ 01 42 22 23 82). Ernest Hébert (1817–1908), painter of Italian landscapes and society portraits, and cousin of the writer Stendhal, lived in this aristocratic mansion typical of the second half of the 19C.

Musée Maillol

From Rue de Varenne, Rue du Bac leads north, crossing Rue de Grenelle, where to the right (No 57–59) is the **Fontaine des Quatre-Saisons**, built by Bouchardon in 1739, to feed the water supply of the *quartier*. To maximise the limited space in this narrow street, the fountain is designed in a semi-circle. The sculptures represent the City of Paris with the Seine and Marne at her feet, with bas-reliefs of the Seasons. The *hôtel particulier* was built on land which once belonged to the Couvent des Récolets. Alfred de Musset (1810–57) lived here from 1824 to 1840 and in this century, jazz enthusiasts frequented the Cabaret de la Fontaine des Quatre Saisons.

The Fondation Dina Vierny has endowed this building with the Musée Maillol which opened in 1995. This charming and well-presented museum also has a delightful small restaurant in the basement. The buildings still reveal traces of the past including the cellars of the old convent and renovation of the fourth wing of the building is planned. Open 11.00–18.00, closed Tues and public holidays, ☎ 01 42 22 59 58. Métro: Rue du Bac.

Dina Vierny met Aristide Maillol (1861–1944) in 1934, when she was 15 and he 73—and in her he recognised the ideal figure he had been modelling all his life. Their association lasted for ten years, during which Vierny began collecting. She opened a gallery in St-Germain-des-Prés after the war and, a native of Russia, launched avant-garde Russian artists such as Poliakoff. Vierney created the Foundation after donating a number of Maillol's sculptures to the Tuileries Gardens in 1964.

The concept of a museum developed over 15 years and the skilful adaptation of the old buildings is due to Pierre Devinoy. The visit starts on the site of an old Poissonerie. The gallery **008**, with exposed original timbers, is dedicated to Maillol's Monumental works, including *La Rivière*, 1938–43 and versions of those exhibited in the Tuilleries.

A spiral staircase takes you to the upper floor, where the wing is mainly devoted to all aspects of Maillol's work. The first room (**110**) contains the bronze sculpture, *La Méditerranée*, 1902–05, pensive and serene, which early established him among the great Modern sculptors. A painter first, his work in crayon, pastel, chalk and charcoal, and paintings in oils is exhibited in rooms **111–114**, and includes *Portrait of Dina*, 1940, and *Dina with a Scarf*, 1941. Examples of Maillol's diverse talents—ceramics, wood and stone carvings—are on show in room **119**.

In rooms **216–219** on the second floor are earlier works such as the Impressionistic painting, *Seated Woman with Sunshade*, 1895, and tapestry designs. Room **218** is a bright white space with nine bronzes of between 1900 and 1931 including *Pomone*, 1910.

Dina Vierny's private collection comprises modern and contemporary art, including work by Odilon Redon, Renoir, Maurice Denis and Gauguin. There is a gallery of Matisse drawings (room **127**), drawings and watercolours by Dufy (room **129**), as well as carvings and watercolours by Gauguin (room **118**). Vierny was an early supporter of naive artists, here represented by Douanier Rousseau (1844–1910), Louis Vivin (1861–1936) and Camille Bombois (1883–1969) among others in rooms **120,123,128,130–1**. The collection also includes works by each of the Duchamp brothers: Marcel Duchamp (1887–1968), one of the original Dadaists, Raymond Duchamp-Villon (1876–1918), and Jacques Villon (1875–1963).

Russian non-figurative art includes works by Poliakoff, Kandinsky, Charchoune, Boulatov, Yankilevski and Oscar Rabin, and the Constructivist Jean Pougny. Ilya Kabakov, one of the first proponents of Installations, built for the museum *The Communal Kitchen* which is located below the ground floor. There are also sculptures by Gilioli, Couturier and Zitman, and a vast collection of drawings by Degas, Picasso, Bonnard, Ingres, Cézanne, Suzanne Valadon, Foujita, and others. The museum mounts temporary exhibitions and some of the works in the permanent collection are exhibited in rotation.

Half-left across Blvd St-Germain, the government offices occupy two early-18C houses: No. 246, the Hôtel de Roquelaure (1722), by Lassurance and Leroux, has a fine courtyard. Guillaume Apollinaire (1880–1918) lived and died at No. 202. To the right of the junction, Rue St-Guillaume, crosses the boulevard. At No. 27 is the 16C Hôtel de Mesmes, enlarged in 1933, now the Institut National d'études politiques; No. 16, the Hôtel de Créqui, built in 1660–64, and extended in 1772, was for a time the home of poet, statesman and historian Alphonse Lamartine (1790–1866).

Across the Boulevard, the continuation of Rue du Bac leads north to the Seine. It took its name from the ferry operating there before the construction of the Pont Royal. No. 46 Rue du Bac, is the stylish Hôtel de Boulogne, c 1740.

To the east is the former Dominican church of **St-Thomas-d'Aquin**, begun in 1682 by Pierre Bullet in the Jesuit style, and completed, with the construction of the monks' choir in the east, behind the altar, in 1722 and façade, in 1765–69. The light interior with pale stained glass, has recently been cleaned and restored to great effect. *The Transfiguration* on the vaults of the choir was painted by Lemoyne, and the organ of 1771 was restored in the 19C and again in the 20C.

11· Les Invalides

■ Arrondissements: 75007, 75015.
■ Métros: Invalides, Varenne, La Tour-Maubourg, St-François-Xavier.
RER: Invalides.

Restaurants

Chez l'Ami Jean, 27 Rue Malar, ☎ 01 47 05 86 89. Traditional Basque cuisine. £
Du Coté 7e, 29 Rue Surcouf, ☎ 01 47 05 81 65. Traditional with Thirties decor. £
Le Bellecoure, 22 Rue Surcouf, ☎ 01 45 55 68 38. Traditional. £££
D'Chez Eux, 2 Av Lowendal, ☎ 01 47 05 52 55. Bistrot. ££
Chez Françoise, Aérogare des Invalides, ☎ 01 47 05 49 03. Traditional. ££
Paul Minchelli, 54 Blvd Latour Maubourg, ☎ 01 47 05 89 86. Haute cuisine, specialising in fish dishes. Art Deco style. ££
La Source, 49 Blvd. de Latour Maubourg, ☎ 01 47 05 51 34. Traditional. £

The districts to the west of Faubourg St-Germain have wider, more spacious avenues than the faubourg, dominated by the magnificent building of Les Invalides, which contains the burial place of Napoléon I, the Dôme des Invalides, and the church of St-Louis, as well as the Musée de l'Armée. Further west is the skeletal Tour Eiffel and the massive block of the Tour Montparnasse not far to the east.

From the Right Bank, **Pont Alexandre-III** is an appropriately grand approach and, gleaming after a recent total restoration, enhances the sweeping panorama of Les Invalides at the end of its esplanade. This walk combines well with a return via the Palais de Chaillot.

Esplanade des Invalides, 487m by 250m, was laid out in 1704–20 by Robert de Cotte and planted with rows of elms, but it subsequently deteriorated and it was not until 1978 that the whole area was replanted with lawns and scented lime trees. At its north-east corner is the Aérogare.

To the west, Quai d'Orsay extends as far as Pont de l'Alma. At No. 63 on the Quai is the American Church, built in a Gothic style in 1927–31. The public entry to the **Egouts de Paris** (sewers) is opposite 93 Quai d'Orsay, next to the Pont de l'Alma, open summer: 11.00–17.00, winter to 16.00, closed Thurs, Fri and last 3 weeks of January (☎ 01 47 05 10 29). James Joyce lived, from 1935 to 1939, at 7 Rue Edmond-Valentin, a short distance south west off Av. Bosquet.

From Pl. des Invalides, south of the Esplanade, Av. de la Motte-Picquet leads south west past the front of the Ecole Militaire (see Ch. 12); in the angle is a small garden, the Square Santiago de Chili, matched on the east side by the Square d'Ajaccio adding a touch of colour in spring. The Blvd des Invalides skirts this side of the Hôtel des Invalides, whose formal façade contrasts with the domestic architecture opposite. To the left runs the Rue de Grenelle and the Rue de Varenne; at the corner of the latter is the Musée Rodin (see p 116). On the

opposite side of the Invalides is the **Jardin de l'Intendant**, a fine formal garden based on plans by Robert de Cotte but carried out only in 1980. It is organised around a large pool and the border are punctuated by cone-shaped yews; the architect Jules Hardouin-Mansart (1646–1708) is remembered in a 19C statue by Ernest Dubois.

The Hôtel des Invalides

The Hôtel des Invalides (Pl. 12; 4; headquarters of the military governor of Paris) was founded by Louis XIV in 1671 as a home for disabled soldiers, the first enduring institution of its kind; at one time it housed between 4000 and 6000 pensioners or *invalides*. At present about 80 war veterans live here and the hospital is one of the most modern in Paris.

Statue of architect Jules Hardouin-Mansart which stands in Jardin de l'Intendant

The buildings, which form a majestic ensemble, were erected from the designs of Libéral Bruant (died 1697), and J. Hardouin-Mansart continued the work. During the Revolution it was known both as the Temple de l'Humanité and Temple de Mars. It was restored under Napoléon I, who was later buried beneath its Dôme. The buildings encompass four museums: the Musée de l'Armée; Musée de l'Histoire Contemporaine, Musée de l'Ordre de la Libération, the Musée des Plans et Reliefs; also the Eglise St-Louis and the Eglise du Dome, and Napoléon's Tomb; see below.

■ Tickets cover three museums and entry to Napoléon's Tomb (the main entrance to which is in the Pl. Vauban). Musée de l'Armée, daily, summer:10.00–18.00, winter to 17.00, closed 1/1, 1/5, 1/11, 25/12 (☎ 01 44 42 37 72); Musée des Plans et Reliefs, daily, summer 10.00–12.30, 14.00–17.45, closed 01/01, 01/05, 01/11, 25/12, winter to 16.45 (☎ 01 45 51 95 05); Musée de l'Ordre de la Libération, open Mon–Fri 14.00–17.00 (☎ 01 47 05 04 10).

Between the Esplanade and the Invalides are fortifications in the style of Vauban, with a ditch and bossed walls. Facing out are two artillery batteries: the unmounted Batterie Trophée, and the Batterie Triomphale, whose salvoes announcing victory were last heard at the end of the First World War. The Batterie Triomphale was removed by the Germans in 1940. Made for Frederick the Great in 1708, these eight pieces were captured by Napoléon in 1805.

The dignified **north façade**, is 200m long and four storeys high, with a pavilion at each end surmounted by stone trophies and flags. The remaining decoration is concentrated in the attic storey where the dormer windows, here and elsewhere, take the form of different trophies. Flanking the main entrance are copies of the original statues of *Mars* and *Minerva* by Guillaume Coustou (1735). Above the central door, the equestrian bas-reliefs of *Louis XIV accompanied by Justice and Prudence*, by Pierre Cartellier, in 1815 replaced the original design by Coustou, destroyed during the Revolution.

Opposite the entrance to the Cour d'Honneur (102m by 64m) is the door of the church of St-Louis, above which are Seurre's original bronze statue of Napoléon, which formerly topped the Vendôme Column (see p 193), and an astronomical clock (1781).

On the east side of the courtyard is the main entrance to the Musée de l'Armée; see below. At the foot of the staircase to the right of the entrance to the church, is one of the Renault cars (the 'Marne taxis'), which, commandeered by Général Gallieni, carried troops to the Front in September 1914, so saving Paris from the advancing Germans.

Eglise St-Louis (the chapel of Les Invalides or the Soldiers' Church) was built (c 1679–1708) by Bruant and Hardouin-Mansart. The imposing interior, decorated with captured regimental colours, has a gallery built at the same level as the dormitories of the disabled. In 1837 it resounded to the first performance of Berlioz's *Grande Messe des Morts*. The organ (1679–87) is by Alexandre Thierry, with a case possibly designed by Hardouin-Mansart. Concerts still take place here. A sheet of plain glass behind the high altar separates the chapel from the Dôme des Invalides. The chapel contains several memorials to those who fell on the field of battle, and the coffin and pall used in the translation of Napoléon's ashes in 1840. In vaults below (no admission) are the graves of numerous French marshals and generals.

On leaving the chapel, turn left along the Corridor de Metz to reach the entrance of the Dôme. Visitors approaching from the Pl. Vauban, to the south, will find a ticket-office near the main entrance (Pl. 12; 4).

The **Dôme des Invalides**, begun by J. Hardouin-Mansart in 1677 and finished in 1706, was added to the church of St-Louis as a chapel royal. In the niches on either side of the entrance are statues of *Charlemagne* and *St Louis* by Coysevox and Nicolas Coustou. The **ribbed dome**, the most splendid in France, roofed with lead, stands on a balustraded base and attic storey. In each bay are trophies, regilded in 1989 with 12kg of gold, and it is crowned with a lantern and short spire rising to a height of 107m.

The admirably proportioned interior, 56m square, is in the form of a Greek cross, with an ornate Baroque decoration of paintings, sculpture and mosaic paving. The focus of attention, however, is the sumptuous **Tomb of Napoléon**, designed by Visconti, in which the Emperor was placed in April 1861, 40 years after his death at St Helena (see Château de Bois-Préau, see p 314). His remains were brought to Les Invalides in December 1840 (see Arc de Triomphe). His body lay in the Chapel St-Jérome while the sarcophagus of dark red porphyry (from Finland), resting on a pedestal of green Vosges granite, was being prepared.

The tomb, 4m by 2m and 4.5m high, is surrounded by a gallery with ten bas-reliefs after Simart representing the benefits conferred on France by the Emperor. Facing the sarcophagus are 12 figures by Pradier symbolising his greater victories, between which are six trophies of 54 colours taken at Austerlitz. The statue of *Napoléon in his Coronation Robes* is also by Simart. The main altar, has a baldaquin of the mid-19C and paintings by N. Coypel in the vault. Steps either side lead to the Crypt from where a more imposing view of the tomb is obtained than from above. The inscription at the entrance is taken from Napoléon's will, '*Je désire que mes cendres reposent sur les bords de la Seine, au milieu*

de ce peuple français que j'ai tant aimé', translates as: 'I desire that my mortal remains rest on the banks of the Seine, in the midst of the French people whom I have loved so dearly'.

The chapels on the upper level, going in an anti-clockwise direction from the south east, contain the **tombs** (some enshrining only hearts) of *Joseph Bonaparte* (d. 1844), Vauban (d. 1707), tomb of 1847 by Antoine Etex; Ferdinand Foch, Marshal of France (d. 1929), tomb by Landowski; Lyautey, soldier and colonial administrator (d. 1934), tomb by Albert Laprade; La Tour d'Auvergne (d. 1800), the first grenadier of the Republic; and Turenne, soldier (d. 1675), first buried at St-Denis, his remains were saved from destruction, and his tomb is by Le Brun, Tuby and Marsy. The last chapel, St-Jérome, stands empty. Relics of the Roi de Rome (1811–32), Bonaparte's only son, who died prematurely of phthisis and was originally buried in Vienna, were brought here by the Germans in 1940, but since 1969 have lain in the vaults of the crypt (see above).

Les Invalides, Eglise du Dôme, 1675–1706

Musée de l'Armée

The Musée de l'Arme comprises a most extensive and well-displayed collection of arms and armour, weapons, uniforms and military souvenirs. The building also houses the Musée des Plans-Reliefs (see below), a library and a small cinema.

From the **main entrance** (east side of the Cour d'Honneur), you can first visit the Salle Turenne (right), in which colours of French regiments from the First Republic to the present have been re-hung, and fine frescos, variously attributed to J.-B. Martin des Batailles (1659–1735) or pupils of Van der Meulen. There is an interesting maquette of Les Invalides, made before 1757. To the left is the Salle Vauban, containing cavalry uniforms and equipment and more frescos.

From the vestibule, stairs take you to the **second floor**. On the right is the entrance to a series of rooms devoted to the military exploits of the Ancienne Monarchie (1618–1792), set out in chronological order. Most figures are displayed to be seen in the round as are the suits of armour in the west wings. Among the numerous plans, engravings, prints and portraits, are macabre curiosities such as the cannon-ball that killed Turenne and the perforated back plate of his cuirass. Note also the colours of the Irish Clancarty regiment (1642).

Another room contains souvenirs of Général la Fayette (1757–1834), followed by compartments concentrating on the Revolutionary, Directory and Consulate periods, with numerous Napoleonic souvenirs, including one of Bonaparte's grey coats; his tent and furniture, and the stuffed skin of his white horse, Vizir, which outlived the Emperor by eight years. Among portraits of his marshals, that of Ney, by Gérard, is notable. A further series of cabinets devoted to Napoléon at St-Helena, and the period 1830–52, bring you back to the stairs. See also Malmaison and Bois-Préau, Ch. 35.

On the **third floor** are sections devoted to the Second Empire, Crimean War and Franco-Prussian War of 1870, with early photographs, and paintings by Alphonse de Neuville and Edouard Detaille.

On the **attic floor** of the east wing are the important collections of the autonomous **Musée des Plans-Reliefs**, with a collection of some 120 relief models (apart from those dismounted or in reserve), and it is known that another 41 existed in 1697. The majority were built to the scale 1:600 and, together with maquettes, maps and plans, represent the form of fortresses—both inside France and on her frontiers—since the time of Vauban.

The idea of constructing them is attributed to Louvois (1641–91), Louis XIV's minister of war. Secreted until 1776 in the Louvre, they were then moved to Les Invalides, where they have for the most part remained. The models date from the period 1668–1870, although many of them have since been restored.

On the west side of the Cour d'Honneur are the extraordinarily rich **Collections of Arms and Armour**, with weapons of all periods, many of artistic interest and masterpieces of damascening and chasing. To the right, the Salle François I. A small room near the entrance, contains arms dating from before the 9C.

To the left of the entrance to this wing is the Salle Henri IV, concentrating on jousting armour. Note the diminutive 'sample' suits. Straight ahead of the vestibule are galleries containing the important **Collection Pauilhac**. Among the numerous medieval and Renaissance pieces are suits belonging to Henri III, Louis XIII, Henri IV and Louis XIV. The **Collection of Firearms**, showing the evolution of such weapons, is outstanding.

There are also collections of **Oriental** arms and armour from Turkey, Persia, India and China. Among individual helmets of interest is that of the Ottoman sultan Bajazet II (1447–1512). La Galerie de l'Arsenal recaptures the atmosphere of arsenals of the past.

From these galleries there is a view into adjacent courtyards and a number of artillery pieces, while the walls of the Cour d'Angoulême (north) are embellished by the Danube Chain, which the Turks used to hold their vessels in position during the Siege of Vienna in 1683.

On the **second floor** are galleries devoted to the 1914–18 and the 1939–45 War, illustrated by documents, scale models, and films, describing the movements of troops during the principal campaigns. Occupied France, France during the Liberation, and the sad history of deportations are also covered, as are the Normandy Landings.

A room on the **third floor** is devoted to artillery. The collection of scale models, dating back to the end of the 16C, is presented in the Gribeauval Room.

12 · The Ecole Militaire and Tour Eiffel

■ Arrondissements: 75007, 75015.
■ Métros: École Militaire, Cambronne, Bir-Hakeim, Champ-de-Mars, La Motte Picquet-Grenelle. RER: Champs-de-Mars/Tour Eiffel.

This walk continues the exploration of the 7e arrondissement from Les Invalides to the Eiffel Tower, its familiar profile and great height dominating the district and set in one of the great vistas of Paris, stretching from Ecole Militaire across the Champ des Mars gardens and the Seine to the Trocadéro. In the 15e are two recent innovations, the fairground museum and Parc Citroën.

Restaurants and cafés

7e arrondissement

Altitude 95, Eiffel Tower 1st Floor, ☎ 01 45 55 00 21. Brasserie, Zeppelin decor. £

Au Bon Acceuil, 14 Rue de Montessuy, ☎ 01 47 05 46 11. Good value bistrot. £

Le Bourdonnais, 113 Avenue de la Bourdonnais, ☎ 01 47 05 47 96. £££

Le Chevert, 34 Rue Chevert, ☎ 01 47 05 51 09. Traditional cuisine in rustic setting. £

Duquesnoy, 6 Av. Bosquet, ☎ 01 47 05 96 78. Haute cuisine. £££

Le Jules Verne, Eiffel Tower 2nd Floor, ☎ 01 45 55 61 44. Haute cuisine —for high flyers. £££

Le Petit Troquet, 28 Rue de l'Exposition, ☎ 01 47 05 80 39. Seafood and the rest. £

Le Samovar d'Or, 59 Av. de Suffren, ☎ 01 43 06 37 36. Traditional. £

La Terrasse de l'École Militaire, 2 Pl. de l'Ecole Militaire, ☎ 01 45 55 00 02. Art Deco decorations. £

Thoumieux, 79 Rue St.-Dominique, ☎ 01 47 05 49 75. Large bistrot.

15e arrondissement

L'Amanguier at 46 Rue du Théatre (M. Dupleix), ☎ 01 45 77 04 01, and at 46 Blvd. du Montparnasse, ☎ 01 45 48 49 16. Traditional. £

Le Belisaire, 2 rue Marmontel (M. Convention), ☎ 01 48 28 62 24. Traditional. £

Bistrot d'André, 232 Rue St.-Charles (M. Balard), ☎ 01 45 57 89 14. £

Café du Commerce, 51 Rue du Commerce (M.E.-Zola), ☎ 01 45 87 03 27. Bistrot. £

La Cantine des Photographes, 76 Rue de la Processions (M. Volontaires), ☎ 01 40 61 09 91. Traditional. £

Les Celebrités, Hôtel Nikko, 61 Quai de Grenelle, ☎ 01 40 58 20 20. Haute cuisine. View of the Seine.

La Dinée, 85 Rue Leblanc (M. Balard), ☎ 01 45 54 20 49. Traditional bistrot. ££

Morot-Gaudry, 8 Rue de la Cavalerie, ☎ 01 45 67 06 85. Haute cuisine with view of Eiffel Tower.

L'Os à Moëlle, 3 Rue Vasco-de-Gama (M. Balard), ☎ 01 45 57 27 27. Traditional bistrot. £

Chez Quinson, 5 Pl. Etienne Pernet (M. Félix-Faure), ☎ 01 45 32 48 54. Bouillabaisse. ££

Rebuzzi & Co., 131 Rue Saint Charles (M. Bir-Hakeim), ☎ 01 45 75 99 99. Italian deli. £

Le Suffren, 84 Av. de Suffren (M. La Motte Picquet-Grenelle), ☎ 01 45 66 97 86. Brasserie. £

From the semi-circular Pl. Vauban (Pl. 12; 4), south of the Les Invalides, Av. de Villars, running south east, shortly meets the southern section of Blvd des Invalides by the neo-Renaissance façade of the church of St-François-Xavier (1875). The avenue becomes Blvd des Invalides and continues as far as Rue de Sèvres, where it meets Blvd de Montparnasse.

At this latter junction are the buildings of the Institut National des Jeunes Aveugles (Blind), founded in 1793 by Valentin Haüy. South of Rue de Sèvres are the Hôpital des Enfants-Malades (founded 1724) and Hôpital Necker, once a Benedictine nunnery, founded in 1779 by Louis XVI, and rebuilt in 1840. Also radiating from Pl. Vauban is the wide tree-lined Av. de Breteuil.

If heading for UNESCO, École Militaire and the Tour Eiffel, take Av. de Tourville west from Pl. Vauban. Alternatively, to avoid the large avenues, from Pl. des Invalides the more varied and interesting Rue de Grenelle will lead you to the Champ de Mars. Rue de Grenelle meets Rue Cler to the south, a pedestrianised street with a market.

South west of Pl. Vauban between Avenues Ségur, Lowendal, Suffren and next to Pl. de Fontenoy, are the buildings of UNESCO, the headquarters of the UN's Organisation for Education, Science and Culture, open Mon–Fri 09.00–12.30, 14.30–18.00. The main **UNESCO Building**, designed by an international team of the French and American architects Bernard Zehrfuss and Marcel Breuer and the Italian engineer, Pier Luigi Nervi, was begun in 1954 and inaugurated in 1958. The number of member states of UNESCO has increased from the original 37 to 184, and its multi-national character is reflected in all aspects of its design.

This large complex consists, in fact, of three main buildings. The square building to the west has, on an exterior wall, a mosaic by Bazaine next to which is a delightful **Japanese Garden** designed by Noguchi. Recent additions to the garden are the five sculptures, *Signaux Eoliens*, by Vassilakis Takis. The Conference Building has fluted concrete walls and an accordion-pleated concrete roof covered in copper. It contains a vast mural by Picasso and a fresco by Rufino Tamayo. The main building is the Y-shaped Secretariat of seven floors in concrete and glass, and the Ségur façade enlivened by an extraordinary spiral fire escape. Supported by 72 pylons, the huge ground-floor hall is tiled with Norwegian quartzite and decorated with works by Afro (Italy) Apper (Netherlands) and Matta (Chili), and the French photographer Brassaï.

On the vast Piazza, between avenues Lowendal and Suffren, are works by Alexander Calder, Henry Moore, Giacometti, Miró and Llorens Artigas. Other works include a bronze relief by Jean Arp, painting by Victor Vasarely, a tapestry by Le Corbusier and in the Miollis building, an installation by Soto.

To the north is the **Ecole Militaire** (Pl. 12; 3–5), a handsome structure covering part of the former farm and château of Grenelle, built by J.-A. Gabriel, and enlarged in 1856.

18C railings separate the Pl. de Fontenoy from the elegant Cour d'Honneur, profusely embellished with Corinthian columns and pilasters. The figure of Victory on the entablature is in fact modelled on Louis XV, but this seemingly went unnoticed by Revolutionary iconoclasts.

The school was founded in 1751 by Louis XV for the training of noblemen as army officers. It was opened in 1756 and completed in 1773. In 1777 its rigid rules for entry were modified to accept the élite of provincial military academies and thus in 1784 Bonaparte was chosen from the Collège de Brienne. It is now occupied by the École Supérieure de Guerre, or staff college.

On written application to the Commandant, 1 Pl. Joffre, a guided tour of the interior can be arranged. The most impressive room is the Salon des Maréchaux, with its fine *boiseries*. The chapel (1768–73), decorated with nine paintings of the *Life of St Louis*, is open to the public daily. Bonaparte was confirmed in the chapel during his training.

Off Pl. Cambronne to the south west is Rue Frémicourt and its extension, Av. Emile-Zola, leading due west to Pont Mirabeau: see below.

Between the Ecole Militaire and the Seine lies the **Champ-de-Mars**, almost 1km long, laid out in 1765–67 as a parade ground on the market-gardens of the old Plaine de Grenelle.

The ground was the scene of several early aeronautical experiments by J.-P. Blanchard in 1783–84 and others. It was the theatre of the celebration to mark the first anniversary of the storming of the Bastille, the *Fête de la Fédération* (14 July 1790), and of Napoléon's *Champ de Mai* on his return from Elba. Used as a racecourse after the Restoration, the parade ground was transformed and reduced in 1860 and became the site of five universal exhibitions. In 1908 work, lasting 20 years, was begun to create the park that we see now with central lawns, avenues of trees and less formal areas either side. The fountains have recently been renovated, there is a bandstand, marionette theatre, and other amusements. Among the sculptures is the *Monument of the Rights of Man*, near the Rue de Belgrade (south east) commissioned for the bicentenary of the Revolution from Yvan Theimer. Captain Alfred Dreyfus was publicly degraded here in December 1894, the start of *l'affaire Dreyfus* in which he was falsely accused of delivering documents concerned with the national defence to a foreign government.

The Eiffel Tower

The Tour Eiffel (Pl. 11; 7), at the river end of the Champ-de-Mars, a masterpiece of 19C engineering, is still one of the tallest structures in the world (319m high including the television installation). An inseparable part of the Paris landscape, it remains the most emblematic monument of the city.

Built in 1889 for the Universal Exhibition, the Tour Eiffel aroused as much controversy then as the Pompidou Centre or the Louvre Pyramid do today. Originally granted only 20 years of life, its new use in radio-telegraphy in 1909 saved it from demolition. The creation of the engineer Gustave Eiffel (1832–1923), the tapering lattice-work tower is composed of 18,000 pieces of metal weighing over 7000 tonnes (total weight 10,100 tonnes), fastened by 2,500,000 rivets, while its four feet are supported by masonry piers sunk 9–14m into the ground. It is repainted every seven years, and the

17th application began in 1995. The Eiffel Tower brown, exclusive to the monument is, in fact, gradated from a lighter tone at the summit to a darker one at the base to enhance the impression of perspective.

The first and second platforms are reached by lift and stairs, and the third, 276m from the ground, by lift only. On a clear day, particularly about one hour before sunset, the extensive views are remarkable. Ascent by lift 09.30–23.00, July–Aug. 09.00–24.00; ascent on foot, 09.00–18.30, July–Aug 09.00–24.00. An all-time favourite, there can be a long wait for the lift at peak times.

Platform 1 has a reasonably-priced brasserie, **Altitude 95**, bars, shops and a post office as well as Cineiffel, with audio visual presentations and a history of the Tower. On Platform 2 is a display of technical information about the Tower and the old hydraulic lifts, as well

The Eiffel Tower

as an up-market restaurant, **Le Jules Verne**, with an exclusive lift from the south pillar. Platform 3 offers a reconstruction of Gustave Eiffel's office.

Pont d'Iéna spans the Seine to the Palais de Chaillot: see p 266.

Quai Branly, south west of Av. de Suffren, brings you into the 15e arrondissement, a densely populated residential area, with numerous recent parks and gardens, which remains mainly unknown by the visitor. Further on is Pont de Bir-Hakeim, crossed by the métro, and from it Blvd de Grenelle leads south east. On No. 8 a plaque records the round-up of thousands of Parisian Jews in the *vélodrome* (cycle-track) here in July 1942 before their deportation.

Quai de Grenelle continues south west past Sq. Bella Bartok, a little verdant valley created in 1981 in the concrete-jungle flanking the Seine. On the opposite bank is the Maison de la Radio (see p 263). Stretching between Pont de Bir-Hakeim and Pont de Grenelle is an artificial island, the **Allée des Cygnes**, with a pleasant, tree-lined walk. At the western extremity is a scale replica in bronze of Bartholdi's Statue of Liberty, a gift from the Parisian community in the United States in 1885 in return for the original presented by France to New York.

Further still is Pont Mirabeau (1895–97), leading to Auteuil, and to the south east, at 25–35 Rue de la Convention, is the Imprimerie Nationale (founded 1640), moved here in 1925 from the Hôtel de Rohan (visits by written application). East of the print works at 50 Rue de l'Église is the new **Musée des Arts Forains** (fairground), a heaven for children, open Sat, Sun, 14.00–19.00 (☎ 45 58 65 60), métro: Félix-Faure. An informal museum, it has a diverse collection of roundabouts, stalls and other fairground attractions.

On the riverside beyond Pont Mirabeau the site of the former car factory was transformed in 1992 into the **Parc André-Citroën**, open 07.30–18.00, Sat, Sun and public holidays, 09.00–18.00 (métros: Lourmel, Pl. Balard; RER: Blvd Victor). Rigorous, architectonic, it is the creation of Alain Provost and Gilles Clément working in association with three architects, Patrick Berger, Jean-Paul Viguier and François Jodry. There are three principal sections: the White Garden to the east, the Black Garden to the south, and the main park dominated by two huge rectangular greenhouses. The principal perspective descending towards the Seine, is flanked by banks of evergreen magnolias and beech hedges, with box and yew, trimmed into disciplined shapes. Water is a determining element of the park—a large fountain, canals, lily-ponds, water courses and *jets d'eau* account for about a hectare of the total. On the north-east side are a series of parallel rectangular gardens each planted to a different colour scheme. Opposite each is a small high greenhouse.

The plants in the Jardin des Métamorphoses, on the other side, evoke alchemical transmutations. In contrast to the formal gardens, closer to the river there are stretches of wild gardens described as Jardin des Roches and Jardin en mouvement.

At the opposite end of the arrondissement (métros: Convention, Porte de Vanves) close to Blvd Lefebvre and between Rues des Morillons, des Périchaux and Brancion, the **Parc Georges-Brassens**, laid out 1977–85 and one of the most successful recent gardens, takes the name of the poet-singer who lived in the *quartier*. This was the former hamlet of Vaugirard, until the end of the 18C an important vineyard. The vineyards became market gardens in the 19C and abattoirs until 1974. Some vestiges of the old buildings have been integrated into the gardens. Among its attractions are a pond and fountain, an aromatic and medicinal garden, and vines.

Beyond Blvd Victor and Pont du Garigliano, is the Blvd Périphérique (Quai d'Issy; with the Porte de Sévres further east), on the far side of which is the Héliport de Paris, while adjacent to the east are various buildings of the Armée de l'Air and other Service departments, exhibition areas and Palais des Sports.

The Right Bank

13 · Place de la Concorde to Place du Carrousel

■ Arrondissements: 75001/75008.
■ Métros: Concorde, Tuileries, Palais-Royal.

Restaurants and cafés

Les Ambassadeurs, Hôtel de Crillon, 10 Pl. de la Concorde, ☎ 01 44 71 16 16. Haute cuisine. £££
La Dame Tartine, Jardin des Tuileries, ☎ 01 47 03 93 00. Open sandwiches, snacks. £

Place de la Concorde

The Place de la Concorde (Pl. 7; 7) is one of the world's most impressive squares, next to the Seine and midway between the Etoile and the Ile de la Cité. Even the traffic constantly swirling around it does not detract from the great perspectives and the skilful landscaping of this huge open space, devoid of buildings on three sides. Its design dates from the First Empire, but its present appearance dates from 1852, when Jacques-Ignace Hittorff (1792–1867) redesigned the *Place*. In 1995 the 18 green-bronze and gilded *colonnes rostrales* made for the July festivities of 1838, were renovated and reinstalled. Decorated to resemble the prow of a ship, they symbolise, like the city's coat of arms, the importance of the river to the history of Paris.

In 1757, the then empty site to the west of Paris was chosen to receive a bronze statue of Louis XV commissioned by the *échevins* (magistrates, see Hôtel de Ville, Ch 19). The statue, by Bouchardon and Pigalle (model in the Louvre) was unveiled in 1763 and the surrounding square, the creation of Jacques-Ange Gabriel (1698–1782), named Place Louis XV. The celebrations with fireworks to mark the marriage of the Dauphin Louis and Marie-Antoinette in 1770, resulted in 133 crushed to death in a ditch. In 1792 the statue was replaced by a huge figure of Liberty, designed by Lemot and the square was renamed Pl. de la Révolution. In the same year the robbers of the crown jewels (cf. below) were executed here by guillotine. On 21 January, 1793, the same fate befell Louis XVI on the site now occupied by the fountain nearest the river, and between May 1793 and May 1795 the blade claimed 1119 victims. The square received its present name in 1795 at the end of the Terror, was subsequently renamed Place Louis XV at the Restoration (1815) and finally reverted to Concorde under Louis-Philippe (1830).

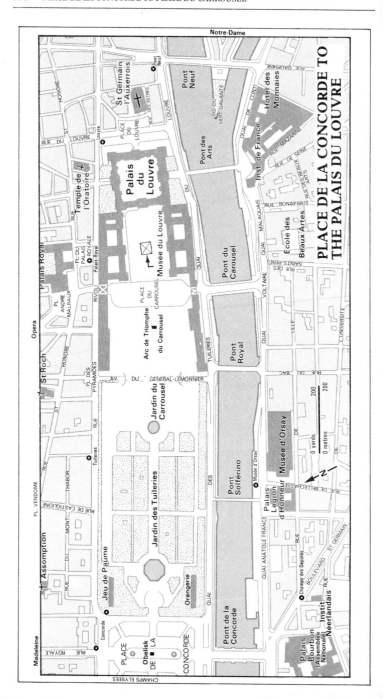

PLACE DE·LA CONCORDE TO
THE PALAIS DU LOUVRE

On the north side of the square are two handsome colonnaded mansions designed by Gabriel in 1763–72, with pediment sculptures by M.-A. Slodtz and G. Coustou the younger, originally intended as official residences. The one on the right, from which the crown jewels were stolen in 1792, is now the Naval Ministry. The left-hand building has long been shared between the Automobile Club and the prestigious Hôtel Crillon.

Between these buildings Rue Royale leads to the church of the Madeleine (see p 238), while the southern perspective opposite is completed by its architectural counterpart, the assertive façade of the Palais-Bourbon (see p 114).

To the west of Pl. de la Concorde, the Av. des Champs-Elysées (see p 251) rises gently towards the Arc de Triomphe, the vista framed by **replicas of the Marly Horses** (originals at the Louvre), two groups by G. Coustou, which were brought from the Château de Marly in 1794. The winged horses are mirrored at the west entrance of the Tuilerie Gardens, opposite, by replicas of Coysevox's equestrian groups (originals in the Louvre) Across the gardens the view extends as far as the Louvre.

Pont de la Concorde, on the south side of the Place, with magnificent views up and down river, was built by Perronet in 1788–90 and widened in 1932. Stone from the Bastille was used in the construction of the upper part (so that Parisians could feel they were treading upon the relics of tyranny!).

> In the centre of the *Place*, the site of Louis XV's statue and then Liberty, rises the **Obelisk of Luxor**, a monolith of pink syenite, almost 23m high and c 230 tonnes in weight. It originally stood before a temple at Thebes in Upper Egypt and commemorates in its hieroglyphics the deeds of Rameses II (13C BC). It was presented to Louis-Philippe in 1831 by Mohammed Ali (the donor of Cleopatra's Needle in London). The pedestal, of Breton granite, bears representations of the apparatus used in its erection in 1836 (see also Musée de Marine, p 267). The two fountains, by Hittorf, copies of those in the piazza of St. Peter's at Rome, are embellished with figures symbolising inland and marine navigation.

The eight stone pavilions round the Square, built by Gabriel in the 18C, which originally gave access over the ditches filled in in the 19C, support statues (restored in 1989) personifying the eight provincial capitals, by Caillonette, Cortot and Pradier. Strasbourg (as capital of Alsace, lost to France in 1871) was hung with crêpe and wreaths until 1918.

The gateway opening from the Pl. de la Concorde has pillars crowned by replicas of equestrian statues of Fame and Mercury, by Coysevox (brought from Marly in 1719). Inside the gates, north and south of the western end of the Jardin des Tuileries are two public galleries, the Jeu de Paume and the Orangerie.

The Musée du Jeu-de-Paume and the Orangerie

The **Musée du Jeu-de-Paume** is so-named because it was accommodated in a real tennis-court built in 1851. The building, which used to contain the Impressionist collections transferred to the Musée d'Orsay in 1986, has been revamped by Antoine Stinco to hold temporary exhibitions of works from 1960 to the present day. Open Tues 12.00–21.30, Wed–Fri 12.00–19.00, Sat, Sun 10.00–19.00, closed Mon (☎ 01 47 03 12 50). There is a small café.

In the **Orangerie**, open 09.45–17.00, closed Tues, 01/01, 01/05, 25/12 (☎ 01 42 97 48 16) to the south across the Tuileries gardens, is Monet's sensational series of mural paintings, **Les Nymphéas** (see also Musée Marmottan, p 268), installed here in 1927. Since 1984 it has been the permanent home of the Jean Walter and Paul Guillaume collection of some 144 Impressionist and early 20C works, including vibrant works by Cézanne, Renoir, Douanier Rousseau and Picasso.

The exhibits start with examples of the impasto Expressionist paintings of Chaïm Soutine (1893–1943), the Lithuanian member of the School of Paris, such as *Le Petit Pâtissier* (c1922) and *La Table* (c 1925). Among the 14 works by Cézanne in the collection are *Apples and Biscuits* (c 1880), the *Portraits of Paul Cézanne*, the artist's son, and *Madame Cézanne* (1885); also *In the Park of the Château Noir* (c 1900) and *The Red Rock*, c 1895, constructed from small planes of colour.

There are two rooms with paintings by Renoir, including several studies of young girls, such as a version of *Young Girls at the Piano* (1892) and *Yvonne and Christine Lerolle at the Piano* (c 1897–98), studies of his children, *Gabrielle and Jean* (c 1895), *Claude Playing* (c 1809), and *Claude Dressed as a Clown* (1909). There are also several lush nudes. Alongside the Renoirs are Monet's *Argenteuil* (1875), contrasts of red boats against bright green waterweed; and Sisley's *The Montbuisson Road at Louveciennes* (1875). The 28 examples of works by André Derain are mainly dark and monumental nudes from his post-Fauves period including *The Artist's Niece* (1931) and *Portrait of Mme Guillaume* (c 1929). In the museum are portrait tributes to the art dealer collector, Paul Guillaume, by Modigliani and van Dongen as well as Derain.

Several of the paintings by Matisse are typical decorative interiors with odalisques painted during the 1920s in Nice. By Henri Rousseau (le Douanier) are *The Wedding* (c 1908), and *Père Junier's Cart* (1910) which the Surrealists raved about. Picasso's blue tendency is represented by *The Embrace* (1903), and his rose period by *Les Adolescents* (1906), while his later monumental nudes are exemplified in *Bathers* of 1921 and 1923. There are also works by Utrillo and by Marie Laurencin.

Stairs descend from the central gallery to the two oval rooms designed with the approval of Monet for the famous waterlily murals, *Les Nymphéas* of c 1914. Drenched in colour and reflected light, the panels submerge the onlooker in vibrating lilacs and blues, intense greens and acid yellows.

Jardin des Tuileries

The Jardin des Tuileries, the best known and oldest of all the gardens of Paris, covering over 28 hectares, still retains the basic formal layout that Le Nôtre designed in 1664. Re-landscaping work was undertaken recently with the aim of returning the garden to something like its original character and glory. With about 100 statues beneath some 2800 trees (mainly chestnuts and limes, but also maples, planes and elms) the garden extends eastwards to the Pl. du Carrousel, uninterrupted now that Av. du Gén.-Lemonnier has gone underground.

At the beginning there were vineyards and fields, and then in the 12C the site, beyond the city walls, was occupied by tile-kilns (*tuileries*). The area was requisitioned by François I in the 16C for his mother, but it was not until Catherine de Médicis assumed power in 1564 that the palais and the gardens took shape. Enclosed in walls, this garden, in the Italian style, was the work of a team probably including Philibert Delorme (1500–70), architect of the Tuileries Palace (see below), Pierre Le Nôtre (grandfather of André), Bernard Palissy and others. Later, during the reign of Louis XIV, important alterations were undertaken by André Le Nôtre (1613–1700), notably the enlargement of the main alley and the creation of the two large pools and terraces.

From the 17C dances, concerts and firework displays took place in the garden, it was a fashionable promenade until the Palais-Royal took over this privilege, and from the Revolution it was even more popular when cafés and restaurants opened. The major changes in the 19C were the construction of the Orangerie (1853), Jeu de Paume (1861), and the creation of the Carrousel Garden (1871).

Terraces extend along both sides of the gardens. On the south, overlooking the Quai des Tuileries is the Terrasse du Bord-de-l'Eau. A new footbridge, Pont de Solférino, crosses to the Quai Anatole-France. On the north side, the Terrasse des Feuillants, skirting the Rue de Rivoli, is named after a Benedictine monastery. To the east, nearly opposite the Rue de Castiglione, was the site of the Manège, the riding-school of the palace, where the National Assembly met from 1789 to 1793, and where Louis XVI was condemned to death.

The Tuileries Garden has three distinct parts: the octagon to the west, the wooded central area and, to the east, the formal gardens and Round Pond of the Grand Carré.

The **octagon** is an open, largely paved, area determined by the large Octagonal Pond. Around it are replicas of 17C–18C statuary, some of the oldest in the garden (originals in the Louvre), by N. and G. Coustou and Van Cleve. On the steps to the south is *Hommage à Cézanne* by Maillol and to the north, a copy of Coysevox's bust of Le Nôtre (original in St-Roch). The wide central avenue leading to the Round Pond is flanked by chestnut and limes in echelon, which shade cafés and various amusements for children.

The **Grand Carré**, from the Round Pond to Av. du Gén.-Lemonnier, was the original Palace garden with the *jardins réservés* or private gardens of Louis-Philippe, and some of its original railings still survive. Turned into informal English-style gardens by Napoléon III, the formal gardens were recreated in 1989 at the Bicentenary of the Revolution. The flower beds are densely populated by statues notably by G. and N. Coustou, Coysevox and Le Pautre.

A **terrace** designed by Ming Pei in 1993, marked by two huge late 17C vases by Robert and Legros, has been built over Av. du Gén.-Lemonnier linking the Tuileries and the Carrousel Gardens and enhancing the perspectives of the historic site.

The **Carrousel Garden**, on Le Nôtre's old garden, is the stage for Dina Vierny's donation of 18 bronzes by Aristide Maillol, which have been in the gardens since 1964–65. The yew hedges have been shaped to provide an all-year-round structure to this area.

The restored and regilded **Arc de Triomphe du Carrousel**, a copy on a reduced scale of the Arch of Septimus Severus at Rome (14.60m high instead of 23m), is enhanced by pink and white Corinthian columns. It was begun in 1806 from designs by Fontaine and Percier to commemorate the victories of Napoléon I in 1805, depicted in the marble bas-reliefs on the four sides. It is surmounted by figures of Soldiers of the Empire and a bronze chariot-group by Bosio (1828) representing the Restoration of the Bourbons. The original group incorporated the antique horses, looted by Napoléon from St Mark's, Venice, in 1797 but returned in 1815.

The Arc de Triomphe du Carrousel

The main west wing of the former Palais des Tuileries no longer exists, except for the **Pavillons de Flore** and **de Marsan** (to the south and north respectively), both of which have been restored or rebuilt. They now form the western extremities of the wings of the Palais du Louvre; see below. The Pavillon de Marsan accommodates the Musée de la Mode (see p 263).

The Palais des Tuileries was begun in 1564 by Philibert Delorme for Catherine de Médicis. Delorme was succeeded by Jean Bullant (c 1520–78) and then, in 1595, by Jacques du Cerceau, responsible for the Pavillon de Flore. The Pavillon de Marsan was built in 1660–65 by Louis le Vau and his son-in-law François d'Orbay (1631–97). Both pavilions were partly rebuilt and restored in 1875–78 by Lefuel.

Louis XVI was confined here after being brought from Versailles until 10 August 1792. It was the headquarters of the Convention. The Tuileries became subsequently the main residence of Napoléon I, Louis XVIII (who died here), Charles X, Louis-Philippe and Napoléon III. In May 1871 the Communards set fire to the building which, like the Hôtel de Ville, was completely gutted. Its charred remains stood until 1884, when the main wing was razed, and the site was converted into a garden in 1889.

The Arc du Carrousel was the main entrance to the courtyard of the Tuileries from the Cour du Carrousel. The Pl. du Carrousel, which derives its name from an equestrian fête given here in 1662 by Louis XIV, lies to the east of the arch. Until the middle of the 19C this was a small square surrounded by a labyrinth of narrow alleys, almost encircled by the royal palaces (see history of the Louvre, p 137).

The archways to the north lead to the Rue de Rivoli and beyond to the south end of the Av. de l'Opéra; those on the south give onto the Quai des Tuileries opposite the Pont du Carrousel.

To the east lies the Cour Napoléon, and the main entrance to the Musée du Louvre, below its glass pyramid; (see Chs 14 and 15). To the west is a distant view towards the Arc de Triomphe and the towers of La Défense beyond.

Underground is the shopping mall, the **Carrousel du Louvre** (see p 140), which opened in 1993, with specialist boutiques, restaurants, car park and alternative entrance to the Louvre.

14 · Palais du Louvre

■ Arrondissements: 75001.
■ Métros: Palais-Royal-Musée du Louvre, Louvre-Rivoli, Tuileries, Pont-Neuf.

The following chapter describes the history and architecture of the Louvre Palace. The Palais du Louvre (Pl. 13; 2) occupies an extensive site between the Rue de Rivoli and the Seine. This was one of the most magnificent of the world's palaces, and the Grand Louvre project, initiated by President Mitterand in 1981, has revitalised and re-enhanced the most majestic public building in Paris.

The Musée du Louvre is described in Ch. 15, and the Musée des Arts Décoratifs in Ch. 16.

Despite its apparent homogeneity, the Louvre as we see it now is the result of many phases of building, modifications and restoration. It can be divided into two main parts: the Old Louvre, comprising the buildings surrounding the Cour Carrée to the east; and the long gallery along the bank of the Seine; and the New Louvre, the 19C buildings north and south of the Cour Napoléon, together with their extensions to the west which were originally part of the Tuileries Palace.

The derivation of the name is unclear, but it was already in use when it first appears in history as one of Philippe Auguste's fortresses (1190–1202), which stood at the south-west corner of the Cour Carrée. A fascinating outcome of the Louvre project is the incorporation of the remains of the old fortress into the museum (see Ch. 15). Charles V (1364–80) made the castle one of the official royal residences, endowed it with his famous library and carried out improvements, including new buildings and a handsome staircase.

Subsequent monarchs preferred other palaces until François I (1515–47) planned the total demolition and reconstruction of all the west and south sides of the fortress. The west side of the Cour Carrée, to the south of the Pavillon Sully, part of the early 16C palace, is the oldest visible elevation. The work was begun by Pierre Lescot (c 1500–78) shortly before the king's death, and was continued under Henri II. Jean Goujon (active 1540–62) was responsible for the sculptural decorations. Their elegant classical style set the tone for all later additions.

Under Charles IX, Henri II's son, the Petite Galerie was begun and a long gallery planned, to connect the Louvre with his mother Catherine de Médicis' new palace outside the Paris wall, the Tuileries. At the time of Henri IV, Luis Métezeau and Jacques II Androuet du Cerceau built the grande galerie from 1594–1606, the first part of the royal design (*Grand Dessein*) to enlarge the Louvre and the Tuileries. The Pavillon de l'Horloge (later called Pavillon de Sully) and the north half of the west façade were the work of Lemercier, 1639–42, but the pavillon was the only part decorated, with large caryatids from the workshop of Jacques Sarazin (17C).

From 1654, during the minority of Louis XIV, work proceeded mainly in the court apartment of the queen mother, decorated by Romanelli and Angier, under the supervision of Lemercier. In 1661 the destruction of the second floor of the Petite Galerie and the royal decision to renew the Grand Dessein of Henri VI resulted in the Apollo gallery, the main floor of the Petite Galerie, and new buildings on the west. The quadrangle was extended and from then on could be described as the Cour Carrée. Several architects, including Bernini and Le Vau, submitted projects for the main façade to the east. However, the great Colonnade of 52 Corinthian columns and pilasters that now forms the exterior east façade (facing St-Germain l'Auxerrois; see p 202) was the work of Claude Perrault, and Le Vau. (The decorations of the Cour Carrée were not completed until the 19C.) But Louis XIV, preoccupied with his new palace at Versailles, soon lost interest in these buildings, which were left in a state of disrepair and occupied by the academies. It was not until 1754 that Louis XV commissioned Gabriel to renovate and restore the palace.

Under Napoléon I part of the North Gallery along Rue de Rivoli was begun and in 1810 the wedding feast of Napoléon and Marie-Louise of Austria was celebrated in the Salon Carré. The building was attacked during the revolutions of 1830 and 1848 and the building of the New Louvre was undertaken at the time of Napoléon III by Visconti in 1852. The Galerie du Bord de l'Eau was largely rebuilt in 1861–68. After Visconti's death the work was continued by Lefuel, who made several radical modifications to its decoration, and completed in 1871. In 1871 it was set on fire by the Communards, though serious damage was limited to the library (see Palais des Tuileries, p 136). The Pavillon de Marsan, part of the Tuileries Palace, was rebuilt by Lefuel.

The Louvre's history is well illustrated and explained in several rooms devoted to the subject, which lie east of the Hall Napoléon (see p 142).

In 1793 the Musée de la République was opened in the Louvre, which, with a change of name, has remained the national art gallery and museum ever since.

By 1981 it was decided that the museum lacked sufficient space for both visitors and workshops, so the north wing, occupied by the Ministry of Finance since 1871, was handed back in 1989. The ambitious Grand Projet du Louvre has been underway since 1983 when President Mitterand approved the plan proposed by Ieoh Ming Pei (a Chinese-born American architect) to construct a glazed pyramid, as the new entrance to the museum. An elegant and innovative if controversial structure, it symbolises the metamorphosis of the Musée du Louvre.

The alterations to the buildings included the excavation of the Cour Carrée to expose the foundations of the medieval fortress and the palace of Charles V, now called the Medieval Louvre. The north side, known as the Richelieu Wing was, until 1989, occupied by the Ministère des Finances which has been transferred to a new building at Bercy. This wing has been extensively rebuilt and adapted to accommodate the enlarged Musée du Louvre.

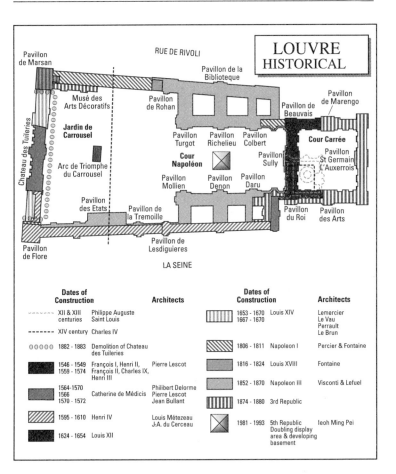

The Pyramid

The Pyramid, 30m square and 20m high, has transparent walls supported by a trussed steel frame. Designed to overcome problems of light and space, aggravated by the proximity of the Seine which makes deep excavations impossible, the glass reflects and refracts light as well as permitting uninterrupted views of the mellow façades of the palace. It takes up less space than conventional building shapes and, now that the lengthy restoration of the fabric and façades of the Palais du Louvre is reaching its finale, shines like a crystal in a stone showcase.

Centrally placed in the Cour Napoléon between the Pavillon Richelieu and the Pavillon Denon, it is flanked by three subsidiary pyramids and seven fountains with triangular basins of Brittany granite. Between it and the Carrousel Arch is an equestrian statue of Louis XIV, a lead copy of 1988 after Bernini's original at Versailles. The statue, but not the Pyramid, is on the same axis as the Tuileries and the Champs-Elysées and the Arc de Triomphe.

The Pyramid (west side) is the main entrance to the Museum with steps and an escalator descending into a spacious well or vestibule, Hall Napoléon (free entry; see p 142) clad in pale stone and flooded with light from the glazed elevations of the Pyramid. From here passages lead to the basements, to the Cour Carrée, and to the South and North Wings. On the central column, is a plaque commemorating the fact that on 18 November 1993, President Mitterand dedicated the whole Palace du Louvre to the museum. In this area are the Information Desk, the Auditorium Group Reception Desk, the Museum Bookshop, restaurants and cafés.

The **Carrousel du Louvre**, is the smart and trendy underground shopping precinct reached from the métro: Palais Royal-Musée du Louvre, or from escalators descending from 99 Rue de Rivoli. Another glass pyramid, this time inverted, provides daylight for this area. It includes a large food hall with a wide variety of cafés. From here passages lead directly to extensive underground car and coach parks. A section of the fortifications planned by Charles V and rebuilt at the beginning of the 16C, which came to light during excavations here, has been preserved.

Below the Pl. du Carrousel and Cour Napoléon is a complex providing space for the reserves of the Louvre, studios for the restoration of works of art, service areas and other facilities.

Three bridges cross the Seine from the Louvre to the Quai Voltaire. To the west is the Pont Royal, a five-arched bridge by Père F. Romain (1685–89); the last pillar on either bank has a hydrographic scale indicating the low-water mark (zero; only 24m above sea-level), besides various flood-marks. The Pont du Carrousel (1834; rebuilt in 1939) retains four seated figures by Petitot and Pradier from the original structure.

The pedestrian Pont des Arts, built of cast iron by Cessart and Dillon in 1801–03, derived its name from the Palais des Arts as the Louvre was then called. It was dismantled for several years then rebuilt in a similar style to the original in 1983–84.

15 · The Musée du Louvre

■ Arrondissement: 75001.
■ Métro: Palais-Royal-Musée du Louvre.

The background to the Louvre Museum and practical information for visiting is given below, while the exterior of the Palais du Louvre, and its architectural history, is described in Ch. 14.

The Musée du Louvre, extended and rejuvenated, is an exciting but rather daunting experience. The Grand Projet du Louvre aims not only to provide better facilities for receiving 5 million visitors a year, but also to create more exhibition space to improve the presentation of works as well as grouping the collections into more coherent themes or schools and logical chronological order. Those familiar with the old Louvre will notice many improvements, especially to the lighting, both artificial and natural. The project is due to be completed by the end of 1998.

Restaurants and cafés at the Louvre

Le Café Marly, entrance on the north side of Cour Napoléon, ☎ 01 49 26 06 60, is a fashionable watering hole which overlooks Cour Marly on the inside the museum. £

In the **Carrousel du Louvre** is a large food hall with a wide variety of cafés.

There are restaurants and cafés under the Pyramid which can be reached without buying a ticket for the museum: **Le Grand Louvre Restaurant** (☎ 01 40 20 53 20), the **Café du Louvre**, the **Café Napoléon**, and a self-service cafeteria.

Café Richelieu is on the first floor of Richelieu pavillon and **Café Mollien** on the first floor of Denon.

There are several ways of tackling a visit and it is probably advisable to start with a preconceived plan tailored to individual preferences or time available. All the old favourites are on view, albeit frequently rearranged—80 per cent of the objects have been or will be moved from their previous positions. Many pieces not previously on view have come out of storage, and there has been a considerable programme of restoration.

On 18 November, 1993, the Grand Louvre Project inaugurated 21,500m² of new exhibition space in the Richelieu Wing, and modernisation has been carried out in the Denon and Sully Wings. To give some indication of the staggering size and scope of the project, when finished, the museum will have doubled its exhibition surfaces, from 30,000 to 60,000m², and increased the number of works exposed by 25 per cent, from 22,000 to 30,000.

The nucleus of the royal art collection was formed by François I at whose request Leonardo da Vinci spent the last few years of his life in France (d. 1519, Amboise). Henri II and Catherine de Médicis carried on the tradition and Henri IV (1589–1610) created a room for antiquities in the Palace; Louis XIV added to the Cabinet des tableaux du roi and the Cabinet des desseins which became the basis of the present collection; Louis XVI acquired some important paintings of the Spanish and Dutch Schools and planned the opening of a museum in the Louvre. During the 18C the Académie de Peinture et de Sculpture (founded 1648) had a permanent exhibition and also held biennial exhibitions of the works of its members here which, during the years 1759–81, were the subject of Diderot's Salons.

In 1793 the Musée de la République was opened to the public, and during the next few years a large number of the most famous paintings of Europe—spoils of conquest by the victorious Republican and Napoleonic armies—were exhibited here; after 1815 the French government was obliged to restore some works of art to their former owners. Under Louis XVIII, the Vénus de Milo and over a hundred pictures were acquired.

The **main entrance** of the Musée du Louvre is situated on the west side of the glass Pyramid sited in the centre of the Cour Napoléon. The Pyramid can be reached at street level from the west, from the east via the Cour Carrée and from the north via the Passage Richelieu. An alternative route of entry is from the

underground shopping precinct, the Carrousel du Louvre (entered from the underground parking, below the Jardins du Carrousel, access Rue du Général Lemonnier); from 99 Rue de Rivoli; or from the métro Palais Royal-Musée du Louvre). In Passage Richelieu (between the Cour Marly and Cour Puget) there is an entrance for ticket-holders and for the disabled.

Cour Napoléon is flanked by three blocks of buildings which are named on the orientation plaques inside the museum: **Sully** (the four sides of the Cour Carrée) to the east; **Denon** (to the south); and **Richelieu** (to the north); see plan.

Pavillon Richelieu, Palais du Louvre

■ The galleries of the Musée du Louvre are open Wed–Mon 09.00–18.00; until 21.45 on Mon (short tour) and Wed (the whole museum) and closed on Tues and certain public holidays (recorded message in English, ☎ 01 40 20 51 51; information desk, ☎ 01 40 20 53 17; Internet: http://www.louvre.fr/). Reduced entrance fee after 15.00 and Sundays; free to persons under 18, and to everyone on the first Sunday of each month. At peak times there can be a long wait to enter the Pyramid, also to buy tickets in the Hall Napoléon. This can be avoided by using a Carte Musées et Monuments, buying your ticket in advance at FNAC department stores (☎ 01 49 87 54 54), or through Minitel 3615 Louvre. Scheduled to open in the second half of 1998 is a second entrance, Porte des Lions, on the Seine side of Denon. All groups have to book in advance, ☎ 01 40 20 57 60, fax 01 40 20 58 24.

Once inside the Pyramid, a spiral stair, an escalator and a lift (for the handicapped) descend from the Pyramid entrance to the spacious **Hall Napoléon**. It is a help to remember that the Hall Napoléon, the main reception area, is below ground when orientating yourself. From here escalators (and lifts) ascend to the entresol, which provides access to the three main wings, Richelieu, Sully and Denon.

In the Hall Napoléon is an information desk giving details of times of lectures, guided tours (in English), etc. Free orientation leaflets (handbooks) in English and six other languages are available at the information desk. (All the English information is signalled in red.) Behind the desk are two large display boards with 14 video screens giving information on the permanent collections and daily activities. The collections are colour coded according to category, e.g. purple for Objets d'Art, green for Egyptian Antiquities.

■ Tickets for the permanent and temporary exhibitions may be purchased at three ticket desks (not always all open). Audio-guides (in English) with a commentary on 180 works can be hired at the entresol level of the three museum wings. There are also cloakrooms, a post office, exchange facilities and an auditorium. The museum mounts about 10 temporary exhibitions a year, and holds lectures, films and concerts in the Auditorium. Virtually the whole museum is accessible by wheel chair (which can be hired free), and an area for blind and partially sighted visitors exists in the foreign Sculpture section of the Denon Wing.

■ Many galleries have broadsheets in several languages, with information on what is exibited there. For those who have limited time but want a whistle-stop tour of the best known works, the Louvre publishes in English a small *First Visit* guide; in addition, a pamphlet *Les nocturnes du lundi*, is in French only and is designed for a visit of the highlights of the collections on Monday evenings, when the museum stays open until 21.45.

■ Hand cameras are admitted without charge. The use of flash and tripods is prohibited.

■ On the south-west corner of the reception area is the museum bookshop selling catalogues, books, videos and CD ROM. These include information on the Louvre and art history in general. Adjacent is a section selling postcards and slides of objects in the Musées Nationaux and nearby is the Chalcographie du Musée selling an extensive range of prints, many of them from the original plates. On the entresol level you can purchase *moulages* or casts—in bronze, resin or plaster—together with replicas of jewellery (of very fine quality and fairly pricey), and copies of other objects from the national collections.

Visits. The seven departments of the Louvre are distributed throughout the three wings. Each level is subdivided into ten sections and each section consists of several galleries. In outline, the collections are arranged as follows:

Paintings: French School, 14C–17C, the second floor of RICHELIEU and 17C–19C, SULLY second floor (Richelieu escalator); Large paintings, 19C, DENON first floor. Northern Schools-Dutch/Netherlandish, Flemish, German, RICHELIEU second floor. Italian and Spanish Schools, DENON first floor (partly open and due for completion in 1998) and English School, temporarily in DENON first floor (being reorganised, and due for completion in 1999).

Graphic Arts (Prints and Drawings) are or will be grouped in accordance with paintings from the corresponding countries, and in part displayed by rotation, i.e.: Northern Schools, RICHELIEU second floor; French School, SULLY second floor; Italian School, DENON first floor; the Consultation and Documentation Rooms will be located at the west of Denon (by written application only).

Greek, Etruscan and Roman Antiquities. This department is laid out in chronological order on the entresol and ground floor of DENON and SULLY ground floor and first floor. Roman and other copies of Greek sculpture are in the reno-vated Salle du Manège, DENON ground floor. Smaller objects are in SULLY first floor: glass, west part, Salle de Boscoréale; ceramics, in the south part, the Campana Gallery; and bronzes in the west part, the Salle des Bronzes.

Egyptian Antiquities has been reorganised and is in the east and south parts of Sully, ground floor and first floor.

Oriental Antiquities: Richelieu, Assyrian and Mesopotamian sections on the ground floor and around Cour Khorsabad. Near Eastern section (Iran, Levant, pre-Islamic Arabia, and Cyprus) in the north and west of Sully ground floor. Islamic Art (some 1000 works in 13 rooms), at the east end of Richelieu entresol.

Objets d'Art: in the northern half of Richelieu first floor (including the Apartments of Napoléon III), and Sully first floor. The Crown Jewels, Apollo Gallery, Denon first floor.

Sculptures: French sculptures from the Middle Ages to the 19C, Richelieu entresol and ground floor, including the Cours Marly and Puget. Italian (11C–15C) and Northern (12C–16C) sculptures, north-west corner of Denon entresol; Italian (16C–19C) and Northern (17C–19C) sculptures, Denon ground floor.

As well as the seven departments listed above, the museum presents a section devoted to the History of the Louvre, including the Medieval Louvre, since the moats constructed by Philippe Auguste in 1190 were excavated during work on the Grand Louvre Project. This area, in the entresol of Sully, adds an exciting new dimension to understanding the Louvre Palace's history with the aid of paintings, sculptures and models.

Medieval Louvre

From the Hall Napoléon below the Pyramid, take the escalator opposite the information desk up to the entresol of Sully and follow the passage leading east to a central point with massive reliefs of 1559–65, attributed to Jean Goujon, taken from the facade of the Louvre. Rooms either side, beginning in the right-hand room, are devoted to the History of the Louvre. Maquettes explaining the growth of the fortress and palace are supplemented by drawings, fragments of masonry, engravings and paintings as well as a reproduction of the Très Riches Heures of the Duc de Berry (1413–16) showing the castle at the time of Charles V. The continuation of the passage leads to the Medieval Louvre.

Passing through a massive rusticated wall by Le Vau (17C) (re-sited), you reach the sombre vaulted galleries below the west part of the Pavillon Sully. Here the site of the Tour de la Fauconnerie, built by Philippe Auguste, is traced on the floor in black. In 1367, Charles V transferred his library to three floors of the tower, and its name changed to the Tour de la Librairie. Various displays explain the excavations of 1983–84, when 16,000m³ of earth was moved, and include archaeological finds from the debris.

The next section brings you to the moat surrounding the massive foundations of the two surviving walls of the medieval fortress, forming its north and east sides excavated below the south-west corner of the Cour Carrée. This outer moat was filled in by Lemercier in 1624 and by Le Vau in 1660. The Tour du Milieu (12C) like the Tour de la Taillerie beyond, shows signs of considerable battering. Between this and the next tower is the base of the drawbridge support and a well of 1660. The basements of the twin towers formed the eastern entrance of the Château du Louvre, and the support for its drawbridge.

The circular donjon (keep) of the earlier fort, established at the turn of the 13C by Philippe Auguste to form a quadrilateral 70m x 77m, was razed and in 1528 the surrounding moat was filled in. On the left you pass a well, probably 14C. Skirting the foundations of this keep (15m in diameter and 7m high, formerly 30m high), are some of the additions made at the time of Charles V. The area was excavated and the walls strengthened in 1984–87, and the moats given ceilings to sustain this south-west corner of the Cour Carrée.

Shuttered concrete passages lead to a vaulted basement room below the present Salle des Cariatides, once the Salle des Gardes, called the Salle St-Louis. Archaeological finds extracted from this site and from the Cour Napoléon reveal life in the old castle. Some 900 objects or fragments were discovered in the well of the keep and 169 of them have been painstakingly reassembled to reveal items of Royal ornamental apparel.

At the far end of the moat is the entrance to the Crypte du Sphinx, and to Egyptian Antiquities.

Paintings

French School

The rooms (including 18 new ones with about 200 additional works) devoted to the French School of painting, displayed in historical order, are arranged as follows: 14C–17C, RICHELIEU second floor, 17C–19C SULLY second floor. The large scale 19C French paintings are in DENON first floor. To reach the start of the French School paintings, take the Richelieu escalator (or lift) up to the second floor.

The first three rooms, opposite the escalator, display Northern European and French Schools of the end of the 14C and beginning of the 15C, when Franco-Flemish artists, working at Paris, Dijon and Bourges, developed the International Gothic style.

Rooms 1–3. Anon. (c 1350), *Portrait of Jean, Le Bon* (1319–64) is a rare 14C easel painting and the only existing French portrait of this period; grisaille on silk of the *Liturgical Cloth of Narbonne* (c 1375), probably for use during Lent, with Charles V depicted in the border; the *Calvaire* by **Beaumetz**, the *Large Round Pietà*, attributed to **Malouel**, and **Henri Bellechose** *Retable of St-Denis* (1415–16) were commissioned by Philippe le Hardi for Champmol, Burgundy. French, Flemish and Italian influences combine in **Jacquemart de Hesdin**, *Carrying of the Cross*.

After room 3, paintings from the Northern Schools continue in the galleries to the left and French painting to the right.

Rooms 4 and 5 School of Avignon, seat of the papal court in the 14C, which produced such brilliant works as the *Thouzon Retable* (two sections) (c 1410). **Barthélémy d'Eyck**, *Crucifixion*, and **Enguerrand Quarton**, *Pietà* of Villeneuve-les-Avignon, a masterpiece of drama and pathos. New currents were introduced from the north by **Nicolas Froment** (active 1461–83), *Matheron Diptych*, and **Josse Lieferinxe** *Crucifixion and Visitation*.

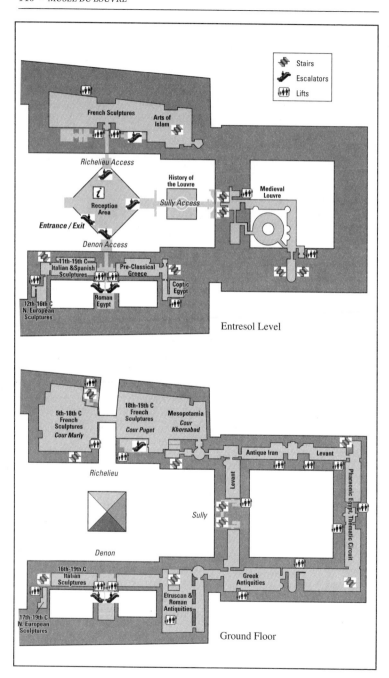

Stairs

Escalators

Lifts

French Sculptures

Arts of Islam

Richelieu Access

i

Reception Area

History of the Louvre

Sully Access

Medieval Louvre

Entrance / Exit

Denon Access

11th-15th C Italian & Spanish Sculptures

Pre-Classical Greece

Coptic Egypt

12th-16th C N. European Sculptures

Roman Egypt

Entresol Level

5th-18th C French Sculptures *Cour Marly*

18th-19th C French Sculptures *Cour Puget*

Mesopotamia *Cour Khorsabad*

Antique Iran

Levant

Richelieu

Levant

Pharaonic Egypt, Thematic Circuit

Sully

Denon

16th-19th C Italian Sculptures

Etruscan & Roman Antiquities

Greek Antiquities

17th-19th C N. European Sculptures

Ground Floor

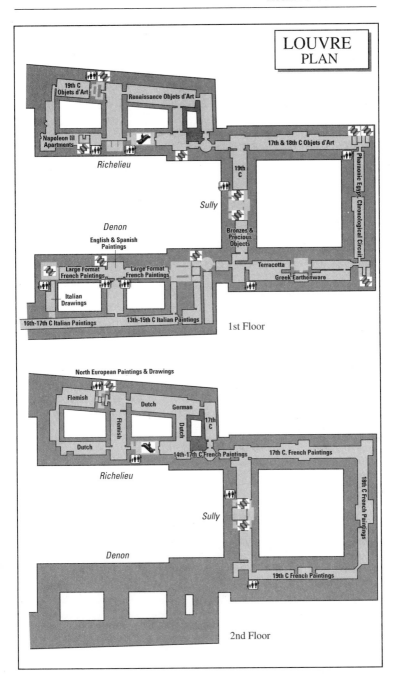

LOUVRE
PLAN

19th C
Objets d'Art

Renaissance Objets d'Art

Napoleon III
Apartments

17th & 18th C Objets d'Art

Richelieu

19th
C

Pharaonic Egypt: Chronological Circuit

Sully

Denon

Bronzes &
Precious
Objects

English & Spanish
Paintings

Large Format
French Paintings

Large Format
French Paintings

Terracotta

Greek Earthenware

Italian
Drawings

16th-17th C Italian Paintings

13th-15th C Italian Paintings

1st Floor

North European Paintings & Drawings

Flemish

Dutch

German

Flemish

Dutch

17th
C

Dutch

14th-17th C French Paintings

17th C. French Paintings

Richelieu

18th C French Paintings

Sully

Denon

19th C French Paintings

2nd Floor

Room 6. **Jean Fouquet** (c 1420–80) was significant for his bold and simpli-
fied forms in both miniatures and full-scale portraits, such as *Charles VII* and
Guillaume Juvenel des Ursins. His influence is seen in the (anon.) *Retable of the
Parlement of Paris* (c 1455)—note the view of the Louvre in the background.
From the centre of France, **Jean Hey** (the Maître de Moulins), fragments of a
Retable of the Bourbons.

16C portraiture in **rooms 7 and 8** is dominated by **Jean Clouet** (c 1485–c
1541). The attribution of his celebrated *Portrait of François I* (c 1530) was the
subject of long debate; **François Clouet** (c 1510–72), *Portrait of Pierre Quthe,
Apothecary* (1562); *Elisabeth of Austria* (wife of Charles IX, painted in 1571);
attributed to **François Quesnel** (c 1543–1616), *Portrait of Henri III*; and
several works by followers of F. Clouet. Among small portraits, largely anon. are
portraits of *Jean Babou de la Bourdasière, Michel de l'Hospital, Catherine de Médicis*,
and also *The Ball at the Wedding of Anne, Duc de Joyeuse*; several by **Corneille de
Lyon** (1505–74) or his school, including Pierre Aymeric.

The First and Second Schools of Fontainebleau, **rooms 10 and 11**. Italian
artists brought to Fontainebleau by François I in the 16C introduced the
Mannerist style and profoundly affected the art of the period Among the main
exponents in the First School were **Jean Cousin the Elder** (c 1490–c 1560)
whose *Eva Prima Pandora*, was one of the first nudes painted in France; and
Antoine Caron (1521–99) *The Tiburtine Sibyl*. The elegant, *Diana the Huntress*
(c 1550) (anon.), is possibly an idealised portrait of Diane de Poitiers, mistress of
the king. Of the Second School (late 16C), a *Portrait of Gabrielle d'Estrées* and one
of her sisters; others introduced a decorative character to their work, see
Dubreuil's *Hyante et Climène offrant un Sacrifice à Vénus*.

The Caravaggist painters are in **room 11**: **Valentin de Boulogne** (1591–
1632), *The Concert with Antique bas-relief, Tavern scene, The Innocence of Suzanne,
The Judgement of Solomon*; **Nicolas Régnier** (1591–1667), *The fortune-teller*;
Claude Vignon (1593–1670) *The Young Singer* and *The Death of St Anthony*;
Simon Vouet (1590–1649), *St William of Aquitaine*; **Nicolas Tournier**
(1590–1639), *Crucifixion*.

Large works by the Court painters of Louis XIII are in **room 12**. **Simon
Vouet**, *Presentation at the Temple* (1641), a strong and confident painting, one of
his many altarpieces, this one commissioned by Richelieu for the Jesuit church
of St-Paul-St-Louis. Vouet's delight in golden yellows is revealed fully in *Allegory
of Wealth, Celestial Charity* and *Virtue* (previously known as Victory); **Jacques
Blanchard** (1600–38) *Charity*; **Eustache le Sueur** (1616–55), *Reunion of
Friends*; one of several portraits by **Philippe de Champaigne** (1602–74), of
Richelieu, and *Louis XIII crowned by Victory*, commemorating the siege of La
Rochelle (1628); also some early works by Poussin (see below).

There follow rooms (**rooms 13, 14 and 16–19**) filled with the work of **Nicolas
Poussin** (1594–1665); the Louvre owns 38 of his paintings, a quarter of the
total in existence. Born in Normandy, Poussin spent most of his life in Rome. The
evolution of his rigorous, intellectualised style can be followed through these
galleries. From the large scale of *Apparition of the Virgin to St James Major* (1629)
(room 12), he turned to a smaller format and recreated antiquity for the
cognoscenti. Among paintings of his first Roman period (1624–40) are:

Bacchanals, Echo and Narcissus, Inspiration of the Poet; and the philosophical themes and Arcadian scenes of his mature years: the celebrated *Arcadian Shepherds* and the grave *Self-portrait*. **Rooms 16–18** with noble landscapes: *The Seasons series* (1660–64), and finally his last work, *Apollo and Daphne*.

Less well represented (**room 15**) is Poussin's artistic opposite **Claude Gellée**, called **Le Lorrain** or Claude in English (c 1600–82), painter of atmospheric landscapes and ports who also spent most of his working life in Rome: *Seaport in the Setting Sun, View of a Port with the Capitol*, and *Ulysees returning Chryseis to his Father* (1644), *Arrival of Cleopatra at Tarsa* (1642–43).

Room 17 presents a changing exhibition of the Painting of the Month.

Room 19 has large scale altar paintings (17C) by the founders of the Académie Royale in 1648, the major contributors being **Eustache Le Sueur** (1616–55), *St Paul at Ephesus*; **Poussin**, *The Miracles of St Francis Xavier*; **Laurent de La Hyre** (1606–56), *The Apparition of Christ to the Three Marys*; **Philippe de Champaigne**, *St Philip*; and **Sébastien Bourdon** (1616–71).

To the south, in **rooms 20–23**, are fine 17C drawings by **Charles Le Brun** (1619–90), and the preparatory cartoons for the Escalier des Ambassadeurs at Versailles, 1674–79, which employ all manner of *trompe l'oeil* and tricks of perspective to create an impression of space. The decoration was subsequently destroyed by order of Louis XV.

Rooms A, B, C leading out of room 19 contain three collections: Beistegui, Lyon and Cröy (see below).

The series of 22 paintings of the life of St Bruno, founder of the Carthusian order, by **Eustache Le Sueur**, fill **room 24**. Completed in 1648, these have recently been taken out of storage.

The decoration of 17C Parisian houses is evoked in **room 25**. Small scale (*du cabinet*) religious paintings, by a variety of painters, including the greatest, along with still lifes, are found in the side galleries, **rooms 26, 27**.

Room 28. Georges de la Tour (1593–1652) deliciously anecdotal *The Card-sharper*, and the sensitive image of *St Thomas* are both lit with natural light in contrast to *St Irene nursing St Sebastian, The Adoration of the Shepherds* and *Mary Magdalen watching a Candle* where the effect of candlelight throwing dramatic shadows plays a key role.

The genre scenes of the **Le Nain brothers** (**room 29**), Louis (c 1600–48), Antoine (c 1588–1648), and Mathieu (c 1607–77) range from subdued colours and quiet dignity, thought to be the work of Louis, to more Baroque works by Mathieu. Among their works are *The Travellers' Rest, The Peasants' Meal, The Forge, The Hay-wain, The Corps de Garde*.

Room 31. Portraits and religious works of the 17C. These include **Philippe de Champaigne**, *The Prévôt des Marchands, Portrait of a Man, Portrait of Jean-Antoine de Mesme*, and *The Last Supper*. His masterpiece of 1662, *The Artist's daughter with Mère Catherine-Agnès Arnauld*, was painted in thanksgiving for the miraculous cure of his daughter. Compare with the sumptuous Equestrian portrait of Chancellor Séguier, by Le Brun, 1661. In room 32 are **Le Brun's** *Battles of Alexander*.

Room 33 has religious paintings by **Jean Jouvenet** (1644–1717). **Rooms**

34–35 are dedicated to the painters of Louis XIV: Le Brun, Mignard, Rigaud. The celebrated full-length likeness of *Louis XIV* in 1701, by **Hyacinthe Rigaud** (1659–1743), is the Baroque portrait of absolute monarchy. **Nicolas de Largillière** (1656–1746), a popular portraitist among the upper bourgeoisie: *The Artist with his Wife and Daughter*, also painted religious subjects such as *The Finding of Moses*. Other painters in this group include **Pierre Mignard** (1612–95), *Self-Portrait*; and **Antoine Coypel** (1641–1722).

Rooms 36 and 37. **Antoine Watteau** (1684–1721) painted the monumental but enigmatic *Pierrot* (also known as *Gilles*), also *Portrait of a Gentleman*, *The Two Cousins* and *L'Indifférent*. The term *fête galante* was coined for his vision of a lazy, melancholic day of late summer, *Pilgrimage to Cythera* (1717). Gems of 18C elegance from the La Caze Collection of 1869 by Watteau, Boucher, Chardin, Lancret (1690–1743), and Jean-Baptiste Pater (1695–1736).

Rooms 38–40. 18C paintings created for the domestic market. Typical of **Jean-Baptiste-Siméon Chardin's** (1699–1779) marvellous still lifes are *Le Buffet*, where perilously perched dishes and fruit form a pyramid of reds and greys; also *The Skate and Hare and Powder-flask*. Studies of children include *Le Souffleur, Young Man with a Violin*; and genre scenes, *Le Bénédicité*. Paintings of pure pleasure by **François Boucher** (1703–70) are pertly pink half-dressed ladies: *Renaud and Armide* (1734), *Diana getting out of her Bath* (1742); also *Venus asking Vulcan for arms for Aeneas* (1732).

Room 41: the Couloir des Poules, with a view of the Seine: ***room 42*** 18C pastels and miniatures (shown in rotation), including work by Chardin; there are more pastels in **rooms 44 and 45**, several by Maurice-Quentin Delatour (1704–88). **Room 43** overlooking the Cour Carée, has large mid-18C paintings by Restout (1692–1768) and Pierre Subleyras (1699–1749), and a portrait by Chardin.

In the following ***room 46***, the Boucher Gallery, are **Jean-Baptiste Oudry** (1686–1755), *Bittern and Partridge Watched by a White Dog*; Louis Tocqué (1696–1772), *Marie Leszczynska* (1740); **Claude-Joseph Vernet** (1714–89), *View of Naples*; **Jean-Baptiste Perronneau** (1715–83), *Mme de Sorquainville*; **Boucher** landscapes: *Le Moulin* and *Le Pont* (1751).

Room 47: *Portrait of Denis Diderot* (1767) by Louis-Michel Van Loo (1707–71); Chardin Still lifes, Vernet and Jean-Baptiste Greuze (1725–1805), such as *The Agreement of the Village* and *The Dead Bird*.

Rooms 48 and 49: **Jean-Honoré Fragonard** (1732–1806), made his name in Paris with *The High Priest Coroesus sacrificing Himself to save Callirhoe*, 1765, in a grand style from which he soon turned to lighter themes dashed off with rapid, vibrant brushstrokes: Fantasy figures, of which the Louvre owns eight, include *Music* and *Portrait of Marie-Madeleine Guimard*; other paintings are *Women Bathing* (c 1770), *Adoration of the Shepherds* (c 1775) and *Le Verrou* (c 1777) oppose sacred and profane love. **Hubert Robert** (1733–1808) painted large picturesque ruins: *Le Pont du Gard* (1787), *The Triumphal Arch at Orange*, *The Maison Carrée*, and *Temple of Diana* (Nîmes). Among works by **Joseph Vernet**, *The Entrance to the Port of Marseilles* (1754), *The Ponte Rotto*; **Elisabeth Vigée-Lebrun** (1755–1842), *Portrait of Hubert Robert*.

In *room 51* are examples of portraits as well as the moralistic and sentimental work of **Jean-Baptiste Greuze** (1725–1805). Room 52: **Vigée-Lebrun** was encouraged to paint by Vernet, whom she painted in 1778; also portraits of women and children. The work of two other women, Anne Vallayer-Coster, 1744–1818, and Adélaïde Labille-Guiard (1749– 1803) is exhibited here.

Salle Vien, *room 53*. classical and religious themes, large format, including *Three Graces*, 1794, by **Baron Jean-Baptiste Régnault** (1754–1829) and **Baron François Gérard** (1770–1837), *Psyche and Cupid*, 1798. The butterfly above Psyche's head symbolises inconstancy.

Examples of **Jacques-Louis David**'s (1748–1825) work are shown together with paintings by his followers in *room 54*. David's rigorous, Neoclassical style influenced all French painting via his pupils Gros, Gerard and Ingres. Jacques-Louis David (1748–1825), *Madame Trudaine* (unfinished); in the same vein, **Baron Antoine-Jean Gros** (1771–1835), *Portrait of Madeleine Pasteur*; **Baron François Gérard** (1770–1837), *Portraits of his wife*, of *Comtesse Regnauld de Saint-Jean d'Angély*; **Marie-Guillemine Benoist** (1768–1826), *A Black Woman*, also Louis Girodet (1767–1824) and Pierre Guérin (1774–1833).

Room 56 has works by **Pierre-Paul Prud'hon** (1758–1823), *Young Zephyr balancing above the Water*; *Bath of Venus*.

Rooms 55, 57, 58, 59, landscapes and genre paintings of around 1800. The 125 studies of Italy by Pierre de Valenciennes (1750–1819) are exhibited in rotation; Eugène Isabey (1803–86), *The Wooden Bridge*. Genre paintings include works by Louis Boilly (1761–1845).

Room 60, **Jean-Auguste-Dominique Ingres** (1780–1867), pupil of David, consummate draughtsman and one of the great portraitists, *Portraits of L.-F. Bertin*, senior, and of *C.-J.-L. Cordier*; also *The Turkish Bath*, *La Baigneuse de Valpinçon*, and the composer *Cherubini*.

The next two *rooms 61 and 62*. are devoted to the great Romantic painters, Géricault and Delacroix. **Théodore Géricault** (1791–1824), *The Mad Woman*, *The Vendéen*; studies for *Officer of the Chasseurs de la Garde*, and for *The Raft of the Medusa*. **Eugène Delacroix** (1789–1863), *Self-portrait*, *Hamlet and Horatio*, *Portrait of Chopin*; *Algerian Women in their Apartments*.

Brought together in *room 63* are the followers of Ingres, and Orientalists, such as Théodore Chassériau (1819–56), *Toilette d'Esther*; Léon Bénouville (1821–59), Hippolyte Flandrin (1809–64) and Paul Flandrin (1811–1902).

Rooms 64–72. Two major collections: Moreau-Nélaton, donated in 1906, and Thomy-Thiery donation of 1902. Among them are many by **Jean-Baptiste Camille Corot** (1796–1875) especially in rooms 68 and 73, such as the *Pont de Mantes* (c 1868), *View of the Colosseum*, and the gentle *Souvenir of Castelgandolfo* (c 1865), *La Femme à la Perle* and the *Mother Superior Mère Marie-Héloïse des Dix Vertus* (1852). Also works by **Delacroix** including *Rebecca carried off by the Templar* (1858); **Jean-François Millet** (1814–75), *Les Botteleurs de Foin* (1850); Eugène Isabey and Thomas Couture. Landscapes by the **Barbizon artists**: Théodore Rousseau (1812–67), Nino Diaz de la Peña, Daubigny (1817–78), Decamps, Huet, Troyon, and Eugène Fromentin. (The Impressionist works from the Moreau-Nélaton collection are at the Musée d'Orsay.)

The **Beistegui collection**, *room A* (between the staircases Henri II and Henri IV), donated in 1953 on the condition that the works are always exhibited together, has a range of works mainly of the 18C–19C, including a 14C *Virgin and Child* (Flemish) and a late 15C *Portrait of the Dauphin Charles Orlando* (son of Charles VIII and Anne of Brittany) by the Maître de Moulins. There are numerous portraits by Largillière, Fragonard, *Portrait of a young artist* and others, Jean-Marc Nattier (1685–1766), van Dyck, Thomas Lawrence (1769–1830), Zuloaga (1870–1945) Carlos de Beistegui, Meissonier (1815–91), David; Ingres' likeness of his friend *Bartolini*, the sculptor; and work by Gérard. Also Rubens' *The Death of Dido*, and Goya's magnificent *portrait of the Marquesa de la Solana*.

Two more collections, **Cröy** and **Lyon**, donated in 1930–32 and 1971 respectively, are in *rooms B and C*. The large donation of 3800 drawings and paintings, by the Princess Louis de Cröy, consists mainly of paintings of the Northern schools with landscapes by Valenciennes. The Hélène and Victor Lyon donation, of 17C–18C Northern and Venetian paintings includes landscapes by Jan van Goyen (1596–1656), Bernardo Strozzi (1581–1644), Canaletto (1686–1768); Giandomenico Tiepolo (1727–1804), and a cross section of late-19C French works by Cézanne, Degas, Jongkind, Monet, Pissarro, Renoir and Toulouse-Lautrec.

For later paintings of the French School, see Musée d'Orsay, Ch. 9.

Large 19C French paintings (under reorganisation) are in three rooms in **DENON** first floor. Take the escalator from Hall Napoléon and then the staircase towards Winged Victory; turn right halfway up these stairs, to start in Salle Daru (room 75). The theatrical works of **J.-L. David**, inspired by antiquity, include *Andromache Mourning Hector* (1783), *Brutus* (1789), *The Sabine Women* (1799), and *The Oath of the Horatii* (1784), widely seen as extolling republican virtues although commissioned for the Crown; the brilliant historical record of *The Coronation of Napoleon I by Pope Pius VII in Notre-Dame, 2 December 1804* (1805–07). David's genius as a portrait painter is demonstrated in *M. Sériziat, His wife and son*; *Madame Récamier*; *The Marquise d'Orvillers*; *Pope Pius VII*; and in his *Self Portrait*. **Baron Gros**, *Christine Boyer*, first wife of Lucien Bonaparte, **Prud'hon** a rather wistful *Empress Joséphine at Malmaison* (1805).

Jean-Dominique Ingres (1780–1867): *Romulus Conqueror of Acron* (1812), *La grande Odalisque* (1814), Portraits of the *Rivière Family* (1805), *The Apotheosis of Homer, Oedipus and the Sphinx*, and *Roger and Angelique*. More sentimental are works by **Pierre-Narcisse Guérin** (1774–1833) *L'Aurore et Cephale* (1810) and by Vigée-Lebrun.

Great Romantic paintings, in Salle Mollien, *room 77*, full blown and slightly sentimental include **Baron Gros** *Bonaparte visiting the Plague-striken at Jaffa* (1804). **Géricault**, *Raft of the Medusa*, treated with the highest drama; **Delacroix**, *Dante Crossing the Styx, Massacre at Chios* (1824), *Liberty leading the People* (1831), *Women of Algiers* (1834); **Chassériau** *The Two Sisters* and *Portrait of Lacordaire*. Also work by Paul Delaroche (1797–1856), Alexandre Descamps (1803–60), Ary Scheffer (1795–1858) *Paolo and Francesca*, and Victor Schnetz (1787–1870).

(The temporary presentation of English and Spanish Paintings is in Salle Denon (room 76) between these two rooms.)

Northern Schools

The 36 new rooms, designed by I.M. Pei and devoted to the Northern Schools of painting—Dutch/Netherlandish, Flemish, and German, with some 840 works, are in RICHELIEU second floor; Northern Prints and Drawings are also found in Richelieu second floor.

> To reach the Northern School galleries, take the Richelieu escalators (or lift) to the second floor, pass through the first rooms and stop in the third, all three common to Northern and French Paintings.

Room 3. The style known as **International Gothic**, developed throughout Europe between about 1370 and 1450, especially in paintings from Bohemia, Lombardy, Burgundy and France, characterised by elegance, decorative refinement and a celebration of courtly life. *Retable from the Chapelle Cardon* (c 1400), the 15C *Virgin Writing*, and a *Virgin and Child* from Bohemia. Turn left.

Rooms 4 and 5. **15C Dutch and Flemish paintings**. A deliberate breakaway from the brilliant but superficial qualities of International Gothic, by Robert Campin and Jan van Eyck, occurred in the southern Netherlands c 1420–25. By a pupil of Campin, **Rogier van der Weyden** (1399/1400–64), the *Braque Family Triptych* (c 1450), a work of intense colour and feeling, and the *Annunciation* with sparkling details; **Jan van Eyck**, *Virgin with Chancellor Nicolas Rolin*; Rolin, donor of this exceptional painting, was the rich and powerful Chancellor of Burgundy. Petrus Christus, *Pietà*.

Many artists followed Van Eyck's innovations in Bruges including **Hans Memling**, of German origin, *The Mystic Marriage of St Catherine* (Virgin and Child surrounded by Saints), *Portrait of an Old Woman, triptych of the Resurrection with the Martyrdom of St Sebastian, the Virgin of Jacques Floreins, triptych of the Flight into Egypt*; **Gérard David** (c 1465–1529), *Triptych of Mary of the Sedano Family, Marriage at Cana*; **Cornelis van Dalem**, *Farmyard in Winter*; **Brueghel the Elder** (1525–69) *Beggars, Sacrifice of Abraham*; **Lucas van Leyden** (1494–1533), *The Card-dealer, Lot and his Daughters*; the last and strangest painter represented is **Hieronymus Bosch** (c1450–1516), with his famous *The Ship of Fools*.

Room 6 is described as the **Studiolo d'Urbino**. With work by Juste de Gand (Justus of Ghent, active 1460) and Pedro Berruguete is a series of 28 portraits of illustrious or wise men: saints and sages, of poets and scholars, including Dante, commissioned by Federico da Montefeltro for the Ducal Palace at Urbino.

15C German works from Cologne and other artistic centres are presented in **room 7**: the dramatic and sensual oeuvre of the **Master of the St Bartholomew Altarpiece** (active c 1500), *Descent from the Cross*, painted for an Antonite community; narrative cycles by the **Master of the Legend of St Bruno** and by the **Master of the Legend of St Ursula** (dressed in sumptuous costume, Ursula is shown departing on a pilgrimage to Rome, spurning the pagan king who demands her hand in marriage); **Master of St Germain-des-Prés**, active in Paris c 1500, *Pietà*, with a view of the Louvre and St Germain-des-Prés.

Room 8. important **German paintings of the Renaissance period**, between 1495 and 1550, characterised by a remarkable original fusion of

German, Netherlandish and Italian art. **Albrecht Dürer** (1471–1528), *Self-Portrait* (1523), *The Grieving Christ*; **Lucas Cranach the Elder**, *Venus in a Landscape*, *St Peter and St Paul*, part of a retable, portraits presumed to be of *Magdalena Luther* and of *Frederick the Wise*, and *The Effects of Jealousy*; five portraits by **Hans Holbein the Younger** (1497–1543), purchased by Louis XIV: *Sir Henry Wyatt, Anne of Cleves, Erasmus* (painted for Sir Thomas More), *Nicolas Kratzer* (Henry VIII's astronomer), and *William Warham, Archbishop of Canterbury*; representative of the Danube School, Wolf Huber (1480–1553) and Hans Sebald Beham (1500–50).

Room 9 and the small gallery, *room 10* has works by Netherlandish painters of the first half of the 16C, from Bruges and Antwerp. **Quentin Metsys** (1465–1530), *Moneylender and his Wife* (note the reflection in the round mirror), a small *Pietà*, and *Virgin and Child*, with a bunch of grapes before an open window; **Jan Gossaert** (Mabuse) (c 1478–c 1532), the beautiful *Diptych of Jean Carondelet* (*Chancellor of Flanders*) and the Virgin; **Joos van Cleve** (1485–1541), *Virgin with Dominican Offering his Heart* (c 1510–15), and *The Last Supper*; Joachim Patinier (c 1475/80–1524), *St Jerome in the Desert*; Barent van Orley (c 1488–1541), *Holy Family*. Small works by Lucas van Leyden (1494–1533); **Pieter Brueghel the Elder** (c 1525–69); **Jan van Sorel** (1495–1562).

Room 11. 16C Netherlandish painters, known as the Romanists, who were influenced by studying antiquity, often during a stay in Italy. **Jan Massys** (c 1509–c 1575), *David and Bathsheba*; **Jan van Hemmessen** (c 1500–63/67), *The Young Tobias Restoring his Father's Sight* (1555); **Pieter Bruegel the Younger** (1564–1638), *Parable of the Blind Men*, a 17C copy of the work of 1568 by Brueghel the Elder.

Room 12. Rotating exhibition of Graphic Arts of the Northern Schools. **Rooms 14 and 16** are small-scale landscapes and still lifes of end 16C–beginning 17C: **Jan Brueghel (Velvet)** (1568–1625), *The Battle of Arbela*; Jacob Fopsen van Es (c 1596–1666), *Still Life*.

The **Dutch and Flemish works of the late 16C and early 17C**, *rooms 13 and 15* are grouped under the heading Mannerist, and exhibit the exaggerated tendencies of this style which spread throughout Europe from Italy. The main exponents of landscape are **Paul Bril** (1554–1626) and **Jan Brueghel**, *Virgin and Child with a garland of flowers*, and *Air* and *Earth* (part of a series of the four Elements); there is also an early **Rubens** *Landscape*. A virtuoso *Still Life* by **Georg Flegel** (1566–1636), sports a fly on the loaf of bread.

Rooms 17–26. 17C Flemish painting, dominated by **Peter-Paul Rubens** (1577–1640). Early paintings (room 17) by Rubens include *Ixion deceived by Juno, Hercules and Omphale* (c 1602–05), and *Adoration of the Magi*; in the same room, **Anthony van Dyck** (1599–1641), *Martyrdom of St Sebastian*; and other contemporaries of Rubens.

Room 18. The Medici Gallery, is the recent and vastly enhanced presentation, against light-green walls, of **Rubens'** resplendent series of 24 huge allegorical works depicting the *Life of Marie de Médicis*. Designed in 1622–25 to decorate the Luxembourg Palace, this was the painter's greatest single achievement and the new gallery is one of the major successes of the Louvre Project. These paintings glorify the life and achievements of the Queen in an appropriately exuberant and eulogistic manner, in chronological sequence. Running from left to right, each canvas represents a major event of Marie's life, starting with her birth in April 1575. Other scenes include her arrival at Marseilles on 3 November 1600, the birth of her son Louis, her coronation at St Denis and the series ends with the reconciliation with her son, Louis XIII, in 1619. Above the door, between portraits of her parents, is Marie de Médicis as Reine Triomphante. This great series influenced later French artists as different as Watteau and David.

Room 19 at the other end of the Medici gallery, overlooking Cour Napoléon, has huge, mainly religious, paintings: **Jacob Jordaens** (1593–1678); **Jacob van Oost** (1637–1713); **Gaspart de Crayer** (1584–1669); **Van Dyck**, *Crucifixion*; **Philippe de Champaigne**, *Assumption of the Virgin*.

Return through the Medici gallery and across Escalier Lefuel (room 20), to **rooms 21–22** for further works by **Rubens**, including a tenderly executed portrait of his wife *Hélène Fourment with two of her Children*, *Baron Henri de Vicq* (c 1625), a portrait of the ambassador who obtained for the artist the commission to paint the Medici canvases; among landscapes by Rubens is the unforgettable *Kermesse*—the village wedding. **Room 22** contains the Rubens' sketches. Also a study for the *Head of an Old Man* by Van Dyck.

Rooms 23 and 25. Mainly David Teniers (1610–90); also small 17C Flemish genre paintings by his contemporaries such as Brouwer, Sorgh, and Craesbeeck, and Pieter Meulener (1602–54).

Rooms 24–26. Works by **Van Dyck** (1599–1641), and **Jacob Jordaens** (1593–1678), *Jesus Banishing the Merchants from the Temple*. Works by Van Dyck include two religious works, *Virgin with Donors* (1630–32), and the moving *St Sebastian supported by the Angels*. An example of his mythological paintings is *Venus and Vulcan* (1626–32) painted just before his departure for England; portraits executed during his Antwerp and Italian periods (before 1632) of *Marchesa Spinola-Doria*, *A Lady of Quality and her Child* and its counterpart *A Gentleman and his Child*; and from his years in England is *Charles I of England* (c 1637). Also in this gallery is **Jan Davidsz de Heem** (1606–1683/84), *The Dessert*, and **Sir Peter Lely** 1618–80), *Portrait of a Man* (c 1658).

The last 12 rooms are devoted to Dutch paintings arranged by genre, rather than around a single artists, with the exception of Rembrandt. The paintings follow more or less chronologically, emphasising the variety and wealth of the Dutch School.

Rooms 27–29. Works from the first half of the 17C, a transition between two schools: **Frans Hals** (1581/85–1666), of Flemish origins, represented by majestic portraits of *Paulus van Berestyn*, and of his third wife, *Catherine Both van der Eem*; his growing preference for restrained colours is found in *Old Woman* and *Buffoon with a Lute*. Other portraitists include **Verspronck** (1606/09–62), *Portrait of Anna van Schoonhoven*; Willem van der Vliet, *Portrait of a Man Seated*; Miereveld (1567–1641), *Portrait of Jan van Oldenbarneveld*;

Landscape, characterised by a limited palette, is dominated by **Van Goyen** (1596–1656), *Two large Sailing Boats and Animals* and *View of Dordrecht*, and **Solomon van Ruysdael** (1600/03–70), *The Landing-stage*, whose compositions often consist mainly of sky, brilliantly painted. Other landscapists are Pieter de

Nyn (1597–1639), Abraham de Verweer (1617–1650); and the painter of Brazil, Frans Post (1608–69).

Among painters specialising in architecture are Saenredam (1597–1665), *Interior of a Church Haarlem*; and **Steenwyck** (c 1580–1649) *Jesus at the House of Martha and Mary*. The influence of Italy is seen, among others, on Cornelis van Poelenburgh (c 1586–1667). Dutch genre scenes are typified by Adam van Breen (1599–1665), *Skaters*. Still Life has a privileged place in Dutch painting, and certain works recall clearly its Flemish origins, e.g. *Flowers* by Bosschaert and Van der Ast.

Large history or genre painting, notably that by the Caravaggist artists, are exemplified by **Gerard van Honthorst** (1590–1656), *The Concert* and *The Lute Player* are fine examples of this style. More sober is **Ter Brugghen** (1588–1629) from Utrecht; also **Frans Hals**, *The Bohemian* and **Judith Leyster** (1600/10–60) *Joyful Company*, **Jan Woutersz** (Stap) (1599–1663), the *Old Man*, and Pieter de Grebber, *Tattooing Lesson*.

Room 30. Further examples of landscapes in the refined greys and browns of Van Goyen, Van Ruysdael and Heda, and the more colourful Italianate works of Berchem, Both and Asselyn.

Room 31 is devoted to **Rembrandt van Rijn** (1606–69), and includes the two introspective *Self-Portraits* of 1633, one *Bareheaded* the other, *Wearing a Toque and Chain* using a rich palette and play of light; the decor of *Self-Portrait with an Architectural Background* (1647) has been reworked by another hand; a fourth self-portrait is of the *Artist in his Old Age at his Easel* (1660). From the 'Baroque' years 1630–40, are *The Philosopher in Meditation*, the *Archangel Raphael taking leave of the Family of Tobias*, and *Holy Family*. From his more mature and mystical period come *Christ at Emmaus* (1648), the stunning *Bathsheba* (1654) and *St Matthew and the Angel* (1661). Perhaps the best known of all Rembrandt's work in the Louvre is the monumental *Bathsheba Bathing*, with copper tones, soft and tangible flesh, and deep velvety shadows. A more violent note is struck by *The Slaughtered Ox* (1655), whereas the imaginary *Landscape with Castle* (c 1640) is an enchanted vision.

Room 32. Works by the pupils, imitators and followers of Rembrandt. His most able pupils were: **Flinck** (1615–60), *Announcement to the Shepherds, Young Shepherdess*; **Ferdinand Bol**, *The Trip Children, Couple, The Mathematician*; **Victors** (1620–76), *Isaac Blessing*; and **Eeckhout** (1621–74). Later pupils of the years 1645–70 include **Barent Fabritius** (1624–73), *Man Reading*; **Drost** (c 1630–c 1680) *Young Scholar* and *Bathsheba*.

Rooms 33–39. **Dutch paintings from the middle to the end of the 17C.** Room 33. *The Fish Market* by **Adriaen Van Ostade**; **Isaac Van Ostade**, *Frozen Canal*; and the **Van der Helst's** *Reepmaker Family* as well as works by Ferdinand Bol and Jacob Van Ruisdael. Room 34 contains **Cuyp's** *The Walk*, **Berchem's** *Landscape and Animals*; the *Oudekerk at Delft* by **VanVliet**, and *View of Amsterdam* by **Backhuiysen**. Room 35 revolves around the work of **Gerard Dou** (1613–75), including *The Bible Reading* and the *Trumpet*. Also in this room are *The Ford* by **Berchem**, *Flowers in a Crystal Jug* by **Mignon** and more landscapes. Room 36 has Still Lifes by **Metsu** (1629–67) and work by **Steen** (1626–79). There is more landscape, genre and still life in room 37.

Room 38. Two works by **Jan Vermeer** (1632–75), the *Lacemaker* (c 1679), with perfect colour and light used to convey intense concentration, and another intimate interior scene of a small group using cool blue tones, called *The Astronomer*. Nearby are **Pieter de Hooch's** *The Drinker*, and the favourite *Courtyard of a Dutch House*; **Ruisdael**, *The Ray of Sunshine*. The last room. ***Room 39*** is dedicated mainly to the 15 works by Wouwerman, along with Jan Weenix, and Hobbema.

Spanish School

The Spanish School, DENON, first floor, is not a very large collection, but is notable for a fine series of masterpieces acquired relatively recently. More magnificient was the collection belonging to Louis-Philippe which, after being exhibited in the Louvre 1838–48, followed the King in exile to London and was dispersed at a public sale in 1853. The Spanish paintings are due to be in their permanent position in the western section of Denon—part of the former Rubens gallery and Petits cabinets—by the end of 1998. Therefore, it was not possible at the time of writing to describe their arrangement. The main paintings in the collection are listed below.

Master of Burgo de Osma (early 15C), retable with the *Virgin and Child, St John the Baptist and St Ambrose*; **Jaime Huguet** (1415–92), *Flagellation* and *Entombment*; **Barnat Martorell**, *Four episodes from the Life of St George* (c 1430–35); **El Greco** (1541–1614), a characteristic work of heavy pathos, *Crucifixion with two Donors* (signed in Greek characters) c 1580, *St Louis, King of France*; **José de Ribera** (c 1591–1652), the fine *Adoration of the Shepherds, St Paul the Hermit, Entombment*, and *Club-footed Boy* (1642); **Francisco de Zurbarán** (1598–1664), *St Bonaventura at the Council of Lyon, St Bonaventure's Corpse Exposed*, and *Sta Apollina*; Francisco Collantes (1599–1656), *The Burning Bush*; **Diego Velázquez** (1599–1660), *Queen Mariana of Austria, Infanta Margarita*, and attributed to Velázquez, *Infanta María Teresa*; **Juan Carreño** (1614–85), *Foundation of the Trinitarian Order*.

Bartolomé Estabán Murillo (1618–82), *Legend of San Diego*, known as *The Angels' Kitchen*, is one of a series of 16 painted for the Franciscan convent at Seville and *Birth of the Virgin*. Known for his sweet Madonnas, Murillo also produced a number of paintings on the theme of picturesque urchins, of which *Young Beggar* (1650), is one of the best. **Luis Meléndez** (1716–80), *Self-Portrait* and *Still-life*; **Francisco Goya** (1746–1828), who absorbed varied influences (Tiepolo, English portraitists, Velázquez) to become the most original artist of his period and, according to André Malraux, the father of modern painting. Works include the striking portrait of *Ferdinand Guillemardet* (c 1798), *The Unequal Wedding, Christ in the Garden of Olives, Woman with a Fan* (c 1810), and *portraits of Mariana Waldstein, Marquesa de Santa Cruz, Evaristo Pérez de Castro*.

Portuguese School

Anon. (mid 15C), *Man with a Glass of Wine*.

English School

Also to be rehoused by 1999 are the works belonging to the English School, which include **Ramsay**, *Lord Elcho*; **Gainsborough**, *Conversation in the park, Lady Gertrude Alston*; **Reynolds**, *Master Hare*; **Romney**, *Sir John Stanley*; **Wright of Derby**, *The Lake of Nemi*; **John Linnell**, *Hampstead Heath*; **Lawrence**, *Charles William Bell, John Julius Angerstein and his wife*; **Raeburn**, *Capt. Robert Hay of*

Spott; **Bonington**, *The Adriatic*; and examples of the work of John Hamilton Mortimer, Fuseli, Constable, Turner (including watercolour view of St-Germain-en-Laye), and Angelica Kauffmann.

Italian Schools

The well endowed Department of Paintings of the Italian Schools 14C–18C, **DENON** first floor, Rooms 1–7 and 11, is being renovated and reorganised and should be completed by mid 1998. This entails a revised circuit in chronological order, starting in the east of Denon and progressing through Salon Carré (Room 3) the room called Sept Mètres (Room 4), the grand Galerie (Rooms 5, 7) and the Salle des Etats (Room 6). The circuit will end in the former Rubens gallery (Room 11), due to open in mid 1998, at the west of the Grande Galerie. Room 6 contains the Mona Lisa.

Room 1, Salle Percier et Fontaine, contains frescos by Botticelli (1445–1510), *Venus and the Graces offering Presents to a Young Girl* (1480/83) and in **Room 2**, is the large *Crucifixion* by Fra Angelico.

Room 3, **Salon Carré** contains about 30 large works by Florentine masters of the 13C–15C. 14C works include the large altar painting *Madonna with Angels* by **Cimabue** (c 1240–1302), is an early attempt to bring a certain naturalism and depth to a fundamentally Byzantine composition. Note in the painted frame the 26 medallions of Christ, angels, prophets and saints. The far freer, more lifelike interpretation of figures by **Giotto** (c 1266–1337) is obvious in *St Francis Receiving the Stigmata*.

The great 15C Florentine painter, **Fra Angelico** (c 1387–1455), in his triumphant *Coronation of the Virgin*, handles a traditional religious subject with novel use of perspective; by the same artist, *The Martyrdom of St Cosmas and St. Damian*; **Sano di Pietro** (c 1405–81), *Five Episodes from the Life of St Jerome*, where the central scene depicts the saint extracting a thorn from the lion's paw; **Master of the Observance**, *St Anthony*, part of a polyptych.

Paolo Uccello (c 1396–1475), *Battle of San Romano*, 1432, is one of three panels on the same theme (others in Florence and London). Combined with brilliant colours, the result is a charmingly decorative if oddly wooden battle scene.

School of Fra Filippo Lippi, a large and sophisticated *Nativity*. **Sandro Botticelli** (1445–1510) was the most important Florentine artist of the second half of the Quattrocento (15C), admired for his refined and delicate approach. The intense and compact composition, set off in a fine carved frame, is a moving painting of a youthful *Madonna and Child*, surrounded by Angels who resemble fresh-faced adolescents; also *Portrait of a Young Man, The Madonna of the Guidi of Faenza, Madonna and Child with St John the Baptist*.

Room 4. The 13C *Painted Cross* by the **Master of San Francesco** and the larger 14C *Crucifixion*, from the workshop of Giotto, originally suspended above an altar, are important works from 13C Siena and Florence. At the extreme of each arm of the latter are St John the Evangelist and the Virgin, the Pelican at the top symbolising the Resurrection.

Small works include: **Simone Martini** (1284–1344), from Siena who worked for a time in Avignon, *Christ bearing the Cross* (c 1340–44), a small section of a polyptych of the Passion; **Guido da Siena** (active 1260–70), *Nativity*, and *Presentation at the Temple*; **Pisanello** c 1395–1454), *A Princess of* *the House of Este*; **Gentile da Fabriano** (c 1370–1427), *Presentation at the Temple*—note the detailed attention to the architectural setting and materials; **Jacopo Bellini** (c 1400–71), father of Gentile and Giovanni and father-in-law of Andrea Mantegna, *Madonna and Child with Donor*.

By the Sienese painter **Sassetta** (1400–50) are five of the 34 scenes parts of the polyptych painted (1437–44) for the church of San Francesco, Sansepolcro, the majority of which are in London: *Madonna and Child with Angels, St Anthony of Padua, John the Evangelist, The Miraculous Deliverance of the Poor from the Prisons of Florence*, and the *Damanation of the Soul of the Avaricious Man of Citerna*.

Small works of the period include **Fra Angelico**, *Angel in Adoration*; School of Fra Angelico, *Herod's Feast*. **Pesellino** (c 1422–57), *St Francis of Assisi Receiving the Stigmata*, and *St Cosmas and St Damien nursing the sick*; **Luca Signorelli** (c 1441/50–1523), *Birth of St John the Baptist*; **Giovanni Bellini** (c 1430–1516), *Crucifixion, Blessing, Portrait of two Men*.

Piero della Francesca's (c 1416–92) *Portrait of Sigismondo Malatesta* reveals his intellectually rigorous style with sharp profiles.

***Room 5*, Grande Galerie**. The precise draughtsmanship of **Andrea Mantegna** (c 1430–1506) produced such works as his *Crucifixion*, and *St Sebastian*. The exaggerated perspective of *Virgin of Victory* (1496) suggests it was intended to be viewed from below.

Painters of the Venetian School in the 15C include **Antonello da Messina** (1430–79), a Sicilian who spent several vital years in Venice: *The condottiere*. **Giovanni Bellini**, the greatest artist of his family, who raised Venetian art to the same heights as that of Florence; his calm, personal vision is seen in *Portrait of a Man*. **Carpaccio** (1437–1525), *St Stephen Preaching in Jerusalem*, note the use of colour and architecture; **Jacopo de Barbari** (1440–1516), *Madonna at the Fountain*; **Cima da Conegliano** (c 1459–c 1518), *Madonna and Child with St John the Baptist* and *the Magdalen*; **Marco Palmezzano**, *Christ supported by angels*; **Catena (c 1495–1531)**, *Portrait of Giangiorgio Trissino*.

Florentine painters of the 15C include: **Ghirlandaio** (1449–94), *The Bottlenosed old Man and his Grandson, The Visitation*; pupil of Ghirlandaio, **Bartolommeo di Giovanni** (active end 15C), *Marriage of Thetis and Peleus*, and *Wedding Procession*; **Piero di Cosimo** (1462–1521), *Madonna and Dove*.

From Perugia, Pietro di Cristoforo Vannucci, called **Perugino** (1445–1523), who strongly influenced his pupil, Raphael; *Madonna with Saints and Angels*, and *Tondo showing the Madonna and Child with St Catherine and St John the Baptist*.

The end of the Quattrocento and first quarter of the Cinquecento (16C), called the Italian **High Renaissance**, when harmony and proportion seemed to have been finally achieved, produced some of the greatest Italian painters.

An air of mystery and sensuality envelopes **Leonardo**'s *The Virgin of the Rocks* (1482), probably earlier than the London version; the *Madonna and Child with St Anne* is an extraordinarily vital yet closely knit group of three generations expressing tenderness and compassion. Also by Leonardo are an *Annunciation* and *St John the Baptist*. From the School of Leonardo, *La Belle Ferronnière* (because of the metal chain around her forehead).

Raphael (1483–1520), *La Belle Jardinière* (1507) is one of several such groups, each a version of the Baptist's visit, using pyramidal composition Leonardo had pioneered. The *Portrait of Baldassare Castiglione* (poet and diplomat) was purchased by Louis XIV from the heirs of Cardinal Mazarin in 1661. *Self-Portrait with a Friend*, presents the artist standing behind another figure who turns towards him. Other works by Raphael include *St George* and *St Michael* and the large *Holy Family* of François I.

Room 6, Salle des Etats. The Louvre is rich in works by **Leonardo da Vinci** (1452–1519), the most celebrated is the portrait traditionally assumed to be of *Mona Lisa Gherardini* (correctly Monna, the Italian for lady), third wife of Francesco di Zanobi del Giocondo, therefore also known as La Gioconda, in French La Joconde. Now in a specially protected niche and brightly lit, this innovative yet enigmatic portrait using soft tonal modelling, positively glows. Leonardo worked on it intermittently between 1503 and 1506 and brought it to France when he came at the invitation of François I in 1516. Purchased by the king, it became the most valued piece in the royal collection. In August 1911 it was stolen but was recovered in Florence in December 1913.

The dynamic use of colour in the Venetian tradition, was brought to its zenith by **Titian** (c 1485–1576) in such works as: *Lady at her Toilet, Allegory representing the Wife of Alfonso d'Avalos being entrusted to Chastity and Cupid, Venus of the Pardo*. The gentle *Concert Champêtre*, the first in the tradition of *fêtes champêtres*, was for long attributed to Giorgione, by whom Titian was heavily influenced, but is now considered to be an early Titian. Religious works include *Supper at Emmaus, The Entombment*; and portraits: *Man with a Glove*, from Louis XIV's collection, and *François I* (taken from an image on a medal).

The Venetian **Tintoretto** (1518–94) combined the 'colour of Titian and the drawing of Michelangelo' to produce a highly personal style; works include *Paradise*, a preparatory work for the Doge's Palace. The huge painting by **Paolo Veronese** (1528–88), *Marriage at Cana* was painted for San Giorgio Maggiore, Venice and the intensity of its colours were rediscovered when it was restored in 1989–92. Others by Veronese are the so-called *La Belle Nani, Supper at Emmaus*, and *Jupiter striking down the Vices* with its tumbling giants.

Rooms 7 and 11. Giulio Romano (c 1499–1546) trained with Raphael, was also an architect and a creator of Mannerism. He produced the sumptuous *Portrait of Joanna of Aragon* (the face by Raphael); **Andrea del Sarto** (1486–1530), *Charity*; and the early Mannerist, **Jacopo Pontormo** (1494–1557), *Holy Family*.

Correggio (1489?–1534), associated with an extreme use of sfumato and a tenderly voluptuous quality, as in *The Mystic Marriage of St Catherine of Alexandria, Jupiter and Antiope, Allegory of the Vices and Virtues*. **Lorenzo Lotto** (c 1480–c 1556), *The Woman taken in Adultery, Christ bearing the Cross*.

The greatest Italian painter of the 17C was **Caravaggio** (c 1499–1546), whose life and work were conducted with passion, and whose artistic influence spread throughout Europe. The message in *The Fortune-Teller* is clearly legible. *Death of the Virgin* (1605–06) was considered scandalous at the time because of the earthy realism of the figures and the heightened contrasts of light and shade. There is also *Portrait of Alof de Wignacourt*.

The most talented of the **Carracci family**, from Bologna, was Annibale (1560–1609): *The Virgin appearing to St Luke and St Catherine, Hunting and Fishing*. **Guido Reni** (1575–1642), who was influenced by the Carracci, went out of fashion in the 19C but is now considered a great colourist: *St Sebastian, Ecco Homo*. Domenichino (1581–1641), pupil of Annibale Carracci: *Herminia among the Shepherds, St Cecilia*; Guercino (1591–1666), *The Raising of Lazarus*.

Pietro da Cortona (1596–1669), one of the founders of the Roman High Baroque: *Venus as a Huntress Appearing to Aeneas*. Bernardo Strozzi (1581–1644), the leading Genoese painter of the 17C, was influenced by Rubens and Van Dyck: *Holy Family*; Salvator Rosa (1615–73), from Naples, was the prototype Romantic artist: *Landscape with Hunters*; Aniello Falcone (1607–56) also Neapolitan, specialised in battles.

Giuseppe-Maria Crespi (1665–1747) was the most individual Bolognese artist of the time, best known for his genre scenes, such as *Woman with Flea*; **Giovanni Paolo Panini** (c 1692–1765), *Concert in Rome* (26 November 1729); **Michele Marieschi**, *View of Santa Maria della Salute*, Venice. **Francesco Guardi** (1712–93) produced views of Venice in a freer and more expressive mood than Canaletto such as the eight scenes depicting festivities organised for *The Coronation of the Doge Alvise IV Mocenigo, View of the church of SS Giovanni e Paolo*. **Pietro Longhi** (1702–85), *Presentation*; **Batoni** (1708–84), *Portrait of Charles John Crowle*; **Giovanni Battista Lampi**, *Count Stanislas Felix Potocki and his sons*.

Perhaps the greatest painter of the 18C, **Giambattista Tiepolo** (1696–1770), was the last in the line of fresco artists and produced exuberant yet delicate work: *The Last Supper*. His son and assistant, **Giandomenico Tiepolo** (1727–1804) painted *Carnival Scene*, and *The Charlatan* and *The Tooth Puller*.

Graphic Arts

The Department of Graphic Arts has been entirely reorganised and divided between the departments of paintings according to the appropriate schools where the works will be exhibited, in rotation. Therefore, drawings and engravings of the French School (**SULLY** Second floor), Northern Schools (**RICHELIEU** Second Floor), Italian School (**DENON** First floor, Mollien Wing Rooms 8–10). Due to be rehoused in Denon are the Consultation Room (by prior written appointment only; for information, ☎ 01 40 20 52 51); the Edmond de Rothschild Collection by appointment (☎ 01 40 20 50 31); and Documentation and Library (☎ 01 40 20 50 25 or 51 94). The reorganisation is due for completion in 1998.

The superb collections, comprise some 1200 miniatures, 40,000 engravings and 130,000 drawings. Although drawings had already existed in the Bibliothèque du Roi, it was not until 1671, when Louis XIV acquired the 5542 drawings (in addition to important paintings) collected by Everard Jabach (d. 1695) that the main nucleus of the Royal Collection was formed. To this were added drawings by Le Brun, Mignard and Coypel. By 1730 an inventory included some 8593 works, plus some 1300 drawings collected by the great connoisseur Pierre-Jean Mariette which were purchased in 1776. By 1792 some 11,000 drawings were listed, and in the following decades the figure almost doubled with the acquisition of the Saint Maurice au Comte d'Orsay collections, and the collections of the Dukes of Modena and of Filippo Baldinucci.

The Codex Vallardi (including a number of drawings by Pisanello) was acquired in 1856 and Jacopo Bellini's sketchbook in 1884. The collection was further enriched by a number of important donations in succeeding years.

Among the approximately **200 pastel portraits** are: Leonardo da Vinci, *Isabella d'Este, Duchess of Mantua*; Charles le Brun (1619–90), *Three portraits of Louis XIV*; several by Robert Nanteuil (c 1623–78); Joseph Vivien (1657–1734), the sculptor François Girardon, and the architect Robert de Cotte. Rosalba Carriera (1657–1757), who did much to popularise the technique in France, *Young girl with a monkey* (the model may have been the daughter of financier John Law); Maurice-Quentin Delatour (1704–88), Hermann-Maurice, Comte de Saxe, Philibert Orry, Jacques Dimont, and the Marquise de Pompadour; Perronneau, Abraham van Robais, The engraver Laurent Cars; Chardin, *His second wife, Self-portraits*, with spectacles, with a green eye-shade, and at his easel.

Greek, Etruscan and Roman Antiquities

This department encompasses all types of antique art from the origins of Hellenism to the last days of the Roman Empire. Its layout has, in part, been revised and extended in two directions, into rooms in **SULLY** first floor previously occupied by Egyptian Antiquities, and into new space in **DENON** entresol. The circuit is in chronological order, starting in Galerie Daru (DENON entresol), and on DENON ground floor, Galerie Borghese, and then continues onto SULLY ground floor and first floor.

From Hall Napoléon, the Denon escalator brings you to DENON entresol. On the left you find the entrance to ***Room 1* Galerie Daru**, the start of the visit. It contains objects illustrating Pre-Hellenic civilisations from the 3rd to the 1st millennium BC such as: pithoi from Knossos (Crete; 1700–1600 BC) and from Thera and Rhodes (14C BC); marble idols from the Cyclades (2500–2000 BC); terracotta and bronze figurines and painted ceramics (Minoan) from Crete (14C–12C BC); a large crater depicting the combat of Hercules and Antaeus; and funerary objects.

This gallery also contains **Archaic Greek Art** from the 10C to beginning of the 5C BC. These include the *Dame d'Auxerre* (c 630 BC), of Cretan origin (part of a collection near Auxerre) a small, compact figure with her hand on her chest, and an Egyptian style wig; the elegant and delicately modelled *Koré of Samos* (c 570–550 BC), one of the oldest and best authenticated works of island sculpture, inscribed 'Cheramues'; the *Rampin Head* (6C BC), a finely modelled piece which was originally part of the statue of a horseman; bas-reliefs from the architrave of the Temple of Assos (near Troy, Turkey) representing *Hercules battling against the Triton*, a banquet, a procession of animals and centaurs; the upper part of the stela, *Exaltation of the Flower*; the torso of Apollo (Miletus, Turkey; 5C BC).

From the entrance to the Galerie Daru take the escalator on the left to the **Salle du Manège, *Room A*** (ground floor) built by Lefuel (1855–57) as the riding school of the stable complex of Napoléon III's new Louvre. It was taken over by the museum in 1879, when it took its present name and still has part of its original decor of 1861—note the stone capitals carved with animals and hunting attributes. This is now used to display coloured marbles such as *Old Fisherman*, *Seneca Dying* and *Romulus and Remus fed by the Wolf*; also items from the Borghese collection, and two huge Albuni basins. From here you move into the DENON Vestibule (off which leads Salle Michel-Ange to the west: Italian Sculptures).

On DENON ground floor to the east of the Vestibule is **Galerie Borghese, Room B**, with antique sculptures from royal and other major historic collections including the *Borghese Crater*, the *Borghese Gladiator* (now completely restored), the late Hellenistic *Borghese Warrior*, signed on the tree-trunk by Agasias (c 100 BC), found at Anzio, Italy, in the 17C, and the reliefs from the temple of Zeus at Olympia (460 BC).

Cross the rotunda (Room 5) on SULLY ground floor, to Greek antiquities, **Rooms 6–17**. The **Corridor of Pan and Parthenon, Apollo, Pallas Athena and Praxiteles Rooms** contain originals and antique replicas: fragments of the east frieze of the *Parthenon at Athens* (5C BC; the greater part of the frieze, which represents the Panathenaic procession, is in the British Museum); the *Laborde Head*, from the pediments of the Parthenon. The **Venus de Milo** found in five fragments by a peasant in 1820 on the island of Melos in the Greek archipelago and now regarded as a 2C BC copy after a 4C BC original. The so-called *Kaufmann Head*, and *Apollo Sauroktonos* (about to kill a lizard), both after Praxiteles; *Athena* (Minerva) *with a Necklace*, copy of the Athena Parthenos of Phidias (438 BC); the *Aphrodite of Cnidos*; and the *Venus of Arles*.

The very fine **Salle des Cariatides, Room 17**, SULLY ground floor, the oldest surviving room in the palace, was built by Pierre Lescot for Henri II, who commissioned Jean Goujon to execute the caryatids supporting the gallery at the far end. Other decoration and the chimneypiece at the near end are by Percier and Fontaine (c 1806). It contains antique replicas of works from the 4C BC to the Hellenistic period (3C–1C BC) by Lysippe: *Hermes fastening his sandal*, and *The Alexander Azara; Artemis, the Huntress*, known as the *Diana of Versailles*, acquired from Rome by François I, is after an original reputedly by Leochares. Among several Aphrodites is *Aphrodite Crouching*, from Vienne.

Etruscan and Roman antiquities are displayed on DENON ground floor, **Rooms 18–30**. Among Etruscan items of great interest are five terracotta plaques from Cerveteri, Italy, (c 530 BC); the remarkable **terracotta sarcophagus** (also discovered at Cerveteri, by Campana, in 1850), depicting the lifelike figures of a man and his wife reclining on a funeral couch, as if alive and conversing. The woman wears a cap (tutulus) and a small gorget; the man, bare-footed, is draped. Further examples of Etruscan antiquities include cinerary urns from Chiusi, bronze vessels and figurines, mirrors, jewellery and ceramics.

DENON ground floor. **Rooms 22–26** show Roman portraits and reliefs, and busts, among which those of Agrippa (63–62 BC) and Livia (58–29 BC), in black basalt, are outstanding; also frescos, mosaics, cameos, sarcophagi.

On the floor of **Room 31**, of the Cour du Sphinx, with a façade by Le Vau, is a huge mosaic of *The Seasons* (c AD 325) from a villa near Antioch. On the walls, a frieze from the temple of Artemis at Magnesia on the Meander, depicting a battle between Greeks and Amazons (2C BC); also the god *Tiber*, a colossal piece found in the 16C.

Take the monumental Escalier Daru at the top of which stands the **Victory of Samothrace** or Winged Victory. This imposing statue of Parian marble, found in 1863, originally stood on a terrace overlooking the Cabeiri sanctuary on the island of Samothrace in the Aegean. The figure stands at the prow of a galley with wings spread, the draperies of her tunic clinging as if flattened by the wind. Further excavations in 1950 led to the discovery of the mutilated right hand (in a case nearby) which was probably held high to announce a naval victory, and established the probable date of the statue as c 190 BC. The breast and left wing are of plaster.

On SULLY first floor, **Room 34**, the **Grand Cabinet du Roi Louis XIV**, built by Le Vau c 1660 is dedicated to some 100 pieces of Greek and Roman glass. Never previously exhibited, these include bottles in a variety of forms and colours, objects for the table and containers, and demonstrates the various techniques used. **Room 33, Salle Henri II,** is devoted to silverwork which includes the **Treasure of Boscoreale**, a collection of superbly decorated silver objects discovered in 1895 in a fine state of preservation in a villa overwhelmed by the eruption of Vesuvius in AD 79; two silver masks from the Gallo-Roman Treasure of N.-D. d'Allençon; the silver *Treasure of Graincourt-lès-Havrincourt*; and jewellery and goldsmiths' work from all periods and regions.

Greek and Roman bronzes, in a new presentation, are in **Room 32**, the **Salle des Bronzes**, and include jewellery, arms and utensils arranged in chronological and geographical groups. Outstanding among them are Archaic Greek Art: a minotaur; statuette of Athene; a warrior; and Silenus dancing (all 6C BC); also Pan and his Syrinx. There are mirrors, including some in their boxes decorated with scenes in relief. Classical Greek statuettes (5C BC): group of Lycurgus and the Maenads; a stag; Hercules fighting; Zeus; Athlete's head, said to have been found at Benevento, Italy, probably from Herculanum 1C BC. Roman Gaul: Statuettes and busts: note eyes; bull; boar; a cock found at Lyon, and the bronze and silver plated Fortuna, first quarter of 3C. Also on display are a winged helmet encircled by a gold crown; gladiator's armour; the *Apollo of Piombino*, a 1C BC bronze figure, with copper encrustations—lips and nipples—which was retrieved from the sea near Piombino, Italy.

Rooms 35–38, Salles Charles X, are three rooms devoted to terracotta figurines, which include objects from Tanagra.

Rooms 44–47, on the same floor, incorporate five chronological and one thematic room (plus three study rooms), for the display of the superlative collection of Antique Pottery from the 10C BC to the 4C BC. Among these are examples of the Geometric style; Attic vases found in the Dipylon cemetery (c 800 BC); pottery from the Greek islands; vessels in the orientalising style; pottery from Corinth; Tyrrhenian amphorae, kraters and other vessels; black-figure Attic ceramics; vases in the Attic style, including both black and red figures; coloured terracottas; Attic red-figure pottery (c 500 BC) including a kylix on which are Eros and Memnon, and an amphora showing Croesus on a Pyre; figurines of the Hellenistic period, especially from Myrina; and antique glassware.

Egyptian Antiquities
The first curator of the Egyptian Antiquities department was Jean-François Champollion (1790–1832), who in 1826 acquired the collection of Henry Salt (1780–1827), and further collections have been added. This richly endowed

department is in three sections: Pharaonic, Roman and Christian (Coptic) Egypt. The Pharaonic section, in **Sully**, is made up of a series of thematic presentations on the ground floor, and a suite of rooms arranged chronologically covering 3000 years of Egyptian art on the first floor. The sections devoted to Roman and Coptic Egypt are in **Denon**. Begin the visit by taking the Sully escalators from Hall Napoléon and cross the Medieval Louvre to arrive opposite the large sphinx in the Crypt of the Sphinx.

Pharaonic Egypt

In the **crypt, *room 1***, is the *Large Sphinx* of great beauty carved from polished red granite. Its date remains uncertain, but the oldest inscription on it goes back to the Middle Kingdom, showing traces of the name of Amenmhat II, 1898–1866 BC. Either side are two bas-reliefs representing *Ramesses II in Worship* before the largest sphinx of all, found in front of the pyramids of Giza. Take the staircase on the left to ***room 2*** on the ground floor of the south wing of the Cour Carrée (or the escalator to the left of the Crypt). A large *Statue of Nakhthorheb*, an important figure of the 26th Dynasty, marks the entrance to the department. The circuit through Rooms 3–10 follows the south side of the Cour Carrée.

Room 3*: the Nile**, is the first of the series of thematic presentations and introduces Egypt through its river, evoked by a long display cabinet which contains models of Boats of the Middle Kingdom, and figurines of fish, crocodiles, hippotamii, and frogs from all periods. The limestone *Akhethetep mastaba* (tomb), ***room 4, found at Sakkara, is decorated with vivid scenes in bas-relief of the life of a dignitary in his rural domaine the highlight of which is the depiction of the master's meal, enlivened with music and dancing. Opposite this materialistic scene of the Old Kingdom is a representation of a chapel of the New Kingdom: paintings of the *Tomb of Ounsou*. These introduce the rest of the exhibits on the theme of Agriculture: tools, papyrus accounts and legal documents, and scale models.

Part of ***room 5*** is concerned with **cattle breeding, hunting and fishing**. Food is the other theme, centred around the Ideal Menu for the Dead, sculpted on the walls of a tomb of the Old Kingdom complete with the names of the delicacies. The displays in ***room 6*** revolve around **writing and scribes**. The principles and evolution of writing can be seen, together with the tools of the scribes and their patrons. There is also a display of weights and measures.

Room 7 addresses the **arts and crafts** through the materials and techniques used: wood, stone, ceramics and metal. Among the exhibits are: the *Stela of the Chief of Craftsmen*, which recalls the pride of these men; the fine bronze statue, arms extended, of the *Horus, the Falcon-God, Making a libation*, was once covered in precious metals.

Room 8 is dedicated to **dwellings and furnishings**, with domestic objects found in tombs: chairs, baskets, brooms and floor coverings, and amphorae are used to evoke a wine cellar. ***Room 9*** contains **objects of adornment**, with beautiful examples of jewellery made of combinations of precious stones, faïence and metal. The rarest in the collection are: gold Necklace of pendant Fishes; Necklace of Pinedjem I, of gold and lapis lazuli; and the Ring of Horemheb. A high point in the collection are the cosmetic objects, particularly the superb Spoons for Cosmetic Creams carved in wood, ivory and faience.

Musical instruments, including the harp, lyre, tamborine, sistrum and castanettes, are exhibited in *room 10*, together with games such as draughts. This brings you to the south-east angle of the Cour Carrée.

Room 11 represents the **Forecourt of the Temple** and the **Alley of the Sphinxes**. From the Serapeum come six limestone sphinxes evoking the long processional alleys called dromos. Four large cynocephali (baboons) in red granite, adoring the rising sun, formerly decorated the base of the Obelisk (see Ch. 13, p 133), at the entrance of the Temple of Luxor.

> The grand staircase in the angle pavilion leads to the first floor and to room 27 of the Egyptian Department, the start of the chronological presentation. If you wish to see the whole of the collection do not, therefore, take this staircase. There is an escalator near room 28.

The Temple, *room 12*, presents large sculptures and pieces of architecture to evoke a temple. The **first court**, bordered by a portico of fine columns of pink Granite with palm-leaf capitals (5th Dynasty); statues of deities including *Sekhmet*, the lion-headed goddess; colossal statues of the kings and statues of privileged individuals: very beautiful *Statue of Ouahibre*. In the **second court** are the great deeds of the Pharaohs: the Wall of the Annales of King Thutmosis II; festivals: bas-relief of the *Jubilee of Osoron II*. This brings you to the heart of the temple: around the naos or chapel sheltering the statue of the god are the chapels of the 'invited' gods. Also here are the *Naos of the reign of Amasis* in pink granite; a processional boat; and the Low-relief of the *King Osorkon I Offering an image of the Goddess Mat*.

Room 12a contains **objects from the Chapels**. The large circular sandstone zodiac, showing the sky, planets and constellations in 50 BC, was the ceiling of the chapel on the roof of the temple of Hathor at Dendera. A large stela dedicated by Queen Hatschepsut to her father *Thothmes I* in her temple of Deir el-Bahari. The walls of a chapel from Karnak, called the Room of the Ancestors, with a list of kings preceding Thutmosis III, is a major document of Egyptian history.

From here, at the end of the Galerie Henri IV, a staircase descends to the **Crypt of Osiris** and **Royal Tomb**, **room 13** (or elevator at the end of the gallery on the left). These two themes are linked as deceased kings were revered as gods, just as the Egyptians believed that Osiris had reigned in the world before becoming sovereign of the dead. The descent towards the magnificent *Sarcophagus of Ramesses III* in pink granite gives a good idea of the hypogeum of the Valley of the Kings. On the walls is the noctural voyage of the sun which reappears triumphant every morning. The same scenes are found again on the massive *Sarcophagus of Djedhor* in black stone. The cult of *Osiris* is represented by the statue in wood, framed by his two faithful companions, Isis and Nephthys.

Room 14 has a splendid display of **wooden mummy cases**; also **stone sarcophagi** like the magnificent limestone *Sarcophagus of Abu-Roash* (Old Kingdom) in the palace-façade style, and the sarcophagus brought from Djedhor by Champollion. Behind the staircase is the small *room 15*, with a display of **embalming and burial**. This contains a *Mummy* of the Ptolemaic period, with an intricately painted 'cartonnage' (moulded linen and plaster) protection. Return via room 14.

Room 16, tombs, has displays containing **objects from burial chambers** of four different periods: Old Kingdom: *Tomb of Isi* at Edfou; Middle Kingdom: *Tomb of Nakhiti* at Assiout; New Kingdom: *Tomb of Gournet Mourrai*; and Third Intermediate Period, from Karnak. These show the evolution in funerary customs over 1000 years.

From the end of room 15, it is possible to reach the long gallery, Galerie de Delphes. ***Room 17***, **funerary equipment**. The full extent, more than 25m, of the papyrus *Book of the Dead of Hornedjitef*, is exhibited unrolled.

Room 18, **magic**, in relation to Egyptian deities which include the small stela of *Honus standing on a crocodile*, figurines of sorcery and execrable texts, and the fearful statue of *Bes*, God of Healing, found at the Serapeum. This leads on to **room 19**, **animals, sacred and mummified**, and the **Serapeum of Memphis**, animals in a long display representing Egyptian gods: the Goose of Amon, the Bull of Montou, Bastet, the cat-faced goddess of Bubastis; plus stelae and bas-reliefs of other divine animals, such as the *Crocodile of Sobek*. There is also an astonishing display of mummified animals, and the magnificent *Statue of the Bull Apis*.

Take the north stairs (or lift) to the first floor. A chronological display, divided into panels representing 1000 years each, introduces the following rooms which cover some 3000 years of Egyptian history and art.

Room 20, **the period of Nagada**, c 4000–3100 BC, the end of the Predynastic era. The highlight of this display is a Knife from Gebel-el-Arak with a carved handle, representing both the beginnings of relief sculpture and an historic event in the depiction of a battle; also, finely sculpted schist palettes.

Room 21. **Thinite Period** (c 3100–2700 BC). *Stela of King Zet Ouadji*, known as the Serpent King, sums up the two great phenomena of this period: the unification of Egypt under a single crown, and the birth of writing. The name of the king is written with the hieroglyphic of the serpent. The art of low-relief was perfected and luxury objects were made in ivory, as were splendid vases in coloured stone.

Room 22. **Old Kingdom** (c 2700–2200 BC), the period of the great pyramids: the development of the personality of the king and his funerary monument reaches its peak in the 3rd Dynasty. Finds from the pyramid of Didoufri, son of Cheops, include a small highly coloured limestone figure of a scribe seated cross-legged, known as the *Scribe accroupi*, with eyes of white quartz and rock crystal; a red quartzite head of *King Didoufri*. The painted stone *Stela of Nefertiabet*, seated before a table with a remarkable array of offerings.

Room 23, **the Middle Kingdom** (c 2033–1710 BC), the classical period for the Egyptians, the time of the great King Sesostris. On the right is the elegant Libation Carrier. Two large statues of contemporaries of Sesostris in wood are the *Chancellor Nakhti*, one of the largest wooden funerary effigies known of this period, and of the *Governor of Hapydjefai* province. In the second half of the room are notable Portrait statues of *Sesostris III* and of his son, *Amenemhat III*. The limestone Lintel from Medamoud represents the king making an offering of bread to the hawkheaded god Montou.

A small corridor contains the most beautiful stelae of this period.

Room 24 contains portraits of the dignitaries of the glorious period of the **New Kingdom** (c 1550–1353 BC) and the various objects on display show a change in style from the rigid archaism of the statue of Prince Iahmes to the sensual portraits of the *King Amenophis III* or *Queen Tiy*. Note the bust of *King Tuthmosis IV*, the Gold Dish given by Tuthmosis III to General Dejehuty and the life-size statues of *Seny Nefer* and his wife *Hatchepsut*.

Room 25 is devoted to the **New Kingdom at the time of Akhenaton and Nefertiti** (c 1353–1337 BC). The famous heretic *Amenophis IV* only reigned about 15 years, his memory later being held in loathing by the Egyptians. Nevertheless, from his time come examples of outstanding art, such as the Colossal Statue in which the stylistic revolution is fully apparent. The display cases contain some of the most beautiful pieces in the Louvre: a torso, probably of *Queen Nefertiti*, in red quartzite; limestone *Head of the Princess*, young yet haughty; and a statuette of *The Young King with his Wife Nefertiti* holding each other by the hand.

Room 26, the **New Kingdom around the time of Tutankhamun** (c 1337–1295 BC). In the first part of the room, the 'Salt' Head probably represents someone who lived during or just after the Amarna period. A very delicate Head in glass of two different blues also shows characteristics of this period. *Tutankhamun*, short-lived successor of Akhenaton, became famous in the 20C when his tomb was discovered almost intact.

You now arrive at the upper landing of the south staircase, dedicated to the civilisation of Ancient Nubia. To the west is the first room of the old Egyptian Museum created at the time of Champollion, in 1827.

Room 27. New Kingdom at the time of **Ramesses** and other **New Kingdom Pharaohs** (c 1295–1069 BC). There is a magnificent fragment of painted relief depicting *Sethi and the Goddess Hathor*. The *Stela des colliers* takes up the theme from El Amarna, the Distribution of rewards from the Window of the Royal Palace. One display is devoted to the son of Sethi I, Ramesses II, whose long reign saw much building. **Room 28**. **New Kingdom** (c 1295–1069 BC). The great gods are represented by a very fine statuette in stone of *Amon and his Wife Mout*; and lesser, by the small *Stela of the Goddess Qadech*. A wall display is devoted to the Serapeum of Memphis; and there are pectorals in gold inlaid with faience.

Room 29. **King-Priests of the Saite period** and the Persian domination (c 1069–404 BC). The finest Egyptian bronze, the statue of *Karomama 'Divine Worshipper of Amon'*, is sumptuously decorated with inlays of gold and silver. The golden jewel representing the Triade Osiris-Isis-Horus; statuette of a *Nude Woman* in ivory is another masterpiece. The painted wood *Stela of Taperet*, with two faces. There are also examples of the most beautiful statuary of the 26th Dynasty, such as the *Statuette of Iahmessaneith*.

Room 30. From the last Pharaohs of Egypt to Cleopatra (404–30 BC). A fine *Torso of Nectanebo I*, and a limestone *Statue of a Falcon protecting the King*. Hellenistic influences are seen in the clinging drapes on the body of the Goddess Isis. Local funerary customs maintained a strong hold, as seen in the *Coffin of Tacheretpaankh* in Gilded Cartonnage, the abundant decorations recalling the mural reliefs of the large temples rebuilt at this time.

This room ends the visit to the Department of Egyptian Antiquities. The following room, the Salle des Colonnes, is the meeting point between the Galerie Campana (Greek vases) and the Gallery of Greek terracottas, and a rest area.

Further on, a lift links this sector to French Paintings (2nd floor) or to Greek Sculptures (ground floor). Across the Salle des Caryatides is a staircase descending to the Medieval Louvre.

Egyptian Antiquities of the Roman Period and the early Christian Period (Coptic Art) is part of a section dealing with late Antiquity in the Eastern Mediterranean, beneath and around the Cour Visconti in DENON entresol. From the Hall Napoléon, take the DENON escalators to the ground floor, and cross an antechamber with a brief introduction to the civilisations of late Antiquity in the eastern Mediterrannean, which brings you to a room devoted to Funerary Objects in Egypt during the Roman period (1C–4C AD).

The theme is set by a painted shroud opposite the entrance, showing the deceased between Anubis and his mummy deified in Osiris. The coffin of Chenptah, the group of Ouahpare, and a funerary papyrus, illustrate the late Ptolemaic period. The Mummy of Padijmenemipet, of the Soter family, a member of which was Archon of Thebes during the reign of Trajan (98–117 AD), is accompanied by his coffin decorated with a zodiac.

Chronological displays include Portraits painted on Wood with wax or tempera, of Roman origin; and the Plastron-masks in plaster, wood or fabric, stuccoed and painted in the ancient Egyptian tradition, all produced during the same period.

The Coffin of Chelidona was brought to France by Champollion: the cover is decorated with symbols of air and water, necessary for the survival of the deceased. A large Shroud (3C–4C AD) shows the deceased making a journey by boat to the underworld. Finally, the objects which accompany the deceased to the tomb: funerary statues, stelae, figurines and offerings to assure life after death.

Coptic Art is presented in the eastern wing of Cour Visconti on DENON ground floor. Coptic art denotes Egyptian art from the 3C AD onwards. It appeared in the pagan environment strongly influenced by Roman Egyptian art and among the Christian community, in particular in relation to the development of monasticism. After the Arab conquest in the mid-7C it was enriched with developing aspects of Muslim art. The most recent works in the Coptic collection at the Louvre date from the 14C. The 580 works showing diffferent aspects of this art are presented both chronologically and thematically.

The emergence of Coptic art which combined Roman and Pharaonic elements is demonstrated in the Horus Horseman. The Shawl of Sabine, slightly more recent, retains themes from pagan mythology associated with a decor of the Nile region. Coptic art of the 5C–8C, such as beautiful weavings and objects from daily life, is exhibited alongside thematic and iconographic displays of Christian imagery, writing and the Coptic language, and magic. Illustrations of the influence on Coptic art of the Islamic domination of Egypt include a very fine Censer in bronze, surmounted by an eagle clasping a serpent; textiles woven in iridescent colours and decorative objects in bone, wood, metal and glass.

At the end of the Coptic section is the **Salle de Bawit**, installed in the former amphitheatre of the Ecole du Louvre, from where you look down on a display centred around a reconstruction of part of the monastery church of Bawit. This monastery, founded in the 4C and abandoned in the 12C, was excavated by French archaeologists at the beginning of this century. In 1903 Egypt made France the generous gift of part of the finds—paintings, sculptures, fragments of architecture, archaeological documents. A section of the monastery has been reconstructed here, its decor of wood and limestone placed on a concrete statue.

In 1998 a model of the Bawit monastery will be installed in the gallery.

Oriental Antiquities and Islamic Art

This department, containing objects from the Middle East apart from Egypt, was inaugurated in 1847 and has benefited from its move into larger galleries. The Department is divided between Oriental Antiquities: Mesopotamian and Iranian, on RICHELIEU and SULLY ground floor; these lead on to the collections from the Levant, SULLY ground floor. Islamic Art is displayed on RICHELIEU entresol. (Antiquities from the Far East may be seen in the Musée Guimet, Ch. 27, p 264.)

From Hall Napoléon, take the Richelieu Escalator to the ground floor. The visit starts in **rooms 1a, 1b, 1c** on the south of Cour Puget with objects remarkable for both their age and beauty, mainly from the ancient city states of Mesopotamia: Tello and Mari, dating from before 3000 BC.

Room 1a. **Archaic Mesopotamia, Sumerian Culture** (3900–2900 BC): follows the development of civilisation in Mesopotamia, from neolithic village origins to the Sumerians' primitive urban culture towards the end of the 4th millennium. Most finds from the periods come from Tello, formerly Girsu (Iraq). Among remarkable small objects are: fragment of a Vessel from Qul'at Jarmo, Kurdistan (c 7500 BC), fragments of Obeid period Painted Ceramics (6th–4th millennia) and Primitive Figurines from Tello.

Early urban culture in Sumer (c 3500–2900 BC) marked the beginnings of social hierarchy and architectural activity, towards the end of which writing was invented. The Cylinder of Uruk (c 3100 BC) is one of the earliest examples of a seal-cylinder used to 'sign' documents. The Jemdat-Nasr period (3100–2900 BC) is represented by vessels in marble or alabaster.

During the early dynastic period (c 2900–2340 BC), writing spread and historic inscriptions appeared: see cabinet 3 concerning hieroglyphics. Among other exhibits are: Foundation Nails which symbolically fixed a building to the ground and repelled evil spirits; bas-reliefs of a plumed figure, Mace of King Mesilim (c 2750 BC) found at Tello and of Ur-Nanshe, prince of Lagash, carrying a basket of bricks on his head for the foundation ceremony; Silver Vase with a frieze of incised animals and the Lagash 'crest', consecrated by Entemena, Prince of Lagash; the Cone of Entemena in terracotta, carved all round with hieroglyphics; bronze Bull's Head.

The first Lagash dynasty, founded c 2500 BC by Ur-Nanshe, is represented on a Large Perforated Relief. The grandson of Ur-Nanshe is commemorated in one of the oldest known historical documents, the magnificent limestone *Stela of the Vultures*, c 2450 BC (restored), from Tello. Carved on both faces, it records the victory of Eannatum, King of Lagash.

Room 1b. The expansion of Mesopotamian culture spread in particular to Mari, on the modern Iraq-Syria border. Important excavations at the temple of the goddess Ishtar (c 2500 BC), produced an alabaster statue of the Intendant of Mari, *Ebih-II*, and mother-of-pearl silhouettes of the *Standard of Mari*. The small **Room 1c**, contains sculptures and precious objects of the archaic dynasties of Sumer (c 2900–2340 BC) including a Votive Relief representing musicians, the Statuette of Ginak, and gold pendants.

Room 2 open to the east side of Cour Puget, contains larger exhibits from Mesopotamia (c 2340–2000 BC), Empire of Akkad, and the last Sumerian dynasties of Gudea and of Ur: Art of the Akkadian period is represented by objects from Susa (the capital, Akkad never having been found), where they were taken in the 12C BC, and from Tello. The glory of the King and empire is idealised in royal diorite monuments: *Stela of Sargon, Stelae of Victory; Statues of King Manishtusu* (seated and standing), *Obelisk of Manishtusu*. The most beautiful is the *Stela of the Victorious Naram-Sin*, king of Akkad, grandson of Manishtusu. In cabinet (2) Judicial documents in Akkadian, which took over for a while from Sumerian as the official language. Note the fine quality of workmanship in the display (1) of seal-cylinders carved in marble, chlorite, and porphyry, along with their 'print-outs' in clay.

The brilliant second **Dynasty of Lagash** (2150–2100 BC) prince, Gudea, represented by nine diorite statues in this room, one of which shows him holding a vase gushing with life-giving waters; also large Clay Cylinders recording, in cuneiform, Gudea's achievements as a builder; fascinating smaller objects include the Goblet belonging to Gudea, decorated with serpents and winged dragons with scorpion tails; alabaster *Statuette of Ur-Ningirsu*, son of Gudea; *Woman with a Scarf*, from Girsu; terracotta Figurines (one with geese); objects concerning the construction of a temple, such as terracotta Foundation Nails; and furnishings from temples and tombs; late cuneiform documents.

Room 3. **Mesopotamia** (2000–1000 BC), Amorite Kingdom and first Babylonian Dynasty from the sites of Larsa Eshnunna, Mari and Babylon: from Eshunna, *statue of a Bull-headed man*. From Larsa, Vase of Ishtar with engraved design.

The ruins of the **Amorite Palace of the King Zimri-Lim, Mari**, revealed exceptional installations including two mural paintings—*Ishtar Investing the King with Regal Powers* and a *Sacrificial Scene*; a Bronze Lion from the temple of Dagan; *Statue of Ishtar*. Terracotta moulds from the palace kitchens. Also to see are models of the ruins and a reconstruction of the Palace. From the Temple of Dagan, a (headless) *Statuette of Idi Ilum, Prince of Mari*; the Disk of Ladun-Lim, the head of a foundation nail.

The **first Babylonian Empire** developed under the Hammurabi, (1792–1750 BC) starting a brilliant period: the freestanding *Codex of Hammurabi*, carved in black basalt, 1792–1750 BC, covered with closely written text, is one of the earliest compilations of laws. The 282 laws embrace practically every aspect of Babylonian life of c 1800 BC. Nearby are the *Royal Head*; bronze, *Worshipper at Larsa*, on bended knee, the face and hands covered in gold leaf; bronze group of *Three Rampant Ibex*, with horns interlaced.

After the death of Hammurabi, Babylon declined, and the Kassites assumed power: texts of charters of donations were engraved on huge Kudurrus or boundary-stones, with symbolic images of gods.

Babylon's brilliance revived in the **neo-Babylonian Empire**, whose greatest king was Nebuchadnezzar II (605–562 BC), famous for capturing Jerusalem and deporting the Jews, as well as being a great builder: the coloured glazed-brick frieze, Lion Passant, decorated a processional route between temples; the *Esagil Tablet*, from the great temple of Marduk; *Astrological Calender* of Uruk; series of alabaster *Statuettes of Female Nudes* reveal the influence of Hellenic culture (Babylon was conquered in 331 BC by Alexander the Great).

Turn right out of room 3 to room 4 for the Cour Khorsabad (see below).

***Room 5.* Anatolian, Cappadocian and Hittite civilisations** (origins to 1000 BC): small *Statuette of Female Nude* (mid-6th millennium BC) is considered among the first figurative symbols of a primitive fertility cult; early bronze age (3rd millennium) objects include idols and vases from the necropolis of Yortan, Votive Horns, a Musical Rattle, Chariot Terrets and Painted ceramics. The period of Assyrian colonies in Cappadocia, c 2000 BC; Cappadocian Tablets, archives in cuneiform script of business negotiations.

The Hittite Empire became in the 14C and 13C BC one of the great powers of the Near East, rivalling Egypt and the Mittani Empire: Figurines in bronze; gold Pendant in the form of a God; Bronze casket (8C–7C).

***Rooms 4 and 6.* Assyria: Cour Khorsabad**, at the east end of the ground floor of Richelieu contains the celebrated **reliefs from the great Assyrian palace of Khorsabad**. The Assyrian Empire reached its peak between the 9C and 7 C BC, and its rulers built great palaces to exalt their achievements.

The impressive presentation against the walls of the courtyard is designed to evoke the original massive scale of the Palace of Dur-Sharrukin, Sargon II's fortress (Khorsabad). The five huge *Winged Bulls* with human heads, or lamassu, which stood at the entrances to protect the palace from evil spirits. Three of these majestic sculptures, which have five feet, so that viewed from the front they are in repose and from the side they appear in motion, are original, and one a 19C copy. The last, a plaster cast from the original in Chicago, has its head turned towards the reliefs associated with it of Two Gigantic Heros Taming a Lion. Other reliefs (4m high), forms of official propaganda, protected and deco-rated the base of the mud-brick walls: Bearers of the King's Furnishings, and the Frieze of the Transportation of Cedar Wood, from Lebanon by land and by sea. Among smaller items are tablets in copper, gold, and silver recording the foun-dation of the Palace of Khorsabad.

Artefacts which have survived from the provincial palaces (***room 6***): Til Barsip (present Tell Ahmar, Northern Syria) rare Mural Paintings one featuring a Blue Goat; an exceptional collection of carved ivories from Arslan Tash. Kalhu (Nimrud), chosen by Assurbanipal II as his capital: Reliefs from the throne room in gypseous alabaster, c 865 BC, include a *Genie with a Bird's head* and *Scorpion's tail*; Reliefs from the palace of Ashur at Nineveh (668–627 BC).

The neo-Assyrian period (9C–7C BC) is represented by bronze Door Plaques from Imgur-Enlil (Balawat); the Annales of Tukulti-Ninurta II; figurine of the Assyrian demon Pazuzu.

Iran and the Levant

The geographic subdivision of exhibits groups from **Iran**, from the origins to the 2nd millennium, in Rooms 7–10, and the 1st millennium in Rooms 11–16. The **Countries of the Levant**—countries on the Mediterranean coast of Asia: Syria, Lebanon, Israel and Cyprus, from the origins to the end of the 2nd millennium BC, are in Rooms A, B, C, D on the west of SULLY. The continuation of exhibits from the Levant (Syria, Lebanon, Israel, Jordan and Turkey) is in Rooms 17–21 on the north of SULLY.

Room 7. **Ancient Iran** (up to the 4th millennium BC). Susa, capital of the western part, was founded c 4200 BC. Three main artistic periods produced varied artefacts: Susa I (4200–3800 BC): Painted Ceramics; Susa II or the period of Uruk (3800–3100 BC) first attempts at metallurgy; Susa III (3100–2800 BC) birth of proto-Elamite writing.

Room 8. Susa (3rd millennium): Vase '*à la cachette*', with treasure hidden inside it. **Room 9**. **Iran and Bactriana** (3rd–beginning 2nd millennia BC): the highlands of the plateau were invaded by Iranians. Bronze Arms and vessels from Luristan to the north of Susa (c 2600–1800 BC); objects from tombs at Tepe Giyan. Bactriana (Afghanistan) produced a wide range of objects, such as the remarkable statue of the *Lady of Bactriana* (c 1800 BC); bronze Wheel Band.

Room 10. **Iran at the Middle-Elamite period** (c 1500–1100 BC): Royal Monuments of the reign of King Untash-Napirisha; headless bronze *Statue of Queen Napir Asu*, wife of King Untash-Napirisha, a considerable work weighing 1750 kg; King Shutruk Nahhunte (12C BC) and his descendants were warrior kings and great builders, responsible for the Acropolis of Susa from which are several Architectural Elements: Votive tray in bronze representing cult scenes of serpents and divinities; furnishings from temples, such as the Sit Shamshi, with a ritual scene celebrating the sunrise; Moulded Brick Panel with Goddesses and Man-bull protecting a Palm tree.

Rooms A, B, C, D. The Countries of the Levant. **Room A**. **Cyprus** (origins to the Iron Age): its important seams of copper and its connections with the Hellenic world, gave rise to a characteristic style. Chalcolithic *Statuette of a Seated Female* (4th millennium); other delightful models, including *Boat with Figures* (end 3rd millennium); *Statuette of a Seated God* from Enkomi; undeciphered Tablet in Cypro-Mycenean; late Bronze Age Luxury and Cult Objects.

Room B. **Coastal Syria, Ugarit and Byblos** (origins to Iron Age): Furnishings from Royal tombs and luxury items from Byblos; Ceramics from Ras Shamra (ancient Ugarit); Furnishings from the tombs of Minet el Beida; ivory Pyxis carved with a goddess and two ibex; Golden Cup from the Temple of Baal (c 1250–1150 BC); *Stela of the God Ba'al*. Phoenician sculptures and collections of objects; embossed gold peg, known as The Hunt, from Ras-Shamra; Bust of the *Pharaoh Osorkon* (924–895 BC) with a Phoenician dedication from the King of Byblos.

Room C. **Inland Syria** (origins to Iron Age), subjected to influences from Mesopotamia as seen from the seal-cylinders, copper statuettes and the use of cuneiform writing: *Idol with Eyes*, in terracotta (c 35,000 BC); Statue Menhir in basalt from Tell Braq (2000–1600 BC); furnishings from the Tomb of Til Barsip, from the Temple of Ninegal, Qatna, and from other temples; *Stela of Zakkus* commemorating the taking of the throne of Hamath by King Zakur; funerary stelae from Neirab or Tell Atis.

Room D. Palestine (7000 BC–1150 BC). Neolithic Plaster statue from Jericho; Ivories from Beersheba (Negev); Bronze Age Tomb Furnishings from Jericho, Lakish, Ay and Farah; an Ossuary in the form of a House; Israelite Dynasty period (1200–1150 BC), Model of a Sanctuary; *Stela of Shihan*; the Moabite Stone, or **Stela of Mesha**, King of Moab (842 BC), discovered in 1868 in a remote village east of the Dead Sea. The 34-line inscription, recording victories over the Israelites in the reigns of Omri, Ahab and Ahaziah, is one of the most important, if not the earliest, examples of alphabetic writing.

The last 11 Rooms, known as the **Sackler Wing**, on the north side of Sully, opened in mid-1997. Rooms 11–16 complete the circuit of Iranian art, from the 14C BC to the 1st millennium BC.

Room 11. 14C–6C BC, Iron Age Iran and neo-Elamite dynasties: Vase in the Form of a Bull in red terracotta and a decorative bronze plaque originally attached to horse bits. Rooms 12–15. 6C–4C BC, the Persian Achaemenid Empire: elements from the Palace of Darius I at Susan including the glazed brick *Frieze of Persian Archers*—the Immortals', and the *Frieze of Lions*. Rooms 16. 3C BC–7C AD, Parthian and Sassanian empires: Harp Player mosaic.

Rooms 17–21 continue the theme of the **Levant** (following on from rooms A, B, C, D), encompassing today's Syria, Lebanon, Israel, Jordan and Turkey, during the 1st millennium BC. Room 17, the Phoenician kingdoms, 8C–2C BC: numerous sarcophagi and funerary monuments from the royal necropolis of Sidon; sarcophagus in basalt of Eshmunazar II, King of Sidon, in Egyptian style; the *stela of Amrit* (7C/8C BC). Room 18. The Mediterranean world, Carthage and Punic North Africa, 8C–1C BC and the Phoenician expansion to the west (8C–2C BC): marble sarcophagus of a Priest; *stela Tophet of Constantine*; objects in glass.

Rooms 19, 20. Arabia Felix and the Arabian desert (7C–3C BC) notably the Yemen, the fringes of the Arabian peninsula; the caravan cities of Palmyra and Dura Europos: stelae in alabaster from Yemen including one with a human mask; the *Lintel of the Judgement of Paris* (2C BC) 3m long, from southern Syria.

Room 21. Cyprus, 9C–1C BC, a complex mixture of cultures. In the centre of the room the monumental *Vase of Amathonte* carved from a single piece of limestone (3.2m in diameter) used as a water reservoir for the sanctuary of the great goddess at the summit of the acropolis of Amathonte (4C BC). Different works demonstrate the diversity of cultures of Cyprus, such as the nude statuette of *Heracles*, and the enigmatic bust of a *Veiled Woman*.

Islamic Art

The new and very beautiful display of **Islamic Art**, in RICHELIEU entresol, to which 13 rooms have been dedicated, is shown in chronlogical order, from the first centuries of the Hegira (622) to modern times. The works represented come from Muslim territories extending from Spain to India, with the exception of North Africa (see Musée des Arts Africains and Oceaniens). Despite conceived ideas to the contrary, there are several representations of humans and animals.

Rooms A and B. **Information and introduction to the Muslim World**; and an explanatory survey of Architecture in Islamic countries.

Room 1. **First Appearance of Islamic art** (7C–8C): Christian, Hellenistic and Sassanid (Persian) elements synthesised into an original style. Three-legged Perfume Burner in bronze; Blown glass Vase with Multiple Handles; stucco Panel with Leaves and Duck; an important series of small Decorated Glass Flasks and Recipients; and capitals influenced by Roman Antiquity.

Room 2. **The Abbassid World** (8C–10C). An imperial art derived from Graeco-Roman Sassanian traditions. The objects in this room come mainly from Iraq, but also from western Iran and Egypt: Dish '*au porte-étendard*' (standard-bearer), with stylised caricatures of figures typical of 10C lustre ceramics. Metallic lustre decoration was the creation of Iraqi potters in the 9C–10C. Wooden Panel with Stylised Birds: the style of sculpted decoration with a bevelled edge was developed in Egypt under the influence of Samarran art.

Room 3. **The Fatimids** (909–1171) and the Islamic West (10C–15C). The Fatimids developed a brilliant and refined culture and a varied, often picturesque iconography: Small flask in the form of a lion in rock crystal; gold Bracelet decorated with Musicians; Quadruped (Hare?) in cast bronze and engraved; Fragment of applied Ivory Ornament with Luth Player; wooden Plaquette with Dancer (11C–12C), from Egypt; Bowl Decorated with a Giraffe; Bowl with Rosace (12 C) from Syria.

Islamic West (8C–15C). Outstanding Pyxis (small box) carved in ivory in 968 for al-Mughira, son of the Calif Abd al-Rahman III (912–961); Peacock Ewer; Bronze lion, probably part of a small fountain.

Room 4. **Eastern Iran** (10C–12C). Dishes with Epigraphic Decor, reading: 'Science, its taste is bitter at the beginning, but at the end sweeter than honey'; 'good health' (to the owner); the famous Shroud of St Josse, from Khorasan, a large silk cloth (10C) decorated with elephants, camels and an inscription, brought to France after the first Crusade (1096–99) by Etienne de Blois, protector of the Abbey of St-Josse (Pas de Calais); Plate with a Scene of Labour.

Rooms 5 and 6. **Iran of the Seljuks** (11C–13C). The quality, diversity and quantity of production make this period a high spot in the history of ceramics in the Muslim Orient.

Room 5. Interesting Series of 'Provincial' ceramics decorated with champlevé and engraved slip; Large Basin with Lion design, Basin with Hare, and Plate with Donkey. This room has a display dedicated to the sciences: Celestial Sphere in Brass Inlaid with Silver (1144) is the oldest known of Arabic manufacture.

Room 6. has a fine Series of Ceramics manufactured in urban centres using new processes; Bowl with Falconer on Horseback; the Chandelier with Ducks is a technical virtuoso; Ewer with a Cock's Head, the outer surface pierced and decorated with a turquoise slip.

Room 7. Funerary Stelae and Sculpted Stones arranged to represent a small rural cemetery (9C–18C).

Room 8 and 9. **Egypt, Near East, Anatolia** (12C–13C), the **Ayyubids** (1071–1250) and the **Mamluks** (1250–1517). Objects from Anatolia, Jezirah and the Syro-Egyptian world, including the first examples of enamelled and gilded glass; pearlised Goblet; important collection of silver encrusted metal— chandeliers, bowls, vases; the Barberini Vase from the name of the Pope Urban VIII Barberini to whom this object was presented in the 17C.

One of the masterpieces of the Islamic collection (displayed separately), is the **Baptistère de Saint-Louis**, a hammered brass bowl, incised and inlaid with silver and gold (c 1300), first kept at the Sainte Chapelle of the Château of Vincennes, and placed in the Louvre in 1852. Collection of lamps from Mosques in enamelled and gilded glass; Collection of albarelles and spice jars, shapes developed later in the West; Basin with the name Hugues IV de Lusignan (1324–59), King of Cyprus, with an inscription in Arabic and in French.

Room 10. **Mongol Iran** (13C–14C). For the first time China, Iran and the West were in direct contact with each other: Dish with Gilded Fish with a pale green base reminiscent of Chinese celadon glaze; Panels with Stars and Crosses in lustreware (on the wall); note the Astrological motif of the Lion and the Sun which became an national emblem in Iran in the 19C.

Room 11. **Timurid, Safavid, Qajar Iran** (14C–20C) and **Mughal India** (16C–19C). This vast room (beneath Cour Khorsabad) evokes, among others, the Timurid Period (14C–15C) which took its name from its founder, a Turk known in the West as Tamerlane, a pitiless conqueror. To improve the status of his homeland, Transoxiana, he systematically deported the cultural elite of towns he conquered. His greatest descendant was his son, Shahruk (1407–47). The whole dynasty patronised the arts, and the early 15C in Iran is known as the Timurid Renaissance: Fine jade cup carved with floral scroll and a poetic inscription.

The **Safavid period** (1501–1736). In 1501, Shah Isma'il, after taking Azerbaïdjan, conquered Iran and led a dynasty which dominated the country until 1732. In a land open to traders, western influences began to penetrate local art: the large and precious **Mantes Carpet** (because it was once at the Church of Mantes) is decorated with animals and hunting scenes; carpet with animals; a rare kilim (tapestry in silk and silver thread) with storiated scenes. (The numerous rugs will be exhibited in rotation because of their fragility.) **Qajar Period** (1779–1924): in 1779 power passed to Qajars who moved the political centre of the empire to Teheran (from Isfahan). Even stronger European influences penetrated and, from the mid-century, in addition to miniatures, via lithography and photography, an important school of easel painting developed. Hence the rather surprising large oil portrait of the celebrated ruler, Fath Ali Shah Seated on the Peacock Throne, received as a gift by Napoléon I.

Mughal India (1526–1858). Among arms on display is Dagger with Horse's Head, and armoury known as Quatre Miroirs; Hookah (narghileh) in enamelled and gilded glass with a floral decor; Large Velour Carpet with a vegetal motif.

Room 12. **The Ottoman world** (14C–19C). The Louvre has many Ottoman ceramics and all the important stages of production from Iznik are represented, showing a widening palette from blue and white, through turquoise, leaf green, mauve, then greenish black, before perfecting the famous Iznik red. The motifs vary from arabesques to bunches of grapes of far-Eastern origin, indented and curved foliage, and floral decoration perfected in the design studios of Topkapi Palace: Large Dish, blue and white; the famous Peacock Dish; and Dish with Grapes; Spandrels with floral decor; Panel from the Mausoleum of Selim II.

Room 13. **Art of the Book**: this room exhibits (in rotation) examples of Arabic, Iranian and Mughal miniatures.

Objets d'Art

The department of Objets d'Art contains a glittering array of artefacts, displayed to advantage in the new, more spacious area alloted to it. The department contains ecclesiastical and secular objects, ranging from jewellery to furnishings, made from a huge range of materials. The works come from France and from other countries, and date from the end of Antiquity to the first half of the 19C. A total of 5500 objects are presented in the 55 Rooms of RICHELIEU (excluding Napoléon III's apartments), plus those in the other 30 or so rooms.

The works from the Middle Ages to Louis XIII (mid-17C) are in *rooms 1 to 33*, on RICHELIEU first floor. The circuit continues chronologically with 18C objects in *rooms 34–61*, SULLY first floor (north). The early 19C exhibits are in *rooms 67–73* near the apartments of Napoléon III, RICHELIEU first floor. Items dating from the Restoration and the reign of Louis-Philippe (which will in due course be transferred to the Rohan wing) are at present in *Rooms 62–65*, SULLY west. The Royal Regalia is in the Apollo Gallery, DENON, Room 66. Totally new to the public are the Apartments of Napoléon III, which miraculously escaped the fire in May 1871, and have been conserved and restored in *Rooms 74–84* of RICHELIEU.

The start of Objets d'Art is reached by taking the RICHELIEU escalators or lifts to the first floor and heading west.

Rooms 1–11. Middle Ages, covers a period of about ten centuries from the end of Antiquity (476) to the Renaissance and has been the object of a new presentation, organised chronologically and geographically.

Room 1. Two porphyry columns from the 4C basilica of St. Peter at Rome flank the door. 5C. Italian metalwork and ivories, such as the Ivory plaque of *Three Miraculous Cures of Christ*. Under the Merovingians (481– 751), the goldsmiths' art flourished, as shown by the Jewellery and Adornments of Queen Aregond, found at St-Denis in 1959. The Carolingian Renaissance produced fine work, such as Two plaques from the binding of the Psalter written by the Scribe Dagulf (783) and the bronze horseman, known as the *Statuette of Charlemagne* (9C), from Metz Cathedral.

Among **Byzantine pieces** are many beautiful ivories: 6C diptych known as the *Barberini Ivory*, the *Harbaville Triptych* (10C), *Triptych of the Nativity* (10C); also lapis lazuli Plaque with figures of Christ and the Virgin (12C); the *Reliquary of the Stone of St-Sepulchre*, from the Sainte-Chapelle is a beautiful piece of 12C Byzantine metalwork; mosaic icons of the *Transfiguration of Christ* (11C–13C) and of *St George and the Dragon* (14C).

Room 2. **Ottonian** openwork Ivory Plaques from the Cathedral of Magdeburg (10C) and Plaque of St John (10C) from St-Denis. From Aix-la-Chapelle, the Mozan Reliquary of the Arm of Charlemagne (c 1170); Ewer from the Treasure of St-Denis, in rock crystal, carved in Egypt around the end of the 10C. The **Treasure of St-Denis** includes many superb ecclesiastical ornaments commissioned or acquired by Abbot Suger, Abbot of St-Denis (1122–51): Suger's Eagle, an antique porphyry vase mounted in silver gilt in the form of an eagle; Vase of Eleanor of Aquitaine in rock-crystal given by the queen to Louis VII, who gave it to Suger; Antique Sardonyx Ewer, mounted c 1150.

Examples of **Limoges enamel work**, finely detailed and colourful: the Large Casket of St Thomas à Becket (end 12C); the Ciborium of Alpais (early 13C).

Early Gothic, developing by 1200, is characterised by increasing naturalism: Cross of St Vincent of Laon.

Room 3. Exceptional **enamel work from the Limousin** in the early 13C is represented by the *Reliquary of St Francis of Assisi*. The Sainte-Chapelle workshop, founded by St Louis in 1239, produced the ivory *Large Virgin*. Gothic ivories include the *Descent from the Cross* (mid 13C). A typical example of the refinement in art of the reign of Philippe le Bel (1285–1314) is the ivory Box with a Mirror, decorated with a Couple playing Chess. Second-half 13C silver-gilt *Polyptych of Floreffe* (French Ardennes). A highlight of the next period is the silver-gilt *Statuette of the Virgin*, presented in 1339 to St-Denis by Jeanne d'Evreux; the Italian *Arm Reliquary of St Louis* of Toulouse (1337) in crystal and enamelled silver gilt.

Room 4. The so-called Ring of St Louis (14C) from St-Denis; Gold Sceptre of Charles V with a statue of Charlemagne; a huge ivory altarpiece by the Embriachi (Italy, c 1400), presented to the abbey of Poissy by Jean, Duc de Berry; Tapestry, possibly from Arras, c 1400, L'Offrande du Coeur.

Room 5. An impressive collection of Hispano-Moorish lustreware (15C–16C). **Room 6**. 15C metalwork: outstanding medallion with Self Portrait of Jean Fouquet (15C); this important period for the art of tapestries is demonstrated by the Legend of St Quentin, Miracle of the Loaves, and other wovenworks. **Room 7**. 15C–16C Italian ceramics and enamels. Faenza pioneered the development of storiated faience: Votive Plaque with Saints. **Room 8**. Flemish tapestries, c 1500, in particular the *Life of St Anatole de Salins* (1501–06). **Room 9** has tapestries and precious metalwork including the *Reliquary of the Hand of St Martha* (late 15C) and **Room 10** is called the Salle des Millefleurs, after the delightful medieval tapestry scattered with flowers. **Room 11** has samples of the technique of painted enamels developed in Limoges at the end of the 15C, and stained glass.

Rooms 12–33. The Renaissance period. The Italian Renaissance, which inspired the French Renaissance, is illustrated in **Rooms 12, 13 and 14**, by Italian bronzes of the 15C and first half of the 16C: Florentine and Paduan Schools.

Rooms 15 and 16. French art at the time of François I: painted enamels, tapestries and furniture. **Room 17** has a bronze *Boy with a Thorn in his Foot* after the Antique, and **room 18**. French and Venetian glass.

Room 19 was specially arranged to display the magnificent scenes of **Maximilian's Hunts** (1531–33) which, ever since entering Louis XIV's collection, have been considered a great masterpiece and remarkably are still complete. The twelve tapestries of the months are after cartoons by the painter Bernard Van Orley (1488–1541) and are a unique document of court life and of rural landscapes. An outstanding collection of Italian 16C and 17C majolica ware of different types.

Room 20 the Scipio Gallery, has eight Gobelins tapestries of the Life of Scipio (1688–90), from designs by Giulio Romano; French painted enamels (15C–16C), including superb examples from the workshops of Léonard Limosin, Jean and Suzanne de Court, Pierre Courteys, J. Pierre Reymond. On the landing, Armoury (c 1556–59) which belonged to Henri II.

Rooms 21–22. French Renaissance articles: door with the initial and emblem of Henri II and Catherine de Médicis; thirteen pieces of pottery from the

St-Porchaire workshop (second half 16C), the largest existing collection; painted enamel *Portrait of the Constable Anne de Montmorency* (1556), a masterpiece by Léonard Limousin; Brussels tapestry of the *Resurrection*. **Room 23**. 16C–17C jewellery, clocks and watches, in enamel, gold and precious stones, including the watch of Jacques de la Garde, gilded copper (Blois, 1510).

Room 24. Salle Charles V (1519–58) has works from **Germany, Flanders and Spain**, such as the Tapestries of the Labours of Hercules produced in Audenarde, and characterised by large cabbage leaves called aristoloches; the Charles V Ewer and Basin (1558–59), silver gilt and enamel, from Antwerp. Medals and plaquettes in bronze, wood or lead, from Flanders, Spain and Germany.

Room 25. Adolphe de Rothschild Room, has a painted coffered ceiling typical of Venetian Mannerism and Italian Renaissance items and one of the group of small bronzes is *Atlante* by Zoppo (Padua, mid-16C); Medicis porcelain and German and Italian Renaissance jewellery. **Room 26**. Notable **bronzes** from the workshops of Jean Bologne and Pietro Tacca (16C–17C) and tapestries from Ferrare (1545). Jean Boulogne's (Giambologna) (1529–1608) most famous bronze is the dynamic *Nessus carrying off Deianeira*.

Rooms 27 and 28. **Treasure of the Order of Saint-Esprit** and the reconstruction of the Chapel of the Order of the Holy Spirit. Henri III founded the Order of Chivalry of St Esprit in 1578: reliquaries, censer, mace, covered goblets, ciborium and pair of rock crystal candlesticks and embroidered vestments. Also, enamelled gold Shield and Helmet of Charles IX (1560–74); some of the oldest tapestries, two episodes from the Story of Artemis (rewoven several times since the reign of Henri IV).

Room 29 contains rare pieces of **Renaissance furniture and tapestries**: *Sacrifice of Lystra*; and a tapestry woven at Mortlake c 1630, of the Acts of the Apostles after Raphael. **Room 30**, has a remarkable collection of the singular art of the ceramicist, **Bernard Palissy** (c 1510–89), the 'inventor of rustic figurines for the king', in the form of perfectly imitated animals and rustic basins with high relief decoration; the art of enamelled pottery from the little village of Avon: figurines and decorative pieces.

Room 31. Tapestry woven in Paris, by Flemish weavers, of Achilles at Scyros (c 1630–40); Barthélemy Prieur (1536–1611), small bronzes; choir stalls from Toulouse Cathedral, 1610–12, designed by Pierre Monge; and a remarkable French armoir dated 1617.

Room 32. Pre-Gobelins tapestries, after Simon Vouet; the beginning of the 17C was fundamental to the history of French furniture, as the new technique of *ébénisterie* (cabinet making) appeared: a fine 17C Parisian ebony cabinet; a remarkable ensemble of bed (with hangings) and six armchairs with original embroidered velvet from the 17C Château of Effiat.

Room 33. Painting on silk outlined in embroidery of the Story of Debora; the exquisite piece known as the Coffer of Anne of Austria, second half of the 17C.

Rooms 34–65, 17C, 18C, Restoration, and the July Monarchy (1814–48); (some of these displays will be relocated in the Rohan Wing to the west).

Room 34. Ceiling painting by Carolus Duran (1878) (restored) representing *Apotheosis of Marie de Médicis*, and a pedestal table with a porphyry top. It is also the **Salle Boulle**, illustrating the work of the cabinet-maker, André-Charles Boulle (1642–1732) with examples of ornate Louis XIV furniture.

Room 35. Collection of ivories including elements of a 17C frieze by van Obstal; tortoiseshell pieces with amber, stones and metal inlay; 17C and 18C tableware and wine glasses.

Rooms 36–41. 18C French faience and porcelain from Vincennes and Sèvres, Marseille, Moustiers and Rouen. On display in **room 42** is a large part of the Grog Carven donation of 18C furniture. In **room 43** a remarkable collection of boiseries and furniture from the Château d'Abondant, Paris c 1750.

Room 44–45 and 49. Sparkling donations of the **goldsmith's and silversmith's art**, the David-Weill and Niarchos collections: a surtout by Jacques Röettiers, made for the Prince of Condé, depicting a stag hunt; the *nécessaire* of Marie Leszczynska (1729); parts of a service ordered by the Empress Catherine II of Russia (late 18C). **Room 48**. Gobelins tapestries illustrating of the *Story of Moses*, after designs by Poussin and watches and clocks.

Room 50. Savonnerie carpet made for the Apollo Gallery (1667); French Regency furniture by Charles Cressent (1685–1768): flat-topped bureau, cupboard and chest of drawers; group of 18C chairs. **Room 51**. Flat-topped bureau by Max-Emmanuel de Bavière and consoles in gilded wood (c 1715); oriental porcelain; large vases from the India Company with the arms of the Duke of Orleans.

Rooms 52–56. Outstanding examples of **Louis XV furniture** (1715–74). The Schlichting room has Gobelins tapestries and furniture by the ébéniste Jean-François Oeben (c 1720–63); and Salle Edmond de Rothschild has exceptional pieces inlaid with plaques of Sèvres porcelain.

Rooms 58–61. Lebaudy room contains **Louis XVI furniture** (1774–91) and is decorated with and gilt and white boiseries from the Hôtel de Luynes (c 1770-75); among furniture which belonged to Louis XVI and Marie-Antoinette is a flat-topped bureau by Hauré and G. Beneman (1787); armchairs by J.-B. Senné (1748–1803). The taste for chinoiserie is seen in the Chinese wallpaper, lacquered corner-pieces and chests by Martin Carlin (c 1730–85); there is also Marie-Antoinette's writing table by Weisweiler (1784). The cabinets contain several small furnishings and precious objects which belonged to the Queen.

Rooms 62, Salle Claude Ott: **toilette in crystal and bronze** made by Escalier de Crystal for the Duchess of Berry. **Room 63**. The **King's bedroom at the Tuileries** with the bed belonging to Louis XVIII by Jacob Desmalter. **Rooms 64 and 65**: end 18C and 19C furniture (temporary presentation).

Room 66. Apollo Gallery contains items originally in the **French royal collection**, including semi-precious vessels of lapis lazuli, jade, amethyst, amber, red and green jasper, agate, sardonyx, basalt, etc. Individual objects include: the crown of of Louis XV (1722); after his coronation the gems were replaced by coloured stones, according to custom; the Crown Jewels retained when the rest were sold in 1887, including the Regent diamond (137 carats), discovered in India and bought by the Regent in 1717; the Côte de Bretagne ruby, which had an illustrious list of owners and was later cut into the shape of a dragon as a decoration of the Order of the Golden Fleece.

Rooms 67 and 68. Salles Valadier and Jacob Frères contain **late-18C and early-19C furniture** and objets d'art. Georges Jacob (1739–1814), who usually signed his work 'G. Jacob', had two sons, who marked their work 'Jacob Frères' until 1804, after which François-Honoré-Georges Jacob Desmalter worked on his own for another decade. The latter's son, Alphonse Jacob, who signed his work 'Jacob', flourished in the 1840s.

Room 68 is the famous **Salon of Madame Récamier** by Jacob Frères. **Room 69**. A representation of the **bedroom of Madame Récamier**. In 1798 the banker, Jacques Récamier, puchased the old Hôtel Necker and the architect, Louis Berthault, was given the task of redecorating it. He designed the furniture which was made by Jacob Frères. Juliette Récamier's original taste in interior design was the prototype for the Empire Style. During the early years of the 19C, the house became one of the great sights of Paris, especially Madame Récamier's bedroom.

Rooms 70–73. Style Empire: *room 70*. Salle Biennais is named after Biennais (1764–1843), personal goldsmith to Napoléon I. In 1810, he delivered the prestigious silver-gilt Tea Service of 28 pieces, ordered by Napoléon for his marriage with Marie-Louise, of which half is conserved at the Louvre; a *nécessaire* by Biennais and Lorillon, given by Napoléon to Tsar Alexander I in 1808.

Room 71. Brogniart assured the collaboration of the architects Percier, Théodore Brongniart (1733–1813) and Vivant Denon. Porcelain at this time consisted of simple forms with for an elaborate, all-over, painted designs and gilding. Le Cabaret Egyptien is a **Sèvres** porcelain coffee-service decorated with views of Egypt, made for the wedding of Napoléon and Marie-Louise, which the Emperor took with him to St. Helena.

Rooms 72 and 73. Severe, monumental **furniture of the Empire period** (1804–15), made by Jacob-Desmalter (1770–1841) and Thomire (1751–1843).

Rooms 74–84. The **Apartments of Napoléon III** have retained their original, and somewhat ostentatious, aspect and furnishings and constitute a unique ensemble of the period. They were created during the Second Empire to house the Ministry of State, during the project to link the Tuileries Palace to the Louvre. The work was carried out by Hector Lefuel from 1857–61 and the apartments miraculously escaped the fire of 1871. The same year, they were made over to the Ministry of Finance, who remained there until the Grand Projet du Louvre in 1989. Completely renovated, they opened as part of the Richelieu wing in 1993.

The reception rooms are in a sumptuous Louis XIV style. From Cour Marly, the apartments can be reached by the grand staircase (alternatively, through the early 19C rooms, or on the south, past Café Richelieu). The Large Antechamber (**room 81**), has walnut panels sculpted by Nelli. Adjacent is the Introduction Gallery (**room 80**), with two landscapes by Daubigny. (**Rooms 85–88** have rest areas and documentation.) This opens into **room 82**, Salle Thiers or the family salon which links both the small rooms (**rooms 83 and 84**) and the large reception rooms. The first is the Salon-théâtre (**room 77**), which has a charming floral and musical decoration, and off it opens the Petit salon de la terrasse (**room 78**).

In the angle, **room 79**, the Grand Salon, is the largest and most sumptuous of the rooms, glittering with gold, adorned with putti, and draped in crimson velvet. The ceiling painting by Charles-Raphaël Maréchal represents the Linking of the Louvre and the Tuileries by Napoléon III. The rather more sedate tones of seagreen marble and darkened wood in the Small dining room (**room 75**) are enlivened by gilding and trompe l'oeil painted wallpaper. The Large dining room has a painted ceiling. **Room 74**, is a corridor alongside the dining rooms.

Sculpture

French sculpture

The collections of French sculpture have arguably benefited more than any other department from the Grand Project du Louvre, which transformed the Richelieu Wing from government offices to magnificent galleries and court-yards, inaugurated in November 1993. French Sculpture is on RICHELIEU entresol and ground floor, organised around Cour Marly and Cour Puget, glazed and terraced courtyards which ascend from the entresol to the first floor. This well lit section sets off to advantage larger pieces of sculpture originally designed for royal gardens or public places.

> Take RICHELIEU escalator to the entresol. Straight ahead is Crypte Girardon leading to the two courtyards. To make the the visit in chronological order, take the staircase to the left just before Crypte Giradon, and start with Room 1, on the south side of Cour Marly. French Early Medieval to Renaissance sculpture is on three sides of Cour Marly.

Rooms 1–6. **6C–12C Romanesque sculptures**, dominated by the 5C/6C columns and capitals from Notre-Dame de la Daurade, Toulouse, and the deco-rated early 12C doorway from the priory of St-Cecile, Estagel (Gard); also capi-tals from Moissac (Languedoc) and Parthenay (Poitou). In the display cabinet is a *Christ* (painted wood), early 12C; a remarkable *Head of St Peter*, with eyes of inlaid lead, from the tomb of St Lazarus, Autun; and the eagle from the tympanum of Cluny.

A statue column from Avignon; a relief of *St Michael and the Dragon*, from Nevers; a carved wooden seated *Virgin and Child*.

Room 3. **Sculpture from mid-12C to early-13C**, Romanesque to early Gothic, in the Ile de France. This intermediary period is represented by the capital of the *Annunication* and *Visitation* from the Paris area, and two extraordi-nary historiated spiral columns, with tumbling figures, from the abbey of Coulombs; the large relief from Carrières-sur-Seine is probably one of the oldest retables left in France; notable is a group of Heads from the voussoirs of the west door of the Abbey of Saint-Denis, erected 1135–40, during the abbacy of Suger and the turning point from Romanesque to Gothic sculpture.

Room 4. **Gothic (13C) sculpture** typical of the elegance of Chartres and the Paris area, including samples from Notre-Dame de Paris and St-Germain-des-Prés. *St Matthew Dictated to by the Angel* is thought to be a fragment of the jubé of Chartres Cathedral.

Room 5. Mainly devoted to **14C retables**: the retable of the Sainte-Chapelle in black and white marble; scenes from the marble retable of the abbey of Maubuisson attributed to Evrard d'Orléans; on the wall, fragments of the Choir enclosure of Notre-Dame de Paris, including the remarkable relief of *Canon Pierre de Fayel* (d. 1344).

Room 6. **14C religious sculpture** and funerary monuments characteristic of 14C French sculpture, including many tender *Virgin and Child*, some with traces of colour. One of the most typical of work from Basse-Normandie of the mid-century is the *Blanchelande Virgin and Child*—the first medieval work acquired by the Louvre in 1850. Also characteristic of this period are recumbent Gothic statues. This room looks out over the newly laid-out Tuileries Gardens.

Room 7. Funerary statues and sculptures, given considerable importance in the 14C, such as the burial stone of Jean Casse, Canon of Noyon Cathedral; and **room 8**, tympanum possibly from St-Denis (13C–14C) with an exuberant green man in trefoil tracery.

Room 9. Sculptures of the time of Charles V and Charles VI from the Ile de France and Berry. These include small statues for the tomb of the entrails of King Charles IV (le Bel; d. 1324) and his queen, Jeanne d'Evreux (d. 1371) by Jean de Liège.

Rooms 10–11. 15C sculpture from Burgundy and the Loire, two important artistic centres which developed along different lines. The celebrated tomb of Philippe Pot, died 1493, Grand Seneschal of Burgundy, formerly in the abbey of Cîteaux, supported by eight *pleurants* (weepers).

The later Middle Ages and early Renaissance in France are represented by the superb marble high-relief of **St George and the Dragon** (1504–09), commissioned from Michel Colombe (c 1430–c 1512) by Georges d'Amboise for the Château of Gallon. The influence of Michel Colombe is seen in the sculptures of *St Peter, St Suzanne and St Anne teaching the Virgin* (c 1500), and the *tomb of René d'Orléans-Longueville* (d. 1515); and the *Virgin of Olivet* and the *Virgin of Ecouen*, possibly from the workshop of Guillaume Regnault, nephew of Colombe; also by Regnault the tomb of Louis de Poncher from St-Germain-l'Auxerrois (1523).

Room 12. Partial reconstruction of the Funerary chapel of Philippe de Commynes. **Room 13**, described as the Passage de la Mort Saint Innocent, has early 16C sculpture from the Ile de France and Champagne. The hugely ornate Flamboyant retable of the *Resurrection* has traces of polychrome. Death statue from the Auvergne, of *Jeanne de Bourbon*, Comtesse d'Auvergne, 1521, showing her being devoured by worms.

Rooms 14–17 (overlooking Rue de Rivoli). Mainly major **16C sculptors** commissioned by royalty to work both on royal residences and on funerary monuments. Their inspiration was drawn from antiquity and from the Italian Renaissance. **Pierre Bontemps** (c 1505–c 1568), **Jean Goujon** (c 1510–64/69), **François Marchand** (c 1500–c 1553) are the most important figures of this period: *Monument of Charles de Maigny* (1556) by Bontemps, and by Goujon for the base of *Fountain of Innocents*, 1547–49, rue St-Denis. **Germain Pilon** (c 1531–90): a remarkable survival from a commission by Queen Catherine de Médicis for the projected Valois chapel at St-Denis is a terracotta model for the *Virgin of Sorrows*.

Barthélemy Prieur succeeded Pilon, continuing his style but more soberly; for example the recumbent marble effigies of the *Constable Anne de Montmorency and his wife*; the upper part of the *Fontaine de Diane* from the Château of Anet is the oldest surviving garden sculpture in France. **Ligier Richier** (c 1500–c 1566) from Lorraine: *Child Jesus sleeping in his Crib*.

Among examples of 16C work, *room 18* is Guirand Mellot's Porte de la Salle du Grand Consistoire du Capitole de Toulouse, ordered in 1552, taken down in 1880. The first part of Louis XIII's reign (1610–43) produced little French sculpture, but from 1630 it was animated by Jacques Sarazin (1592–1660) and the Anguier Brothers, notably Michel (1614–86).

Room 19. Overlooking Cour Marly are 17C sculptures including **Simon Guillain**'s masterpiece, the *Monument of the Pont-au-Change*, which once dominated the busy crossroads opposite the Cité at the time of Louis XIII.

Cour Marly is named after the sculptures from the Parc de Marly, an estate acquired by Louis XIV in 1676 as a more private retreat than Versailles. Jules Hardouin-Mansart, responsible for the architecture and the landscape, used water to embellish the gardens were further adorned with sculptures by the finest artists in the Rococo style. Among those in the courtyard (middle level) are *Seine, Marne, Neptune* and *Amphitrite* intended for the cascade, the work of Antoine Coysevox (1640–1720), also responsible for the equestrian groups, *Mercury and Fame* (1699–1702) (upper level), moved to the Tuileries in 1719. These were superseded at Marly by the magnificent *Horses of Marly* (1743–45) (opposite), of Guillaume 1er Coustou (1677–1746) which were subsequently placed at the end of the Champs-Elysées and brought to the Louvre in 1984. (Reproductions now stand on the Champs-Elysées and the Tuileries.)

Between the two courtyards is ***room 20***. **Crypte Girardon** contains sculptures of the 17C–18C, by Giradon, Puget, and Coysevox. Centrally placed is the small model for the *Equestrian statue of Louis XIV* by **François Girardon** (1628–1715), and at the end of the gallery, **Pierre Puget** (1620–94), marble relief of the *Meeting of Alexander and Diogenes* (1671–89), made for Louis XIV. Grandiose busts of bewigged men include Coysevox's marble bust of Jean-Baptiste Colbert and and a bronze (posthumous) bust of Louis II de Bourbon 'Le grand Condé'; J.-L. Lemoyne (1665–1755) marble *bust of Jules Hardouin-Mansart*. There is also a *bust of Marie Serre* (1706), mother of Hyacinthe Rigaud, by Coysevox.

A disparate collection of **17C–19C French sculpture** is exhibited in and around **Cour Puget**. Dominating the lower part of the courtyard, the four bronze *Captifs*, designed (1679–85) for the Place des Victoires by Desjardins (1637–94), plus four bronze reliefs and eight circular medallions, to commemorate glorious episodes during the reign of Louis XIV. Notable on the middle level are Pierre Puget's Baroque *Milon of Crotona* (1671–82) and *Perseus and Andromeda* (1687–94), made for Louis XIV's Versailles, transferred to the Louvre in 1819. Also Termes and other statues from various parks by Legros (1629–1706), Barois (1656– 1726), and Raon (1631–1707), Flamen (1647–1717), Marsy (1647–81), and Regnaudin (1622–1706).

Beneath the bower of trees are 17C sculptures destined for Versailles and transferred to the Tuileries in 1722, by Sébastien Slodtz (1655–1726) and Nicolas Coustou (1658–1733). Coysevox's lighthearted piece, *Marie-Adelaide de Savoie, Duchesse de Bourgogne*, portrays the mother of Louis XV as Diana (1710) while Jean-Baptiste Pigalle (1714–85) *Madame de Pompadour en Amitié*, marble, 1753, depicts Louis XV's favourite with flowers of all seasons. On the walls at the end are fine stucco friezes by Clodion (1738–1814) and on the upper level, is Pigalle's *Mercury*, in lead, 1753.

French sculpture for the open-air from the mid-18C through to the 19C continues around the terrace, whereas the first-floor galleries on the north side of the Cour Puget, rooms **21–29** and back through **rooms 31–33**, contain small format works.

Room 21. Projects and **models in plaster and terracotta** for 18C tombs and funerary monuments by Bouchardon (1698–1762), Chaudet (1763–1810), Vassé (1716–72), and by Houdon (1741–1828), the marble mausoleum for the heart of Comte d'Ennery (1781). The design by Pigalle, for the mausoleum of Marshall Saxe, Strasbourg, St Thomas, in its architectural setting, is exceptionally elaborate.

Rooms 22–28. Small 18C works in a variety of materials by Falconet (1716–91), Robert le Lorrain (1666–1743), Michel-Ange Slodtz (1705–64) and Marie-Anne Collot (1748–1821), pupil of Falconet; Jean-Baptiste II Lemoyne (1704–78); and Guillaume Coustou (1677–1746), a terracotta of his brother *Nicolas in a Turban*.

Room 24. J.-B. Pigalle's skill in portraiture is seen in such works as *L'Enfant à la cage; Voltaire Nu* in marble, 1776, the fine head added to a realistic decrepit body. Group of male portrait busts includes a bronze of *Diderot* (1777), and *Self Portrait* in terracotta. ***Room 25***. A swirling profusion of qualifying works, high in drama but small in scale, for acceptance at the Académie royale de Peinture et de Sculpture from 1704 to 1791, by a variety of artists: Sébastien Adam (1705–78), Lemoyne, Paul-Ambroise Slodtz, Thierry, Guillaume II Coustou, Monot.

Returning through the parallel galleries overlooking Rue de Rivoli there is work by Jean-Jacques Caffieri (1725–92), *Corneille*, and by his rival Augustin Pajou (1730–1809), *Allegory of Queen Marie Leszczynska*.

Room 28. The preceding portraitists were eclipsed by Jean-Antoine Houdon (1741–1828). Busts of his his contemporaries include *Voltaire*, the singer *Sophie Arnould, Jean-Jacques Rousseau, Diderot, Benjamin Franklin* and *George Washington*.

At the end of the gallery ***room 29***, is Houdon's bronze of Diana the Huntress (1790). This area is, however, called the **Gallery of Grands Hommes**, with statues of illustrious men commissioned in 1776 from Academicians during the reign of Louis XVI: *Molière* and *Corneille* by Caffieri; *Jean de La Fontaine* and a marble of *Nicolas Poussin* (1804), dressed in a toga, by Pierre Julien (1731–1804).

The small ***room 30*** is dedicated mainly to **Clodion**. ***Room 31***. Period of the Revolution, the Empire and the Restoration. Characteristic works are the statue of Peace (silver and bronze), conceived by Vivant Denon, Director of the Louve and modelled by Chaudet (1763–1810); *Napoleon I in Coronation Robes*, marble, 1813 by Ramey (1754–1838); a mosaic by Belloni (1772–1863), *The Genius of the Emperor, Controlling Victory, brings back Peace and Abundance*, 1810, designed for the floor of Salle de la Melpomène at the Louvre.

Rooms 32 and 33. French sculpture from the **Romantic era, 1820–50**, virtuoso pieces in a sentimental vein, are represented by James (Jean-Jacques) Pradier (1790–1852): *Niobe Wounded, Psyche with a Butterfly*, the *Three Graces*; Cortot (1787–1843), *Immortality*, and Jacques-Edme Dumont (1761–1844), *Genius of Liberty*. Works by the great Romantic sculptor, François Rude

(1784–1855), include *Mercury* and *Young Neapolitan playing with a Turtle*. David d'Angers (Pierre-Jean David) (1788–1856) shows a new approach in *Child with the Bunch of Grapes* (1845); in the show cases are bronzes and plasters by the successful sculptor of animals, Antoine-Louis Barye (1795–1875), including the famous *Jaguar devouring a Hare*.

On the **upper level of Cour Puget** are monumental works of the first half of the 19C, among them: Barye's *Roger and Angelique riding the Hippogriffe*; large portrait heads in marble at which David d'Angers excelled; centrally placed, a bronze by Bosio of *Hercules fighting Achelous*; Rude's *Joan of Arc Hearing Voices*, commissioned in 1845 for a series of illustrations of women for the Luxembourg Gardens.

If satiated of French Sculpture, you could veer off to Oriental Antiquities, which begin on the south side of Cour Puget with Ancient Mesopotamia.

Italian Sculpture

The collection of Italian sculpture is in **DENON**, divided between 6C–15C on the entresol and 16C–19C on the ground floor. Take the DENON escalator to the entresol and turn right. (On the right of Donatello gallery, is an area for the visually handicapped with works that may be touched.)

Room 1 (a to f). **Gallerie Donatello** was a stable, built 1857–59 by Lefuel, and contains Italian sculpture from the 6C–15C: *Head of the Empress Ariadne* (early 6C); Armenian stela, beginning of the 14C, in red tuff, with crosses and interlacing; marble Antependium (8C–9C), with animal and vegetal decoration; two Atlantes (second half 13C) archaistic in style; a mid-13C, *Descent from the Cross* in painted wood; *Personification of the Four Cardinal Virtues: Prudence, Fortitude, Justice and Temperance*, 14C, from a funerary monument. *St Stephen* (1390–96), from the west front of Milan Cathedral demolished in 1587, the head replaced at some unknown date, holding a stone, symbol of his martyrdom. Various pieces on the theme of the *Annunciation*.

Versions of the Madonna and Child, in a variety of materials, mainly reliefs: life-size, seated *Madonna and Child*, in painted wood by **Jacopo della Quercia** (c 1374–1438). Dominating Italian sculpture in the 15C with works both elegant and sensual was the great, **Donatello** (c 1386–1466), inspired by Antiquity: *Madonna and Child*, in coloured and gilded terracotta, the half figure of the Virgin of great delicacy and pathos, probably one of the last works produced by Donatello before his departure for Padua (1443); Donatello and his studio: *Madonna Worshipping the Child* (the Piot Tondo), a roundel of terracotta with wax medallions (under glass, partly restored); after a lost original by the master, *Madonna of Verona*, in *cartapesta* (papier mâché). The *Virgin surrounded by four angels*, by **Agostino di Duccio** (1418–81), made for Piero de Medici, is a virtuoso example of marble low relief; the three reliefs of the *Madonna and Child*, by **Mino da Fiesole** (1418–81), give a masterly effect of transparent fabrics.

Notable is the marble roundel of the *Young Christ and St John the Baptist*, by **Desiderio da Settignano** (1428–64), carved to give an astonishing impression of depth.

Among portrait busts: by **Benedetto da Maiano** (1442–97) vigorous bust of *Filippo Strozzi*; and from a Florentine workshop (late 15C), *La Belle Florentine*. Two decorative panels in marble by Fiesole and Giovanni Dalmata came from the lower part of the Mausoleum of Paul II in the old basilica of St-Peter's, Rome.

Room 2. La Bottega des della Robbia (15C–16C): is a small gallery devoted to a collection of enamelled earthenware, in characteristic blue and white, and yellow and green, of the Florentine workshop of the della Robbia (Andrea, 1435–1525), Giovanni (1469–c 1530), Luca (1475–c 1548) and Benedetto Buglioni (1459–1521), including *St Sebastian, Madonna and Child with Three Cherubims*, and *Christ on the Mount of Olives*.

> **Room 3** to the left contains the Spanish collection. For the continuation of Italian sculptures take the Mollien Staircase up to Denon ground floor. On the landing is the large *Nymph of Fontainebleau*, a bronze bas-relief by Benvenuto Cellini (1500–72), made for the Porte d'Orée at Fontainebleau but placed, until the Revolution, above the gateway of the Château d'Anet.

Room 4. Michelangelo Gallery: with low vaults and polychrome marble floor, is a suitably grand setting for Michelangelo's Slaves, with works from 16C–19C. Pass first through the monumental portal of the Palazzo Stanga at Cremona, attributed to Pietro da Rho.

This leads to the most celebrated works in the department, the *Two Slaves*, 1513–15, by Michelangelo Buonarotti (1475–1564): *The Captive*, struggling for his freedom, and the sensuous *Dying Slave*. Both were both intended for the tomb of Pope Julius II, but given to Henri II in 1550 by Robert Strozzi, were placed for some time at the Château of Ecouen (see Ch. 38, p 326) and then transferred to Cardinal Richelieu's collection.

Among several works by (or attributed to) Gian-Francesco Rustici (1474–1554) is *Apollo's Victory over the Python*, marble; *The Young River*, by Pierino da Vinci (1531–54), related to Leonardo; examples of work in bronze by Northern sculptors who spent most of their working life in Italy: Jean Bologne (French), *Mercury Flying* (1580), and Adrien de Vries (Dutch, 1545–1626), *Mercury Carrying off Psyche*, made (1593) for the castle of Prague, but ending up in French royal parks.

Of the high Baroque period, works by **Bernini** (1598–1680) include *Angel carrying the Crown of Thorns* (terracotta, Rome c 1667); and the bust of *Cardinal Richelieu*, modelled on the triple portrait of Richelieu by Philippe de Champaigne in London.

At the end of the gallery are works by Antonio Canova (1757–1822), *Psyche revived by the Kiss of Cupid*, and *Cupid and Psyche standing*; and Bartolini (1777–1850), *Nymph with a Scorpion* (marble, 1837).

Spanish Sculpture

The small collection of Spanish Sculpture, 12C–18C, is squeezed between the Italian and the Northern sculpture collections in *room 3* on Denon entresol and contains examples of capitals from the Visigothic and Mozarab periods. Also works in alabaster from royal tombs of the Catalan Monastery of Poblet; monumental Gothic doorway, richly decorated with vegetal motifs and a Annunciation; an extraordinary work illustrating a Franciscan legend, of the *Dead St Francis*, in polychrome wood with eyes of glass, teeth of bone, and cord of hemp, probably mid-17C.

Northern Sculpture

Continue through the Spanish section to Northern Sculpture, 12C–16C, in the west of **DENON** entresol.

Room A. **English 15C**, alabasters from Nottingham. **Room B**. Virgins (12C–15C) in **International Gothic style**, from the Rhenish lands, Netherlands, Baveria, Germany, Salzburg and Lorraine. Notable is the 12C *Bavarian Crucifixion* carved in lime wood, the emaciated and touching figure of Christ wearing a long pleated perizonium. Go around the Grand-Ecuyer staircase to reach the celebrated and monumental *Virgin and Child* from Isenheim, near Colmar, originally the central part of retable carved in lime wood which lends itself well to complicated drapery.

Room C. **German and Dutch works** from the later Gothic period, 15C–16C, among the reliefs and sculptures is a *Virgin of the Annunciation*, kneeling, in painted alabaster, by Riemenschneider (c 1460–1531); a naked Magdalen (*La Belle Allemande*), in painted lime wood, Augsburg (c 1515) by Gregor Erhart (d. c 1540); a *Crucifixion* in oak from the Brabant, end 15C; *Retable of the Passion*, in polychromed oak, Antwerp, c 1510.

Renaissance sculpture is represented by the *Tombstone of Jean de Coronmeuse*, Abbot of St Jacques de Liège (c 1525–30); and, attributed to Schro (active 1545–68), bust of the *Elector Ottheinrich von der Pfalz*, in alabaster.

Northern Sculpture, 17C–19C continues in Rooms D and E on DENON ground floor.

16 · The Museums of Decorative Arts and Fashion and Textiles

■ Arrondissement: 75001.
■ Métros: Tuileries, Palais Royal-Musée du Louvre, Pyramides. RER: Châtelet-Les-Halles.

Musée des Arts Decoratifs

The autonomous Musée des Arts Decoratifs is in the north-west wing of the Palais du Louvre (Pl. 8; 7), and the main entrance is at 107 Rue de Rivoli. It contains an outstanding collection of French decorative and ornamental art from medieval times to the present. The exhibits range from Italian primitives, tapestries, porcelain, furniture from the Middle Ages to the present. It is especially rich in 17C, 18C and 19C objets d'art and has some splendid examples of Art Nouveau and Art Deco interiors. Open Wed–Sat 12.30–18.00, Sun 12.00–18.00, closed Mon, Tues, 01/01, 01/05, 25/12 (☎ 01 45 55 57 50).

Rather overcrowded, the museum has been undergoing a programme of restoration and expansion as part of the Grand Louvre project, and will extend into a section of the Rohan wing. The Medieval and Renaissance and First Empire collections have been reopened. The permanent collection as a whole, arranged in chronological sequence, is due to reopen in autumn 1998, with the exception of the 20C exhibits, scheduled for 1999. The new layout will include period rooms or series of objects, such as ceramics, silverware and jewellery. The

20C (from 1900 to contemporary) will range from the ground to the ninth floor in the Pavillon de Marsan. The important Library of Decorative Arts will be modernised and two new rooms will be reserved for periodicals.

> The history of the collection is bound up with the Union Centrale des Beaux-Arts appliqués à l'Industrie and the Société du Musée des Arts Décoratifs (founded in 1864 and 1877 respectively), which in 1882 merged to become the Union Centrale des Arts Décoratifs. In 1901 work began on the rehabilitation of the interior of the Pavillon de Marsan, and the Musée des Arts Décoratifs was inaugurated in May 1905. Today, its inventory lists over 80,000 items.

The museum is affiliated with the Musée des Arts de la Mode (see below), and the Musée Nissim de Camondo, 63 Rue de Monceau, 8e; see Ch. 26. It also houses the Musée de la Publicité (posters) temporarily closed, due to reopen on the third floor of the Rohan wing in autumn 1998.

A new departure is the department selling replicas of choice objects from the collections themselves, or of contemporary design, their reproduction undertaken in collaboration with French manufacturers and craftsmen of noted quality.

Temporary exhibitions, usually in the fields of design and decoration, are held here throughout the year.

The newly reorganised museum will be arranged around the central hall, between the Rue de Rivoli and the Jardins des Tuileries, providing access to all the exhibition spaces. On the ground floor will be the boutique, the bookshop and a cafeteria. Until the transformation is complete, it is only possible to give an idea of what there is to see in the museum.

The **Gothic and Renaissance periods** are represented by 13C–16C tapestries, among them the *Romance of the Rose* (Arras, 15C), and *Le Festin* (Brussels, early 16C), and *Scenes from the Life of Christ* (Flemish, c 1500). A 14C painted chest is the oldest known in France. There are examples of furniture of the period, medieval metal work and Renaissance bronzes. Religious works include a number of International Gothic carved and painted retables, and representative examples of German woodcarving. Among smaller works is an anon. *Portrait of a Young Girl* (Bruges c 1550) and a *Portrait of Mary Tudor with the attributes of Mary Magdalen*. There is also a version of *Venus and Cupid, The Honey Thief* by Cranach the Elder (1472–1553).

The **arts of Spain** are represented by Catalan painted panels (Aragon, second half 15C), and the *Retable of St John the Baptist* (c 1415–20) by Luis Borrassá; also stalls from Rueda (Valladolid, early 16C); and embossed leather panels or *guadameciles*.

Decorative arts from the time of **Louis XIII to the Second Empire period** (17C–early 19C), include examples of panelling of c 1707 from 7 Pl. Vendôme, and oak-panelling of c 1735; a ceiling of c 1710 by Claude Audran (1658–1734) from the Hôtel Bertier de Flesselles, Rue de Sévigné, and another of c 1715 from the Hôtel de la Comtesse de Verrie in the Rue du Cherche-Midi; also decorative panels by N. Coypel and by Hubert Robert; painted panels in the Etruscan style (c 1780); and a number of carved wood brackets, panels, picture-frames and mirrors.

In the **furniture collection** are 17C–18C chairs arranged to show the evolution of styles; a fine marquetry cabinet of c 1670; a marquetry *armoire* attributed to Boulle of c 1680 and another by Charles Cressent (c 1725); and examples in the Chinese taste, together with other Chinoiserie objects. Also chairs by members of the Jacob family; a boat-shaped bed by F. Baudry (1827).

Among the **paintings** are a *Portrait of the Chancellor d'Anguesseau* by Robert Tournières; a pastel of Molière; *Venetian Scenes* by Michele Marieschi (1710–43); and monastic scenes by Alessandro Magnasco; garden scenes by Pillement; flower studies (1614–15) by G. Pini; watercolours by Lavreince, J.-B. Huet, Debucourt and Mallet; an early work (c 1806) by Ingres, *The Casino of Raphael at Rome*; and *Houdon's Studio*, and the *Gohin Family*, both by Louis Boilly. Note also a series of wax-portrait moulds, some by G.-B. Nini (c 1717–80), and a collection of portrait-miniatures.

Among the extensive **ceramic collections** are examples from St-Cloud, Moustiers, Strasbourg, Rouen (some exhibiting surprisingly strong Chinese influence), Sceaux, Sinceny, Marseille; *faïences en trompe-l'oeil* and *fine blanches*; ware from Vincennes, Sèvres, Mennecy and Chantilly; biscuit figures, and a curious terracotta of a girl playing with her pet dog, by Clodion (1738–1814); an important collection of Chinese cloisonné; and Delft and Meissen porcelain.

Complementary are such diverse fine quality objects such as door furniture; bronze appliqués, and ornaments (and also a coiffeuse used by Joséphine at the Tuileries); silverware; mathematical instruments; pewter; clocks and watches; ivory boxes; snuff grinders; rings; cutlery; *nécessaires*; embroidered purses; shuttles; walking-sticks; paperweights; pipes; plaster plaques; statuettes; glass ornaments; decorative embossed leather cases; and book-bindings. There are also toys.

Also to see are Charles le Brun's projects for tapestries of *The Months* and furniture and furnishings in the Louis-Philippe taste, and in the style of the Second Empire (Napoléon III).

In the late **19C, 20C and Contemporary collections** are complete interiors, including three rooms (boudoir, bedroom and bathroom) designed for Jeanne Lanvin by Armand Rateau, in 1920–22; as well as applied arts: metal, ceramic and glass including glass by R. Lalique, and paintings by Marie Laurencin, Maurice Denis and Matisse, among others. There are also displays of jewellery of the period. Notable among the Art Nouveau exhibits is a room with woodwork by Georges Hoentschell (1855–1915), furniture by Hector Guimard (1867–1942), Emile Gallé, Louis Majorelle and A. Charpentier. Among smaller objects are a lamp by L.C. Tiffany, glass by Lalique, Dammouse, and Gallé, ceramics by Carriès, Chaplet, Delaherche, and others and metalwork by Hirtz, Dunan and Gaillard. Leading artists and designers from 1945 to the present are represented by such objects as a table by Giacometti and chair by Niki de Saint-Phalle.

Musée de la Mode et du Textile

The Musée de la Mode et du Textile (☎ 01 44 55 57 50) is on two floors of the Rohan wing of the Louvre. The collection of costumes, from the 17C to the 20C, accessories and textiles is, for the first time, on permanent display. These are presented thematically and changed every six months.

The collection had its origins in the Union Française des Arts du Costume, established in 1901, since when its collections of costumes and accessories have been very considerably increased, partly due to donations. A proportion has been acquired with the participation of several famous fashion houses—among the more notable names being Balenciaga, Chanel, Dior, Fath, Givenchy, Lanvin, Patou, Ricci, Rochas, Saint-Laurent, Schiaparelli, Ungaro and Worth. The growth of the industry was spectacular during the latter half of the 19C; the Bottin directory of 1850 listed some 158 couturiers in Paris. By 1872 this had risen to 684 and in 1895 to 1636 (six of whom employed 400–600 workers each), not including small independent dressmakers.

The holdings, being increased continually, include 20,000 costumes and 35,000 accessories of all types (including a rare collection of umbrellas, Second Empire hats, costume jewellery, fans, shoes, handbags and gloves); some 21,000 samples of textiles (prints, tapestries, laces, embroideries, braids); and patterns and pattern-books. To complete the museum, one further floor is made over to a Fashion and Textile Documentation Centre. This holds a photographic library of 215,000 images, a slide library with 300,000 images, 15,000 commercial catalogues of the second half of the 20C to the present day, 6,500 books, 250 periodical titles (about 100 complete series), and a collection of 50,000 drawings and engravings. The museum also contains a textile laboratory.

17 · North of the Rue de Rivoli

■ Arrondissements: 75001, 75002.
■ Métros: Concorde, Tuileries, Pyramides, Palais-Royal. RER: Auber.

Included in this chapter are some of the best known streets of Paris: Rue de Rivoli, Rue St-Honoré and Rue de la Paix; also the beautiful square Place Vendôme, as well as the theatre best known as the Comédie-Française, the gardens of the Palais Royal and the church of St-Roch.

This district, so centrally placed, between the Louvre, Place de la Concorde and the Opéra, is a strange mixture of Parisian elegance and tourist trash. Some of the finest and most luxurious hotels are to be found here, but also more modest establishments. Likewise, there is an abundance of grand and not-so-grand, restaurants, cafés and teashops. In the district are two well-established English bookshops (see below); and prestigious boutiques selling jewellery, fashion and antiques jostle with souvenir stalls selling models of the Eiffel Tower and T-shirts emblazoned with Paris.

Rue de Rivoli

Constructed in 1811–56 and named in honour of Napoleon's victory over the Austrians in 1797, Rue de Rivoli runs east from Pl. de la Concorde (Pl. 7; 7; see p 131) following the Tuileries Gardens and the Louvre. Its western half is flanked by uniform ranges of buildings above an arcade. On the opposite side, at No. 99 is the entrance to the new shopping precinct, the Carrousel du Louvre,

Restaurants and cafés

Angélina, 226 Rue de Rivoli, ☎ 01 42 60 82 00. Tea shop. £

Gérard Besson, 5 Rue du Coq-Héron, ☎ ☎ 01 42 33 14 74. Haute cuisine. Exclusive. £££

Carré des Feuillants, 14, Rue Castiglione, ☎ 01 42 86 82 82. £££

Les Deux Ducs, 95 Rue de Richelieu, ☎ 01 42 96 83 87. £

Drouant, 18 Rue Gaillon, ☎ 01 42 65 15 16, Traditional, Art Deco. £££

L'Echelle (Hotel Normandy), 1, Rue d'Argenteuil, ☎ 01 42 60 30 21. Traditional. £

L'Espadon, Hôtel Ritz, 1 Pl. Vendôme, ☎ 01 42 60 38 30. Haute cuisine. £££

Le Grand Véfour, 17, Rue de Beaujolais, ☎ 01 42 96 56 27. Haute cuisine. 18C decor. £££

A la Grille St-Honoré, 15, Place du Marché St. Honoré, ☎ 01 42 61 00 93. Traditional. £

Le Gutenberg, 64, Rue Jean-Jacques Rousseau, ☎ 01 42 36 14 90. Café. £

Restaurant Lescure, 7, Rue de Mondovi, ☎ 01 42 60 18 91. Rustic bistrot. £

Le Louis XIV, 1 bis, Place des Victoires, ☎ 01 40 26 20 81. Traditional Lyonnais cuisine. ££

Aux Lyonnais, 32 Rue St.-March, ☎ 01 42 96 65 04. Traditional, Art Nouveau bistrot. £

Le Meurice, Hôtel Meurice, 228 Rue de Rivoli, ☎ 01 44 58 10 50. Haute cuisine. £££

Ostréa, 4, Rue Sauval, ☎ 01 40 26 08 07. Brasserie, seafood. £

The Palais Royal terraces, la Gaudriole, la Muscade, ☎ 01 42 97 51 36, £

Pierre au Palais Royal, 10, Rue de Richelieu, ☎ 01 42 96 09 17. Traditional. ££

Pile ou Face, 52bis Rue Notre-Dame des Victoires, ☎ 01 42 33 64 33. ££

Tarte Julie, Passage des Princes, 101 Rue de Richelieu, ☎ 01 42 96 17 80. £

Vaudeville, 29 Rue Vivienne, ☎ 01 40 20 04 62. Brasserie Flo chain. ££

and at No. 107 the Musée des Arts Décoratifs (see Ch. 16). A bronze-gilt statue of *Joan of Arc* by Frémiet stands in Place des Pyramides.

No. 224 is **Galignani's Bookshop**, established here since 1855, but with a history that goes back to 1815. M. Galignani and his English wife, Anne Parsons, started out by publishing an English newspaper, a Guide to Paris with English and German descriptions, and reprints of English books. The shop stocks English and French books, glossies and literature. At No. 226 is the smart place for tea or, even better, hot chocolate, the *salon de thé Angélina*.

At Hôtel Meurice, 228 Rue de Rivoli, General von Choltitz, commander of the German forces in Paris, allowed himself to be captured (25 August 1944), having refused orders to destroy the capital's principal buildings. At 248 Rue de Rivoli is a branch of the British booksellers, WH Smith.

At the western extremity, at the corner of Rue St-Florentin, stands the 18C Hôtel de la Vrillière, or de Talleyrand, built to designs by Chalgrin, where the statesman, Charles Maurice de Talleyrand-Périgord (1754–1838) died. The design of the American Embassy (see p 252) was inspired by this building, and completes the symmetry of the north side of Pl. de la Concorde.

Return to Rue Cambon, where at No. 5 (previously No. 3) Stendhal lived between 1810 and 1814. It crosses Rue du Mont-Thabor on its way north to Rue St-Honoré, a street with a totally different atmosphere from, and running parallel to, Rue de Rivoli. At the junction with Rue Cambon stands the Church of the Assumption, built in 1670 as the chapel of the convent of the Haudriettes and now used by the Polish community.

Turn east on Rue St-Honoré to arrive shortly at Rue de Castiglione. The Hôtel Lotti at No. 7 was described in George Orwell's *Down and out in London and Paris* (1933).

Place Vendôme

This street leads north into the octagonal Place Vendôme (Pl. 7; 8), an outstanding example of Louis XIV style, designed by Hardouin-Mansart. Construction began in 1687, and was completed in 1699, after his death to his design. Originally called Pl. des Conquêtes, it owes its present name to an *hôtel particulier* built here in 1603 by César, Duc de Vendôme, son of Henri IV and Gabrielle d'Estrées. A number of these grand buildings are now luxury hotels (the **Bristol** at No. 3; the **Ritz** at No. 15), or high-class jewellers and chic boutiques. Nos 11–13 is the Ministère de la Justice (since 1815). Frédéric Chopin died at No. 12 in 1849. The uninterrupted splendour of the Place has to some extent been restored by the sinking of the car parking spaces underground; like so much of Paris, it is resplendent at night.

The centre of the Place is dominated by the **Colonne de la Grande Armée** (or the **Vendôme Column**), constructed by Gondouin and Lepère in 1806–10 in the style of Trajan's Column in Rome to replace an equestrian statue of Louis XIV by Girardon (of which the left foot survives at the Musée Carnavalet).

Encircling the column (43.50m high) is a spiral band of bronze bas-reliefs, designed by Bergeret and made from the metal of 1250 Russian and Austrian cannon captured at the Battle of Austerlitz, in 1805. The statue of Napoléon at the summit is a copy by Dumont (1863) of the original by Chaudet torn down by the royalists in 1814. The present statue narrowly escaped destruction in 1871 when a group of Communards, encouraged by the artist Gustave Courbet, demolished the column. Courbet went into exile in Switzerland after being condemned to finance the re-erection of the column in 1875. He died in Switzerland in 1877.

The once fashionable Rue de la Paix (now lined with travel agencies and airline offices) leads north to the Pl. de l'Opéra (see Ch. 22).

Turn right down Rue Casanova towards the Place du Marché-St-Honoré for an alternative route back to Rue St-Honoré and yet another aspect of the *quartier*. On the corner of Rue du Marché-St-Honoré is the site of a Dominican convent where the Jacobin Club met in 1789–94 (it is now a restaurant).

St-Roch

To the east, on Rue St-Honoré, steps ascend to St-Roch (Pl. 7; 8). Hemmed in by buildings and on a narrow street, the impact of this fine Baroque church is lost yet it is one of the largest churches in Paris and rich in paintings and monuments.

It was begun in 1653 to plans by Jacques Lemercier. Work was interrupted in 1660 until in 1719 a generous donation from the banker John Law enabled its completion. The elegant façade was the work of Robert de Cotte, 1736–38, and in 1706–10 Jules Hardouin-Mansart added the Chapel of the Virgin, to the north. The church was consecrated in 1740 and further extensions were added to the north in 1717 and 1754. Having lost many religious works at the Revolution, it was radically altered in the 19C and given a new decor and many monuments and paintings from churches that had been destroyed.

The **interior** has been the project of restoration since 1993. Its total length is an impressive 126m. The body of the church originally had a classical layout, but the additional 18C circular chapels and the Chapel of the Calvary produce a dramatic sequence of Baroque spaces. Between 1750 and 1770, at the initiative of Curé Jean-Baptiste Marduel, the church was endowed with a grandiose ensemble of painted and sculpted decoration only a sample of which remains. But new works were commissioned in the 19C and it contains many furnishings of interest. The organ case dates from 1752, while the instrument has been modified several times. The stalls and the upper part of the pulpit are also 18C.

To the left of the entrance is a medallion of *Corneille* (1606–84), who is buried in the church. In the first chapel in the east aisle (right) are a *bust of François de Créquy* (d. 1687) by Coysevox and the *tomb of the Comte d'Harcourt* (d. 1666) by Renard. The second chapel contains a statue of *Cardinal Dubois* (d. 1723) by G. Coustou and a monument, by Huez, to the astronomer *Maupertuis* (1698–1759). In the dome of the Chapel of the Virgin is a restored painting of the *Assumption* by Jean-Baptiste Pierre, 1756, and *Glory*, by Falconet (1756), in stucco against the arcade, was part of a group replaced by the marble *Nativity* by Michel Anguier, from Val-de-Grâce. There are also 17C paintings by E. Le Sueur and Claude Vignon, and 18C works by Germain Drouais and Jean Restout. The Communion Chapel has a curious tabernacle inspired by the temple in Jerusalem (c 1840), and some fine stained glass depicting St Denis the Areopagite (1849) by Régnier.

Continuing around the church, on the west side, on the last pillar of the ambulatory, is a *bust of Le Nôtre* (d. 1707) by Coysevox. In the transept is a plaster of *St Andrew* by Pradier (1823), and a statue of *St Augustin* by Huez (1766); also a canvas of *St Denis Preaching* by Joseph-Marie Vien, 1767 and 19C murals. The next chapel contains a monument to the *Abbé de l'Epée* (see beginning of Ch. 7). The 3rd chapel (beyond the transept) contains the remains of a monument to *Pierre Mignard* (1610–95) by Jean-Baptiste II Lemoyne, 1744. And in the last chapel is a painting by Théodore Chassériau.

Going east along Rue St-Honoré, where Napoleon suppressed the Royalist rising of 5 October 1795, you soon reach Pl. André-Malraux (Pl. 8; 7) formerly Pl. du Théâtre-Français, with a view north west towards the Opéra. The two fountains are by Davioud. To the south the short Rue de Rohan meets Rue de Rivoli opposite the arch leading to Pl. du Carrousel. On the east of the Place stands the restored **Théâtre Français**, built in 1786–90 by Victor Louis, but largely remodelled after a fire in 1900. (Occasional visits with the CNMHS.)

As an institution the Théâtre-Français (or Comédie-Française) dates from the amalgamation in 1680 of the Hôtel de Bourgogne actors with Molière's old company, which had already absorbed the Théâtre du Marais. In 1812 Napoléon signed a decree (at Moscow) reorganising the Comédie-Française, which is still a private company although controlled by a director nominated by the government and enjoying a state subsidy.

In the foyer is the admirable seated statue of *Voltaire* by Houdon and the chair in which Molière was sitting when acting in *Le Malade Imaginaire* and taken fatally ill. The theatre also owns various statues of actors and dramatists, including *Talma* by David d'Angers, *Dumas fils* by Carpeaux, *Mirabeau* by Rodin, and a statue of *George Sand* by Clésinger; also the portrait of *Talma* by Delacroix and other paintings by Lemoyne, Caffieri, Van Loo, Mignard and Coypel. The auditorium ceiling was painted by Albert Besnard (1913).

An inscription high up on the corner of Rue de Valois (on the eastern side of the Palais-Royal) marks the site of the Salle de Spectacle du Palais-Cardinal, occupied by Molière's company from 1661 to 1673, and by the Académie Royale de Musique from 1673 until a fire in 1763.

The Palais-Royal

Adjoining the Théâtre Français, the Palais-Royal and its surroundings form one of the most attractive and interesting areas of Paris. The name Palais-Royal is now applied not only to the original palace but also to the extensive range of buildings and galleries surrounding the gardens to the north. This pedestrian thoroughfare, entered from neighbouring streets by several passages, is now a delightful backwater.

The Palais-Royal proper, originally known as the Palais-Cardinal, was designed by Jacques Lemercier in 1634–39 for Richelieu, who, as chief minister, wished to be near the Louvre. He died there in 1642. Bequeathed to Louis XIII, it was first called Palais-Royal during the residence of Anne of Austria (d. 1666), then regent, and her sons Louis XIV and Philippe d'Orléans. During the Fronde in 1648 they had to beat a hasty retreat from it and when Louis XIV returned to Paris he lived at the Louvre. Queen Henrietta Maria, widow of Charles I of England, and her daughter lived in the palace, which was altered by Mansart.

In 1763 a fire destroyed the east wing and the theatre. The houses and galleries around the gardens, the work of the architect Victor Louis, were built as a speculative venture in 1781–86 by Philippe-Egalité, the Regent's great-grandson, under pressure of debt, and let out as shops and cafés. He also built the Théâtre-Français. The Théâtre du Palais-Royal, in the northwest corner, dates from the same period.

The cafés became a rendezvous for malcontents, since the police were excluded from entry, and on 13 July 1789 Camille Desmoulins delivered in the gardens the fiery harangue which precipitated the fall of the Bastille the following day.

The name Palais-Royal was changed to the Palais-Egalité, and it was used as government offices. In 1814 it was returned to the Orléans family and reverted to its earlier name. It was the residence of Louis-Philippe until

1832 but in 1848 it was plundered by the revolutionaries. The palace was rebuilt by Chabrol in 1872–76 after damage during the Commune. It is now occupied by the Conseil d'Etat and the Ministère de la Culturel.

The buildings in the Cour de l'Horloge, facing Pl. du Palais-Royal, were erected by Constant d'Ivry (1763–70), with sculptures by Pajou (left wing) and Franceschi (right; 1875). The façade on the north side, overlooking the Cour d'Honneur, was begun by d'Ivry, continued by Louis, and completed by Fontaine, who also restored the east and west wings. The so-called **Galerie des Proues**, on the east side of the court, is the only relic of Lemercier's 17C building. To the north, the Cour d'Honneur is separated from the gardens by the Galerie d'Orléans, a double Doric colonnade by Fontaine (1829–31), which was restored and cleared of its shops in 1935.

The gardens of the Palais-Royal are surrounded on three sides by arcades and buildings with shops and dwellings that form an altogether charming and harmonious ensemble. Past residents include the writers Colette and Jean Cocteau. From the south, you enter the Cour d'Honneur, to the north is the Galerie Beaujolais, on the west side is the Galerie de Montpensier, and opposite the Galerie de Valois. Nos 79–82 Galerie de Beaujolais, the **Grand Véfour**, was the fashionable rendezvous of writers in the Second Empire and is now a restaurant of high repute (see below). In 1785, 17 Galerie de Montpensier was a museum of waxworks, founded by Curtius, the uncle of Mme Tussaud. The Café du Caveau (Nos 89–92) was the meeting place of the partisans.

The large rectangular **gardens**, less frequented than others in the centre of Paris, were renovated in 1992. Straight avenue of limes, planted in 1970, flank a formal garden with parterres and a fountain. The Petit Canon, which used to fire at midday, was installed in 1786 on the Paris meridian and moved to the parterre in 1799, but stopped functioning in 1914. Since 1990 it has again been in working order. In 1985–86, Daniel Buren's 250 puzzling truncated black-and-white fluted columns of differing heights, above and below ground, were installed in the Cour d'Honneur; and Pol Bury's mobile steel spheres have animated the pools of the Galerie d'Orléans since 1985.

Immediately east of the Palais-Royal is the Rue de Valois, with (Nos 1–3) the Pavillon du Palais-Royal (1766, by D'Ivry and Moreau); at Nos 6–8, once the Hôtel Melusine, the first meetings of the French Academy took place in 1638–43. The ox sculptured above the door recalls its period as the restaurant Boeuf à la Mode from 1792 to 1936.

In the parallel street to the east, Rue Croix-des-Petits-Champs, is the entrance to the **Banque de France** (Pl. 8;7), founded in 1800 and moved here in 1811. The buildings incorporate the former Hôtel de la Vrillière, built by Mansart in 1635–38 and restored by Robert de Cotte in 1713–19, later known as the Hôtel de Toulouse from its occupancy by the Comte de Toulouse, son of Louis XIV and Mme de Montespan. Within the bank is the profusely decorated Galerie Dorée, one of the first of its kind in the 17C (occasional visits organised by the CNMHS).

At the corner of Rue de la Vrillière and Rue Croix-des-Petits-Champs is the 18C Hôtel Portalis (by Ledais). At 33 Rue Radziwill, on the north side of the Banque de France, is an unusual double staircase.

To the north east of the Bank lies the circular **PL. DES VICTOIRES**, laid out by Jules Hardouin-Mansart in 1685; the surrounding houses were designed by Pradot. The *equestrian statue of Louis XIV* by Bosio (1822) replaces the original, destroyed in 1792; the bas-reliefs on the pedestal depict the *Passage of the Rhine*, and *Louis XIV Distributing Decorations*.

Immediately north west is the surprisingly provincial-looking Pl. des Petits-Pères, and **Notre-Dame-des-Victoires**, or the church of the Petits-Pères, dedicated in 1629 by Louis XIII to commemorate the capture of La Rochelle from the Huguenots in the previous year. On the site of a former chapel, it was begun by Pierre Le Muet in 1629–32; Libéral Bruant designed the transept and last bay of the nave 1642–66, and it was completed only in 1740 by Sylvain Cartault. The plan of the interior derives from the Gesù in Rome, with communicating chapels around the nave. Every interior wall is plastered with ex-voto tablets and the organ case and carved stalls date from 1740. The second chapel on the left contains the *tomb of the composer Jean-Baptiste Lully* (1633–87) by Pierre Cotton, with a bust by Gaspard Collignon; in the choir are seven paintings (1746–55) by Carle van Loo.

The adjoining street leads north to the **Bourse des Valeurs** or Stock Exchange (guided visits weekdays 11.00–13.00). Built by Brongniart and Labarre in 1808–27, it is a typical neo-classical building of the period with a grandiose Corinthian peristyle. The north and south wings were added in 1903.

Rue Feydeau, to the north, built on Louis-XIII fortifications, and the Rue des Colonnes, to the west, retain some interesting houses in an old district through which Rue du Quatre-Septembre was driven in 1864. Rue Vivienne leads south from the Bourse along the east side (right) of the Bibliothèque Nationale (see Ch. 18), and includes several 17C–18C houses.

On the left, at the corner of Rue Colbert, stands part of the Hôtel de Nevers, built by Mazarin in 1649 to house his library (see below). Further on is a fountain of 1708, and beyond (right) in the Sq. Louvois (Pl. 8; 5–7), the Fontaine Louvois, by the younger Visconti (1844).

The Square was laid out in 1839 on the site of a theatre (the Salle Louvois) built in 1794, which housed the Opéra until 1820. For the Bibliothèque Nationale, on the east side of the square, see p 198. No. 12 Rue Chabanais, immediately to the west was the setting of Toulouse-Lautrec's painting *Au Salon* (1894).

Continue south on Rue de Richelieu passing at the corner of Rue Molière the Fontaine Molière by Visconti (1844): the dramatist is by Seurre and the figures of Comedy by Pradier. The street ends at the Pl. André-Malraux.

18 · The Bibliothèque Nationale de France-Cardinal de Richelieu

■ Arrondissement: 75002.
■ Métros: Bourse; Pyramides, 4 Septembre. RER: Auber.

Restaurants

Canard d'Avril, 5 Rue Paul Lelong, ☎ 01 42 36 26 08. South west France/duck specialities. ££
Le Grand Colbert, 2 Rue Vivienne, ☎ 01 42 86 87 88. Brasserie. £
Coup de Coeur, 19 Rue St-Augustin, ☎ 01 47 03 45 70. Traditional. £
Rôtisserie Monsigny, 1 Rue Monsigny, ☎ 01 42 96 16 61. Traditional cooking by Jacques Cagna. ££

The Bibiliothèque Nationale

On the east side of the Sq. Louvois rises the western façade of the Bibliothèque Nationale de France-Cardinal de Richelieu (with its entrance at 58 Rue de Richelieu, ☎ 01 47 03 81 26).

A high proportion of the contents of this library, which, with the British Library, is one of the two largest in Europe, is moving in 1998 to the new Bibliothèque National de France-François Mitterand, east of Gare d'Austerlitz (see p 84). However, the Richelieu-Vivienne site will keep several of the special collections, among them manuscripts, prints, photographs, maps and plans, music, coins, medals, antiquities, and the collection from the performing arts.

The areas open to the public include the Musée du Cabinet des Médailles et Antiques and the temporary exhibition rooms, Galerie Mansart and Galerie Mazarine.

The buildings of the Bibliothèque Nationale de France consist of a group of 17C hôtels particuliers added to and amended until the end of the 19C. In 1666 Colbert installed the Bibliothèque du Roi in one of his houses on Rue Vivienne, next to the Hôtel Mazarin which had been added to by Mansart in 1654. It was first opened to the public for two days a week in 1692. In 1724 the buildings were extended by Robert de Cotte and in 1826 the library spread into Galerie Mazarin, the former Hôtel Chevry and Hôtel Tubeuf, built by Le Muet in 1635, up to Rue des Petits-Champs. Between 1857 and 1873, Henri Labrouste carried out a number of modifications to the building, including the delicate cast- and wrought-iron frame supporting a cluster of domes suspended over the Main Reading Room.

Formerly known as the Bibliothèque Royale and the Bibliothèque Impériale, it originated in the private collections of the French kings. Largely dispersed at the end of the Hundred Years War, the Library was refounded by Louis XII and moved to Blois. During the next two centuries it was at Fontainebleau, and then Paris, before finding its present home in Rue de Richelieu. Guillaume Budé (c 1468–1540) had earlier been appointed the first Royal Librarian. It was enriched by purchase or by gift of many famous private libraries and smaller collections (including that of Colbert), and at the Revolution its range was further increased with the confiscation of books from numerous convents and châteaux. In 1793 it was enacted that a copy of every book, newspaper, etc printed in France should be deposited by the publishers in the Bibliothèque Nationale.

The main entrance vestibule is on the right of the Cour d'Honneur. The Reading Room (seen through glass doors opposite), covered by nine faience cupolas, seats 360 readers (as against the 2000 which the new Bibliothèque Nationale-F. Mitterand will accommodate). Galerie Mansart, to the right at the foot of the stairs, was formerly Mazarin's sculpture gallery—note his arms above the door and the carved foliage and paintings by Grimaldi. The Cabinet des Estampes beyond contains about 11 million items varying from master prints to postcards, posters and wallpapers samples.

The Department of Music contains two million works including collections of musical scores, books on music, and MSS (among them Mozart's *Don Giovanni*) previously in the Library of the Conservatoire de Musique. The Manuscripts department has an awesome collection, with more than 530,000 MSS, of which some 10,000 are illuminated, ranging from the oldest book, an Egyptian manuscript c 2000 BC, to manuscripts, by authors such as Marcel Proust and Jean-Paul Sartre. The Department of Maps and Plans has 90000 items, including 104 globes.

Musée du Cabinet des Medailles et Antiques

The Musée du Cabinet des Medailles et Antiques (☎ 01 47 03 83 30), beyond the iron gates on the first floor landing is reached by stairs to the left of the main entrance. The collection, founded in the 16C, but containing objects known to be in royal hands some time before that date, contains over 500,000 coins and medals, from Antiquity to the present day, in addition to antiquities of outstanding quality, only a small proportion of which are on display.

Near the entrance is a Parian marble torso of Aphrodite (Hellenistic period), while in showcases on this and on the mezzanine floor are examples of French and foreign coins and medals, engraved cameos and jewels. Notable is the Grand Camée, from the Sainte-Chapelle, representing the Apotheosis of Germanicus, with Tiberius and Livia—the largest antique cameo known; the aquamarine intaglio of Julia, daughter of Titus, a particularly fine carved portrait; an engraved Chaldaean stone (1100 BC), found near Baghdad; the agate nef (incense boat) from St-Denis; the Dish of Chosroes II, king of Persia (c 600 AD); the sardonyx Cup of Ptolemy; the Patère de Rennes (a Roman gold dish found in 1774); a Merovingian chalice and oblong paten (6C), from Gourdon, in the Charollais; a bust of Constantine the Great, once the head of the cantor's wand at the Sainte-Chapelle; and a series of ivory chessmen (11C–12C), once reputed to have belonged to Charlemagne (d. 814).

Other cases contain Renaissance medals and bronzes; Egyptian terracottas and painted limestone statuettes; Roman bronze statuettes; ancient arms and armour, and domestic utensils; Greek and Etruscan vases, including a red-figured amphora, signed Amasis; cyclix of Arcesilaus, king of Cyrene; vase of Berenice (239–227 BC), from Benghazi, and other ceramics; gold objects from the tomb of Childeric I, at Tournai; ivory consular diptychs, and Byzantine diptychs; gold bullae of Charles II of Anjou, king of Naples (1285–1309), of Baldwin I, Emperor of Constantinople in 1204–06, and of Edmund, Earl of Lancaster, titular king of Sicily, 1255–63; gold coins found at Chécy (Loiret); a Celtic bracelet (Aurillac; 5C–6C); a silver hoard from the temple of Mercurius Canetonensis (Berthouville, Eure), including silver figurines and vessels of the 2C BC and others of the best Greek period.

Also displayed is the so-called Throne of Dagobert, on which the kings of France were crowned: a Roman curule (seat of office) chair of bronze, with arms and back added in the 12C by Suger. The restored Salon Louis XV, decorated by Van Loo and Natoire, with *dessus de portes* by Boucher, has its original coin cabinets.

Behind the Bibliothèque, in the recently renovated Galerie Colbert (1826), off Rue des Petits Champs, is the commecial showcase of the Library. The adjacent Galerie Vivienne (1823) (between Rues Vivenne and des Petits Champs) is a smart shopping arcade.

19 · Place du Palais-Royal to Place de la Bastille

- Arrondissements: 75001, 75002, 75004.
- Métros: Palais Royal-Musée du Louvre, Louvre-Rivoli, Les Halles, Etienne-Marcel, Châtelet, Rambuteau, St-Paul, Sully-Morland, Bastille. RER: Châtelet-les Halles.

This chapter includes important old churches such as St-Germain-l'Auxerrois, St-Eustache and St-Merri as well as the tawdry modern quarter of Les Halles with its subterranean concrete bunker and major RER intersection. As always in Paris, the picturesque and historic abut the crass and commercial, a case in point being Rue St-Denis. Rue de Rivoli skirts the two large squares, Chatelet and Place de l'Hôtel de Ville, and its extension, Rue St-Antoine, runs through the Marais district to end at the increasingly popular Bastille district dominated by the new Opéra Bastille.

Walking east from Pl. du Palais-Royal, with the façade of the Palais-Royal on your left (see Ch. 17), follow Rue St-Honoré along the north side of the **Louvre des Antiquaires** (☎ 01 42 97 27 00). This building of 1852, formerly the department store of the Grands Magasins du Louvre, was acquired in 1975 by the British Post Office Staff Superannuation Fund as an investment, and gutted. Since 1978 it has accommodated, on three floors, some 250 professional antique-dealers' stalls, open to the public daily from 11.00–9.00, except Monday (also closed on Sunday from mid July-mid September). They can also organise transport, settle customs formalities and provide certificates of authenticity, etc. Lectures and exhibitions are frequently held here.

A short distance to the east is (right) the **Temple de l'Oratoire**, designed by Clément Métezeau the younger and Jacques Lemercier, and built in 1621–30 for Cardinal Bérulle as the mother church in France for his Congregation of the Oratory. In 1811, Napoléon assigned it to the Calvinists. The façade is 18C.

Restaurants and cafés

L'Alsace aux Halles, 16 Rue Coquillière, ☎ 01 42 36 74 24. ££
L'Assiette Lyonnaise des Halles, 14 Rue Coquillière, ☎ 01 42 36 51 60. £
Benoit, 20 Rue St-Martin, ☎ 01 42 72 25 76. Traditional. ££
Bistrot du Louvre, 48 Rue d'Argout, ☎ 01 45 08 47 46. ££
La Boucherie, 10, Rue Coquillière, ☎ 01 42 36 03 14, chain of steak restaurants. £
Le Brin de Zinc et Madame, 50 Rue Montorgeuil, ☎ 01 42 21 10 80. £
Bistro Caveau François Villon, 64 Rue de l'Arbre Sec, ☎ 01 42 36 10 92. Bistrot. £
Au Chien qui Fume, 33 Rue du Pont-Neuf, ☎ 01 42 36 07 42. Traditional. £
La Cloche à Fromage, 25 Rue de la Reynie, ☎ 01 42 36 12 52. Cheese specialities/dishes. £
Le Lazare, 68 Rue Quincampox, ☎ 48 87 99 34. Seafood. £
Diable des Lombards, 64 Rue des Lombards ☎ 01 42 33 81 84. Brasserie. £
Pain, Vin, Fromage, 3 Rue Geoffroy l'Angevin, ☎ 01 42 74 07 52. Cheese dishes/fondues. £
Le Panorama, 14 Quai du Louvre, ☎ 01 42 33 32 37. Brasserie. £
Le P'tit Gavroche, 15 Rye Ste-Croix-de-la-Bretonnerie, ☎ 01 48 87 74 26. Reasonably priced. £
Pharamond, Rue la Grande Truanderie, ☎ 01 42 33 06 72. Traditional bistrot, Art Nouveau decor. ££
Au Pied de Cochon, 6 Rue Coquillière, ☎ 01 42 36 11 75. Brasserie. £
Les Rivolines, 46 Rue de Rivoli, ☎ 01 42 78 65 87. Traditional. £
Les Trois Axes, 150 Rue du Fb. St Martin, ☎ 01 42 74 68 34. Traditional. £
Le Cheval Vert, 50 Rue François Miron, ☎ 01 42 71 15 01. ££
Le Maraîcher, 5 Rue Beautrellis, ☎ 01 42 71 42 49. Bistrot. £
La Perla, 26 Rue François-Miron, ☎ 01 42 77 59 40, Mexican bar. £
Louis Philippe Café, 66 Quai de l'Hôtel de Ville, ☎ 01 42 72 29 42. Provençal cuisine. £
Le Trumilou, 84 Quai de l'Hôtel de Ville, ☎ 01 42 77 63 98. Bistrot. £

Against the apse is a monument of 1889 by Crauk to Admiral Coligny (1519–72), the chief victim of the massacre of St. Bartholomew, who was wounded in a nearby house now replaced by 144 Rue de Rivoli.

Further east in Rue-St-Honoré are several well-preserved 17C houses. The **Fontaine du Trahoir**, its stalactites and shells surrounding a nymph, sculpted by Boziot, was rebuilt by Soufflot in 1778, replacing an earlier fountain by Goujon.

A short distance east of the Oratoire, Rue-St-Honoré is intersected by Rue du Louvre. By turning right here, and crossing Rue de Rivoli, with a view of the east façade of the Palais du Louvre, you reach PL. DU LOUVRE. This supposedly is the area where Caesar's legions encamped in 52 BC. Opposite stands the Mairie of the 1st Arrondissement (1859) which, according to Viollet-le-Duc, was intended as a caricature of the adjoining church. The conspicuous Neo-Gothic north tower was added the following year.

St-Germain-l'Auxerrois

St-Germain-l'Auxerrois (Pl. 14; 1), a Gothic church of the 13C–16C, was drastically altered in the 18C and restored (1838–55), under the direction of Lassus and Baltard. A major programme of renovation was recently undertaken.

The most striking exterior feature is the **porch**, by Jean Gaussel (1435–39), with a rose window, and above it, a balustrade which encircles the building. The transeptal doorways (15C) and Renaissance doorway (1570) (seen from the neighbouring school yard), north of the choir, are noteworthy. Nothing remains of the cloister.

> The church, dedicated to the 5C St Germanus, Bishop of Auxerre, stands on the site of a Merovingian sanctuary. A second church replaced it in the 11C, which was replaced by the present building in the 13C. The ringing of its bells for matins on 24 August 1572 was the signal to commence for slaughter of Huguenots, known as the Massacre of St Bartholomew. The building was desecrated during the Revolution and sacked by a mob in 1831.
>
> Royal artists and architects of the Valois Court were buried in St-Germain: the poets Jodelle and Malherbe; the architects Lemercier, De Cotte, Gabriel and Le Vau; the artists Coypel, Boucher and Chardin; the sculptors Coysevox, N. and G. Coustou; and the engraver Israël Silvestre.

The **interior** (78m by 39m) is double-aisled. The alterations of 1745, mingled the classicism of the 18C with 14C–15C architecture and converted the piers into fluted columns and heightened their capitals. The organ case, from Sainte-Chapelle, was designed by Pierre-Noël Roussel and and made by Lavergne in 1756. Opposite the entrance are two 17C white marble holy water stoups.

The **royal pew** (1682–84), in the north aisle, a tour de force of wood carving, was designed by Le Brun and executed by François Mercier. The wood is worked to represent a baldaquin with draperies above fretworked panels and supported by Ionic columns and pilasters. Behind it is a 16C Flemish sculptured triptych with painted wings and, in the aisle-chapel opposite, is another altarpiece (1519) in carved wood, from Antwerp. The pulpit is 17C. The outer south aisle is occupied by the Chapel of the Virgin, late 13C, the with a Tree of Jesse designed by Viollet-le-Duc and above it a 14C Virgin of the Champagne School. The 15C St Mary of Egypt and the 13C St Germanus (Germain), were originally in the porch.

Fragments of the destroyed rood-screen, sculpted by Jean Goujon, are preserved in the Louvre, and the wrought-iron choir-railings date from 1767. On the left at the choir entrance is a wooden statue of *St Germanus*, seated; on the right a stone figure of *St Vincent* (both 15C). Only the transepts have their original 15C–16C stained-glass. The font was designed by Mme de Lamartine.

Above a small door in the ambulatory (south side) is a late-15C polychrome Virgin. The first inner bay, the oldest part of the church, is the base of the 12C belfry. In the 4th chapel are marble statues of *Etienne d'Aligre and his Son*, both Chancellors of France (d. 1635; 1677); 6th chapel, a relic of a Pietà by Jean Soulas (1505); and in the 7th chapel, effigies from the tomb of the Rostaing family (1582 and 1645). There are several 19C frescos by Guichard, and windows by Lusson.

Rue du Louvre leads north from Rue-St-Honoré to the small Pl. des Deux-Ecus. Off Rue Jean-Jacques-Rousseau to the south west is the once fashionable but now rather run-down **Véro-Dodat arcade** (1822), named after Messieurs Véro and Dodat. To the east of Pl. des Deux-Ecus is the refurbished circular mid-18C building, the **Bourse du Commerce** (Pl. 8; 8). Formerly the Corn Exchange, it received its metal dome in 1811, was destined for demolition in 1880, but was spared and remodelled in 1888. It can be visited on weekdays. The upper part of the interior hall is decorated with a fresco representing international commerce (due for restoration). There is a curious double spiral opposite the entrance.

A fluted Doric column adjoining its south-east side was once part of the Hôtel de la Reine (later Hôtel de Soissons, in the garden of which stock-jobbing (brokering) took place from 1720), built for Catherine de Médicis in 1572 on the site of the earlier Hôtel d'Orléans which had belonged to Blanche of Castile (d. 1252). The column may have been used as an astrologer's tower.

Les Halles

The Bourse de Commerce is now the only remaining evidence in Paris of the Halles Centrales, which by mid-1969 had been moved to extensive modern markets at Rungis (c 11km south of Paris and north of Orly airport). Markets had stood here since the early 12C, but the ten huge pavilions constructed by Victor Baltard (1805–74) in the 1850s immediately to the east, together with two additional market halls completed in 1936, were demolished by 1974 (with the exception of No. 8, which was re-erected at Nogent-sur-Marne, see Ch. 41). What Zola described as *Le ventre de Paris* is no more, although it is still referred to as the *trou* or hole. For the area immediately to the north, see below.

The radical redevelopment of the whole area of Les Halles, has been much criticised on aesthetic grounds, but the technical problems posed and resolved were prodigious. These included the siting of the important underground railway-station a major intersection of the RER system at the bottom of the *trou*; the provision of road tunnels and underground parking facilities; air-conditioning plants, skilfully disguised behind the façades of houses; and the erection of new blocks of buildings, which to some extent harmonise with the old. A number of architects took part in the project, including for a time Ricardo Bofill.

The vaunted **Forum des Halles**, its ribbed and glazed courtyard forming the sunken lid to the *trou*, and embellished by curious pink marble statuary entitled Pyègemalion (sic), by the Argentinian sculptor Julio Silva, has had a very mixed reception since it was inaugurated in September 1979. Most of the building is on three subterranean floors, and although partially lit from the central square and supplied with numerous escalators and lifts, it can induce both claustrophobia and agoraphobia. Certain walls, ceilings and pillars in passages are decorated with examples of pop art; there are several cinemas, and plenty of shops.

To the north and east of the Forum are terraces on which mirrored mushroom-shaped pavilions have sprung up. **Gardens** covering nearly 5 hectares have been laid out to the west, planted with 600 trees while plants trail over metal structures and 11 fountains play along. For children, there is a garden of six fantasy worlds designed by the sculptor, Claude Lalanne.

Seen across the the flattened area and gardens, St-Eustache (see below) comes into its own, as does the Bourse du Commerce and the astrological tower. Nearby the restored Fontaine des Innocents (see below) is also now set off to advantage. Large areas have been designated pedestrian precinct, both east and west of the transverse Blvd de Sébastopol, and the improvements in communication and notable revival of local trade have made this district a hub of activity of every kind.

From the western side of the Bourse du Commerce, Rue du Louvre continues north, on the right of which is the **Hôtel des Postes** (1880–84), the main Post Office of Paris: opposite, in the elegant Hôtel d'Ollone (built in 1639 and altered in 1730), is the Caisse d'Epargne (or Savings Bank).

> From the 13C to the 18C the University of Paris was responsible for the postal service for private citizens, while from 1461 the royal mail was carried by relays of post riders. In 1719 the University lost its privilege and all mail was controlled by the royal service. In 1757 the postal headquarters was in the Hôtel d'Hervart.

From just north of the Bourse du Commerce, heading east, is Rue Coquillière with a remarkable shop selling kitchen utensils and numerous restaurants, including *Au Pied de Cochon* where all-night revellers used to eat oysters for breakfast when the old market was in full swing.

St-Eustache

Just beyond, and dominating the area, is the splendid silhouette of St-Eustache (Pl. 8; 8). Begun in 1532, perhaps by Pierre Lemercier, it was consecrated in 1637. It appears to be a Gothic structure with supporting flying buttresses but, typical of this transitional period, on closer inspection it is seen to have Renaissance details and decorations.

> The Neo-Classical main west doorway, completed only in 1754–88, is totally out of keeping with the rest of the church, but both transepts have round-headed doorways (c 1638–40), the decoration restored. A passage from Rue Montmartre leads to the north transept. The open-work bell-tower, known as the Plomb de St-Eustache, above the crossing, has lost its spire, and above the Lady Chapel in the east is a small tower built in 1640 and rebuilt in 1875.
>
> The church was the scene of the riotous Festival of Reason in 1793, and in 1795 became the Temple of Agriculture. St-Eustache has always been noted for its music. Here Berlioz conducted the first performance of his *Te Deum* (1855) and Liszt his *Messe Solenelle* (1866) and it is now the venue of an organ festival in June and July.

The **interior** is a striking combination of Gothic plan and Renaissance decorative motifs. The nave is short and the double aisles and chapels continue round the choir, while the wide transepts do not extend beyond the chapel walls. Square piers are flanked by three storeys of superimposed orders, the vaulting is Flamboyant with heavy pendant bosses, and above the high arcades is a small gallery. In the chapels are restored paintings from the time of Louis XIII and the 11 lofty windows of the apse were executed by Soulignac (1631), possibly from cartoons by Philippe de Champaigne. The churchwardens' pew was designed by Pierre le Pautre and carved by Carteaux, c 1720 and the unadorned stalls were acquired from the convent of Picpus. The organ, with an ornate case by Victor Baltard (1854), is one of the most important in Paris.

The second chapel on the south, the musicians' chapel, commemorates Rameau, Franz Liszt and Mozart's mother. On the trumeau of the transept doorway is a 16C statue of *St John* and the second choir chapel has a *Pietà* attributed to Luca Giordano (1632–1705). The glass of the fifth chapel, which features St Anthony, was given by the Société de la Charcuterie de France. On the altar of the Lady Chapel is a *Virgin* by Pigalle (1748) accompanied by murals by Thomas Couture (1856).

As you return by the north aisle, in the first choir chapel is the very fine but incomplete *tomb of Colbert* (d. 1683), designed by Le Brun, with statues of Colbert and Fidelity by Coysevox, and of Abundance by Tuby. In the next chapel is a painting of the *Supper at Emmaus*, school of Rubens, a 17C French painting of the burial of a martyr. *The Ecstasy of the Virgin* (c 1627) in the third chapel is by Rutilio Manetti. Above the north-west door is the *Martyrdom of St Eustace* by Simon Vouet.

Rue de Turbigo leads north east from St-Eustache towards Pl. de la République, soon reaching Rue Etienne-Marcel, in which, to the left (at No. 20), rises the Tour de Jean-sans-Peur, a graceful defensive tower of c 1400 once incorporated in the Hôtel de Bourgogne. Part of this mansion (see No. 29) was used from 1548 until the turn of the 18C as a theatre, where plays by Corneille and Racine were performed.

The next street to the east, RUE ST-DENIS, is one of the oldest routes in Paris. Parallel to the old Roman road, now Rue St-Martin, it leads to the Royal necropolis of St-Denis (see Ch. 36). Partly pedestrianised, this narrow, bustling, street is lined with sandwich bars and seedy shops. At No. 135, in its north section, an inscription indicates the former position of the Porte St-Denis or Porte aux Peintres, a gateway in the walls of Philippe Auguste. No. 142 is the Fontaine de la Reine (1730). On No. 133 are statues from the medieval Hôpital de St-Jacques, once on this site.

You then reach on the left **St-Leu-St-Gilles**, built in 1235, the nave reconstructed after 1319. The aisles were added in the 16C; the choir, still partly Gothic, in 1611 (and reconstructed in 1858–61 to make way for the adjacent boulevard). The façade and windows were remodelled in 1727 and a crypt excavated in 1780. The church contains three Nottingham alabaster reliefs (in the sacristy entrance) and a sculptured group of *St Anne and the Virgin*, by Jean Bullant (second south chapel). The organ gallery is by Nicolas Raimbert (1659).

Continue south and you reach the small Sq. Joachim du Bellay, on part of the site of the medieval Cimetière des Innocents, the main burial ground of Paris until 1785, when the remains, probably including those of La Fontaine, were transferred to the catacombs (see Ch. 7). Traces of the arches of the cemetery galleries are still to be seen on Nos 11 and 13 in the Rue des Innocents.

The restored Renaissance **Fontaine des Innocents** was originally erected in 1548 in the neighbouring Rue St-Denis by Pierre Lescot, with bas-reliefs by Jean Goujon (now in the Louvre). It was remodelled and set up here by Payet c 1788, the south side (for it had earlier abutted a building) being decorated by Pajou.

Across the ugly Blvd de Sébastopol (left), the narrow Rue Quincampoix (parallel to the east), is another ancient street, although most houses date from the 17C–18C.

To the east opens Pl. Edmond-Michelet (or Sq. de la Reynie). Diagonally from here, looking across Rue St-Martin, is a view of the Centre Pompidou, with its large, sloping Piazza. Just north at the junction of Rue Bernard-de-Clairvaux, leading east into this redeveloped Quartier de l'Horloge, and Rue Brantôme, is an imaginative modern clock, with automata, by Jacques Monestier (1979). For the Centre Pompidou (see Ch. 20).

> This area, known as the **Beaubourg** from the 11C when it was a small rural community surrounded by vineyards, came within the boundaries of the city of Paris when Philippe-Auguste's walls were constructed in the 13C. The main artery was Rue Beaubourg, and the focus the church of St-Merri. This ancient quarter, still boasting some fine 17C and 18C houses, was carved up in the 19C with the building of Rue Rambuteau and Blvd Sébastopol, fell into neglect and was partly demolished in the 1930s. Its character radically altered when the Centre Georges Pompidou opened in 1977.

Immediately south of the Centre, is Pl. Igor-Stravinsky (recently renovated), flanked by relics of the Rue Brisemiche. A novel installation is the **fantasy fountain** with amusing coloured mobile sculptures by Nikki de St Phalle and Jean Tinguely, in keeping with the Pompidou centre but setting up a cruel visual contrast with its neighbour, the church of St-Merri (or St-Merry).

St-Merri

St-Merri (1515–52), stands at the intersection of the two major Roman axes, the present Rue St-Martin and Rue de la Verrerie. The dingy exterior of the church belies a noble **interior** which has retained many original furnishings. It replaced at least two older churches which covered the grave of St Médéric of Autun (d. c 700), and was built in Flamboyant Gothic at a time when Renaissance styles were taking over. The porch, albeit mutilated, is carved with pinnacles and friezes. In the 18C the interior was given a Baroque decor. From 1796–1801 it became the Temple of Commerce (much of which in this area was of the carnal kind). The west front is notable for its rich decoration, but the statues are mostly poor replacements of 1842. The north-west turret claims the oldest bell in Paris (1331); the south-west tower lost its top storey in a fire.

The nave and choir, like Notre-Dame, are the same length, and have simple quadripartite vaults except over the crossing which has lierne vaults and a pendant boss. A frieze of animals, leaves and figures runs around the nave above the arcades. The window tracery has flame-like curves. There is a double aisle on the right (south)—one for the canons and one for the public, and a single on the left. The church lost its 16C wooden jubé early in the 18C. The Slodtz brothers undertook the sculptured embellishments in the 18C: Michel-Ange Slodtz designed the pulpit (1753), the gilded Glory above the main altar and added marble veneer and stucco to the choir chapels. The dark oak organ case dates from 1647, modified in the 18C and in 1857. Saint-Saëns was organist here.

Immediately to the right of the entrance is a Renaissance screen, and in the first outer chapel of the south aisle are the remains of the 13C church. Further on is a large chapel by Boffrand (1743–44), with three oval cupolas, beautiful bas-reliefs by Paul-Ambroise Slodtz (1758), and a *Supper at Emmaus* by C. Coypel. The 17C painting above the choir's south entrance of the *Virgin and Child* was one of a pair by C. Van Loo, but its opposite number was stolen.

In the left aisle, the first chapel contains a 15C tabernacle; the third a *Pietà* attributed to Nicolas Legendre (c 1670); the 4th, a painting by Coypel (1661). From the fifth, a staircase descends to the crypt (1515), which has grotesque corbels and the tombstone of Guillaume le Sueur (d. 1530). The church was decorated with murals in the 19C, some by Chassériau, in the third chapel north of the choir. The painting of *St Merri Liberating Prisoners* in the north transept is by Simon Vouet.

There is some good stained-glass contemporary with the church in the upper windows, although much was taken out in the 18C, and the lower windows are mainly 19C. The nave windows belong to the early 16C; outstanding are the two west windows, depicting the life of *St Nicholas of Myre* and of *St Agnes*. The stained glass of the choir and transept is attributed to Pinaigrier and dated c 1540.

The quarter around St-Merri, with its narrow and picturesque alleys, retains several characteristic old houses which survived the rage for demolition during the Halles-Beaubourg redevelopment scheme.

According to tradition, the writer Boccaccio (1313–75), whose mother was French, was born near the junction of the adjacent Rue des Lombards and Rue St-Martin, in which there is a 17C bas-relief of the *Annunciation* on No. 89. Rue des Lombards, named after the Italian bankers and money changers who frequented it in the Middle Ages, continues to the east by the Rue de la Verrerie.

You meet Rue de Rivoli again just south of St-Merri. This eastern section of the street was laid out under Napoléon III to allow rapid access for troops to the Hôtel de Ville in case of emergency.

Across Rue de Rivoli is Sq. St-Jacques, a public garden since 1856 and the first of a series of green areas created by Haussman who was busy transforming the district at the time. In the centre rises the flamboyant Gothic **Tour St-Jacques**, dating from 1508–22. Since 1797 this is the only relic of a series of churches standing on this site from the 9C dedicated to St Jacques-la-Boucherie. It was a rallying point for pilgrims on the road to Santiago de Compostella in Spain. From 1836 it was used as a shot-tower until creatively restored in 1858 by Ballu, and since 1885 as a meteorological station.

Adjoining to the south west is the hectic **Pl. du Châtelet** (Pl. 14; 2), bounded by the Seine, here crossed by the Pont au Change: see Ch. 1. The Place is named after the vanished Grand Châtelet, a fortress gateway leading to the Cité, once the headquarters of the Provost of Paris and the Guild of Notaries. It was begun in 1130, and demolished between 1802 and 1810. There is a plan of the fort on the front of the Chambres des Notaires on the north side of the square.

On the east side is the Théâtre de la Ville, restored after a fashion and reopened in 1980, only to be severely damaged by fire in 1982. To the west is the Théâtre du Châtelet (1862), in which the Communards were court-martialled in 1871.

In the centre is the Fontaine du Châtelet (or de la Victoire or du Palmier) dating from 1808 and 1858. An inscription indicates the position of the Parloir aux Bourgeois, the seat of the municipality of Paris from the 13C until 1357 (see below).

From the north side of the Place, Av. Victoria, named in honour of Queen Victoria's visit to Paris in 1855, leads east to another large square, the **PL. DE L'HÔTEL-DE-VILLE** (Pl. 14; 2), known until the Revolution of 1830 as Pl. de Grève, for here, since the 11C, ships had moored on the strand or *grève*. This square was the location for public executions, many incredibly barbarous, of Protestants, assassins, sorceresses, highwaymen, murderers, revolutionaries, and the like. It was often a rendezvous for unemployed or dissatisfied workers, who were said to *faire grève*, which came to mean to go on strike.

The **Hôtel de Ville**, on the eastern side of the square, stands on the site of its historic predecessor, begun c 1532 and burnt down by the Communards in 1871. This caricature replica, in the style of the French Renaissance, was built (on a larger scale) in 1874–84 from the plans of Ballu and Deperthes. Its over-decorated façades are embellished with statues of eminent Frenchmen; its interior is also lavishly adorned in the official taste in architecture of the period, with sculpture, elaborate carvings and murals, including Puvis de Chavannes' *The Seasons*. The platforms of the métro station, Hôtel de Ville, are decorated with illustrations of the old building and its splendid interior.

At 29 Rue de Rivoli, on the north side of the building, is the Municipal Tourist Office (☎ 01 42 76 43 43).

In 1264 Louis IX created the first municipal authority in Paris by allowing the merchants to elect magistrates (*échevins*), led by the *prévôt des marchands*, who was also head of the Hanse des marchands de l'eau. This merchant guild, which had the monopoly of the traffic on the Seine, Marne, Oise and Yonne, took as their emblem a ship, a device which still graces the arms of the city. Their first meeting-place was known simply as the Parloir aux Bourgeois; later they met at the Grand-Châtelet itself; and finally, in 1357, the Provost Etienne Marcel bought the Maison aux Piliers or Maison du Dauphin, a mansion in Pl. de Grève, for their assemblies. In 1532 plans for an imposing new building were adopted but work was stopped at the second floor, and the new designs were not completed until 1628.

This was where in 1789 the 300 electors nominated by the districts of Paris met. On 17 July, Louis XVI received the newly-devised tricolour cockade from the hands of Jean Sylvain Bailly, the Mayor. On 10 August 1792, the 172 commissaries elected by Paris gave the signal for a general insurrection. In 1794 Robespierre took refuge here, but was arrested on 27 July and, his jaw smashed by a bullet, dragged to the Conciergerie. In 1805 it became the seat of the Préfet de la Seine and his council, and was the scene of numerous official celebrations.

The Swiss Guards put up a stout defence of the building during the July Revolution of 1830. In 1848 it became the seat of Louis Blanc's provisional government and witnessed the arrest of the revolutionary agitators

Armand Barbès and Louis-Auguste Blanqui. The Third Republic was proclaimed here in 1870 (4 September) and, in the following March, the Commune. On 24 May 1871 the building was evacuated before being set ablaze by its defenders.

In 1944 the Hôtel de Ville was a focus of opposition to the occupying forces by the Resistance movement who, by 19 August, had established themselves in the building repelling German counter-attacks until relieved by the arrival of Général Leclerc's division five days later.

Just across Rue de Rivoli from the north-east corner of the Hôtel de Ville, is the **Temple des Billettes**, at 22 Rue des Archives. It was built in 1756 for the Carmelites, but since 1812 has been used as a Lutheran church. Adjoining it to the north is the cloister, completed in 1427, with Flamboyant vaults. This is the only medieval cloister extant in Paris and is a relic of an older convent. The cloister is regularly used for exhibitions, and the church for concerts.

Rue de Rivoli and Rue St-Antoine

Rue de Rivoli, and its eastern extension, Rue St-Antoine, split the ancient Marais district into two unequal sections; the smaller, to the south, is described below; for the area to the north, see Ch. 21.

To the east of the Hôtel de Ville, between two of its annexes, lies **PL. ST-GERVAIS**, with its elm tree, a reminder of the famous elm of St-Gervais, beneath which justice used to be administered; the proverbial expression for waiting for Doomsday is, ironically, *Attendre sous l'orme* (the elm). This was one of the first inhabited areas on the Right Bank, and Rue François-Miron follows the course of a Roman road which led from Lutetia to Senlis.

St-Gervais-St-Protais

Dominating the eastern side of Pl. St-Gervais is St-Gervais-St-Protais (Pl. 15; 1–3). One of the oldest parishes on the Right Bank, its history goes back to the 6C. It is thought that the sanctuary was rebuilt in the 13C. Despite the classical façade, the body of the present church is a late Gothic structure begun at the end of the 15C.

The original plans are attributed to Martin Chambiges, whose work was continued by his son Pierre. The lower stages of the tower are an early 15C survival. The façade (1616–21), recently renovated, by Clément II Métezeau is proposed as the earliest example in Paris of the correct sequence, of the three Classic orders: Doric, Ionic and Corinthian. The choir and transepts date from rebuildings of 1494–1578 and the nave was continued in Flamboyant Gothic between 1600–20, with lierne and tierceron vaults, despite the strength of Italian Renaissance influence at this time. Work on some of the chapels and tower went on until 1657.

Philippe de Champaigne (1602–74), Scarron (1610–60) and Crébillon the Elder (1674–1762) are buried here. François Couperin (1668–1733) and seven members of his family served as organists from 1653 to 1830. Their instrument, restored, survives, while the case was rebuilt in the 18C.

The **interior**, impressive for its loftiness and unity of style, is remarkably rich in works of art. The high windows of both nave and choir contain much painted glass of c 1610–20 by Robert Pinaigrier and Nicolas Chaumet.

In the **south aisle**, the third chapel has an altar commemorating some 50 victims of the bombardment of Good Friday 1918, when a German shell struck the church. In the fourth are seven low 17C painted panels of the *Life of Christ*. Painted glass of 1531 by Pinaigrier, restored in the 19C represents, in the fifth chapel, the *Martyrdom of St Gervais and St Protais*, and in the sixth the *Judgement of Solomon*. The eighth chapel contains the *tomb of Michel le Tellier* (d. 1685), by Mazeline and Hurtrelle; the bearded heads supporting the Chancellor's sarcophagus are from the tomb of Jacques de Souvré (d. 1670), by François Anguier, the rest of which are in the Louvre. The Lady Chapel, a heady example of Flamboyant Gothic (1517) with complicated vaults and a bravura pendant boss, also retains fine original glass (restored in the 19C) of the *Life of the Virgin*.

In the **north aisle** is a plaque commemorating the consecration of an earlier church, 1420. All that remains are the first two levels of the belfry above the sacristy, which retains a good iron grille of 1741. In the north transept is a restored mid-16C Flemish painting of the Passion. From the next chapel you can enter the Chapelle Dorée (1628) with its original decoration; in the adjacent chapel are a 13C high relief of the *Dormition of the Virgin* (below the altar), and a portrait by Pajou (1782) of Mme Palerme de Savy. (At the time of writing, these chapels were under restoration.)

In the **choir**, the first seven stalls in the upper row were remade in the 17C; the rest are mid-16C with interesting misericords. The 18C bronze-gilt candelabra and cross were designed by Soufflot. Against the north entry-pillar is a 14C Virgin, known as N.-D. de Bonne-Délivrance; and on either side of the altar, wooden statues of the patron saints, by Michel Bourdin (1625).

The **south façade** of the church can now be seen since the area has been the subject of clearance and restoration. The façades of some houses in Rue des Barres, behind the building, are worth looking at, and the surrounding streets, in the pleasing *quartier* of St-Paul have some fine 17C and 18C elevations and details.

The stepped RUE FRANÇOIS-MIRON, leading north east from St-Gervais, is one of the more imposing streets in the district. Nos 2–14, built c 1735, are adorned with wrought-iron work with an elm motif (see above); Nos 30, 36 and 42 all have good features.

No. 26 Rue Geoffroy-l'Asnier (right) is the **Hôtel de Chalons-Luxembourg** (1608), with a magnificent doorway (1659) and an attractive Louis XIII pavilion in the courtyard. No. 22 is a handsome 17C elevation, and at No. 17, is a Jewish Study Centre with, on the angle with Rue Grenier-sur-l'eau, a memorial to an Unknown Jewish Martyr.

Further east in Rue François-Miron, Nos 11 and 13 are late medieval houses timber-framed houses. Outstanding is No. 44, **La Maison d'Ourscamps** (1585), occupied by the l'Association de Paris historique, built around a timbered and jettied courtyard and over a vaulted 13C cellar. The former townhouse of the Abbey of Ourscamps (near Noyon), it provided accommodation for students of Notre-Dame school as well as serving as a warehouse for produce from the country property. (Open Mon–Sat 14.00–18.00, occasionally Sun.)

No. 68 is the badly neglected **Hôtel de Beauvais**, by Le Pautre, with an interior courtyard, ornate circular vestibule and carved staircase (closed at present). The balcony of the Hôtel du Président Hénault (No. 82) is also worth noting. Around the corner, at 5–7 Rue de Fourcy, is the gallery of the **Maison Européenne de la Photographie** (☎ 01 44 78 75 08), with a café.

To the right in Rue de Jouy, No. 7, the **Hôtel d'Aumont**, by Le Vau (1648) and François Mansart (1656), has some of its original decoration, including work by Le Brun.

Beyond, Rue du Figuier leads right to the **Hôtel de Sens** (Pl. 15; 3), built 1475–1519 for the archbishops of Sens, when the bishopric of Paris was suffragan to the metropolitan see of Sens (before 1623); it is older than the Hôtel de Cluny (see p 75), the only other important example of 15C domestic architecture in Paris. Unfortunately, after long neglect, the Hôtel de Sens was poorly restored; since 1911 it has housed the Bibliothèque Forney, a reference library for the fine arts.

To the east, Quai des Célestins commands attractive views of the Ile St-Louis. On the left, at No. 32, the site of the Tour Barbeau. This completed, on the river bank, the northern perimeter of Philippe Auguste's defensive wall, one of the best sections of which is be seen from the adjacent Rue des Jardins-St-Paul across the school playground.

The neighbouring Rue St-Paul had acquired its name before 1350; at No. 32, a fragment of the belfry of the vanished church of St-Paul-des-Champs survives. See below for the eastern end of the Quai des Célestins.

Between Rue des Jardins-St-Paul and parallel Rue St-Paul, the former gardens of King Charles V were restored and rearranged in 1970–81 in a series of courtyards perfect for browsing, called the **Village St-Paul**, with craft boutiques and cafés.

The north end of Rue des Jardins-St-Paul brings you to Rue St-Antoine, an ancient thoroughfare retaining several elegant façades.

A few paces to the west is **St-Paul-St-Louis** (Pl. 15; 3), or the Grands-Jésuites, built for that Society by Louis XIII in 1627–41 to replace a chapel of 1582. The Jesuits were suppressed in 1762, and St-Paul was added to the original name in 1796 to commemorate the demolished St-Paul-des-Champs.

Building work, including the handsome Baroque portal, was supervised by Martellange until 1629, and François Derrand saw it through to its completion in 1641, while Turmel was responsible for the interior decorations. Its florid style, inspired by 16C Italian churches, is a good example of Jesuit architecture in France. The clock on the façade came from the church of St-Paul. The church was restored by Baltard in the 19C and the statues on the façade are 19C (by Lequesne, Etex and Préault). Richelieu said the first mass here.

The ornate interior is imposing but light, retaining the original clear glass with floral friezes. The 55m high dome over the crossing, was the third to be built in Paris (after the Petits Augustins and the Carmes). In the pendentives are medallions of the four Evangelists and, in the drum, trompe l'oeil paintings of Clovis, Charlemagne, Robert le Pieux and St-Louis (19C). Most furnishings have been dispersed, some to the Louvre, and the tomb of Henri II to Chantilly (see Ch. 39). The suspended silver angels carrying the embalmed hearts of Louis XIII and XIV have, of course, long gone.

However, the church still contains some fine works. In the north transept, is the beautiful painting **Christ in the Garden** by Delacroix, and opposite *St Louis Receiving the Crown of Thorns*, school of Vouet (1639); and in the south, *Louis XIII offering a Model of the Church to St Louis* by Vouet. There is also good wood carving and 17C ironwork. Buried here are Bishop Huet of Avranches (d. 1721), and Louis Bourdaloue, confessor to Louis XIV.

Turning east along Rue St-Antoine, you shortly reach (left; No. 62) the most elegant and prestigious *hôtel particulier* in the Marais, the **Hôtel de Sully** (or de Béthune-Sully). It is occupied by the Caisse Nationale des Monuments Historiques et des sites (CNMHS), who can give information about guided tours to the sites and monuments of Paris (booklet Visites Conférences available in most museums, ☎ 01 44 61 21 69/01 44 61 21 70) and has an excellent book-shop, open Tues–Sun. They publish Monuments Historiques, a review devoted to the restoration of architecturally important buildings. (Their publications are also available at Porte C of the Grand Palais, Ch. 25.)

The mansion, thought to be by Jean du Cerceau (1624–30), was acquired by Sully, the minister of Henri IV, in 1634. The courtyard, a fine example of Louis-XIII style, abounds in carved decorations, notably around the dormers and six bas-reliefs in niches, the females representing the Elements and the males Autumn and Winter. Spring and Summer are on the garden façade, a subdued echo of the courtyard. The entrance pavilions and the interior, extensively restored, still have their 17C ceilings and panelling. Extended by an orangery, the Petit Sully, in 1634–41, it is possible to walk through the garden out into Place des Vosges.

The Photographic Archives of the Caisse Nationale, invaluable to the student of French art and architecture, are at 4 Rue de Turenne, adjacent to the west.

From just east of the Hôtel de Sully, the short Rue de Birague approaches the southern entrance of the Pl. des Vosges (see Ch. 21); Nos 12 and 14 have elegant features.

Opposite, from the south side of Rue St-Antoine, leads Rue Beautreillis. Beneath the carriage-entrance of No. 22, the Grand Hôtel de Charny, are some woodcarvings in purest Louis XIII style. No. 10 was the Hôtel des Princes de Monaco, built c 1650, but altered in the 18C–19C. To the right in Rue Charles V is the imposing Hôtel d'Aubray (No. 12) of 1620. No. 10, the Hôtel de Maillé, retains its Louis XIII façade and No. 15, opposite, dates from 1642. Nos 7 and 9 Rue Beautreillis, late 16C, are fine bourgeois houses.

On reaching Rue des Lions, with a number of 17C–18C mansions, including No. 10 and No. 11, in which Mme de Sévigné lived in 1645–50, turn left and then right to regain the Quai des Célestins.

No. 4 Quai des Célestins, the stately **Hôtel de Fieubet**, formerly Hôtel de St-Pol, with an interesting courtyard, was renovated and decorated by Le Sueur and Vicotte after plans by Jules Hardouin-Mansart for Gaspard de Fieubet, Chancellor to Anne of Austria. Unfortunately in 1857 it was transformed into a pastiche of Italo-Spanish Baroque. Since 1877 is has accommodated the Ecole

Massillon. The Hôtel de Nicolai, No. 4, is also of the late 17C.

At No. 1 Rue de Sully, on the far side of Blvd Henri-IV, in the Quartier de l'Arsenal (named after the arsenal established here by Henri IV), stands the **Bibliothèque de l'Arsenal** (Pl. 15; 4).

The library, opened to the public in 1797, was founded in 1757 by Antoine-René, Marquis de Paulmy d'Argenson (1722–87), and sold by him to the Comte d'Artois in 1785. It is partly installed in the former residence of the Grand Master of Artillery, built in 1594 for Sully. The façade in the parallel Blvd Morland (facing the starkly functional Préfecture de Paris) is by Boffrand (c 1723). Noteworthy are the Salon de Musique, by Boffrand, with superb Louis-XV woodwork, and the Apartment of the Duchesse de La Meilleraie, with a ceiling by Vouet. (Occasional visits with the CNMHS.)

This important library has been a department of the Bibliothèque Nationale since 1977. It possesses some 15,000 MSS, one million printed volumes and 100,000 engravings, musical works and maps. It is known particularly for its incomparable series of illuminated MSS, and almost complete collection of French dramatic works. The Gordon Craig collection was acquired in 1957. Among its archives are the papers of the Bastille; documents relating to the 'Man in the Iron Mask', and the 'Affair of the Diamond Necklace'; letters of Henri IV to the Marquise de Verneuil; also Louis IX's Book of Hours and Charles V's Bible, among others. Nodier, Hérédia, Mérimée and Anatole France were librarians here.

Turning north east (right) past the Caserne des Célestins (barracks of the Gendarmerie Mobile, built on part of the site of the famous Celestine monastery founded in 1362, but suppressed in 1779), you shortly bear left off Blvd Henri-IV, to regain the Rue St-Antoine (via the Rue Castex). On the corner is the circular Temple de Ste-Marie, originally the chapel of the Convent of the Visitation, and now a Protestant church. It was built by François Mansart (1598–1666) in 1632–34. The unscrupulous Surintendant des Finances, Nicolas Fouquet (1615–80) and Henri de Sévigné (Mme de Sévigné's husband, killed in a duel in 1651) were buried here. Vincent de Paul was almoner of the convent for 28 years.

A few paces to the west, at No. 21, is the Hôtel de Mayenne (or d'Ormesson), with a turret and charming staircase. Now the Ecole des Francs-Bourgeois, it was built by Jean or Jacques II du Cerceau in 1613–17, and modified by Boffrand in 1709.

To the east, a tablet on 5 Rue St-Antoine marks the position of the court of the Bastille (see Ch. 21), by which the Revolutionary mob gained access to the fortress. Near the junction of this street and the Pl. de la Bastille was the site of the great barricade of 1848, and also the last stronghold of the Communards in 1871.

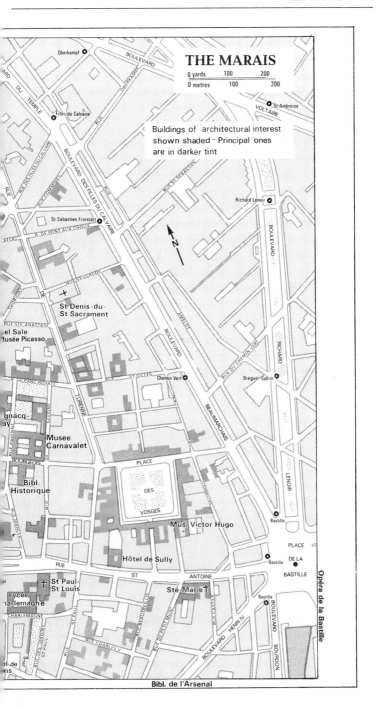

THE MARAIS

0 yards	100	200
0 metres	100	200

Buildings of architectural interest
shown shaded – Principal ones
are in darker tint

Oberkampf

St Ambroise

Filles du Calvaire

St Sebastien Froissart

Richard Lenoir

St Denis-du-
St Sacrament

el Sale
Iusée Picasso

Chemin Vert

Breguet-Sabin

Musee
Carnavalet

Bibl.
Historique

PLACE

DES

VOSGES

Mus. Victor Hugo

Bastille

Hôtel de Sully

PLACE
DE LA
BASTILLE

Bastille

St Paul-
St Louis

Lycée
harlemagne

ANTOINE

Ste-Marie

Bastille

Opéra de la Bastille

el de
ns

Bibl. de l'Arsenal

20 · Centre Pompidou

■ Arrondissement: 75004.
■ Métros: Rambuteau, Hôtel de Ville, Châtelet; RER: Châtelet-Les Halles.

> **Restaurant du Centre**, ☎ 01 48 04 99 89, terrace.

The Centre Georges Pompidou (Pl. 14; 2), renowned for its building, the first great modern architectural project in Paris, contains the national collection of modern art, one of the most important in the world. Officially called the **Centre National d'Art et de Culture Georges-Pompidou**, it was named after the former president who, in 1969, conceived the idea of a centre covering all aspects of modern culture. It is also known simply as the Pompidou Centre.

■ The centre is open Mon and Wed–Fri. 12.00–22.00, Sat, Sun and bank holidays, 10.00–22.00. Closed Tues and 1 May; (☎ 01 44 78 12 33). There are three types of tickets: either for the National Museum of Modern Art, or for Major Exhibitions, or a One-Day pass which includes the museum, exhibitions and all guided visits. Guided visits of different aspects of the Centre are available in English from 15 June–15 September. (There will be limited access to the Centre until 1 January 2000, due to renovation works—see below.)

The Centre consists of four main departments: Le Musée National d'Art Moderne has recently merged with the Centre de Création Industrielle (MNAM/CCI) to make one museum; Le Département du Développement Culturel (DDC) which aims to offer the public the widest possible range of 20C culture; La Bibliothèque Publique d'Information (BPI), a multi-media free-access public library; and L'Institut de Recherche et Coordination Acoustique-Musique (IRCAM), musical research and creation bringing together composers and scientists. The Centre also hosts activities such as theatre, dance, music, cinema and new technology.

The superstructure of this astonishing metal cage, arguably the most controversial building since the Eiffel Tower, is 166m long from north to south, 60m wide, and 42m in height. It uses 15,000 tonnes of metal and has a glazed surface of 11,000m². The functional and structural elements are in full view and mainly on the exterior—some picked out in red and blue. This leaves maximum space inside on eight open-plan levels totalling 60,000m². The Anglo-Italian team which won the competition for the design of the Pompidou Centre (out of 681 entries) included the architects Richard Rogers and Renzo Piano, in association with G. Franchini and the Ove Arup group.

The building, inaugurated 31 January 1977, was designed to accommodate 5000 visitors per day but the number has been far exceeded (it received 6 million in the first year) causing immense wear and tear. A complete facelift not only of the exterior, but of all the surroundings, started in 1995. The surroundings will be enhanced with planting and sculptures. The completion date is 31 December 1999.

The Centre is approached from the west by the lively **Piazza Beaubourg** which slopes down from Rue St-Martin to the main entrance on the ground floor. Here varied performances and exhibitions—both impromptu and organised—take place (beware of pick-pockets). On the south side the Millennium Clock is counting down the seconds to the turn of the century. There is another entrance on Rue du Renard-Beaubourg to the east. One of the most daring features of the building is the external escalator running up a glazed tube which writhes

A section of the outside of the Pompidou Centre

up the façade to a series of platforms, providing access to each of the upper five floors. It is one of the most popular areas for the remarkable views it offers over Parisian rooftops (free access).

The forecourt and all the areas adjacent to the Centre have been improved and landscaped. On the north of the Piazza Beaubourg is an extension which opened in January 1997, designed by Piano, enclosing a garden and the Studio of Constantin Brancusi (1876–1957) moved from 11 Impasse Ronsin. (The number of visitors admitted to the studio is limited to 75 at any one time.)

During the revamp of the interior of the Centre certain limited areas will be open to the public. The new **Brancusi Studio** in the piazza will be open. The escalators will continue to run so that the panorama from the fifth floor terrace can be enjoyed. There will be a permanent exhibition space in the southern gallery of the present contemporary area. On the piazza, a large temporary construction will house an information centre, a bookshop and other activities. There will also be a giant screen projecting future events and a series of exhibitions of works from the collection will be held in Paris (and elsewhere). The Centre's reopening is scheduled to coincide with the millennium celebrations on 1 January 2000.

The proposed major rearrangement of the interior will liberate more space for the permanent collection of the Musée National d'Art Moderne over the whole of the third and fourth floors, while the exhibition space on the 5th floor will also be extended.

The first basement is used for conferences, cinema, theatre, dance and other events. Also accommodated in the building are sections of the library (BPI), with over 350,000 volumes, 250,000 transparencies, 12,000 records, reference material, films, video-cassettes, etc. IRCAM (acoustics and music) is happily muffled in sound-proof bunkers (below Pl. Igor-Stravinsky, between the Centre and St-Merri). During the transitional period, there will alternative library facilities in the neighbourhood.

Musée National d'Art Moderne

The some 40,000 works in the collection date from 1905 to the present, and provide an overview of all types of visual arts and all major movements and artists of the 20C. It is not possible to exhibit the entire collection; about 1500 works may be on view at any one time, changing three times a year, apart from the most important works. A selection of the highlights of the museum is discussed here.

The first modern movement of the 20C, **Fauvism** (*fauve*, wild beast), a term coined in 1905 as a criticism of the violent, impasto colour and contorted forms of a group of young artists, is well represented: **André Derain** (1880–1954), *Le Pont de Chatou, Les deux Péniches;* **Georges Braque** (1882–1963), *Paysage de L'Estaque* and *L'Estaque* (c 1906), and *Paysage des Carrières St-Denis, Cinq Bananes et Deux Poires,* both 1908; **Raoul Dufy** (1877–1953), *Les Affiches à Trouville;* **Maurice de Vlaminck** (1876–1958), *Les Arbres Rouges* (1906).

Other artists briefly involved with Fauvism were: **Camoin** (1879–1965), *Portrait of Marquet;* **Albert Marquet** (1875–1947), *La Plage de Fécamp, Portrait d'André Rouveyre,* 1904, *Bassin du Havre;* **Othon Friesz** (1879–1949), *Portrait de Fernand Fleuret,* 1907.

The numerous works in the collection by **Henri Matisse** (1869–1954) cover the major developments in his art. From his Fauve period, *Algerienne* (1909), and early experiments with simplification of forms *La Blouse Roumaine, L'Odalesque à la Culotte Rouge,* and *Le Luxe I* (1907) and expressive colour *Grand Intérieur Rouge;* an interlude with Abstraction, *Porte-fenêtre à Collioure* (1914) contrasts with the highly decorative *Figure Décorative sur Fond Ornemental* (1925–26). Several examples of his cut-outs are also in the collection: *Deux Danseuses* (1937–38), *Polynésie, Le Ciel* (1946), *Nu Bleu II and III* (1952), *La Tristesse du Roi* (1952) as well as projects for the chapel at Vence. Bronzes include *Nu Couché* (1907), *Deux Negresses* (1908), *Jeanette I and IV* (1910–13) and *Nu de Dos I, II, III, IV* (1930).

A member of the **Nabis** group, **Pierre Bonnard** (1867–1947), moved to the Côte d'Azur c 1925 to concentrate on interpreting light, forms and character exclusively with colour: *L'Atelier au Mimosa* (1939–46), *Nu à la Baignoire* (1931), *Nu de Dos à la Toilette* (Nu Jaune) (1934).

The development of **Cubism** is followed through the works of its creators, Braque and Picasso, between 1907 and 1914, from Analytical, c 1908–11, to the Synthetic phase with collages, c 1911–14, alongside masks and carvings from Gabon and the Ivory coast which deeply influenced Cubist vision: **Braque**: *Les Usines de Rio-Tinto Zinc à l'Estaque* (1910), *Le Guéridon, Composition au Violin, L'Homme à la Guitar, Compotier et Cartes, Nature Mort e sur une Table* (Gillette), and two portraits; **Picasso**: *Etude d'une des Demoiselles d'Avignon* (1907), *Femme Assise* (1910), *Tête de Femme* (pastel), and *Femme à la Tête Rouge* (gouache), *Le Violin, Portrait d'un Jeune Fille, Tête d'Homme au Chapeau, Le Guéridon Noir.*

Among other important artists to experiment with Cubism was **Juan Gris** (1887–1927): *La Guitar* (1913), *Verre et Damier* (1914), *Le Petit Déjeuner* (1915) *Pierrot à la Grappe* (1917). **Amédée Ozenfant** (1886–1966), **Jeanneret** (**Le Corbusier**) (1888–1965), with **Fernand Léger** developed an ordered form of Cubism kown as **Purism**. So for a time did Francis Picabia: *Udine* (1913).

A three-dimensional interpretation of Cubism was attempted by **Raymond Duchamp-Villon**: *Le Cheval Majeur* (1914-66); **Henri Laurens**: *Construction, Bouteille et Verre* (1917); and **Alexander Archipenko** (1887–1964). Also from just before the First World War are works by the brilliant young **Henri Gaudier-Brzeska** (1891–1915).

La Section d'Or group, combined Cubism with light and colour (known as

Orphic Cubism) in a celebration of modern life, to create such compositions as: **Robert Delaunay** (1885–1941), *La Fenêtre* (1912–13), the first completely abstract painting by a French artist, *La Ville de Paris*; and *Eiffel Tower*; and **Sonia Delaunay** (1885–1979), *Prismes Electriques* (1914).

The large group of works by **Fernand Léger** (1881–1955) ranges from and lyrical *La Noce* (1911–12) to a rigorous personal interpretation of Cubism: *Contraste de Formes* (1913). Returning to a figurative style after the First World War, Léger produced strictly unsentimental works such as the large *La Lecture* (1924), and *Élément Mécanique* (1924) a tribute to the machine age; also the huge *Composition aux Deux Perroquets* (1935–39), and combined dynamic flat decorative forms with free colour in *Les Grands Plongeurs Noirs* (1944).

There are **Picassos** of all periods: monumental, *La Liseuse* (1920); Neo-Classical, *Nature Morte à la Tête Antique* (1925); Surrealist, *Figure* (c 1927); mythological, *Minotaure* (1927); a tapestry cartoon, *Confidences* (1934); also, *L'Aubade* (1942), and *Portraits of Mme Paul Eluard*, and of *Dora Maar*. The metal assemblages of the Catalan, **Julio Gonzalez** (1876–1942), a friend of Picasso, are represented by *Femme à la Corbeille* (c 1930–33) and *Petite Danseuse* (1934–37).

Varied approaches to non-figurative art include **Suprematism**, an extreme form of abstract art invented by Kasimir Malévich (1878–1935), as in *La Croix Noire* (1915); **Constructivism**, geometric abstraction, a development of collage in Russia around 1917–21, by Antoine Pevsner, *Masque* (1923), Naum Gabo, Tatlin, Rodchenko and El Lissitsky; the **de Stijl** group of Dutch artists associated with the magazine of the same name (1917–32) who produced the pure abstraction of Van Doesburg, *Composition* (1920), and Piet Mondrian, *New York City I* (1942). Frantisek Kupka (1871–1957) was another pioneer of abstract art, as in *Planes by Colours* (1911).

Other forms of abstraction are found in the sculpture of **Constantin Brancusi**: *La Muse Endormie* (1910), *Le Coq* (1935). Many of the above artists, plus Hans Arp, Herbin, Sophie Taeuber-Arp, Vantongerloo, Gerit Rietveld, belonged to an association of about 400 artists, called **Abstraction-Création** founded in 1931.

Futurism, a celebration of modernity whose adherents wanted to represent simultaneous phases of movement, emerged in Italy led by the poet Filippo Marinetti. Examples include Luigi Russolo (1885–1947); Alberto Magnelli, *Explosion Lyrique No. 8*, *Florence* (1918); the Russian Michel Larionov (1881–1964), launched a version of Futurism called **Rayonism**, as in *Promenade—Vénus de Boulevard* (c 1912–13).

Montparnasse artists of the 1910–30 era, include **Marc Chagall**: *Double portrait with a Glass of Wine* (1917–18), *The Acrobat, Guerre* (1943); **Chaïm Soutine**, *Le Groom* (1928), and *Portrait of Miestchanioff*; **George Rouault** (1871–1958) *The Wounded Clown*, and religious paintings such as *La Sainte Face* (1933); **Amedeo Modigliani**, *Tête rouge* (1915); **Otto Dix**, *Portrait of Sylvia von Harden* (1926) an uncompromising portrait of a journalist, a woman and an era.

The museum has many works by the Russian-born **Wassily Kandinsky** (1866–1944). From early Fauvist-type landscapes he moved to the floating, detached shapes of *Sans Titre* (1910), *Avec l'Arc Noir* (1912) and titles such as Impressions, Improvisations and Compositions (c 1911–14), later creating more dynamic, explosive, compositions such as *Sur blanc II* (1923). A member, with Kandinsky, of the Blaue Reiter group in Munich, and then of the Bauhaus (1922–33), was **Paul Klee** (1879–1940) among whose works are *Villas at Florence* (1926) and *En Rythme* (1930). Expressionism is represented by member of the German Die Brücke group such as **Ernst-Ludwig Kirchner**, *La Toilette* (1913–20).

Dada was born in 1916 in Zurich out of the horrors of the First World War. Anti-art, provocative and funny if sometimes obscene, it was taken up by George Grosz, *Remember Uncle August, the Unhappy Inventor* (1919); Kurt Schwitters, *Merz* (1926), Man Ray, *Cadeau* (1921–63); Picabia, *L'Oeil Cacodylate* (1921); Hausmann and Marcel Duchamp and Max Ernst.

Surrealism had its roots in Dada, literature, Freud's theories and the hallucinatory paintings of **Giorgio di Chirico**, *Premonitory Portrait of Guillaume Apollinaire*. Its poet-painters, led by André Breton, had a far-reaching effect on all aspects of art. Members of the group represented include: **Max Ernst** (1891–1976) *À l'Intérieur de Vue* (1929), *Loplop Présente une Jeune Fille* (1930); **René Magritte** (1898–1967), *Le Double Secret* (1927), *Le Modèle Rouge*; **Yves Tanguy**, *A Quatre Heures d'Eté, l'Espoir* (1929), and **Salvador Dali** (1904–89), *Hallucination Partielle, Six Images de Lénin sur un Piano* (1931). The individual, poetic style of **Joan Miró** (1891–1983), *La Sieste* (1925), and the montage, *L'Objet du Couchant* (1937), has strong ties with Surrealism. So equally does the work of sculptors such as **Hans Arp**, *Danseuse* (1925), and the chilling works of **Alberto Giacometti**, *La Pointe à l'Oeil* (1931), and **Hans Bellmer**, *La Poupée* (1934–37), who both came under its spell.

Among **sculpture** of the 1920s onwards are works by: **Lipchitz**, *Head of Gertrude Stein* (1920), *Figure* (1926–30); Gargallo, *Statue of the Prophet*; the highly personal three-dimensional work of **Alexander Calder** (1898–1976): in wire, *Josephine Baker* (1926); mobiles—*Disque Blanc, Disque Noir* (1940–41); in wood Requin et Baleine (c 1933). Also the mechanised sculptures of **Jean Tinguely**: Sculpture *Méta-Mécanique-Automobile* (1954); and the figurative visionary sculptress, **Germaine Richier** (1904–59), *L'Ouragane* (1948–49).

Post-Second World War art is represented by the **art brut** (raw art) of **Jean Dubuffet**, for example: *Dhô tel Nuancé d'Abricot, Le Métafisyx* (1950), *Le Voyageur sans Boussole, 8 juillet 1952*. Other figurative painters of the post-war period are: **Alberto Giacometti**, *Portrait de Jean Genet* (1955); **Francis Bacon** *Van Gogh in a Landscape* (1957), *Three People in a Room*; Balthus, *Cathy's Toilet*; *The Painter and his Model* (1980–81). Later members of the School of Paris include abstract painters such as Maria Elena Vieira da Silva, *La Bibliothèque* (1949); Nicolas de Staël, *La Vie Dure* (1946), Jean Fautrier, *Femme Douce* (1946), Antoni Tàpies (b. 1923), and Pierre Soulages (b. 1919), whose huge canvases trace a form in space. The great master of **op art** is Victor Vasarély (1908–1997), *Hô II* (1948–52).

Among American painters represented in the museum are the **Abstract-Expressionists**, Willem de Kooning, *Woman* (c 1952) and Barnett Newman, *Shining Forth* (to George) (1961); Mark Rothko's modern icons; colour field painting of Frank Stella, *Parzeczew II* (1971); and Jackson Pollock, drip technique painting '*Number 26 A*', *Black and White*. Pop Artists include Jasper Johns, Andy Warhol, Claes Oldenburg and Robert Rauschenberg.

The **Nouveau Réaliste** group, founded in Paris in 1960, reinterpreted the ready-mades of Marcel Duchamp. Arman (b. 1928), *Home Sweet Home* and *Chopin's Piano*; Yves Klein is known above all for his monochromatic works in blue; Niki de Saint-Phalle and Martial Raysse create bizarre and colourful assemblages. Joseph Beuys (1921), *Homogeneous Infiltration for Grand Piano* (1966), is a mysterious work made for a Happening.

From the 1960s to the 1980s, there are **Compressions** by César; **Assemblages**, by Ben; **Minimalist** or Cool Art, art devoid of all rhetoric; **Conceptual Art** by Daniel Buren, Robert Ryman, Mario Merz; Process Art, Land Art and Arte Povera; Supports/Surfaces, conceived by Claude Viallat, François Rouan, Toni Grand; and Figurations, by Valerio Adami and Georg Baselitz. And added to this is Photomontage.

21 · The Marais

■ Arrondissements: 75003, 75004, 75012.
■ Métros: Bastille, St-Paul, Hôtel-de-Ville, Rambuteau, Temple, Arts-et-Métiers, Réaumur-Sébastopol.

Restaurants and cafés

L'Ambroisie, 9 Pl. des Vosges, ☎ 01 42 78 51 45. Haute cuisine. £££
Baracane, Bistrot de l'Oulette, 38 Rue des Tournelles, ☎ 01 42 71 43 33. Bistrot. £
Au Bascou, 38 Rue Réamur, ☎ 01 42 72 69 25. Bistrot. £
Bofinger, 5 Rue de la Bastille, ☎ 01 42 54 13 67. Brasserie with Art Nouveau decor. ££
Ma Bourgogne, 19 Pl. des Vosges, ☎ 01 42 78 44 64. Café/bistrot. £
Brocco, 180 Rue du Temple, ☎ 01 42 72 19 81. Tea room. £
Le Cristal, 18 Rue du Temple, ☎ 01 42 72 69 62. Grills. £
Le Dômarais, 53bis Rue des Francs-Bourgeois, ☎ 01 42 74 54 17. Dinner concerts. £
Le Dos de la Baleine, 40 Rue des Blancs Manteaux, ☎ 01 42 72 38 98. *Cuisine de marché.* £
Les Enfants Gâtés, 43 Rue des Francs-Bourgeois, ☎ 01 42 77 07 63. Bar. £
Jo Goldenberg, 7 Rue des Rosiers, ☎ 01 48 87 20 16. Deli/Central European. £
La Guirlande de Julie, 25 Pl. des Vosges, ☎ 01 48 87 94 07. £
Le Grand Bleu, opposite 46 Blvd de la Bastille, ☎ 01 43 45 19 99. Fish. £
Les Grandes Marches, 6 Pl. de la Bastille, ☎ 01 43 42 90 32. ££
Café l'Industrie, Rue St-Sabin/Rue Sedaine (Bastille). Café-bar. £
Chez Jenny, 39 Blvd du Temple, ☎ 01 42 74 78 78. Game and seafood. £
Majestic Café, 34 Rue Vielle du Temple, 'Bar Rock'. £
Au Marais Gourmand, 26 rue Charlot, ☎ 01 48 87 63 08. Traditional. £
La Taverne du Nil, 9 Rue du Nil, ☎ 01 42 33 51 82. Lebanese cuisine. £
La Truffe, 31 Rue Vieille du Temple, ☎ 01 42 71 08 39. Vegetarian. £

The Marais, one of the most interesting districts of old Paris, is bounded by the Grands Boulevards on the north and east, by Blvd de Sébastopol to the west, and by the Seine to the south. In spite of past neglect, demolition and some rebuilding, it remains substantially as developed in the 17C. Numerous buildings of outstanding architectural interest, many of them restored in recent years, offer a fascinating reminder of the elegance of this period. In the Marais are several important museums, among them the Musée Carnavalet, Musée Picasso and Musée Cognacq-Jay.

The southern sector of the Marais and the Beaubourg are described in Chapters 19 and 20.

So called from the marshy land (*marais*, marsh or morass), the district only became habitable with the arrival of the Knights Templar and other religious houses who settled here in the 13C and converted the marshes into arable land. Royal patronage began with Charles V, who, anxious to forget the associations of the Palais de la Cité with the rebellion of Etienne Marcel in 1358, built the Hôtel St-Paul here. In the 16C, the Hôtel de Lamoignon and Hôtel Carnavalet were built, but the seal of royal approval came with the construction of the Pl. Royale (1605; later known as the Pl. des Vosges, see below).

Courtiers built themselves houses as near to the Pl. Royale as possible, and the Marais remained the most fashionable residential area of Paris until the creation of the Faubourg St-Germain in the early 18C. The Revolution ended its long reign of splendour, the nobles fled, the State confiscated their property and sold it to craftsmen, mechanics and merchants who flooded into the area, bringing a totally different aspect to the *quartier* while the grand buildings fell into neglect. Much of the Marais is still animated by trade and commerce and it is again a fashionable place to live, while its museums and picturesque streets draw many visitors.

Place de la Bastille

Immediately east of the Marais lies Pl. de la Bastille (Pl. 15; 4), laid out in 1803.

The ground plan of the famous fortress prison is marked by a line of pavingstones in the Place beneath which some of its cellars are said to survive. Its keep (a model of which is in the Musée Carnavalet) stood on the west side, across the end of Rue St-Antoine, and the main drawbridge was slightly north of the junction with Blvd Henri-IV. The July Column (see below) stands approximately in the centre of what was the east bastion. The Canal St-Martin now runs beneath the Place, appearing to the south in the Port de Plaisance de l'Arsenal which flows into the Seine. The area between the port and Blvd de la Bastille was turned into a garden in 1982–83, and the **Grand Bleu restaurant** is installed in a glass building.

The **Bastille** (more correctly the Bastille St-Antoine), originally a bastion-tower defending the eastern entrance to Paris, developed under Charles V into a fortress with eight massive towers, immensely thick walls, and a wide moat. Nevertheless, prisoners managed to escape. By the reign of Louis XIII, the Bastille had become almost exclusively a state prison for political offenders, among whom were the mysterious Man in the Iron Mask

(1698–1703) and Voltaire (twice). The arbitrary arrest by *lettre de cachet*, imprisonment without trial, made the Bastille a popular synonym for oppression. Many illustrious names are among those held here, often for obscure reasons: the Duchesse du Maine and Mme de Tencin; John Vanbrugh the playwright/architect for most of 1692; another inmate was the notorious Marquis de Sade, who wrote Justine and other lubricious works here.

On 14 July 1789, the Revolutionary mob, aided by a few troops, attacked and overwhelmed its defenders, murdered the governor, the Marquis de Launay, and freed a handful of prisoners. Work on its demolition was immediately put in hand.

The **July Column** (Colonne de Juillet) is not connected with the storming of the Bastille, but was erected by Louis-Philippe in 1840–41 to commemorate the 504 victims of the three days' street-fighting of July 1830, who are buried in vaults beneath the circular base of the column. The victims of the Revolution of February 1848 were subsequently interred here, and their names added to the inscription. The bronze-faced column, 51.5m high, is surmounted by a bronze-gilt figure of Liberty.

To the south east of the Place, on the site of the former Gare de la Bastille, is the **Opéra de la Bastille**, a sophisticated, costly and somewhat unwelcoming structure with a convex façade. It was built to celebrate the bicentenary of the Revolution with the intention—so far unfulfilled—of 'bringing opera within the reach of the masses'. Its design, by Carlos Ott, a Uraguayan-born Canadian, was chosen from 744 projects.

Incorporating the latest technical equipment, the opera house is noted for its excellent acoustics and troubled history for actual performances. The building covers a large area and comprises a main auditorium with seating for 2700, a so-called *Salle modulable* for 600 to 1000, and a studio seating 280. Granite, wood and glass are used in the uncluttered decor of the main auditorium which has excellent sightlines. In addition, there are several rehearsal rooms for the orchestra, chorus and ballet, apart from numerous studios, extensive workshops and store rooms for scenery and costumes, and two restaurants. The scene changes are made by bringing into position any of six separate platforms, including the stage, without needing to make any specific, and often noisy, scene shifting behind the scenes. There are guided visits lasting just over an hour at certain times, ☎ 01 40 01 19 70; box office: information, ☎ 01 43 43 96 96, reservations, ☎ 01 44 73 13 00.

For the Faubourg St-Antoine, to the east, see Ch. 31.

Nos 2–20 in Blvd Beaumarchais, leading north from Pl. de la Bastille, are built on the site of a luxurious mansion and garden belonging to the dramatist Caron de Beaumarchais (1732–99).

Rue de la Bastille leads north west from Pl. de la Bastille, north of and parallel to Rue St-Antoine, to Rue des Tournelles, No. 28 in which is the **Hôtel de Mansart-Sagonne**, built for himself in 1674–85 by Jules Hardouin-Mansart and decorated by Le Brun and Mignard. Rue du Pas-de-la-Mule leads left to Pl. des Vosges; beyond, No. 50 has a splendid façade.

Place des Vosges

Pl. des Vosges (Pl. 15; 2-4) is one of the most attractive squares in Paris (1606–11). At the heart of the Marais, it is a large quadrangle surrounded by 39 houses built on a uniform plan with brick, stone and stucco façades, arcaded ground floors and simple dormers. Trees were not planted in the central gardens until 1783, damaging the overall symmetry, so the ideal time to visit is in winter when the leaves have fallen.

The main approach to Pl. des Vosges, from Rue St-Antoine, is by Rue de Birague, passing through the Pavillon du Roi (see below).

> The Place occupies the site of the royal Palais des Tournelles, the residence of the Duke of Bedford, English regent of France in 1422 after the death of Henry V. In 1559 this was the scene of the fatal tournament when Henri II was accidentally killed by Montgomery, and it was in consequence abandoned by his widow, Catherine de Médicis. The square in its present form was laid out for Henri IV, probably by Baptiste du Cerceau, as the Place Royale and opened in 1605. The slightly taller king's pavilion was built above the gateway in the centre of the south side, and the queen's was the corresponding building on the north (No. 28). In the earlier part of the reign of Louis XIV this was one of the most fashionable addresses in Paris, and the centre of the Nouvelles Précieuses satirised by Molière. It only acquired its present name in 1799, the department of the Vosges having been the first to discharge its liabilities for the Revolutionary Wars.

At the corners of the square are fountains (1816), and in the centre an indifferent *equestrian statue of Louis XIII* (1825) set up to replace one destroyed in 1792.

No. 6 is the **Maison Victor Hugo**, open 10.00–17.40, closed Mon and public holidays (☎ 01 42 72 10 16), in which Victor Hugo (1802–85) lived in 1832–48 (second floor), perhaps of more interest for his numerous pen and wash drawings (c 350) than for the memorabilia. The upper rooms provide an opportunity to enjoy the view over the Place.

Things to see include the *bust of Hugo* by Rodin; *Portrait of Juliette Drouet* by Bastien-Lepage; *The Première of Hernani* by Besnard; *Portrait of Adèle Foucher*, the poet's wife, by Louis Boulanger; *Hugo on his Death-bed* by Bonnat; and works by Célestin Nanteuil and Delacroix. There is also furniture and woodwork, designed or carved by Hugo.

No. 7, the Petit-Hôtel de Sully, was built by Jean Androuet du Cerceau. The writers Théophile Gautier (in 1831–34) and Alphonse Daudet lived at No. 8, the Hôtel de Fourcy (1605) and No. 21 was the mansion of Cardinal de Richelieu.

From the north-west corner of Pl. des Vosges you cross Rue de Turenne (where to the left, in the court of No. 23, is the Hôtel de Villacerf, of c 1660, with a fountain), and enter **RUE DES FRANCS-BOURGEOIS**. One of the principal streets of the Marais, it takes its name from the citizens who, being vassals to a feudal lord, were exempt from municipal taxes. (For the north part of the Rue de Turenne see p 235.)

Musée Carnavalet

The Musée Carnavalet, or Musée de l'Histoire de Paris (Pl. 15; 1; métro: St-Paul), at the corner of Rue des Francs-Bourgeois and Rue de Sévigné is an important collection illustrating the history of Paris from prehistory to the early 20C through paintings, sculpture, furniture and interiors. Especially charming are the reconstructed interiors saved from mainly 18C Parisian mansions when Haussmann was demolishing so many buildings in the 19C. Open 10.00–17.40, closed Mon and certain public holidays (☎ 01 42 72 21 13).

The museum is housed in the imposing **Hôtel Carnavalet**, begun in 1548 for Jacques de Ligneris, President of the Parlement, built around a court-yard adorned with sculptures by Jean Goujon. It was altered in 1660 by François Mansart, who built the present façade, but retained the 16C gateway with its Goujon sculptures. Further alterations were made in 19C and 20C. In 1989 the museum was extended into the Hôtel le Peletier de St-Fargeau, built by Pierre Bullet for Michel de Peletier in1687–90, and linked to the main building by a gallery on the first floor.

Mme de Sévigné lived here from 1677 until her death in 1696; her apartments were on the west side, opposite the entrance. The building was acquired by the municipality in 1866 and the museum was inaugurated in 1880.

The bronze *statue of Louis XIV* in the centre of the courtyard is by Coysevox. Of the sculptures in the courtyard, the best are those by Jean Goujon on the entrance arch and above the door on the left. The reliefs of *The Seasons*, on the side opposite the entrance, were probably done under his direction. On the right, the relief above the door is a 19C copy of the one opposite; those on the first storey are by Van Obstal (1660).

In the spring of 1996 the wraps were taken off a total renovation of the Hotel Carnavalet. The most eye-catching result of the restoration are the 60 or so rooms with Louis XV and Louis XVI decor, stunningly revamped to return them to their original state.

The entrance to the museum is to the right of the courtyard. After passing through a vestibule, off which is a bookshop, you turn left into the **Salles des Enseignes**, with shop and tavern signs of the 15C–19Cs. Maquettes of Paris during the last century are exhibited here. Beyond these rooms is the foot of the Escalier de Luynes. On the ground floor are Archaeological, Renaissance and 18C sections. The recently restored period rooms are on the first floor. The Hôtel le Peletier de St-Fargeau has displays relating to Paris from the Revolution to the 20C.

Ground floor

The colonnaded Pavillon de Choiseul, between the Cour de la Victoire (right) and Cour des Drapiers, brings you to the section (**rooms 1–4**) devoted to the early history of Paris, with maquettes of Gallo-Roman Lutetia, and its extent during the Merovingian period; fragments of masonry and collections of glass, terra-cottas, bronze figurines and coins. Also displayed are bronze objects, jewellery, ceramics, buckles and arms, together with parts of a sarcophagus.

Returning through the colonnade, you find on the right the Renaissance rooms (**5–10**). As well as a maquette of the medieval Cité there are several interesting paintings: an anon. mid-16C Flemish painting of the *Prodigal Son in the Company of Courtesans*, with a view of Paris in the background; a *Portrait of Mary Stuart in 1561*, wearing a white mourning veil (School of Clouet); and an anon. 16C *View of the Cimetière des Innocents*; a *Portrait of the Duc de Guise* (known as Le Balafré from his scar) attributed to François Quesnel, and of *Catherine de Médicis* (School of Clouet), with an anon. *Portrait of Henri III*, and an anon. late 16C *View of the Procession of the League* in the Pl. de Grève. The Salle Bleu has early views of Paris, including a Dutch painting of *Skaters on the Seine* and 16C prints.

The **Salon Ledoux** has panelling of 1762, designed by Claude-Nicolas Ledoux (1736–1809), saved from the Café Militaire (formerly in Rue St-Honoré). Here also are Martin Drolling's *Portrait of Ledoux*, attributed TO Callet, *Portraits of Ledoux and his Daughter*, and an anon. portrait of *Ledoux's Wife*. **Room 31** contains some magnificent gilt panelling of 1767 from the Hôtel d'Uzès, Rue Montmartre, also from designs by Ledoux.

First floor

Now that the whole of this floor is open, it is possible to make the visit in any sequence. However, to follow the exhibition chronologically, begin with **rooms 24–26**, the former apartment of Mme de Sévigné, now known as the **Salles des Échevins**, devoted to Paris during the Ancien Régime. The first room contains a monumental chimneypiece of the Louis-XIII period. There are several portraits of aldermen by de Troy and Duplessis, and one by Largillière of *Françoise Boucher d'Orsay* in 1702.

The **Salles Sévigné**, **rooms 21–23**, with late 17C panelling, were lived in by Mme de Sévigné's son. Room 21 was used as a portrait gallery, and contains a pastel portrait of her by Nanteuil, and a portrait by Mignard of her daughter, Mme de Grignan. Among souvenirs is the japanned desk Mme de Sévigné brought from the Château des Rochers near Vitré and a collection of faience.

Rooms 12–20 describe the transformation of Paris during the reigns of Louis XIII and Louis XIV, recorded in views of the city and evoked by the interiors of grand town houses. In the first room, *Pont Neuf*, c 1633; **room 13**, *Views of the Place Royale* (now Pl. des Vosges), and of the Cité from the Quai de la Tournelle, c 1646, and several views by Abraham de Verwer. **Room 14** has engravings of buildings, and **room 15** further views, including the *Observatoire* by Pierre-Denis Martin and also his *View from the Quai de Bercy*. **Room 16** contains early 18C panelling from the Hôpital de la Pitié, and views of popular scenes. **Room 17** displays richly painted and gilded *boiseries* of c 1656 from the Hôtel Colbert de Villacerf at 23 Rue de Turenne; in **Room 19** is panelling from the *grand cabinet doré* by Le Brun from the Hôtel de la Rivière, 14 Pl. des Vosges, with ceiling painting by Le Brun. **Room 20** contains another ceiling painting (1651), also by Le Brun, from the same mansion and recently restored.

The remainder of the rooms are in Louis XV and Louis XVI styles. These rooms contain interiors from *hôtels particuliers* originally situated in smart *quartiers* such as the Faubourg St-Germain and Faubourg St-Honoré. Two have been meticulously redecorated using the 18C technique *peinture à la colle*. The colour schemes, all of which are different, vary according to the period, and were scrupulously researched. The panelling has relief decoration in both wood and

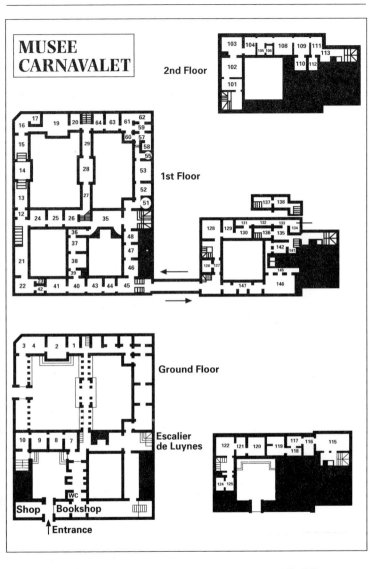

MUSEE CARNAVALET

2nd Floor

1st Floor

Ground Floor

Escalier de Luynes

Shop   Bookshop   WC

↑ Entrance

stucco. Fabrics were specially woven to match the decor, carefully differentiating between what is authentic and what is remodelled. The antique furniture comes from various collections including the important collection of furniture donated in 1965 by Henriette Bouvier.

Rooms 27–29 contain views of Paris between 1720 and 1760, notably those by Charles-Léopold de Grevenbroeck, and Nicolas Raguenet (1715–93). Picturesque among those by the latter is *The regatta near the Pont Notre-Dame*, showing the houses that formerly flanked the bridge.

Room 32 is a reconstruction of a stairwell from the Hôtel de Luynes, decorated with trompe-l'oeil paintings of people on balconies, by P.A. Brunetti (1748). In **room 39** is a collection of wax portraits and a beautiful study by Boucher, *Le Pied de Mlle O'Murphy*; **room 41** Chardin's *Game of Billiards*, and Etienne Jeaurat (1699–1789), the *Transport* 'filles de joie' *to La Salpêtrière*. **Room 46** contains a portrait of the *Abbé Tournus Praying* by Restout. **Room 47** is devoted to the theatre during the reign of Louis XV. **Room 48** contains a portrait of D'Alembert by Catherine Lusurier and a *Portrait of Voltaire* after Nicolas de Largillière and Voltaire's Armchair.

Rooms 49–64 also depict aspects of Paris during the later years of the reign of Louis XV and that of Louis XVI. **Room 53** contains two genre paintings by Michel Garnier (1753–1819), of interest for their depiction of costume; **Rooms 56–57** display several more topographical and architectural paintings, while Room 57, decorated by Boucher and Fragonard c 1765, comes from the house of the engraver Gilles Demarteau in the Rue de la Pelleterie. **Rooms 59–64** contain more paintings by de Machy, Hubert Robert (including his *Demolition of the Houses on the Pont Notre-Dame in 1786* and on the *Pont au Change in 1788*), J.-B. Lallemand, Debucourt, Alexandre Noël and others.

From room 45, you pass along a passage (which may contain exhibitions) to the **Hôtel le Peletier de St-Fargeau**, and then up a staircase. This brings you to the first of a dozen rooms devoted to the French Revolution but glossing over the bloody period when the Terror was at its height. It is a strange coincidence that the building, once the home of Michel Etienne le Peletier de St-Fargeau, great-grandson of the founder, and who was assassinated on the same day as a member of the Convention, should now be devoted to this era.

Rooms 101–104 contain *La Fête de la Fédération*, a large painting by Thévenin, and *La Déclaration des Droits de l'Homme*. Also an anon. *Portrait of Mirabeau*, and a view of the *Revolutionaries in the Jeu de Paume, Versailles, 20 June 1789*, school of David; the keys of the Bastille; *The Storming and Destruction of the Bastille* by Hubert Robert; and a model of the prison cut from one of its stones under the direction of Palloy, the demolition contractor, and other souvenirs of the event; historical scenes of events preceeding the fall of the Bastille by J.-B. Lallemand; a Self-portrait Bust, attributed to Curtius, a relation of Mme Tussaud; and an anon. *Portrait of Dr Guillotin*.

Rooms 105–106 depict life in the Prison du Temple from 10 August 1792, and a *Portrait of young Louis XVII* painted there in 1793 by J.-M. Vien le fils. Two paintings by Jean-Jacques Hauer: *Louis XVI's Fairwell to his Family*, and *Louis XVI taken away from His Family*; paintings of the *Execution of the King* and of *Marie-Antoinette*. **Rooms 107–108** are devoted to the Convention and the Terror, with prison scenes by Hubert Robert and anonymous portraits of main political figures of the period; scenes by de Machy and Hubert Robert (*The Prison of St-Lazare*). **Rooms 109–113** are concerned with the Directoire and the period of the Revolutionary wars. **Room 13** contains numerous colourful gouaches by Pierre-Etienne le Sueur, and **room 14** a collection of Sèvres porcelain depicting revolutionary emblems.

Stairs and a lift descend to the **ground floor** and **room 115**, devoted to the Consulate and First Empire, with Gérard, portraits of *Mme Récamier seated* and of the actress *Mlle Duchesnois*; Pierre-Paul Prud'hon, *Portrait of Talleyrand in*

1807; Robert Lefèvre, *Portrait of Napoléon in 1809*; the Death-mask of Napoléon and his Nécessaire de Campagne, among other souvenirs.

Room 116. Restoration period. Gérard, *Portrait of Charles X*.

Rooms 117–118 contain paintings of Paris, notably by E. Bouhot, *View of the Palais des Tuileries seen from the Quai d'Orsay*; Corot, *The Pont St-Michel* and *Quai des Orfèvres*.

Rooms 119–120 are devoted to the Revolution of July and the July Monarchy, with a maquette depicting the arrival of the Duc d'Orléans at the Hôtel de Ville, 31 July 1830; a plaster model by F. Rude of the *Departure of the Volunteers*, for his relief on the Arc de Triomphe; François Dubois, *The Erection of the Obelisk of Luxor* in the Pl. de la Concorde, together with a painting of the scene by Geslin.

Room 121. The Second Republic. Horace Vernet, *Portrait of Arago*; anon., *Portrait of Pierre-Joseph Proudhon* and several paintings by H.-V. Sebron and J.J. Champin. **Rooms 122, 124–25** concern the Romantic period, with portraits by Henri Lehmann of *Liszt*, and of *Marie d'Agoult*; of the divas *Marietta Alboni* and *Malibran* by A.-J. Péignon and Henri Decaisne respectively. A collection of miniature caricature sculptured busts in bronze or plaster of famous artists and musicians by Jean-Pierre Dantan, notably those of Berlioz, Verdi and the Duke of Wellington.

At the top of the adjacent stairs, designed by Pierre Bullet, **rooms 126–127**, are a number of views of Paris. Retrace your steps, and from the landing you have a view of two huge bird's-eye *Panoramas of Paris* c 1852 by Victor Navlet.

Rooms 128–129 are devoted to the Second Empire, with the Prince Imperial's cradle (1856); a *Portrait of Baron Haussmann* attributed to Henri Lehmann; a pastel *Portrait of Mérimée* by Simon Rochard; anon. *Arrival of Queen Victoria at the Gare de l'Est to attend the Universal Exhibition of 1855*; *View of the levelling of the Colline de Chaillot in 1867 for the Exhibition*, and a panoramic view of that exhibition.

Room 130 covers the Siege of Paris in 1871, with a view of the artillery in the Jardin des Tuileries in late September 1870; Gambetta leaving Paris by Balloon; sketches by Puvis de Chavannes for his *The Pigeon*, and *The Balloon*; and Corot, *Paris Burning*. **Room 131**. *The Commune*, illustrated by G. Boulanger.

Passing through room 132 you enter **room 133**, with a *Portrait of Blanqui* by Eugène Carrière; and views by Victor Dargaud and E.-M. Lansyer. **Room 135** contains several Parisian views, among them Lépine, *The Seine at Passy*; Jongkind, *The Rue St-Séverin at night*; Guillaumin, *The Seine at Bercy*; and Lebourg, *Notre-Dame under Snow*.

Room 136 is devoted to portraits of literary figures, among them, P.L. Mita, Nadar; Eugène Carriere (1849–1906), Edmond de Goncourt; L. Montegut, Daudet Writing; Boldini, a pastel of 'Gyp'; Gustave Doré (1832–83), Charles Philipon. **Room 137–138** depict the Belle Epoque, with several works by Jean Béraud (1849–1935).

Room 141 contains the Art Nouveau decoration of a private room from the Café de Paris, which stood at 39 Av. de l'Opéra (1899; by Henri Sauvage), until demolished in 1954. In adjoining **rooms 142–143** is the reassembled decoration of 1900 for the jewellery shop of Fouquet, in Rue Royale, designed by Alphonse Mucha (1860–1939).

You pass into **room 146**, with the reassembled Baroque decoration of the ballroom of the Hôtel de Wendel, designed in 1924 by the Catalan artist Josep Maria Sert (1876–1945), the theme of which is the Procession of the Queen of Sheba.

Room 147 contains sections displaying furniture and mementoes from the homes of Paul Léataud, Marcel Proust, and Anna de Noailles, all of whom used to write in bed. Among portraits here are Countess Greffulhe, the Abbé Mugnier; J.-E. Blanche, Princesse Jean de Broglie, Cocteau in 1913, and René Crevel; Foujita, Jean Rostand (the biologist son of Edmond); and Romaine Brooks, Natalie Barney.

On leaving this room, turn to look at the caryatids from the Café de Paris (see room 141 above) and the *Portrait of André Wormser* by Albert Besnard.

By continuing ahead along the passage (room 148) and descending the stairs you return to the entrance.

No. 48 Rue de Sévigné, the Hôtel de Jonquières, retains the relief (1810) from an old fountain; No. 52, built by Pierre Delisle-Mansart for himself, has been much altered.

In Rue Payenne, immediately west of the Hôtel Carnavalet, No. 11, the Hôtel de Polastron-Polignac, houses the Swedish Cultural Centre and **Musée Tessin**, containing paintings by Alexander Roslin (1718–93), and others. No. 13, the Hôtel de Lude, is another good example of an early 18C mansion. There is a small lapidary collection in the Sq. Georges-Caïn opposite.

South of the Hôtel Carnavalet, on the corner of the Rue Pavée, No. 24 is the fine **Hôtel Lamoignon**, built in 1584 for Diane de France, the legitimised daughter of Henri II, but named after Lamoignon, a 17C occupant. Possibly the work of J.-B. Androuet du Cerceau, it has colossal Corinthian pilasters and curved pediments. It now houses the Bibliothèque Historique de la Ville de Paris, containing over 400,000 volumes and 100,000 manuscripts relating to the history of the city, and to the Revolution.

The Statue of 'Flore et son Char', Square Georges-Caïn

Rue Pavée brings you to **RUE DES ROSIERS**, the old Jewish quarter (parallel with Rue des Francs-Bourgeois), an atmospheric street with some interesting restaurants.

On the south side of Rue des Francs-Bourgeois, No. 31 is the Hôtel d'Albret, built c 1640 by François Mansart, with an 18C street façade. At the end of the courtyard of No. 33 is a fragment of the walls of Philippe Auguste. The Hôtel de Guillaume Barbès (No. 35) was built in the second half of the 17C.

Musée Cognacq-Jay

At 8 Rue Elzévir, leading north, parallel to the Rue Payenne, is the Hôtel de Donon, since 1990 the home of the Musée Cognacq-Jay (Pl. 15; 1). The restored mansion, dating from 1575, was built for Médéric de Donon, but several alterations were made in the mid 17C. The museum was started by Ernest Cognacq (1835–1928), founder of the Magasins de la Samaritaine, and was inaugurated in 1929. Open 10.00–17.40, closed Mon and public holidays (☎ 01 40 27 07 21)

This is an intimate and perfectly maintained museum, entirely devoted to the 18C, with a profusion of objects in 20 small rooms on four floors and in the impressively beamed attic. Many of the rooms contain beautiful panelling with rocaille decoration, some removed from the Château d'Eu (Normandy), and some original 17C panelling.

Among outstanding pieces of **furniture** are a Beauvais tapestry covered set of chairs by J.-B. Lelarge; marquetry work by Denizot, Weisweiler; a bureau by Boulle in ebony inlaid with a variety of materials; a small desk in holly by Oeben; a Louis XVI bed *à la polonaise*. The collection of ceramics and porcelain includes a colourful pair of Kien-Lung Cranes (porcelain); also terracotta busts by J.-B. Lemoyne of the Maréchal de Saxe and the Maréchal de Lowendal; Meissen porcelain and French terracotta figures, including Clodion, Project for the tomb of Mme Dubarry's dog; a rare collection of enamelled and jewelled boxes and other small objects. It has an unusually large collection—for Paris—of English paintings of the period.

A pick of the outstanding **portraits** includes: Boucher, *Mme Baudouin, his Daughter*; Gérard, *Mme Bauquin du Boulay and her Niece*; Marguerite Gérard, *Claude-Nicolas Ledoux*, the architect; Hugh Douglas Hamilton, *Lady Carhampton (?)*; Adélaïde Labille Guiard, *Comtesse de Maussion*; Largillière, *The Duchess of Beaufort (?)*; Maurice Quentin Delatour, *Mme la Présidente de Rieux, Self-portrait, Man in a Blue Waistcoat*, and *The Marquis de Bérenger*; Thomas Lawrence (1769–1830), *Princess Clémentine de Metternich*; Nattier, *Madame Henriette, Marie Leszczynska*; Perronneau, *Charles Lenormant du Coudrey*; Reynolds, *Lord Northington*; attributed to Romney, *Female portrait*; John Russell, *Miss Power*; Mme Vigée-Lebrun, *The Vicomtesse de Mirabeau Playing a Guitar*, and *A Dancer*;

Other works include Boucher, *La belle Cuisinière*, Canaletto, two *Venetian scenes*; Chardin, *Still Life with a Copper Cauldron*; Morland, *The First Steps*; Wright of Derby, *The Young Bird-Catchers*; Rembrandt, *Balaam's Ass* (1626; an early work); Ruisdael, *The Old Oak*; G.-B. Tiepolo, *Cleopatra's Banquet*; Watteau, *Assembly in the Park, Gilles à l'Orée du Bois*, and *Return from the Hunt*, one of a set of four, two of which are in the Wallace Collection, London; also works by Fragonard, Greuze, Guardi and Hubert Robert.

Among the *galante* scenes are a number by Boilly, Pierre-Antoine Baudouin (1733–69), Nicolas-Ren, Jollain (1732–1804), Nicolas Lavreince (1737–1807) and J.-B. Mallet (1759–1835).

Returning to Rue des Francs-Bourgeois, you pass at No. 26 the Hôtel de Sandreville (late 16C–18C); No. 30, the Hôtel d'Alméras, a red-brick mansion of the Henri IV period, merits a glance. The Allée des Arbalétriers (No. 38) was one of the entrances to the Hôtel Barbette (see below), and led to the field alongside the walls, once a practice ground for crossbowmen.

On the corner of the transverse Rue Vieille-du-Temple (right; No. 54) survives the pretty turret (c 1510; restored) of the heavily restored Hôtel Hérouët.

A short distance south is the **Hôtel des Ambassadeurs de Hollande** (No. 47), built by Cottard in 1657–60. On this site stood the house of the Maréchal de Rieux, in front of which on his return from Isabeau de Bavière's residence (see below), the Duc d'Orléans was assassinated in 1407 by the hired bravos of Jean sans Peur (Duke of Burgundy).

For the north half of Rue Vielle-du-Temple, see below.

On the left you pass **N.-D. des Blancs-Manteaux** (deriving its name from the white habits of an order of mendicant monks established here in 1285 by Louis IX); the 18C door came from St-Barthélemy in the Ile de la Cité, demolished in 1863. The church contains a rococo pulpit in the Flemish style (1749).

At 55 Rue des Francs-Bourgeois are the offices of the Crédit Municipal, formerly the Mont-de-Piété (a government pawnbroking establishment), founded by Louis XVI in 1777. Architecturally notable are Nos 54, the Hôtel de Camus; 56, the Hôtel de Fontenoy (early 18C); 58, and 58 bis, the Hôtel d'Assy (early 17C).

Beyond is the imposing portal of the **Hôtel de Soubise** (former Hôtel de Clisson) (No. 60; Pl. 15;1), the greater part of which was built by Delamair in 1706–12 on the site of the mansion of the Duc de Guise. The Archives Nationales have been housed here since 1808, ensuring the survival of the interior decoration (1712–45) by Natoire, Boucher, Van Loo, Restout, Lemoyne and others. The splendid Cour d'Honneur, with its colonnade, has copies of *The Four Seasons* by Robert le Lorrain on the façade.

The earlier entrance, the turreted Gothic gateway of 1380 (at 58 Rue des Archives), was part of the Hôtel de Clisson, built in 1372–75 by the Constable Olivier de Clisson, a supporter of Charles V against the English. Bolingbroke (later Henry IV) gave a farewell banquet here in 1399 before setting out for England. With its purchase in 1553 by Anna d'Este, wife of François de Lorraine, Duc de Guise, it became the Hôtel de Guise, remaining in the family until 1696, when Anne de Soubise bought it. It contains the Museum of the History of France. The chapel bears traces of the Chapelle de Clisson of 1375 transformed in 1533 for the Guise by Primaticcio. The Oval Room is a masterpiece of the transitional style from Louis XIV to Louis XV. Original documents which show the development of French institutions from the outstanding collection are exhibited in rotation. Open 13.45–17.45, closed Tues (☎ 01 40 27 61 78)

From Rue des Archives, skirting the west side of the Hôtel de Soubise, leads Rue de Braque, in which Nos 4–6, the Hôtel Le Lièvre de la Grange, is a fine late-17C mansion; No. 7 belonged to the Comte de Vergennes (1717–87), foreign minister to Louis XVI and supporter of American Independence.

At the corner of Rue des Archives and Rue des Haudriettes, further north, is a fountain, with a naiad sculpted by Mignot (1765).

Diagonally opposite is the very fine **Hôtel de Guénégaud** (60 Rue des Archives) by François Mansart (c 1650), containing a Musée de la Chasse et de la Nature and an exclusive Hunting Club. Open 10.00–12.30, 13.30–17.30, closed Tues, ☎ 01 42 72 86 43.

The museum contains a variety of hunting weapons, from the 16C–19C, from France and other parts of Europe; powder flasks, daggers, crossbows, etc. and stuffed big game, swords, porcelain decorated with hunting scenes and Mexican terracotta animals. Among the paintings are *Philip the Fair* (Philip I of Spain; father of the Emperor Charles V) in falconer's costume, and *La Chasse de Diane* by

'Velvet' Brueghel and van Balen. There are also a number of works by François Desportes (1661–1743); and by Chardin, Oudry, Carle Vernet and Monet.

At No. 62, adjacent, the Hôtel de Montgelas (1709), and the fine doorway at No. 20, Rue des Quatre-Fils are worth looking at.

In Rue Charlot, leading north east from Rue des Quatre-Fils, is St-Jean-St-François, built as a Capuchin chapel on the site of a *jeu de paume* and completed in 1715. No. 7, opposite, the Hôtel de Brévannes, is partly 17C.

Further along Rue des Quatre-Fils you regain Rue Vieille-du-Temple, in which, at No. 87, a few paces to the right, stands the magnificent **Hôtel de Rohan**. It was known also as the Hôtel de Strasbourg, and was begun in 1704 by Delamair.

It was successively inhabited by four cardinals of the Rohan family, all of whom were bishops of Strasbourg. From 1808 to 1925 the mansion was occupied by the Imprimerie Nationale, after which it was thoroughly restored to house certain departments of the Archives Nationales not accommodated in the neighbouring Hôtel de Soubise (see above). In the second courtyard is a fine relief of the *Horses of Apollo* by Robert le Lorrain; the **Cabinet des Singes** contains paintings by Christophe Huet (1745–50).

From the intersection of Rues Vieille-du-Temple (in which No. 90 was the site of the Jeu de Paume des Marais, used as a theatre from 1634–73) and des Quatre-Fils, you can make a detour towards the north-eastern section of the Marais via the Hôtel Salé (see below). Its garden façade is approached by turning right off the former street along Rue des Coutures-St-Gervais, flanked by several 17C houses.

Alternatively, you can follow Rue de la Perle south east to the tastefully redeveloped Pl. de Thorigny, passing (right; No. 1) the restored **Hôtel Libéral-Bruant**, built in 1685 for his personal use by one of the architects of Les Invalides. It has a perfectly harmonious pedimented elevation, decorated with four busts in niches. It now houses the **Musée de la Serrure** (or Musée Bricard). Eugène Bricard, was the 19C collector of this splendid decorative door-furniture, including locks, keys, handles and plaques of all periods. Open 10.00–12.00, 14.00–17.00, closed Sat, Sun, ☎ 01 42 77 79 62.

A few paces to the south east bring you to RUE DU PARC-ROYAL. No. 4, was built c 1620. No. 10, the restored Hôtel de Vigny, of the same date, is now the offices of the Centre National de Documentation du Patrimoine—Inventaire Général. The Rue Payenne leads back towards the Hôtel Carnavalet.

Musée Picasso

By turning north east up Rue de Thorigny, you reach at No. 5 (left) the **Hôtel Salé** (Pl. 15; 1) an elegant mansion also known as the Hôtel Aubert de Fontenay and the Hôtel de Juigné, but became known as the Hôtel Salé on account of the huge profits its owner made out of the salt tax. The largest house in the Marais, it is a prime example of a *hôtel particulier* of the 17C between court and garden.

The whole building was thoroughly restored before receiving the collection of works by Picasso (1881–1973), acquired by the State in lieu of death duties. From the entrance hall across the courtyard, a majestic staircase sweeps you up to the collections.

■ Open summer: 09.30–18.00, winter 09.30–17.30, closed Tues 1/1, 25/12, (☎ 01 42 71 25 21). Free guided visits for individuals and groups in English (not summer) Fri 14.30. Facilities for the disabled include the loan of wheelchairs.

This is a favourite visit for anyone who loves both modern art and fine houses. It has an extensive collection of works by Picasso and a number of canvases by other artists which he owned. The large collection of drawings and prints is displayed in rotation. The galleries are arranged in approximately chronological order to show Picasso's development from 1894–1972.

The collection includes from his early period, just after his first visit to Paris, his haunting **Blue Period** *Self-portrait* (1901) painted when he was 20; and *Celestina* (1904). Between the Rose Period *The Two Brothers* (summer 1906) and *Self-Portrait* (autumn 1906), after his discovery of Iberian art, there is a change of direction. The culmination of this was his seminal work of 1906–07 now in New York (*Les Demoiselles d'Avignon*) for which the Museum has some preparatory works. Representative of his **Cubist era** (1907–15) are the well-known *Still-life with Chair Caning* (1912), his first collage, made with rope and oil-cloth printed with a design of chair caning; a three-dimensional interpretation of Cubism is *Sculpted Female Head* of his companion Fernande Olivier; the synthesis of collage and sculpture produced the witty construction of 1915, *Violin;* in total contrast he began to make Ingresque portraits such as *Portrait of Olga Khoklova* seated (1917), the Russian dancer who became his wife in 1918.

Bathers (Biarritz, 1918) recalls summer by the sea; from his **Classical Period** come *Jug and apples; Women Running along a Beach* (1922); *The Pipes of Pan* (1923). *Paul as a Harlequin* and *Paul as a Pierrot* show his small son in fancy dress. Although Picasso was never part of the Surrealist group, its influence plus the impact of his personal problems at the time emerge in the aggression of *The Kiss* (1925), *Large Nude in a Red Armchair* (1929) and *Figures by the Sea* (1931).

In early 1930, Picasso painted a Crucifixion and worked on a series of sculpted female heads. Paintings of the period include the voluptuous *Sleeping Nude* (1932) and a portrait of his model and then lover, *Marie-Thérèse Walter*. The themes of the bull fight and the Minotaur recur throughout Picasso's art: *Corrida* (1933) and the drawing *Minotaur* (1936). Towards the end of the 1930s there was a new focus in the artist's life, represented in *Portrait of Dora Maar* (1937); and in 1938, he painted his small daugher, *Maya and her Doll* (1938). His political anguish later in the decade is reflected in *Cat with a Bird* (1938).

During the war, Picasso assembled and sculpted: the cryptic *Bull's Head*, from bicycle parts, and large *Man with a Sheep* (1943). His stays in Antibes with Françoise Gilot from the summer of 1946 inspired *Skull, Sea Urchins and Lamp on a Table* (1946). He became passionately interested in ceramics while in the south of France: *Vase: Woman with a Mantilla* (1949). Animals and birds played an important role in his work, as in *Nanny-Goat* (1951). Later works include: *Massacre in Korea* (1951); *Dejeuner sur L'Herbe* (both burlesque and tribute to Manet; 1960); *Woman with Open Arms* (1961) and *The Young Artist* (1972).

Among **works collected by Picasso** now belonging to the State, are: Balthus, *The Children*; Cézanne, *Château Noir*; Corot, *Little Jeannette*; Miró, *Self-portrait*; Modigliani, *Seated Girl*; Henri Rousseau, *Self-Portrait with Lamp, The*

Artist's Wife, and *The Sovereigns*; Renoir, *Seated Bather*; and works by Braque, Matisse and René-Hilaire de Gas (1770–1858; grandfather of Edgar Degas).

Rue Ste-Anastase leads right off Rue de Thorigny into Rue de Turenne, where (right) Nos 52–54 form the 17C Hôtel de Montrésor. No. 60 is the Hôtel du Grand-Veneur, with a fine boar's head on the façade, while No. 66 retains traces of the Hôtel de Turenne, built for the great marshal's father. On the site of the chapel of the convent later installed here, the church of St-Denis-du-St-Sacrement was built in 1835 in the neo-Greek style, by Godde. At the junction of Rue Debelleyme, leading north west, and Rue Vieille-du-Temple is the **Hôtel d'Espinay**, No. 110, with a remarkable staircase. This *quartier* has a number of art galleries.

Rue des Archives

No. 78 Rue des Archives (the next main street to the south west), was built by Bullet (c 1660), with a beautiful staircase by Le Muet.

Further north is **Sq. du Temple** (Pl. 9; 7), at the centre of the densely populated Quartier du Temple, one of the 24 squares created during the Second Empire. Until the late-12C this was the site of the stronghold of the Knights Templar. The headquarters of their order in Europe until 1313, it was then occupied by the Order of St John. Today this garden boasts many different trees and a lake and cascade made with rocks from the Forest of Fontainebleau.

The area owned by the Templars lay for the most part between this point and Pl. de la République to the north east (see latter part of Ch. 22). Before the Revolution it was occupied by wealthy families, artisans who did not belong to the corporations and therefore were free from many restrictions, and debtors who were protected here from legal action.

The palace of the Grand Prior of the Knights of St John was renowned for its luxuriousness but, with the Revolution, the Tour du Temple (1265) was transformed into a prison, and in August 1792 Louis XVI and the royal family were taken from the Tuileries and incarcerated here. (Objects from the prison are now in the Musée Carnavalet.)

A short distance to the north (195 Rue du Temple) is **Ste-Elisabeth**, founded in 1628 by Marie de Médicis. The main feature is the *boiseries* including, in the ambulatory, 17C carvings of scriptural scenes from the abbey of St-Vaast at Arras.

The Musée National des Arts et Métiers-Techniques and the Abbey Church of St-Martin-des-Champs

Rue Réaumur leads west from Sq. du Temple, passing (left) RUE VOLTA, in which No. 3, of c 1300, is possibly the oldest surviving house in Paris. Rue Réaumur crosses Rue de Turbigo to meet Rue St-Martin (the original Roman road to the north from Lutetia) between the former priory of St-Martin-des-Champs (right) and (left) St-Nicolas-des-Champs. The exterior of the church is best seen from Rue Réaumur, to the south.

> The priory of St-Martin-des-Champs, founded in 1060 by Henri I and presented to the Abbey of Cluny by Philippe I in 1079, stood outside the city walls until the early 14C. During the Revolution it was taken over by an educational institution. Its dependencies were later used as a small-arms factory and in 1798 were assigned to the Conservatoire des Arts et Métiers, which had been founded in 1794. The collections of Vaucanson and other scientists were assembled here and in 1802 it opened as the Musée des Techniques. Its administrator was Joseph-Michel Montgolfier (1740–810), who with his brother Jacques-Etienne (1745–99, a paper-manufacturer) were the inventors of the air-balloon (1783).

The **Musée National des Arts et Métiers-Techniques**, described as the museum of the Industrial Revolution, has its entrance at 292 Rue St-Martin (Pl. 9; 7). The museum has been undergoing considerable renovation and is due to reopen in 1998 (recorded information ☎ 01 40 27 23 31). Incorporated in the museum is the **Abbey Church of St-Martin-des-Champs**, restored in 1854–80. The fabric of the choir, with its apse chapels, is perhaps the earliest Gothic vault in Paris (1130–40), while the aisleless nave dates from the 13C.

To the right of the entrance courtyard is the former refectory, a 13C master-piece, built by Pierre de Montreuil (architect of the Sainte-Chapelle). This remarkable hall (42.80m by 11.70m), its vaulting supported by a central row of columns (recalling those of the Eglise des Jacobins at Toulouse), and with a reader's pulpit at the east end, now accommodates the library. The external side of the southern doorway is a good example of decorated Gothic, and the sole relic of the original cloisters. Further south is the restored 13C portal of the church (not entered from here; see below). The turret is a comparatively recent addition.

The museum contains models of locomotives and rolling-stock; an extensive collection of astronomical and surveying instruments; clocks (by Berthoud, Lepaute, Bréguet, Janvier and other famous 18C horologists); and a collection of elaborate automata, including Marie-Antoinette's Joueuse de Tympanon. It also has printing machinery; apparatus used by Daguerre, Niepce, Lumière and others, in the pioneering days of photography and cinematography; and histor-ical equipment illustrating the development of recording, television and radio-astronomy. There is a section devoted to domestic lighting and heating; models of machines, including the Machine de Marly (see end of Ch. 35) and cars and planes.

Among the prototypes of the motor car are Cugnot's steam-carriage of 1770 and one by Serpollet (1888); petrol-driven vehicles include a Panhard (1896), Peugeots of 1893 and 1909, a Berliet phaeton (1898), a De Dion-Bouton (1899) and a Renault of 1900. Among the aeroplanes are those of Ader (1897), Esnault-Pelterie (1906), the plane in which Blériot made the first flight across the Channel (1909) and a Bréguet of 1911.

At the north-west corner of the building is the Fontaine du Vertbois (1712) which, with the adjoining tower, has been restored.

Adjacent is **St-Nicolas-des-Champs**, with a square tower, built in 1420 but enlarged in 1541–87, when the choir was rebuilt and the outer nave aisles added. The north façade is 15C, the east door is framed by a Flamboyant arch (19C statues). The original west doors have survived, and the fine south portal (c 1576), after Philibert Delorme, also retains its contemporary doors.

There is good woodwork in the nave vestibule. Paintings include a *Baptism of Christ* by Gaudenzio Ferrari, and *Madonna and Saints* by Amico Aspertini (both c 1500). The ambulatory chapels have 17C wall-paintings; also *Our Lady of Victories* (c 1610–20) and *The Apostles at the Tomb of the Virgin* and the *Assumption* (on the 17C high-altar), are by Vouet.

Return to **Rue du Temple** by turning east along Rue des Gravilliers (just south of St-Nicolas-des-Champs). 13 Rue Chapon (the first turning right, going south), has an interesting court. Nos 101–103, the Hôtel de Montmorency, the residence of Fouquet in 1652, has its entrance at 5 Rue de Montmorency. No. 51 in this street, the Maison du Grand-Pignon, restored in 1900, was built in 1407 by Nicolas Flamel.

Rue Michel-le-Comte, parallel to the south, retains a number of early 17C houses, including the Hôtel Le Tellier (No. 16), with a fine courtyard. Nos 67–87, on the west side of Rue du Temple, provide a charming ensemble of 17C houses, of which Nos 71, 73 and 75 form the Hôtel de St-Aignan, built by Le Muet in 1640–50; the courtyards and gate are particularly elegant. No. 79, c 1620, altered after 1751, the Hôtel de Montmor, has a fine gateway and attractive pediment in the courtyard. No. 41, the Auberge de l'Aigle d'Or (17C), is the last remaining example in Paris of a coaching inn of the period. The square turret on No. 24 dates from 1610; and an inscription on No. 17 indicates the site of the house of du Guesclin (1372–80).

Rejoin the Rue de Rivoli at the Hôtel de Ville (see Ch. 19).

22 · The Grands Boulevards

■ Arrondissements: 75002, 75004, 75008, 75009, 75010.
■ Métros: Concorde, Madeleine, Opéra, Richelieu-Drouot, Rue Montmartre, Bonne-Nouvelle, Strasbourg-St-Denis, République. RER: Auber.

The district known as the Grands Boulevards combines commerce with entertainment—opera, theatre, cabaret and cinema—and has historic links with developments in art and cinema in the 19C and at the beginning of the 20C.

The **Grands Boulevards**, a succession of wide thoroughfares extending in a curve from Pl. de la Concorde to the Bastille, were laid out in 1670–85 on the site of the inner ramparts, demolished in previous decades. These had constituted the eastern part of the *enceinte de* Charles V, erected after 1370, and the

Restaurants and cafés

L'Amanguier, 20 Blvd de Montmartre,☎ 01 47 70 91 35. Traditional. £
Charles Baudelaire, Hôtel Burgundy, 8 Rue Duphot, ☎ 01 42 60 34 12. £
Café de la Paix, 12 Blvd des Capucines, ☎ 01 40 07 30 20, Decor by Garnier, architect of the Opéra. £
Chez Clement, 17 Blvd des Capucines, ☎ 01 47 43 00 25. Seafood. £
Bistrot de Gala, 45 Rue du Fb. Montmartre, ☎ 01 40 22 90 50. Traditional bistrot. £
La Ferme des Mathurins, 17 Rue Vignon, ☎ 01 42 66 46 39. Traditional. £
Sam Kearny, 100 Rue St-Lazare, ☎ 01 42 80 31 41. American style food.
La Taverne Kronenbourg, 24 Blvd des Italien, ☎ 01 47 70 16 64. Brasserie. £
Ladurée Royale, 16 Rue Royale, ☎ 01 42 60 21 79. Tea shop. £
Léon de Bruxelles, 8 Pl. de la République, ☎ 01 43 38 28 69. Chain specialising in mussels. £
Leonidas, 6 Rue de la Michodière, ☎ 01 47 42 78 71. Greek. £
Lucas-Carton, 9 Pl. de la Madeleine, ☎ 01 42 65 22 90. Haute cuisine; decor by Majorelle, the Art Nouveau cabinet maker. £££.
Royal Madeleine, 11 Rue Richepance, ☎ 01 42 60 14 36. Traditional. £
Chez Maxim's, 3 Rue Royale, ☎ 01 42 65 27 94. Haute cuisine. £££
Les Muses, Hôtel Scribe, 1 Rue Scribe, ☎ 01 44 71 24 26. Traditional. ££
Auberge Nicolas Flamel, 51 Rue Montmorency, ☎ 01 42 71 77 78. Ancient building. £

new fortifications to the west built by Louis XIII in 1633–37. Although the Western Boulevards are no longer so fashionable, they are still busy shopping and commercial districts.

RUE ROYALE makes a convenient approach to the Boulevards from the Pl. de la Concorde (see p 131). As far as Rue St-Honoré, it is lined with uniform 18C houses and shops of quality. No. 16, *Ladurée Royale*, is the classy stop for tea and macaroons. At No. 11 is *Lalique*. René Lalique (1860–1945), also a goldsmith and jeweller, caused a sensation when he displayed his designs in glass at the International Exhibition of 1900. No. 9 contains the **Musée Bouilhet-Christofle**, devoted to the art of the silversmith (see also end of Ch. 36), and No. 3, *Chez Maxim's* was a haunt of high society in the 1890s.

The street is dominated by Ste-Marie-Madeleine, or simply **La Madeleine** (Pl. 7; 6), built in the style of a Greco-Roman temple, and surrounded by a majestic Corinthian colonnade, echoed by the Assemblée Nationale across the river.

Two earlier churches had been demolished unfinished, in 1777 and 1789, before Pierre-Alexandre Vignon (1763–1828) started work in 1806 on the orders of Napoléon, who, before he had thought of the Arc de Triomphe, intended it as a Temple of Glory for the Grande Armée. It was finished by Huvé in 1842. In the pediment is a relief of the Last Judgement by Lemaire (recently restored); the bronze doors are adorned with bas-reliefs of the Decalogue by Triqueti (1838).

The interior abounds in gold leaf and coloured marble, paintings, mosaics and sculptures, and a fine Cavaillé-Col organ. The nave is covered by three coffered domes and the east end by a half dome, with an enfilade of columns around the sanctuary. In chapels on either side of the entrance are the *Marriage of the Virgin*, by Pradier, and the *Baptism of Christ* by Rude; the group of the *Ascension of the Magdalen*, on the high-altar, is by Marochetti.

On the eastern side of the **PL. DE LA MADELEINE** is a small **flower market**. At No. 2 stood the Café Durand, where Zola wrote *J'Accuse*, an open letter denouncing the army and defending Dreyfus, published in *L'Aurore*, on 13 January 1898. On Rue de Sèze is **Fauchon**, the most famous of all Parisian grocery stores, whose window displays are a mouth-watering work of art.

The southern is section of Blvd Malesherbes, leading north-west from the Madeleine, is dominated by **St-Augustin**, an early example of the use of iron in church construction (1860–71), by Baltard, architect of the former Halles. Marcel Proust spent much of his youth at No. 9 Blvd Malesherbes.

BLVD DE LA MADELEINE, the westernmost of the Grands Boulevards, leads north east. Off it to the south east Rue des Capucines takes you towards Pl. Vendôme (see p 193) while the boulevard itself becomes Blvd des Capucines, which crosses Pl. de l'Opéra (see below). Off its north side the Rue Edouard-VII leads to a small *place* containing an *equestrian statue of Edward VII* (by Landowski), a frequent visitor to Paris as Prince of Wales and king, and a promoter of the Entente Cordiale which was established between Britain and France in 1904.

At 14 Blvd des Capucines a tablet records the first exhibition of a cinema film given by the brothers Lumière (28 December 1895), and a few days later the first demonstration of X-rays, a discovery of Dr Roentgen, took place in the same room. No. 35 was once the studio of Nadar (Félix Tournachon; 1820–1910), the portrait-photographer and aeronaut. The first Impressionist Exhibition was held here in 1874, with paintings by Renoir, Manet, Pissarro, Monet, etc. Included in this exhibition of 1874 was Monet's *Impression Soleil levant* (1872) (depicting the port of Le Havre in mist) which gave the group its name. (See Musée Marmottan, p 263.)

Opéra Garnier

The focal point of the busy Pl. de l'Opéra (Pl. 7; 6) is Garnier's opera house to the north. From the terrace of the fashionable *Café de la Paix*, on the north west, you have a good view of the façade of the opera.

■ Open 10.00–17.00 every day (☎ 01 40 01 22 63); there are also guided visits (closed 1/1, 1/5 and during matinées).

The grandiose Opéra Garnier, an appropriately lavish monument to the extravagant and brilliant period of the Second Empire, was built in 1861–75 from the designs of Charles Garnier (1825–98). Although covering a huge area, it contains only around 2150 seats, few in comparison with some other large theatres. The Opéra-Garnier was recently overhauled and renovated, and the public areas can be visited (auditorium when not in use), The first opera-house in Paris was established in 1669 by

Perrin, Cambert and the Marquis de Sourdéac on the Left Bank, between the Rue de Seine and the Rue Mazarine. The first director was Lully (from 1674), under whom it acquired its secondary title of Académie Royale de Musique.

The façade, flanked by a flight of steps, is lavishly decorated with coloured marbles and sculpture. On either side of the arcade opening into the vestibule are allegorical groups, including (right) *The Dance* by Carpeaux (a copy, the original now graces the interior of the Musée d'Orsay). Above are medallions of composers; and bronze-gilt statues of other composers and librettists are seen between the monolithic columns of the loggia. Behind the low dome of the auditorium is a triangular pediment crowned by a statue of *Apollo of the Golden Lyre*.

At 8 Rue Scribe is the entrance to the **Museum of the Opera**. This mounts permanent and temporary exhibitions. The museum contains a complete collection of the scores of all operas and ballets performed here since its foundation, and over 100,000 drawings of costumes, scenery and photographs of artistes. Open 10.00–18.00, winter to 17.00, 01/01, 01/05, 08/05 (☎ 01 47 42 07 02).

The Hall d'Acceuil contains a shop selling souvenirs and books. The second vestibule contains the box-office, beyond which is the Grand Staircase, with its white marble staircase 10m wide, and with a balustrade of onyx and rosso and verde antico lit by elaborate chandeliers. On the first floor, where the staircase divides, is the entrance to the stalls and the amphitheatre, flanked by caryatids, and on each floor are arcades of monolithic marble columns. The Avant-Foyer leads to the Grand Foyer; glass doors communicate with the Loggia overlooking the Pl. de l'Opéra, and by the middle door is a bust of Garnier by Carpeaux.

The auditorium is resplendent in red plush and gilt, and with five tiers of boxes. The dome, resting on eight pillars of scagliola, was painted in 1964 by Chagall with murals inspired by nine operas, in curious contrast to the rest of the decor. The huge stage is 60m high, 52m wide and 37m deep, behind which is the Foyer de la Dance (the scene of many paintings of ballet dancers by Degas; see Musée d'Orsay), with a mirror measuring 7m by 10m.

Av. de l'Opéra leads south east to Pl. André-Malraux (see Ch. 17), and is crossed by Rue Louis-le-Grand. Napoléon and Joséphine Beauharnais were married in 1796 at 3 Rue d'Antin (the next cross-street), which was then the Mairie of the 2nd arrondissement. The Fontaine Gaillon (1828), just to the east in the Rue St-Augustin, is by Visconti and Jacquot.

Immediately behind the Opéra, facing Pl. Diaghilev, are the department stores of *Galeries Lafayette* (1898) and, to the west, *Du Printemps* (1889; but remodelled after a fire in 1921, and since), with huge and remarkable central halls.

Just east of the former is Rue de la Chaussée-d'Antin, leading north to La Trinité (see p 245). At No. 5 Mozart stayed in 1778 and Chopin in 1833–36.

Blvd des Italiens (the continuation north east of Blvd des Capucines), whose many cafés have been largely replaced by cinemas and commercial buildings, derived its name from the Théâtre des Italiens (1783), where Donizetti's *Don Pasquale* was first performed in 1843. Sir Richard Wallace (1819–90), who collected many of the works of art now in the Wallace Collection, London (see also Ch. 28), had a home in Rue Taitbout (north side of the boulevard).

The next street, RUE LAFFITTE, was named after Jacques Laffitte, 1767–1844, the financier (see Maisons-Laffitte, p 318). At the far end of the street you can see N.-D.-de-Lorette with Sacré-Coeur in the background (pp 244 and 249 respectively). At Nos 39 and 41 stood Ambroise Vollard's art gallery, the dealer who strongly supported avant-garde artists. He was the first to display the work of Gauguin and Cézanne and organised the first exhibitions in Paris of works by Picasso and Matisse (1901 and 1904 respectively).

It was in the parallel RUE LE PELETIER (to the east) that Orsini tried unsuccessfully to assassinate Napoléon III in 1858, but killed or injured 156 other people. No. 3 was the Café du Divan, frequented by Balzac, Gautier, Nerval and Baudelaire. On the site of No. 6 stood the Salle Le Peletier, an opera-house from 1821 until 1873, when it was burned out.

In Rue de Marivaux (opposite) stands the **Opéra-Comique-Salle Favart** (entrance, 2 Rue Boïeldieu) with a bijou auditorium. The Opéra-Comique originated in a company which produced pieces during local fairs, and in 1715 purchased from the Opéra the right of playing vaudevilles interspersed with ariettas. Discord between the two theatres continued until in 1757 Charles Favart (1710–92) finally established the rights of the Opéra-Comique, which moved to this somewhat confined site in 1783, since rebuilt.

At the junction of the boulevard with that of Blvd Montmartre and Blvd Haussmann (only extended to this point in 1927), Rue Drouot leads north past (No. 6) the Mairie of the 9th arrondissement in a mansion of 1746–48, and No. 9 (left), the Hôtel des Ventes de Paris, or **Nouveau Drouot**, rebuilt in the 1980s, the main auction-rooms of Paris, where important sales are held from February to June. Since 1801 it has occupied the same place in Parisian life as Christie's or Sotheby's in London. Pissarro painted 13 views of Blvd Montmartre from a window of the Grand Hôtel de Russie, which stood at 1 Rue Drouot.

To the south, Rue de Richelieu leads to the Bibliothèque Nationale (see Ch. 18). The short Blvd Montmartre, in spite of its name, is some distance from Montmartre. At No. 10 (left) is the **Musée Grévin** (☎ 01 36 68 33 23), a waxwork collection equivalent to Mme Tussaud's in London. On the right is the Rue Vivienne, leading to the Bourse. The Théâtre des Variétés was the scene of several of Offenbach's successes.

The Rue Montmartre, so named since 1200, leads south east towards St-Eustache (see p 204).

RUE DU FAUBOURG-MONTMARTRE, heading north west towards the former suburb of Montmartre, recalls the time when the boulevard formed the city boundary. Rue Geoffroy-Marie, a turning off to the right, leads through a mainly Jewish quarter, towards the Rue Richer. Here at No. 32 is the cabaret known as the *Folies-Bergère* (originally the Café Sommier Elastique, founded in 1869 to produce vaudevilles). Manet's *The Bar at the Folies-Bergère* was painted in 1881.

Continuing east from Blvd Montmartre is Blvd Poissonnière. To the north, at 2 Rue du Conservatoire (beyond the Rue Rougemont), is the Conservatoire National d'Art Dramatique, a small theatre of 1802, reputed for its acoustics.

The boulevard is now crossed by Rue Poissonnière (right) and its northern extension, the Rue du Faubourg-Poissonnière, both named after the fishmongers who used to pass by on their way to the Halles. Beyond this junction, the line of boulevards is continued by Blvd de Bonne-Nouvelle, on the northern side of which is the façade (1887) of the Théâtre du Gymnase. To the south, steps lead up to N.-D. de Bonne-Nouvelle, rebuilt in 1824.

The short Blvd St-Denis (Pl. 9; 5) lies between the Porte St-Denis and the Porte St-Martin, beyond which Blvd St-Martin continues as far as Pl. de la République. The **Porte St-Denis**, a triumphal arch 23m high, designed by Blondel, was erected in 1674 to commemorate the victories of Louis XIV in Germany and Holland. The bas-reliefs were designed by Girardon and executed by the brothers Anguier. It faces Rue St-Denis, or Voie Royale, once the processional route of entry into Paris, and last so used on the occasion of Queen Victoria's visit in 1855.

On the far side of Blvd de Sebastopol, which with its northern extension, Blvd de Strasbourg, stretches from Pl. du Châtelet to Gare de l'Est, you pass the **Porte St-Martin**, another triumphal arch in honour of Louis XIV, c 18m high, built in 1674 by Bullet, and decorated with bas-reliefs of contemporary campaigns, by Desjardins and Marsy (south side) and Le Hongre and the elder Legros (north).

Rue St-Martin (the original Roman road leading north from Lutetia) leads south to the Musée National des Techniques and St-Nicolas-des-Champs (see Ch. 21), off which the Rue N.-D. de Nazareth runs left. The façades of Nos 41–49 are of interest.

You pass two famous theatres in Blvd St-Martin, just east of the arch, the **Théâtre de la Renaissance**, managed by Sarah Bernhardt in 1893–99, and the **Théâtre de la Porte-St-Martin**, both rebuilt after being burnt down during the Commune.

PL. DE LA RÉPUBLIQUE (Pl. 9; 8), on the site of the Porte du Temple, and the junction of seven important thoroughfares, was laid out in 1856–65 by Haussmann for strategic reasons, but it has maintained a political role as the scene of radical demonstrations. The pedestal of the Monument de la République (1883; 25m high), has bronze bas-reliefs by Dalou.

At the corner of Rue Léon-Jouhaux (previously Rue de la Douane) leading north east from the Place, was Daguerre's workshop in 1822–35. The Théâtre Lyrique was one of many (including Des Funambules, 1816–62) which stood on a section of Blvd du Temple demolished by Haussmann.

Beyond Pl. de la République the boulevards are of slight interest, and change their character. Blvd du Temple, with its continuations, leads south east to Pl. de la Bastille (see Ch. 21).

23 · Gare de l'Est to Gare St-Lazare

■ Arrondissements: 75003, 75009, 75010.
■ Métros: République, Gare de l'Est, Gare du Nord, Poissonnière, N.-D.-de-Lorette, Trinité, St-Lazare, St-Augustin, Madeleine. RER: Auber.

Although this district is not a main tourist attraction, it is crossed by visitors who have travelled to Paris by train from the north (including Eurostar) or the east, or those on their way to Montmartre; the once fashionable residential parts of the area contain museums in the former homes of Gustav Moreau and Ary Scheffer.

Restaurants and a pub

Androuët, 41 Rue d'Amsterdam, ☎ 01 48 74 26 93. Cheese based dishes. ££

The Cricketer Pub, 41 Rue des Mathurins, ☎ 01 40 07 01 45. English pub. £

Brasserie Flo, 7 Cour des Petites Ecuries, ☎ 01 47 70 13 59. 1886 brasserie. ££

Julien, 16 Rue du Fb. St-Denis, ☎ 01 47 70 12 06. Brasserie with Art Nouveau decor. ££

Mollard, 115 Rue Saint-Lazare, ☎ 01 43 87 50 22. Brasserie. £

Le Petit Café, 14 Blvd de Strasbourg, ☎ 01 42 01 81 61. Basque cuisine. £

Le Petit Duc, 14–16, Blvd Bonne Nouvelle, ☎ 01 47 70 30 46. Traditional. £

Le P'tit Quinquin, 150 Rue Lafayette, ☎ 01 40 34 74 64. £

Le Saulnier, 39 Blvd. de Strasbourg, ☎ 01 47 70 08 31. £

BLVD DE MAGENTA leads north west from Pl. de la République to meet the outer boulevards beyond the Gare du Nord. Just east of its intersection with Blvd de Strasbourg is the often altered church of **St-Laurent**, on the site of a 6C basilica near the old Roman road.

The present building, begun before 1429 but retaining an older north tower, was continued in the 16C–17C, the nave having been vaulted and the choir remodelled in 1655–59, with a high-altar by Antoine le Pautre. The Lady Chapel dates from 1712. The 17C façade was demolished in 1862–65, when the Flamboyant west front was built and the spire erected.

Just to the north, the courtyard of the **Gare de l'Est** (Pl. 9; 3) the future terminus of the projected TGV line to Strasbourg and Germany, occupies the site of the medieval St Lawrence fair. To the west of the boulevard at this point stood the Prison de St-Lazare (rebuilt as a hospital), from 1632 the headquarters of the Lazarists or Priests of the Mission, founded in 1625 by Vincent de Paul (1576–1660).

The boulevard next crosses the Rue La Fayette before passing (right) the **Gare du Nord**, by Hittorff (1863), the terminus of the line from Calais, Boulogne, etc. (Pl. 9; 3), and also of a rapid shuttle service to the Charles de Gaulle airport. The station is the terminus of the TGV Eurostar, TGV Nord and TGV Thalys to Brussels, Amsterdam, and Liège (and Cologne in 1997). The future RER EOLE line (due for completion in 1999) will be sited in the underground Gare du Nord-Est between the two stations.

In the thickly populated cosmopolitan Quartier de la Chapelle to the north of the main-line stations, there stands **St-Denis-de-la-Chapelle** (13C, but much restored), where Joan of Arc received communion in November 1429 before besieging Paris. Adjacent is a modern basilica, **Ste-Jeanne-d'Arc**, begun in 1932, but the main part of reinforced concrete completed later by Pierre Isnard and consecrated in 1964. Further north is one of the last covered markets in metal, the Marché de la Chapelle, 1885.

Turning south west along the Rue la Fayette, you pass **St-Vincent-de-Paul**

(1824–44), by Jacques Hittorff, inspired by Roman basilicas. With two square towers dominating a pedimented portico of 12 Ionic columns, it is approached by a monumental flight of steps. The interior frieze was painted by Hippolyte Flandrin (1809–64) and the dome by Picot. On the altar is a Crucifixion by Rude and the main organ is the work of Cavaillé-Col.

Via Rue d'Hauteville, leading south, you reach Rue de Paradis, where at No. 30 *bis* is the shop of the glass-maker **Baccarat**, replacing one existing since 1764, with a museum adjoining (☎ 01 47 70 64 30).

Return to Rue la Fayette (to the west) which crosses Rue Cadet where, at No. 16, is the Musée du Grand Orient de France, with material relating to European Freemasonry (☎ 01 45 23 20 92). At this intersection, the Rue de Châteaudun leads west to pass **N.-D.-de-Lorette**, another basilican church, built in 1823–36 by Hippolyte Lebas, with a portico of four Corinthian columns. The grandiose interior has coffered vaults and colonnade.

RUE DES MARTYRS, from behind the church, is the old route up to **Mont-martre**, a lively *quartier*, full of eating places, and already well known for its cabarets in the 18C. North west from the church, Rue N.-D.-de-Lorette ascends to the small Pl. St-Georges. The *lorettes*, or *demi-mondaines*, who formerly inhabited the area in the 19C, were a favourite subject of the caricaturist Gavarni (1801–66), and are represented on his monument here by Denys Puech.

27 Pl. St-Georges is the **Fondation Dosne-Thiers**. The residence of President Thiers (1797–1877) from 1822 to 1871, it contains the Bibliothèque Thiers—80,000 volumes on the history of France since the Revolution; and the Napoleonic collection of Frédéric Masson, of 30,000 volumes; drawings by David; and a bust of Joséphine by Houdon. Temporary exhibitions are held here; apply for permission to visit the Masson collection. Opposite, at No. 28, is an over-ornate neo-Renaissance mansion. This was at the centre of an area developed in the 19C by Lapeyrière and dubbed *la Nouvelle Athènes*—so named by Dureau de la Malle in the *Journal des débats* in 1823. The luxury buildings, designed by Auguste Constantin among others, attracted businessmen, bankers, writers such as the brothers Goncourt and artists.

At the top of Rue St-Georges is a small theatre of the same name, the façade decorated in trompe l'oeil. The street runs downhill, and in the parallel Rue de la Rochefoucauld, to the west (via Rue d'Aumale) is the **Musée Gustave Moreau**, containing a collection of some 18,000 paintings and drawings left by Moreau (1826–98) to the State. Open Mon, Wed 11.00–17.15, other days, 10.00–12.45, 14.00–17.15, closed Tues, 1/1, 1/5, 25/12 (☎ 01 48 74 38 50).

The walls of this creaking, atmospheric studio on two floors are covered with paintings by the leading Symbolist whose use of colour and surprisingly liberal teaching methods deeply influenced the next generation of artists. A former pupil, George Rouault, was the first curator of this museum. Among the works on display are *The Apparition and Salome*, of 1874–76), *Mystic Flower* (1890), *Hésiode et la Muse, Jupiter and Semele* (1895). A picturesque spiral staircase leads to the upper floor where watercolours are exhibited by rotation and drawings can be viewed in cases with movable panels. Degas' *Portrait of the Artist*, dated 1867, also hangs here. On the first floor it is possible to see the tiny apartment in which Moreau and his parents lived, full of family souvenirs.

To the west, off Sq. de la Trinité, stands **La Trinité**, built in 1863–67 by Ballu in a hybrid, unappealing style characteristic of the Second Empire, with a tower 63m high. It was erected on the site of the disreputable Cabaret de la Grande Pinte, later Les Porcherons. In front of the church is a welcome patch of greenery, with fountains also by Ballu and sculptures by Duret.

From a point north east of the church, Rue Pigalle and Rue Blanche climb north east and north towards Montmartre. Between the two, a short distance north, is Rue Chaptal. Tucked away at the end of a cobble courtyard at No. 16 is the **Musée de la Vie Romantique**, in the Maison Renan-Scheffer, with collections devoted to George Sand and Ary Scheffer; it is also used for temporary exhibitions. Scheffer brought together here the artistic glitterati of the era and his great niece, daughter of the philosopher Ernest Renan, carried on the tradition. The house remained in the family for about 150 years. As well as the house, the studios built by Scheffer for teaching and receiving guests, contain paintings and memorabilia. Open 10.00–17.40, closed Mon (☎ 01 48 74 95 38).

To the west of La Trinité Rue Clichy climbs gently north to Pl. de Clichy. No. 16 is the **Casino de Paris**, a famous music-hall. To the south, Rue de Mogador leads to the Opéra.

Rue St-Lazare leads west from Sq. de la Trinité to **Gare St-Lazare** (Pl. 7;4), a terminus of the western region of the SNCF. Its interior was the subject of paintings by Monet in 1877 (see Musée d'Orsay p 105). To the west of the station, the Rue de Rome leads north west (through the Pl. de l'Europe, painted by Caillebotte in 1877).

Rue du Havre leads south from Gare St-Lazare, where No. 8, the Lycée Condorcet, founded in 1804, occupies the former buildings (with a Doric cloister court) of a Capuchin convent; on the site of its chapel (in the parallel street to the east) is St-Louis d'Antin by Brongniart (1782). The street is continued south of the Blvd Haussmann by Rue Tronchet to the Madeleine (see p 238).

The **BLVD HAUSSMANN**, one of the main streets in the area, commemorates Eugène-Georges, Baron Haussmann (1809–91) who, as Préfet de la Seine, initiated extensive urban development in central Paris. Work began here in 1857 as part of a scheme to construct an unbroken thoroughfare from the Blvd Montmartre to the Arc de Triomphe, and was only completed in 1926.

A short distance to the west, on the south side of the Blvd Haussmann, is the **SQ. LOUIS XVI** (Pl. 7; 5), formerly the Cimetière de la Madeleine. Here lie the bodies of the victims of the panic of 1770 in the Pl. de la Concorde (see p ???), together with the Swiss guards massacred on 10 August 1792 and all those guillotined between 26 August 1792 and 24 March 1794. In the square stands the **Chapelle Expiatoire** (CNMHS) erected in 1815–26 from the plans of Percier and Fontaine in the style of a classical funeral temenos. Built by order of Louis XVIII, it was dedicated to the memory of Louis XVI and Marie-Antoinette, whose remains, first interred in the graveyard on this site, were removed to St-Denis in 1815; see Ch. 36.

Inside are two marble groups: *Louis XVI and his confessor Abbé Henry Essex Edgeworth* (1745–1807) by Bosio (below which is inscribed the king's will, dated

25 December 1792) and *Marie-Antoinette supported by Religion*, by Cortot, the latter figure bearing the features of Mme Elisabeth. (Below is inscribed a letter said to have been written by the queen to her sister-in-law from the Conciergerie on 16 October 1793.) The bas-relief by Gérard above the doorway represents the removal of their remains.

24 · Montmartre

■ Arrondissement: 75018.
■ Métros: best approached from the stations of Clichy, Lamarck-Caulaincourt or Anvers.

Restaurants and cafés

L'Assommoir, 12 Rue Girardon, ☎ 01 42 64 55 01. Next to Moulin de la Galette. £
Le Basilic, 33 Rue Lepic, ☎ 01 46 06 78 43. Traditional. £
Le Buffet, 18 Rue des Trois Frères, ☎ 01 42 62 22 15. Bistrot. £
Charlot Roi des Coquillages, 12 Pl. de Clichy, ☎ 01 48 74 49 64. Shellfish. ££
Chartier, 7 Rue du Fb.-Montmartre, ☎ 01 47 70 86 29. Big and busy. £
Chez la Mère Catherine, 6 Pl. du Tertre, ☎ 01 46 06 32 69. Bistrot founded 1793. £
Au Clocher de Montmartre, 10 Rue Lamarck, ☎ 01 42 64 90 23. Auvergne cuisine. £
Le Cottage Marcadet, 151bis Rue Marcadet, ☎ 01 42 57 71 22. ££
Le Montmartre, 74 Rue des Martyrs, ☎ 01 42 64 74 28. Traditional. £
Le Perroquet Vert, 7 Rue Cavallotti, ☎ 01 45 22 49 16. Traditional. £
Le Restaurant, 32 Rue Véron, ☎ 01 42 23 36 16. ££
Le Sancerre, 35 Rue des Abbesses, ☎ 01 42 58 08 20. Café/bar. £
La Table d'Anvers, 2 Pl. d'Anvers, ☎ 01 48 78 35 21. Haute cuisine. ££
Brasserie Wepler, 14 Pl. de Clichy, ☎ 01 45 22 53 29. Traditional brasserie. £

Montmartre is a must for almost every visitor to Paris, drawn by numerous associations: the old village atmosphere, the Moulin Rouge, chansonniers, cabarets, bohemians, its reputation as a centre of artistic and political fement in the 19C, its situation high above Paris and the Sacré-Coeur basilica which seems so mystical from the distance. Surprisingly, despite its popularity, the *quartier* has retained a distinct atmosphere, best discovered by walking up there, and an hour or two may be pleasantly spent wandering around the 'Butte', familiar from the paintings of Utrillo, among others. But first of all, there is Clichy to negotiate.

Pl. de Clichy (Pl. 7; 2) was the site of the Barrière de Clichy, which on 30 March 1814 was defended against the approaching Prussian troops by pupils from the Ecole Polytechnique and the Garde Nationale under Marshal Moncey. The action is commemorated by a bronze group by Doublemard (1869).

To the east lies the wide **BLVD DE CLICHY**, forming, with its continuation Blvd de Rochechouart, the southern boundary of Montmartre proper. The Place and Blvd de Clichy were frequently painted by Renoir, Van Gogh (in 1887), Signac and many other artists working in the vicinity.

The first turning right off Blvd de Clichy is Rue de Douai: which shortly crosses Pl. Adolphe-Max (formerly Pl. Vintimille), a district formerly much frequented by artists and writers: Dickens, George Sand, Bonnard, Vuillard, Zola among others.

Blvds de Clichy and de Rochechouart are the focus of the sleazy night life where colourful crowds congregate around Pl. Pigalle and Pl. Blanche, on the northern side of which is the Moulin Rouge, founded by Joseph Oller, which was inaugurated on 1 May 1889. Yet close to these seedy centres there are residential districts and more salubrious nightlife.

Pl. Pigalle was the site of the Café de la Nouvelle Athènes, long an artistic rendezvous, notably of Manet and Degas.

Over a century has passed since Montmartre was made more accessible by the construction of new streets ascending through the northern slums, and poor artists, migrating there because it was both picturesque and cheap, made it an artistic centre for about 30 years. Among those who vividly depicted this bohemian era was Henri de Toulouse-Lautrec (1864–1901), whose studio was at 5 Av. Frochot, near the Pl. Pigalle.

About 1881 the famous 'Le Chat Noir' (84 Blvd de Rochechouart; closed in 1897) was opened, advertising the attractions of the district and inviting a tide of pseudo-bohemians, tourists and less desirable hangers-on, before which the serious artists gradually retreated and have now all but vanished.

Seurat had a studio at 128 bis Blvd de Clichy from 1886, and died nearby; Signac's studio in 1886–88 was at No. 130 in the Boulevard, where Picasso lived in 1909. Degas died at No. 6 in 1917, where his protegée, Mary Cassatt, had painted.

Cimetière de Montmartre

The short Av. Rachel, the first turning on the left off Blvd de Clichy going east, leads to the main entrance of the Cimetière de Montmartre, on the western slope of the Butte (Pl. 7; 2), partly spanned by a viaduct.

Although not quite as famous as that of Père-Lachaise, it is nevertheless fascinating both for its tombstone art (by Bartholdi, David d'Angers, Falguière, Rodin and Rude) and the celebrities buried there. It extends over 11 hectares under the shade of some 750 trees and opened in 1825. Plans of the graveyard indicating where the illustrious are buried is available at the main entrance. Among the avenues of tombs are memorials to 18C–20C writers, such as Gautier, De Vigny, the Goncourt brothers, Alexandre Dumas fils, Stendhal, Heine, Murger, Zola (a huge red marble monstrosity), Feydeau, Maxime du Camp, Renan and Giraudoux; or composers: Berlioz, Delibes, Offenbach, Halévy, Adam and Ambroise Thomas; also Adolphe Sax; the artists remembered here include Fragonard, Greuze, Delaroche, Carle Vernet, Horace Vernet, Diaz de la Peña and Degas; the actors Frédéric Lemaître and Louis Jouvet; the dancers Vestris, Taglioni and Nijinsky; Mme Récamier, Pauline Viardot and Marie Duplessis ('La Dame aux Camélias'); as well as Waldeck-Rousseau, Marshal

Lannes (heart only), Hittorff. Fourier, Ampère, Dr Charcot and Miles Byrne, the United Irishman.

From Pl. de Clichy, Rue Caulaincourt is carried over the cemetery by a viaduct, which is the most convenient approach to Montmartre by car. Toulouse-Lautrec kept a studio for a decade prior to 1897 at No. 21 and Renoir at No. 73 c 1910, where the Swiss artist Steinlen (1859–1923), died.

Continuing along Blvd de Clichy, you pass (left) the once-famous **Moulin Rouge**, now a cabaret-restaurant, facing the Pl. Blanche and turn left up the steep Rue Lepic towards the rebuilt Moulin de la Galette. Vincent van Gogh and his brother, Théo, lived at No. 54 in 1886; the dancer La Goulue began her career here, and it was painted by Renoir in 1876 and Bonnard in c 1905, among others. In Av. Junot, off Rue Lepic, is the Modern Movement house built in 1926 by Adolphe Loos, the Viennese purist, for the Dadaist writer, Tristan Tzara.

Rue Norvins brings you to the legendary **Pl. du Tertre** (Pl. 8; 1–2) with its rapid-portrait artists always touting for business, much commercialisation, and crowded cafés, maintaining a holiday atmosphere summer and winter. (Alternative means of ascending to Montmartre are by funicular, between Rue Tardieu and Rue St-Eluthère, every 5 minutes all day; or by Montmartrobus, from Pigalle and the Marie du 18e, every 12 minutes).

To the east of Pl. du Tertre stands **St-Pierre-de-Montmartre**, the successor of an earlier church built to commemorate the martyrdom of St Denis, a relic of a Benedictine nunnery founded in 1134 by Adélaïde de Savoie (d. 1154). It was consecrated in the presence of her son Louis VII by Pope Eugenius III in 1147 and is one of the oldest churches in Paris.

The severe façade dates from the late 17C and the bronze doors (1980) were made by T. Gismondi. Inside, against the west wall, are two ancient columns with 7C capitals; two other capitals, one at the apse entrance and another in the north aisle, are of the same date. The Romanesque nave has 15C vaulting; the north aisle dates from 1765 and the south c 1838, both vaulted 1900–05. The transept and the choir retain Romanesque elements with, over the choir, one of the earliest examples in Paris of a ribbed vault (1147). The apse was rebuilt in the late 12C. The tomb of the foundress lies behind the altar. The altar itself is the work of J.-P. Froidevaux, consecrated in 1977, and the glass installed in 1954, is by Max Ingrand.

In the adjacent Jardin du Calvaire (closed) are Stations of the Cross executed for Richelieu. Foundations of a Roman temple have been discovered to the north of the church, while in the derelict graveyard (open only on All Saints Day) is the tomb of the navigator Bougainville (1729–1811); also buried here is the sculptor Pigalle (1714–85).

The Butte Montmartre

The Rue Azais, to the south, leads to the terrace below the Basilique du Sacré-Coeur, which affords a rare opportunity for a panoramic view of Paris—with a rash of skscrapers erupting on the skyline—without suffering vertigo.

An obvious vantage point, the history of the Butte Montmartre is one long series of sieges and battles. The Butte was occupied by Henri of Navarre in 1589 when besieging Paris, and the final struggle between the French and the Allies took place here in 1814. On 18 March 1871, at 6 Rue des Roses to the north east of the Butte, Generals Thomas and Lecomte were murdered by insurgents when attempting to seize cannon entrusted to the National Guards. Their deaths precipitated more drastic government action against the Communards.

The Butte Montmartre rises 130m above sea-level and 104m above the level of the Seine, and is thought of as the highest point in Paris (although Belleville in the 20th arrondissement is, in fact, slightly higher; see Ch. 29). Various derivations of the name include Mons Mercurii, Mons Martis or Mons Martyrum; the two first presuppose the existence of a Roman temple on the hill; the last the probability that St Denis and his companions, SS. Rusticus and Eleutherius, were beheaded at the foot of the hill, and according to tradition, St Denis then walked to the site of the Basilica of St-Denis (see Ch. 36), carrying his severed head. The site of the martyrdom is said to be where the Chapelle du Martyre stands, in the convent at 9 Rue Yvonne-le-Tac, just east of the Métro Abbesses. It was in the crypt of the chapel built here that Ignatius de Loyola and his six companions, including Francisco Xavier, taking the first Jesuit vows, founded the Society of Jesus (1534). (Metro: Abbesses one of the last two surviving constructions by Hector Guimard in cast iron and still glazed.)

Sacré-Coeur

In 1873 the National Assembly decreed the building of a basilica here as an expiatory offering after the Franco-Prussian War of 1870–71. The result, the Sacré-Coeur, visible from almost every part of Paris, is a conspicuous white stone edifice in a Romanesque-Byzantine style derived from St-Front at Périgueux.

> The cult of the Sacred-Heart became popular after the first pilgrimage in 1873 to Paray-le-Monial in Burgundy, the site of a 17C revelation. Work on the church began in 1876 from the plans of Abadie (who had recently restored St-Front), and although used for services in 1891, it was not consecrated as a basilica until 1919. It is built of Château-Landon stone which whitens with age.

The two statues at the front of the basilica depicting *Joan of Arc* and *St Louis* are by Hippolyte Lefebvre. The bronze doors with a delicate vegetal design lead inside. It is hard to reconcile the radiant white exterior with the unremitting gloom of the interior. 100m long and 75m across the ambulatory, it is surmounted by a dome 83m high, and abutted by a square campanile in which hangs the Savoyarde, one of the world's heaviest bells: 19 tons.

Inside, this pilgrimage church is extensively decorated with mosaics, executed by Luc-Olivier Merson, the huge (largest in the world) one above the high altar depicting Christ and the Sacred Heart worshipped by the Virgin, Joan of Arc and St Michael. The glass is 20C.

Both the crypt and the dome can be visited for a fee. The dome, not surprisingly, provides more views—inside and out; from the external gallery you can see the 80 columns (each with a different capital).

Flights of steps descend the steep slope of the Butte through the gardens of Sq. Willette (the funicular runs on the west side). Rue de Steinkerque continues downhill to Blvd de Rochechouart and Pl. d'Anvers.

Au Lapin Agile, Montmartre

Not a great deal remains of **Old Montmartre**, with its cottages and little gardens, although it still has something of a village atmosphere. In Rue des Saules, leading north from Rue Norvins, the Clos Montmartre was created in 1933 and planted with vines which are harvested each October and vinified in the Marie du 18e Arrondissement. No. 4 in this street is *Au Lapin Agile* (named after the rabbit of M. André Gill, who commissioned the sign), made famous by its artistic clientele. Maurice Utrillo (1883–1956) is buried in the nearby Cimetière St-Vincent.

At No. 42 Rue des Saules is the **Musée d'Art Juif** (closed Fri, Sat) and at 17 Rue St-Vincent, to the right beyond the vineyard, steps climb to the **Musée de Vieux-Montmartre** (12 Rue Cortot), installed in a 17C building. It contains, apart from ephemera and material of very local interest, a small collection of Clignancourt (or Montmartre) porcelain, made in 1767–99 in a pottery at the junction of the Rues du Mont-Cenis and Marcadet. This house was occupied by Renoir in 1875, and later by Emile Bernard, Suzanne Valadon, her son Maurice Utrillo, and Dufy, among others.

Not far south of Rue Norvins, Pl. Emile-Goudeau was a favourite artistic area c 1910. No. 13 was the famous **Bateau-Lavoir** (rebuilt since a fire in 1970), the ramshackle residence at different times of Picasso, Modigliani, Van Dongen, Derain, Gris, and Max Jacob. It is where Picasso conceived his ground-breaking *Demoiselles d'Avignon* and where a banquet was held in honour of Douanier Rousseau.

At the foot of the Butte Montmartre, in a Pavilion built by Baltard, is the **Musée d'Art Naïf-Max Fourny**, open 10.00–18.00 every day (☎ 01 42 58 72 78). It has a restaurant.

25 · Avenue des Champs-Elysées

■ Arrondissement: 75008.
■ Métros: Concorde, Champs-Elysées-Clemenceau, Franklin D. Roosevelt, George-V, Charles de Gaulle-Etoile, RER: Charles de Gaulle-Etoile.

Restaurants and cafés

Arc de Triomphe, 73 Av. Marceau, ☎ 01 47 20 72 04. Traditional. £
Cap Vernet, 82 Av. Marceau, ☎ 01 47 20 20 40. Brasserie. £
Cercel Ledoyen, Ground Floor, Carré des Champs-Elysées, ☎ 01 47 42 76 02. ££
Chiberta, 3 Rue Arsène Houssaye, ☎ 01 45 63 77 90. Haute cuisine. £££
Chez Clement Elysées, 125 Champs Elysées, ☎ 01 47 20 01 13. £
Les Elysées du Vernet, Ho Vernet, 25 Rue Vernet, ☎ 01 44 31 98 00. Haute cuisine. Belle Epoque. ££
Fouquet's, 99 Champs-Elysées, ☎ 01 47 23 70 60. The names of stars in brass. ££
Café Georges V, 120 Av. des Champs-Elysées, ☎ 01 45 51 13 21. Traditional. £
Lasserre, 17 Av. Franklin-Roosevelt, ☎ 01 43 59 53 43. Haute cuisine. £££
Laurent, 41 Av. Gabriel, ☎ 01 42 25 00 39. Haute cuisine. In the gardens. £££
Ledoyen, First floor, Carré Champs-Elysées, ☎ 01 47 42 23 23. Haute cuisine. South-facing gardens. £££
Le Matignon, 1 Av. Matignon, ☎ 01 42 25 26 26. Seafood. £
Le Petit Yvan, 1bis Rue Jean Mermoz, ☎ 01 42 89 49 65. £
Restaurant de Paris, 38 Rue de Ponthieu, ☎ 01 42 56 50 86. Reasonably priced. £
Pub Renault, 53 Champs-Elysées, ☎ 01 42 56 18 40. The pub/restaurant in a car showroom. £
La Table du Gouverneur, 10 Champs-Elysées, ☎ 01 42 65 85 10. ££
Taillevent, 15 Rue Lamennais, ☎ 01 46 63 39 94. Haute cuisine. £££

The Champs-Elysées

To the west of the Pl. de la Concorde extend the Champs-Elysées, through which the Av. DES CHAMPS-ELYSÉES, probably the most famous avenue in the world, gently ascends to the Arc de Triomphe. Half-way along the avenue on the south side is the Musée du Petit Palais and, opposite it, the Ground Palais.

At the beginning of the 17C, this low-lying area was still marshland, but in 1667 a decree was issued to create a promenade in the same perspective as the Tuileries gardens and it was drained and planted in 1670 according to Le Nôtre's designs. The Marquis de Marigny (brother of Mme de Pompadour) had it replanted in 1765 and the avenue extended to the Pont de Neuilly in 1774. Cossacks encamped there in 1814, as did English troops in the following year after Waterloo. It was fashionable under the Second Empire, and in 1858 the gardens were re-landscaped *à l'anglaise*. The gardens are virtually unchanged since then.

It consists of two parts; the first, forming a park, extends to the Rond-Point des Champs-Elysées; the other is the commercialised avenue, flanked by offices and showrooms, cinemas and banks, and expensive cafés, which continues north west towards the striking silhouette of the Arc de Triomphe.

Although the impressive perspectives remain and it is still popular, time has treated the Avenue des Champs-Elysées harshly and its former elegance has faded. However, the recent planting of about 300 additional trees has helped to redress the balance a little, and lit up at night (especially Christmas) it still looks magical.

Running parallel to the north side of the Champs-Elysées is Av. Gabriel, with the American Embassy (1931–33) at the corner of Rue Boissy-d'Anglas. Further on (right) are the gardens of the British Embassy and then those of the Palais de l'Élysée (see Ch. 26).

From the Pl. Clemenceau, Av. de Marigny leads north, passing (left) the Théâtre Marigny, and an open-air stamp market (Thursday and Sunday) to reach the walled gardens of the Palais de l'Élysée (see p 256), but mere mortals are forbidden to tread the flanking *trottoir*.

On the south side, between the Petit (left) and Grand Palais, both built for the Exhibition of 1900, is Av. Winston Churchill, creating a typically grand Parisian vista. The avenue leads to the splendid **Pont Alexandre-III** (1896–1900) a single steel arch 107.50m in length, recently spruced up and restored, and across the Seine to Les Invalides (see Ch. 11).

Detail from Pont Alexandre III

The Musée du Petit Palais

The Petit Palais, or Musée des Beaux-Arts de la Ville de Paris (Pl. 7; 7), with its domed entrance in the Av. Winston Churchill, was built by Girault. With interesting **collections of paintings**, donated to the city, it often overlooked by the visitor and therefore never crowded.

■ Open 10.00–17.40, closed Mon and some public holidays, ☎ 01 42 65 12 73.

Three or four temporary exhibitions are held here each year, often based on works in the collection. The galleries are arranged in a semi-circle around an interior garden linked by two large galleries either side of the main entrance. To follow the collection chronologically, begin in the large south gallery.

The collection which stretches from Antiquity to 1925, is arranged to demonstrate different types of artistic expression in particular periods. It divides roughly into two sections. The first is Ancient Art, encompassing everything from Egyptian and Classical Antiquities to 18C European, made up mainly of four bequests: Dutuit, Tuck, Ocampo and Marie. The other, French 19C–20C comprises purchases and commissions by the Ville de Paris in the 19C and a considerable number of bequests.

The **Dutuit Collection**: Gallo-Roman bronzes; Egyptian statuettes; and an extensive collection of Greek ceramics; an impressive collection of Grolier bindings; Gubbio and Urbino majolica; ceramics from the school of Bernard Palissy and from the Saint-Porchaire workshops; a remarkable 17C finial; Limoges enamels; ivories; German and Burgundian wood carvings; among the paintings, Cranach the Elder, *The Burgomaster's Daughter*; Velvet Brueghel, *Wedding*; and Cima de Conegliano, *Madonna and Child*, and other works of the Italian Renaissance.

The **Edward Tuck Collection**: Chinese porcelain of the K'ang-Hsi period (1662–1722); Battersea enamels; Meissen figures; 18C Beauvais tapestries, after Boucher and Huet, paintings by Greuze, *Portrait of Benjamin Franklin*; Poussin, *The Massacre of the Innocents*; Largillière, Hubert Robert, terracotta bust of Franklin by Houdon; sculptures by Puget, and a representative collection of Louis XV furniture.

Paintings of the **Dutch school** include: Willem van de Velde (1611–93), *Marine views*; Hobbema (1638–1709), *Mills, Forest scene*; Ter Borch, *The Fiancée*; Adriaen van Ostade, *The Gazette, Woman with a Letter, The Analyst*; Metsu, *The Toilet, Woman Playing the Virginal*; Rembrandt, *Self-Portrait in Oriental Costume*; Neefs, *Church Interior*; Isaak van Ostade, *Farmyard*; Teniers the Younger, *Tavern Scenes*; Jan Steen, *Idiot Begging Alms*; Wouwerman, *Gypsies, The Cavaliers' Halt*; Jordaens, *Diana's Repose*; Adriaen van de Velde, *Landscape*; Berghem, *The Watering-place*.

19C–early 20C **French painting**, with a fine cross section of works from the Rococo to the Impressionists and beyond. Fragonard, *Portrait of Lalande*, the astronomer; two commissions for the old Hôtel de Ville by Jean-Victor Schnetz (1787–1870), and Paul Delaroche; Géricault, *Italian Landscape in Stormy Weather*; Gustave Doré, *The Valley of Tears* (1883), *The Assumption* and *Ecce Homo*; James Tissot, *Departure and Return of the Prodigal Son*; Courbet's large, dark and smoky *Fireman Running to a Fire* (1851).

Portraits include Leon Bonnat (1833–1922), *Mme Ehrler*; Baudry, *Mme Singer*; Marie Bashkirtseff, *Self-portrait*; and Sargent, *Mme Allouard-Jouan* and Courbet of *M. Corbinaud*, of his Father, of *Pierre-Joseph Proudhon and his Children*, and *Self-Portrait with his Dog*. There is Ingres *Henri IV Playing with his Children* (1817) and the *Death of Leonardo da Vinci* (1818), being embraced by François I. Also the vital and energetic *Combat du Giaour and du Pacha* (1835), along with work by academic artists such as Chassériau, Boulanger, Granet, and Alphonse Legros Le Lutrin.

The 19C section continues in the **Zoubaloff Gallery** (opposite side to the main entrance). Courbet's Realist masterpiece *Girls on the Banks of the Seine* (1856), *Sleep* (1866); and in the same category, Daumier and Jules Breton. Changes in landscape painting can be followed through Corot, Boudin, Rousseau, and Jongkind, *View of Notre-Dame from the Quai de la Tournelle* to Sisley, Pissarro; Monet, *Sunset at Lavacourt*; two women artists of the 19C, Mary

Cassatt, *Head of a girl* (pastel), *Portraits of Lydia Cassatt* and of *M.D.*; Berthe Morisot, *A Young Girl, In the Park*. Portraits include: Manet, *Portrait of M. Duret*; Renoir, *Portrait of A. Vollard, Woman with a Rose*; Cézanne, *Portrait of Ambroise Vollard*; and others by Vuillard and Bonnard. Other works by Cézanne, wall-panels of the *Seasons* (signed 'Ingres' in derision); as well as the *Three Bathers* (c 1879–82) which once belonged to Matisse, and *Rocks and Branches at Bibémus* (c 1904); Gauguin, *Old Man with a Stick*; Toulouse-Lautrec, *The Nice Mail-coach, Portrait of André Rivoire*.

19C sculpture, interspersed among the paintings and in the Grande Galerie nord, includes Denis Puech's *La Pensée*, in multi-coloured marble, and works by Dalou, Carpeaux, Renoir and Rodin. There are ceramics by Gauguin, and jewellery and glass by Lalique, Tiffany, Gallé and Georges Fouquet (1862–1957).

The **Grand Palais** (☎ 01 44 13 17 17, recorded information), facing the Petit, with a classical façade, surmounted by a lofty portico, houses important exhibition-halls. It has a café. Its western half contains a planetarium and the **Palais de la Découverte**, devoted to spreading scientific knowledge, is open 09.30–18.00, Sun 10.00–19.00, closed Mon, 1/1, 1/5, 14/7, 15/08, 25/12 (☎ 01 40 74 80 00).

Publications of the *Caisse Nationale des Monuments Historiques* and those of the *Inventaire général des Monuments et des Richesses artistiques de la France*, are available from Porte C.

Six avenues radiate from the Rond-Point des Champs-Elysées, with its six fountains. To the south west extends the wide Av. Montaigne.

Two streets beyond, at 107 Rue La Boétie, are showrooms of the **Institut Géographique Nationale**, where a large range of French maps may be bought.

At No. 127 (left) beyond the upper end of the Av. George-V, is the **Office de Tourisme de Paris**, open 09.00–20.00 all year except 01/01, ☎ 01 49 52 53 54.

Twelve avenues radiate starwise from PL. CHARLES-DE-GAULLE (formerly **Pl. de l'Etoile**, and still commonly known as such: Pl. 6; 5), around which traffic roars alarmingly. The uniform façades facing it between each avenue were designed by Hittorff in 1854–57.

The Arc de Triomphe

In the centre stands the grandiose Arc de Triomphe (CNMHS), the largest triumphal arch in the world (almost 50m high, and 45m wide), erected to the glory of the French army, and recently restored.

Designed by Chalgrin, and begun in 1806, it was not completed until 1836. The main façades of the arch are adorned with colossal groups in high relief. Facing the Champs-Elysées are (right) the *Departure of the Army in 1792* or La Marseillaise by Rude (the most dynamic composition of the four) and (left) the *Triumph of Napoléon in 1810*, by Cortot. Facing the Av. de la Grande-Armée are (right) the *Resistance of the French in 1814*, and (left) the *Peace of 1815*, both by Etex.

The four spandrels of the main archway contain figures of Fame by Pradier, and those of the smaller archways have sculptures by Vallois (south side) and Bra. Above the groups are panels in relief of incidents in the campaigns of 1792–1805. On the row of shields in the attic storey are inscribed the names of 172 (victorious) battles of the Republic and the Empire, including some claimed to be French victories, but in fact not so! Below the side arches are the names of some hundreds of generals who took part in these campaigns, those who fell in action being underlined. A discreet silence is maintained about the other hundreds of thousands of Frenchmen who fought and died for the Emperor, both in victories and defeats.

Beneath the arch is the **Tomb of the Unknown Soldier**, symbolic of the dead of both World Wars. Its flame has burnt constantly since 11 November 1923. At its foot is a bronze plaque representing the Shaef shoulder-flash, and dated 25 August 1944, the day of the liberation of Paris from the German occupation. It contains a museum of the history of the monument, and on the summit is a platform from which you can see the star pattern in the street below and wonder at the swirling traffic, as well as the panoramic views.

■ Open Apr–Sept, Thurs–Sat 09.30–18.30, Sun, Mon to 18.30; Oct–March, Thurs, Sat 10.00–22.30, Sun, Mon 09.30–18.00. Closed 1/1, 1/5, 8/5, 14/7, 11/11, 25/12. ☎ 01 43 80 31 31.

Since 1840, when the route was followed by a cortège bearing Napoléon's body, watched, despite the intense cold, by 100,000 people, the Champs-Elysées has been used for state processions on a number of occasions, funereal, triumphal and in celebration of liberation.

To the west, the Av. de la Grande Armée leads gently downhill to Porte Maillot, with the towers of La Défense rising some distance beyond: see latter part of Ch. 28.

26 · Rue du Faubourg-St-Honoré to Parc Monceau

■ Arrondissements: 75008, 75017.
■ Métros: Concorde, Madeleine, St-Philippe-du-Roule, Pl.-des-Ternes, Villiers, Monceau, Charles de Gaulle-Etoile. RER: Charles de Gaule-Etoile.

This chapter crosses one of the most luxurious *quartiers* of Paris, around the Elysées Palace, liberally sprinkled with embassies, expensive hotels and restaurants, upmarket boutiques, jewellers and fashion houses and two important art collections at the Musée Jacquemart-André and the Musée Nissim de Camondo; nearby is Parc Monceau.

Rue du Faubourg-St-Honoré is the north-west continuation of Rue St-Honoré, extending from Rue Royale (leading from the Pl. de la Concorde to the Pl. de la Madeleine, see Ch. 22) to Pl. des Ternes (north east of the Arc de Triomphe), following the course of the medieval road from Paris to the village of Roule. It

Restaurants and cafés

L'Ampère, 1 Rue Ampère, ☎ 01 47 63 72 05. *Cuisine de marché*. £

L'Amanguier, 43 Av. des Ternes, ☎ 01 43 80 19 28. Traditional. £

Comtesse du Barry, 23 Av. de Wagram, ☎ 01 46 22 17 38. Périgordian style cuisine. £

Billy Gourmand, 20 Rue de Toqueville, ☎ 01 42 27 03 71. Traditional. ££

Le Bistrot d'à Côté Flaubert, 10 Rue G. Flaubert, ☎ 01 42 67 05 81. Bistrot Rostang. ££

Le Bistrot d'à Côté Villiers, 16 Av. de Villiers, ☎ 01 47 63 25 61. Bistrot Rostang. ££

Le Bistrot de l'Etoile-Niel, 75 Av. Niel, ☎ 01 42 27 88 44. Bistrot Savoy. ££

Le Bistrot de l'Etoile-Troyon, 13 Rue Troyon, ☎ 01 42 67 25 95. Bistrot Savoy. ££

Espace Dégustation, 39 Rue Laugier, ☎ 01 47 54 05 02. Lyonnais cuisine. ££

Le Grenadin, 44 Rue de Naples, ☎ 01 45 63 28 92. Haute cuisine. ££

La Marée, 1 Rue Daru, ☎ 01 43 80 20 00. Haute cuisine. Fresh seafood. ££

Michel Rostang, 20 Rue Rennequin, ☎ 01 47 63 40 77. Haute cuisine. £££

La Rotisserie d'Armaillé, 6 Rue d'Armaillé, ☎ 01 42 27 19 20, Bistrot Cagna. ££

Guy Savoy, 18 Rue Troyon☎ 01 48 80 36 22. Haute cuisine. £££

Paul Scarlett's, 7 Av. de la Porte de Clichy, ☎ 01 42 26 78 13. Potatoes in every form. £

became fashionable at the end of Louis XIV's reign, and in the 18C its splendid mansions made it a rival to the Faubourg St-Germain as an aristocratic quarter.

On the left in Rue du Faubourg St-Honoré is the exclusive Cercle Interallié (No. 33; of 1714), the Russian Embassy during the Second Empire; and adjacent (No. 35), the Hôtel de Charost, since 1825 the **British Embassy** (Pl. 7; 5), formerly at the Hôtel de Sagan in the Faubourg St-Germain, to which its earlier history refers.

> The 4th Duc de Charost commissioned Antoine Mazin to build the mansion in 1722. In 1785 it was let to the Comte de la Marck, during whose tenancy much of its interior decoration was completed, and the jardin à l'anglaise laid out. It was bought in 1803 by Pauline Bonaparte (later Princess BorghEse), much of whose furniture remains, and was sold by her to the Duke of Wellington in 1814 for £32,000, the figure including numerous clocks, chandeliers, candelabras and chimneypieces. Berlioz and Harriet Smithson were married in the chapel in 1833, with Liszt as best man.

No. 41 is the Hôtel Pontalba, built by Visconti and restored by E. de Rothschild. The **Palais de l'Elysée** (no admission), stands at the corner of Av. de Marigny. This heavily guarded mansion was built by Molet as the Hôtel d'Evreux in 1718 but has been greatly altered and enlarged since.

It was occupied by Mme de Pompadour, Murat, Napoléon I (who signed his second abdication here in 1815), Wellington and Napoléon III, who lived here as Président from 1848 until he moved, as Emperor, to the Tuileries in 1852. It then reverted to its use as a residence for visiting heads of state (including Queen Victoria in 1855 and Elizabeth II in 1957). Since 1873 it has been the official residence of the President of the Republic.

To the right, No. 11 Rue des Saussaies was the Gestapo headquarters in Paris during 1940–44. Passing (right) the Ministère de l'Intérieur (Home Office), built in 1769–84 flanking Pl. Beauvau, continue along Rue du Faubourg-St-Honoré. Beyond Av. Matignon on the right, stands **St-Philippe-du-Roule**, built in 1769–84 by Chalgrin on the site of the parish church of Roule and later enlarged. The sculpture of *Religion* on the pediment is by Duret, and the basilical style interior contains Chassériau's ceiling painting, *Descent from the Cross*.

At 45 Rue La Boétie (to the right) is the **Salle Gaveau**, one of the more important concert-halls in Paris.

Rue du Faubourg-St-Honoré soon meets the wide Av. de Friedland, which leads west to the Arc de Triomphe (see p 254). At 208 Rue du Faubourg-St-Honoré, beyond Av. Friedland, are the buildings of the old Hôpital Beaujon (1784); opposite, at 11 Rue Berryer, is the former Hôtel Salomon de Rothschild and Honoré Balzac died in 1850 where 12 Rue Balzac now stands.

Just beyond the intersection with Av. Hoche is the **Salle Pleyel** (1927), the largest concert-hall in Paris, radically revamped in 1981. In Rue Daru, parallel to the north, is the exotic neo-Byzantine Russian Orthodox church of St-Alexandre-Nevsky (1859–61).

From behind St-Philippe-du-Roule (see above) Rue de Courcelles crosses Blvd Haussmann. At 38 in Rue de Courcelles (then 48) Dickens lodged in 1846; from 1901–05 Proust lived at No. 45, with his cork-lined sound-proof room, before moving to 102 Blvd Haussmann where he remained until 1919. The Galerie Ching Tsai Loo at No. 48 is a unique red building in Chinese style commissioned in 1926 for an Oriental art dealer.

The Musée Jacquemart-André

The Musée Jacquemart-André (Pl. 6; 4) at 158 Blvd Haussmann contains a remarkable collection of French 18C art and Italian Renaissance art in a beautiful setting. Following extensive renovations, the museum reopened in 1996 and for the first time the public can enter the Italian Museum and the private apartments. There is a delightful Salon de thé on the ground floor in the former dining room complete with a G.B. Tiepolo fresco and tapestries, *The Legend of Achilles*. Open 10.00–18.00 daily (☎ 01 42 89 04 91) and each visitor is issued with an autoguide.

The house was built c 1870 by Edouard André (d. 1894), who in 1881 married the painter Nélie Jacquemart, and in 1912 she bequeathed the collection to the Institut de France.

Ground floor

In the entrance hall is a Winterhalter, *Portrait of Edouard André*, who came from a rich Protestant family and built the house c 1870. In the first room are two oval paintings by Boucher, *Toilette of Venus* and the *Sleep of Venus*, Nattier,

Portrait of the Marquis d'Antin, Canaletto, *St Mark's Square* and *The Rialto, Venice*; Chardin, *Still life*; and a bust of Pigalle. This leads to the spacious **Grand Salon**, with magnificent 18C woodwork and mirrors, four Gobelins tapestries, and busts by Coysevox, Hudon, and Henri IV by Barthélémy Tremblay.

The first in a suite of small rooms off the Grand Salon contains a Beauvais tapestry called Russian Games, after Le Prince, a Savonnerie carpet (1663), a Louis XIV fireplace and a Guardi painting. The Cabinet de Travail, with a painted ceiling attributed to Tiepolo, has works by Greuze, Fragonard and Lancret and, on the desk, a *portrait of Nélie Jacquemart* who painted Edouard André's portrait in 1872. The Boudoir contains Vigée-Lebrun's, *Countess Skravonska* and paintings by David, Reynolds and Hubert Robert.

The **Library** contains Egyptian antiquities, and gems of Flemish and Dutch paintings such as Rembrandt, *Amalia von Solms, Pilgrims at Emmaus, Dr Arnold Tholinx*; Van Dyck, *Count Henry of Peña, Time Cuts the Wings of Love*; Franz Hals, *Portrait of a Man*; Ruysdael, *Landscape*: also Philippe de Champaigne's *Portrait of A Man* and the *Boucicaut Book of Hours*, which belonged to Diane de Poitiers.

The other large reception room opposite, in sumptuous Second Empire style, has a different atmosphere, with red damask walls and ebony furniture. This was used as Music Room. It contains a small Fragonard *Head of an Old Man*; works by Vigée-Lebrun and Largillière and a Beauvais tapestry from a cartoon by Boucher, called Autumn.

The **Winter Garden** is an unusual oval space at the end of the building with a beautiful swirling double staircase designed by Henri Parent with antique sculptures. On the staircase is a fresco by Tiepolo, *Henri III welcomed by Federigo Contarini to the Villa de Mira*.

The Smoking Room has objects brought back from the Orient by Mme André, including 14C lamps from a mosque. There are also the pictures from England by Joshua Reynolds, Gainsborough and John Hoppner (1758–1810).

First floor

On the first floor are the three rooms dedicated to the Italian Renaissance. The prodigious collection includes 82 14C and 15C paintings and a handful from the 16C. Major works include Lorenzo Monaco (1370–1425), *Virgin and Child*; Giovanni dal Ponte, a coffered ceiling decorated with *Four Couples in a Garden*; a miniature *Annunication* (1430–40), by Mariano d'Antonio; a banner (1444) by Pietro di Giovanni di Ambrogio; Giorgia Schiavone, *Profile of a Man*, on parchment and *Virgin and Child*; Uccello, *St George and the Dragon*; Perugino, *Virgin and Child* (c 1470); Vittore Carpaccio, *The Embassy from Hippolytos* (1493–95) and *Six Saints from a Coronation of the Virgin* (1493), by Carlo Crivelli; large retable by Francesco Botticini (1446–97), *The dead Christ with the Virgin, Saints and Others*, painted in rather acid clours and in its original frame. Bernadino Luini, *Virgin with SS. Margaret and Augustine*; a brilliant little *Virgin and Child* by Cima da Conegliano (end 15C); oval painting by Signorelli (1441–1523) of the *Holy Famly with St John the Baptist*; also Giovanni[?] Bellini, *Virgin and Child*, Mantegna, *Mocking of Christ*.

Italian sculpture includes works by Laurana and Jacopo Sansovino. A number of 15C marble doorways have been re-erected and among terracottas from the della Robbia workshops, is a Madonna and Child by Luca della Robbia. There is a Florentine wood and marquetry bench with the Strozzi arms (end

15C) and marquetry choir-stalls, c 1505 (Northern Italian).

Descend to visit the three intimate rooms of the private apartments.

The Rue de Téhéran, a few paces to the east, climbs north across Av. de Messine to meet Rue de Monceau.

The Musée Nissim de Camondo

The Musée Nissim de Camondo, 63 Rue de Monceau (Pl. 7; 3) is an annexe to the Musée des Arts Décoratifs which was bequeathed by Count Moise de Camondo (died 1935) as a memorial to his son Nissim, killed in 1917 (his daughter and grandchildren died at Auschwitz). The mansion itself dates from 1911–14, but the interior decor uses 18C panelling or reproductions, such as the wrought-iron balustrade of the staircase, to create the setting for the outstanding collection of antique furniture, carpets, tapestries and tableware. The house has been almost completely restored and fabrics remade to replicate the original. Open 10.00–17.00, closed Mon and Tues, ☎ 01 53 89 06 40.

From the entrance hall, with a red marble fountain (1765) from the Château de St-Prix, Montmorency, and a flat-topped desk by J-H. Riesener, stairs lead up past a pair of corner cupboards decorated with Japanese lacquer attributed to B.V.R.B., and a pair of armchairs upholstered in Savonnerie tapestry.

First floor

The **Grand Bureau** has a pair of low cabinets by Leleu; a roll-top desk and secretaire by Saunier, the latter from the Château de Tanly; desk-armchair of 1778; a white marble-topped table by M. Carlin from the Château de Bellevue; two low chairs known as voyeuses, designed for watching the gaming tables, by Séné; chairs by N.Q. Foliot covered in Aubusson tapestry (scenes from La Fontaine); Aubusson tapestries with six fables from La Fontaine after Oudry; a Beauvais screen with the fable of the Cock on the Dunghill; bronze bust of *Mme Le Comte* by Coustou; Vigée-Lebrun, *Bacchante*.

The **Grand Salon**, overlooking the garden, has white and gold panelling from a private town house at 11 Rue Royale; a pair of covered vases carved from petrified wood, from the collection of Marie-Antoinette; marquetry cabinet and tables by Riesener; round table and bureau de dame (with Sèvres porcelain plaques) by Carlin; a pair of low tables by A. Weisweiler; oval table by D. Roentgen and one by R.V.L.C. (R. Vandercruse, called Lacroix); suite of furniture (which belonged to Sir Richard Wallace), including two sofas and an armchair by G. Jacob; a six-leaved Savonnerie screen; *L'Eté* (Hubert Robert's daughter), a marble bust by Houdon; Vigée-Lebrun, *Mme Le Coulteux du Molay*; La Pêcheuse, a Beauvais tapestry, after Boucher; and among Savonnerie carpets, one (L'Air) woven for the Grande Galerie of the Louvre (1678) and one made in 1660.

Salon Huet: seven panels and three dessus de portes of Scènes pastorales painted by J.B. Huet, dated 1776; marquetry roll-top desk by Oeben; pair of cabinets by Garnier and Carlin; sofa, *bergères* and chairs by Séné; a folding screen by J.B. Boulard, delivered in 1785 for Louis XVI's Salon des Jeux at Versailles.

Salle à Manger, with a view of the Parc Monceau: console and a pair of ebony and chased and gilded bronze serving tables by Weisweiler; pair of small cabinets by Leleu; silver, including two tureens by Auguste and Roettiers (the latter's work was ordered by Catherine II of Russia for Orloff). Cabinet des Porcelaines, with a table set of Sèvres porcelain, known as the Buffon set, decorated with birds. Galerie: sofa and chairs by P. Gillier; Aubusson tapestries, after Boucher, La Danse Chinoise.

Petit Bureau: furniture by Topino, Riesener and R.V.L.C., among others; snuffboxes, clocks, Chinese porcelain (Kien-Loung); terracotta medallions by J.B. Nini; marble *bust of Mme le Comte* by Coustou; four *Views of Venice* by Guardi; *portrait of Necker* by Duplessis; Oudry, sketches for Gobelins tapestries of *Les Chasses de Louis XV*; three paintings by H. Robert. On the stairs leading to the second floor, two Aubusson tapestries in the Chinese style, after Boucher.

Second floor

Galerie: sofa and chairs by Nogaret; a series of engravings after Chardin; 18C Chinese porcelain. Turning right into the **Salon Bleu**: pair of tables attributed to Riesener; low bookcase by Weisweiler; red morocco casket embossed with the arms of Marie-Antoinette; views of Paris by Bouhot (1813), Canella (1830), Demachy (1774) and Raguenet (1754); a family portrait by Gautier-Dagoty (c 1770); watercolour of the Quai Malaquais by T. Boys; Chinese porcelain of the 17C–18C.

Bibliothèque, an oak-panelled oval room, contains a drop-front desk by Leleu; two bronzé and Sèvres biscuit candelabras by Blondeau after Boucher; two paintings by H. Robert; Aubusson tapestry screen (1775). Chambre à Coucher: furniture by Cramer, Topino and G. Jacob. Among paintings: Danloux, Rosalie Duthé; Lavreince, *The Singing Lesson*; Lancret, *Les Rémois*; Drouais, *Alexandre de Beauharnais as a Child*; Houdon, presumed *Portrait of Anne Audeoud*, a plaster bust; Savonnerie carpet (1760) for the chapel at Versailles. Deuxième Chambre: secretaire attributed to Riesener; screen by Canabas; Scènes de Chasse by de Dreux, Shayer, Fontaine (J.F.J. Swebach) and H. Vernet. The Bathroom and Dressing Room of the early 20C are also open to the public.

At 7 Av. Vélasquez, a parallel street to the north, is the **Musée Cernuschi**, bequeathed to the city in 1895 by the collector (of Maltese origin). In many ways it complements the more comprehensive collections of Oriental art in the Musée Guimet and Musée d'Ennery (see pp 260 and 272 respectively). Open 10.00–17.40, closed Mon, ☎ 01 45 63 50 75.

Of particular interest are the funerary figurines of the T'ang and Wei dynasties, neolithic terracottas, and bronze vases of the Chang dynasty (14C–11C BC), while outstanding are the paintings on silk of horses and grooms of the T'ang period (8C). Note also the collections of clasps, mirrors, and jade amulets. On the first floor is an extensive collection of bronze objects from Louristan and Iran (8C–7C BC), a bronze basin of 5C–3C BC and porcelain of various periods.

Parc Monceau

The neighbouring Parc Monceau (Pl. 6; 4; 88 hectares) is an appropriately elegant garden for this smart district. It derives its name from a vanished village, and is a remnant of a private park laid out by Carmontel in 1778 for Philippe-Egalité d'Orléans, Duc de Chartres, and father of Louis-Philippe. Its gardener was Thomas Blaikie (1750–1838), a Scotsman. It was then known as the 'Folie de Chartres', and certain picturesque details remain.

Near the north-east corner is the Naumachie, an oval lake with a graceful Corinthian colonnade, which may have come from either the Château du

Raincy or from the projected Valois chapel at St-Denis. To the east of the lake is a Renaissance arcade from the old Hôtel de Ville; to the west is the Rotonde de Chartres, a toll-house (by Ledoux) of the 18C city wall erected by the Farmers-General. Used as a keeper's lodge, the building was disfigured in 1861 by fluting its columns and adding a dome. The four monumental gates are by Davioud, and scattered among the ornamental trees and shrubs and colourful flowerbeds are several statues, including *Ambroise Thomas* by Falguière (1902), *Guy de Maupassant* by Verlet (1897).

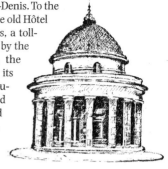

*The toll house by Ledoux
in Parc Monceau*

There are a number of imposing mansions in the streets to the north, including those in Rue de Prony, leading north west. Off this street, Rue Fortuny turns north east to the renamed Pl. du Gén. Catroux (formerly Pl. Malesherbes but still métro Malesherbes). Slightly to the north is the Salle Cortot, a concert-hall (78 Rue Cardinet).

Batignolles

Further north east, in the Batignolles, some picturesque areas still survive the pressures of modernisation, and deserve exploration. In 1989 the **Promenade Pereire**, a promenade plantée, was created on top of the RER line between Rue Bayen (Porte Maillot) and Pl. Maréchal-Juin. This clever camouflage consists of open gardens alternating with enclosed squares in a continuous walkway. The *quartier* gave its name to a school of Impressionist painters under the leadership of Manet (see the painting by Fantin-Latour in the Musée d'Orsay).

In the **Cimetière des Batignolles** (best approached by the Av. de Clichy, and some distance north west of the Cimetière de Montmartre) lie Verlaine, André Breton and Léon Bakst.

The Av. de Villiers leads north west from the Pl. du Gén. Catroux, in which No. 43 is the Musée Henner, devoted to the work of Jean-Jacques Henner (1829–1905). Some distance further west, near the Porte de Champerret, stands Ste-Odile (1938–46), with a flattened dome and rocket-like tower. Nearby, at 41 Blvd Berthier, John Singer Sargent had his studio c 1883–86, which was taken over by Giovanni Boldini.

27 · Chaillot, Passy and Auteuil

■ Arrondissement: 75016.
■ Métros: Concorde, Alma-Marceau, Iéna, Trocadéro, Passy, Muette, Porte-d'Auteuil.

The 16e arrondissement is a smart residential area characterised by large 19C and 20C apartment blocks, several pleasant gardens and an expensive shopping district around Rue de Passy; the *quartier* also boasts the best view of the Eiffel Tower. Also in the 16e are the Musée Marmottan, the Musée d'Art

Moderne de la Ville De Paris, the Musée Guimet and, in the Palais de Chaillot, the Musée de Monuments Français, the Musée de la Marine and the Musée de l'Homme.

Restaurants and cafés

Angelina, Hotel Rond Point de Longchamp, 10 Pl. de Mexico, ☎ 01 47 04 89 42. Traditional. ££
Le Bistrot de l'Etoile Lauriston, 19 Rue Lauriston, ☎ 01 40 67 11 16. Bistrot Savoy. £
La Butte Chaillot, 112 Av. Kleber, ☎ 01 47 27 88 88. Bistrot Savoy. £
Le Grand Chinois, 6 Av. de New-York, ☎ 01 47 23 98 21. £
Faugeron, 52 Rue de Longchamp, ☎ 01 47 04 24 53. Haute cuisine. £££
Malakoff, 6 Pl. du Trocadéro, ☎ 01 45 53 75 27. Rustic. £
Le Petit Rétro, 5 Rue Mesnil, ☎ 01 44 05 06 05. Traditional. £
Port Alma, 10 Av. de New York, ☎ 01 47 23 75 11. Seafood. ££
Presbourg, 3 Av. de la Grande Armée, ☎ 01 45 00 24 77. £
Prunier Tmaktir, 16 Av. Victor Hugo, ☎ 01 44 17 35 85. Seafood, art deco decor. £££
Le Relais du Parc, Hôtel Le Parc, 58 Av. Raymond-Poincaré, ☎ 01 44 05 66 66. ££
La Salle à Manger, Hôtel Raphaël, 17 Av. Kléber, ☎ 01 44 28 00 17. Traditional. ££
Sous l'Olivier, 15 Rue Goethe, ☎ 01 47 20 84 81. Traditional. Rustic. £
Le Vivarois, 192–193 Av. Victor Hugo, ☎ 01 45 04 04 31. Haute cuisine. £££

From Pl. de la Concorde (see p 131), the Cours la Reine with its extension, Cours Albert-1er (No. 40 has glass doors by Lalique, whose home it was), leads west to the Pl. de l'Alma. It was laid out in 1616, and followed the old road to the villages of Chaillot, St-Cloud and Versailles, and the Roman canal which brought water from Chaillot.

The parallel Port de la Conférence, flanking the Seine, takes its name from the Porte de la Conférence (demolished in 1730), through which the Spanish ambassadors entered Paris in 1660 to discuss with Mazarin the projected marriage between Louis XIV and María Teresa.

Pont des Invalides (west of the Pont Alexandre-III) dates from 1827–29, but was rebuilt in 1879–80 and enlarged in 1956. Pont de l'Alma (1970) retains the figure of a *zouave* (a member of the French light infantry corps originally formed of Algerians) from its predecessor, which was long used as a gauge in estimating the height of the Seine in flood.

Immediately east of the south end of Pont de l'Alma is the public entrance to the **sewers** (*égouts*) of Paris, a formidable system laid out by the engineer Eugène Belgrand (1810–78). Part of it may be visited between 11.00–17.00 except Thurs and Fri; and it is closed when raining. The total combined length of the sewers of Paris which may be entered has been estimated at 2100km.

Several handsome streets radiate north from Pl. de l'Alma (Pl. 11; 6), many of the mansions being the showrooms of haut-couturiers. At 13 Av. Montaigne, leading north east, is the **Théâtre des Champs-Elysées**, by A. and G. Perret (1911–13), with bas-reliefs by Bourdelle. On the west side of Av. George-V, leading northwards, is the **American church of the Holy Trinity** (1885–88), built in a Gothic style by G.E. Street.

Av. de New York, with its continuations, follows the north bank of the Seine for some distance before bearing west to the Porte de St-Cloud. Parallel to the long narrow Allée des Cygnes (Isle of Swans) lying mid-stream south of Pont de Bir-Hakeim, is the cylindrical **Maison de la Radio** (or de l'ORTF), designed in 1960 by Henri Bernard, impressive in size even if its tower is out of proportion to the rest of the building (Pl. 10; 8). The Musée Radio-France, devoted to radio, is at 116 Av. du Président-Kennedy, but it may only be visited with a guided tour starting hourly from 10.30–16.30 (but not 12.30) closed Sun, ☎ 01 42 30 33 83.

On the southern extremity of the Allée des Cygnes, crossed here by the Pont de Grenelle (rebuilt 1875), and facing downstream, is a reduced size bronze replica of Bartholdi's *statue of Liberty*, presented to France by the United States, where the original stands at the entrance to New York harbour.

Av. DU Président-Wilson leads west from the Pl. de l'Alma, from which Av. Marceau immediately ascends right towards the Arc de Triomphe, passing (left) **St-Pierre-de-Chaillot** (1937), built in a bogus Byzantine/Romanesque style by Emile Bois. It replaced the 18C parish church.

To the right in Av. du Président-Wilson, behind gardens, is the Hôtel Galliéra (1888), built to house the collections of the Duchesse de Galliéra (d. 1889), who subsequently changed her mind and bequeathed the majority of them to the city of Genoa. At present it houses the **Musée de la Mode et du Costume** (of the Ville de Paris), with its entrance at 10 Av. Pierre-1er de Serbie. Parts of the extensive collections, enriched by numerous donations, are usually shown in rotation in a series of temporary exhibitions covering specific themes or periods. Open 10.00–17.40, closed Mon, ☎ 01 47 20 85 23.

Normally there is a display of dresses, designs, costume and fashion-plates, photographs and an astonishing variety of accessories, lingerie and other forms of clothing, from costume jewellery to shoes, as well as dolls and wigs.

Musee d'Art Moderne de la Ville de Paris

On the south side of the avenue stands the **Palais de Tokyo** constructed for the Universal Exhibition of 1937 (by Aubert, Dondel, Viard and Dastugue) on the site of a military bakery, itself replacing the old Savonnerie (see also Gobelins, p 85). The wall of the terrace is decorated with bas-reliefs by Janniot; and here, with other statues by Bourdelle, is a bronze of *La France*, installed in 1948, with the inscription 'Mother, here are your sons who fought so long and hard' (Charles Péguy).

The building consists of two wings, that to the east housing the Musée d'Art Moderne de la Ville de Paris. Frequent temporary exhibitions are held here, in which case the permanent collection may in part be on view. There is a café-restaurant in the building. Open 10.00–17.30, Sat–Sun 10.00–18.45, closed Tues, ☎ 01 53 67 40 00.

The museum was inaugurated in 1961 to house the municipal collection of

20C works built up from donations since 1930, plus acquisitions. It owns important works drom the School of Paris and other European artists and a growing contemporary collection.

There are several large works, including murals by the Delaunays, *Rythmes*, and by Gleizes and Villon; the vast wall decoration of 250 panels, *Fée Éléctricité*, painted by Raoul Dufy for the Pavilion of Light at the 1937 Exhibition; two versions of Matisse's *Dance* (1931–32) designed for the Barnes Foundation in the USA, in a specially designed setting. The Fauves are represented by Matisse, *Pastoral* (1905), Derain, *Three Figures seated on the Grass* (1906), Dufy, *The Aperitif*, as well as Vlaminck and Rouault.

Among works by Picasso are *L'Evocation*, a tribute to his friend Casagemas, donated by Vollard, *Still Life with Pipe* (1914) and *Pigeon with Peas* (1911). Other artists represented in the collection include Bonnard, *Nude in the Bath*, Braque, *Tête de Femme* (1909); Léger, *Disks* (1918); and Gris. Orphic Cubists such as Robert Delaunay, *The Cardiff Team*; also Modigliani, *Woman with a Fan*; Chagall, *Le Rêve*, and Zadkine, *Orpheus and Foujita*. There are also works by Lhote, Soutine, Friez, Marie Blanchard, Gromaire, Lurçat, Gruber, Buffet and Soulages. And by Oppenheim, Alechinsky, Motherwell and Keith Haring. The engravings by Derain, Le Satyricon Suite and by Picasso, Vollard Suite, are not on permanent display.

To the west is the Pl. d'Iéna (Pl. 11; 5), from which seven streets diverge. 2 Av. d'Iéna is the residence of the US ambassador. To the north of the Place stands the Musée Guimet (see below).

The Musée Guimet

The Musée Guimet at 6 Pl. d'Iéna, with its annex at 19 Av. d'Iéna, was founded at Lyon in 1879 by Emile Guimet (1836–1918), presented by him to the State, transferred to Paris and inaugurated in 1889. In 1945 it officially became the Département des Arts Asiatiques des Musées Nationaux, Guimet's original collection having been considerably augmented, and now includes those of the Asiatic department of the Louvre, illustrating the arts of India and the Far East. The museum is closed for restoration and likely to be so until 1999 or even longer.

The only section currently open, the **Galeries du Panthéon Bouddhique**, are housed on two floors in the former Hôtel Heidelbach, at 19 Av. d'Iéna. These galleries largely concentrate on sculptures related to the Buddhist cult in Japan (some 250) and—to a lesser extent—in China. Its garden has been laid out in the Japanese style.

Major works in the museum are listed below by country. **Cambodia**: Khmer sculpture, including a statue of Hari-Hara (pre-Angkorian style; late 6C), uniting in one person the two gods Siva and Vishnu; lintel of 7C–12C; sculpture of 9C–10C; Female divinity (early 9C); Vishnu in the Kulen style; Brahma in the Koh Ker style; pediment from the temple of Banteai Srei (967); seated·Buddha in the style of Angkor Wat (early 12C); carvings of a lion, an elephant and of the magic serpent, Naga (12C). Also sculptures in the Bayon style (12C–13C); each meditative statue wears the enigmatic 'Angkorian smile'; portrait of King Jayavarman VII; frieze of dancing *apsaras*.

Champa Art of Assam (**central Vietnam**): a head of Buddha (9C) and a dancer with two young elephants (10C). Java: : heads of Buddha (8C–9C); lintel decorated in the Prambanan style (9C); bronzes (7C–9C), and statuettes of Avalokitesvara and Kubera, gods of riches—note the seven treasure-pots at his feet; leather marionettes for a shadow-theatre; a painted fabric calendar from Bali.

Siam (Thailand): stuccoes from P'ra Pathom (c 8C); Buddhas of the Schools of Sukhodava and U-Thong (14C–15C); head of Buddha (16C); painted and worked leather hangings. Laos: Buddha with a begging-bowl. Burma: lacquered wooden Buddha and illuminated MSS.

Tibet: statue in gilded bronze of Dakini; and statuettes decorated with coloured stones; religious objects, jewellery and silverwork. Paintings illustrating the life of Buddha, gods and saints. **Nepal**: Buddhist paintings and statues of wood and gilded bronze.

India: funerary furniture and stone sculpture from near Pondicherry; clay sarcophagus, pottery and jewellery. Mathurâ and Amarâvatî sculpture (2C–4C); serpent-king (sandstone); marble bas-reliefs; Buddhas. Among objects of the 'classical' period (4C–8C), a Buddha in the Gupta style; Torso of a finely sculpted sandstone Buddha (mid 5C); steles of Pâla Art (8C–12C); South Indian stone sculpture; bronzes of Siva; beautiful gouaches and watercolours of the Mogul, Rajput and Pahâri period (16C–18C), including one of Louis XIV when young.

Pakistan and Afghanistan: examples of Græco-Buddhist Gandara sculpture (1C–5C); decorative bas-relief (schist); figurines from the Buddhist monastery of Hadda, including a Genie carrying a floral offering and a demon in a fur; fragments of frescos from the monastery of Kakrak (c 5C); the Treasure of Begram (1C–2C): Græco-Roman and Syrian objects, Indian ivories and Chinese lacquer-work discovered together by the French archaeological mission to Afghanistan in 1937 and 1939–40.

China: carved bone objects of the Chang Dynasty (16C–11C BC) and important collections of archaic bronze implements, ritual vases and arms, from Ngan-Tang, capital of the dynasty; ritual vase in the shape of an elephant; a 'p'an' bowl of the Chou Dynasty (11C–5C BC); the Treasure of Li-Yu, a remarkable find from the Warring Kingdoms Dynasty (5C–3C BC), notably a jade, turquoise and gold-ornamented sword. Jades: the earlier ones in the form of symbols (Pi, the sky; Tsong, the earth; Kwei, the mountain, etc.) and bronzes. Tombstone (Han Dynasty; 206 BC–AD 220); Buddha from Yun-Kang (5C); heads of Bodhisattva and Kasyapa, from Long-men (early 6C); Ananda and Kasyapa, disciples of Buddha (Suei Dynasty; 561–618), marble with traces of polychrome; Dvarapàla, guardian of the temple and funerary statuettes of the T'ang Dynasty (618–906); gilded bronzes of the Wei, Suei and T'ang dynasties (5C–10C), including a small stele representing Sakyamuni and Pradhutaratna, dated 518; lacquer-work; polychrome bowls of the Han Dynasty and Sung Dynasty (960–1279); black lacquer cabinet decorated in gold (17C).

Japan: Jômon and Yayoi pottery (2000–1000 BC and 1C BC–3C AD respectively); figurines (Haniwa) of the era of the Great Tombs (5C–6C); wooden Buddhas (8C–9C); carved masks of the Nara Dynasty (8C); portraits of bonzes (14C–15C); pottery for the Tea Ceremony ('Cha-no-yu'); Imari Kakiemon and Satsuma porcelain; sword-furniture (kozukas); screens, one illustrating the arrival of the Portuguese in Japan (16C). Also, from Korea: Gilded bronze crown and silverware from the kingdom of Silla (5C–6C); and ceramics.

The museum also has an important collection of **Chinese porcelain**, formed principally from the Calmann Collection—'three colour' ware (T'ang Dynasty), celadon, black and white wares (Sung Dynasty)—and from the Grandidier Collection: Ming (1368–1643) and Ch'ing (1644–1912) dynasties. **Central Asia**: Buddhist paintings from Touen-houang; votive banners, one representing Kasyapa in old age, dated 729.

To the south west is the Palais du Conseil Economique et Social, by Auguste Perret (1937–38), originally designed for a Musée des Travaux Publics. The north wing was added in 1960–62 to house the Western European Union.

Av. du Président-Wilson ends at **Pl. du Trocadéro** (Pl. 10; 6), on the former colline de Chaillot (named after a fort near Cádiz occupied by the French in 1823), semi-circular in shape, from which six thoroughfares fan out. In the centre stands an equestrian statue of Maréchal Foch (1851–1929). It is flanked to the south east by the dull Palais de Chaillot (see below). The terrace descends to gardens, fountains and to the Seine, crossed by the Pont d'Iéna, to lead the eye to a breathtaking view of the Eiffel Tower and beyond, across the Champ-de-Mars, to the Ecole Militaire and the Unesco buildings, see Ch. 12.

> Catherine de Médicis built a country house on this hill, later embellished by Anne of Austria. In 1651 Henrietta Maria established the Convent of the Visitation here, which was destroyed during the Revolution. Napoléon planned to use the site for a palace for his son which would eclipse the Kremlin, but the disasters of 1812 intervened.

To the west, steps ascend to the small **Cimetière de Passy**, where Debussy, Gabriel Fauré, Manet and Berthe Morisot are buried.

The Palais de Chaillot

The Palais de Chaillot, on the south-east side of the Pl. du Trocadéro, was erected for the Paris Exhibition of 1937 and replaced the earlier Palais du Trocadéro, designed for the 1878 Exhibition. The building (by Carlu, Boileau and Azéma) encases in its two curved extensions the two wings of the original structure, from the terrace between which, flanked by a battalion of statues, there is a panoramic treat.

Below the square, adorned with gilded bronze statues, is an aquarium and the **Théâtre de Chaillot**, seating over 2000, the home of the Théâtre National de Chaillot (decorated by Bonnard, Dufy and Vuillard, among others). The third General Assembly of the United Nations took place here in 1948.

The **Trocadero Gardens**, on the slopes descending to the river, flank fountains which include a battery of 20 jets shooting almost horizontally towards the Seine. After Pont d'Iéna (1806–13, since widened twice), the next bridge downstream is Pont de Bir-Hakeim (formerly Pont de Passy, 1903–06), a double bridge, the upper part used by the métro, named after a French victory in North Africa in 1942.

The Palais de Chaillot at present houses four museums: in the Paris wing (east), the Musée des Monuments Français and Musée du Cinéma-Henri Langlois; in the Passy wing (west), the Musée de la Marine and the Musée de l'Homme.

The **Musée des Monuments Français** is due for an overhaul and will be closed until early 1999. The museum was founded by Viollet-le-Duc in 1879 as the Musée de Sculpture Comparée, and contains faithful replicas of masterpieces of French sculpture, architecture, murals and stained-glass. The renovations will allow an increase in the number of exhibits on display and extend the chronology from the 12C through to the period between the Wars. To those familiar with the great French monuments *sur place*, it is a strange experience to find them grouped together here.

Devotees of the cinema will find much of interest in the **Musée du Cinéma** located in the basement of this wing, established by Henri Langlois (1914–77). Over 3000 items are displayed in 60 sections, vividly presenting diverse aspects of the history of the film during its earlier decades.

On the ground floor of the west wing of the Palais de Chaillot is the **Musée de la Marine**, worth a visit even for the most convinced land-lubber, open 10.00–18.00, closed Tues (☎ 01 45 53 31 70). It has a remarkable collection of material illustrating French naval history through to the 21C, including and series of models of ships and a number of fine paintings of maritime subjects include Vernet's Ports of France. A team of restorers can be observed at work, and consulted if desired.

The main gallery, right of the entrance, is dominated by the richly carved poop of the Reale (1690–1715), some of the sculpture of which is attributed to Puget. Note the paintings (Nos 61 and 62) of the *Embarkation of Henry VIII for the Field of Cloth of Gold* by Bouterwerke (a copy of the original by Vincent Volpi) and a *View of Amsterdam* by Bakhuysen (1664). Four anonymous views of Malta (Nos 138–9) and two views of Port Mahon (Nos 147 and 416, the latter by Joseph Chiesa) are also of interest, and a number of marine paintings by Jean-François Hue (1751–1823).

In the centre of the gallery are displayed 13 (of the 15 completed of the original 24 commissioned) views of the Ports of France painted between 1754–65 by Claude-Joseph Vernet (1714–89), depicting Dieppe, Antibes, tuna-fishing near Bandol, Rochefort, La Rochelle, Cette, two views of Toulon, two of Bordeaux, two of Bayonne, and Marseille.

You pass the richly ornamented Emperor's Barge (1811) before entering a section devoted to lighthouses and leading to the area used for temporary exhibitions. Along a parallel gallery are further sections displaying thematic topics, such as navigation and voyages of discovery, 18C shipbuilding, the merchant navy, and early steamships. The history of the French Navy includes the first armoured frigate *La Gloire*, launched in 1859, and continues through to the present with the nuclear aircraft carrier Charles de Gaulle due to join the French Fleet in the early 21C.

The **Musée de l'Homme**, housed on the first and second floors of this wing, was formed by the amalgamation of the Galerie d'Anthropologie and the Musée d'Ethnographie du Trocadéro. A comprehensive library, photographic library, cinema and various technical services are also housed here. Open 09.45–17.15, closed Tues and public holidays; ☎ 01 44 05 72 72, recorded message, ☎ 01 44 05 72 72.

The sections devoted to Anthropology, Paleoanthropology and Prehistory,

Africa, the Near East and Europe are found on the first floor. On the second are rooms displaying exhibits from the Arctic, Asia, Indonesia and Oceania, and America.

Rue Franklin (No. 8 was Clemenceau's residence from 1883 to 1929) leads south west from Pl. du Trocadéro, and is continued by Rue Raynouard. From their junction at Pl. de Costa Rica, Rue de Passy, high street of the old village of **Passy**, runs west to the Jardin du Ranelagh (see below).

Steps descend to the left in Rue Raynouard to Sq. Charles Dickens, in which the vaulted medieval cellars of the **Musée du Vin** may be visited (10.00–18.00 every day); it has a restaurant, ☎ 01 45 25 63 26, in the 14C cellars.

No. 47 Rue Raynouard is the **Maison de Honoré de Balzac** (admission 10.00–17.40, closed Mon), the author's home in 1841–47, where he wrote *La Cousin Bette* and *La Cousin Pons* among other novels. The ivy-covered **RUE BERTON**, behind the house, is one of the more charming lanes which survive and were once characteristic of Passy.

Rue des Vignes also leads to the Chaussée de la Muette and the east end of the **Jardin du Ranelagh** (Pl. 10;7), part of the ancient royal park of La Muette. It was designed to emulate its fashionable namesake in London, and just before the Revolution was a favourite resort. It is graced with a statue of *La Fontaine* (1984) by Corréla. The first balloon ascent in France was made nearby in 1783 by Pilâtre de Rozier and the Marquis d'Arlandes.

The royal Château de la Muette, originally a hunting-lodge, improved by the Regent Orléans and restored by Louis XV for Mme de Pompadour, has completely disappeared. The present mansion, just north of the Jardin du Ranelagh and east of the Porte de la Muette, was built by Baron Henri de Rothschild, and is now the property of the Organisation for Economic Cooperation and Development.

Statue of La Fontaine in the Jardin du Ranelagh

Musée Marmottan

Tucked away on the edge of the 16e arrondissement, at 2 Rue Louis-Boilly, leading off the west side of the Ranelagh gardens, is the Musée Marmottan (Pl. 10; 5/7). This pleasant and intimate museum in a 19C *hôtel particulier* never appears to get crowded. The basis of the museum was the Marmottan Collection of Empire paintings, furniture and bronzes but it is best known for its celebrated works by Monet and other Impressionists. Less well known is the eclectic display including several donations, among them medieval miniatures and 19C paintings. Temporary exhibitions are mounted in the museum, recently renovated. Open 10.00–17.30, closed Mon (☎ 01 42 24 07 02).

From the original collection are Flemish, German and Italian paintings, including *Resurrection of Lazarus*, School of Lucas Cranach, and *Descent from the Cross*, Hans Muelich (1515–73). To this were added the **Wildenstein Collection of 228 medieval illuminated miniatures** assembled in one room. This gallery, on the left of the entrance, is due for restoration. Among the French illuminations are a page from the *Hours of Étienne Chevalier* by Jean Fouquet (c 1420–c 1481), *Alchemy* by Jean Perreal (1455–1530), the depiction of a boar-hunt (late 15C); some by Jean Colombe (c 1430–1529), Jean Bourdichon (c 1475–1521), *The Kiss of Judas*. Examples of Italian illuminations include several by Lucchino Giovanni Belbello da Pavia (fl. 1430–62); and the remarkable Renaissance page of parchment *The Baptism of Constantine* by Giovanni dei Corradi with the intial 'P' made up of elements of classical architecture. There are also some Flemish works of the period. An outstanding 15C French tapestry illustrates the Story of St Susanne.

The collection of First Empire works is made up of **decorative and fine arts**: furniture by Jacob Frères and Pierre-Antoine Bellangé; an extraordinary geographical clock, designed in 1813, inlaid with painted Sèvres porcelain medallions representing time zones, later altered; and a surtout de table by Thomire, in gilded bronze; there is also porcelain of the period. Paintings include a *portrait of Désirée Clary* by Gérard; the *Duchesse de Feltre and her Children* by François-Xavier Fabre; *A Young Woman* by Lawrence; a *View of Fontainebleau* by Bidault and Boilly, and by the latter, *Portrait of a Captain of the First Company of Musketeers*. There are also drawings by Fragonard and Hubert Robert.

The **Impressionist works** came from three donations, Donop de Monchy, Michel Monet and Duhem. The most notorious of all Impressionist works, *Impression Sunrise* by Claude Monet, was part of the de Monchy donation. First shown in 1874, this painting gave its name, albeit derisive at the time, to the most important artistic movement of the 19C. In 1985 this priceless canvas and others were stolen from the Marmottan, but happily all were recovered five years later in Corsica.

Grouped together, these works provide a fine overview of the development of 19C painting from Corot, *The Lake at Ville-d'Avray seen Through Trees*, to late Monets. Carolus Duran, *Portrait of Monet*; of *Monet and his Wife* by Renoir and, by Monet himself, *The Beach at Trouville*, *Walking near Argenteuil*, *A Train in the Snow*, *Argenteuil in the Snow*, *The Pont de l'Europe Gare St-Lazare*, *Vertheuil in the Mist*, one of the series of *Rouen Cathedral, Effects of Sunlight—Sunset*, the two atmospheric renditions of *The Seine at Port-Villez*, and *London, the Houses of Parliament* reflecting on a glinting Thames; also sketches for his later canvases and several caricatures. Most haunting are variations on the theme of the gardens at Giverny: Waterlilies, willows, wisteria and the Japanese Bridge and their reflections in the ponds. The Giverny works form a complementary collection to those in the Orangerie (see p 134).

The wealth of this small museum does not end here: there is the glowing *Bowl of Tahitian flowers* by Gauguin; Berthe Morisot's sensitive *Small Girl with a Basket* and *At the Ball*; Sisley, *The Canal du Loing in Spring*; Renoir, *Girl in a White Hat* (pastel); and paintings by Caillebotte, Guillaumin, Jongkind, Pissarro and Le Sidaner, *Daybreak at Quimperlé*. Also drawings by Constantin Guys, Boudin and Signac, among others. There are also paintings by the collector Henri Duhem (1860–1941) himself.

To the south is the residential district of **Auteuil**, bordering the Bois de Boulogne. Henri Bergson (1851–1941) lived at 47 Blvd de Beaséjour, skirting the Jardin du Ranelagh, and the Goncourt brothers (Edmond 1822–96 and Jules 1830–70) lived and died at 67 Blvd de Montmorency.

From Blvd de Montmorency, turn left into Rue de l'Assomption and right into Rue Docteur-Blanche. At 8–10 Sq. Dr-Blanche are two villas designed in 1923 by by Le Corbusier (Charles-Edouard Jeanneret; 1887–1965), **Villas Jeanneret and La Roche**. The former contains the library of the Le Corbusier Foundation which holds a large part of the Le Corbusier archives.

Villa La Roche is open to the public and can be visited Mon–Thur 10.00–12.30, 13.30–18.00, Fri to 17.00, closed Sat, Sun, public holidays and August (☎ 01 42 88 41 53). Villa La Roche is a prime example of the spirit of Le Courbusier and an essential visit for anyone interested in the Modern Movement. The house, built for a Swiss banker, Raoul La Roche, is designed around a main hall leading to two different sections of the house—private and public. The overall impression is of light and carefully articulated space.

At the southern end of Blvd de Montmorency is the Porte d'Auteuil, the south east entrance to the Bois de Boulogne (see p ???), and an approach to the A13 autoroute and the Blvd Périphérique. From Pl. de la Porte d'Auteuil, Blvd Exelmans swings south east to reach the Seine at Pont du Garigliano. South west of the Porte d'Auteuil is the **Jardin des Serres d'Auteuil** (Municipal Nursery Gardens), part of Louis XV's botanic gardens, with remarkable glasshouses. Nearby are the Roland-Garros tennis courts and south of the gardens are the restored Piscine Molitor and several stadiums.

Rue d'Auteuil leads east to N.-D. d'Auteuil, built in the Romanesque-Byzantine style (1877–92) on the site of the 12C parish church; in front is a monument to Chancellor d'Aguesseau (d. 1751) and his wife.

In the small **Cimetière d'Auteuil**, in the Rue Claude-Lorrain (south of and parallel to the Blvd Exelmans), lie Hubert Robert, Mme Helvétius, Carpeaux, Gavarni and Gounod.

28 · Bois de Boulogne, Neuilly and La Défense

■ Arrondissements: 75016, 92200, 92060.
■ Métros: Porte-d'Auteuil, Muette, Porte-Dauphine, Porte-Maillot, Les Sablons, Esplanade de La Défense. RER: Grande-Arche de la Défense.

Two great contrasts come together in this chapter: the lung of Paris, the Bois de Boulogne with its famous rose gardens, the Parc de Bagatelle, and the concrete jungle of La Defense. Adjacent lies the residential suburb of Paris, Neuilly-sur-Seine, with the Musée National des Arts et des Traditions Populaires.

Restaurants

L'Auberge du Bonheur, Allée de Longchamp, Bois de Boulogne, ☎ 01 42 24 10 17. £

Le Bistrot d'à Côté Neuilly, 4 Rue Boutard, Neuilly, ☎ 01 47 45 34 55. Michel Rostang. £

Le Chalet des Îles, Lac du Bois de Boulogne, ☎ 01 42 88 04 69. ££

La Grande Cascade, Allée de Longchamp, Bois de Boulogne, ☎ 01 45 27 33 51. Haute cuisine. £££

Les Jardins de Bagatelle, Bois de Boulogne, ☎ 01 40 67 98 29, 19C stables, terrace.

L'Orée du Bois, 1 Allée de Longchamp, Bois de Boulogne, ☎ 01 40 67 92 50. £

Le Pavillon des Princes, 69 Av. de la Porte d'Auteuil, ☎ 01 47 43 15 15. Seafood. £

Le Pavillon Royal, Rte. de Suresnes, Bois de Boulogne, ☎ 01 40 67 11 56. ££

Pré-Catalan, Rte. de Suresnes, Bois de Boulogne, ☎ 01 45 24 55. £££

Toit de Passy, 94 Av. Paul Doumer, ☎ 01 45 24 55 37. ££

The Bois de Boulogne

The Bois de Boulogne (Pl. 10; 1–3), at 845 hectares, is slightly smaller but better known than its counterpart at the other end of the city, the Bois de Vincennes. It is the tiny remnant of the old Forest of Rouvray, part of the band of forest once surrounding ancient Lutetia. Tamed, landscaped, subdivided, it encompasses gardens, lakes and the Longchamp racecourse. It lies immediately to the west of the 16e arrondissement of Paris (Chaillot, Passy and Auteuil: see Ch. 27), and was originally bounded on the east by part of the peripheral fortifications of the city. Now the Blvd Périphérique tunnels below the east and south edges of the Bois, which is bounded on the north by Neuilly; the suburb of Boulogne-Billancourt to the south, and by the Seine to the west, on the far side of which rise the hills of Mont Valérien, St-Cloud, Bellevue and Meudon. (Warning: Do not stray into the Bois at dusk or after dark.)

Although the châteaux of La Muette, Madrid and Bagatelle, and the abbey of Longchamp were erected on its borders, the Bois was neglected until the middle of the last century. Much timber was cut down for firewood during the Revolution, and a large part of the Allied army of occupation bivouacked here after Waterloo. It was the haunt of footpads and often the scene of suicides and duels. In 1852 it was handed over by the State to the City, was transformed into an extensive park and became a favourite promenade of the Parisians. The model was Hyde Park in London, which had so impressed Napoléon III. More trees were felled in 1870 to prevent them giving cover to the Prussians. The equestrian scenes which were such a favourite subject of Constantin Guys (1805–92) often had the Bois in the background.

There are four main entrances to the Bois from central Paris, namely the **Porte Maillot** (at its north-east corner); the **Porte Dauphine** (at the western end of the Av. Foch); the **Porte de la Muette** (at the south end of the Av. Victor-Hugo); and the **Porte d'Auteuil** (at its south-east corner). Between the last two is the subsidiary **Porte de Passy**.

The *Bois* is divided diagonally by the long **Allée de Longchamp**, leading south west from the Porte Maillot towards the Carrefour de Longchamp and a popular equestrian rendezvous. It is intersected by the **Route de la Reine Marguerite** (from the Carrefour de la Porte de Madrid to the Porte de Boulogne, on the south side of the Bois).

The usual approach to the Bois is by the imposingly wide, garden-flanked Av. Foch (opened in 1855 as the Av. de l'Impératrice), leading west from the Étoile to the Porte Dauphine, later known as the Av. du Bois de Boulogne. Note one of the original Art Nouveau entrances to the métro on the north side of the avenue here, designed by Hector Guimard.

Not far from the Etoile is a monument to Adolphe Alphand (1817–91), who laid out the Bois and many other parks in Paris in their present form.

At 59 Av. Foch, on the left, is the **Musée d'Ennery**, with a small but important collection of Oriental art formed by the dramatist Adolphe d'Ennery (Eugène Philippe; 1811–99); the building also houses a collection of Armenian art. No. 80 Avenue Foch was the home of Claude Debussy (1862–1918). South west of the park entrance is a huge building (1955–59) constructed for NATO but now housing university faculties. Open Thurs, Sun 14.00–18.00, ☎ 01 47 23 61 65.

To approach the Porte de la Muette directly from the Etoile, follow Av. Victor-Hugo, in which Hugo (1802–85) died in a house on the site of No. 124.

Musée National des Arts et des Traditions Populaires

Of particular interest in the northern section of the Bois is the Musée National des Arts et des Traditions Populaires (Pl. 10; 1), easily reached from either Porte Maillot or Porte Dauphine, or, more directly, from the métro: Les Sablons. The museum is housed in a not unattractive functional building by Jean Dubuisson, completed in 1966, standing just west of the Carrefour des Sablons. Open 09.45–17.15, closed Tues, ☎ 01 44 17 60 00.

The museum is a fascinating tribute to French craftsmanship and country life. The huge range of the collections is exceptionally well displayed. It also has vast documentary resources and a research centre focussing on the study of French contemporary culture, and an auditorium. Several rooms are devoted to temporary exhibitions.

The extent of the collections is apparent in the **Galerie Culturelle**, laid out in a series of sections covering aspects of rural life in the pre-industrial periods, in which some 5000 objects are seen in context or grouped ecologically. Among these are objects with sheepfarming; baking; the smithy; stone-splitting; forms of rural transport; wood-turning and furniture carving; viticulture; the fabrication of horn and wood objects; the embellishment of metalwork; ceramic production; and sections devoted to peasant costumes and coiffes, with a charming painting of an Arlesienne.

North west of the museum is the **Jardin d'Acclimatation** (linked to Porte Maillot by a little train), with a small-scale zoo (its former inmates were eaten in 1870), a playground, and the Musée en Herbe, which has temporary exhibitions and workshops for children. To the west, near the Porte de Madrid, stood the Château de Madrid, built in 1528 by François I, who is said to have named it in memory of his captivity in Spain, after the Battle of Pavia. It was gradually demolished between 1793 and 1847.

Parc de Bagatelle
Further west, skirted by the Route de Sèvres à Neuilly, are the walls of the Parc de Bagatelle (24 hectares). It is open to the public until dusk (fee), and there is a restaurant (expensive).

This delightful and well-tended oasis is made up of several gardens in different styles, but is most famous for its rose-garden, at its best in mid-June, when the annual International New Rose competition takes place in the Orangerie. Concerts are also held here. Landscaped with a wide selection of trees, and with follies, streams, waterfalls and lakes, the planting shows the influence of the Impressionists' preference for massed blooms—the Garden Conservator in 1905, J.-C.-N. Forestier, was a friend of Monet. As well as the roses, there are iris, wisteria, clematis and water lilies.

The elegant little **Château de Bagatelle**, replacing an earlier residence, was built for a wager within 64 days by Bélanger for the Comte d'Artois, later Charles X, in 1779. The dome was added in 1852. It was acquired by the Ville de Paris in 1904.

During the Revolution it was turned into a tavern and later became the residence of Sir Richard Wallace (1818–90), supposed natural son of the Marquess of Hertford. Wallace had a town house at 25 Rue Taitbout where he collected art treasures (now in the Wallace Collection, London) in addition to those he had inherited from his half-brother the eccentric Richard Seymour Conway, 4th Marquis of Hertford (1800–70), who had bought the mansion in 1835 and died here. Hertford's own brother, Lord Henry Seymour (1805–59), was founder of the exclusive Jockey Club. Wallace was also a great benefactor of Paris, which he provided with drinking fountains, and he helped to equip ambulances during the 1870–71 war. He founded the Hertford British Hospital in Paris (opened 1879) and built the Anglican church of St-George (1887–88; Rue Auguste-Vacquerie, off Av. d'Iéna).

To the west are various sports grounds (including polo and *tiercé*); to the south west is the Hippodrome de Longchamp, opened in 1857. On the north side is a windmill (restored), almost the only relic of the Abbey of Longchamp, founded in 1256 by St Isabel of France, sister of Louis IX.

From the Carrefour de Longchamp (just east of the windmill), a road leads due east past the Grande Cascade (an artificial waterfall) to skirt the enclosure of the Pré-Catelan (according to legend, name after the troubadour Arnaud Catelan, murdered here c 1300), with a huge copper beech. The **Jardin Shakespeare**, has specimens of plants and trees mentioned in Shakespeare's plays.

Further east are buildings of the Racing Club de France, flanking the west bank of the Lac Inférieur, with two linked islands. Boats may be hired on the east bank. Further south is the Lac Supérieur, beyond the Carrefour des Cascades; in the south-east corner of the Bois, is the Hippodrome d'Auteuil (steeplechasing).

N.-D.-des-Menus, in Av. J.-B. Clément, leading south west from the Porte de

Boulogne, although frequently restored (by Viollet-le-Duc among others) still has its 14C nave. Beyond (right) are the **Jardins Albert Kahn** (including one laid out in the Japanese style). Open daily April–November.

In the RUE DENFERT-ROCHEREAU is a series of buildings in the Modern Movement style of 1926–27, by L.-R. Fischer, Le Courbusier and Robert Mallet-Stevens; also at the angle of Rue des Arts and Allée des Pins are two *résidences-ateliers* of 1924, by Le Corbusier and Pierre Jeanneret. There are more examples of experimental architecture of the 1920s by Auguste Perret, and André Lurçat in Rue du Belvédère and in Rue Nungesser-et-Coli (near Parc des Princes), an apartment block (1932) by Le Corbusier.

From the Arc de Triomphe (see p 254), Av. de la Grande Armée descends north west to the **Porte Maillot** (Pl. 10; 2), a great meeting of principal routes and the site of extensive blocks of buildings in recent years commanded on the north side by the International Centre and the Palais des Congrès and one of the Aérogares (or air terminals) of Paris.

A short distance to the north west, near Pl. du Gén. Koenig (Pl. de la Porte des Ternes), stands **N.-D. de la Compassion**, a mausoleum in the Byzantine style (1843).

Neuilly-sur-Seine

Beyond Porte Maillot, the wide Av. Charles-de-Gaulle bisects Neuilly-sur-Seine, once the most fashionable suburb of Paris. It was partially laid out in what was formerly the park of Louis-Philippe's château (built in 1740 and burnt down in 1848), and later developed as a colony of elegant villas, but the construction of blocks of flats has overwhelmed the distinctive character of the neighbourhood.

Its southern half retains the attraction of being adjacent to the Bois de Boulogne. In the old cemetery, lie Anatole France and André Maurois and in the **Cimetière de Lavallois-Perret**, the suburb north of Neuilly, lie Louise Michel (1830–1905), the revolutionary, and Maurice Ravel (1875–1937).

Av. Charles-de-Gaulle leads to **Pont de Neuilly**, a stone bridge by Perronet (1768–72, almost entirely rebuilt in 1935–39), which replaced an earlier bridge erected in 1606 after Henri IV and Marie de Médicis were almost drowned in the Seine here. The central section of the bridge stands on the northern extremity of the Ile de Puteaux; to the north is the Ile de la Grande Jatte, painted by Seurat in 1884.

La Défense

The distinctive silhouette of the high-rise buildings of La Défense ominously looming beyond the péripherique to the north west is familiar to most visitors to Paris. The district's best known building, the Grande Arche, is already over-shadowed by a taller one behind it.

La Défense, named after a monument commemorating the defence of Paris against the Prussians in 1871, designates an extensive area of 760 hectares, which has been developed since 1958 by the Etablissement Public pour l'Aménagement de la Région de la Défense, or EPAD, to create a business centre outside Paris proper. The first building of consequence was the triangular-shaped flat-domed exhibition hall, known as the CNIT Centre

(1958), with the largest concrete vaulted roof in the world. The construction of the RER line in 1970 has brought La Défense within rapid reach of central Paris and the tower blocks keep rising. One of the first was the Tour Roussel-Hoechst (then known as the Tour Nobel), a mere 34 storeys, immediately south of the far end of the Pont de Neuilly.

La Défense is impressive. It is also controversial. There are plans to rebuild the ESSO building, one of the earliest erected and recently demolished, further west on the north side of the main axis of La Défense. It has been mooted that this was because it was not an aggressive enough example of the high-rise structures which have since mushroomed, housing a variety of national and international companies and corporations—and turning the area into a concrete jungle, in spite of the claims of architects and town-planners. There are some 30,000 residents and over 140,000 people work there.

Rail and road traffic is sited underground, making this a car-free zone, but the warren of passages leading from the car parks (with 26,000 spaces) and the RER station to the offices, commercial areas, banks, hotels, restaurants, fast-food establishments and residential blocks is unalluring. The vast expanse of main esplanade is broken up with a variety of sculptures, fountains and murals, and about 10 per cent (and increasing) of the surface area is given over to urban gardens. An obvious setting for contemporary art, some 50 monumental works have been installed by artist such as Calder, Miró, Takis, Moretti, Venet, and Agam.

The whole area has been divided into 11 sectors and it is wise, if you are heading somewhere in particular, to know in advance the number of the sector you wish to visit. Emerging directly from the RER station or métro (line 1), you will find yourself (in sector 4) on the Parvis close to **La Grande Arche**. This gigantic arch can be visited, 1 Apr–30 Sept, Mon–Fri 09.00–19.00, Sat, Sun, 09.00–20.00; 1 Oct–31 March, 09.00–18.00; the roof stays open for one hour after closing time.

The unusual design, by the Danish architect Johann Otto von Spreckelsen (1929–87), chosen by M. Mitterrand from 424 projects, was completed in mid 1989. Although called an arch it might well be described as a colossal hollow cube or, from the distance, a marble picture frame. It sits on 12 huge piles, sustaining a weight of 300,000 tonnes, is 110m square, and is open on two sides and pivoted slightly from the main axis of La Défense. Below the arch (now housing several ministries and other offices), is suspended a cloud-like structure. A series of exterior elevators rise to the summit, which provides an awesome view over the surrounding chaos of buildings. Among these, several of which have façades of mirror-glass, the following stand out: to the south of the arch are the angular Pascal Towers; to the east, the dark monolithic Framatome Tower (46 storeys), 235m high—so far the tallest—reflecting the prismatic ELF Tower adjacent. Further east rises the Descartes Tower; and beyond, the GAN Tower and triangular-shaped ASSUR Tower, and facing it, on the other side of the main axis, is the sharp-angled PFA Tower.

It is planned to exploit an extensive area further west, which will be flanked to the north by an extension of the main axis, and will incorporate the Parc André Malraux, the largest park to be created in Paris since the beginning of the century, covering 25 hectares, using the soil extracted from the commercial district. This is part of an ambitious scheme to improve Nanterre, the préfecture of the département of Hauts-de-Seine, further north west, under which the new A14 motorway will tunnel to meet the A13.

29 · Place de la République to La Villette

■ Arrondissements: 75010, 75019.
■ Métros: République, Colonel Fabien, Jaurès, Porte de la Villette, Porte de Pantin, Buttes-Chaumont, Jourdain, Télégraphe.

Restaurants and cafés

Café de la Musique, Cité de la Musique, ☎ 01 44 84 45 45. £
Restaurants and Cafés in the Cité des Sciences et de l'Industrie, ☎ 01 40 05 82 00: Restaurant de la Grande Halle, Level S2; Croq'cité, next to the aquarium; Bar Ariane, next to the Ariane rocket; Bar de la Santé, Level 2 next to the Life and health exhibition; Bar de la Géode, in the Geode. And in the Park de la Villette, cafés in Folies P7 and L2. £
Le Pavillon du Lac, Park des Buttes Chaumont, ☎ 01 42 02 08 97. and ☎ 40 40 00 95. £
Le Vieux Belleville, 12 Rue des Envierges, ☎ 01 44 62 92 66, Traditional. £

La Villette is synonymous with the Cité des Sciences et de l'Industrie, the huge centre devoted to modern technology set in a large park, and the more recent (1996) Cité de la Musique. To the south are two small, lesser-known parks, Parc des Buttes Chaumont and Parc de Belleville.

Rue de Lancry, the first main turning right off Blvd de Magenta (leading north from Pl. de la République), soon crosses the Canal St-Martin, close to a treelined lock, beyond which Rue Bichat leads right to the entrance of the **Hôpital St-Louis** (Pl. 9; 6), founded by Henri IV and built by Claude Vellefaux in 1607–12. It is an excellent and now rare example of the early Louis XIII style, and its courtyards and chapel may be visited on application at the porter's lodge; the chapel is open most afternoons (except Saturday).

Follow Rue de la Grange-aux-Belles (which skirts its north side). Near here stood the Gibet de Montfaucon, the Tyburn of Paris, set up in the 13C and finally removed in 1790. The gallows proved fatal to three Surintendants des Finances: Enguerrand de Marigny, who erected it; Jean de Montaigu, who repaired it; and Semblançay, who tried to avoid it.

La Villette

Further to the north is Pl. du Colonel-Fabien, from which Blvd de la Villette leads to Pl. du Stalingrad. Here, in the shadow of the overhead métro line, on a small island site, stands the **Rotunde de la Villette**, built as a toll-house by Ledoux in 1789, and now a repository for archaeological finds in the Paris area.

Parc de la Villette

At 44 Rue de Flandre, leading north east from the northern side of the Place, is a relic of the old Portuguese Jewish Cemetery, in use between 1780 and 1810. The district of **La Villette** was known until the early 1970s for its cattle-market and abattoirs and formerly had an iron-foundry run by two English engineers, Davidson and Richardson. The ambitious project of converting the extensive site of some 55 hectares into a public park lying on both sides of the Canal de l'Ourcq, and the building of a science museum in its northern half and a museum of music in the south was realised between 1980 and 1996.

The south entrance to the park and the Cité de la Musique is best approached from the métro: Porte de Pantin, while the Cité des Sciences (see below) is more conveniently reached from the métro: Porte de la Villette.

The Cité de la Musique

The south entrance to the park and the Cité de la Musique is best approached from the métro: Porte de Pantin, while the Cité des Sciences (see below) is more conveniently reached from the métro: Porte de la Villette.

A complex of dynamic and varied buildings designed by Christian de Portzamparc is laid out on either side of the south entrance to the park. On the west side, at 211 Av. Jean-Jaurès, stands the new **Conservatoire de Paris**, ☎ 01 40 40 45 45, whose history goes back to 1765, containing practice and recording studios, three concert halls, a database library and many other facilities.

The larger building on the east side, the **Cité de la Musique** at 221 Av. Jean-Jaurès, is designed for a variety of events in connection with music. It includes the Musée de la Musique with its amphitheatre, flexible concert hall (with the possibility of a variety of seating configurations), a music and dance resource centre, and various facilities for educational music associations.

■ Open Tues–Thur 12.00–18.00, Fri and Sat until 19.30, Sun 10.00–18.00, closed Mondays, ☎ 01 44 84 44 84. Guided visits for groups Tues–Sat 09.00–12.00 by prior reservation only, ☎ 01 44 84 46 46.

The main entrance to the Cité de la Musique is opposite the Fontaine aux Lions next to which there is a café-restaurant (open 08.30–02.00) where musical interludes include jazz on Wednesday evenings. There is an extensive boutique-bookshop in the centre.

The museum exhibits some 900 instruments, paintings, sculptures and works inspired by music, and will hold temporary exhibitions. As well as collecting and conserving, the museum aims to give visitors the opportunity both to see and to hear musical instruments. The Cultural Service programmes various types of guided tours, concerts, diverse meetings, conferences, workshops and shows for the young. The 230-seat amphitheatre within the museum is the focus for concerts of historic instruments.

The museum boasts some exceptional and even unique sets of instruments, notably 17C Venetian archlutes, guitars by Voboam; an outstanding collection of French stringed instruments from the 18C and 19C; Cremona violins by Amati, Stradivarius and Guarnerius del Gesù; recorders by Hotteterre; Flemish harpischords by the celebrated Rucker dynasty; 18C French harpischords; pianofortes by Erard and Pleyel; an exceptional collection of brass instruments by Adolphe Sax; 20C instruments, including an electronic violin by Max Mathews, a MIDI saxophone and Frank Zappa's E-Mu synthesizer; also unique instruments from around the world, such as a 17C Sàrangi from northern India and a 19C chest drum from Zaire,

The **park** itself, designed by Bernard Tschumi, is an innovative exercise in urban renewal with areas particularly appealing to children. Between the Place de la Fontaine aux Lions (Cité de la Musique) and the Cité des Sciences et de l'Industrie, a covered passageway parallel to the western side of the Grande Halle leads across the park and crosses the Canal de l'Ourcq (the south bank of which is skirted by another transverse passageway) to enter the northern sector. Alternatively, there is a path which takes you on a winding route across most of the 35 hectares through prairies and picnic areas, gardens with themes such as *Miroirs, Vents et Dunes, Brouillards, Bamboo*, and past 24 follies of bright red enamelled metal, laid out on a grid pattern. There are canal trips, between la Villette and Pl. Stalingrad, Métro: Jaurès. ☎ 01 42 39 15 00 or general information ☎ 01 40 03 75 03.

The Cité des Sciences et de l'Industrie
The northern half of the park is dominated by the spherical Géode (see below), beyond which is the huge rectangular building of the Cité des Sciences et de l'Industrie, entered more conveniently from the Porte de la Villette at 30 Av. Corentin-Cariou. Near this is the restored rotunda of the Veterinary Surgeon, the only 19C building left, now housing a small museum devoted to the history of the abattoirs.

■ The Cité is normally entered from the north and most of the facilities and amenities, including a science bookshop, are grouped on the main entrance level. Opening times (including the Géode): Tues–Sun 10.00–18.00, closed Mon and 1/5, 25/12. There are various restaurants.

The impressive Cité des Sciences et de l'Industrie was inaugurated in March 1986. It was built on the site of the auction-hall of the slaughter-house, but this structure was never completed. It consisted of 20 reinforced concrete piers supporting 16 lattice girders each 65m long, which formed the basis of the present building, radically adapted by Adrien Fainsilber, and employing several new technologies.

Among unusual features are the three glazed sections of glass wall on its southern side, each 32m square, rising to the roof and in fact forming conservatories or hot-houses; the two rotatable roof cupolas, each 18m in diameter; and—within the conservatories—the transparent lifts (elevators) ascending within a stainless steel framework. The whole structure is surrounded by a moat.

The Cité offers a panorama of science and technology, communication, environment, health, astronomy, and computers, through exhibitions, models and interactive games. The **Cité des Enfants**, is designed specially for children of 3 to 12. A leaflet in English is available at information desks, specifying the whereabouts of the displays and exhibitions, both permanent and temporary.

The main hall is 100m long and 40m high, below which are two levels from which the Géode is reached (see below), accommodating a multimedia library, conference centre, etc. Escalators, with their mechanism visible, ascend to the upper three floors (on the second of which is the Planetarium) devoted to the permanent exhibitions, known as Explora.

Among the several scale models which may be entered are the latest *Nautilus*, which can plunge to a depth of 6000m; a model of *Ariane 5* 1:5 scale, which is nevetherless 13 metres high; and a mock-up cockpit of an A320 airbus, which simulates flight conditions. Several different types of robots are shown, and another section is devoted to computers and communications technology, among other sciences touched on.

Immediately to the south of the main building is the **Géode**, a spherical dome of 36m diameter, its 630 tonne double shell composed of 6433 preformed triangular plates of polished stainless steel, with an inner framework of c 1600 triangles constructed with 2580 steel tubes linked by 835 assembly knots. The interior houses some 395 tiered seats facing a huge hemispheric cinema screen of 1000m² and 26m in diameter, on which a series of specially adapted films using the omnimax technique are shown, projecting an image at an optical angle of 180°.

Pl. du Colonel-Fabien, Av. Mathurin-Moreau leads to the west entrance of the **Parc des Buttes Chaumont** (south west of La Villette), one of the most picturesque and least known of Parisian parks (23 hectares), in the midst of the district of Belleville. This was created during Haussmann's régime in 1866–67 by Alphand and Barillet from a decidedly unpromising terrain. The bare hills (*monts chauves*) of extensive gypsum (plaster of Paris) quarries, where rubbish was dumped, were transformed into craggy scenery. Lawns slope down to a lake spanned by a suspension bridge leading to a rocky promontory topped off with a tiny classical temple. Among the well-tended flowerbeds are two restaurants and various entertainments for children.

Le Temple de Sybille at the Parc des Buttes-Chaumont

Belleville

Belleville in the 20th arrondissement is not an area often visited by the tourist, but for the adventurous there are finds to be made. Near the south-east side of the park, the Rue Fessart leads east, crossing the Rue de la Villette (where at No. 51 the artist Georges Rouault was born in 1871) to Gothic-revival **St-Jean-Baptiste** (by Lassus, 1854–59). South of the church, the Rue de Belleville continues east, passing a developing area to the north, to the **Cimetière de Belleville**. An inscription to the right of the entrance in the Rue du Télégraphe records that Claude Chappe experimented here with the aerial telegraph that was to announce the victories of the French Revolutionary Wars. Originally called Tachygraphe, it was set up in 1792 on this site and was the base of lines to Lille and Strasbourg.

In the opposite direction, is the highest point in Paris (128m) around which a garden, the **Parc de Belleville**, was created in 1988, with an impressive rocky terrace providing a truly panoramic view of Paris. Belleville harbours a number of artists, who have contributed to the conservation of this cosmopolitan quartier, and whose workshops are opened in May during several days of Portes Ouvertes. From métro: Belleville or Pyrénées is a direct line to Chatelet.

30 · Père-Lachaise Cemetery

■ Arrondissement: 75020.
■ Métros: Père-Lachaise, Alexandre-Dumas, Philippe-Auguste.

Restaurants

La Bastide, 74 Rue Amelot, ☎ 01 40 21 20 00. Traditional. £
Le Saint Amour, 2 Av. Gambetta/32 Blvd Ménilmontant, ☎ 01 47 97 20 15. £

From Pl. de la République, Av. de la République leads east-south-east across Blvd Richard-Lenoir, built over the Canal St-Martin in 1860 by Haussmann. Blvd R. Lenoir continues to the north-west corner of Père-Lachaise. The main entrance is in Blvd de Ménilmontant.

The Cimetière de l'Est, better known as Père-Lachaise, is the largest (47 hectares) and long the most fashionable cemetery in Paris, and its tombs display the work of many 19C French sculptors, funerary and otherwise, several of which are of importance and some outrageous kitsch. Regrettably, a number of graves and statues have been vandalised or covered in graffiti.

Père François de La Chaise (1624–1709) was the confessor of Louis XIV, and lived in the Jesuit house rebuilt in 1682 on the site of a chapel. The property, situated on the side of a hill from which the king, during the Fronde, watched skirmishing between Condé and Turenne, was bought by the city in 1804 and laid out by Brongniart, and later extended. But this cemetery is not reserved for Roman Catholics, and buried side-by-side are Jews, Buddists, Muslims and non-believers.

The first interments were those of La Fontaine and Molière, whose remains were transferred here in 1804. The monument to Abélard and

Héloïse, set up in 1779 at the abbey of the Paraclete (near Nogent-sur-Seine), was moved here in 1817, its canopy composed of fragments collected by Lenoir from the abbey of Nogent-sur-Seine.

The plan on pp 282–83, will help you track down some of the tombs of the illustrious dead interred here and when you are exhausted, there are pleasant areas for sitting or admiring the view of Paris. Either side of the main alley, the **central sector** (24 hectares) is classed an historic site, and the eastern part of this (9.5 hectares), where Chopin and Géricault are buried, is classed as **Secteur Romantique**. The tomb of Oscar Wilde (his body was moved here nine years after his death in 1900), designed by Jacob Epstein, vies in popularity with the simpler grave of the rock star Jim Morrison, who died accidentally in Paris in 1970. Huge mausoleums such as that of the Princess Elisabeth Deminoff contrast with the realistic bronze by Dalou of the young journalist Victor Noir shot in cold blood by Pierre Bonaparte in 1870.

*Tomb of Oscar Wilde,
Père-Lachaise Cemetery*

In the eastern corner of the cemetery is the **Mur des Fédérés**, against which 147 Communards were shot on 28 May 1871; and here also is a monument to the many thousand Frenchmen who died either in German concentration camps or during the Resistance of 1941–44 and other deeply moving tributes to victims of Nazism. Thousands of Parisians still visit the cemetery on 1 and 2 November, All Saints' Day (Toussaint) and the Day of the Dead.

The list of the famous seems endless. Among **writers** are Beaumarchais, Victor Hugo, Béranger, Proust, Balzac, Benjamin Constant, Gérard de Nerval, Alfred de Musset, Daudet, Apollinaire, Henri de Régnier, Barbusse, Bernardin de Saint-Pierre, Villiers de l'Isle-Adam, Colette and Eluard.

Composers and musicians buried here include Grétry, Boieldieu, Hérold, Pleyel, Rossini (later removed to Florence), Cherubini, Bellini (removed to Catania), Bizet, Reynaldo Hahn, Chausson, Kreutzer, Chopin, Lalo, Gustave Charpentier, Auber, Poulenc and so on, as well as the singer Adelina Patti.

Artists and sculptors are also numerous: David, David d'Angers, Pradier, Pissarro, Corot, Doré, Ingres, Gros, Daumier, Daubigny, Clésinger, Guillaume Coustou, Alfred Steven, Barye, Prud'hon, Delacroix, Géricault, Seurat and Modigliani.

There is a representative selection of **Napoléon's marshals**: Davout, Kellermann, Lefèbvre, Masséna, Ney, Murat, Victor, Macdonald, Suchet, and generals Foy, Junot, Reille, Savary, Marbot and Baron Larrey.

Other **celebrities** include Talma, Isadora Duncan, Sarah Bernhardt and Yvette Guilbert, Marie Walewska, Champollion, Parmentier, Blanqui, Baron Haussmann, Percier, Fontaine, René Lalique, Saint-Simon, Lammennais, Michelet, Arago, Monge, and Branly.

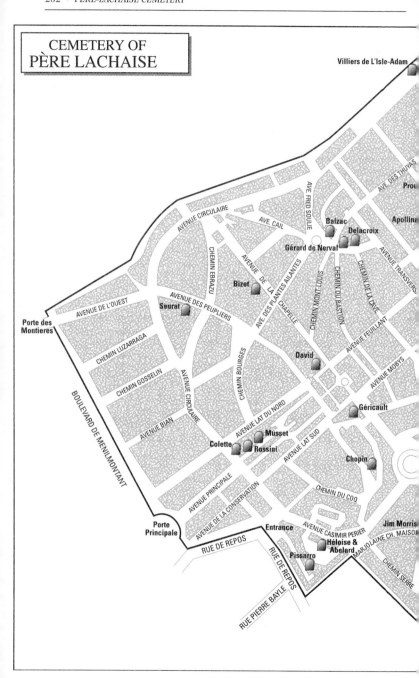

CEMETERY OF PÈRE LACHAISE

Villiers de L'Isle-Adam

AVE. DES THUYAS

Prou

Apollina

AVE. FRED SOULIE

AVENUE CIRCULAIRE

AVE. CAIL

Balzac

Delacroix

Gérard de Nerval

CHEMIN ERRAZU

AVENUE DE LA CHAPELLE

AVE. DES PLANTES AILANTES

CHEMIN MONTLOUIS

CHEMIN DU BASTION

CHEMIN DE LA CAVE

AVENUE TRANSVERS

Bizet

AVENUE DES PEUPLIERS

AVENUE DE L'OUEST

Seurat

Porte des
Montieres

CHEMIN LUZARRAGA

CHEMIN GOSSELIN

CHEMIN BOURGES

AVENUE CIRCULAIRE

AVENUE BIAN

David

AVENUE FEUILLANT

AVENUE MOBYS

Géricault

AVENUE LAT DU NORD

Musset

Colette

Rossini

AVENUE LAT SUD

Chopin

BOULEVARD DE MENILMONTANT

AVENUE PRINCIPALE

CHEMIN DU COQ

AVENUE DE LA CONSERVATION

Entrance

AVENUE CASIMIR PERIER

Jim Morris

Porte
Principale

Héloise &
Abelard

MARJOLAINE CH. MAISON

Pissarro

RUE DE REPOS

RUE DE REPOS

CHEMIN SERRE

RUE PIERRE BAYLE

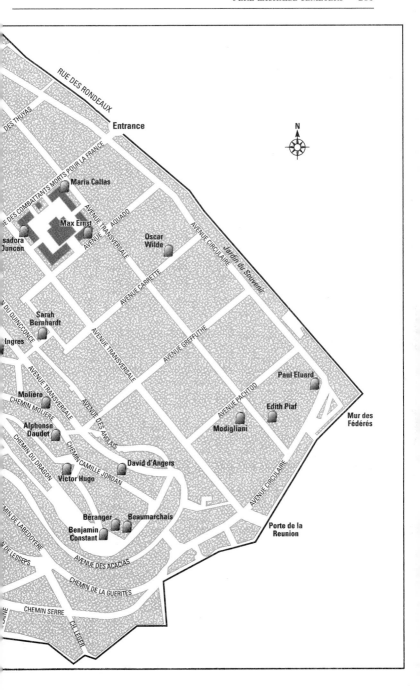

Among the British names are Sir William Keppel (1702–54), second Earl of Albemarle; Gen. Lord John Murray (1711–87); Adm. Sir Sidney Smith (1764–1840); Gen. Sir Charles Doyle (1770–1842); and Sir Richard Hertford-Wallace (1818–90), the connoisseur and benefactor of Paris (see p 273) and Mary Clarke (Mme Mohl; 1793–1883).

North of the Rue de la Roquette, opposite the main entrance of the cemetery, stood the Prison de la Grande-Roquette, itself on the site of the convent of the Hospitalières de la Roquette, founded in 1639, replaced in 1899 by the Petite-Roquette (for women). From 1853 to 1899 condemned prisoners were held at La Roquette while awaiting execution. Here in 1871 50-odd Commune hostages were shot, although c 130 were also released. Thiers' victorious government forces 'of law and order' then proceeded to round up thousands of Communards—both repentant and defiant—and in two days shot out-of-hand 1900 of them in retaliation or 'in expiation'.

To the south east of the cemetery, approached by Blvd de Charonne (forking off Blvd de Ménilmontant) and Rue de Bagnolet, stands **St-Germain-de Charonne**, a rustic church of the 13C–14C, restored in the 19C, retaining its village cemetery (the only other in Paris being St-Pierre-de-Montmartre). St-Jean-Bosco (1937), of concrete and with a lofty tower, stands a short distance south east of the junction of Blvd de Charonne and Rue de Bagnolet.

31 · Faubourg St-Antoine

Arrondissements: 75011, 75012.

Métros: Bastille, Nation, Gare de Lyon (Bercy, Dijon, Météor Line). RER: Gare de Lyon, Nation.

This off-the-beaten-track *quartier* around Place de la Nation and Gare de Lyon has two recent innovations, the Viaduc des Arts, with its trendy shops, and the Promenade Plantée, a series of planted areas and gardens.

From Père-Lachaise (see above), Blvd de Ménilmontant, with its continuation south, Av. Philippe-Auguste, leads south east to Pl. de la Nation, also reached direct from Pl. de la Bastille by métro. **RUE DU FAUBOURG-ST-ANTOINE** leads east-south-east from Pl. de la Bastille to Pl. de la Nation through an area memorable in the history of the Revolutions of 1789 and 1848. It was also the scene of skirmishing during the Fronde (1652), when Turenne defeated Condé.

Since the late 13C it has been a centre of cabinet-making, and many courtyards and passages still hide busy workshops behind 18C façades. The whole area is being spruced up and a number of antique shops and galleries now flourish here.

At No. 1 Rue du Faubourg-St-Antoine, leading away from Pl. de la Bastille (see p 222) and the new opera-house, Joseph Fieschi in 1835 hatched his plot to assassinate King Louis-Philippe (see Blvd du Temple)—it failed, but 18 others were killed. At No. 61 (left), at the corner of Rue de Charonne, is the Fontaine Trogneux (1710). Further on (right) Sq. Trousseau occupies the site of the

Restaurants and cafés

Les Allobroges, 71 Rue des Grand Champs,☎ 01 43 73 40 00. Traditional. £
A La Biche au Bois, 45 Av. Ledru Rollin, ☎ 01 43 43 34 38, Traditional. £
Brasserie l'Européen, 2 Rue de Lyon, ☎ 43 43 99 70. Traditional and fish. £
La Flambée, 4 Rue Taine, ☎ 01 43 43 21 80. Cassoulet, rustic. £
Les Fleurs du Berry, 197 Av. Daumesnil, ☎ 01 43 43 24 61. Rustic. £
La Gourmandise, 271 Av. Daumesnil, ☎ 01 43 43 94 41. Traditional. £
Chez Paul, 13 Rue Charonne, ☎ 01 47 00 34 57. Bistrot.
Le Phonographe, 181 Rue de Charenton, ☎ 01 43 47 59 91. Burgundian. £
La Sologne, 164 Av. Daumesnil, ☎ 01 43 07 68 97. Traditional. £
La Tour de Lyon, 1 Rue de Lyon, ☎ 01 43 43 34 38 . Cuisine de marché. £
Le Train Bleu, Pl. Louis Armand, Gare de Lyon, ☎ 01 43 43 09 06, 1900s decor. £
Le Saint Pourcain, 234 Rue du Fb. St-Antoine, ☎ 01 43 70 83 22, Auvergne. ££
Les Zygomates, 7 Rue Capri, ☎ 01 40 19 93 04. Bistrot. £

Hospice des Enfants-Trouvés, in the graveyard of which the Princesse de Lamballe, the close companion of Marie Antoinette, was buried after her corpse had been paraded through the streets in 1792.

To the left, Rue St-Bernard leads to **Ste-Marguerite**, built in 1634 but many times altered since. Behind the high altar is a *Pietà* by Girardon. It is believed that the 10-year-old Louis XVII, who in all probability died at the Temple (see p 235), was buried in the graveyard here in 1795, together with other victims of the Revolution.

South of Rue du Faubourg-St-Antoine at this point is the Hôpital St-Antoine, rebuilt in 1905 but retaining part of Lenoir's 18C building for the former Abbaye de St-Antoine-des-Champs.

Several thoroughfares converge on the spacious **PL. DE LA NATION**, at the centre of which is a colossal bronze group representing the *Triumph of the Republic*, by Dalou (1899). It was known formerly as the Pl. du Trône (named after the throne erected for Louis XIV's triumphal entry in 1660 with Maria Thérèsa); in 1794 no fewer than 1306 victims of the Terror were guillotined here. Between 1793 and 1880 it was known as the Pl. du Trône-Renversé.

To the east of the cirque are two **pavilions**, built as toll-houses by Ledoux in 1788, each surmounted by a Doric column 30.50m high; one with a statue of Philippe Auguste (by Dumont), the other, of Louis IX, by Etex.

Cours de Vincennes—once the scene in Easter Week of the Foire aux Pains d'Épice, a festival dating back to the 10C, when bread made with honey and aniseed was distributed by the monks of the Abbey of St-Antoine—leads directly east from Pl. de la Nation to Porte de Vincennes, and beyond to the Château de Vincennes (see Ch. 32), also reached direct by métro.

Rue Fabre-d'Églantine leads south to Rue de Picpus, where, at the end of the garden at No. 35, a convent of Augustinian nuns, is the little **Cimetière de Picpus** (open 14.00–16.00 or 18.00, except Monday), a private burial ground for emigrés and descendants of victims of the Revolution, the most famous of whom are La Fayette and the families of Chateaubriand, Crillon, Gontaut-Biron, Tascher de la Pagerie, Choiseul, La Rochefoucauld, Du Plessis, Montmorency, Talleyrand-Périgord, Rohan-Rochefort, Noailles, Quélen and Salignac-Fénelon; also members of the house of Salm-Kyrbourg and those guillotined in the Pl. du Trône-Renversé.

A short distance south east of the Pl. de la Bastille, in Rue de Charenton, is the rebuilt Hospice des Quinze-Vingts, founded as an asylum for 300 blind people by Louis IX in 1260.

In the parallel Av. Daumesnil are two imaginative new installations making use of the old elevated railway line. The **Viaduc des Arts**, consists of arty boutiques built into the brick and stone arches of the railway viaduct, including copper and silver workshops and a museum. Above the viaduct is a walkway called the **Promenade Plantée**, a series of planted areas and gardens from the Bastille (close to Rue Ledru-Rollin) to Vincennes (Rue Edouard-Lartet), has been made on the old tracks giving views of a little-known district of Paris. There are a number of access points and four new gardens along the way: Jardin Hector-Malot, the Jardins de Reuilly, the Jardin de la Gare de Reuilly, and the Jardin Charles-Péguy.

Rue de Lyon leads south from Pl. de la Bastille to the modernised **Gare de Lyon** (Pl. 5; 6), terminus of lines to Dijon, Grenoble, Lyon, the south of France and Italy, including TGV. It preserves a fin-de-siècle buffet called *Le Train Bleu*.

Opposite the station once stood the Mazas Prison, where 400 Communards were rounded up and massacred by Thiers' troops in 1871. On its south side the station is now overlooked by tower blocks, including the Tour Gamma A, 195 Rue de Bercy, containing offices of the Observatoire économique de Paris (Institut National de la Statistique et des Etudes Economiques), a mine of such information.

Rue Van Gogh leads south east from the station across the new Pont Charles- de-Gaulle, spanning the Seine to provide direct access to the Gare d'Austerlitz (see p 84).

Not far south east of the station rises the new block of offices housing the Ministère de Finances, flanking Blvd de Bercy, which leads to the widened Pont de Bercy (1864). On the far side of the boulevard stands the hexagonal **Palais Omnisports** (1984), a stunted pyramid topped by a tubular platform supported by four cylindrical towers. The structure accommodates 17,000 spectators.

The area to the south east is the new **Parc de Bercy**, due to be completed in 1998, where the bonded warehouses and cellars once stood. Three of the old buildings have been integrated into the gardens, namely the Pavillon de Bercy, the Maison du Jardinage and the Maison du Lac. A path follows the former transportation route of wine from the Seine to the warehouses, and a small vineyard serves as a reminder of the previous activity of the *quartier*. Some areas are planted with trees rarely found in Paris.

At the far end of the park, between Pont de Tolbiac (1884) and Pont National

(1852; enlarged 1942), will be **Bercy Village**, a commercial centre carrying on the traditional activity of the district around the wine industry. An international trading centre, the Quartier International des Vins et de l'Alimentaire, has opened here.

Immediately beyond the Pont National is the bridge carrying the Périphérique, and the Porte de Bercy, the gateway to the A4 motorway to the east.

A few paces to the west is the new road bridge Charles de Gaulle, between Gares de Lyon and Austerlitz, and further still, Pont d'Austerlitz. Dating from 1802–07, but rebuilt in stone in 1855 and widened in 1886, it spans the Seine to Pl. Valhubert and Gare d'Austerlitz.

32 · Vincennes

■ Arrondissement: 94300.
■ Métro: Porte de Vincennes. RER: Vincennes.

Restaurants and cafés

Le Restaurant du Plateau de Gravelle, Bois de Vincennes, ☎ 01 43 96 99 55. £
Le Chalet de la Porte Jaune, 1 Av. de Nogent, Lac des Minimes, Bois de Vincennes, ☎ 01 43 28 80 11. £
Le Chalet des Îles, Ile de Reuilly, Bois de Vincennes, ☎ 01 43 07 77 07. £
Le Chalet du Lac de Saint-Mande, Orée du bois de Vincennes, ☎ 01 43 28 09 89. £
La Chesnaie du Roy, Route de la Pyramide, Bois de Vincennes, ☎ 01 43 74 67 50. £

Vincennes is best known for its château and for the Bois de Vincennes and gardens. In the same area is the Musée National des Art Africains et Océaniens.

Château de Vincennes

Approximately 2km east of the Porte de Vincennes, reached directly by métro to Château de Vincennes, RER to Vincennes, or on foot by the Promenade Plantée (see Ch. 31) stands the impressive bulk of the historic Château de Vincennes (CNMHS), rectangular in plan, and flanked by nine square towers. All except the entrance tower, the finest and largest, which lost only its statues, were reduced to the level of the walls in the 19C. Michelet called it 'the Windsor of the Valois'.

■ The chateau is open 10.00–18.00 (winter to 17.00), closed 1/1, 1/5, 01/11, 11/11, 25/12. ☎ 01 48 08 31 20. The keep is at present closed for renovations.

The present castle, succeeding an earlier hunting-lodge fortified by Louis IX, was begun by Philippe VI in 1337. Its fortification was completed by his grandson Charles V (1364–73), who also started work on the Chapel, which was not finished until 1552. An idea of how it once looked may be gained from the illustration of December in the *Très Riches Heures of the Duc de Berri*, or Fouquet's panel of *Etienne Chevalier*. The foundations of the Pavillons du Roi and de la Reine (to the south) were laid in the 16C, but these buildings were not completed for nearly a century, when the château, then in Mazarin's possession, was altered and decorated by Le Vau.

With the completion of the palace at Versailles (c 1680), Vincennes was deserted by the court, and the château was occupied in turn by a porcelain factory (1745; transferred to Sèvres in 1756), a cadet school and, in 1757, a small-arms factory. Offered for sale in 1788, it found no purchaser, and in 1791 La Fayette rescued it from destruction by the Revolutionary mob. In 1808 Napoléon converted it into an arsenal, when the surviving 13C buildings were demolished. In 1840 it was made into a fortress and much of Le Vau's decoration was destroyed or masked by casemates.

During the Second World War, German occupying forces had a supply depot here, and the Pavillon de la Reine was partially destroyed by an explosion in 1944 during their evacuation of the building. Restoration continues to be undertaken sporadically, but much work is still to be done.

There are numerous historical associations with Vincennes: Louis X died here in 1316, Charles IV in 1328, Charles IX in 1574 and Mazarin in 1661; and Charles V was born here in 1337; Henry V of England died here in 1422, seven weeks before the death of Charles VI, whom he was to succeed as king of France.

During the reign of Louis XIII, the keep was used as a state prison. In March 1804 the Duc d'Enghien (son of the Prince de Condé), after arrest on Napoléon's orders, was here tried by court-martial and shot the same night. Général Daumesnil, governor of the château from 1809 to 1814, during the Hundred Days, and from 1830 until his death in 1832. When summoned to surrender to the Allies in 1814, his answer was 'First give me back my leg' (which he had lost at Wagram). In 1830, when the mob broke into the building, he dispersed them by threatening to blow up the powder-magazine. Mata Hari was shot here in 1917. In 1944, three days before evacuating it, the Germans shot some 30 hostages against the interior of the ramparts.

Cross the moat to enter the fortress beneath the imposing Tour du Village, 48m high, and pass between a range of tawdry buildings in military occupation to reach the central courtyard. The **keep**, 50m in height, a square tower flanked with round turrets, is enclosed in a separate turreted enceinte, and is the finest of its type in France (since the Château de Coucy—north of Soissons—was blown up by the Germans in 1917). It is at present undergoing restoration. The two doors on the ground floor facing the postern came from the prison of Louis XVI in the Temple. A wide spiral stair ascends to the first and second floors (third floor closed), supported by vaults springing from a central column; the corbels at each corner of the first floor room symbolise the Evangelists. Note the oak beams between the ribs.

The **second floor**, a favourite residence of Charles V, contains a fine chimneypiece, and an oratory in the north-west turret. Henry V (of England) and Charles IX died here. The main landmarks of central Paris are easily discerned to the west. The kitchen, with its internal well, is shown on the ground floor.

The **chapel** opposite was founded by Charles V in 1379 and, retaining the Gothic style, was only completed in 1552. The Flamboyant façade has a magnificent rose-window surmounted by an ornamental gable filled with tracery. The bare interior contains graceful vaulting, and at the east end, seven stained-glass windows by Beaurain (16C), restored after an explosion in 1870. A monument to the Duc d'Enghien (see above; by Deseine, 1816) may be seen in the oratory.

To the south, approached through a portico, lies the immense Cour d'Honneur, and beyond, the monumental Tour du Bois. To the right stands the Pavillon du Roi (now containing military archives), and opposite, the Pavillon de la Reine, where Mazarin died in 1661. Both were completed by Le Vau in 1654–60.

The **Bois de Vincennes** (995 hectares), first enclosed in the 12C, was replanted in 1731 by Louis XV and converted into a park for the citizens of Paris. It was further enlarged in 1860.

Within the Bois, to the south east of the château, is the Parc Floral of 1969, the largest green area to be created in Paris since the second half of the 19C. The flat terrain was given a contoured relief and two irregular shaped lakes provide a focus. Within the 31 hectares are thematic gardens, rhododendrons and water plants and further animation is provided by modern sculptures and various buildings. Beyond are stadiums and sports grounds. Further east is the Lac des Minimes, a Jardin Tropical and an Indo-Chinese pagoda.

Towards the south-west end of the Bois, approached directly from the château by the Av. Daumesnil, is the Parc Zoölogique de Vincennes, the main zoo of Paris. Beyond it is the Lac Daumesnil, south of which is a Buddhist temple.

The Musée National des Arts Africains et Océaniens

The Av. Daumesnil leaves the Bois at the Porte Dorée (or Porte Picpus), just north of which stands the Musée National des Arts Africains et Oceaniens (75012), with an ornately sculpted façade.

■ Opening times: 10.00–12.00, 13.30–17.30, Sat, Sun 12.30–18.00, closed Tues, 1/5. ☎ 01 44 74 84 80. Métro: Porte Dorée.

The building was erected in 1931 for a Colonial Exhibition. It also contains an aquarium. As its name implies, it concentrates on the arts of the former French colonies rather than their ethnography, for which see Musée de l'Homme, p 267.

Ground floor: left, the Oceanian Collection: masks, wooden drums and statues from the New Hebrides; to the right, naïf bark paintings from Australia.

First floor: left, arts of the West African coast, including gold figurines etc., from Akan; brass and gold powder figures from Ghana and the Ivory Coast; note also the carved wood woman and child from Kran (Liberia). To the right, work from the Niger and Congo basins, Yoruba (Nigeria) and the Cameroons; Benin bronzes; nail-studded magic statues from the Congo; Bembe figurines, masks, jewellery, and pottery.

Second floor: left, Moroccan jewellery, including a fine necklace from Fez (16C–17C); arms; and a section devoted to fabrics, brocades, embroidery, caftans, etc. To the right, the arts of Tunisia and Algeria, including bonnets, pendants, and fibulas.

Some 3.5km north east—as the crow flies—in the **Parc de Montreau** (to the east of Montreuil), at 31 Blvd Théophile Sueur (91300), open Wed–Fri 14.00–17.00, Sat 14.00–18.00, Sun 10.00–18.00, is the Musée de l'Histoire Vivante, open Wed–Fri 14.00–17.00, Sat 14.00–18.00, Sun 10.00–18.00, largely devoted to the Socialist ethic and the history of the revolutions of 1830 and 1848, the Paris Commune and other proletarian movements.

Around Paris

33 · From Paris to Versailles

■ **By road**. Versailles is easily reached by taking the A13 motorway and turning left at the first exit after passing through the tunnel at St-Cloud. A road leads south west towards the Château of Versailles (see Ch. 34, closed on Mondays, although the gardens are open every day; parking in the Pl. d'Armes). An alternative is the N10, bearing south west from the Porte de St-Cloud over the Pont de Sèvres, which our route follows.

■ **By rail**. A convenient route is the RER line C, from Paris-Austerlitz, with stations at, for example, St-Michel, Musée d'Orsay, Invalides, Champ-de-Mars or Javel to the terminus nearest the palace, **Versailles-Rive Gauche**. There are also lines from the Gare St-Lazare to Versailles-Rive Droit, and from the Gare Montparnasse to Versailles-Chantiers.

    Alternatively, take the métro to the Pont de Sèvres, then bus 171.

Restaurants and cafés

Le Boeuf a la Mode, Pl. du Marché N-D., 4 Rue au Pain, ☎ 01 39 50 31 99. Traditional. £

Brasserie du Théâtre, 15 Rue des Réservoirs, ☎ 01 39 50 03 21. £

Brasserie La Fontaine, Trianon Palace, 1 Blvd de la Reine, ☎ 01 30 84 38 47. £

La Flotille, in the Park of the Château, ☎ 01 39 51 41 58. Traditional. £

Les Manèges Hotel Sofitel, 2bis Av. de Paris, ☎ 01 39 53 30 31. Traditional. £

La Marée de Versailles, 22 Rue au Pain,☎ 01 30 21 73 73. Seafood. £

Le Potager du Roy, 1 Rue du Maréchal-Joffre, ☎ 01 39 50 35 34. Cuisine de marché. £

Le Quai No. 1, 1 Av. de St-Cloud, ☎ 01 39 50 42 26. Seafood. £

Rôtisserie Ballester, 30 bis Rue des Réservoirs, ☎ 01 39 50 70 01. Reasonable. £

Les Trois Marches, Trianon Palace, 1 Blvd de la Reine, ☎ 01 39 50 13 21. Haute cuisine. £

The N10, on leaving the Porte de St-Cloud (south-east corner of the Bois de Boulogne, with fountains by Landowski), crosses the suburb of Boulogne-Billancourt before reaching the Pont de Sèvres (rebuilt 1963). **Sèvres** itself is famous for the porcelain factory founded in 1738; the **Musée National de Céramique de Sèvres** (métro: Pont de Sèvres) on the edge of the Park of St-Cloud, also displays ceramics and porcelain from other factories and countries. The museum is open 10.00–17.00, closed Tues (☎ 01 41 14 04 20).

    The factory was moved here from Vincennes in 1756 at the request of Mme de Pompadour, and since 1760 has been State-controlled. Among designers of

Sèvres porcelain were E.-M. Falconet (1716–91) and J.-B. Pigalle (1714–85).

On the first floor are Islamic ceramics (8C–15C) and ceramics from Anatolia (16C–18C); historical collections, mostly from France; Italian majolica; Hispano-Moresque ware. from the Middle Ages to the 18C. Second floor, North Gallery: Delft ware; faience from Nevers; from Moustiers, Rouen, Strasbourg, Marseille and Sceaux; and copies of Oriental pieces manufactured at St-Cloud, Mennecy, Meissen and Chantilly. South Gallery: porcelain from Vincennes and Sèvres, and Saxe (Meissen).

Some distance to the west, in the suburb of **Ville d'Avray**, the 'Villa des Jardies' was the country retreat of Balzac in 1837–41. It was later the home of Léon Gambetta (1838–82), one of the proclaimers of the Republic in 1870, and from 1879 to 1882 president of the chamber. He died at Villa d'Avray. The 18C church contains frescos by Corot, who often painted the lakes in the Bois de Fausses Reposes, further south west.

Immediately south east of Sèvres is **Meudon** (Celtic *Mellodunum*), whose benefice Rabelais enjoyed in 1551–52 and where Wagner wrote *The Flying Dutchman* in 1841. The Villa des Brillants, the **Rodin Museum** at Meudon, was the sculptor's home from 1895 until his death in 1917. Recently renovated, the property can be visited between 1 May and 30 September (Fri, Sat, Sun, 13.30–18.00, ☎ 01 45 34 13 09). On display are casts of Rodin's major works and the sculptor's collection of antiquities in the garden.

Further south is the **Observatoire d'Astronomie Physique**. The building, formerly the Château Neuf, was built for the Grand Dauphin (Monseigneur, the son of Louis XIV), by Hardouin-Mansart, but a fire in 1870 reduced it to a single storey. The terrace commands a wide view and the Forêt de Meudon extends to the south and west.

St-Cloud, 2km north of Sèvres, was also the site of a porcelain factory from 1695 until 1773, when it was destroyed by fire. The royal castle was burned down during German occupation, 1870–71, the ruins cleared away in 1891. The **park** (392 hectares), with its cascades, fountains and views over Paris, is open to the public. On a height some 3km north is the fort of Mont Valérien (1830). Off Blvd Washington is an American Military Cemetery.

From Sèvres, the N10 continues south west (through the suburbs of Chaville and Viroflay) to (c 8km) Versailles.

Versailles

■ **Tourist Information Office**: 7 Rue des Réservoirs. 78000-Yvelines. ☎ 01 39 50 36 22 (guided visits of the town).

Préfecture of the *département* of Yvelines, Versailles lies in a low sandy plain between two lines of wooded hills. With its regular streets and imposing avenues converging on the palace, it seeks to retain its royal cachet although the château, with which the history of the town is inextricably entwined, over-shadows it in interest; see p 295.

Versailles makes a pleasant base outside Paris for those who choose to take

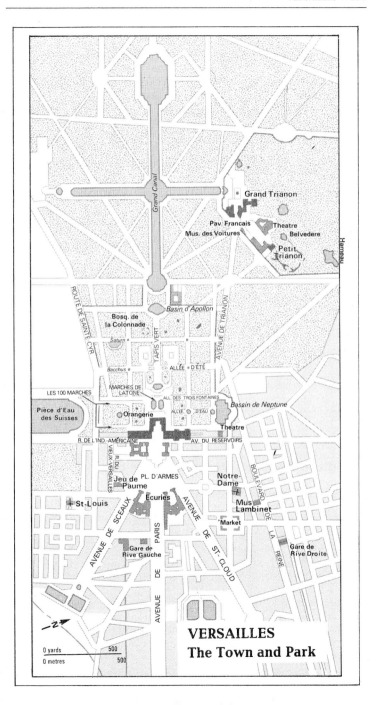

VERSAILLES
The Town and Park

Grand Canal

Grand Trianon

Pav. Francais
Mus. des Voitures

Theatre
Belvedere

Petit
Trianon

Hameau

ROUTE DE SAINTE CYR

Bosq. de
la Colonnade

Basin d'Apollon

AVENUE DE TRIANON

Saturn

TAPIS VERT

Bacchus

ALLÉE D'ÉTÉ

LES 100 MARCHES

MARCHES DE
LATONE

ALL. DES TROIS FONTAINES

Pièce d'Eau
des Suisses

Orangerie

ALLÉE D'EAU

Bassin de Neptune

Theatre

R. DE L'IND. AMÉRICAINE

AV. DU RESERVOIRS

R. DU VIEUX VERSAILLES

Jeu de
Paume

PL. D'ARMES

Notre-
Dame

BOULEVARD DE

St-Louis

Ecuries

Mus
Lambinet

Market

AVENUE DE SCEAUX

AVENUE DE PARIS

AVENUE DE ST-CLOUD

LA REINE

Gare de
Rive Gauche

Gare de
Rive Droite

AVENUE DE

0 yards   500
0 metres   500

advantage of the variety of musical entertainment on offer or to see the fountains play on summer evenings. Also, the town contains some buildings of importance, described below. There are hotels of all categories and several restaurants (see p 291) in the town, and many sites of interest in the *département*.

The Tourist Information Office north of the château, is housed in the Hôtel des Réservoirs, built by Lassurance for Mme de Pompadour (but much altered), still bearing the marquise's arms. Proust isolated himself here for almost five months in the latter half of 1906. The Théâtre Montansier (No. 13), founded by the actress Mlle Montansier, was built by Heurtier and Boulet in 1777, and since restored.

A few minutes' walk to the north east is the **Musée Lambinet**, housed in a mid-18C mansion (at 54 Blvd de la Reine) and containing sculptures by Houdon. The collection of early prints and views of Versailles is of interest.

At No. 1 Blvd de la Reine (further west) is the *Trianon Palace*, a luxury hotel built by René Sergent, the architect of the Plaza Athénée in Paris, in 1910. During the First World War it was a hospital for British troops and in April 1917 the Allied Military Committee installed its permanent War Council here. It was chosen by Allied politicians for meetings preceding the signing of the Treaty of Versailles in the château. In the dining room is a plaque recording the handing of conditions for peace by Georges Clemenceau to the German High Command on 7 May 1919. In 1939 the Trianon Palace was requisitioned by the Royal Air Force, by the Luftwaffe in 1940 and by the Americans in 1944 when it was again the meeting place for decisions that settled the peace.

Today the Trianon Palace Hotel has been restored. The hotel's original architectural splendours, façades, entrance hall, gallery and salons have been elegantly refurbished. If you can't afford to stay, pop in for a cup of tea.

A short distance south east stands **Nôtre-Dame**, by Jules Hardouin-Mansart (1684–86), with a pulpit of the period. To the south east are the restored market halls of Versailles

Hardouin-Mansart also designed the **Grand-Commun**, immediately south of the Château, built to accommodate court functionaries, with some fine bas-reliefs. Adjacent is the former Hôtel de la Guerre (1759) and Hôtel de la Marine et des Affaires Etrangères (1761), now the municipal library, with Louis XV decoration.

From here Rue du Vieux-Versailles (left) leads to the **Jeu de Paume**, the royal tennis-court (1686) (admission July–Aug, Sun pm only). On 20 June 1789, the deputies of the Third Estate, finding themselves locked out of the States-General, adjourned here, and with the astronomer Bailly as their president, swore not to separate until they had given France a proper constitution.

To the south stands a rare example of a church of the period of Louis XV, **St-Louis** (1742–54; by Jacques Mansart de Sagonne). A restrained version of Baroque, it was designated a cathedral in 1802.

To the west is the former royal kitchen-garden, now a landscape college (occasional visits).

To the south east is Pl. du Marché-St-Louis, with 18C houses. Further on, at 4 Rue St-Médéric, was the Parc-aux-Cerfs, purchased in 1755 by Louis XV for entertaining his mistresses.

In Av. de Paris, leading directly east from the château, No. 21 occupies the

Hôtel de Mme du Barry (1751; admission on application), with contemporary *boiseries*. Comte Robert de Montesquiou (1855–1921), on whom Proust based his Baron Charlus and Huysmans his Jean des Esseintes in *A Rebours*, lived at No. 53. Further on at Nos 57–61 is an old *laiterie* (dairy); and No. 111, the Pavillon de Musique, was built by Chalgrin in 1781, in emulation of the *hameau* (hamlet) at the Petit Trianon, for Joséphine-Louise de Savoie, Comtesse de Provence, wife of the future Louis XVIII.

34 · The Château and Gardens of Versailles: the Trianons

When planning your visit, bear in mind that it is almost impossible to see more than a part of the immense ensemble of Château, Trianons and Gardens in one day, especially at the height of the season. To appreciate everything fully would take at least two days.

■ **Admission**: the **château** is open every day May–Sept. 09.00–18.30; Oct–Apr 09.00–17.30, **except** Monday, certain public holidays and during official ceremonies.

■ **Guided and non-guided visits**. There are a variety of visits, some independent, some guided, and some only available at certain times. **Non-guided visits**: the State Apartments, permanently open (audioguide available); the 17C Historical Galleries and Hall of Battles (not continuously open). Independent visit with audioguide to the King's Chamber and Apartments of the Dauphin and Dauphine. **Guided visits**: (among some of the most interesting) include Private Apartments of: Louis XV and Louis XVI and the Opera; of Marie-Antoinette; of Madame de Pompadour and Madame du Barry; the Opera and the Chapel; a Day of Louis XIV. In summer, an exterior visit is Uncovering Groves.

The ticket to all guided and audioguided visits includes admission to the State Apartments. Tickets are valid all day. There is a reduced rate after 15.30 every day, and all day Sunday.

To check availability and openings, it is worth enquiring in advance from the Bureau d'Action Culturelle, ☎ 01 30 84 76 18. Individual reservations can be made on the spot for the same day. (Group reservations for visits without guide for State Apartments, ☎ 01 30 84 75 43, weekends ☎ 01 30 84 76 50.) There are also visits (in French only) from October to April, Histoire du Château, Cycle du Mardi, and Cycle de Visites Approfondies, ☎ 01 30 84 76 41.

The visitors' entrance for individuals for the non-guided visit, general information, currency exchange and hire of audioguide is **Entrance A**, in the Cour de la Chapelle; for the visit to the King's Chamber with audioguide or with a guide, **Entrance C**; and for the guided visits, buy tickets at **Entrance D**. Groups enter at **Entrance B** on the north side of the Cour Royale and there are facilities for the handicapped at **Entrance H**. There are various information and ticket offices, cloakrooms (obligatory for umbrellas, parcels) and bookstalls.

As the State Apartments tend to get saturated throughout the morning, an alternative is to visit the Grand and Petit Trianons first before returning to the main building.

■ See p 307 for the **gardens and park** (open year-round 07.00–dusk); and p 309 for the **Grand and Petit Trianons** (closed Mon, May–Sept 10.00–18.30; Oct–Apr 10.00–12.30, 14.00–17.30).

■ There is a **café** (Cour de la Chapelle, near Entrance A) and a **restaurant**, *La Flotille*, in the gardens opposite the Grand Canal.

Versailles emerged from obscurity in 1624, when Louis XIII built a hunting lodge here, which was subsequently developed into a small château, with a garden laid out in 1639. The royal estate originally covered an area of 6614 hectares, surrounded by a 43km-long wall and entered by 22 gates. The domain was reduced to 815 hectares after the Revolution. The real creator of Versailles was Louis XIV, who in 1661 conceived the idea of building a lasting monument to his reign. Louis le Vau was entrusted with the renovation and embellishment of the old building around the Cour de Marbre, while Le Nôtre laid out the park. After Le Vau's death in 1670 the work was continued by his pupil François d'Orbay, and the interior decoration was supervised by Charles le Brun. In 1682 Louis XIV transferred the court and seat of government here from St-Germain. Jules Hardouin-Mansart, appointed chief architect in 1676, radically remodelled the main body of the château and built the two huge north and south wings, giving the immense façade (with its 375 windows) a total length of 580m, and began work on the chapel.

The workforce employed on the building and in laying out and draining the grounds was impressive. Dangeau noted in August 1684 that: 'Each day there were 22,000 men and 6000 horses at work'. The cost, impoverishing France (though not as much as the Bourbons' endless wars did), amounted to over 60 million livres. In 1687 Mansart started work on the Grand Trianon. La Bruyère compared the Court itself to marble for, like the building, it was 'composed of men who are very hard but highly polished'. The life at Court, where its members would orbit, moth-like, around the imperious figure of the *Roi soleil*, was a superficially scintillating scene disguising monotonous routine, rigid protocol and ceremonious etiquette which, coupled with intrigue and hypocrisy, governed the daily drama of Versailles. The Duc de Saint-Simon's Memoires describe it all inimitably.

The main wings would have been compartmented into numerous diminutive suites to house individual courtiers and their families. Under Louis XV a series of royal apartments, decorated in the current style, were incorporated; and one of the colonnaded pavilions in the entrance court, the interior of the opera-house and the Petit Trianon were built by Jacques-Ange Gabriel. Louis XVI redecorated a suite of apartments for Marie-Antoinette and built the rustic village or Hameau.

The independence of the United States was formally recognised by Britain, France and Spain in the Treaty of Versailles, signed in 1783. The meeting of the Assembly of the States-General was held in Versailles in

1789, where on 20 June the deputies of the Third Estate formed themselves into the National Assembly. On 6 October an angry mob, some 7000 strong, led by the women of Les Halles, marched to Versailles and forced the royal family to return with them to Paris, where they were confined to the Tuileries. The place was then pillaged.

The château was the birthplace of Louis XV (1710–74), Louis XVI (1754–93), Louis XVIII (1755–1824) and Charles X (1757–1836).

By 1792, Versailles was denuded of its finery, the Grand Canal quite dry, having been uninhabited for over two years. In 1814 the palace was occupied by Tsar Alexander I and Friedrich Wilhelm III of Prussia. Under the Restoration, the second colonnaded pavilion was completed by Dufour, but the building later deteriorated from neglect. Louis-Philippe did irreparable damage to the château by housing a museum here.

In the Franco-Prussian War Versailles became the HQ of the German armies operating against Paris. The château was used as a hospital and Moltke occupied No. 38 Blvd de la Reine. On 18 January 1871, King Wilhelm I of Prussia was crowned German Emperor in the Galerie des Glaces; on 26 January the peace preliminaries were signed at Bismarck's quarters at 20 Rue de Provence. In 1871–75 the National Assembly sat in the opera-house, and here the Third Republic was confirmed on 25 February 1875. The general restoration of the complex began after the appointment of Pierre de Nolhac as curator in 1887.

During the First World War Versailles was the seat of the Allied War Council, and the Peace Treaty with Germany was signed in the Galerie des Glaces on 28 June 1919. Further extensive restorations were made in 1928–32, thanks largely to the donations of the Rockefeller Foundation, and were continued after the Second World War under the curatorship of Gerald van der Kemp. During that war, the Allied GHQ was at Versailles from September 1944 until the following May, and many buildings were requisitioned by the military.

The wide Avenues de St-Cloud, de Paris and de Sceaux converge on Pl. d'Armes, east of the château, bounded to the east by the **Grandes Ecuries** (south) and the **Petites Ecuries** (north), the royal stables, built by Mansart in 1679–85 to accommodate 200 carriages and 2400 horses. Communards were incarcerated here in 1871. Their façades have been restored, and converted into a **Carriage Museum**, containing Louis XVIII's hearse. It is advisable to check opening hours (☎ 01 30 84 76 18); the museum is due to open permanently in 1998.

The Château de Versailles
Flanking the gateway to the château, with Mansart's original grille, are groups of sculpture: (right) *France Victorious over the Empire* by Marsy, and *Victorious over Spain* by Girardon; and left, *Peace* by Tuby and *Abundance* by Coysevox. The Avant-Cour or Cour des Ministres is flanked by detached wings once assigned to secretaries of state. Beyond the *Equestrian Statue of Louis XIV* (erected 1836) is the Cour Royale, between two colonnaded pavilions dating from 1772 (right) and 1829.

In the time of Louis XIV, only those who possessed the 'honours of the Louvres'—called 'cousin' by the king, and who had the right to bring their coach or chair or liveried servants into the great Courtyard of the Louvre—could enter this court in a similar fashion.

Walk over to the **Cour de Marbre**, a deep, marble-paved recess at the end of the Cour Royale; this was the courtyard of Louis XIII's château and the nucleus of the whole, before being transformed by Le Vau and Mansart.

Non-guided or auto-guided tours ~ Entrance A

Ground floor. Adjacent to the Entrance Hall is the Vestibule de la Chapelle, with handsome carved and gilded doors and containing a marble relief by Nicolas and Guillaume Coustou of Louis XIV crossing the Rhine.

The visit begins on the first floor in the upper **Vestibule de la Chapelle**, decorated with Virtues by various sculptors, and a striking view of the Chapel and Royal Gallery, the door of which has a chased lock by Desjardins.

The **Grands Appartements du Roi** (King's State Apartments) have kept their original decorations of marble inlay, sculptured and gilded bronzes, carved doors and painted ceilings, executed under the supervision of Charles le Brun. The original furniture, however, has been lost.

The **Salon d'Hercule**, one of the most impressive in the château, was fitted up by Louis XV in the Louis XIV style and inaugurated in 1739. The decoration revolves around the great work by Paolo Veronese, *Dinner in the House of Simon* (recently restored) given to Louis XIV in 1664, and placed in a grand moulded frame (Jacques Verberckt), as was the other Veronese, *Eliezer and Rebecca*. On the ceiling is the *Apotheosis of Hercules* by François Lemoyne (1733–36) and Antoine Vassé (1729–34) was responsible for the elaborate bronzes.

The **Salon de l'Abondance** was used as a refreshment room at royal receptions. The ceiling-painting here is by Houasse (restored). The portraits are those of Louis XIV's eldest son, The Dauphin, and of his grandsons, *Duc de Bourgogne* and *Philip of Anjou* (later V of Spain), all by Rigaud; and those of *Louis XV* by J.-B. van Loo.

The **Salon de Vénus**, the main entrance to the State Apartments, and named after its painted ceiling (also by Houasse), is noteworthy for its marble decorations in early Louis XIV style. The carved doors are by Caffieri; above are bronze bas-reliefs. The mural decorations of this salon (and the succeeding one) are original. In the central alcove is a statue of *Louis XIV in Antique Costume* by Jean Warin; on either side of the room are trompe-l'oeil paintings by Jacques Rousseau.

The **Salon de Diane**, the former billiard room, is named after the ceiling painting by Gabriel Blanchard and contains a bust of Louis XIV (then aged 27) by Bernini (1665).

The **Salon de Mars**, once the Guardroom, later a gaming-room and subsequently a ballroom and concert-room, has a ceiling by Audran, Jouvenet and Houasse. The paintings above the doors are by Simon Vouet and the portraits of Louis XV and Marie Leszczynska are by Carle van Loo.

The **Salon de Mercure**, a card-room at the time of Louis XIV and where after his death that monarch lay in state for eight days, has a ceiling by J.-B. Champaigne. The tapestry, by Le Brun, is one of the earliest woven at the

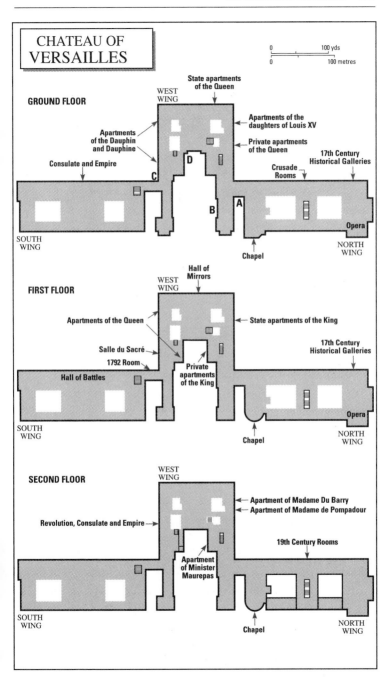

CHATEAU OF
VERSAILLES

0   100 yds
0   100 metres

GROUND FLOOR

State apartments
of the Queen

WEST
WING

Apartments of the
daughters of Louis XV

Apartments
of the Dauphin
and Dauphine

Private apartments
of the Queen

D

17th Century
Historical Galleries

Crusade
Rooms

Consulate and Empire

C

B   A

Opera

SOUTH
WING

NORTH
WING

Chapel

FIRST FLOOR

Hall of
Mirrors

WEST
WING

Apartments of the Queen

State apartments of the King

Salle du Sacré

1792 Room

17th Century
Historical Galleries

Hall of Battles

Private
apartments
of the King

Opera

SOUTH
WING

NORTH
WING

Chapel

SECOND FLOOR

WEST
WING

Apartment of Madame Du Barry

Apartment of Madame de Pompadour

Revolution, Consulate and Empire

19th Century Rooms

Apartment
of Minister
Maurepas

SOUTH
WING

NORTH
WING

Chapel

Gobelins (1668–72); the clock, with automata, of 1706, is by Antoine Morand.

The **Salon d'Apollon**, the former throne-room (in which the thone was silver), is the last room of the King's State Apartments. In the centre of the ceiling is Charles de la Fosse's masterpiece, depicting *Louis XIV* (the *Roi Soleil*) *as Apollo in a Chariot Escorted by the Seasons*. The portrait of the king in royal regalia is Rigaud's copy of that in the Louvre.

The Galerie des Glaces, together with its antechambers, the Salons de la Guerre and de la Paix, form a grandiose decorative ensemble. The **Salon de la Guerre**, completed in 1678, keeps its original decoration of coloured marble and bronze and still has three of the six busts of Roman emperors, bequeathed by Mazarin. Over the mantlepiece is a superb stucco medallion of Louis XIV on horseback by Antoine Coysevox. The ceiling painting, the first of a series designed by Charles le Brun, represents *France Victorious, Bearing on her Shield the Portrait of Louis XIV*.

The sparkling **Galerie des Glaces**, or Grande Galerie, 73m long, 10.5m wide and 12.3m high, is a masterpiece of the Louis XIV style. It was begun by Jules Hardouin-Mansart in 1678 and its decoration, from designs by Le Brun, was completed in 1686. Among the artists employed were Caffieri, Coysevox, Le Comte and Tuby, for the sculptures; Cucci for the mirror frames; and Ladoireau for the trophies on the walls.

The gallery is lit by 17 windows looking on to the park, and facing these are an equivalent number of bevelled mirrors of equal size, altogether an installation of excessive luxury in the 17C. The red marble pilasters have bronze capitals decorated with cocks' heads, fleurs-de-lys and suns. The cornice of gilded stucco is adorned with crowns and the collars of the Orders of the Saint-Esprit and St Michael. The marble statues of Venus, Paris, Mercury and Minerva in the niches are copies from the Antique; some other statues are also copies of originals. Twenty silvered bronze and Bohemian glass chandeliers illuminate the gallery. It is easy to imagine the the scene, at the time of Louis XIV, with candlelight falling on the lavish furnishings and fabrics.

The central ceiling-painting represents *Louis XIV Omnipotent*, while the numerous other paintings depict the subjection of Holland, the Empire and Spain, the Peace imposed by Louis on his enemies, his embassies abroad, the Protection of the Arts and of the People, and the great Foundations established during his reign.

You now enter the **Salon de la Paix**, the queen's card-room. The ceiling completes Le Brun's scheme, depicting *France Bringing the Benefits of Peace to Europe*. Over the chimneypiece (left unfinished by Le Brun) is a painting by Lemoyne (1729), showing *Louis XV Offering Peace*, following his great-grandfather's example.

The **Chambre de la Reine**, the first of the Grands Appartement de la Reine (Queen's State Apartments), has been lavishly restored to its appearance when Marie-Antoinette fled from it on the morning of 6 October 1789. The chimneypiece has been brought back from the Trianon; the silk hangings were copied at Lyon from pieces of the original material supplied by Lyon in 1787. The balustrade is a reconstruction. Both Marie-Thérèse and Marie Leszczynska died in this room (1683 and 1768, respectively), and the confinements took place here of the queens of France. The jewel cabinet of Marie-Antoinette is by

Schwerdfeger (1787); her bust was executed by Félix Lecomte. Above the doors are allegorical paintings of the *Children of Louis XV* by Natoire and de Troy; the grisaille panels of the ceiling are by Boucher.

The **Salon des Nobles**, or **Salon de la Reine**, was the queen's presence-chamber. The ceiling is by Michel Corneille (d. 1708); the tapestry portrait of Louis XIV is by Cozette (after L.-M. van Loo).

The **Antichambre**, where the king and queen dined in public, was formerly the Queen's Guardroom. The portrait of *Marie-Antoinette* in 1779 is by Mme Vigée-Lebrun, who also painted that of the queen with her children (1787). Three other portraits, by Adélaïde Labille-Guiard, depict the *Duchess of Parma*, and *Mesdames Elizabeth, Adélaïde and Victoire* (Louis XIV's aunts). It was in this room on 1 January 1764 that Mozart, not quite eight years old, was invited with his father to attend the Grand Couvert.

The **Salle des Gardes de la Reine**, with marble decoration of the period of Louis XIV, retains its ceiling by Noël Coypel. It was here that the revolutionary mob, having mounted the adjacent staircase, burst in, and where three of the Swiss Guards died in the queen's defence.

Following on from the Salles des Gardes is **Salle du Sacré** (Coronation Room), previously referred to as the Grande Salle des Gardes. This room has been restored since its alterations by Louis-Philippe. The ceiling-painting is by Callet and the *dessus de portes* (above the door) are by Gérard; on the walls are huge paintings by David depicting *Napoléon Presenting Eagles in the Champ-de-Mars* (1804), and his *Crowning of the Empress Josephine at Notre-Dame* (a copy of that in the Louvre); and *Murat at the Battle of Aboukir* (1799) by Gros.

A small room leads to the **Salle de 1792**, containing military portraits, and originally the Salle des Marchands, to which vendors of goods were admitted for the convenience of the inmates of the palace. The **Escalier des Princes**, by Mansart, gave access to the south wing, once reserved for the princes of the blood.

Beyond this extends the **Galerie des Batailles** (not permanently open), nearly 120m long, constructed at the time of Louis-Philippe by combining most of the rooms on the first floor, which displays a dull selection of huge canvases representing French military achievement—perhaps the only one of note being *The Battle of Taillebourg*, by Delacroix.

The visit to the **Appartements de Louis XIV, du Dauphin, de la Dauphine** is with audioguide, and starts from **Entrance C**. You then ascend the Queen's Staircase to the First Floor and through the Guard Room.

To the right is a suite of four rooms known as those of Mme de Maintenon (1635–1719), who later became Louis XIV's confidante. As his morganatic wife, she occupied the suite from 1684 to 1715. Most of the business of state was transacted in her bedchamber. No trace remains of the former decoration of Mme de Maintenon's apartments, which are now occasionally used for temporary exhibitions.

The first room of the Appartements du Roi is the **Salle du Gardes du Roi**, and from there you enter the **Première Antichambre** in which Louis XIV supped in public at 10 o'clock, with his back to the fireplace. The Seconde Antichambre, adjacent, is known as the **Salon de l'Oeil-de-Boeuf** since 1701 because of its oval bull's-eye window. It was in this room that the courtiers would wait for admission to the king's *lever*. The decorations are original, including the stucco frieze showing children's games on a gold background by Van Cleve, Hurtrelle and Flamen, among others. A curious picture by Nocret represents the Olympian gods and goddesses with the features of the royal family. Three doors open onto the **Hall of Mirrors**; and another on the left leads into the Queen's Apartments.

Stairs behind a mirrored door descend to the **Apartments of the Dauphin(e)** (see below).

The lavishly restored **Chambre du Roi**, Louis XIV's bedchamber (in which he died on 1 September 1715), overlooks the Cour de Marbre. Here the ceremonious *lever* (rising) and *coucher* (retiring) of the king, who used to lunch daily at a little table placed before the middle window, took place. It was from the balcony of this room that Marie-Antoinette and Louis XVI, at La Fayette's suggestion, showed themselves to the mob on 6 October 1789. The decorations of carved wood and the balustrade separating the (reconstructed) bed from the rest of the room have been regilded, but are in part original: most of the rich brocades and other fabrics are of recent manufacture, woven at Lyon, scrupulously copying the original materials. The sculpture of gilded stucco above is by Nicolas Coustou. The chimneypieces date from 1761, with bronzes by Caffieri; the bust of Louis XIV is by Coysevox. There is a self-portrait by Van Dyck.

The adjacent **Cabinet du Conseil**, dates in its present form from 1755, with boiseries by Antoine Rousseau. Note the two Sèvres vases and the table on which the Treaty of Versailles was signed.

From the Cabinet du Conseil you return through part of the Galerie des Glaces (see above) back to the Oeil-de-Boeuf room, with paintings by Lancret, and descend to the ground floor, to the **Apartments of the Dauphin and Dauphine**, the restoration of which was completed in 1986. The rooms look out onto the gardens and were occupied by eight dauphins and their wives. They have been repeatedly altered and much of the original decoration was spoiled or even destroyed by Louis-Philippe.

The Antichambre gives access to the Dauphin's **Seconde Antichambre** which contains some of Nattier's masterpieces: *Marie Leszczynska in a Houserobe*; *Madame Adélaïde*, and a sketch for *Madame Adélaïde Disguised as Air*, part of a decoration for the Large Drawing Room.

The **Chambre** with green decoration, later the bedroom of the Dauphin Louis (1729–65), son of Louis XV, with Tocqué, Marie-Thérèse-Antoinette-Raphaelle d'Espagne; Louis-Michel van Loo, Felipe V of Spain and Elisabeth Farnese; Nattier, Louise-Elisabeth de France (Duchess of Parma). Note the various works of art of importance: *boiseries* by Verberckt, the magnificent red lacquer cabinet of Bernard van Rysenburgh, and the marble chimneypiece with figures by Caffieri; also the copy, made by Marie Leszczynska, of a painting of a farm by Oudry, signed Marie, Reine de France.

The **Grand Cabinet** (Dauphin's Study), at the corner of the building, has a splendid view of the gardens. Regilt, and with chairs by Georges Jacob and a flat-topped desk by van Rysenburgh, it also contains portraits of the Daughters of Louis XV by Nattier and a Terrestrial and Celestial Globe by Mancelle, 1781. The **Small Library**, has four seascapes by Joseph Vernet.

The **Cabinet de la Dauphine** (Inner Room) retains part of its charming woodwork decoration and over the doors are Oudry, *The Four Seasons*, and Nattier, *Marie-Josèphe de Saxe*. The **Chambre de la Dauphine**, has a *lit à la polonaise* (with four columns and an ornate canopy). Louis XVI, Louis XVIII and Charles X were born in this room, which was also the bedroom of Marie-Antoinette on her arrival in France from Vienna in May 1770.

In the **Grand Cabinet** are paintings by, Jean-Baptiste van Loo, *Stanislas Leszczynski and Catherine Opalinska, Queen of Poland*; Belle, *Marie Leszczynska and the Dauphin*; Rigaud, *Samuel Bernard the banker*; Stiemart (after Rigaud), *Cardinal Fleury*; School of Rigaud, *Philibert Orry*; Tocqué, *Marquis de Matignon*.

The **Seconde Antichambre** has several portraits by Alexis Simon Belle, among them *Marie-Anne-Victoire* (Maria-Anna-Victoria; Infanta of Spain, betrothed to Louis XV when she was three, who in 1729 married the future José of Portugal); attributed to Pierre Gobert (after Nattier), *Peter the Great of Russia* (who visited Versailles in May 1717); François Stiemart, *Marie Leszczynska*; J.-B. van Loo and Parrocel, *Louis XV on Horseback*; J.-L. Lemoyne, *Bust of Philippe, Duc d'Orléans*. The **Première Antichambre** or Guard Room contains Rigaud *Louis XV as a child*; Santerre, *The Regent Orléans*; Largillière, two unknown members of the Parlement; Pierre-Denis Martin (le Jeune), *Departure of Louis XV from the Lit de Justice* and *The Consecration of Louis XV at Reims*.

Guided visits

The Chapel, Opéra and Private Apartments of Louis XV and Louis XVI can only be visited on a guided tour—the chapel is open once a month for services (enquire at the information desk). The **Chapel**, with its colonnade of Corinthian columns, was begun by Jules Hardouin-Mansart in 1699 and completed in 1710 by Robert de Cotte. The high altar is of marble and bronze with sculptures by Van Clève, above which is the organ. François Couperin was one of the great organists who played here. The central ceiling-painting is by Antoine Coypel, and above the royal pew is a *Descent of the Holy Ghost* by Jouvenet.

The **Opéra**, or **Salle de Spectacles**, at the far end of the North Wing, is reached through two galleries. The Foyer de l'Opéra, retains its 18C decoration by Pajou. The Opéra, although planned in the 1680s, was built for Louis XV by Gabriel in 1753–70. It was first used on the occasion of the marriage of the Dauphin (Louis XVI) and Marie-Antoinette, when Lully's *Perseus* was performed. It was repainted under Louis-Philippe, and in 1855 was the scene of a banquet given in honour of Queen Victoria.

Modelled on the King of Sardinia's theatre in Turin, it is a perfect example of Louis XV decoration, having been skilfully restored (1955–57) by Japy, even the upholstery being copied from the original specifications. Seating 700 spectators and with a stage second in size only to the Paris Opéra Garnier, it is now reserved for rare gala performances.

On the first floor of the north side of the Coin de Marbre, you visit the **Cabinets du Roi** or Petits Appartements du Roi (private apartments of the king), known as the Inner Apartments in Louis XIV's day, where the king kept his most precious art treasures. This series of rooms was transformed by Louis XV in 1735 to provide a retreat from the tedious etiquette of his court.

The **Chambre de Louis XV** is the bedroom in which the king died of smallpox on 10 May 1774; with *boiseries* by Jacques Verberckt and a bust of his mother, the Duchesse de Bourgogne, by Coysevox. The **Cabinet de la Pendule**, derives its name from Passemant's clock, placed here in 1754, executed by Dauthiau, with chased designs by Caffieri, surmounted by a crystal globe marking the phases of the sun, moon and planets: note also the barometer by J.-B. Lemaire.

Cabinet des Chiens, with a frieze of hunting scenes and decorated with flower-paintings, was occupied by lackeys and the king's favourite hounds. Adjacent is the **Salle à Manger des Retours de Chasse** overlooking the much-altered Cour des Cerfs.

The **Cabinet Intérieur du Roi**, in the angle, is the grandest room in the apartment, with panelling and mirror frames considered the finest made by Verberckt. The original furniture of the time of Louis XV is still in place, with the famous rolltop desk by Oeben and Riesener (1760–68). The Arrière Cabinet or Private Study, where Louis XV met his secret agents, led into the apartments of Madame Adélaïde.

The **Cabinet de Musique de Mme Adélaïde**, also with fine gilded *boiseries* by Verberckt, is where, in December 1763, Mozart played the harpsichord before Mme Adélaïde (1732–1800, 4th daughter of Louis XV) and other members of the family. The **Bibliothèque de Louis XVI** (with Louis-XV furniture) was decorated by Antoine Rousseau. The chimneypiece is by Boizot and Gouthière, and the candelabrum is attributed to Thomire.

The **Salle à Manger** took its present shape in 1769. Sometimes known as the Porcelain Room, as an exhibition of Sèvres was held here each Christmas in Louis XVI's time, it is elegant with blue drapes and Sèvres porcelain plaques of hunting scenes. The chairs, 1786, are by Sené and Boulard. The Salle de Billiard and Salon des Jeux, where Louis XIV's collections of paintings and gems were displayed, became part of Mme Adélaïde's suite.

The guided tour of the **Petits Appartements de la Reine Marie-Antoinette**, starts on the first floor of the south side of the Coin de Marbre, after ascending the Queen's Staircase and crossing the Guardroom via an access made especially for today's visitors.

The small and cramped private suite of Marie-Antoinette, situated between the state rooms and courtyards, give a fascinating insight into the private life of the court. The apartment retains its superb decoration of the time of Marie-Antoinette. Among the rooms visited are the **Salle de Bains** and the **Nouvelle Bibliothèque** used by the ladies-in-waiting. In the **Salon de la Reine**, with elaborate decoration by the brothers Rousseau, she received her intimate friends, and her musicians, Gluck and Grétry, and sat to Mme Vigée-Lebrun for her portraits. Next is the **Bibliothèque**, with imitation bookshelves over the doors and adjustable shelving. The **Petite Méridienne** or Sofa Room, is an octagonal room redesigned by Mique in 1781, with the Queen's day bed, the original pedestal table and two armchairs by Georges Jacob with replica uphol-stery. Then there are two very small rooms, the second the former boudoir of the Duchesse de Bourgogne with its wood panelling of 1701.

The visit continues with exquisite rooms (recently renovated) used by the Queen for informal entertaining. These include the **Salle à Manger**. Next to this is a bijou **salon** (Billiard Room, it can only hold a maximum of 10 people) for withdrawing after the meal, the fabrics copied from the original. There was a direct and discreet route between the King's and Queen's bedroom along back corridors, looking over the Dauphin's rooms.

The tour then descends to the ground floor to the part of a three room apartment adapted in 1784 for Marie-Antoinette, comprising a charming pale blue and white **Salle de Bains**, recently restored, with a Louis XVI bed, and a Bibliothèque, its decor lost in the 19C. Cross the **Galerie Basse**, two parallel galleries below the Galerie des Glaces, between courtyard and garden. Completely altered since Le Vau designed it in 1669, the steps between the two compensate for the difference in level between the Old and New Châteaux. This was where Molière gave several of his plays, including the first performance of *Tartuffe* (1664); it has recently been remodelled and contains several false arches. This brings you to a **chambre**, in pale green, with Georges Jacob bed and chairs and a dressing table by Riesener. It contains the last state portrait of Marie-Antoinette (1788) by Vigée-Lebrun.

The four rooms—the Grand Cabinet, Inner Cabinet, Antichambre and Chambre—which make up the **Appartements du Capitaine des Gardes**, also part of this visit, contain some important paintings by Duplessis and Hubert Robert; also a painting of Marie-Antoinette, aged ten, dancing at Schönbrunn. On a chest-of-drawers is a copy of the famous diamond necklace which was the subject of a scandal in 1785. A scheming woman, calling herself Countess de la Motte-Valois, perusaded Cardinal de Rohan to buy the necklace to give to Queen Marie-Antoinette. When the necklace subsequently disappeared the Cardinal was arrested at Versailles. The scandal which ensued brought discredit on the Queen despite the fact that she was not at all implicated in the affair.

The **Appartements de Mme de Pompadour et de Mme du Barry**, which are adjacent rooms, are on the attic floor of the North Wing (guided visit). Mme de Pompadour (1721–64) occupied her diminutive suite from 1745 to 1750 when, no longer the king's mistress but still his confidante, she moved to the ground floor. Mme du Barry (1743–93), lived in these apartments from 1769–74 only. The beautiful *boiseries* have been restored and repainted in their original colours.

The following rooms may be visited independently but are not permanently open. The **Salles des Croisades**, on the ground floor of the North Wing, are five rooms installed by Louis-Philippe. The route to them takes you through a gallery with plaster casts of royal effigies from St-Denis. Decorated in the Troubadour style of the Romantic era, they contain paintings of the important events in the Crusades.

Salles du Dixseptième Siècle (17C Gallery), North Wing, ground and first floors, is open intermittently as a non-guided visit and consists of 21 rooms. There is an impressive collection of portraits and historical paintings from the accession of the Bourbons to the throne of France to the death of Louis XIV: Anon., *Henri IV in Armour*; Rubens, *Mary de Médicis*; Philippe de Champaigne, *Cardinal Richelieu*, *Mère Agnès Arnauld*; and there are Portraits of the sculptors, artists and writers of the period. These rooms also include *Views of Versailles* by Pierre-Denis Martin; Portraits of *La Grande Mademoiselle*, *Henriette d'Angleterre* and several court beauties painted by the Beaubrun brothers; Nocret, *Anne of Austria*; and Le Brun, *Turenne*.

The mid 19C **Questel Staircase** ascends to the first floor, with battle scenes by Van der Meulen and an *Equestrian portrait of Louis XIV* in 1672, by Houasse. Views of royal châteaux: St-Germain and Vincennes by J.-B. Martin, Marly and Trianon by P.-D. Martin, St-Cloud by Allegrain; also a fine bust by Nicolas Coustou of Colbert. Portraits and self-portraits by Antoine Coypel, Largillière, Rigaud, Mignard, and Ferdinand Elle; Antoine Benoist, wax portrait of Louis XIV aged 68.

The **18C rooms and Appartments des filles de Louis XV, Mesdames Victoire and Adélaïde** may only be visited by appointment (for groups or individuals at group rates). These rooms are on the ground floor adjacent to the Royal Apartments, and include the Hall of the States General.

The **Première Salle**, once part of the former Bathing Apartment (a suite of bathrooms), was later occupied by Mme Victoire, an accomplished musician to whom Mozart dedicated his first six harpsichord sonatas in 1784. The paintings are: Barthémy Olivier, *The English Tea-Party*, with Mozart at the harpsichord, and J.-B. Charpentier, *The Cup of Chocolate*; there also works by L.-M. van Loo and Tocqué. In the following rooms are above door paintings of the *Fables of La Fontaine* by Oudry, and a commode by Riesener. There are also a harpsichord by Blanchet, some good *boiseries* and furniture, and portraits such as Nattier, *Mme Adélaïde*.

The first room of **Mme Adélaïde's Apartments**, has *dessus des portes* by J.-B. Restout of the The Seasons. The **Chambre** in which Mme de Pompadour died has fine chairs by Foliot and the bust of the Dauphin by Pajou. The **Grand Cabinet** is endowed with a Gagliano violin belonging to Mme Adélaïde.

Adjoining the landing of the Escalier de la Reine is the Escalier de Stuc, which ascends to the second floor where, in the Attique de Chimay and Attique du Midi, are displayed an outstanding **Collection of Historical Paintings** illustrating the early Napoleonic period. Visits by appointment only.

Several rooms contain views of the many battles fought in the Revolutionary and Napoleonic wars, among them works by Louis-François Lejeune, Giuseppe-Pietro Bagetti, Nicolas-Antoine Taunay, Gén. Bacler d'Albe and Carle Vernet. Other fine paintings include Gros, *Napoléon at Arcole*; one of five copies made by David of his *Napoléon crossing the Alps*; J.-F. Hue, *Napoléon visiting camp at Boulogne*. War at sea is also illustrated, including George Healy's copies of Hoppner's portraits of *Lord Nelson* and *Lord St Vincent*, and of Lawrence's *William Pitt*.

Portraits of the imperial family are dominated by Gérard's *Napoléon as Emperor of the French*, also his *Madame Mère*; Robert Lefèvre, *Portrait of Napoléon*; F.-A. Lethière, *Josephine*; Vigée-Lebrun, *Portrait of Marie-Annunciade-Caroline Bonaparte*. Notable among other portraits of the period are an unfinished pastel of *Marie-Antoinette* by Alexandre Kucharsky; Girodet, *Chateaubriand* and *J.-B. Bellay*, Deputy for St. Dominique; David, *Pope Pius VII*; Gérard, *Comte Regnaud de St. Jean d'Angely* and *Murat*.

Other rooms, devoted to the Restoration of the Bourbons, the July Monarchy, Second Empire and Third Republic are on the second floor of the North Wing.

The Gardens of Versailles

The vast formal gardens are reached by passages leading north and south of the Cour Royale. Carefully planned vistas, straight tree-lined walks, artificial lakes and ponds are laid out with geometrical precision. Interspersed among the groves and clumps of trees, lawns and terraces, are statues and vases of marble and bronze. The ultimate embellishment is the famous fountains. Some of the more fragile or damaged original statues have been placed in the *écuries* (stables) for safety, and replaced by casts.

André le Nôtre (1613–1708), the celebrated landscape-gardener, designed the gardens for Louis XIV. The fountains and hydraulic machinery were the work of Jules Hardouin-Mansart and the engineer François Francini, while the sculptural decoration was carried out under the supervision of Le Brun and Mignard.

The gardens were first laid out in 1661–68. The preliminary work of levelling and draining the site was prodigious, and thousands of trees were brought here from all parts. Inspired by Italian originals, but interpreted on a scale hitherto unknown, Versailles represents the masterpiece of French gardening. In their general lines and their classical sculptural decoration, the gardens remain as planned, but it was not until the 18C that trees were planted to the present extent, so that what we now see are really the gardens of Louis XV and Louis XVI.

The park and gardens were very seriously damaged in the storm of February 1990, when some 1500 trees were blown down. The entire restoration is in hand, but the replanting of trees (possibly as many as 20,000) will take 20 years.

■ The gardens and park are normally open from 07.00 until dusk to pedestrians (no picnics); cars are admitted to the park on payment, and to the Trianons (via Blvd de la Reine, north of the château).

■ The **fountains** play on certain Sundays in May–October only. For further information contact the Bureau d'Action Culturelle, ☎ 01 30 84 76 18. For information on the **Grandes Eaux Musicales** and the **Grandes Fêtes de Nuit**, contact the Tourist Office (see above). A Mini-Train provides transport around part of the gardens and to the Trianons, ☎ 01 39 50 55 12.

The most direct pedestrian approach to the **Grand Trianon** is to follow the Allée d'Eau (see below), leading north from the terrace behind the central block of the palace to the Grille de Neptune, then turn left and veer slightly north west along the Av. de Trianon, approximately 20 minutes' brisk walk. But taking this route only, you see little of the main gardens. An alternative route is to bear half left (north west) on reaching the Grand Canal (see below and on plan).

The central axis of the main terrace commands wonderful **views**, and the terrace itself is adorned with bronze statues after the antique, cast by the Keller brothers, amongst them, *Apollo, Bacchus* and *Silenus*; also marble vases of *War* by Antoine Coysevox, and *Peace* by Tuby.

Beyond the Parterre d'Eau, two large ornamental pools decorated with bronzes (1690), are the **Marches de Latone**, monumental flights of steps, with an impressive view of the château and, in the opposite direction, a famous vista of the gardens. Flanking these steps are the **Fontaines de Diane** (right) and **du Point-du-Jour** (*Dawn*). By the former are statues of *Air* by Etienne le Hongre, and *Diana the Huntress* by Martin Desjardins.

On the right (north) of the terrace extend the **Parterre du Nord**, where the original design of Le Nôtre has been largely respected. Just beyond is the **Fontaine de la Pyramide** (in lead) by François Girardon, and among the sculptures in the cross-walk (left) is *Winter*, also by Girardon. The **Allée d'Eau**, designed by Perrault and Le Brun (1676–88), leads directly to the **Bassin de Neptune** (1740), the largest fountain-basin in the gardens. The **Bosquet des Trois Fontaines** (parallel to the Allée d'Eau), leads back to the main axis, passing (right) the **Bains d'Apollon**, within a grove laid out by Hubert Robert under Louis XVI, in a romantic spirit very different from Le Nôtre's formal symmetry.

The Marches de Latone (see above) descend to the oval **Bassin de Latone** (Latona, or Leto, mother of Artemis and Apollo, insulted by Lycian peasants, had them turned into frogs by Zeus.)

Further west extends the so-called **Tapis Vert** (or Allée Royale), a lawn 330m long and 36m wide, lined with marble vases and statues, many of them copies from the Antique. On the left is *Venus* by Pierre le Gros and *Achilles at Scyros* by Vigier. Towards its far end (right) is the entrance to the **Bosquet des Dômes**, with several statues, including *Acis and Galatea* by Tuby.

Almost opposite, beyond the far side (south) of the Tapis Vert, in the **Bosquet de la Colonnade**, is a circle of marble arches by Mansart (1685–88), in the centre of which once stood the Rape of Proserpine by Girardon, now in reserve.

At the far end of the Tapis Vert is the **Bassin d'Apollon**, in the centre of which is the impressive group of *Apollo's Chariot* by Tuby. To the right is the Petite Venise, where Louis XIV's Venetian gondoliers were housed.

Beyond the Bassin d'Apollon, and separated from the gardens by railings, is the Petit Parc, divided by the **Grand Canal**, 1650m long and 62m wide, the scene of Louis XIV's boating parties. Almost at its central point it is crossed by a transverse arm (c 1070m), extending from the Grand Trianon, to the north, to the few remaining buildings of the former royal menagerie.

To return to the château, cross the (so-called) **Salle des Marronniers**, a chestnut grove behind the Colonnade, to pass the Bassin de Saturne or de l'Hiver. South of this is the Bassin du Miroir, followed by the Bassin de Bacchus or de l'Automne, with sculptures by Girardon and Marsy and then, right, the glade known as the **Bosquet de la Reine**.

The Parterre du Midi leads from here to the château. To the right (south) two flights of steps, known as the Cent Marches, descend alongside the **Orangerie** by Mansart, into which Communards were herded in 1871 prior to their imprisonment.

Further south, beyond the St-Cyr road, is the **Pièce d'Eau des Suisses** (682m long by 134m wide), excavated in 1678–82 by the Swiss Guards, many of whom are said to have died of malaria during the operation.

The Grand Trianon

The Grand Trianon, a miniature palace designed by Jules Hardouin-Mansart and Robert de Cotte, was built for Louis XIV in 1687 as a retreat from the formality of court life, although with sumptuous marble decorations comparable with those of Versailles itself. It replaced a flimsy summer-house for picnics, tiled inside with blue and white Delftware, and known as the 'Porcelain Trianon', erected on the site of the village of Trianon, which had been razed in 1663.

The buildings, sacked at the Revolution, were redecorated for Napoléon, who frequently stayed there with Marie-Louise, his second wife, and the Empire furniture which he installed still remains. In the 1960s, accurate work of reproduction of fabrics of the period was undertaken and more recently the Grand Trianon was renovated to receive heads of state on official visits.

On the left of the courtyard, with the open colonnade or peristyle ahead, is the visitors' entrance. Off the entrance, the **vestibule** contains views of Versailles and Chambord by Allegrain and Pierre-Denis Martin respectively, and a console table by Jacob-Desmalter.

In the **left wing** a corridor leads to Empress Josephine's Boudoir, containing a gondola-shaped sofa, to the right of which is the splendidly mirrored **Salon des Glaces**, furnished with a handsome set of white and gilt chairs covered with Beauvais tapestry. The **Salon des Colonnes**, is one of the most beautiful rooms in the Trianon, with Napoléon's bed (1809) from the Tuileries, later enlarged. The Antichambre de la Chapelle was transformed in 1691, but still contains a small sanctuary. Beyond is the open **peristyle** of Languedoc marble pillars.

Cross the peristyle (originally an open loggia) to the **right wing**, first entering the Salon Rond, with paintings entitled *Flowers and Fruit of America* by Desportes. At the time of Louis XIV, this served as a vestibule opening onto a theatre which stood here until 1703, then the apartment was further transformed in the 18C and 19C. The Salon de Musique has a bronze table with Vosges granite top, two consoles by Jacob-Desmalter, and the Beauvais tapestry-covered set of chairs. You next visit the Grand Salon and Salon des Malachite, the latter with a malachite bowl given by Alexander I of Russia after the Treaty of Tilsit in 1807.

From the adjoining Salon Frais, built to protect fragile blooms in the upper garden, with four *Views of Versailles* by J.-B. Martin, you turn left into the gallery, decorated by Mansart, with good views south over the terrace. It contains views of the *Gardens of Versailles and Trianon*, at the time of Louis XIV, 21 by Jean Cotelle (1645–1708), two by Allegrain and one by J.-B. Martin. The Salon des Jardins looks out onto the Grand Canal. The suite of rooms beyond is not open to the public. Adjacent to the Salon Frais is the Salon des Sources, with *Views of Versailles* by P.-D. Martin (1663–1742) and Charles Chastelain (1672–1740).

The next five rooms which make up the **Appartement de l'Empereur** are visited only with a guide. They once formed the Apartments of Mme de Maintenon, and were later occupied by Stanislas Leszczynski, former king of Poland (1741), Mme de Pompadour, and Napoléon with Marie-Louise.

The **gardens** were laid out by Mansart and Le Nôtre. To the west is the **Water Buffet** (the main fountain), also designed by Mansart, with bas-reliefs and figures of *Neptune* and *Amphitrite*. A bridge leads from the Jardin du Roi, behind the palace, to the gardens of the Petit Trianon.

The Petit Trianon

To the east is the Petit Trianon (1762–68), with two floors and an attic storey. It was built by Ange-Jacques Gabriel for Louis XV as a country retreat for himself and Mme de Pompadour, who did not live to see it completed. Mme du Barry then occupied it. It was a favourite residence of Marie-Antoinette, and was subsequently occupied by Pauline Borghese, Napoléon's sister. To the left of the courtyard is a chapel.

Many of the rooms in the Petit Trianon retain their original decoration, including chimneypieces by Guibert in the Dining Room and Grand Salon. In the dining room, traces of a trap-door, through which it was intended that tables would appear ready-laid, are still visible in the floor. The entrance is in the former Billiard-Room and the first floor is open to the public for a non-guided visit of ten rooms all containing paintings and furnishings of quality. The attic storey may be visited on a guided tour (☎ 01 30 84 76 18).

The **gardens** of the Petit Trianon were originally a ménagerie and botanical garden laid out by Bernard de Jussieu for Louis XV, a passionate botanist, but were altered for Marie-Antoinette in the English style (1774–86). Louis XVI had a little garden here where he liked to pick his own herbs.

To the west of the main building is the **French Garden Pavilion**, built in 1750 by Gabriel, with a good view of the façade of the palace. To the north is the **theatre** (1780; by Richard Mique), where Marie-Antoinette made her début in court theatricals, beyond which is the octagonal **Belvedere** (also by Mique), with charming interior decoration by Le Riche, overlooking a small lake. The queen was resting in a grotto here when, on 6 October 1789, she was told the news that a revolting mob had broken into Versailles.

The Hameau, Versailles

Some few minutes' walk to the north east, on the far side of a larger lake, are remains of the **Hameau**, a theatrical hamlet built in 1783 for Marie-Antoinette to indulge her taste for nature, as popularised by Jean-Jacques Rousseau. The ensemble was, in fact, a working farm whose produce was used at the Château. It comprises a mill, the Maison de la Reine (with a dining-room, drawing room, and Chinese cabinet room, plus a billiard-room), the boudoir on the right; a pigeon-cote and the Tour de Marlborough.

You can return past the Temple d'Amour (1778; by Mique), with its Corinthian colonnade and Mouchy's copy (1780) of Bouchardon's statue of *Cupid cutting his bow from the club of Hercules*, to return to the courtyard of the Petit Trianon, and the exit.

35 · Malmaison
Rueil-Malmaison

■ **Getting there**. Reuil-Malmaison is reached either by road (N13; 7.5km) from the Pont de Neuilly, or on the RER Line A from Auber via Etoile to La Défense. At La Défense take the 258 bus to within a few minutes' walk of the château. Alternatively take the RER to Rueil-Malmaison, and the 144 or 467 bus to the town centre, then a ten-minute walk across the park of Bois-Préau.

   Tourist Information Office, 160 Avenue Paul-Doumer (13), 92500-Rueil-Malmaison, ☎ 01 47 32 35 75.

Restaurants and cafés

El Chiquito, 126 Avenue Paul-Doumer, ☎ 01 47 51 00 53. Fish and seafood. ££
Le Plat d'Etain, 2 Rue des Marroniers, ☎ 01 47 51 86 28. Fish. ££
Le Relais de Saint-Cucufa, 114 Rue-de-Général Miribel, ☎ 01 47 49 79 05. Seafood. ££
L'Arc en Ciel, 5 Rue Béquet, ☎ 01 47 52 11 00. Fish. £
Chanteric, 1 Place Richelieu, ☎ 01 47 08 46 91. Regional. £
Le Jardin Close, 17 Rue Eugène-Labiche, ☎ 01 47 08 03 11. Traditional. £

Rueil 2000
Les Alizés, 2 Place des Impressionnistes, ☎ 47 51 27 69. Traditional cooking. On the banks of the Seine. £
L'Entre-Mers, 6 Place des Impressionnistes, overlooking the Seine, ☎ 01 47 32 91 32. Crêpes. £

Reuil-Malmaison, to the west of Paris, on the banks of the Seine, has close associations with the early Empire period at the Châteaux of Malmaison and of Bois-Préau.

The town which acquired its suffix Malmaison in 1928, is a pleasant and prosperous place with walks on the banks of the Seine and a Japanese and rose garden near the Tourist Office. In the **church** of Rueil, 1584, with a west façade by Lemercier of 1635, is the tomb of the Empress Joséphine (1825); that of Hortense de Beauharnais in the chapel opposite was erected in 1858 by her son, Napoléon III, who also donated the 15C Florentine organ-case by Baccio d'Agnolo. In the former Mairie is a Museum of Local History.

The Château de Malmaison

■ Open 10.00–12.00, 13.30–17.00; winter, 09.30–12.00, 13.30–16.30; closed Tues, 1/1, 25/12. ☎ 01 41 29 05 55; combined ticket with Bois-Préau.

The château was built c 1620 and became, from 1799, the country residence of Napoléon and Joséphine, who chose it because of the park, then covering 800 hectares, with the intention of rebuilding the house. The work of transforming the interior was entrusted to Fontaine and Percier. Malmaison's interesting collections concentrate on the earlier Napoleonic period, the Consulate and on Joséphine and her children Eugène (1781–1824) and Hortense (1783–1837). Its annexe (see below) is devoted to Napoléon in exile and the Napoleonic legend. The Empire period (1804–15) is covered by the Musée Napoléon I at Fontainebleau; see Ch.40.

Joséphine (Marie-Joséphe Rose) Tascher de la Pagerie (1763–1814), born in Martinique, the daughter of a nobleman, had married Alexandre, Vicomte de Beauharnais, in December 1779; he was guillotined in 1794. In 1796 she married Bonaparte, who crowned her Empress in 1804. Josephine retired here, with her children after her divorce in December 1809, and continued to develop her interest in botany and gardening. She died at Malmaison five years later of a chill caught while entertaining visiting allied sovereigns.

Malmaison was later bought by María Cristina of Spain, and in 1861 was acquired by Napoléon III. Despoiled of most of its contents, it was sold in 1896 to the philanthropist Daniel Osiris (1828–1907), who refurnished it and presented the château to the State as a Napoleonic museum.

The house contains superb collections of furniture and fittings, carpets, porcelain, silver, clocks (all in working order), and a variety of objets d'art of the early Napoleonic period: among the furniture are several pieces made specifically for the Consul and his wife by Jacob Frères and other ébenistes, and such personal pieces as Joséphine's bed (designed by Jacob-Desmalter), dressing-table, dressing case and embroidery frame. Show-cases display a large number of smaller souvenirs. All the rooms on the ground floor are being returned to their former state according to Fontaine and Percier's original drawings for the interior. Restoration work began in 1985 to recreate the original Neo-classical decor by the painstaking removal of layers (up to eight) of subsequent paint, followed by retouching where necessary.

Ground floor

The enclosed porch or vestibule in the form of a tent was added in 1800. The **Main Hall**, in Antique style, contains marble busts of members of the Bonaparte family; a number of others are displayed throughout the building. The paintwork in the **Billiard Room** has been stripped back to the original of 1812, and contains some furniture by Jacob-Desmalter from the great gallery and an Empire-style billiard table. In the **Drawing Room** (Salon Doré) are severe Egyptian-style furnishings by Jacob Frères and paintings by Gérard and by Girodet of the *Apotheosis of the French who died in the Revolutionary Wars*, both inspired by Ossian's poems. The **Music Room** (being restored), which at the time of Josephine had a gallery, contains Josephine's harp and the pianoforte belonging to Hortense.

To the left of the Main Hall, the **Dining Room** has frescos of Pompeian dancers by Louis Lafitte and the Council Chamber, the setting for the creation of the Legion of Honour, has recently been returned to its original design by Percier of a military tent. The adjoining **Library**, also by Percier and Fontaine, has books retrieved from Napoléon's personal collection, a travelling chest for books used by him during his campaigns and a the desk from the Tuileries Palace.

Among the many fine portraits in Malmaison are: Gérard, *Napoléon in Grenadier Uniform* (1804/5), *Joséphine Seated*, and *Madame Mère*; Isabey's drawing of *Napoléon as First Consul at Malmaison*; Bacler d'Albe, *Gén. Bonaparte* (1796/7); Girodet, *Queen Hortense*; David's original of *Bonaparte crossing the St-Bernard Pass* (various replicas elsewhere); Gros, the *First Consul after Marengo*; Pierre-Paul Prud'hon, the *Empress Joséphine* c 1809; also paintings collected by Joséphine who had a penchant for Troubadour-style works inspired by the Middle Ages.

First floor

At the foot of the stairs to the first floor is a *Head of Napoléon* by Canova. On this floor were the apartments of Napoléon, of Hortense and Eugène, and of Joséphine. The Emperor's rooms, in part reconstructed, display various memorabilia, and his former **Bedroom** replicates the original as closely as possible. The painting of *Joséphine* (1809) by Gros shows the park of Malmaison. The small rooms of Joséphine's accommodation have altered less. Her **State Bedroom**, restored as it was after 1812 to an unusual but elegant red and gold tent-like oval, is where she died. The Empress's **Ordinary Bedroom**, which she preferred, is brighter and lighter and due to be restored. Other rooms contain the Austerlitz Table, in Sèvres porcelain and bronze, commemorating Napoléon's victory; porcelain including the beautiful Egyptian tea set (Sèvres), Napoléon's last present to Joséphine before the divorce; mementoes of friends of the Empress (including a bust of Charles James Fox by Ann Seymour Damer); a book by Redouté; and exhibits linked with the history of Malmaison.

On the **second floor** are Joséphine's original wardrobes and various court apparel, including two dresses which belonged to her. There is also space for temporary exhibitions.

In the **gardens**, of which only six hectares remain of 200, are beds planted with those varieties of rose grown by Joséphine with the help, until 1805, of her English gardener, Mr Howatson. The gardens were celebrated in their time and her blooms were later drawn and coloured by Pierre-Joseph Redouté.

To the left of the entrance lodge, on your way out, is the **Coach House**, with Napoléon's *landau en berline* used at Waterloo and taken by Blücher, also the St-Helena hearse, presented by Queen Victoria. Behind is the **Pavillon Osiris**, with collections of caricatures, medallions and snuffboxes propagating the Napoleonic legend, and a portrait of *Tsar Alexander I* by Gérard. Beyond the other side of the entrance drive is a summer-house used as a study by Napoléon when First Consul.

From opposite the entrance, a few minutes' walk through the park will take you to the **Château de Bois-Préau**, dating from 1700, and acquired by Joséphine in January 1810 as an annexe in which to accommodate her entourage and visitors, and to house part of her collections. It was later sold and in 1926 bequeathed to the State by its then American owner, the millionaire Edward Tuck (see also Petit-Palais p 252). Open Thurs–Sun 12.30–18.30, winter to 17.30, closed Mon–Wed and public holidays.

Rooms on the first floor are devoted exclusively to the period of Napoléon's years of exile. On 17 October 1815 he disembarked from the Northumberland and settled in his enforced residence at Longwood on the remote south Atlantic island of St-Helena, where—under the eye of Sir Hudson Lowe, the governor—he was to remain until his death on 5 May 1821.

Here, in addition to the camp-bed in which he died, are numerous souvenirs of his years of captivity, among them his *nécessaire* No. 3 (by Biennais), silver flasks and other plate, his grey coat and hat, boots and slippers, apart from furniture; a book given to Napoléon by Lord Holland; Marchand's Sketch of the dead emperor; and his death-mask, moulded by Antommarchi, his Corsican doctor. His remains were brought back to France and placed in Les Invalides in December 1840; see p 122.

The N13 follows the south bank of the Seine, passing at **Bougival**, with a Romanesque church tower, the house where Bizet died (1875) and the datcha built by Turgenev, open Sundays, 10.00–18.00 (groups by appointment only, ☎ 01 45 77 87 12).

36 · St-Germain-en-Laye

■ **Getting there**. St-Germain-en-Laye is easily reached from central Paris by the RER Line A from Auber or Etoile. This line replaces the first railway constructed in France, in 1837, which made the Seine Valley accessible in the 19C to many Parisians, most notably artists, but resulted in the destruction of part of the garden of the château.

   By road, it may also be approached from the Pont de Neuilly by the N13 (taking in en route the Château of Malmaison, see above), or by the N190 branching right off the N13, which passes through the suburb of Le Vésinet.

   Tourist Information Office, 38 Rue au Pain, 78100-Saint-Germain-en-Laye, ☎ 01 34 51 05 12.

St-Germain-en-Laye is dominated by a huge château housing the Musée des Antiquités Nationales, with gardens on the edge of the forest; the district also has links with Impressionist and Nabis painters. Also included in this chapter are the site of the former Château Marly at Marly-le-Roi and the Château de Maisons at Maison-Lafitte.

Between Rueil-Malmaison and St-Germain-en-Laye, on the **Ile des Impressionnistes** (off the N190 or by RER to Rueil-Malmaison), is the last remaining *guinguette* (an out of town café which also offers music and dancing), the **Maison Fournaise**, now a restaurant (☎ 01 30 71 41 91) with a museum (Wed to Sun, 11.00–17.00, ☎ 01 34 80 63 22). As the setting of Renoir's *Le Déjeuner des Canotiers* (1881), this location has been revived as a tribute to the Impressionists who came to paint and eat here. An Impressionist Festival is held one Sunday in June.

Restaurants and cafés

St-Germain-en-Laye 78100
Le Bouchon Goumand, 10 Rue André Bonnefant, ☎ 01 39 73 65 70, wine bar. £
Brasserie du Théatre, Pl. du Château, ☎ 01 30 61 28 00. £
Cazaudehore-La Forestière, 1 Av. Prés. Kennedy, ☎ 01 34 51 93 80. Haute cuisine. ££
Ermitage des Loges, 11 Av. des Loges, ☎ 01 34 51 88 86. Traditional. £
La Feuillantine, 10 Rue des Louviers, ☎ 01 34 51 04 24. £
Pavillon Henri IV, 21 Rue Thiers, ☎ 01 39 10 15 15. Haute cuisine. ££
Le Petit Lyonnais, 11 Rue St-Pierre, ☎ 01 39 21 02 05.
Tarte Julie, 3 Rue Vieil Abreuvoir, ☎ 01 39 73 95 11. £
Le Vieux Fourneau, 31 Rue Wauthier (near Pl. du Marché), ☎ 01 39 73 10 84. £
Chatou 78400
La Maison Fournaise, Île des Impressionistes, ☎ 01 30 71 41 91. Traditional. £

St-Germain-en-Laye is on the edge of the Forest of St-Germain. It has a pleasant centre with well kept 17C–18C mansions and elegant shops. Places to visit—in addition to the Château and its park—are the Maurice Denis Museum (Musée du Prieuré) and the birthplace of Claude Debussy.

The strategically sited royal **Château**, dominating a bend of the Seine, was erected in the 12C by Louis VI and completely rebuilt (except for the keep) by François I in 1539–48. The infant Mary Stuart lived here from October 1548 until her marriage to François II in April 1558. In 1862 Eugène Millet restored the castle to its François I form after it had been used as a military prison for three decades, and adapted it to house a Musée Gallo-Romain. In 1972 an important project was begun to return the château to its former glory.

The so-called Château-Neuf, below the original castle, begun by Philibert de l'Orme for Henri II in 1557 and transformed by Henri IV, was demolished in 1776, except for the Pavillon Henri IV and the Pavillon Sully, at the foot of the steep slope east of the town, in the suburb of Le Pecq.

It was in this 'new castle' that Louis XIV was born in 1638 and it remained one of the principal seats of the French Court until the completion of Versailles in 1682. Large sums were spent on improving it during the years 1664–80. Meanwhile, the Château-Neuf afforded refuge to Henrietta Maria of England (1644–48). After 1688 what was then called the Vieux Château was the residence—and Court—of James II (1633–1701) who died here, as did his wife, Mary of Modena (1658–1710) who helped the impoverished English who filled St-Germain.

In 1962, a century after the setting-up of the earlier museum in the château, the **Musée des Antiquités Nationales** was installed here. The impressive collections, which trace the existence of man from his origins to the Middle Ages, are clearly labelled and described and displayed in chronological order. Open 09.00–17.15, closed Tues, certain public holidays, ☎ 01 34 51 53 65.

On the **ground floor** you can visit the Chapel (1230–38), just predating the Sainte-Chapelle in Paris, also by Pierre de Montreuil. François I and his first wife, Claude de France (1499–1524; daughter of Louis I), Louis XIV and his son, the Grand Dauphin, were baptised here. It has been sadly disfigured over the years and contains copies only of tombs from the Alyscamps at Arles.

Rooms on the **mezzanine floor** are devoted to the Palaeolithic and Neolithic periods; the Bronze Age, with bracelets, torques and other gold objects; the Hallstatt period (1st Iron Age; 800–450) and the La Tène culture (450–52 BC), with a good collection of bronze vessels and jewellery; also a reconstructed chariot burial from La Gorge-Meillet and a maquette of the fortified site of Alèsia.

Stairs ascend to the **first floor**, concentrating on the Gallo-Roman period, with sections displaying Celtic divinities and those from the Graeco-Roman world, including notable figures of Venus and Mercury; ex-votos and their mould; an exemplary display of silver utensils, glassware, bronze lamps, scales, handles, keys and sigillate pottery. Other rooms contain small sculptured objects—birds, boars, horses and human figures: note the charming couple in bed, with a dog at their feet, from Bordeaux; a collection of jewellery, buckles, fibulae, games, and a collection of arms. A large mosaic pavement of the 3C from St-Romain-en-Gal (on the Rhône opposite Vienne) depicts a rustic calendar of the seasons. Adjacent are a variety of agricultural implements. Further collections of jewellery, plaques, glassware, and buckles from the Merovingian period are also to be seen, together with a section devoted to comparative archaeology.

To the north of the château is the **Grand Parterre**, originally part of a remodelling scheme by Le Nôtre between 1662 and 1674, which also included the Jardin de la Dauphine to the east, now planted with rows of elms, and the Grande Terrasse. The Jardin Anglais was created in the 19C. At its south-east corner, at 21 Rue Thiers, is the **Pavillon Henri-IV**, a hotel since 1836, where Dumas wrote *The Three Musketeers* and *Monte Cristo*.

The 1945km of the **Grande Terrasse of St-Germain** extends north east and commands a splendid view of Paris—particularly of La Défense: Notre-Dame is approximately 21km to the east. At the far end is the Grille Royale, the entrance to the **Forêt de St-Germain**, the former royal hunting preserve, of some 3500 hectares with pleasant drives and walks (see IGN map 2214 and TOP25).

The church of **St-Louis** (opposite the château), designed c 1765 by N.-M. Potain, but not completed until early 19C, contains the tomb of James II of England, erected at the request of George IV, and in which his partial remains were re-interred in 1824.

Behind the church, at 38 Rue au Pain, leading south west is the Tourist Information office and, in the same building, the **Musée Claude Debussy** (open Tues–Sat 14.00–18.00).

The composer Claude Debussy (1862–1918) was born on 22 August 1862 at 38 Rue au Pain, and spent his childhood in this fine 17C–18C house arranged around a courtyard. His parents owned a small shop at the same address. The museum contains a collection of memorabilia presented by Madame de Tinan, the composer's daughter-in-law, arranged chronologically, following the development of the composer. On the second floor is a Salon de Musique equipped with a Bechstein c 1915 to reproduce faithfully Debussy's music.

The continuations of Rue au Pain (Rues A. Bonnefant and de Mareil) lead you, after a few minutes' walk to the **Musée du Prieuré**, 2 bis Rue Maurice-Denis (Wed–Fri, 10.00–17.30; Sat, Sun, 10.00–18.30; ☎ 01 39 73 77 87).

A former royal hospital founded by Mme de Montespan in 1678, in 1905 **Maurice Denis** (1870–1943) rented a studio here and from 1914 until his death the property became his home. Denis was co-founder and principal theorist of the Nabis (Prophets in Hebrew), and the museum, inaugurated in 1980, throws an interesting light on the development of Modern art. The bequest by his family and the group of artists known as the Nabis has been increased by acquisition over 15 years.

Among important works by Maurice Denis are *Self Portrait* (1921), with the Prieuré in the background; *Portrait of Paul Sérusier*; *Portrait of his Mother*; *Marthe, his First Wife, in the garden at dusk*; *Ladder in the Foliage*; *Pilgrims at Emmaus*; *Jacques Portelette aged four*; *Mme Ranson and her Cat*. Other artists represented in the collection include: Louis Anquetin (1861–1932), *Self-Portrait, Woman in Black*; Emile Bernard (1868–1941), Portrait of Dom Verkade; Pierre Bonnard (1867–1947), *Screen with Rabbits, My Grandmother*; Thérèse Debains (1907–74), *Woman in a Straw Hat*; Charles Filiger (1863–1928), *Christ in the Tomb* (c 1890); Paul Gauguin (1848–1903), *The Patron's Daughter* (1886); Georges Lacombe (1868–1916), carved wood *Bust of Maurice Denis*; Paul-Elie Ranson (1864–1909), *The Witches*; Paul Sérusier (1864–1927), *Portrait of his Wife, Breton Girl*; Félix Vallotton (1865–1900), *Bookshelves*; Edouard Vuillard (1868–1940), *Garden at l'Etang-la-Ville, The Reservoir*.

Also displayed are several designs by Maurice Denis for wallpapers and stained glass together with furniture and examples of the decorative arts of the period, including ceramics by the Daum brothers of Nancy.

The **Chapel** was decorated entirely by Maurice Denis (who was a devout Catholic) with blue frescos and Stations of the Cross, and he also designed the glass, with the exception of the round Visitation by Marcel Poncet. The adjacent Studio was built by Auguste Perret in 1912 for Maurice Denis when he was working on the frieze for the Théâtre des Champs-Elysées and is now the venue of temporary exhibitions.

Chambourcy

At Chambourcy, 4km west of St-Germain, is the 18C property of **André Derain** (1880–1954) from 1935, La Roseraie, 64 Grande Rue, with his studio intact, is occasionally open to the public (☎ 01 30 74 70 04).

Poissy

North west of St-Germain-en-Laye at Poissy is Le Corbusier's **Villa Savoie** (1929), at 82 Rue Villiers, a 15 minute walk from the RER (Line A) station. One of Le Corbusier's virtuoso designs, the house has remained virtually unchanged. Open Mon to Wed 10.00–12.00, 13.30–17.30, Nov–Apr 10.00–16.30; ☎ 01 39 65 01 06.

Désert de Retz

On the edge of the **Forest of Marly**, c 2km south of Chambourcy, is the secluded **Désert de Retz**, a curious 18C garden with a group of bizarre follies— one in the form of a huge truncated Doric column. Created between 1774 and 1789 by François de Monville, the site was restored in 1986 and can be visited from March to October the fourth Saturday of each month in the afternoon.

Marly-le-Roi

Some 4km south of St-Germain, to the west of the N386, stood the royal **Château of Marly**, its name preserved in the town of **Marly-le-Roi**, built in 1679–86 by Jules Hardouin-Mansart for Louis XIV, and a favourite retreat from the formality of Versailles, while the great château was receiving a much-needed clean. Unlike other royal residences, Marly was planned as a group of 12 guest-houses around the central royal pavilion, and dedicated to carefree conviviality. The buildings and the parkland setting were fully integrated and much use was made of trompe l'oeil and water.

> The famous **Marly horses**, by Coysevox and Coustou, which adorned the pools, were gradually transferred to the Tuileries between 1719 and 1794 (see Louvre). Sold at the Revolution, the château was used as a factory until 1809. Then plundered for its stone, it was finally demolished in 1816. Vestiges remain of the park, where the famous hydraulic Machine de Marly stood. It was originally constructed in 1681 to raise water from the Seine to the Marly aqueduct, which in turn carried it to Versailles. New machinery had been installed in 1855–59, taking its water from an underground source, but the whole thing was dismantled in 1967.

The **church** of Marly-le-Roi was also built by Mansart (1689) and contains some works originally in Versailles. Also in Marly-le-Roi is the Château de Monte Cristo, home of Alexandre Dumas (1 Apr–1 Nov, 10.00–18.00, closed Mon).

For other sites west, south west and north west of St-Germain-en-Laye, see *Blue Guide France*.

Maisons-Lafitte

Some 4km north of St-Germain-en-Laye is **Maisons-Laffitte**, birthplace of Jean Cocteau (1889–1963). A racehorse centre, there are training-stables, a Musée du Cheval de Course and a racecourse. Although the railway station was known as Maisons-Laffitte as early as 1843 (see below) the town adopted the name officially only in 1882.

Its celebrated **Château de Maisons** (CNMHS) was built for René de Longueil (1596–1677), first Marquis de Maisons, a Surintendant des Finances before Fouquet. Recognised as the masterpiece of François Mansart (1642–51), it has remarkable interior decoration. Open summer: 10.00–12.00, 13.30–18.00; winter: to 17.00, closed Tues and public holidays, ☎ 01 39 62 01 49.

> The property was bought in 1777 by the Comte d'Artois (later Charles X) and partly redecorated by Bellanger. It was deserted at the Revolution and its contents dispersed. In 1804 it was acquired by Marshal Lannes, Duc de Montebello, and was sold in 1818 to Jacques Laffitte (1767–1844), a banker

and speculator who had profited out of the Napoleonic Wars. In 1833 he demolished the stables and sold off the estate. Further fragmented by a subsequent owner, Tilman Grommé, a Russian artist, the shell of the château was saved from demolition in 1905, when it was acquired by the State and restored.

From the present entrance, formerly a chapel, a series of rooms on the ground floor may be visited. These include the Salles des Graveurs, with a trompe l'oeil ceiling, and collections of prints and plans; and the Salon des Captifs, with a coffered ceiling, and a fireplace carved by Gilles Guérin. Passing through the Vestibule d'honneur, with reliefs by Jacques Sarrazin, you enter the south wing, redecorated by the Comte d'Artois. The main staircase, embellished with putti executed by Philippe de Buyster, ascends to (left) the Salon d'Hercule, hung with early 18C Gobelins tapestries of the Hunts of Maximilian, among others, a musicians' gallery and another fireplace by Guérin; the Chambre du Roi; the Salon à l'Italienne, containing a portrait by Van Dyck of the *Countess of Bedford*; and the domed Cabinet aux miroirs, with a marquetry floor. In the south wing is the former Queen's suite, transformed by Lannes. Voltaire wrote *Marianne* when a guest here in 1720.

The N308 leads south east across a meander of the Seine towards La Défense (see latter part of Ch. 28) and central Paris. The road passes, after crossing the Pont de Bezons (south of Colombes), the site of a château in which Henrietta Maria (1606–69) died. The widow of Charles I of England, she was buried at St-Denis.

37 · St-Denis

■ **Getting there. By car**, St-Denis is best reached from Paris by turning off the A1 autoroute about 3km north of the Porte de la Chapelle. **By train**, take the métro Line 13 to St-Denis-Basilique or the RER Line D to St-Denis.

■ **Tourist Information Office**, 1 Rue de la République, 93200 St-Denis (☎ 01 55 87 08 70).

The main site in St-Denis is the Basilica, royal mausoleum and birthplace of Gothic architecture; but also to here see is the Musée d'Art et d'Histoire and a successful exercise in urban renewal.

St-Denis is mainly visited for its Basilica (Cathedral since 1966), but it is also a lively and cosmopolitan suburb which has been transformed since the 1980s by imaginative redevelopment. The architects involved in designing the interesting new commercial, domestic and educational buildings (well worth seeing) include Roland Simounet and Oscar Niemeyer. A vast sports stadium, the venue for the World Cup in 1998, has been created at Plaine-St-Denis. As well as the Basilica with its royal tombs, other places to visit are the Art and History Museum and the former Abbey buildings now the School of the Légion d'honneur.

Restaurants and cafés

Les Arts, 6 Rue de la Boulangerie, ☎ 01 42 43 22 40. Traditional. £
Le Boeuf est au 20, 20 Rue Gabriel-Péri, ☎ 01 48 20 64 74. £
Chez Renée, 6 Rue Charles-Michels, ☎ 01 48 20 17 48. Traditional. £
Les Cours de l'Abbaye, 8 Rue des Boucheries, ☎ 01 48 09 84 13. Traditional. £
Le Numidien, 28 Rue Gaston-Philippe, ☎ 01 48 21 58 22. Berber-North African cuisine. £
Phi Long, 32 Rue Gabriel-Péri, ☎ 01 42 43 53 65. Vietnamese cuisine. £
Au Roi du Couscous, 63 Rue du Landy, ☎ 01 42 43 20 25. Algerian cuisine. £
La Table Gourmande, 32 Rue de la Boulangerie, ☎ 01 48 20 25 89. Hauate cuisine. £
La Table Ronde, 12 Rue de la Boulangerie, ☎ 01 48 20 15 75. Traditional. £

An important commercial centre since the Middle Ages, the **Foire** (fair) **de St-Denis** began in the 8C, and the celebrated **Foire du Lendit** (held in the spring) was held from 1050 and received royal recognition from Louis VI until 1552. The present **market** is the largest in the Ile-de-France. The 19C Grande Halle of the market and the 18C Maison des Arbalétriers (drying house) nearby have been restored.

Basilica (Cathedral) of St-Denis

The Gothic Cathedral of St-Denis (CNMHS) was supposedly built over the burial place, c 250, of the missionary apostle of Lutetia, Denis (Dionysius), and his companions Rusticus and Eleutherius at Catolacus, 11km north of Paris, near the ancient Paris-Beauvais route. St Denis was considered the first Bishop of Paris and by the 12C he was ousting St Martin of Tours as national saint.

■ Open 10.00–19.00, winter to 17.00, Sun 12.00–19.00, winter to 17.00, ☎ 01 48 09 83 54.

The abbey of St-Denis was founded c 475, traditionally at the instance of St Geneviève, and enlarged in 630–38 by Dagobert, who also founded a Benedictine monastery. The first substantial church on the site was built by Abbot Fulrad in 750–75, and here in 754 Pope Stephen III consecrated Pepin the Short, his wife and sons, thus establishing them securely on the throne which Pepin had recently usurped. This church was itself replaced by another built by the powerful and influential Abbot Suger (abbot 1122–51)—a momentous occasion in the history of architecture, for the new style adopted was the prototype of what become known as Gothic. The narthex (west porch, c 1135–40), crypt and apse (1140–44) survive from this period of construction. The rebuilding of the nave had barely begun before Abbot Suger's death, and the rest of the building, notably the nave and transepts, dates from 1231–81, following the designs of Pierre de Montreuil (d. 1267). The chapels on the north side of the nave were added c 1375. Already strong links between the Crown and the Abbey were reinforced at the time of Abbot Suger who, from 1127, was adviser to Louis VI and Louis VII, and Regent during the Second Crusade (1147–49).

Dagobert had chosen to be buried close to the saintly relics of Denis and the Abbey Church finally became the sole royal mausoleum. With the exception of Philippe I, Louis XI, Louis-Philippe and Charles X, all the French kings since Hugh Capet were buried here. As well as its role as protector of royal bodies and souls, in 1120 Louis VI accorded it the privilege of keeper of the royal insignia, including the oriflamme (the military standard), and the coronation regalia. Its association with royalty and the fact that 13 bishops attended the dedication of the choir in 1144, assured the spread of its style of architecture throughout northern France.

In 1422 the body of Henry V lay in state at St-Denis on its way from Vincennes to Westminster, and here Joan of Arc came seven years later to dedicate her armour. Henriette d'Angleterre, daughter of Charles I, was buried here in 1670 where her mother, Henrietta Maria, had been buried the previous year.

After injudicious alterations in the 18C, the abbey was suppressed at the Revolution and its roof stripped of lead. During the Terror, the tombs were rifled, their contents dispersed and the corpses of the kings tosssed into a common pit and covered with quicklime.

The best of the monuments were saved from destruction by Alexandre Lenoir, who preserved them in his Musée des Petits-Augustins (Ecole des Beaux-Arts), from where they were later returned and drastically restored. Renovation of the fabric of the basilica was taken in hand in 1805, but in 1837 the north tower was struck by lightning. Debret undertook the rebuilding of the tower, but it collapsed in 1845 and was reconstructed by Viollet-le-Duc who, with Darcy, carried out subsequent restoration to the basilica. The explosion of a nearby bomb-dump in 1915 caused further damage, and additional restoration work was started in 1952. It was designated a Cathedral in 1966.

Exterior

The **west front**, a development from the great Norman churches, notably St-Etienne in Caen, inspired generations of Gothic façades. Mighty buttresses divide the elevation vertically into three sections, corresponding to the internal stucture of the church. An original element is the crenellated caesura between the façade and the set-back tower (originally twin towers). Three west portals, deep and finely profiled, animate the lower part of the facade. The central one is larger than the others and sets up a different rhythm in the central bay. The sculpture in the tympana and voussoirs of all three portals has been terribly abused and was heavily reworked in the 19C.

The *Last Judgement* of the **central tympanum** has a few original elements—the images of God and Christ, and The Dove and the Lamb. The **north door** was possibly decorated with a mosaic in the first instance, representing for the first time on a tympanum a *Virgin in Majesty*. The present 19C carvings show the Story of St Denis. The Signs of the Zodiac on the jambs are 12C.

The **south door** tympanum has scenes from the *Life of St Denis*, mainly 12C but with 19C heads. The *Labours of the Month* on the jambs are 12C. The high relief statues of Old Testament Kings in the jambs, which was a turning point in the integration of sculpture with architecture (coming before those at Chartres), were destroyed in 1771. Another innovative feature of the west façade is the large oculus (it is not known how it was originally subdivided) high in the central bay, the precursor of the rose window of Gothic architecture.

Suger undertook the enlargement of the **east end** in honour of a new shrine and to allow for the increasing number of pilgrims. The exterior of Suger's apse appears less innovatory than the west end, with Romanesque round-headed windows and relieving arches around the crypt, although the windows of the chapels are Gothic. The upper storeys with flying buttresses date from the 1230s. By Suger's death in 1151, the two ends of the church were still linked by the 8C construction. When the rebuilding of the nave and transept was undertaken during the mid-13C, the upper level of Suger's choir was destroyed and whether flying buttresses had originally been used can only be hypothesised. The transeptal portals, each with a pioneering Rayonnant rose window, are mid-13C work.

Interior

Suger added to the west of the existing 8C church the large **narthex** supporting three chapels, an early medieval concept. But characteristic of Early Gothic are the rib vaults which spring from strong piers enlivened by clusters of elongated shafts, and the tall openings between them. Supposedly the oculus in the west was a practical solution to lighting the low central chapel above the narthex. Work to rebuild the 8C **nave** began in earnest in 1231. The junction between the narthex and nave is awkward. In contrast, the overall effect of the wide nave, slender shafts and exceedingly fine tracery, glazed triforium and vast expanses of glass in the clerestory, is elegant and lives up to its comparison with a lantern of light. The transepts are generous to allow for the royal tombs. They are pierced north and south with magnificent **rose windows** squared up to fill the whole of the bay and continuing behind the open triforium below, the first of their kind and emulated at Notre-Dame in 1258. The glass is 19C.

Suger began the reconstruction of the **east end** immediately after the completion of the west, in 1140. The work consisted of enlarging both the crypt and, above it, the choir, and creating the double ambulatory. In 1144, 20 new altars were consecrated. This construction clinches St-Denis's reputation as the birthplace of Gothic: the shallow undulating chapels opening wide into the double ambulatory and linked to it by ribbed vaulting (an ingenious combination of round and pointed ribs), and the enormous ratio of glazed to solid wall. The use of slender columnar supports, rather than compound piers, looks back to Romanesque east ends. This is probably explained by a desire to harmonise the ambulatory with the 8C building still in place. The elegant arrangement of columns allows an uninterrupted view through to the large windows of the radiating chapels, two in each, fulfilling Suger's aim of filling the church with 'wonderful and uninterrupted light'. The axial chapels of the crypt and ambulatory were both dedicated to the Virgin.

From Suger's records, it is known that the central vessel was rib-vaulted. The carved and inlaid High Stalls of the Ritual Choir (1501–07) from the chapel of Georges d'Amboise at the Château de Gaillon; the Low Stalls are 15C work from St-Lucien, near Beauvais. In the choir is a charming 12C Virgin, originally at the abbey of Longchamp.

The **crypt**, entered on either side of the choir, was constructed by Suger around the original Carolingian martyrium built by Abbot Fulrad, the site of the grave of St Denis and his companions. There are some 12C capitals and traces of wall paintings, and excavations have revealed Gallo-Roman Christian tombs and the tomb of Queen Aregonde, Clovis's daughter-in-law, and fragments of earlier churches.

The central chapel was the Bourbon burial vault until the Revolution, and contains the sarcophagi of Louis XVI, and Marie-Antoinette (see Chapelle Expiatore; Ch. 23), and those of Louis XVIII among other 18C–19C sovereigns. The ossuary on the north side contains the bones that were thrown into a pit when many tombs were rifled in 1793. On the south side is a 19C cenotaph in memory of the Bourbon kings, including Henri IV and Louis XIV. The **stained glass** in the Lady Chapel dates from the 12C, placing it among the oldest in France, albeit restored in the 19C. Among the 15 panels which have survived, mounted in modern glass in the east end, is a *Tree of Jesse*, in which Abbot Suger himself is represented. The Baptistry window, designed by J. J. Gruber in 1932, is vividly different.

On the south side of the ambulatory are a copy of the Oriflamme and statues of Louis XVI and Marie-Antoinette at Prayer, commissioned by Louis XVIII.

The tombs

The tombs—described below—are a remarkable collection of funerary sculpture from the mid-12C to the mid-16C. Among tombs in the south aisle, are that of Louis d'Orléans (d. 1407), and Valentine de Milan (d. 1408), an Italian work of 1502–15, commissioned by Louis XII. This combines a figure in repose, in the French tradition, on an Italian-style sarcophagus where the twelve apostles replace the more usual pleurants. Opposite, against the south-west pillar of the crossing, is the heart-tomb of François II (d. 1560), by Germain Pilon and Ponce Jacquiau. Also in the south aisle, the urn (1549–55) by Pierre Bontemps, containing the heart of François I.

In the south transept: the tomb of **François I** (d. 1547) and Claude de France (d. 1524), a masterpiece by Philibert Delorme, begun in 1547, is a classicised version of the tomb of Louis XII (see below), in the form of a triumphal arch. Much use is made of coloured marbles skilfully worked by Bontemps. The royal pair appear kneeling, with their children, on the upper level, and again, recumbent, below. On the east side of the south transept are the tombs of **Charles V** (d. 1380), a remarkable likeness sculpted by André Beauneveu, commissioned before the king's death; the statue of his queen, Jeanne de Bourbon comes from the Célestins church in Paris. Bertrand du Guesclin (d. 1380), High Constable of France, is one of the few commoners buried here. The tomb of Charles VI (d. 1422) also resides in this transept.

At the west end of the choir is the tomb of **Philippe III**, le Hardi (d. 1285) by Jean d'Arras, using black and white marble, one of the first portrait statues. There is also a masterly effigy of his queen, Isabella of Aragón (d. 1271), and the tomb of **Philippe IV**, le Bel (d. 1314). At the left of the steps to the sanctuary is the 13C tomb of **Dagobert** (d. 638), with relief sculptures on three levels in a pinnacled niche, showing the torment and redemption of the king's soul, and a beautiful **statue of Queen Nanthilde** (13C). The figures of Dagobert and his Son are 19C restorations. Nearby is the tomb of Léon de Lusignan (d. 1393).

On the north side of the ambulatory, you pass the tombs of (left) **Blanche and Jean** (both d. 1243), children of Louis IX, a rare example of a tomb in metalwork and enamel. Transferred from St-Germain-des-Prés is a remarkable slab in cloisonné mosaic (11C), of **Frédégonde** (d. 597), queen of Chilperic I; and **Childebert I** (d. 558), of the mid-12C, the oldest funerary effigy in France. In the chapel at the top of the steps, are draped **statues of Henri II** (d. 1559) and **Catherine de Médicis** (d. 1589) by Germain Pilon (1583). In the sanctuary is the **Altar of the Relics** (by Viollet-le-Duc), on which are placed the reliquaries, given by Louis XVIII, of St Denis and his fellow-martyrs.

In the north transept is the temple-like tomb of **Henri II**, part of a grandiose scheme on the part of his queen, Catherine de Médicis, which included a huge rotunda in the Italian style on the north transept. Famous artists linked with its construction were Primaticcio, Lescot, Bullant, and A. du Cerceau. Although the chapel was never entirely completed the tomb, designed by Primaticcio in 1560–73, was placed there by Henri IV. The chapel was, however, demolished in the 18C. The monument, with recumbent and kneeling effigies of the king and queen, was sculpted by Germain Pilon and others. Here also are the tombs of Philippe V (d. 1322), Charles IV (d. 1328), Philippe VI (d. 1350) and Jean II (d. 1364), the last two by André Beauneveu. In the choir are tombs of Louis X (d. 1316) and his son Jean I (d. 1316).

The north aisle contains the tomb of **Louis XII** (d. 1515) and **Anne de Bretagne** (d. 1514), covered by a baldaquin, commissioned by François I and made by Giovanni di Giusto, a Florentine, c 1515–31. On the upper part, the royal pair are represented in life. Below, they are depicted after death in a remarkably sensitive manner (in contrast with the heavy allegorigal figures surrounding them), and the chapel-like tomb enclosing the transi and the transie (the effigies of the dead pair) introduces a new element in funerary monuments. Bas-reliefs illustrate episodes in the king's career.

Among other 13C–14C tombs, are that of **Louis de France** (d. 1260), the eldest son of Louis IX, with Henry III of England as one of the pleurants in the cortege around the base—an early example of this imagery.

To the south of the basilica are restored **monastic dependencies**. Rebuilt in the 18C by Robert de Cotte and Jacques V Gabriel, they were occupied after 1809 as a **Maison d'Education de la Légion d'Honneur**, for the daughters of members of the Legion. This can be visited during term time and weekends, guided tours only; identification is necessary.

Musée d'Art et d'Histoire

Some five minutes' walk further south, at 22 bis Rue Gabriel Péri, the museum of the town's history Musée d'Art et d'Histoire is installed in a Carmelite convent founded in 1625. The chapel (closed for restoration) by Mique, with an Ionic portico, has a fine compartmentalle cupola (1780), built while Louise de France was in residence (1770–87). St-Denis is one of the most researched towns in France since revealing important finds during excavations for the métro in 1972, and the museum was installed in the former convent in 1981. Three wings of the original cloister survived and the fourth has recently been replaced. Pious 18C mottos on the convent walls have been restored.

In the former chapter house is the reconstituted **Pharmacy of the Hôtel-Dieu** (demolished 1907) with other souvenirs of the former hospital. The refectory and kitchen of the Carmelite convent have been converted into an excellent archaeological and historical section explaining the role of the town since the time of ancient Catolacus on the tin route across northern Europe, at the time of medieval St-Denis with its pilgrimage and fairs, in the evolution from monarchic to communist associations, and in modern industries as varied as Pleyel pianos (until 1962), chemicals, Christofle glass, and gas—evoked in André Lhote's painting of the *Usine à Gaz, St-Denis et Gennevilliers*, 1937.

The history of the Carmelites is recorded in the restored cells on the upper floor, one with memorabilia specific to Madame Louise, daughter of Louis XV. Works from the Besson donation, notably by Albert AndréAndré, Albert, are shown in adjacent rooms. On the second floor is a huge and fascinating collection devoted to the Commune de Paris (1870–71). The museum owns some 4000 engravings and lithographs by Daumier (not necessarily on view).

The recent modern wing of the cloister leads to the section devoted to the poet Paul Eluard (1895–1952), born in St-Denis. The exhibits include some of Eluard's manuscripts and works by Zadkine, Picasso, Max Ernst, Cocteau, Giacometti and Françoise Gilot, a *Portrait of Paul Eluard* (1952) by André Fougeron, as well as rare editions illustrated by his painter friends.

Also in St-Denis, but best approached from the métro: Porte de Paris and following the Blvd Anatole France to the south west across the Canal St-Denis, and there turning right, is the **Musée Bouilhet-Christofle** (open during working hours). Here are replicas of historical interest and original pieces of the art of the gold- and silversmith produced by the Société Christofle since its establishment.

38 · Ecouen

■ **Getting there**. Ecouen (95440, Val d'Oise) can be reached by **train** from Gare du Nord (Luzarches or Persan-Beaumont line), to Ecouen-Ezanville station, then the 269 bus (direction Garges Sarcelles) to the Mairie. The Château is reached on foot by a path to the left of the Mairie. An alternative route from the station is by a footpath through the woods.

By road, from the Porte de la Chapelle, take the N16 past St-Denis (see Ch. 37), in the direction of Chantilly. The road crosses a dreary dormitory area between (left) **Sarcelles**, with relics of a 12C church with a Gothic nave and Renaissance façade, and (right) **Villiers-le-Bel**, which belies its name.

The town of Ecouen is of slight interest, but the Musée National de la Renaissance is worth visiting, and the church of St-Acceul includes some interesting stained-glass in its choir (1544).

The Musée National de la Renaissance

■ Open Wed–Mon, 09.45–12.30, 14.00–17.15, ☎ 01 34 38 38 51, recorded information, or ☎ 01 34 38 38 50. The Park is open in the summer until 19.00 and in winter to 18.00.

The town is dominated by the magnificent Renaissance **Château d'Ecouen**, which houses the Musée National de la Renaissance, inaugurated in 1977. This delightful and clearly laid-out museum, less visited than others on the outskirts of Paris, is intended to give an overview of the decorative arts of the Renaissance. The collection follows on chronologically from the Musée du Moyen Age (Cluny) in Paris. One of the main reasons for choosing the Château d'Ecouen as the site for the museum was the need to house the series of large tapestries of David and Bathsheba, stored for a long time at the Hôtel de Cluny.

The construction of the château began c 1538 for the Constable Anne de Montmorency. Among major artists he employed were the sculptor Jean GoujonGoujon, Jean and the architect Jean Bullant (1520–78). The building was put to a variety of uses during the Revolutionary period, and in 1805 became a school for the daughters of members of the Légion d'Honneur. Many of its embellishments, including an altar by Goujon from the chapel, were removed during the Revolution, and reverted to the Duc d'Aumale, who chose to include them in his château at Chantilly.

Built in two stages, beginning 1538 and 1547, the château is arranged around a courtyard with square pavilions on the angles and moats on three sides. The elevations are simply articulated with pilasters and string courses, ornamentation confined to the dormer windows which show a progression in styles from the west to the north wings. After 1547, work began on the interior to provide luxurious apartments for the owners and the King, Henri II, and porticos were added. Those on both sides of the north wing have Henri II's insignia. The south portico, which uses the Colossal Order for the first time in France, is ascribed to Jean Bullant. It was intended as the setting for Michelangelo's Slaves (see Louvre) given to Montmorency by Henri II.

Ground floor

The **entrance** is through the east wing, a replacement, in 1807, of the super-imposed galleries with an equestrian statue of the Constable, designed by Goujon or Bullant, destroyed in 1787 (a fragment of its decorative sculpture is in the museum).

From here, turn left into the **Chapel (room 1)**, with painted Gothic ribbed vaulting and delicately carved Renaissance-style stonework, before walking through a series of rooms on the ground floor. **Room 2** has a profusely decorated mantelpiece in the School of Fontainebleau style, the first of 12 depicting biblical themes, which are a feature of Ecouen. This room contains arms and armour, including stirrups with the emblem of François I, and a collection of enamelled plaques by Pierre Courteys (Limoges; 1559). **Room 4** has a collection of carved Renaissance panels and **room 5** has rare painted leather hangings from Normandy with Roman heroes. The chimneypiece shows *The Tribute to Caesar*.

A series of smaller rooms (**rooms 6–8**) is devoted to collections of magnificent alabaster, carved wood plaques and panels. There are also pearwood and box-wood statuettes, mainly German or Flemish. The outstanding bronze figurines include *Jupiter* by Alessandro Vittoria, *Virgin and Child* by Niccolò Roccatagliata, and fornicating satyrs by Riccio. In **room 9** are metalwork, some damascened, cutlery and a collection of Renaissance door-furniture.

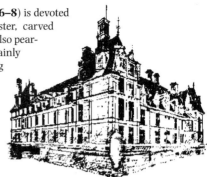

The Château d'Ecouen

Among the mathematical instruments and watches in **room 10** are a Celestial Sphere in gilded copper and an exquisite automated timepiece masquerading as a miniature ship, by Hans Schlotlheim of Augsburg. An unusual piece (**room 11**), is the splendid inlaid silversmith's workbench from Germany (1565), a full-scale working model made for a nobleman's pleasure rather than as a craftsman's tool. **Room 12**, known as that of Catherine de Médicis, with tapestries, is crossed before reaching a room (**room 13**) reserved for concerts and other functions. In the subsequent rooms (**room 14**), are collections of sculpture including work by Luca della Robbia. French sculptures include *The Three Fates*, in marble, by Germain Pilon, and *The Compassion of the Father* in terracotta.

The reconstructed **Constable's Library**, above the Chapel, is reached by a separate staircase from the Constable's antechamber on the first floor. It has its original and unique decor of wooden panels inlaid with gilt arabesques and the monogram of Anne de Montmorency.

First floor

The first floor has been arranged to evoke the owners' and king's residence as it was after 1547. In the South Wing were the apartments of Anne de Montmorency and his wife, Madeleine. In the decor are reminders of his role as commander of the army—his emblem was a sword and blue eaglets feature in his arms. The decorated chimneypiece has a scene of *Esau Hunting* and there are two School of Fontainebleau paintings. The adjacent apartments of Madeleine de Savoie (**rooms 2–3**), mainly a reconstruction, contain a 16C Venetian bureau inlaid with painted mother-of-pearl and and notable carved doors (from elsewhere). In the antechamber is an Italian spinet (1570).

Room 5, the Psyche Gallery, was originally grandly decorated with stained glass and paving (remnants of which are exhibited elsewhere), and murals. The finely carved stone fireplaces are from Châlons-en-Champagne (1562), with reliefs of *Christ and the Samaritan*, and *Actaeon surprising Diana in her Bath*.

This room (with **rooms 4 and 7**) houses the *raison d'être* of the museum, the celebrated series of **tapestries** entitled *The Story of David and Bathsheba* (Brussels c 1510). Possibly Jan van Roome was involved in their creation. Individualistic portrayal of the figures and architectural settings, typically Renaissance, is combined with a foreground reminiscent of medieval millefleurs. Stylised flowers form the border and the colours are still strong. The story, reading from left to right, begins with a scribe before an open book recording the episodes and each of the ten tapestries contains several scenes. David, despised by his wife, brings the ark to Jerusalem, then departs for battle against the Ammonites at Rabbah, with Uriah, husband of Bathsheba. After seducing Bathsheba, David sends Uriah to his death and Bathsheba is received at David's court. The prophet Nathan predicts the death of their child, while allegorical figures put Lust to flight. David and Bathsheba's child dies, and David appeases god's anger by fasting and praying. He then resumes the battle and takes Rabbah. As the story ends the scribe closes the book.

Room 7, Henri II's chamber, has a painted ceiling à la française with the king's monogram and crescent, and a chimneypiece featuring *Saul in Anger Slaughtering Two of his Cattle*.

Beyond a carved wooden staircase, from the Chambre des Comptes of the Palais de la Cité, is **room 8**, the Salle d'honneur, which has the only sculpted marble chimneypiece at Ecouen. Attributed to Jean Bullant, c 1558, the coloured marble was a gift of Cardinal Farnese. The paved floor, originally in the Psyche Gallery, was made by Masséot Abaquesne (mid 16C), who made his name by his work at Ecouen. Displayed in this room are two tapestries of the Fructus Belli series (the other six dispersed elsewhere), woven in Brussels, 1546–48, by Jean Baudouyn from cartoons by Giulio Romano, which show the soldiers' payday and the general's dinner. **Rooms 9–10**, have painted leather panels with scenes from Scipio and a chimneypiece with the Judgement of Solomon. In **room 11** is some fine secular stained glass from Ecouen, with the emblems of Anne de Montmorency, Catherine de Médicis, François I and Henri II.

Second floor

Room 1 is devoted to a remarkable group of ceramics from Iznik (ancient Nicaea, in north-west Turkey), dating largely from 1555–1700. In **room 2** there is stained glass mainly from churches around Paris. Stairs lead up to the Embroideries section. **Room 3** contains 16C French tile panels, and ceramics by Masséot Abaquesne including a magnificent tiled floor of of 1550 and pharmacy pots; also two rare pieces from the Saint-Porchaire workshops, c 1560, and faience attributed to Bernard Palissy. **Rooms 4–5** contain painted panels from 15C Florentine marriage-chests (*cassoni*) depicting the Trojan Horse and other Classical scenes; Limoges enamel plaques and portraits (by Léonard Limousin, Nardon Pénicaud, Pierre Reymond, Pierre Courtois and others); also collections of majolica, glass and among the jewellery, a swan pendant from Germany. There are fine examples of the gold and silversmith in **room 7** notably a Daphne by Wenzel Jamnitzer, a goblet in the shape of a snail (Netherlands; c 1700) and several magnificent examples from Nuremberg and Augsburg.

39 · Sceaux

■ **Getting there**. The N20 leads south from the Porte d'Orléans to (10km) Sceaux, which is also be reached by the RER Line B, stopping at Bourg-la-Reine, Sceaux or Parc de Sceaux.

■ **Tourist Information Office**, Sceaux, ☎ 01 46 61 19 03. 92330, Sceaux (Hauts-de-Seine).

2km south of the Blvd Périphérique the double **Aqueduct de Arceuil** crosses the valley of the Bièvre. The lower part was built in 1613–23 by Marie de Médicis to supply the Luxembourg fountains; it was preceded by a Roman aqueduct, built in the 4C to bring water to the Palais des Thermes. Both Erik Satie and artist Victor Vasarely lived in the suburb of Arceuil.

After 4.5km the broad Allée d'Honneur climbs west from the N20 to the entrance of the **Château de Sceaux**. A 19C building replaced the sumptuous 17C château built for Colbert, which, during the first half of the 18C, was the scene of the literary and artistic court of the ambitious Duchesse du Maine (1676–1753). Voltaire wrote *Zadig* here; and works by Racine, Molière and Lully were performed in the adjacent Orangerie (left), constructed by Jules Hardouin-Mansart (1684; restored). To the right is the Pavillon de l'Aurore, by Perrault.

Since 1937 the **Musée de L'Ile de France** has been installed in the château, which was restored between 1992 and 1994. This illustrates the history and topography of the area around Paris. It is well worth visiting, not only for its site, but for the wealth of interesting material depicting the appearance of, and life in, the environs of the capital in past centuries. It also contains a documentation centre (by prior appointment). Open 10.00–18.00 April–Sept, otherwise 10.00–17.00, closed Tues 1/1, Easter, 1/5, 1/11, 11/11, 25/12. ☎ 01 46 61 06 71 or 01 41 13 70 41.

The museum is now arranged around four main themes. The ground floor is devoted to the History of the Property and its main owners, from the time of Colbert's original château to the one built by Lesoufaché in 1857 for the Duke of Trevise. The **Grand Salon** (room 3) contains portraits of Colbert attributed to Lefebvre, and of the Duchess of Maine by De Troy. The **Small Green Room** (room 5), with a charming view, shows a large collection of Sceaux ceramics. The **Library** (room 7) contains Sevres, St-Cloud and Vincennes ware.

Room 9 on the first floor, the **Royal Residences Room**, displays paintings, engravings and furniture evoking the châteaux of Marly, St-Germain or Choisy, now destroyed. The **Landscape Rooms** (rooms 11, 12, 13 and 17) show the area as it was between the 17C and 20C, with a room dedicated to a number of views by Paul Huet (room 13). Lastly, there are rooms containing works given by artists, such as the watercolours and engravings by Dunoyer de Segonzac and the famous series *Hostages* by Jean Fautrier.

The majestic **park**, laid out by Le Nôtre, forms one of the more attractive open spaces near Paris and contains, south of the château, a series of cascades leading to the Octagon, to the west of which is the Grand Canal. From here you have a view of the Pavillon de Hanovre, moved here in 1934 from the Blvd des Capucines.

A short distance north west of the château, across the park, is the **old churchyard** of Sceaux, where the fabulist Florian (1755–94) is buried. The simple tombs of Pierre (1859–1906) and Marie Curie (née Sklodowska; 1867–1934), the discoverers of radium, are in the local cemetery.

Some 2.5km west, in the Parc de la Vallé aux Loups, is the restored residence of Chateaubriand (in 1807–18).

Further Afield

The following chapters describe three of the more important monuments and collections outside Paris which make pleasant days out to more rural areas. These include the Musée Condé at Chantilly, the attractive town of Senlis, with its 12C Cathedral, and the Château and forest of Fontainbleau.

40 · Chantilly and Senlis

■ **Getting there**. Paris to Chantilly is 41km (25 miles) on the N16. Chantilly may also be reached by the N17 and D924A, a very slightly longer route; Senlis, 10km east of Chantilly, is also reached directly by the A1 motorway. Two routes to Chantilly are briefly described below.

Restaurants and cafés

Chantilly (60500)
Les Balladins, ZAC du Coq Chantant (RN 16), ☎ 03 44 58 13 12. £
Capitainerie du Château, Château de Chantilly, ☎ 03 44 57 15 89. Lunch only. £
Restaurant du Château, 22 Rue du Connétable, ☎ 03 44 57 02 25. £
Le Relais Condé, 42 Av. du Maréchal Joffre, ☎ 03 44 57 05 75. ££
Rôtisserie du Connétable, 75 Rue du Connétable, ☎ 03 44 57 02 91. £
Hotel-Restaurant de la Gare, Place de la Gare, ☎ 03 44 62 56 90. £
Au Lion d'Or, 44 Rue du Connétable, ☎ 03 44 57 03 19. £
Le Tipperary, 6 Av. du Maréchal Joffre, ☎ 03 44 57 00 48. £
Senlis (60300)
Auberge de la Mitonnée, 93 Rue du Moulin St Tron, ☎ 03 44 53 10 05. £
Hostellerie de la Porte Bellon, 51 Rue Bellon, ☎ 03 44 53 03 05. ££
Le Scaramouche, 4 Pl. Notre-Dame, ☎ 03 44 53 01 26 (closes at 21.30). £
La Vieille Auberge, 8 Rue du Long Filet, ☎ 03 44 60 95 50. £

If you are taking the N16 route to Chantilly, you might want to make a detour to **Royaumont**, where there are the considerable remains of a great Cistercian abbey, founded in 1228. Louis IX was married in the church in 1234, and the beautiful refectory, its vaulting sustained by five monolithic columns, contains the tomb by Coysevox of Henri of Lorraine (d. 1666).

If, on the other hand, you choose the N17 route, it leaves Paris by the Porte de la Villette and at 16km passes (left) the airport of **Le Bourget**, with the **Musée de l'Air** and its collection of 140 aircraft, mostly from c 1919, but including earlier flying machines. The first regular flights between Le Bourget and London (Croydon airport) started in 1919. Just beyond on the right is **Roissy-Charles de Gaulle** airport. After 18.5km the D924A forks left for (9.5km) Chantilly, first crossing part of the Fôret de Chantilly (2100 hectares) before reaching the Château de Chantilly; the right fork leads in 9.5km directly to Senlis; see below.

Chantilly

■ Tourist Information Office, 23 Avenue du Maréchal Joffre, 60500 Chantilly (Oise), ☎ 03 44 57 08 58.

Chantilly, the Newmarket of France, where race-meetings have been held since 1834, is principally famous for its château, housing the Musée Condé. It was formerly reputed for its silk lace and for its porcelain, the manufacture of which was established in 1725. The potteries were opened by Christopher Potter (d. 1817), who settled in Paris in 1789.

The Rue du Connétable leads east past Notre-Dame (1692) to the vast **Grandes-Ecuries**, built for Louis-Henri, Duc de Bourbon (1692–1740) by Jean Aubert from 1719. Once stabling 240 mounts, they have been restored to house an equestrian museum.

Musée Condé

Passing through the Porte St-Denis, just north of which is the Jeu de Paume of 1757, you arrive at the Château de Chantilly, two connected buildings on an island in a carp-stocked lake. It houses the Musée Conde, containing unique collections of French paintings and illuminations of the 15C–16C, an important library and other works of art.

The domain came into the possession of the Montmorency family in 1522 and, after the execution of Henri II Montmorency (1595–1632), it passed in 1643 to the Grand Condé (Louis II, Prince de Condé; 1621–86), whose mother was a Montmorency. The Petit Château or Capitainerie was built in c 1560, probably by Jean Bullant, for the Constable Anne de Montmorency (1493–1567), whose adjacent mansion, the Grand Château, was erected in 1528–32 by Pierre ChambigesChambiges, Pierre. Molière's *Les Précieuses Ridicules* was first performed here, in 1659; during the visit of Louis XIV in 1671, François Vatel, Condé's maitre d'hôtel, committed suicide because he thought the fish would be late for Friday dinner (as described by Mme de Sévigné, the great 17C letter writer). The Duc d'Enghien (1772–1804), shot at Vincennes on Napoléon's orders, was born here.

The Grand Château, rebuilt in 1684–91 by Hardouin-Mansart, was virtually razed at the Revolution, although the Petit Château survived. Some repairs were carried out after 1818 by the last of the Condés (who committed suicide in 1830), but it was left to his heir, the Duc d'Aumale (1822–86), fifth son of Louis-Philippe, to rebuild the Grand Château entirely, following the designs of Honoré Daumet. Unfortunately, Aumale also inherited his father's taste in many respects. After the confiscation of the property of the Orléans family in 1853, the château was acquired by the English banking firm of Coutts, but was returned to its rightful owner by a decree of the National Assembly in 1872. Despite being banished to Twickenham, the Duc d'Aumale bequeathed the whole domain, together with his art collections, to the Institut de France in 1897.

Chantilly marked the farthest advance in this direction of German troops in September 1914, but it remained undamaged, and soon after became the general HQ of the French high command, with Joffre and Nivelle in residence.

Go through the iron Grille d'Honneur, to leave on your right the Château d'Enghien (1770; by Le Roy), now the curator's residence. On the Terrasse du Connétable is a statue by P. Dubois of Anne de Montmorency. You then pass between two bronze groups of hounds by Cain, cross the moat and enter the Cour d'Honneur.

The **Galerie des Cerfs** displays the arms of successive owners of Chantilly, and is hung with 17C Gobelins tapestries of hunting scenes; above the chimneypiece is the Vision of St Hubert by Paul Baudry.

Notable in the **Galerie de Peinture** are Poussin, *Massacre of the Innocents*; Trophime Bigot, *Supper at Emmaus*; Fromentin *Hawking in Algeria*; Lancret, *Déjeuner au Jambon*; Philippe de Champaigne, *Mazarin, and Richelieu*; Lampi, *The Tsarina Féodorowna*; Nanteuil, Colbert; *Views of Chantilly* by De Cort; and paintings by Annibale Carracci. The rotunda of the Galerie de Peinture (room 1) formed by the Tour de Senlis, with a mosaic pavement from Herculaneum, contains François Clouet, *Odet de Coligny* (large version); Raphael's beautiful *Madonna of Loreto*; and Piero di Cosimo, *Simonetta Vespucci*.

In the **Galerie du Logis** (**room 4**) are Perrault's copy of Horace Vernet's painting (at Versailles) of *Louis-Philippe and his Sons leaving Versailles*; and in the Salle de la Smalah (**room 6**) Bonnat, *Portrait of the Duc d'Aumale in 1890*.

Among portraits in **room 7**, the Rotonde de la Minerve, formed by the Tour du Connétable, are: Duplessis, *The Duchesse de Chartres watching her Husband's Departure for Ushant* (1778); Nattier, *The Duchesse d'Orléans* (as Hebe), and Carle Vernet, *The Duc d'Orléans and Duc de Chartres* (1788). On display in **room 8**, adjoining, a Greek statuette of Minerva, the Portalés Amphora, bronze ewers from Herculaneum, Tanagra figures and other antiquities, including coins minted within ten years of the eruption of Vesuvius in AD 79, found at Pompeii; also a portrait of Franz I of Austria by Lawrence.

Room 9, Salle de Giotto, contains Enguerrand Quarton (1410–66), *Virgin*; Jacopo del Sellaio, *Madonna*; School of Giotto (Maso di Banco), *Death of the Virgin*; Andrea del Sarto, *A Youth*; Ghirlandaio, *Portrait of Louis de la Trémoille*. Salle Isabelle, **room 10**, landscapes by Théodore Rousseau and seascapes by W. van de Velde the Younger and J. van Ruisdale. Salon d'Orléans. **Room 11**, Bonnat, *The Duc d'Aumale in 1880*; Jalabert, *Queen Marie-Amélie in 1865*; and also 18C Chantilly porcelain.

Room 12, Salle Caroline, has works by Greuze, including *La Surprise*, a study for the *Village Marriage Contract* (in the Louvre); Watteau, *L'Amante inquiète* and *La Sérenade*; Mignard, *The Comtesse de la Suze*; and Marc Nattier (Father) *The Duchesse de Nantes*, daughter of Mme de Montespan; and attributed to Rigaud, *The Princesse des Ursins*.

Room 13, Salle Clouet has many 16C portraits, with works by Jean and François Clouet and Corneille de Lyon, among them. Also, Marc Duval, *Jacques de Savoie*; Jean Decourt, *Henri III* (?) and *Albert de Gondi*; attributed to Corneille de Lyon or his school, *Gabrielle de Rochechouart* (?), and the *Dauphin François* (son of François I); attributed to Jean Clouet or his school, *Jeanne d'Albret, Charles IX, Elisabeth of Austria, Odet de Châtillon, Catherine de Médicis, Marguerite de Valois as a Child, Henri II as a Child*; and further portraits including anonymous, François I, and his sister, Marguerite d'Angoulême.

Return through the Galerie du Logis (room 5) (past portraits by Mierevelt of Hugo Grotius and of Elisabeth of Bohemia) to cross the Galerie de Peinture to enter the Galerie de Psyché, containing 42 of the original 46 **stained-glass windows**, representing the Loves of Cupid and Psyché, made c 1541 for the Montmorency château at Ecouen (see p 326), and probably designed by Michel Coxie. At the end of the room is a bust by Guillaume Dubois of Henri IV (1610).

Room 15, the **Sanctuario**, contains some of the main treasures of the collection, including Raphael, *Madonna of the House of Orléans*, and the *Three Graces*. The *Esther and Ahasuerus*, although catalogued as by Filippino Lippi, is probably by Amico di Sandro, a pupil of Botticelli. Forty of the original 47 precious miniatures ascribed to Jean Fouquet (1415–81), executed for the *Book of Hours of Etienne Chevalier*; the treasurer of France (1410–74) and his patron saint are depicted adoring the Virgin and Child.

Room 16, in the **Tour du Trésor** (view) displays an enamel of Apollo guiding the Chariot of the Sun, attributed to Cellini, and the rose diamond (copy), known as the Grand Condé; a Cross from the treasury of Basel (15C); snuff boxes embellished with views of Chantilly by Roussel (1775); and collections of enamels, miniatures and fans.

Passing a bas-relief of the Departure of Phaethon by Jean Goujon, you enter **room 17**, the **Tribune**, an octagon containing a vase by Clodion; while on panels above the cornice are paintings of residences connected with the Duc d'Aumale: the Collège Henri-IV, Aumale, the Palais-Royal, Ecouen, Palermo, Guise, Villers-Cotterêts and Twickenham. On the walls, in unlikely juxtaposition, hang Reynolds, *Countess Waldegrave and her Daughter* (1761); Ary Scheffer, *Talleyrand*; Watteau, *Plaisir Pastoral*; Van Dyck, *Gaston, Duc d'Orléans*; Memling(?), *Diptych of the Virgin appearing to Jeanne de Bourbon* (daughter of Charles VII), *Christ on the Cross*; Perugino, *Madonna with SS Peter and Jerome*; School of Botticelli, *Autumn*; Flemish School, *Antoine, the Grand Bastard of Burgundy* (brother of Charles the Bold); Sassetta, *Mystic Marriage of St Francis*; Pesellino, *Madonna with SS Peter and Anthony*; Mignard, *Molière, and Mazarin*; Ingres, *Mme Devauçay* (painted in Rome in 1807), and *Self-Portrait*; Philippe de Champaigne, *Angélique Arnaud*; H.-G. Pot, *Andres Hooftman*; after Rigaud, *The Abbé de Rancé*; Rigaud, *Louis XIV*; three portraits by Mme Vigée-Lebrun; also the *Fall of Phaeton* by Goujon, which complements that in the other vestibule.

After the Galerie des Cerfs, turn right to visit apartments in the Petit Château decorated by the Duc de Bourbon and furnished in the French Regency style with Beauvais tapestry, contemporary clocks, ornaments and *boiseries*. **Room 18** has *dessus de portes* by Oudry and Desportes; an enamel of Henri IV by Claudius Popelin; and Sèvres, Rouen and Chinese porcelain. **Room 19**, Van Dyck, *Comte Henri de Bergues*, and *Princesse Marie de Brabançon*; Justus van Egmont, *The Grand Condé in 1658*, and after Nanteuil, in 1662; four enamel portraits by Léonard Limousin; anonymous, *Abraham de Fabert, Maréchal de France and François II de Montmorency, Duc de Luxembourg*. The mosaic above the chimneypiece is from Herculaneum.

The richly decorated **bedroom (room 20)**, with panels by Christophe Huet, contains a commode by Riesener from Versailles, which belonged to Louis XVI, and **room 21, le Grand Cabinet**, chairs by J.-B. Sené and a fine chandelier. an equestrian statue of the Grand Condé by Frémiet. **Room 22**, the **Salon des Singes**, so-named from the chinoiserie panel-paintings (1737) by Christophe

Huet of '*Singeries ou différentes Actions de la vie Humaine*'. (The exquisite Petite Singerie, in a room below, may be viewed when visiting the Private Apartments of the Duc and Duchess of Aumale on a guided visit.) This suite of eight rooms (18C–19C), was decorated by the Duc d'Aumale at the time of his marriage.

Room 23, the **Galeries des Actions de M. le Prince**, contains panels painted in 1686–96 by Sauveur Lecomte of scenes of battles fought by the Grand Condé (including Rocroi, Nördlingen and Lens), whose despatch-case lies on the bureau of the Duc de Choiseul. Over the fireplace is a trophy formed of his swords and pistols; above is his portrait, when only 26 years of age, at Rocroi (by J. Stella); below, a medallion by Coysevox of 1686, the year of the Prince's death. His bust in biscuit de Sèvres on the mantlepiece is by Roland (1785); those in marble of Turenne and of the Grand Condé are by Derbais (1695). Room 24, the Salon de Musique, contains a Portrait of the Duc d'Enghien by Vallain; and a collection of miniatures.

Retrace your steps to enter the **Cabinet des Livres**, containing some 12,500 volumes, many of great rarity or from an important provenance, and many are superbly bound. Perhaps the greatest treasure among some 1493 MSS is the **Très Riches Heures du Duc de Berri**, with its brilliant illuminated pages depicting the months. Exquisitely ornamented they are still, with their realistic rendering of depth and natural detail, far more naturalistic than most International Gothic art. They were begun c 1415 by Pol de Limbourg and his brothers, and completed some 70 years later by Jean Colombe. Only reproductions of the fragile originals are now on view.

You return to the **Grand Vestibule**, on the right of which is the Grand Escalier, with its copper, brass and galvanised iron balustrade, designed by Daumet and executed by the brothers Moreau, with caryatids by Chapu, and Gobelins tapestries after Boucher and de Troy.

The **chapel**, founded in the early 14C and virtually destroyed during the Revolution, was rebuilt by Daumet in 1882. Behind the altar is the mausoleum of Henri II de Condé, with bronze sculptures by Jacques Sarazin. The altar itself (by Jean Bullant and Jean Goujon), the *boiseries* of 1548 and the stained glass (1544, with portraits of Anne de Montmorency's children), were all brought here from Ecouen (see p ???). The flag was captured at Rocroi (1643).

The **park**, with impressive parterres, was laid out mostly by Le Nôtre for the Grand Condé, and is adorned with sculptures and ornamental ponds. Among the buildings which may be seen are the Maison de Sylvie, to the south east behind the Château d'Enghien, to reach which you pass the Chapelle de St-Paul (1552) and the Cabotière (early 17C). 'Sylvie' was the name given to Marie Félice Orsini, Duchesse de Montmorency, by Théophile de Viau who, when condemned to death in 1623 for his licentious verses, was hidden by her in this dwelling, later rebuilt by Condé. Here also, in 1724, the romantic affair of Mlle de Clermont (sister of the Duc de Bourbon) and Louis de Melun, killed in a 'hunting accident', took place.

To the north east stand a group of cottages, the Hameau (constructed by Le Roy in 1774 for the penultimate Condé) being the scene of many *fêtes champêtres* of the period.

Behind the Hameau, you can ascend 80m in an attached balloon (Aérophile) for a remarkable view of the park, château and forest of Chantilly and the town of Senlis. On the Grand Canal, from where the Balloon departs, electric boats provide an alternative view of the ensemble as they glide silently around the park (commentary in French and English).

5.5km north east of Chantilly is the notable 12C church of **St-Leu-d'Esserent**, just north of which are priory cloisters. The local quarry supplied stone for the cathedrals of Chartres and Sens, and later the Château de Versailles. In 1944 they were used for the assembly of V1 and V2 rockets.

Senlis

The D924 leads east from Chantilly via Courteuil, where Abbé Prévost (1697–1763), author of *Manon Lescaut*, died, to approach Senlis (15,300 inhabitants). The town has some attractive old alleys within its Gallo-Roman ramparts. It has a 12C cathedral, which is of interest.

■ **Tourist Information Office**, Pl. du Parvis Notre-Dame, 60500 Senlis (Oise), ☎ 03 44 53 06 40.

> Probably built on the site of Augustomagus, Senlis was a royal residence from the time of Clovis to Henri IV; Hugh Capet was elected 'Duc des Francs' here in 987; in 1358 it was the scene of a massacre of nobles by the Jacquerie. It was briefly in German hands in September 1914, when they set fire to some streets and plundered the town. It was also damaged in 1940.

A stretch of its medieval ramparts survives to the south east, while in the town centre is the Hôtel de Ville, rebuilt in 1495, from which the Rue du Châtel leads into the Gallo-Roman enceinte, of which 16 towers remain, although many are hidden by houses. This street also takes you past the Hôtel des Trois-Pots, first mentioned in 1292, but with a 16C façade, to the entrance to the ruined castle, the Priory of St-Maurice (14C), a hunting museum and the cathedral.

The **Cathedral** was built in 1155–84 (almost coeval with St-Denis and Notre-Dame), its south tower surmounted by a 13C spire. The central door of the west façade is embellished with statues and reliefs. The transepts were rebuilt in the mid 16C after a fire, and display Renaissance tendencies; the five east chapels and the side portals date from the same period.

The interior retains a beautiful triforium gallery, and a splendid 16C vault in the east chapel of the south transept. The late 14C chapter-house, with a remarkable central pillar, and the octagonal sacristy, a relic of the original church, are both notable.

To the east is the former Bishop's Palace, behind which is the former church of St-Pierre (now a market). It has a Flamboyant façade of 1516, one tower with a dome of Renaissance date and the other partly Romanesque, with a spire of 1432.

To the west of the town are the relics of a Gallo-Roman amphitheatre. 2.5km south east are the picturesque ruins of the **Abbaye de la Victoire**, founded by Philippe Auguste to commemorate the Battle of Bouvines (1214), and rebuilt in the 15C–16C.

41 · Fontainebleau

■ **Getting there**. Distance from Paris, 60km (40 miles). From the Gare de Lyon, there are **trains** to Fontainebleau-Avon (45 min) and from there Cars Verts (every 15 minutes) to the château. **By car**, take the A6 motorway (Porte d'Orléans/Lyon exit from the périphérique), then the N37. After the junction where the N37 joins the N7, the road crosses part of the Forêt de Fontainebleau (see below). At 7km after leaving the motorway, a crossroad leads right 1km to the village of Barbizon (see below).

■ The **Tourist Information Office** is opposite the Château at 4 Rue Royale, 77300 Fontainebleau (Seine et Marne), ☎ 01 60 74 99 99. From the Tourist Office, during the main season, are guided walks of the town (in French), rides in horse-drawn *caleche* or by *petit train*; also available for hire are audio-guides (also in English) of the château, interior and exterior.

Restaurants and cafés

Fontainebleau, 77300 (Seine-et-Marne)
Chez Arrighi, 53 Rue de France, ☎ 01 64 22 29 43. Traditional. £
Le Beauharnais, 27 Pl. Napoléon, ☎ 01 60 74 60 00. Haute cuisine. ££
La Carpe d'Or, 21bis Rue Paul Séramy, ☎ 01 64 22 28 64. £
Le Caveau des Ducs, 24 Rue de Ferrare, ☎ 01 64 22 05 05. £
Croquembouche, 43 Rue de France, ☎ 01 64 22 01 57. £
Jardin de Diane, 41 Rue Royale, ☎ 01 64 69 34 34. £
Auberge du Mont-Chauvet, Route des hauteurs de la solle, ☎ 01 64 22 93 30. £
La Route du Beaujolais, 3 Rue Montebello, ☎ 01 64 22 27 98. Bistrot Lyonnais. £
Table des Maréchaux, 9 Rue Grande, ☎ 01 64 22 20 39.
Barbizon, 77630
Auberge du Manoir Saint Hérem, 29 Grande Rue, ☎ 01 60 66 42 42. Haute cuisine. £
Les Allouettes, 4 Rue Antoine Barye, ☎ 01 60 66 41 98. ££
La Clé d'Or, 73 Grande Rue, ☎ 01 60 66 40 96. £
Hostellerie de la Dague, 5 Rue Grande, ☎ 01 60 66 40 49. £
Hostellerie Les Pléiades, 21 Rue Grande, ☎ 01 60 66 40 25. £

Fontainebleau is one of the most pleasant resorts within easy reach of Paris and popular with Parisians who want to live outside the capital. It has the dual attractions of the Château and the forest, both magnificent. Formerly the HQ of NATO, the area is internationally known for its professional and academic institutions such as the international business school, INSEAD, the Office National des Forêts, and the Ecole des Mines.

The Rue Royale and Blvd Magenta (in which there are several old mansions) converge on the Pl. du Gén. de Gaulle, in which the doorway of the Hôtel du Cardinal de Ferrara, built 1544–46, is the only surviving authentic work of architect, painter and theorist Sebastiano Serlio (restored in 1995). At 88 Rue

St-Honoré is the **Musée Napoléonien d'Art et d'Histoire Militaire**
(14.00–17.00, closed Sun and Mon).

Fontainebleau is mentioned as a royal hunting-seat in 1137, and it was
later fortified. Thomas à Becket, then in exile, consecrated the chapel of St-
Saturnin in 1169; and in 1259 Louis IX founded a monastery of
Trinitarians here. Philippe IV (le Bel) (1268–1314) was born and died here.
James V of Scotland spent December 1536 at Fontainebleau, before his
marriage with Madeleine, daughter of François I.

The Château of Fontainebleau was an important royal residence for
centuries and Napoleon also took it over, although he only used it for a short
time. As Charles VII and his successors deserted Fontainebleau for the Loire,
the château's present form is largely due to François I, who found the place
almost derelict. After 1527 he assembled a group of mainly Italian architects and artists to rebuild and decorate it, among them Sebastiano Serlio
(1475–1554), G.B. Rosso, Francesco Primaticcio (1504–70) and Nicolò
dell'Abbate, with Gilles le Breton as the chief French architect. The Italian
Mannerist style naturalised here became known as the School of
Fontainebleau, marked by its often extreme, etiolated elegance. Work
continued during the reigns of Henri II and Henri IV whose son, Louis XIII,
was born and baptised here in 1601. Both François II and Henri III were
also born at Fontainebleau.

In 1657 it was the scene of the the assassination of Monaldeschi, the
favourite of ex-Queen Christina of Sweden (see below and Avon); and Louis
XIV signed the Revocation of the Edict of Nantes here in 1685.

Napoléon I spent 12 million francs on the restoration of the Château. At
the time of his coronation in 1804 he received Pius VII at Fontainebleau;
the second visit by the Pope, from June 1812, was less auspicious, as
Napoleon forced Pius to spend 19 months as his prisoner until he
renounced temporal power. On 6 April 1814 Napoléon signed the act of
abdication here, before departing for Elba on the 20th, when he said
farewell to his Old Guard—only to return on the 20th March 1815 via
Grenoble to review his grenadiers and lead them to the Tuileries.

The château was again restored by Louis-Philippe, at enormous cost, in
neo-Renaissance style. It did not benefit by being occupied for six months in
1870–71 by the Prussians; while from 1941 it was the headquarters of
General von Brauchitsch, until liberated by General Patton in August 1944.
From 1949–66 it was the military HQ of the Allied powers in Europe. The
last important political event at the Château was the European Summit in
June 1984.

The Musée National du Château de Fontainebleau

■ Open summer: 09.30–17.00; July and Aug, 09.30–18.00; Nov–May 09.30–
12.30, 14.00–17.00; closed Tues, 1/1, 1/5. Last entry 45 minutes before
closing (☎ 01 60 71 50 70). Information panels throughout the Château are
printed in five languages. Photos permitted without flash. Access for the
handicapped to the Great Apartments.

The Château is composed of many distinct buildings erected over the centuries, mostly of two storeys. As much of the stone (local sandstone) is unsuitable for sculpture, its exterior is plain when compared to its richly decorated interior, which is described first. The Pl. du Gén. de Gaulle provides a good view of the west front of the château; the massive wrought-iron grille marks the site of a former wing which closed the courtyard. This vast space (152m by 112m), the Cour des Adieux, is where Napoléon made his farewell. Also called Cour du Cheval-Blanc, it has a horseshoe-shaped staircase of 1634 by Jean Androuet du Cerceau (which replaced one by Le Breton begun in 1531) in the main façade which dates from the 16C and is monogrammed with the F of François I. This wing, articulated by pavilions with high slate roofs, is in sandstone and rendered stone. Despite the different building phases and complex alterations, there is, at first glance, a certain conformity in the elevations by the sympathetic use of similar materials. The low wing on the left, also from the time of François I but heavily modified during the intervening time, introduces brick. The south wing, known as the Louis XV wing, which replaced the Galeries d'Ulysse demolished in 1739, is built in brick and stone to harmonise with its neighbours.

The visitors' entrance and Salle d'Acceuil with information on the château (hire of recorded commentary) and region is in the Louis XV wing, to the right of the courtyard. There is a well-stocked shop for books and souvenirs of the Château.

For the Musée Napoléon I, see below.

First floor

Follow the corridor to the Escalier de Stuc with its false marbling and, on ascending to the **first floor**, turn right to enter **room 48**, the **Galerie des Fastes**. Built by Napoléon III on the site of a stairway, it has some of the best furnishings and displays a collection of paintings, some by Oudry, against a red background. The painting by Boulanger of the *Welcome of Pius VII by Napoléon I*, shows the Portail du Baptistère, in fact topographically incorrect as the occasion took place some 5km away.

The **Galerie des Assiettes** (**room 49**), is decorated with 128 Sèvres porcelain plates (1839–44) painted with views of Fontainebleau and other royal residences and, curiously, one with a scene of Niagara Falls and another of Twickenham; the ceiling is decorated with murals on wood by Ambroise Dubois (1543–1614).

The Appartements des Reines Mères (of Pius VII) in this wing are closed for restoration.

Room 50, the **Vestibule du Fer à Cheval** (named after the courtyard), has three original massive oak doors of the Louis XIII period (17C). Off this opens **Room 51**, the gallery or tribune of the **Chapelle de la Trinité** (entirely restored in the 1980s), built for Henri II by Philibert Delorme on the site of Louis IX's foundation. Martin Fréminet, inspired by Michelangelo, was largely responsible for its sumptuous decoration (1608–14), with the vault-paintings set in ornately moulded and heavily gilded stucco frames, while the elaborate altarpiece by Francesco Bordoni (1633) surrounds a painting of the *Deposition* by Jean Dubois, Ambroise Dubois' son. It was the scene of the marriage of Louis XV and Marie Leszczynska in 1725; in 1810 of the baptism of the future Napoléon III;

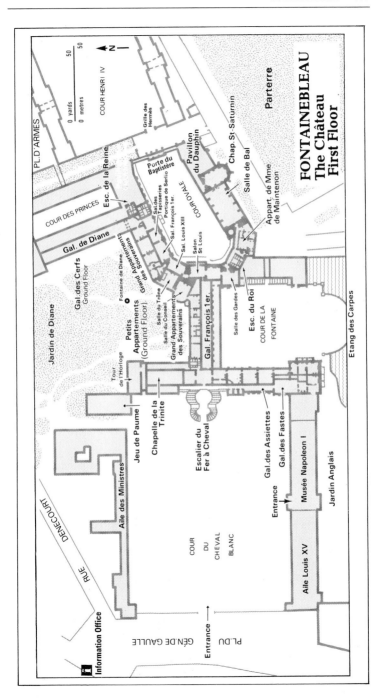

FONTAINEBLEAU
The Château
First Floor

PL.D'ARMES

COUR HENRI IV

Grille des Hermès

0 yards 50
0 metres 50

Porte du Baptistère

Pavillon du Dauphin

Chap. St-Saturnin

Parterre

Salle de Bal

Appart. de Mme de Maintenon

COUR OVALE

Esc. de la Reine

COUR DES PRINCES

Gal. de Diane

Sal. des Tapisseries
Portique de Serlio
Sal. François 1er.
Sal. Louis XIII
Salon St Louis

Jardin de Diane

Gal. des Cerfs
Ground Floor

Fontaine de Diane

Petits Appartements
(Ground Floor)

Grand Appartements des Souverains

Salle du Trône
Salle du Conseil

Grand Appartements des Souverains

Gal. François 1er.

Salle des Gardes

Esc. du Roi

COUR DE LA FONTAINE

Etang des Carpes

Tour de l'Horloge

Jeu de Paume

Chapelle de la Trinité

Escalier du Fer à Cheval

Gal. des Assiettes

Gal. des Fastes

Entrance

Musée Napoleon I

Jardin Anglais

Aile des Ministres

DENECOURT

RUE

COUR DU CHEVAL BLANC

Aile Louis XV

Information Office

PL.D.
GÉN.DE GAULLE

Entrance

and in 1837 of the marriage of Ferdinand, Duc of Orléans (1810–42; eldest son of Louis-Philippe) to Helen of Mecklenburg-Schwerin.

From the vestibule you enter the first of the **Salles Renaissance**, the 64m long **Galerie François I**, with magnificent doors, built in 1528–44, to link the chapel and the donjon. A private gallery, for which the King kept the keys, his initial and salamander device are conspicuous. The decoration is *à la française*, with wood panelling on the lower walls, and stucco, paintings and fresco above. The stucco reliefs by Rosso were completed after his death by Primaticcio, the strongest example of Italian influence in the decoration of the château, and an origin of the First School of Fontainebleau. The frescos represent allegorical and mythological scenes, with reference to the life of the king. This was restored under Napoleon III, but one painting was left to show how the gallery originally looked. Seen from the windows is the carp lake, a novelty created by Henri IV and subsequently a trend setter.

Turn right to the **Salle des Gardes** (**room 63**), completed c 1570, but redecorated in 1836, a combination of Louis XIV and Empire. This, the first of the **Grands Appartements**, retains its original frieze and ceiling (the design of which is reproduced on the marquetry floor) of the time of Henri IV. The woodwork is of the 17C. The chimneypiece, with a bust of Henri IV attributed to Matthieu Jacquet, was made up from several pieces recovered from the Belle Cheminée under the auspices of Louis-Philippe. The original furniture in this and the following suite of rooms was sold and was replaced in the first decades of the 19C. It includes a number of pieces by Alphonse Jacob-Desmalter (c 1840), placed as they were during the Second Empire.

Turn left to visit rooms (**rooms 57–62**), originally the royal suite of François I, and converted by Louis XIV into the **Appartements de Mme de Maintenon**. The Boulle commode and clock by Lepaute in the bedroom are worth examining. It is said that Louis signed the disastrous Revocation of the Edict of Nantes in the Grand Salon in 1685, and the *boiseries* are in part of that date. **Room 62** is the antechamber of the former Salle de Spectacle. This wing had formerly contained the Belle Cheminée, dismantled in 1725 when the rooms were turned into a theatre, burnt out in 1856.

The splendid 30m-long **Salle de Bal**, **room 56**, was begun by Gilles le Breton, but transformed by Delorme. It was originally an open loggia in the Italian style but glazed later, and commands the best view of the Cour Ovale and of the donjon of Louis IX. The design of the elaborate coffered walnut ceiling is reproduced on the parquet floor, a conceit of Louise-Philippe. The decor is generously endowed with the interlaced monograms of Henri II and of the Queen, Catherine de Médicis, C, which somewhat ambiguously, can also be interpreted as the D of Diane de Poitiers, the Royal mistress. Primaticcio designed, and Nicolò dell'Abbate executed in 1552 the now much-restored mythological scenes. The satyrs flanking the fireplace are copies of the originals melted down at the Revolution.

The adjacent Chapelle de St-Saturnin (1541), replacing that consecrated by Becket, and the Pavillon du Dauphin, are closed but visits may be arranged through the Tourist Office.

Return through room 54, a rotunda, and along the landing of the **Escalier du Roi**, the last part of the Château built during the Renaissance. The heavily ornate upper part of the well was formerly the bedchamber of Anne de Pisseleu, Duchesse d'Etampes, the mistress of François. But this was transformed into a staircase after a design by Gabriel in 1749. The sculptures are ascribed to Primaticcio and the frescos, in which the king is depicted as Alexander the Great in eight episodes from the life of the Macedonian hero, were painted by Niccolo dell'Abbate from Primaticcio's designs. The stucco figures are of the period of Jean Goujon. From the windows your look across the Cour Ovale to the doors of the Porte du Baptistère.

Passing through room 64, decorated with mythological scenes by Ambroise Dubois and others, you enter **room 65**, in the original keep of the castle, which was the king's bedchamber until the 17C. It was transformed in 1757, redecorated in 1836 and embellished by paintings of the 1780s depicting episodes in the life of Henri IV. The fine marble bas-relief of Henri IV à cheval (1599; by Jacquet) comes from the above-mentioned Belle Cheminée.

The **Salon Louis XIII** (**room 66**), formerly the Cabinet du Roi or Chambre Ovale, retains some of its early 17C decoration, restored in 1837, and most of its original paintings by Ambroise Dubois of *The Loves of Theagenes and Chariclea*, although three were removed in 1757 when the doors were widened to admit the voluminous dresses of the period. In this room Marie de Médicis gave birth to Louis XIII in 1601.

Room 67, the **Salon François I**, has a medallion of Venus and Adonis by Primaticcio over the chimneypiece, and on the walls are several Gobelins tapestries depicting hunting scenes. Those in the next room (room 68) illustrate the *Story of Psyche*, while the adjoining antechamber contains three of *The Seasons* (Spring is missing).

Room 70, the long (over 80m) **Galerie de Diane**, built c 1600, for Marie de Médicis to take walks during bad weather. Barrel vaulted, it was decorated with paintings illustrating the *Myth of Diana* and the *Victories of Henri IV*. During the Restoration it was transformed and since 1858 has served as a library.

From its vestibule you turn right through **room 71**, the first of the **Appartements de la Reine**, whose 18C decor was refurbished by Napoleon for Joséphine. All the rooms have been entirely restored, the fabrics and carpets rewoven and are, indeed, splendid. **Room 72**, the **Salon des Jeux** (or Salon de l'Impératrice), reproduces the original neo-classical designs of the time of Marie-Antoinette (1786) with stucco by P.-L. Roland, and contains Louis XVI combined with First Empire furniture (among it, several pieces by Jacob Frères and Jacob-Desmalter). The Fleur-de-Lys/Bee symbol chosen by Napoléon still decorates the room.

Room 73, the glitzy **Chambre de l'Impératrice** (or the Room of 19 Queens), has an ornate Louis XIV ceiling and its walls covered by silk manufactured at Lyon. Marie-Antoinette's bed, with her initial 'M', made for this room in 1787 by Sené and Laurent, was fact never used by her. It also has replicas of the the former hangings. The 19 queens who used the room included Marie de Médicis, Marie-Thérèse, Marie Leszczynska, Marie-Antoinette, Joséphine, Marie-Louise, Marie-Amélie and the Empress Eugènie. Napoléon's armchair was made specially for him and adapted to his needs. **Room 74**, the **Queen's Boudoir**, an unrestored delight with delicate painted panels, contains furniture by Riesener and Georges Jacob of 1786.

Former bedroom of Henri IV, the garishly ostentatious **Throne Room** (**room 75**), first used as such by Napoléon in 1808, served previously as the Emperor's bedchamber. This is the only Throne Room left in France with its original trappings, but the juxtaposition of two conflicting styles is somewhat incongruous. Some of the decoration dates from the mid 17C, but most of the boiseries were carved in the 1750s. Very obvious are the Savonnerie carpet, the candelabra in rock crystal by Chaumont, the standards flanking the throne surmounted by the initial N and an eagle, designed by Percier and Fontaine for St-Cloud and moved here in 1808, and the Napoleonic bees on the baldaquin. The portrait of Louis XIII is after Philippe de Champaigne.

Room 76, the richly decorated **Salle du Conseil**, is an exceptional room with a frivolous rococo decor mainly 1751–53. The five ceiling paintings are by Boucher, and represent the *Sun Beginning its Race and Chasing the Night*, and the *Four Seasons*. On the walls are are paintings *en camaïeu* (monochrome painting), framed by gilded panels, in alternate blue and pink, by Carle van Loo and J.-B. Pierre but, in harsh contrast, the furniture is First Empire. A European Summit meeting was held in this room in 1984.

Rooms 77–82, the private **Appartements de l'Empereur**, have been restored to their original splendour after years of renovations entailing the revival of almost forgotten crafts, and are the in-thing to visit at Fontainebleau. These six rooms, used by Napoléon as campaign headquarters, back onto the Grande Galerie of François I and overlook the Jardin de Diane. Originally built for Louis XVI, Napoléon took them over and had them entirely refitted from 1804. The Emperor's Bedroom, dripping with gilt and chandeliers, contains the sumptuously draped ceremonial bed for which the new fabrics are faithful copies of the originals. The **Small Bedroom** of the Emperor, showily bright green and red, contains his desk ordered from Jacob Desmalter, and his camp bed, the only one he could sleep in, with camouflage. The **Salon Particulier** contains all the original furniture of 1808, and is also known as the Abdication Room as it contains the table where he signed the Abdication on 6 April 1814. The **bathroom** is trimmed in orange fabric and the chairs in the Salle des Gardes are upholstered with Beauvais tapestry work and the carpet was remade. The Antechambre contains large paintings.

Stairs descend to the ground floor and to the lower level of the Chapel. The two-sided painting is 16C on one side and 17C on the other, on a 17C display stand.

Petits Appartements de l'Empereur et de l'Impératrice

You can visit these rooms on a guided tour, in French (☎ 01 60 71 50 70). Most of them still have their late 18C decoration and Empire furniture and were occupied by Napoléon and his staff, members of the royal family or royal mistresses. Among the furnishings are the Emperor's richly canopied bed (1804) by Jacob-Desmalter. There are other pieces by Jacob-Desmalter, Jacob-Frères, Boulle, and some attributed to Riesener. The visit also includes the Map Room and the Galerie des Cerfs decorated with stags' heads and paintings of the 1860s, when Napoléon III commissioned Alexandre Denuelle to decorate it. This was the scene of the Marquis de Monaldeschi's assassination in 1657; the chain mail he was wearing and the sword which pierced it, are on view.

Musée Napoléon I

The Musée Napoléon I, installed on two floors of the Louis XV wing (1738–74), on the south side of the Cour des Adieux, is also by guided visit only (09.30–12.30, 14.00–17.00, closed Tues.). This is devoted to the period of the First Empire (1804–15) and complements the collections at Malmaison and Bois-Préau which concentrate on the Consulate and his years on St-Helena (see p 312). Almost every room contains remarkable examples of the furniture of the period by the more eminent cabinet makers.

Evoking the period are busts and portraits of members of the Imperial family, including Gérard's portraits of *Napoléon I* and *Joséphine*, in their coronation robes, surviving regalia, robes and decorations. The Grand Vermeil, the silver-gilt *surtout* of table decoration by Henry Auguste presented by the city of Paris, and porcelain and cutlery, is on display. There are souvenirs of Marie-Louise (1791–1847), whom Napoléon married in 1810. One room concentrates on the Roi de Rome (1811–32) with, among other reminders of his childhood, his cradle, by Thomire-Duterme. Other members of the extensive Bonaparte family to whom the Emperor dispensed favours are not forgotten, and a room is devoted to his mother, Mme Mère, née Maria Letizia Ramolino (1750–1836), widowed with eight children when aged 35.

At the west of this wing, is the Théâtre Napoléon III (1857; by Hector Lefuel) incorporated here after the former theatre burnt out. Visits can be arranged through the Tourist Office.

It is possible also to take a guided visit of the restored **Musée Chinois**, containing a collection of Oriental art and the rooms of the Empress Eugénie, at the east end of this wing.

The exterior of the Château

As is evident from the visit to the interior, the Château is arranged around several main courtyards (described below except for the Cour des Princes, which cannot be visited). Each is a testament to different phases of building, and the complexity of the structure is compounded by the different names given to each courtyard according to successive episodes in its history. Starting off from the north-east corner of the Cour des Adieux, and passing the Jeu de Paume (real tennis court) on your right, the path brings you to the **Jardin de Diane** which was formerly entirely closed by an orangery built by Henri IV in brick and stone, similar to the existing building on the east, the Galeries de Diane and des Cerfs, with busts in niches, c 1600.

In the centre of the garden is a bronze **fountain** with the huntress Diana surrounded by hounds and stags' heads. The original was placed here in 1603, but suffered at the Revolution, and was partially replaced in 1813. The present Diana, unlike the 17C figure, is after an antique original, but the dogs and stags heads, recovered from the Louvre, are by Pierre Biard (1603). At the base of the Tour de l'Escalier of the building on the west side of the garden, is a doorway with Egyptian caryatids and children bearing the arms of François I.

Go around this wing, following the line of the moat, to reach the **Porte Baptistère** (Dauphine), a domed monumental entrance designed by Primaticcio for Henri IV, the entrance to the Cour Ovale. Around the original oval courtyard was the 12C castle whose donjon remains practically unaltered. In 1601, after the Court had fled Paris because of the plague, this was the scene of the baptism of Louis XIII. Opposite is a gateway of 1640, decorated with heads of Mercury by Gilles Guérin, opening onto the **Cour Henri-IV**, 1606–09. Enclosed on three sides by buildings in a combination of brick and render, these were originally the kitchens and staff quarters, distanced from the main building to minimise fire risk. The main entrance to Cour Henri IV is to the north, facing the Pl. d'Armes.

To the south of Cour Henri IV, through the central pavilion with the curved façade, is the **Grand Parterre** (Parterre du Tibre), a formal garden with ornamental ponds designed by Le Vau but divest of its pattern of box hedges. Beyond the round pool of Tiber to the south, and beyond the waterfall and canal to the east, is the Forest. On the right, past the apse of the Chapelle St-Saturnin, is the **Porte Dorée** by Le Breton, an important relic of the building campaign of François I. This, the least altered structure of the time (c 1528–40), gives an idea of the original impact of Italian Renaissance art on French architects and builders. An Italianised fortified gate is flanked by two towers, in the manner of Gaillon (Eure); most innovative are the three superimposed open bays.

A passage leads into the **Cour de la Fontaine** framed by buildings of different eras: the François I gallery, the Henri IV terrace, apartments of Henri II, the elegant building by Primaticcio with double staircase and, opposite, the large pavilion of Gabriel, built in 1750. The large dogs of Fô guard the old entrance to the Chinese rooms of Empress Eugénie. To the south and south west extends the Etang des Carpes, with its island pavilion from the time of Henri IV, rebuilt by Louis XIV and restored by Napoléon. The Jardin Anglais, laid out for Napoléon, reflects 19C fashion.

The 84-hectare **park** extends to the east of the parterre with straight alleys radiating star-shaped from a junction, bordering the canal of about 1200m long, dug by order of Henri IV.

A little way to the east, beyond the walls, is the town of **Avon**, once more important than its neighbour. The 13C–16C church contains a number of interesting tombstones, as well as the tomb of the assassinated Monaldeschi. In the cemetery lies the writer Katherine Mansfield (1888–1923) who died near here.

The Forest of Fontainebleau

The approximately 20,000 hectares Forest of Fontainebleau, known in the past as the Forest of Bière, surrounds, and is the objective of as many, if not more, visitors than the Château. It attracted royalty in the past because of its good hunting, and today it draws the crowds for the sheer beauty of its landscape, for walking and rock climbing, and for its flora and fauna. Made accessible by several good roads, there is also still space to get away. Densely wooded in parts, predominantly with oak, but also with pines, beech and birch; other parts are rocky wildernesses interspersed with sandy clearings. Some of the more picturesque sites are the **Gorges de Franchard**, for the 12C Ermitage and the view; and the **Désert d'Apremont**, for the rock formations, some 4km west and north west respectively of the Carrefour de la Libération. Also the **Heights of the Solle** for the view of the racecourse and the beeches of the Gros Fouteau. The IGN Map 401 includes this area.

Barbizon

Now a sophisticated resort of artists and celebrities, Barbizon lies 8km north-west of Fontainebleau, via the N7 (or take unmarked Routes Forestières through the forest and past the sites mentioned above). This well-manicured village liberally sprinkled with boutiques and bistrots becomes very crowded at weekends. In the mid-19C, it was the headquarters of the Barbizon group, which counted among them Millet, Théodore Rousseau, Corot, Diaz de la Peña and Daubigny. The first two were buried at Chailly-en-Bière, just north of the main road, where Bazille, Monet, Renoir, Sisley and Seurat also painted.

The **Musée de l'Auberge Ganne** opened in 1995 in the *auberge* frequented and decorated by many of these artists during the years 1848–70. The museum is open Apr–30 Sept 10.00–12.30, 14.00–18.00; Oct–30 Mar to 17.00, closed Tues; ☎ 01 60 66 22 38. A modest building, it has been imaginatively transformed into a bright exhibition area around a little garden-courtyard. On the entrance level, is an audio-visual room and three rooms evoking the *auberge* when it was run by the Ganne family. On the first floor the former bedrooms have displays recalling Barbizon at the time of the painters, with photographs, drawings, engravings and paintings. *The Painters in the Forest of Fontainebleau* by Coignet (1798–1860) sums up the importance of the surroundings to the group who pioneered painting en plein air. The walls and furniture in an upper room, decorated by the artists have been restored to make a touching souvenir of the former painter-clients. The Maison Atelier de Théodore Rousseau, further along the street, is used for temporary exhibitions.

42 · Champs sur Marne

■ **Getting there**. The Château de Champs sur Marne (77420, Seine er Marne) is not the easiest place to get to. **By car**, there are two alternatives: follow the N34 beyond Vincennes through Nogent-sur-Marne to Neuilly-sur-Marne, there turning onto the N370 for Champs-sur-Marne; or take the A4 motorway driving east from Porte de Bercy, turning off for Marne-la-Vallée and following signs for Champs.

By train. The RER provides a fast service to Marne-la-Vallée; there change to a bus for Champs-Mairie; or take train from Gare de l'Est to Chelles, there also taking a bus to Champs-Mairie.

If travelling by car, there is little of interest to see en route. The **Château de Beauté** at **Nogent**, in which Charles V died in 1380, was demolished in 1622. Charles VII gave it to Agnés Sorel and it was later occupied by Diane de Poitiers. One of the market pavilions by Baltard (1805–75) which survived the demolition in 1972 of Les Halles Centrales (see Ch. 19), was re-erected here.

The painter Antoine Watteau died at Nogent in 1721. Bry-sur-Marne, further east, was the birthplace of Louis Daguerre (1787–1851), the photographic pioneer who gave his name to the daguerrotype. Etienne de Silhouette (1709–67), the parsimonious controller-general of finances in 1759, is said to have decorated the walls of his château here with outline portraits, subsequently named after him. At Chelles stood a Merovingian palace in the 6C, where Chilperic I was murdered in 584 at the instigation of his wife Frédégone. Nothing remains of the abbey founded there in 660.

The **Château de Champs** was built in 1703–07 by J.-B. Bullet on the site of an earlier structure. It was later the residence of the Princess de Conti (daughter of Louis XIV and Louise de la Vallière) and in 1757 of Mme de Pompadour. Pillaged during the Revolution, it was restored in the 1890s and since 1934 has been used occasionally by visiting heads of state. The gardens were laid out by Claude Despots, a nephew of Le Nôtre.

From the entrance vestibule you ascend to the **first floor** and turn into the Music Room, with a frieze of instruments, and *dessus de portes* by Monnoyer: those in the Guest Room are by Boucher; those in Mme de Pompadour's Bedroom (with its painted woodwork) by Carle van Loo. The next room contains Drouais' Portrait of Mme de Pompadour as *La Belle Jardinière*, and scenes of sheep and goats by Desportes.

The Grand Salon on the **ground floor** contains furniture covered with Aubusson tapestry, and a Coromandel screen. The Dining-room, with *dessus de portes* by Desportes and Oudry, is embellished with pink marble fountains and serving tables, while a large canvas by J.-B. Martin (?) depicts a hunting scene at Champs. The Smoking-Room, with wood panelling, 18C Beauvais tapestries and a Boulle bookcase, displays Van Loo's *Portrait of Louis XV* given by the king to Mme de Pompadour. The Salon Chinois, decorated c 1740 by Christophe Huet, contains a fine chandelier, a Tabriz carpet, furniture covered with Beauvais tapestry depicting La Fontaine's fables and an onyx console table. In the adjoining room hangs Mignard's *Portrait of Louis XIV* in his minority. The Blue Room is also attractively decorated by Huet.

Some 7km further east is the **Château de Guermantes**. Its name was made familiar by Proust—*Le Côte de Guermantes* was published 1920–21 in 2 volumes, but the building, with a wing added by Robert de Cotte, is in no way connected to the novel. Some 3.5km south of Guermantes stands the **Château de Ferrières** (rebuilt in the Renaissance style for the Rothschild family by Joseph Paxton in 1857); and 3.5km east of the last, that of Jossigny, of 1743.

Disneyland Paris

12km due east of Champs, at Marne-la-Vallée is the extensive site of Disneyland Paris, a sophisticated fantasyland with all the accoutrements of rides, hotels, bars, shops, restaurants and so on, which is always open. Close enough to Paris for a day off for children and parents (RER Line A, Marne-la-Vallée-Chessy; by road, A4, exit 14.). For further information, ☎ 01 64 74 40 00 (in the UK, ☎ 0990 030 303).

7km south east of Jossigny lies **Villeneuve-le-Comte**, a planned village of 1230, with a church, standing on the edge of the Forêt de Crécy (not to be confused with that near Abbeville where the battle of 1346 took place).

Glossary of architectural terms

Acajou, mahogany
Arc-boutant, flying buttress
Archivolt, the series of mouldings which form the ensemble of an arch
Ardoises, slates
Autel, altar
Boiseries, decorative woodwork
Caissons, en, coffered
Carrefour, crossroads
Carrelages, floor tiles
Caserne, barracks
Chevet, exterior of an apse; also **abside**
Colonnette, little column for a vaulting shaft
Contreforts, buttresses
Corbels, wooden or stone projections supporting a beam or parapet, and often elaborately carved
Dessus de porte, a painting above a door
Donjon, keep
Douves, moat; wet or dry
Ebeniste, cabinet-maker
Eglise, church
Email, enamel
Escalier, staircase, à vis, spiral
Flèche, spire
Hôtel, mansion
Hôtel de Ville, town hall, also **Mairie**

Hôtel-Dieu, principal hospital in many towns
Jeu de Paume, a real tennis court
Jubé, rood-screen
Mansarde, the roof of which each face has two slopes, the lower steeper than the upper, named after the architect François Mansart (1598–1666)
Nacre, mother of pearl
Narthex, an ante-nave, porch or vestibule to a church or basilica
Nef, nave
Oeil-de-Boeuf, small circular, sometimes oval, window (bull's eye)
Piece d'eau, an expanse of water, usually ornamental
Porte-cochère, carriage gateway
Poutres, beams or joists
Rez de Chaussée, ground floor
Tierceron, curved rib in Gothic vaults springing from the same point as the intersecting diagonal rib, and rising to the end of the ridge-rib
Tympanum, space, often decorated, between door lintel and arch
Vermeil, silver-gilt
Vitrail, stained-glass window
Voussoires, wedge-shaped stones used in constructing arches or vaults

Historical Introduction

The Romans

The foundations of modern France may be said to date from the crossing of the Alps by the Romans in 121 BC and the establishment of the province (Latin provincia; modern Provence) of Gallia Narbonensis. Important remains such as the Pont du Gard and the theatres and amphitheatres at Nîmes, Arles and Orange are still extant. But the whole of France as we now know it did not become subject to Rome until after Julius Caesar's decisive defeat of Vercingetorix at Alésia in 52 BC. In the previous year Caesar had first mentioned—under the name of *Lutetia*—the fortified capital of the Parisii, an insignificant Gallic tribe, confined on islands in the Seine, which he nominated as the rendezvous of deputies from conquered Gaul. Lyon, however, was the Roman capital of Gaul throughout.

In spite of occasional local revolts, Rome gradually imposed her government, roads, speech and culture on Gaul. By c AD 300 the country had become partially Christianised, St Dionysius (Denis) being its first bishop, but by then a series of Barbarian invasions began. In 292 Paris became a base of the Emperor Constantius Chlorus, and then more importantly for the Emperor Julian the Apostate (356–60), although it was not until 360 that the name was applied to the river-port. Barbarian mercenaries (among them Visigoths and Burgundians) were employed to defend the frontiers of the Empire in its decline, but they wearied of their alliance with the degenerate Gallo-Romans, and after the repulse of Attila and his Huns at the Chalon (451) became virtually masters of the land, the most powerful tribe being the Salian Franks under their legendary leader Merovius.

The Merovingians

Merovius's grandson Clovis I (481–511) defeated Syagrius (the Roman governor of Soissons) in 486, and the Alemanni at Tolbiac in 496, after which he adopted the Christian religion. In the following year Paris opened her gates to him (traditionally on the advice of Ste. Geneviève), although he did not make it his official capital until 508. According to Frankish custom, the kingdom was divided on his death between his three sons into Austrasia (between the Meuse and the Rhine), Neustria (the territory to the northwest, from the Meuse to the Loire) and Burgundy (to the south), and although the Merovingians remained in control, the dynasty was weakened by internecine warfare during the next two centuries.

Eminent among the Merovingians was Chilperic I (king of Neustria from 561–84) and Dagobert (king of Austrasia from 622 and of all France from 628 until his death in 638). Paris remained the political centre of conflicting Frankish interests, its growing population overflowing to form suburbs around monasteries situated on both banks of the river; but after the death of Dagobert, who refounded the abbey of St-Denis, most of the power passed into the hands of the '*maires du Palais*', one of whom, Charles Martel (714–41), an Austrasian, was to defeat the invading Moors at Poitiers in 732. In 751 Pepin, Martel's son, deposed Childéric III, the last of the Merovingians, and founded a new dynasty.

The Carolingians

Pepin, le Bref (751–68)
Charlemagne (768–814)
Louis I, the Pious (814–40)
Charles, le Chauve (the Bald;
  840–77)
Louis II, le Bègue (the Stammerer;
  877–79)
Louis III (879–82)
Carloman (882–87)

Charles, le Gros (the Fat; 884–87)
Count Eudes (887–98)
Charles, le Simple (898–923)
Louis IV, d'Outremer (Beyond the Sea;
  936–54)
Lothaire (954–86)
Louis V, le Fainéant (the Lazy;
  86–87)

Although Pepin resided occasionally at Paris, his son Charlemagne, in alliance with the Pope, extended his dominion over Germany and Italy, and was crowned 'Emperor of the West', or 'Holy Roman Emperor'. He moved the seat of government from France to Aix-la-Chapelle (present-day Aachen). Not only a great ruler, Charlemagne also presided over a remarkable revival of learning and education. However, the system of dividing territories on the death of kings was to cause the eventual disintegration of the empire, and in 843, by the Treaty of Verdun, those areas which were to form modern France were transferred to his grandson Charles 'le Chauve'. Further division ensued, and France became little more than a collection of independent feudal states controlled by dukes and counts.

The situation was further disturbed by the invasion of Scandinavian or Norse pirates. By 912 the Vikings had settled in Rouen and had carved out the duchy of Normandy for themselves, in 885 having besieged and pillaged Paris itself from their encampment (possibly on the present site of the Louvre). The Cité had been defended by Eudes, Duc de France and comte de Paris, who in 888 deposed Charles 'le Gros', but the Carolingian dynasty staggered on for another hundred years. It was a century of disunity for France, distinguished politically by the growth of Norman power, and religiously by the foundation in 910 of a Benedictine abbey at Cluny, soon to gain fame and influence.

Capetians

Hugues Capet (987–96)
Robert, le Pieux (996–1031)
Henri I (1031–60)
Philippe I (1060–1108)
Louis VI, le Gros (1108–37)
Louis VII, le Jeune (1137–80)
Philippe Auguste (1180–1223)
Louis VIII, le Lion (1223–26)
Louis IX (St. Louis; 1226–70)
Philippe III, le Hardi (the Bold;
  1270–85)

Philippe IV, le Bel (the
  Handsome/Fair; 1285–1314)
Louis X, le Hutin (the Quarrelsome;
  1314–16)
Jean I (1316; died 4 days old)
Philippe V, le Long (the Tall;
  1316–22)
Charles IV, le Bel (1322–28)

Hugh Capet was elected by the nobles at Senlis in preference to any more incapable Carolingians, and he and his successors proceeded to make Paris the centre of their tiny 'royal domain'—at first only the Ile de France. But this policy frequently brought them into conflict with independent spirits, one of whom, William, duke of Normandy, in 1066 invaded and conquered England. Paris grew steadily in size and importance, particularly on the North Bank, and during the reign of Louis VI, if not earlier, a second town wall was thrown up. The 'Hanse Parisienne', a league of merchants, was established, marking the foundation of the municipality.

The marriage in 1152 of the future Henry II of England to Eleanor of Aquitaine (the divorced wife of Louis VII), whose dowry brought Henry about one-third of France, was to cause a power struggle between the two countries which lasted three centuries. In 1095 Urban II preached the First Crusade at Clermont; in 1198 the Abbey of Cîteaux was founded; in c 1115 Clairvaux was founded by St. Bernard, who in 1146 was to preach the Second Crusade at Vézelay. In 1163 the foundation-stone of **Notre-Dame** was laid and some years later Philippe Auguste built the fortress of the Louvre. This religious enthusiasm was in part the reason for the expulsion of the Jews. The cathedral schools of Paris (at which Guillaume de Champeaux and Abélard had taught) were united to form one **University**, which was granted its first statutes by Pope Innocent III in 1208. This was established on the **Left Bank** of the Seine, where the growing student population settled; the **Right Bank** became the centre of commerce, industry and administration. Some streets were paved; the two ancient wooden bridges were replaced by ones of stone; and the city was enclosed by an extensive line of fortifications.

In the political field **Philippe Auguste** won back a large part of the lost provinces (Normandy and Anjou), inflicting a heavy defeat on the allies of John of England at Bouvines in 1214. The bloody Albigensian Crusade of 1209–13 eventually delivered Languedoc to French rule. During the long reign of **Louis IX**, the **Hospice des Quinze-Vingts** and the theological college of the **Sorbonne** were founded, the latter to become a dominant influence in the University. The **Palais de la Cité** was rebuilt (parts of which, notably the Sainte-Chapelle, still exist), and the office of Provost was reformed; statutes were drawn up for the many guilds, which were to remain in force until the Revolution. Louis, canonised in 1297, was a great crusader, and eventually lost his life at Tunis. With the death of Charles IV in 1328 the direct branch of the Capetian dynasty became extinct.

House of Valois

Philippe VI(1328–50)
Jean II, le Bon (the Good; 1350–64)
Charles V, le Sage (the Wise; 1364–80)
Charles VI, le Bien-Aimé (the Well-beloved; 1380–1422)
Charles VII, le Victorieux (1422–61)
Louis XI (1461–83)

Charles VIII, l'Affable (1483–98)
Louis XII, le Père du Peuple (1498–1515)
François I (1515–47)
Henri II (1547–59)
François II (1559–60)
Charles IX (1560–74)
Henri III (1574–89)

The claim of Philippe de Valois to the throne was disputed by Edward III of England, who invaded France, precipitating the **Hundred Years War**

(1337–1453). He routed the French army at Crécy (1346) and inflicted a further defeat on Jean II at Poitiers in 1356. The ravages and depredations of both French and English soldiery roused the peasants (the Jacquerie) and the burgesses to revolt. In Paris, **Etienne Marcel** (Maire du Palais and provost of the merchants) took advantage of the situation to increase the influence of the municipality, but he offended public opinion by attempting to hand over the city to Charles of Navarre, and was assassinated in 1358. Two years later, by the Treaty of Brétigny, England reduced her claims only to Aquitaine and Calais, but before long desultory warfare between the two countries broke out again and continued until the French had won back a large part of their lost territory, largely due to the tactics of Du Guesclin.

Charles V was able to bring back some order to the kingdom. He built the fortress of the **Bastille**, but anarchy returned during the following reign, when his weak-minded son **Charles VI** provoked the citizens of Paris—at that time numbering some 280,000—by excessive taxation. Although the resulting revolt of the 'Maillotins' was bloodily suppressed, the king became the pawn of rival regents and for the next 40 years France suffered from dissensions between the aristocratic party, the Armagnacs, and the Burgundians, the popular party (Jean II had made his fourth son, Jean sans Peur, Duke of Burgundy).

Seizing the opportunity, **Henry V of England** invaded France, and supported by the Burgundians, defeated a French force at Agincourt (1415). By the Treaty of Troyes (1420) he received the hand of Catherine, Charles VI's daughter, together with the right of succession to the throne. But in 1422 Henry died at Vincennes, only seven weeks before the death of Charles VI. **Charles VII**, by himself no match for the English and Burgundians, found a champion in **Jeanne d'Arc** (Joan of Arc; 1412–31). But the English continued to control Paris until 1436. In 1429 John, Duke of Bedford repelled an assault led by Joan, who, after a brilliant campaign, defeated the English at Orléans in May of that year. Captured at Compiègne by the Burgundians in 1430, she was handed over to the English, condemned as a heretic by a court of ecclesiastics, and burned at the stake in Rouen. But the successful revolt she had inspired continued, and by 1453 only Calais remained of the once extensive English possessions in France. A vivid account of conditions prevailing in Paris during the years 1405–49 is given in the anonymously compiled 'Journal d'un Bourgeois de Paris'. The poet Villon was born here in 1431.

With the reign of **Louis XI** the change from a medieval social system to the modern state was accelerated. A brilliant and unscrupulous politician (and relieved of the menace of England, then occupied with the domestic 'War of the Roses'), he proceeded to crush the great feudal lordships which encroached on his territory, the most threatening being that of **Charles the Bold** ('le Téméraire') of Burgundy. The Peace of Péronne (1468) gave the Burgundians a momentary advantage, but Louis managed to win over Charles' English allies by the Treaty of Picquigny (1475). After Charles' death before the walls of Nancy in 1477, Louis soon overwhelmed his lesser adversaries, and brought Arras, the Franche-Comté, Anjou, and Maine into direct allegiance to the crown. In 1469/70 the first printing-press in France was set up in the Sorbonne; and in 1484 the first meeting of the Estates-General was convened at Tours, near which, in the Loire valley, several châteaux were being rebuilt as royal residences.

The following half century was principally occupied with indecisive campaigns in Italy, the only tangible result of which—particularly during the reign of François I—was the establishment in France of the cultural concepts of the Italian Renaissance. Among the more important literary figures of the period were Marot, Rabelais, Du Bellay, and Ronsard, the last two being members of the poetic circle known as La Pléïade.

Charles VIII and **Louis XII** were successive husbands of **Anne de Bretagne**, whose dowry, the important duchy of Brittany, was formally united to France in 1532 on the death of her daughter, wife of François I. The reign of **Henri II** saw the acquisition by France of the Three Bishoprics (Metz, Toul, and Verdun), while Calais fell to the Duc de Guise in 1558. In 1559 Henri II concluded the treaty of Cateau-Cambrésis with Felipe II of Spain, thus ending the Italian wars. In 1564 an edict fixed the beginning of the year as 1 January, inaugurating the 'new style' of dating.

The short reign of **François II**, who while still dauphin (aged ten) had married Mary Stuart, Queen of Scots, was followed by that of his brother **Charles IX**. At the instigation of **Catherine de Médicis** (1519–89), his bigoted and domineering mother, Charles signed the order for the massacre of protestant Huguenots on the Eve of St Bartholomew (23 August 1572). (Catherine was mother also of Henri III, and of Marguerite de Valois, the first wife of Henri of Navarre.) From 1560 until the promulgation of the Edict of Nantes in 1598, the country was ravaged, sporadically, by the Religious Wars of the League (La Ligue). In 1588 the ultra-Catholic Henri, Duc de Guise, was murdered at Blois by **Henri III**, against whom he had been an overt rebel. The king himself was assassinated at St-Cloud the following year.

House of Bourbon

Henri IV, le Grand (1589–1610)	Louis XVI (1774–92)
Louis XIII, le Juste (1610–43)	Louis XVII (never reigned)
Louis XIV, 'le Roi Soleil'(1643–1715)	Louis XVIII (1814–24)
Louis XV, le Bien-Aimé (1715–74)	Charles X (1824–30)

The parents of **Henri IV** (of Navarre) were Jeanne d'Albret (daughter of Marguerite of Navarre) and Antoine de Bourbon, of the Bourbon branch of the Capetian dynasty, descending from Robert of Clermont, sixth son of Louis IX. A Protestant, Henri eventually defeated the Catholics at Ivry (1590), but was unable to enter the besieged capital until 1594, after he had ostensibly abjured his faith with (it is said) the cynical remark that '*Paris vaut bien une messe*'. Despite his conversion, he granted Protestants freedom of worship by the Edict of Nantes. Among the many who joined in the general recognition of Henri as the legitimate heir to the throne was Montaigne, whose '*Essays*' were published in part in 1580.

Peace established, Henri set about enlarging the **palaces of the Louvre** and the **Tuileries**, planned several squares including the Place Royale, and completed the Pont Neuf. However, with his assassination by Ravaillac in 1610, religious restlessness returned, and the admirable reforms and economies instituted by the **Duc de Sully** (1560–1641), his able minister, were brought to nothing by the extravagant favourites of young **Louis XIII** (whose mother,

Marie de Médicis, Henri had married in 1600 after his divorce from Marguerite de Valois). On Henri's death, Marie became Regent, but in 1624 **Cardinal Richelieu** (1585–1642) took over the reins of government. His main aim was the establishment of absolute royal power in France, and of French supremacy in Europe. He suppressed all Protestant influence in politics, capturing their stronghold, La Rochelle, in 1628. Anyone defying Richelieu suffered severe penalties, and numerous fortresses throughout the country were dismantled in the process of repression. The cardinal then turned his attention to the Habsburg power, which since the reign of Emperor Charles V had surrounded the frontiers of France, and, in alliance with Gustavus Adolphus of Sweden, Richelieu involved France in the Thirty Years War. The campaigns of the Grand Condé (1621–86; a member of a collateral branch of the Bourbons) resulted in the temporary acquisition of Picardy, Alsace and Roussillon.

In 1635 and 1640 respectively, the **Académie Française** and the Imprimerie Royal were founded; a fifth wall was erected around Paris, where several new quarters arose, such as the **Pré-aux-Clercs** (Faubourg St-Germain), the **Ile-St-Louis** and the **Marais**, which became a favourite residence of the nobility. Marie de Médicis built the **Palais du Luxembourg**; Anne of Austria, consort of the king since 1614, founded the church of **Vâl-de-Grace** in thanksgiving for the birth of a son (later Louis XIV) in 1638; and Richelieu built for himself the Palais-Cardinal, later the **Palais-Royal**.

Richelieu had been succeeded meanwhile by **Cardinal Mazarin** (1602–61), who carried on his predecessor's policies. Although France was assured of the possession of Alsace and the Three Bishoprics by the Treaty of Westphalia in 1648, the expenses of campaigning were crippling. Civil war broke out, known as 'La Fronde', from which no one—the insurgents, Mazarin, Condé or Marshal Turenne (1611–75)—emerged with much credit. During the Fronde, Condé (who had defeated the Spaniards at Recroi in 1643), allied himself with Spain (who had not subscribed to the Treaty of Westphalia), but Turenne's victory at the Battle of the Dunes (1658) forced Spain to accept the Treaty of the Pyrenees the following year.

On Mazarin's death in 1661 **Louis XIV**, who had succeeded as a minor in 1643, decided to govern alone, duped by the conviction that '*L'État c'est moi*'. The nobility were reduced to being ineffectual courtiers, and the king selected his ministers from the *haute bourgeoisie*, some, such as **Colbert** (1619–83), being very able. He then launched a series of costly wars of self-aggrandisement, which although they eventually increased the territory of France—its frontiers fortified by Vauban (1633–1707)—were to bring his long reign to a disastrous close. At the same time his indulgence in such extravagant projects as the building of a palace fit for the 'Roi Soleil' at **Versailles** (extended by Hardouin-Mansart, with gardens laid out by Le Nôtre and its lavish decoration supervised by Le Brun), where Louis had chosen to transfer his court in 1672, further beggared the country. At Versailles most of the great artists of this and succeeding reigns were gathered, while among composers Lully (from 1652 until his death in 1687), Couperin and (in the following reign) Rameau provided music to entertain the court.

In Paris, which had now grown to a metropolis containing some 500,000 inhabitants and 25,000 houses, boulevards were laid out on the lines of Etienne Marcel's wall. The **Hôtel des Invalides** was founded in 1671. The University quarters were incorporated within the city, which had become one of the cultural centres of Europe—Corneille, Molière, La Fontaine, Boileau and Pascal (the latter associated with the activities of the reforming Jansenists of Port-Royal) making their home there—while the salons of Mme de Rambouillet and Mme de Sablé, among others, had become the influential intellectual rendezvous of such figures as La Rochefoucauld, the Scudérys, and Bossuet. Meanwhile, in 1685, Louis had revoked the Edict of Nantes, which again imposed Catholicism on the whole country.

The king's preoccupation with 'La Gloire' involved him first in the rapid campaign of 1667–68, which secured the possession of several towns in Flanders; while the Dutch War of 1672–78 ended in the Peace of Nijmegen and the absorption of the Franche-Comté. Less successful were the campaigns against the League of Augsburg (or the Grand Alliance; 1686–97), and of the war of the Spanish Succession (1701–13), in which French forces suffered repeatedly at the hands of Marlborough and Prince Eugène (at Blenheim in 1704; Ramillies in 1706; Oudenaarde in 1708; and Malplaquet in 1709), although Marshal Villars won a victory at Denain (1712) after the withdrawal of the English from the war.

'If greatness of soul consists in a love of pageantry, an ostentation of fastidious pomp, a prodigality of expense, an affectation of munificence, an insolence of ambition, and a haughty reserve of deportment; Lewis certainly deserved the appellation of Great. Qualities which are really heroic, we shall not find in the composition of his character.' Such was Smollett's condemnation. Life at court during the latter part of the reign and subsequent regency (under Philippe, duc d'Orléans; 1715–23) is brilliantly recorded in the 'Mémoires' of the Duc de Saint-Simon. Several bad harvests (particularly in 1726, 1739 and 1740) decimated the peasantry—who formed four-fifths of the population of 20,000,000 in 1700—but colonial trade improved, and merchants thrived in such provincial centres as Bordeaux, Nantes, and Marseille.

The marriage in 1725 of **Louis XV** to Marie, daughter of Stanislas Leszczynski (the deposed king of Poland) drew France into the War of the Polish Succession (1733) and further ruinous wars followed, including that of the Austrian Succession (1740-48) (in which Louis was allied with Frederick the Great of Prussia in opposition to England and Holland, who supported the cause of Maria Theresa, Empress of Austria). In spite of Saxe's brilliant victory at Fontenoy (1745) the French gained little, while the English improved their position as a maritime power, and Prussia likewise gained in strength. The Seven Years War (1756–63), in which France was allied to Austria, was disastrous for France, and saw the loss of flourishing colonies in India, North America and the West Indies. By 1788 the cost of these wars had created a situation whereby three-quarters of the State expenditure was being spent on reducing the national debt and on defence.

Nevertheless, grandiose buildings continued to be erected in Paris, such as the **Panthéon** and the **Palais-Bourbon**; but a sixth wall, raised as a customs-barrier by the powerful and rapacious farmers-general of taxes, only fostered further discontent ('Le mur murant Paris rend Paris murmurant'). In contrast to the general degradation of his court and the corruption and negligence rife among his administrators, the reign of Louis XV was made illustrious by some of the great names in French literature: Voltaire, Rousseau, Montesquieu, Marivaux, the Encyclopédistes (Diderot, Condillac, Helvetius, d'Alembert, et al), who frequented the fashionable salons of the Marquise de Lambert, Mme de Tencin, Mme du Deffand, Mlle Lespinasse, Mme Geoffrin, or Baron d'Holbach, and others of lesser influence. But many of the philosophers vehemently attacked both the establishment and the clergy, and their ideas undoubtedly helped to sow the seeds of revolution. At the same time the expulsion of the Jesuits in 1764, after years of struggle with the Jansenists, removed one of the pillars of the Ancien Régime.

On his succession **Louis XVI** found the populace critical of his predecessor's extravagance and lack of military success, but was too weak to cope with the interminable financial crises (in spite of the reforms initiated by Turgot from 1774 and of Necker from 1777). 'This man is rather weak but not imbecile, but there is something apathetic about both his body and his mind he has no taste for instruction and no curiosity', wrote the Austrian Emperor Joseph I, after visiting his brother-in-law, while he urged Marie-Antointette to abandon 'the vortex of dissipation around her' and seek 'rational company', prophetically remarking that otherwise 'the revolution will be cruel'. Economic problems were precipitated by bad harvests, particularly in 1787–88, when there were grain riots in many French towns, including Paris and Grenoble. These crises inspired reforms, which, if accepted, would have adversely affected the privileged estates ('Les Privilégiés')—the upper ranks of the clergy (the First Estate), and the majority of the nobility (the Second Estate)—who therefore rejected them. Louis' foreign policy, which supported the American colonies in their struggle for independence from England, was not only financially disastrous, but indirectly did much to disseminate democratic ideals.

In an attempt to reform methods of taxation—for Les Privilégiés held innumerable hereditary rights by which they avoided paying taxes, yet levied them to their own advantage—the king convoked an assembly of the Etats généraux. The 1165 deputies elected met at Versailles on 5 May 1789, for the first time since 1614. The first political act of the Third Estate, the Non-Privilégiés (which numbered almost 600) was the creation of a **National Assembly** (17 June), which, meeting separately in the Jeu de Paume on the 20th, swore not to disband until a constitution had been given to the country which would limit royal autocracy and guarantee liberty, equality and fraternity. Three days later Mirabeau defied the king: '*Nous sommes ici par la volonté du peuple etêon ne nous arrachera que par la force des baïonnettes*'; and on 9 July, reinforced by many of the clergy and a minority of the nobility, the renamed Assemblée constituante set to work to frame such a constitution. But two days later Necker, who had promised further financial reforms, was dismissed by the king, and it was feared that this gratuitous act would be followed by the dissolution of the Assembly.

The Revolution

The citizens of Paris—and also in the provinces at Dijon, Rennes, Lyon, Nantes, and Le Havre—were provoked into a more open rebellion, culminating in the storming of the Bastille on 14 July; but while the next few months saw numerous reforms, there was little political or economic stability, and tensions heightened. In an attempt to avoid bankruptcy, church lands were nationalised, which produced some opposition. Many of the nobility—a class shortly, but temporarily, to be abolished—sought asylum abroad. The king and his unpopular consort, **Marie-Antoinette**, were virtually prisoners in the Tuileries; they attempted to flee the country but were arrested (at Varennes in June 1791) and brought back to Paris. On 1 October 1791 a new Legislative Assembly was formed, which in the following April declared war on Austria to forestall foreign intervention. The Assembly was at first led by the moderate Girondins, but the following year the extreme Jacobins under Danton, Robespierre and Marat, seized power and, as the National Convention, meeting on 20 September (the day on which the victory of Valmy turned the tide of war in France's favour), established the Republic.

On 21 January 1793 Louis XVI was executed in the Place de la Révolution, an act followed by the setting-up in March of the dictatorial Committee of Public Safety, which, suspicious of the moderate party, ruthlessly suppressed all those suspected of royalist sympathies. The guillotine was in constant action. In July Marat was assassinated, and even the Dantonists found themselves to be a moderating force, opposed to the even more bloodthirsty Hébertists. But **Robespierre** (1758–94), chief architect of the Reign of Terror, brooked no rivals, and early in 1794 both Hébert and Danton were guillotined. However, after further weeks of ferocious intimidation, the reaction came and on 27 July (9 Thermidor; see below), Robespierre's own head fell.

By 1795 the Girondins were again in control, although the Royalists continued to make determined efforts to change the course of events, particularly in the Vendée, where they were eventually suppressed by Hoche. On 28 October 1795 a Directory of five members assumed power. One of the five was Barras, to whom the young Corsican general, **Napoléon Bonaparte** (1769–1821), owed his promotion as general of the Interior. During the next four years French republican armies under Bonaparte won notable successes abroad, especially in campaigns against the Austrians (whom he was to crush at Marengo on 14 June, 1800). Returning to Paris after his failure to destroy the British fleet at the Battle of the Nile, Bonaparte found the tyrannical Directory generally detested, and with the help of the army and of Siéyès, established the Consulate by a coup d'état on 9–10 November 1799. Bonaparte became First Consul, assisted by Siéyès and Roger Ducos. A new constitution awarded him the consulate for life but such was his personal ambition that he declared himself 'Emperor of the French', and was crowned Napoléon I (1804–15) in Notre-Dame by Pope Pius VII (18 May 1804). A Civil Code, largely retaining the liberal laws of the Revolution, was laid down. Paris was embellished with monuments and bridges, as befitted the capital of an expanding empire, and was further enriched by the spoils of conquest.

First Empire

Faced by a new coalition of Britain, Austria, and Russia, Napoléon shattered the last two at Austerlitz in 1805, and imposed on them the humiliating Peace of Pressburg, but his fleet had been virtually destroyed at Trafalgar only six weeks earlier. In the following year Prussian armies were cowed at Jena and Auerstadt, and a further campaign against Russia was ended by the Treaty of Tilsit, which brought temporary peace to the Czar. Austria attempted to renew the struggle, but suffered disastrous defeats at Essling and Wagram. The subsequent Peace of Vienna (1809) marked perhaps the apogee of the emperor's power.

Meanwhile, his brother Joseph had been imposed on the Spaniards, whose guerrilla methods of carrying on the war in the Peninsula caused a continual drain on Napoléon's reserves of power. Britain sent out two expeditionary forces to assist the incapable Spaniards, and under Wellington they inflicted a series of defeats on the French, among them Salamanca, and culminating in the battles of Vitoria (1813) and—on French territory—Toulouse.

Napoléon himself had just returned from the disastrous invasion of Russia, where the 'Grande Armée' although successful at Borodino, was virtually annihilated by the winter. The Prussians, recovered from their previous defeats, were able to retaliate at Leipzig (October 1813), and with the Russians and Austrians entered France. Paris itself surrendered to the Allies (31 March 1814) after skirmishing on the heights of Montmartre. The emperor abdicated at Fontainebleau, and retired to the island of Elba.

The Monarchy restored

The **Bourbons** were restored, but the Treaty of Paris (30 May 1814) restored the frontiers of 1789. During 'the Hundred Days' (26 March–24 June 1815), Napoléon made a desperate attempt to regain absolute power, having claimed at Grenoble (en route to Paris from Elba) that he had come to deliver France from 'the insolence of the nobility, the pretensions of the priests and the yoke of foreign powers'. His defeat at Waterloo (18 June) and subsequent banishment to St Helena, where he died in 1821, enabled the king—**Louis XVIII**—to resume his precarious throne, which he was only able to retain by repressive measures: the University was supervised by the clergy. The reign of his successor, **Charles X** (1824–30), under whom were passed the reactionary Ordinances of St-Cloud, suppressing the liberty of the press and reducing the electorate to the landed classes, only proved that the Bourbons could 'learn nothing and forget nothing'. The '**July Revolution**' of 1830 lost him his throne.

House of Orléans. **Louis-Philippe** (1830–48; son of Philippe-Egalité d'Orléans of the Revolution) was chosen as head of the 'July Monarchy', and the upper-middle class, who had striven for power since 1789, now achieved it. Most of the urban populace, however, still lived in pestilential conditions: some 19,000 Parisians of a total of about 900,000 died in an outbreak of cholera in 1832. The total population of France was then about 32,500,000. The only other towns of any size were Lyon and Marseille, with about 115,000 each, and Bordeaux and Rouen with about 90,000 each. France was still essentially a country dominated by agriculture and by a rural population.

The king devoted himself, with perhaps more energy than taste, to the further embellishment of the capital, and many pretentious buildings date from this period. Gas lighting had first been installed there in 1814. In 1840 the body of Napoléon was transferred with much pomp to its last resting-place under the Dôme des Invalides. The city was surrounded by a ring of fortifications in 1841–45, but these could not defend the 'citizen-king' against his people. Socialist ideas were spreading, but the conservative policy of Guizot opposed any reforms, and in the '**February Revolution**' of 1848 Louis-Philippe was overthrown. In June 1848, during the brief military dictatorship of Géneral Cavaignac, some 4000 workmen were killed, another 1500 shot, and 11,000 imprisoned or deported to Algeria. In the elections which followed, which introduced universal male suffrage, the electorate leapt from 250,000 to 9,000,000. Among famous literary figures during the first half of the century were Balzac,

Chateaubriand, Hugo, George Sand, Stendhal, Flaubert, Gautier, and Sainte-Beuve.

The Second Republic

A Second Republic was set up by the provisional government, and **Louis Napoléon** (Bonaparte's shrewd and cynical nephew, who as pretender had already made two abortive attempts to regain the throne), was elected Prince-President by almost 75 per cent of those who voted; but such was the sentimental prevalence of the idea of Empire, that in December 1851 a coup d'état (involving the temporary imprisonment of some 30,000 in opposition) led to his election as the Emperor Napoléon III (1852–70) some months later, thus inaugurating the Second Empire.

Having adopted the clever but misleading motto of '*L'Empire c'est la paix*', he proceeded to embroil the country in a succession of wars, firstly in the Crimea (1854–56), and then in Italy, which he undertook to deliver from Austrian oppression, afterwards receiving Savoy and Nice in recompense. But he stopped Garibaldi and his followers capturing Rome. Meanwhile he continued the expedient policy of his predecessor, by clearing the mass of congested, evil-smelling, and tortuous lanes of old Paris, which had so favoured the erection of barricades in 1830 and 1848 and the spread of cholera. In their place Baron Haussmann laid out a number of broad boulevards which are still characteristic of much of the centre, while from 1861 Garnier's Opera-house, representative of the expansive taste of the time, was being built, and the Bois de Boulogne and the Bois de Vincennes were transformed into public parks.

But these peaceful projects were halted abruptly in 1870 when Napoléon III declared war on Prussia. The inglorious campaign ended with the capitulation of Sedan, where the emperor was taken prisoner and deposed. He died in exile at Chislehurst (England) in 1873.

Third Republic

Presidents

1871–73 Adolphe Thiers	1906–13 Armand Fallières
1873–79 Maréchal MacMahon	1913–20 Raymond Poincaré
1879–87 Jules Grévy	1920 Paul Deschanel
1887–94 Sadi Carnot	1920–24 Alexandre Millerand
1894–95 Jean Casimir-Périer	1924–31 Gaston Doumergue
1895–99 Félix Faure	1931–32 Paul Doumer
1899–1906 Émile Loubet	1932–40 Albert Lebrun

Léon Gambetta and **Adolphe Thiers** were largely instrumental in forming the Third Republic, which had been proclaimed (4 September 1870) while German troops advanced on Paris, which was laid siege to on 19 September, its defenders commanded by Trochu. After a four-month siege and much suffering and famine, Paris capitulated on 28 January 1871. At this time the fortified enceinte of Paris almost 34km long, and had 67 entrances or gates. A circle of 17 detached fortresses were built at strategic points beyond this boundary wall. The Louvre had been turned into an armament workshop, the Gare d'Orléans (now Austerlitz) into a balloon factory, and the Gare de Lyon into a cannon-foundry; but the army was ill-prepared. Order was not re-established until the Communard Insurrection (18 March–29 May) had been crushed at the cost of pitched battles in the streets, in which 3000–4000 Communards were killed, and the destruction of parts of the Tuileries and other public buildings such as the Hôtel de Ville. Retaliatory measures included the summary execution of 20,000–25,000 Parisians, including women, mostly of the working classes; and the deportation of a further 4000–5000. Thiers, who was ultimately responsible for these mass killings, was then declared Président. An amnesty bill, introduced by Gambetta, was not adopted until 1880.

By September 1873 the last occupying troops had gone, but France was left to pay a heavy war indemnity and lost the provinces of Alsace and Lorraine. Various political crises, embittered by the reprehensible 'Dreyfus affair' (1894–1906), in which Alfred Dreyfus was falsely accused of betraying France to a foreign government, coloured much of the period up to the outbreak of the First World War. An 'Entente Cordiale' between Britain and France was established in 1904, putting an end to colonial rivalry and paving the way to future co-operation. In 1903 the '*Loi sur les Associations*' was passed, and in 1905 the Church was separated from the State, both essential measures to counteract the powerful influence the ecclesiastics and religious orders still had on education. During these decades building continued apace and the economy continued to grow. The '**Grand Palais**' and '**Petit Palais**', a new **Hôtel de Ville**, the **Gare d'Orsay**, the **Eiffel Tower** and the basilica of **Sacré-Coeur** exemplify the taste of an age, differing facets of which were well described by Zola and later by Proust. In 1910 extensive areas of Paris were inundated by the flooding of the Seine.

Two World Wars

War with Germany broke out on 3 August 1914. French troops were dramatically reinforced at the Marne by some 11,000 men rushed to the front in Parisian taxis: citizens had the satisfaction of hearing the din of battle gradually recede and little damage was done to the capital by air raids or long-range bombardment. But although Paris was saved from another occupation, ten departments were overrun, and the attrition of four long years of trench warfare followed with the Battle of the Somme, culminating in the terrible bloodbath of Verdun in 1916. On 11 November 1918 an armistice was signed. The provinces lost to France through the Treaty of Versailles in 1871 were restored, although **Clemenceau**, the 'Tiger', France's Prime Minister, wanted more. Nothing, however, could compensate for the staggering loss of life during the war years. For every ten Frenchmen aged between 20 and 45, two had been killed—a total of over 1,300,000. Slowly, and only partially, the country recovered her strength, even if politically she showed little initiative. In Paris, Thiers' fortifications were demolished in 1919–24, affording an opportunity to lay out a new ring of boulevards. A number of new buildings were erected for the Exhibition of 1937, including the **Musées d'Art Moderne** and the **Palais de Chaillot**. Meanwhile France's passive defensive policies were concretely expressed in the construction of a costly and supposedly impregnable barrier along the German frontier—the Maginot Line (named after a minister of war)—which, after the outbreak of the Second World War (September 1939), was sidestepped by invading armoured divisions in May 1940.

Demoralised French forces, in no state to resist and not capable of mounting a successful counter-attack, capitulated to the triumphant Reich, while a high proportion of the British army was able to re-cross the Channel from Dunkerque (27 May–4 June 1940) in a fleet of open boats sent to their rescue. The Germans proceeded to occupy the northern half of the country and the Atlantic coast, overrunning the rest of France after 11 November 1942. For the rest of the war, the slowly growing underground Resistance Movement did what it could to thwart the collaborating policies of the 'Vichy Government' (1940–44) presided over by the octogenarian Marshal Pétain, hero of Verdun, and Pierre Laval, among others.

Meanwhile, a provisional government had been set up in London by **Géneral Charles de Gaulle** (1890–1970), and Free French forces co-operated in the liberation of France. Allied troops disembarking in Normandy and in the south of France (6 June and 15 August 1944 respectively) converged on Paris, which was free by late August. France was able to participate in the victory celebrations of May 1945 and even occupy a small 'zone' of Germany as one of the victorious Four Powers.

Fourth Republic

In October 1946 the Fourth Republic was proclaimed, of which Vincent Auriol (1947–54) and René Coty (1954–58) were presidents. Women now had the vote and proportional representation was adopted. Slowly, despite many changes in government and despite defeat in Indo-China and revolt in Algeria, the country was restored to economic prosperity after the physical and moral devastation of war. In 1957 a Common Market (EEC) was established, in which France, West Germany, Italy and the Benelux countries were founder members.

Fifth Republic

1958–69 Charles de Gaulle   1981–95 François Mitterrand
1969–74 Georges Pompidou   1995– Jacques Chirac
1974–81 Valéry Giscard d'Estaing

In 1958 de Gaulle prepared a new constitution, which was approved by a referendum, and the general was elected the first president of the new republic by universal direct suffrage, for a period of seven years. The powers of the head of state were considerably—some would say inordinately—increased: he nominates the prime minister, who in turn recommends the members of the government; he can make laws and refer decisions of major importance to popular vote by referendum; in extreme cases he has the power to dismiss the National Assembly.

In 1962 Algerian independence was proclaimed; reversing earlier immigrations, a remarkable number of Algerians can now be seen in the towns of France. In 1965 de Gaulle was returned to power with enthusiasm but with a reduced majority. In May 1968 a serious 'Student Revolution' took place in Paris, which precipitated overdue educational reforms. The following year de Gaulle resigned and was succeeded by Pompidou, who died in office in 1974. His successor was Giscard d'Estaing whose somewhat cavalier attitude to the mass of his countrymen produced a reaction, and a swing to the Left, with Mitterrand moving into the Elysée. But, Mitterrand immediately alienated many of his supporters by the inclusion of Communist ministers in the government, a devious manoeuvre which in turn provoked reaction, and launched an ill-timed programme of nationalisation. In spite of instituting changes in the electoral system in an attempt to retain Socialist control, they lost the election of March 1986, when Jacques Chirac, who had been the right-wing *maire* of Paris since 1977 (when the title was changed from that of Préfet de la Seine) became Prime Minister, inaugurating what was called a period of 'cohabitation' with the Socialist President. Mitterand in 1988 was re-elected, and the Socialist party returned to power in the National Assemby.

In 1989, the bicentenary of the Revolution was celebrated by the inauguration of a prestigious opera house at the Place de la Bastille. In 1995 Jacques Chirac won the presidential election, beating the Socialist Lionel Jospin (Mitterand, dying of cancer, stood down) but his new right-wing government found itself faced by acute economic and social problems. Partly because of the attempt to meet the financial guidelines for the projected European Monetary Union, unemployment rose to levels not seen since before the Second World War. This, coupled with increasing racial tensions, gave the National Front, the nefascist party led by Jean-Marie Le Pen, an opportunity to increase its vote. The Fifth Republic approaches its 40th birthday amid seemingly insolvable crises.

Museums, Collections and Monuments

A table giving hours of admission is printed below, but it is wise to check opening times by telephone or in the press as during strikes or public holidays there are likely to be unscheduled closures. As a general rule, the **National Museums** are closed on Tuesdays, and the **Municipal Museums** are closed on Mondays; but see below. Some museums have late openings and close early, and may be shut between 12.00 and 14.00, although the large museums tend to stay open. The same guidelines may also apply to other monuments, and churches, except for the major ones, are often closed. In some cases the admission fee is reduced or entrance is free on Sundays. A comprehensive list of Museums and Monuments with detailed information is published by the Office de Tourisme de Paris and sold for around 10 francs.

Museum Pass (La Carte Musées et Monuments). This card gives direct entry to some 65 museums and monuments in Paris and and the region. They can be bought at the Office de Tourisme, and at many museums and métro stations. It is available for 1, 3 or 5 consecutive days. It avoids having to queue in the busier museums and is very advantageous for the Louvre, as it means you can bypass the long queues that gather there, and use it to enter by Passage Richelieu where the wait is never as long. Note that it cannot be used for temporary exhibitions or guided tours. Note also in the section dedicated to the Louvre alternative means of acquiring tickets in advance for that museum.

Lecture tours are organised by several bodies; those promoted by the Caisse Nationale des Monuments Historiques et Sites (CNMHS) (who also publish a number of informative guides, and edit a magazine entitled Monuments historiques) are listed in a bi-monthly brochure entitled *Visites Conférences* obtainable from the Hôtel de Sully, 62 Rue St-Antoine, 75004, directly or by mail, ☎ 01 44 61 21 69/44 61 21 70, from the Mairies of each arrondissement, or from the Paris Tourist Office.

A list of such guided visits can also be found in some newspapers. No advance booking is usually necessary: just turn up at the right place at the time stated, and pay the fee. The group is conducted by a competent official French-speaking guide-lecturer.

Entrance fees. All museums charge an entry fee. The quality of general catalogues of permanent collections is constantly improving, especially in the larger museums, and English versions are quite frequent. Many are published by the Editions de la Réunion des musées nationaux (a list of catalogues in print by this organisation is available from the bookstalls of any of the national museums) or by the Musées et Monuments de France.

Hours of Admission

Some museums will not allow entry some 45 minutes before closing time—even mid morning, before closing for lunch. Sections of some museums may be closed at times other than those indicated. Many are closed on Bank Holidays (*jours fériés*). It is always wise to double-check opening times in advance.

Tourist Offices can provide a museums and monuments guide for Paris and the Ile de France (in English) giving up-to-date admission times. You can also get a *Bulletin des Musées et Monuments Historiques* at most museums.

NB. **GT** indicates guided tour only.

Arabe, Institut du Monde
Quai St.-Bernard, 5e.

10.00–18.00 Tues–Sun.
Closed Mon. Page 80

Archives Nationales
60 Rue des Francs-Bourgeois, 3e,

13.45–17.45. Closed Tues
Page 232

Armée, Musée de l'
see Invalides

Art Moderne de la Ville de Paris
11 Av. du Prés.-Wilson, 16e

10.00–17.30; Sat–Sun
10.00–18.45; closed Tues.
Page 263

Arts Africains et Océaniens
293 Av. Daumesnil, 12e,

10.00–12.00, 13.30–17.30;
Sat, Sun 12.30–18.30; closed
Tues, 1/5. Page 289

Arts Décoratifs
107 Rue de Rivoli. 1er

12.30–18.00 Wed–Sat;
12.00–18.00; closed Mon, Tues &
1/1, 1/5, 25/12. Page 188

Arts et Traditions Populaires
6 Av. du Mahatma-Gandhi 16e
(Bois de Boulogne)

9.45–17.15, closed Tues.
Page 272

Assemblée Nationale
Palais Bourbon, Blvd St-Germain

GT when not in session:
10.00, 14.00, 15.00 on Sat.
Page 114

Balzac, Maison Honoré de
47 Rue Raynouard, 16e

10.00–17.40. Closed Mon.
Page 268

Beaubourg: see Pompidou

**Bibliothéque Nationale,
Cardinal Richelieu
& Cabinet des Médailles**
58 Rue de Richelieu, 4e

See p 198

Bibliothèque Nationale, François Mitterand

GT. Tues–Sat 14.00, Sun 15.00. Page 84

Bourdelle
16 Rue Antoine-Bourdelle

10.00–17.40; closed Mon & public holidays. Page 92

Camondo, Nissim de Camondo
63 Rue de Monceau, 8e,

10.00–17.00; closed Mon & Tues. Page 259

Carnavalet
23 Rue de Sévigné, 3e

10.00–17.40; closed Mon & some public holidays. Page 225

Catacombes
1 Pl. Denfert-Rochereau 14e

GT. Tues–Fri between 14.00 & 16.00; Sat 09.00–11.00, 14.00–16.00. Page 90

Cernuschi
7 Av. Velasquez, 8e

10.00–17.40, closed Mon. Page 260

Chapelle Expiatoire
Sq. Louis XVI, 8e

Page 245

Chasse (hunting)
60 Rue des Archives, 3e

10.00–12.30, 13.30–17.30; closed Tues. Page 232

Cinema/Henri Langlois
Palais de Chaillot, 16e

Page 267

Cluny; see Moyen Age-Thermes

Cognacq-Jay
8 Rue Elzévir, 3e

10.00–17.40; closed Mon & public holidays. Page 231

Conciergerie
1 Quai de l'Horloge, 4e

09.30–18.30; winter 10.00–17.00; closed 1/1, 1/5, 1/11, 11/11. 25/12. Page 56

Delacroix, Musée
6 Rue de Furstenberg, 6e

09.45–17.00; closed Tues & some public holidays. Page 103

Eiffel Tower
Champs de Mars, 7e

lift 09.30–23.00 July–Aug; by foot 09.00–18.30, July–Aug 09.00–24.00. Page 129

Egouts
South end of Pont de l'Alma, 7e

11.00–17.00 summer; 11.00–16.00 winter; closed Thurs, Fri & last 3 weeks Jan. Page 121

d'Ennery (oriental art)
59 Av. Foch, 16e

14.00–18.00 Thur–Sun. Page 272

Gobelins (tapestries)
42 Av. de Gobelins, 13e

GT. Tues–Thurs 14.00 & 14.15.
Page 85

Guimet
6 Pl. d'Iéna, 16e and with
extention at 19 Av. d'Iéna

closed for restoration.
Page 264

Homme, Musée de l'
Palais de Chaillot, 16e

09.45–17.15; closed Tues &
public holidays. Page 267

Hugo, Maison de Victor
6 Pl. Des Vosges, 4e

10.00–17.00; closed Mon &
public holidays. Page 224

Instrumental (musical instruments)
Cité de la Musique
(La Villette)

12.00–18.00 Tues–Thurs;
12.00–19.30 Fri & Sat. 10.00–
18.00 Sun; closed Mon. Page 277

Invalides, Les (army museum)
Esplanade des Invalides, 7e
also **Plans-Reliefs**

tickets for 3 museums and
Napoléon's tomb. 10.00–18.00;
winter 10.00–17.00; closed 1/1,
1/5, 1/11, 25/12. Page 122

Jacquemart-André
158 Blvd Haussmann, 8e

10.00–18.00 daily. Page 257

Jardin des Plantes (Histoire Naturelle)
57 Rue Cuvier, 5e
Grande Galerie d'Evolution

07.30–20.00 (or sunset). Page 81

10.00–18.00 Wed–Mon; 10.00–
22.00 Thurs; closed Tues

Louvre, Musée du
Pyramid (Cour Napoléon)
Palais du Louvre, 1er

09.00–18.00 Wed–Mon; closed
Tues. Page 142

Jeu-de-Paume & Orangerie
Pl. de la Concorde

12.00–21.30 Tues; 12.00–19.00
Wed–Fri; 10.00–19.00 Sat, Sun.
Closed Mon. Page 133

Maillol

11.00–18.00; closed Tues &
public holidays. Page 119

Marine
Palais de Chaillot, 16e

10.00–18.00; closed Tues.
Page 267

Marmottan
2 Rue Louis-Boilly, 16e

10.00–17.30; closed Mon.
Page 268

Mineralogy & Geology
Blvd St-Michel

13.30–18.00 Tues–Fri;
10.00–12.30, 14.00–17.00 Sat;
closed Sun, Mon, public holidays.
Page 268

de la Mode et du Costume
Rue de Rivoli, 1er

10.00–17.40. Closed Mon.
Page 263

Monnaie (Mint)
11 Quai de Conti, 6e

13.00–18.00; closed Mon &
some public holidays. Page 96

Monuments Français
Palais de Chaillot, 16e

closed for restoration until 1999.
Page 267

Moreau, Gustave

11.00–17.15 Mon & Wed; other
days 10.00–12.45, 14.00–17.15;
closed Tues & 1/1, 1/5, 25/12.
Page 244

Moyen Age-Thermes
6 Pl. Paul-Painlevé, 5e

09.15–19.45; closed Tues
& some public holidays. Page 75

Notre-Dame, Cathedral
Crypte Archéologique
Pl. du Parvis Notre-Dame, 4e

09.30–18.30; winter 10.00–17.00;
closed 1/1, 1/5, 1/11,
11/11, 25/12. Page 60

Observatoire
61 Av de l'Observatoire, 14e

GT first Sat of month 14.30.
Page 89

Opéra
Pl. de l'Opéra, 9e

10.00–17.00 daily, closed 1/1,
1/5, Page 239 & 240

Orsay, Musée d'
1 Rue de Bellechasse, 7e

09.00–18.00 Tues–Sun summer;
winter 10.00–18.00,
09.00–18.00 Sun; Thurs until
21.45. Closed Mon & 1/1, 1/5,
25/12. Page 104

Palais de Justice
2 Blvd du Palais, 1er

Page 57

Panthéon
Pl. Ste-Geneviève

10.00–19.30; winter 10.00–18.15;
closed 1/1, 1/5, 1/11,
11/11, 25/12. Page 72

Petit Palais
Av. Winston Churchill, 8e

10.00–17.40; closed Mon & some
public holidays. Page 252

Picasso
5 Rue de Torigny, 3e,

09.39–18.00 summer; winter
09.30–17.30; closed Tues & 1/1,
25/12. Page 234

Pompidou, Centre (CNAC)
4e

12.00–22.00 Mon & Wed–Fri;
10.0022.00 Sat, Sun & bank
holidays; closed Tues & 1/5.
Page 216

Postal Museum
34 Blvd Vaugirard, 15e

10.00–18.00; closed Tues &
public holidays. Page 92

Rodin, Musée
77 Rue de Varenne, 7e

09.30–17.45 summer;
09.30–16.45 winter; closed Mon
& 1/1, 25/12. Page 116

Romantique, de la Vie
16 Rue Chaptal, 9e

10.00–17.40. Closed Mon.
Page 245

Sainte-Chapelle
Blvd du Palais, 4e

09.30–18.30; 10.00–17.00
winter; closed 1/1, 1/5, 1/11,
11/11, 25/12. Page 58

Sciences et de l'Industrie
30 Av. Corentin-Cariou, 19e
(La Villette)

10.00–18.00; Tues–Sun;
closed Mon & 1/5,
25/12. Page 278

Villette, La; see Science et de l'Industries and Instrumental

Vincennes, Château de

10.00–17.00; closed 1/1, 1/5,
1/11, 11/11, 25/12. Page 287

Zadkine Museum
Rue d'Assas, 100 bis

10.00–17.30; closed Mon & public
holidays. Page 103.

Environs of Paris

Barbizon, Musée de l'Aubarge Ganne

10.00–12.30, 14.00–18.00 April–
30/9; Oct–30/3 to 17.00. Closed
Tues. Page 345

Champs, Château de
Chantilly (Musée Condé)

Page 346
Page 331

Défense, La; Grande Arche de

09.00–19.00 Mon–Fri;
09.00–20.00 Sat & Sun; 09.00–
18.00 1/10 to 31/3. Page 275

Ecouen, Château de
Musée de la Renaissance

09.45–12.30, 14.00–17.15
Wed–Mon. Page 326

Fontainebleau, Château de	09.30–17.00; July & Aug 09.30–18.00; Nov–May 09.30–12.30, 14.00–17.00; closed Tues. 1/1, 1/5. Page 337
Maisons-Laffitte, Château de	10.00–12.00, 13.30–18.00; in winter until 17.00; closed Tues & public holidays. Page 318
Malmaison and Bois-Préau	10.00–12.00, 13.30–17.00; in winter 09.30–12.00, 13.30–16.30; closed Tues & 1/1, 25/12. Page 312
St-Denis, Basilique de	10.00–19.00; in winter to 17.00; 12.00–19.00 Sun (winter to 17.00). Page 320
St-Germain-en-Laye Antiquitiés Nationales Pl. du Château	09.00–17.15; closed Tues & some public holidays. Page 316
Preiuré (Nabis) 2bis Rue Maurice-Denis	10.00–17.30 Wed–Fri; 10.00–18.30 Sat & Sun. Page 317
Sceaux, Château de (Musée de l'Ile de France)	10.00–18.00 April–Sept; 10.00–17.00; closed Tues & 1/1, Easter, 1/5, 1/11, 11/11, 25/12. Page 329
Sèvres, Céramique de	10.00–17.00. Closed Mon. Page 291
Versailles, Château de	09.00–18.30 May–Sept; 09.00–17.30 Oct–April; closed Mon & some public holidays. Page 295
Grand Trianon & Petit Trianon	10.00–18.30 May–Sept; 10.00–12.30,14.00–17.30 Oct–April. Closed Mon
Gardens/Parks	07.00–dusk the year round Page 295

The **cemeteries** of Père Lachaise (p 280), Montmartre (p 247), Montparnasse (p 91) and are normally open from 07.30–18.00 in summer, and from 08.00–17.00 in winter; that of Picpus is open during the afternoon only.

Index

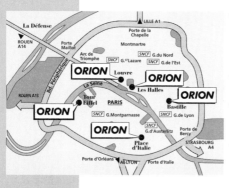

Atlas Contents

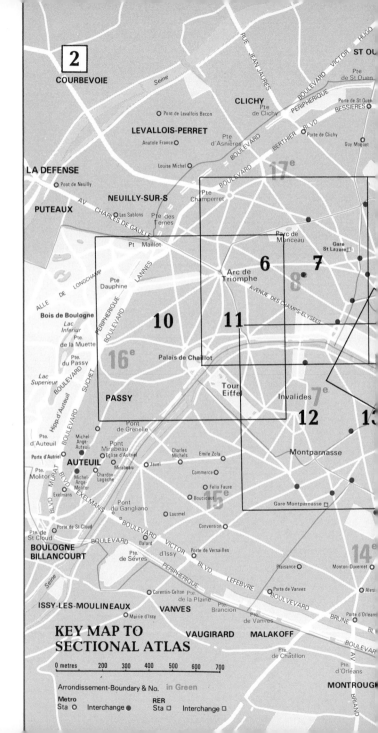

2

COURBEVOIE

Seine

RUE JEAN JAURES

CLICHY
Pte
de Clichy

ST OUEN

Pte
de St Ouen

BOULEVARD PERIPHERIQUE

VICTOR HUGO

BESSIERES

○ Pont de Levallois Becon

LEVALLOIS-PERRET

Anatole France ○

BOULEVARD

BERTHIER

Porte de St Ouen

Porte de Clichy

BLVD

Guy Moquet ○

LA DEFENSE

Pte
d'Asnières

Louise Michel ○

17ᵉ

○ Pont de Neuilly

NEUILLY-SUR-S

PUTEAUX

AV CHARLES DE GAULLE

○ Les Sablons

Pte
Champerret

BOULEVARD

Parc de
Monceau

Gare
St Lazare ▢

Pte des
Ternes

Pt Maillot

LANNES

Arc de
Triomphe

6

8ᵉ

7

Pte
Dauphine

DE LONGCHAMP

ALLE

Bois de Boulogne

*Lac
Inferiur*

PERIPHERIQUE

BOULEVARD

10

16ᵉ

11

AVENUE DES CHAMPS-ELYSEES

Pte.
de la Muette

SUCHET

Palais de Chaillot

Pte.
du Passy

*Lac
Superieur*

BOULEVARD

Hipp d'Auteuil

Tour
Eiffel

Invalides

7ᵉ

PASSY

Pont
de Grenelle

12

13

Pte.
d'Auteuil

BOULEVARD

Michel-
Ange
Auteuil

Pont
Mirabeau

Charles
Michels

Emile Zola ○

Montparnasse

Porte d'Auteuil ○

○ Eglise d'Auteuil

Mirabeau ○

○ Javel

Pte.
Molitor ○

MURAT

BLVD

Michel-
Ange-
Molitor

Chardon-
Lagache ○

Commerce ○

Exelmans ○

EXELMANS

○ Felix Faure

15ᵉ

○ Boucicaut

Pont
du Garigliano

Gare Montparnasse ▢

○ Lourmel

Porte de St Cloud ○

BOULEVARD

○ Convention

14ᵉ

Pte. de
St Cloud

VICTOR

Pte
de Versailles

BOULEVARD

Balard ○

d'Issy

BOULOGNE
BILLANCOURT

Pte.
de Sèvres

BLVD

Plaisance ○

Monton-Duvernet ○

PERIPHERIQUE

LEFEBVRE

Seine

○ Corentin-Celton

Pte.
de la Plaine

Porte de Vanves ○

BOULEVARD

○ Alesi

Pte.
Brancion

ISSY-LES-MOULINEAUX

VANVES

○ Mairie d'Issy

Porte d'Orleam

BRUNE

Pte
de Vanves

KEY MAP TO
SECTIONAL ATLAS

VAUGIRARD

MALAKOFF

BOULEVARD

AV

Pte.
de Châtillon

Pte.
d'Orléans

MONTROUG

BRAND

0 metres	200	300	400	500	600	700

Arrondissement-Boundary & No. in Green

Metro
Sta ○   Interchange ●

RER
Sta ▢   Interchange ▢

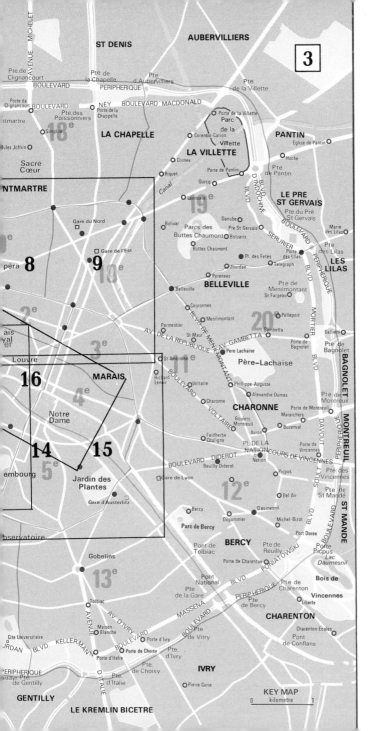

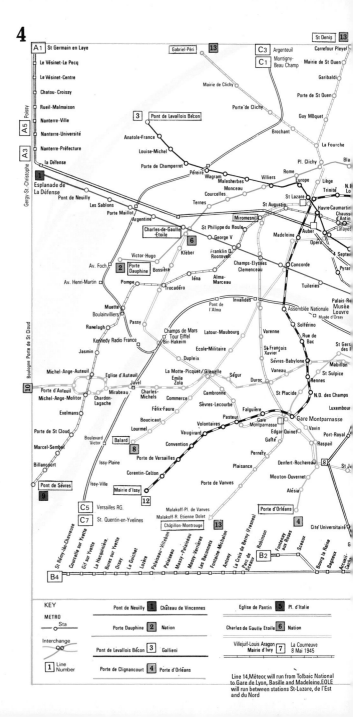

y-la-Ville | D1 | B5 | Roissy Aéroport Ch. de Gaulle

B3 | Mitry-Claye

de Clignancourt

12

Porte de la Chapelle

7 | La Courneuve 8 Mai 1945

Fort d'Aubervilliers

Aubervilliers

Bobigny-Pablo Picasso | 5

Simplon

Porte de la Villette

affrin

Marx Dormoy

Corentin-Cariou

Bobigny-Pantin Raymond Queneau

Lamarck-aulaincourt

Marcadet-Poissoniers

Château Rouge

Crimée

Église de Pantin

esses

Barbès-Rochechouart

Riquet

Hoche

Anvers

Stalingrad

Porte de Pantin

Durcq

La Chapelle

Laumière

Gare du Nord

Louis-Blanc

Jaurès

orges

Poissonnière

Bolivar

Danube

Botzaris

7 | Mairie des Lilas | 11

Cadet

Gare de l'Est

Château Landon

Buttes Chaumont

Pré St Gervais

etier

Colonel-Fabien

Pl. des Fêtes

Télégraphe

Drouot

Château d'Eau

Jacques Bonsergent

Jourdain

Porte des Lilas

Rue Montmartre

Pyrénées

3

Bonne-Nouvelle

Strasbourg-St Denis

Belleville

St Fargeau

Sentier

Goncourt

Couronnes

Pelleport

Réaumur-Sébastopol

Temple

République

Ménilmontant

3 | Gallieni

Marcel

Arts et Métiers

Parmentier

St Maur

Gambetta

Porte de Bagnolet

Filles du Calvaire

Oberkampf

Père Lachaise

Mairie de Montreuil

B | Rambuteau

St Sébastien-Froissart

Richard Lenoir

St Ambroise

Phillippe-Auguste

9

Châtelet-Les Halle

Hôtel de Ville

Chemin-Vert

Voltaire

Alexandre-Dumas

11

St Paul

Bréguet-Sabin

Charonne

Avron

Croix de Chavaux

Robespierre

Cité

Pont-Marie

Boulets-Montreuil | 2

Buzenval

Porte de Montreuil

St Michel

St Michel Notre-Dame

Sully-Morland

Bastille

Ledru-Rollin

Faidherbe-Chaligny

Nation

Porte de Vincennes

Maraîchers

Cluny La Sorbonne

Reuilly Diderot

6

St Mandé-Tourelle

Vincennes

Mutualité

Picpus

Bérault

1

ardinal-Lemoine

Quai de la Rapée

Montgallet

Château de Vincennes

A4 | Marne-la-Vallée

Monge

Jussieu

Gare de Lyon

Bel-Air

Fontenay sous Bois

10 | Gare d'Orléans *Austerlitz

Daumesnil

Nogent sur Marne

r-Daubenton

St Marcel

Bercy

Dugommier

Michel-Bizot

Joinville le Pont

Gobelins

Campo-Formio

Quai de la Gare

Port Dorée

Saint Maur-Créteil

Chevaleret

Porte de Charenton

Le Parc de St Maur

5

Nationale

Champigny

rvisart

Pl. d'Italie

Liberté

La Varenne-Chennevières

Tolbiac

Porte d'Ivry

Boulevard Masséna

Sucy-Bonneuil

Porte de Choisy

Pierre-Curie

Charenton-Ecoles

Boissy St Leger | A2

Maison-Blanche

Porte d'Italie

Kremlin-Bicêtre

Mairie d'Ivry | 7

Alfort Ecole Vétérinaire

Maisons-Alfort Stade

Maisons-Alfort les Juilliottes

Créteil l'Echat Hôpital H. Mondor

Créteil Université

8

Villejuif-Paul Vaillant-Couturier (Hôpital Paul Brousse)

Pont de Rungis | C2

Dourdan | C4

Créteil Préfecture Hôtel de Ville

Villejuif-Louis Aragon | 7

St.-Martin d'Etampes | C6

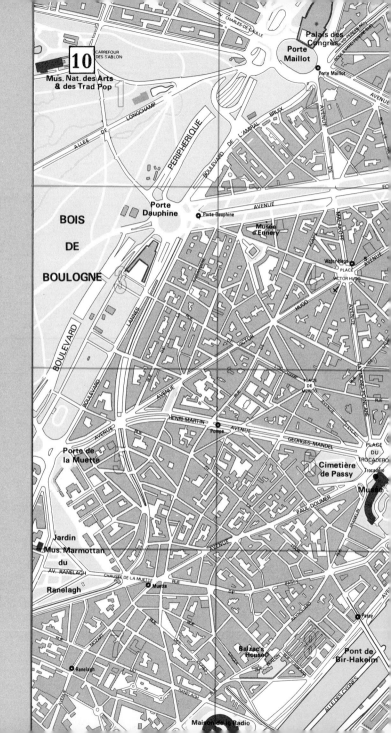

CARREFOUR
DES SABLON

Mus. Nat. des Arts
& des Trad Pop

Palais des
Congrès

Porte
Maillot

Porte Maillot

AV. CHARLES DE GAULLE

ALLÉE DE LONGCHAMP

PERIPHERIQUE

BOULEVARD DE L'AMIRAL BRUIX

AVENUE

Porte
Dauphine

Porte Dauphine

AVENUE

Musée
d'Ennery

BOIS

DE

BOULOGNE

BOULEVARD LANNES

Victor Hugo

PLACE
VICTOR HUGO

HUGO

AVENUE RAYMOND POINCARÉ

MALAKOFF

RUE DE LA POMPE

AVENUE VICTOR

RUE

AVENUE

LONGCHAMP

PLACE
DE
MEXICO

BOULEVARD

AVENUE

HENRI MARTIN

Pompe

AVENUE

GEORGES-MANDEL

PLACE
DU
TROCADERO

Porte de
la Muette

AVENUE

RUE

Cimetière
de Passy

Trocadéro

Musée

PAUL-DOUMER

FRANKLIN

Jardin

Mus. Marmottan

du

AV. RANELAGH

CHAUSSÉE DE LA MUETTE

Muette

AVENUE

RUE

Ranelagh

RUE

RUE

PASSY

RAYNOUARD

Passy

RUE MOZART

RUE

Ranelagh

RUE

RANELAGH

Balzac's
House

Pont de
Bir-Hakeim

ALLÉES DES CYGNES

Maison de la Radio

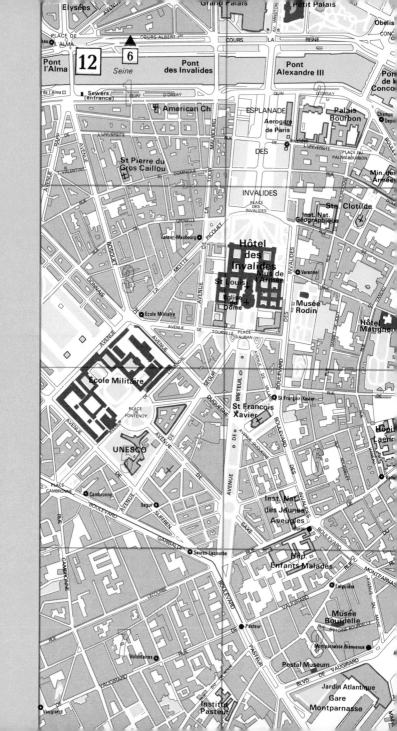

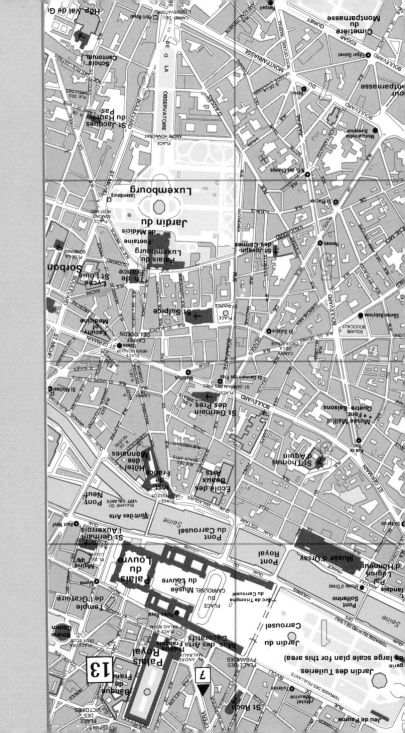

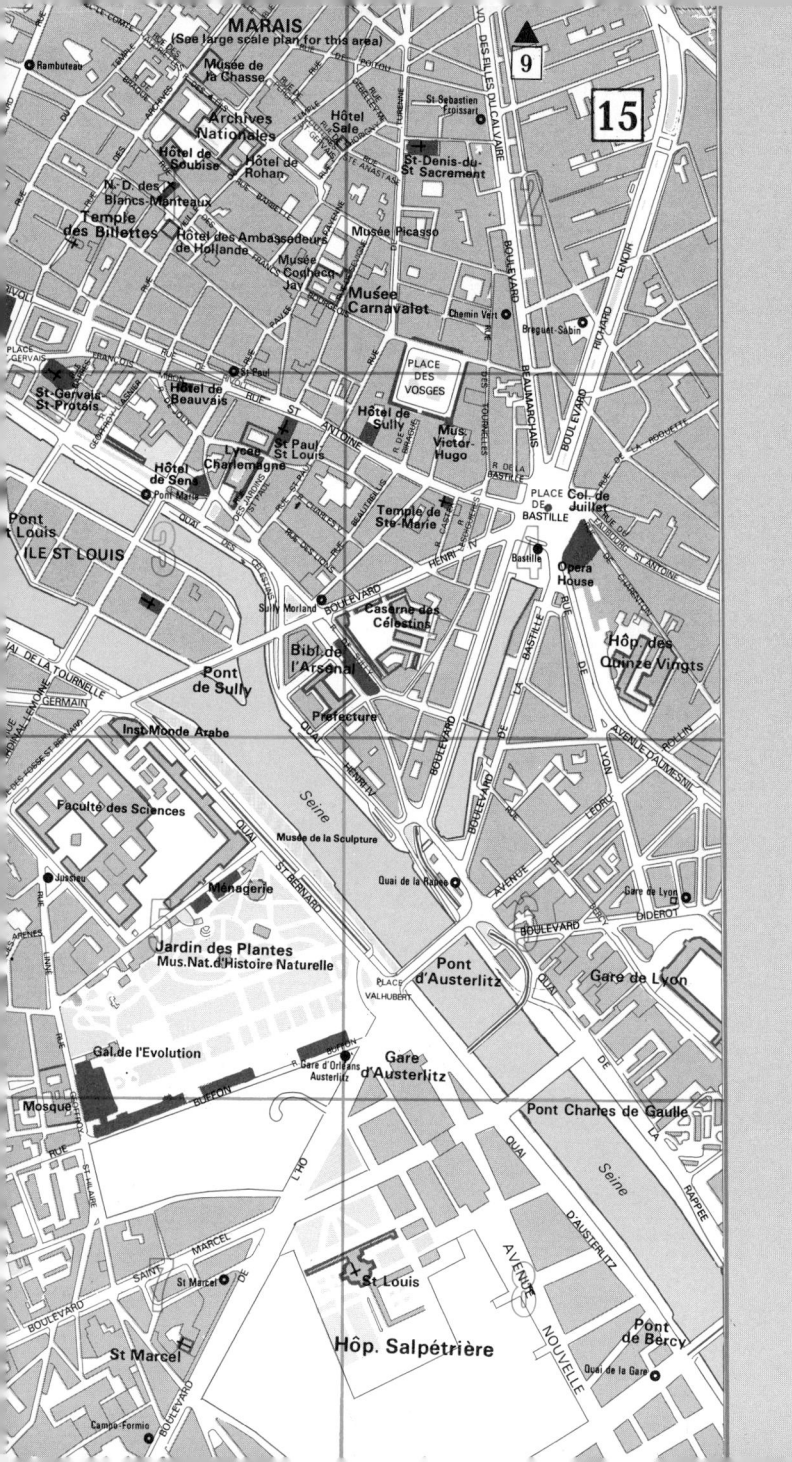